School Psychological
Services

PRENTICE-HALL PSYCHOLOGY SERIES
Arthur T. Jersild, *Editor*

Edited by
JAMES F. MAGARY
University of Southern California

School Psychological
Services
In Theory and Practice
A Handbook

PRENTICE-HALL, INC.
Englewood Cliffs, New Jersey

PRENTICE-HALL INTERNATIONAL, INC., *London*
PRENTICE-HALL OF AUSTRALIA, PTY. LTD., *Sydney*
PRENTICE-HALL OF CANADA, LTD., *Toronto*
PRENTICE-HALL OF INDIA (PRIVATE) LTD., *New Delhi*
PRENTICE-HALL OF JAPAN, INC., *Tokyo*

Editor's Introduction

Thirteen years ago the historic Thayer Conference convened at West Point to take a penetrating look at the functions, qualifications, and training of school psychologists. This conference marked a turning point in the field of school psychological services; furthermore, it served to give a certain unity of purpose to a large group of persons offering disparate services of a psychological nature in various school settings. Since the date of the conference the number of school psychologists has grown very rapidly, as well as the number of techniques and the availability of community referral facilities. Many colleges have established masters and doctoral training programs, and many workshops and regional associations have appeared on the scene.

This book takes the Thayer Conference Report, *School Psychologists at Mid-Century,* as its skeletal structure and is intended to provide a comprehensive body of information which can serve as an introductory text for the graduate student of school psychology. Most aspects of the school psychologist's work are covered in the pages ahead. Each author has developed his topic in as much detail as the allotted space allows, and each has provided the ambitious reader with a list of carefully selected supplementary readings for further exploration of the subject. The text is a symposium of highly qualified psychologists and educators who have in common a deep concern about the quality of school psychological services. This common concern represents perhaps the only consensus among the various contributors, for the field of school psychology, like any young discipline, is beset by conflicts, rifts, and differences of opinion among the experts. The astute reader will discover some of these differences in the reading of this text.

The field of school psychology is not an entitative science but an interdisciplinary endeavor; it draws on the findings and insights of clinical psychologists, counseling specialists, educational psychologists, and special educators, as well as persons in many peripheral fields. Thus, the authors of the various chapters have a number of professional identifications. Eight of these individuals are practicing school psychologists in states ranging from California to New York, while twelve are school psychologist trainers.

Although the school psychologist recognizes his symbiotic relationship with the educator, the point of view of the editor of this text is that the school psychologist is first and foremost a carefully trained behavioral scientist skilled in bringing psychological insight to bear on school-related problems that have resisted the wisdom and good intentions of educators. In the editor's opinion, the task of the school psychologist is to bring an alternative frame of reference from the behavioral sciences to bear upon a set of school-related observations or behaviors, with the end in view of facilitating learning and adjustment for as many school children as possible, both in groups and as individuals. Given this psychological frame of reference, it is important for the school psychologist to remember that the teacher is the central person in the school setting and, whenever possible, he should effect behavioral changes in pupils by working with their teachers. To achieve a productive relationship with the teacher, he needs the skill and diplomacy of a psychological consultant. Several chapters in this text emphasize this aspect of the school psychologist's role—an aspect that seems certain to become increasingly important as time goes on.

Listed here are a number of additional trends which the reader will find developed in the following pages: (1) the school psychologist will in the future attempt to serve all the children in the schools, at least in terms of the implementation of sound mental health programs; he will not work exclusively with the extreme deviates; (2) the school psychologist will work more frequently with small groups than with individual children in various types of diagnostic, remedial, and therapeutic activities; (3) he will serve much more frequently than in the past as an advisor on many more aspects of the total school program, especially that of curriculum development; (4)

there will be an increase in the number of mental hygiene and psychology courses offered by our high schools, and many of these courses will be taught by school psychologists; (5) the importance of findings in developmental, social, and physiological psychology, previously ignored by most school psychologists, will become paramount; (6) the team, or multi-disciplinal, approach will continue to be relied upon in solving the problems of youth and will include the school sociologist and school psychiatrist; (7) individual therapy with seriously disturbed children will be relegated to clinics and professionals outside the school setting; (8) on the other hand, more responsibility will be given the classroom teacher—with the support and guidance of the school psychologist—in working out appropriate solutions to the wide range of problems of individual children; (9) as the specialties of school psychology and special education become more highly developed, the school psychologist will have less responsibility for the administration of special education programs; (10) there will evolve clearer concepts of roles or functions with other pupil personnel workers, such as counseling and guidance specialists, social workers, physicians, school sociologists, psychiatrists, and psychometrists. Hopefully, all school psychological service workers will have a common base of graduate education with additional training in each specialization; (11) although the nomenclature difficulty will be with us for some time because of the diversity of the services offered, attempts will be made at clarification; (12) there will be more careful evaluation of school psychological programs in order to develop the most economical, effective constellation of services for the greatest good of all pupils; (13) the school psychologist will deemphasize his role as test-diagnostician and his responsibility in the group testing program; (14) he will become increasingly data-oriented and will be especially concerned about fostering the cognitive growth of children as perhaps the best aid to ego-building that an educational institution can offer.

The professor and student who use this text will find that it is exceedingly well documented in terms of both historical and contemporary research and writing related to school psychological personnel. Because of limitations in space, references that have been cited in footnotes are not listed in the Selected Supplementary Readings section which follows each chapter. Furthermore, readings which have been selected for one chapter have not been repeated as suggestions in another chapter, even though the content of the suggested reading might be applicable to both. Because of the similarity of content in Chapters 1 and 22, the Selected Supplementary Readings for these two have been grouped together at the end of Chapter 22.

The editor wishes to express his thanks to the following school psychologists and school psychologist trainers who read and criticized parts of the manuscript while in various stages of production and gave professional advice regarding the book: Marcella Bonsall, Janet Bower, Roger Callahan, Earl Carnes, William Culp, Philip Diskin, Gertrude Driscoll, Belle Dubnoff, Paul

Eiserer, Paul Erickson, Marguerite Ford, Marianne Frostig, E. Ellis Graham, Susan W. Gray, Theodore Grubbe, James Hall, Albert J. Harris, Richard Harsh, Robert J. Havighurst, Conwell Higgins, Gertrude Hildreth, Allen Hodges, Kenneth Hopkins, Arthur R. Jensen, Henry Johnson, Elvet Jones, John Jordan, George M. Kaiser, Herbert J. Klausmier, Roy A. Kress, Nadine Lambert, Frederick J. Lighthall, Nicholas Long, August Mauser, Boyd R. McCandless, C. Edward Meyers, Elmer Morgan, Clark Moustakes, T. Ernest Newland, F. Parsons, Keith J. Perkins, Laurence J. Peter, Lafayette S. Powell, Marvin Powell, Mabel C. Purl, Stephen Rauch, Thomas A. Ringness, Jerome Rothstein, Terry Rusk, Sophia T. Salvin, Elnora Schmadel, J. Kirk Seaton, Georgene Seward, Carleton Shay, Marie Skodak, the late Percival M. Symonds, Thelma Thurston, Ralph Tindall, Gilbert Trachtman, Leona Tyler, Gracia Van Daff, Elmer Wagner, Jane Warters, Paul H. Whiteman, Gertrude L. Wyatt, and Thais Yeremian.

The editor wishes to thank the staff of Prentice-Hall, especially William R. Grose and James H. Clark for their kind assistance in making this book a reality. He is also indebted to many other kind spirits who have helped by encouragement, careful typing, and editorial assistance, in particular: Jean F. Arin, Sonia Ervo, Lucy Hino, Jody Hokanson, F. C. Holinko, Roger Holloway, Grace Hume, Mary Lou Jordan, Frances M. Kearns, Eve Kerr, Thelma Koppel, Joan Lacertosa, Karen Lindsay, Ethel E. Magary, Joanne McDaniel, Elizabeth McLaughlin, Maureen McLaughlin, Marianne Meacham, Irving Melbo, Charles Pensinger, Victoria Sahlman, Sharon Spencer, Margaret Starbuck, Jane Tinker, Diane Westergaard, and Peter Wilkins.

The editor feels very strongly that the public school is a dynamic and exciting place for a psychologist to work. He will be gratified if this book contributes to the initial training of the school psychologist by helping him reach a high professional level.

JAMES F. MAGARY

December, 1966
University of
Southern California

The Contributing Authors

ROBERT M. ALLEN, PH.D., is Professor of Psychology, University of Miami. He is a Diplomate in Clinical Psychology, ABEPP; a fellow, Division 12; and a member of Division 22 of the American Psychological Association, the American Academy of Psychotherapists, and the American Association on Mental Deficiency. He is a fellow, Society for Projective Techniques; a certified psychologist in the states of Florida and New York; a research editor of the *Cerebral Palsy Review*; a member of the board of editors, *Psychological Reports*; and an abstractor, *Excerpta Medica*. Dr. Allen is the author of papers and books in the field of psychological assessment of the normal, cerebral palsied, and mentally retarded individual.

GLADYS L. ANDERSON, PH.D. (deceased, 1965). Former Quondam Associate Professor, Research Associate Professor, Research Associate, Department of Psychology, Michigan State University. Previously Research Clinical Psychologist, Judge Baker Guidance Center, Boston; School Psychologist, Montclair, New Jersey; State Director for Northern California, Child Protection Program;

and Field Supervisor for the San Francisco Bay Area Child Protection Program, California Department of Education. She also served as Director of the Cross-National Study of Creativity and Children's Values in eight countries. She was co-editor of *Introduction to Projective Techniques,* and co-author of *Manual of Individual Mental Tests and Testing.*

JACK I. BARDON, PH.D., is Professor of Education and Coordinator of the School Psychology Training Program, Graduate School of Education, Rutgers University. He is a fellow of the American Psychological Association, a member of the executive committee of the New Jersey Psychological Association, and a past president of the New Jersey Association of School Psychologists. He is also an associate editor of the *Journal of School Psychology.*

ELI M. BOWER, ED.D., is Consultant, Mental Health in Education, National Institute of Mental Health. He was formerly Deputy Director, Liaison and Prevention Services, State Department of Mental Hygiene, and Consultant in Mental Hygiene for the State Department of Education in California. He is a fellow of the American Psychological Association, the American Orthopsychiatric Association, and an associate editor of *Psychology in the Schools, Exceptional Children,* and the *American Journal of Orthopsychiatry.*

RUDOLPH J. CAPOBIANCO, ED.D., is Research Scientist II at the Johnstone Training Center in Bordentown, New Jersey. He has been a professor of special education and psychology at various universities, where he played a role in the training of school psychologists. He has contributed chapters to several books. He is a member of numerous professional organizations, including the American Association on Mental Deficiency, the Council for Exceptional Children, and the American Psychological Association.

NORMAN M. CHANSKY, PH.D., is Professor of Education at Temple University. Dr. Chansky is a member of the Divisions of Developmental, Educational and School Psychology of the American Psychological Association, a fellow of the North Carolina Psychological Association, and a member of the American Educational Research Association. His research activities are in the identification of intellectual factors associated with inadequate academic achievement and its rehabilitation.

DONALD G. FERGUSON, ED.D., is Associate Professor and Coordinator of student personnel training programs at Kent State University. Dr. Ferguson is a member of the American Psychological Association and past president of the Ohio School Psychological Association. His publications include the book, *Pupil Personnel Services.*

MAURICE F. FREEHILL, ED.D., is Professor of Educational Psychology, University of Washington, and Area Chairman for Educational Psychology, Guidance and Psychological Services. He has been the Director of a College Psychological Service and Research Center, is a certified psychologist, and is past president of the Washington Personnel and Guidance Association. He is the author of *Gifted Children: Their Psychology and Education.*

WILLIAM ITKIN, PH.D., is Professor of Psychology and Chairman of the Special Education Program, Illinois Teachers College Chicago-North. He was formerly Director of the Chicago Board of Education Cooperative Research Project, and a school psychologist with the Chicago Bureau of Child Study. He is a fellow of the American Psychological Association, the American Association for the Advancement of Science, and the American Association on Mental Deficiency. He was president of the Division of School Psychologists during 1966–67.

DONALD A. LETON, PH.D., is Associate Professor in Educational Psychology at the University of Hawaii. He was formerly the coordinator of the School Psychology Program at U.C.L.A. He is a fellow in the American Psychological Association, and a member of the American Educational Research Association and the American Association for the Advancement of Science. An associate editor of *Psychology in the Schools,* he has contributed to the research and professional literature in this field.

GORDON P. LIDDLE, PH.D., is Director of the Interprofessional Research Commission of Pupil Personnel Services, University of Maryland. Since 1960 he has also directed a project aimed at modifying the school experience of culturally handicapped children in the primary grades through curriculum changes and parent education. He is a member of the American Psychological Association, the Association for Supervision and Curriculum Development, and the American Educational Research Association.

JAMES F. MAGARY, PH.D., is Chairman, Department of Educational Psychology, at the University of Southern California. He was formerly coordinator of Special Education at the University of Southern California, Psychological Coordinator at the Devereux Foundation, as well as Director of Psychological Services at Jersey City State College and its laboratory schools. He has served on the Executive Board of the California Association of School Psychologists and Psychometrists, and is an associate editor of the *Journal of School Psychology.* He is a member of professional organizations, including the American Psychological Association and the Council for Exceptional Children. He has written in the areas of school psychology and special education.

STANLEY S. MARZOLF, PH.D., is Director, Psychological Counseling Service, Illinois State University, and past president of the Illinois Psychological Association and of the American Association of State Psychology Boards. He is a fellow of the American Psychological Association, and a Diplomate in Counseling, American Board of Examiners in Professional Psychology. He has served on various committees of the Division of School Psychology of the American Psychological Association. He is the author of *Psychological Diagnosis and Counseling in the Schools,* and has contributed to other texts and journals in the fields of clinical and educational psychology.

MERLE L. MEACHAM, ED.D., is Assistant Professor of Educational Psychology and Guidance at the University of Washington. He was formerly Director of Guidance and Counseling at Peninsula College. He was for ten years a school psychologist with the Port Angeles and Clallam County Schools in Washington. He is a member of the Washington State Psychological Association, the Western Psychological Association, and is affiliated with Division 16 of the American Psychological Association. He has taught in the training programs for school psychologists at Western Washington State College.

NEWTON S. METFESSEL, PH.D., is Professor of Educational Psychology, and Director, Bureau of Educational Research, University of Southern California. He designed and is principal investigator for "Project Potential," a research project sponsored by the United States Office of Education. A major facet of "Project Potential" is the identification of creative abilities among culturally disadvantaged youth. A former president of the California Educational Research and Guidance Association, he is a member of the American Psychological Association, the American Educational Research Association, the National Council in Measurement in Education, and the American Personnel and Guidance Association.

FRANCES A. MULLEN, PH.D., is the former Assistant Superintendent in charge of Special Education, Chicago Public Schools, Chicago, Illinois. She is a past president of the Division of School Psychologists of the American Psychological Association; Diplomate of the American Board of Examiners in Professional Psychology; a fellow of the American Association on Mental Deficiency, the American Orthopsychiatric Association, and the American Psychological Association; and a member of the Council for Exceptional Children, the American Association of School Administrators, and the Interprofessional Research Commission of Pupil Personnel Services.

HARRIET E. O'SHEA, PH.D., is Emeritus Professor of Psychology, Purdue University, and presently consultant chief psychologist, Franklin County Mental Health Center, Greenfield, Massachusetts. She was a member of the Thayer Conference on School Psychology at Mid-Century. She is a Diplomate in Clinical Psychology of the American Psychological Association, and a fellow of the APA, the American Orthopsychiatric Association, and the Society for Research in Child Development. She is a member of the American Academy of Psychotherapists and other professional societies. She was for a number of years chairman of the Committee on Intellectually Gifted Children of Division 16.

ELLEN V. PIERS, PH.D., is Associate Professor of Psychology and associated with the Psychological Clinic, Pennsylvania State University. She was formerly school psychologist in Nashville, Tennessee. She is a member of the Society for Research in Child Development, the American and Eastern Psychological Associations, and the Executive Committee of the Pennsylvania Psychological Association. She is a certified psychologist in Pennsylvania, and Diplomate in Clinical Psychology, ABEPP.

HENRY PLATT, PH.D., is presently School Clinical Psychologist, Devereux Schools, Devon, Pennsylvania, and Director, Professional Psychological and Educational Training, the Devereux Foundation Institute for Research and

Training. He is also Consultant School Psychologist, Luzerne County Industrial School for Boys; Research Consultant, Professional Examination Service, the American Public Health Association. Dr. Platt is a member of all major organizations related to school and clinical psychology.

HAROLD F. POWELL, PH.D., is Professor of Educational Psychology, Wayne State University. He was formerly a teacher in special education working with behavior problem boys. He also served as a counselor and a school psychologist with the Detroit Public Schools. He is a member of the American Psychological Association and the Michigan Psychological Association. He was a Fulbright lecturer in Italy 1958–59.

WILLIAM J. RUZICKA, PH.D., is a consulting and clinical psychologist in Palo Alto, California. He also teaches part-time in the Department of Psychology at San Francisco State College. He is a member of the American Psychological Association, Divisions of Clinical Psychology and Consulting Psychology.

LOUIS G. SCHMIDT, PH.D., is Professor of Psychology and Chairman of the Psychology Department at California State College, Fullerton. He was Chairman of the Department of Counseling and Guidance at Indiana University from 1952 to 1961. He is a certified psychologist in California and a member of the American Psychological Association.

HIRSCH LAZAAR SILVERMAN, PH.D., SC.D., is Professor of Education, Seton Hall University. He was formerly Professor of Psychology and Chairman of the Department of Educational and School Psychology, Graduate School of Education, Yeshiva University. He is a certified psychologist in New York and New Jersey, and is research clinical and consulting psychologist in the M/R Clinic, New Jersey. He is a fellow of the American Psychological Association, the International Council of Psychologists, the New York Academy of Science, the Gerontological Society, the New Jersey Academy of Science, the American Association on Mental Deficiency, and the American Association for the Advancement of Science. Professor Silverman is the author of eight books and contributes widely to professional magazines and journals both nationally and abroad.

DONALD C. SMITH, PH.D., is Associate Professor of Psychology and Director of the Child Study Center at the Ohio State University. He is also Coordinator of the School Psychology Training Program, editor of the *Journal of School Psychology*, and a member of the Executive Board of Division 16.

VERDUN TRIONE, ED.D., is Director of Research and Instructional Evaluation, Clark County Schools, Las Vegas, Nevada. He was formerly Guidance Coordinator and School Psychologist of Sonoma County and Mendocino County, California. He pioneered school psychology and counseling and testing programs in both counties, and later became Supervisor of Psychological Services, Pittsburg Unified School District in California. He is a member of the American Psychological Association and CASPP. He has a number of publications relating to school psychological services.

J. E. WALLACE WALLIN, PH.D., is a distinguished pioneer in clinical and school psychology and special education in such settings as the Vineland Training School and the St. Louis, Cleveland, and Wilmington school systems. He has established and directed many departments, conducted many research studies, written a multitude of articles and books in these fields, and developed psychological evaluation instruments. He has taught and lectured at many colleges and universities. His professional career—which began in 1900 (PH.D., Yale 1901)—has covered the entire history of these fields in the United States. He is now semi-retired and lives in Wilmington, Delaware.

IRLA LEE ZIMMERMAN, PH.D., is a Diplomate in Clinical Psychology, American Board of Examiners in Professional Psychology. In addition to private practice, she has served as consultant to the California State Department of Education, the Department of Pediatrics at the University of California Medical Center, Los Angeles, and various schools and agencies. Over 25 publications and research studies include work on school phobia, reading retardation, delinquency, and differential diagnosis of emotional and organic impairments.

Contents

7

*Group Appraisal
of School Children,* 171

STANLEY S. MARZOLF

8

*Case Studies and
the Case Conference,* 208

DONALD A. LETON
LOUIS G. SCHMIDT

9

*The School Psychologist and
the Mental Health Needs
of Children,* 234

MAURICE F. FREEHILL

10

*Individual Intellectual Evaluation
of School Children,* 268

IRLA LEE ZIMMERMAN
HIRSCH LAZAAR SILVERMAN

15

16

17

18

School Psychological
Services

J. E. WALLACE WALLIN

DONALD G. FERGUSON

1

The Development
of School Psychological Services

School psychology, now in its second half-century, has
evolved primarily as a consequence of efforts within the
American educational system to develop schools based on
the principle that each learner must be known and
understood and regarded as central in the educative
process. Its evolution demonstrates how American schools
are continuously expanding toward a fuller realization of
the democratic way of life and toward greater service to
the individual and the community. Having a psychologist
to work specifically in the schools stands as a prime example of the inventiveness that has made our nation's
schools the great institutions they are.

This chapter defines the services and discusses the
development of school psychology in light of some major
influences which have contributed to its growth.

Defining School Psychology

No definition of school psychology exists that is
universally acceptable to all in this field even though attempts at definition have long concerned both educators

and psychologists. The American Psychological Association and other professional groups, state departments of education, local boards of education and universities that train specialists in this field are all seeking refined definitions. Each group of definers is motivated by different concerns, has a somewhat different frame of reference, and thus tends to view the role of the school psychologist and the services he should offer somewhat differently.

DEFINITIONS BY PROFESSIONAL ORGANIZATIONS

The American Psychological Association, which is outstanding among the professional groups, looks upon the school psychologist primarily as a psychologist employed by the schools whose job is to apply psychological principles and techniques to school activities. During the 1950's, the APA, Division 16, the Division of School Psychologists, attempted to clarify issues in school psychology. In 1952, the APA identified the school psychologist as a psychologist who practices in an educational setting. He was defined as a person who possessed special skill as both a "clinician and educator." [1] The 1954 Thayer Conference, attended by representatives of many professions, failed to achieve a more adequate definition since the duties of school psychologists at that time were so varied. It was not until 1955 and the publication of the conference report, *School Psychologists at Mid-Century,* that a single definition was achieved. The debate was resolved into the following statement:

> The school psychologist is a psychologist with training and experience in education. He uses his specialized knowledge of assessment, learning, and interpersonal relationships to assist school personnel to enrich the experience and growth of all children, and to recognize and deal with exceptional children.[2]

A more recent statement of the APA appeared in 1958 in another committee report entitled *The Psychologist on the School Staff; Report of the Committee on Reconsideration of the Function of the School Psychologist.* The committee was attempting to determine whether a reasonable consensus as to the function of the school psychologist existed. Also, its purpose was to prepare a clear factual statement in the language of school personnel that would be useful to school staffs in planning and evaluating psychological services. This Division 16 committee, under the chairmanship of T. Ernest

---

[1] American Psychological Association, Division 16, *Annual Report of the Committee on Certification,* mimeographed (December, 1952).

[2] Norma E. Cutts, ed., *School Psychologists at Mid-Century: a Report of the Thayer Conference on the Functions, Qualifications, and Training of School Psychologists* (Washington, D. C.: American Psychological Association, Incorporated, 1955), p. 30.

Newland, is presently working on a revision of the 1958 statement, to be issued in 1967.

The following comment on the training necessary for school psychologists constitutes in effect a definition:

> . . . the school psychologist must be well-trained in the basic concepts of psychology through extensive theoretical and experimental study as well as in clinical techniques. To apply his psychological understandings and skills effectively in the school setting he must also be well-trained in education, thoroughly experienced in work in the school setting, realistic in his understanding of the functions, the methods, and the problems of the school, and appreciative of the present contribution and future possibilities of the teacher in the classroom.[3]

This 1958 report clarifies his role somewhat by outlining twenty types of essential activities carried out by the school psychologist and other pupil personnel workers.[4] The most recent APA Division 16 statement appeared as part of their recommendations to state departments of education for the certification of school psychologists. The statement stresses the need for preparation in both psychology and education. It points out the necessity for training ". . . to develop psychologists who are interested in and knowledgeable about schools, whose contributions are meaningful to and utilized by the teacher because they are based on understanding of the classroom situation and teacher problems as well as on sound psychological knowledge and skills."[5]

In 1966, the California Association of School Psychologists and Psychometrists, the largest state organization in the nation, tentatively defined the practice of school psychology as:

> . . . the application of established principles of learning, motivation, perception, thinking, child development, and emotional relationships to the study of the behavior of school children and their educational concerns. The purpose of such application and study is to facilitate learning and total human development through the prevention, identification, evaluation, and remediation of educational problems and disabilities.

Psychological services were specified as:

> Psychological services are the professional consultation services available from credentialed school psychologists and psychometrists which include, but are

---

[3] American Psychological Association, Division 16, *The Psychologist on the School Staff: Report of the Committee on Reconsideration of the Functions of the School Psychologist,* mimeographed (June, 1958).

[4] American Psychological Association, *Report of the Committee on Relations Between Psychology and Education, Subcommittee on Training of Pupil Personnel Services Staff,* mimeographed (August, 1958).

[5] Division 16 Committee on Training Standards and Certification, "Proposals for State Department of Education Certification of School Psychologists," *The American Psychologist,* 18, No. 11 (1963), 711–714.

not limited to, the individual evaluation of pupils and the subsequent counseling and consulting of parents, pupils, and teachers regarding the prevention, remediation, and placement of children of educational concern or who have learning and behavior disorders.

(a) Psychological services shall emphasize the prevention and early identification of potential learning disorders in children in preschool and primary grades. Psychological services shall be involved in the development of preventive educational programs in consultation with parents and educators.

(b) Psychological services and recommendations shall be based upon the professional observation of pupils behavior, consultation with parents and teachers, the administration, as needed, of tests of general intelligence, perception, specific abilities, educational achievement, personality and motivation, and the integration of all available health and developmental information. Upon the completion of a psychological study of an individual school child the parents shall be requested to meet and consult with the psychologist pertaining to his findings and professional recommendations concerning the child's learning problem and education.

(c) Psychological services should also include . . . the individual psychological evaluation of culturally disadvantaged minors for the purpose of aiding in the planning for providing positive stimulation of their educational and cultural propensities. . . ; the individual psychological evaluation to determine eligibility for early admission to first grade . . . ; identification of the gifted . . . and identification of educationally handicapped minors . . . ; consultation to educators and districts in the selection of particular intelligence and achievement tests and in the development of local testing programs . . . ; the certification of eligibility for admission to classes or schools for the educable mentally retarded . . . and for the trainable mentally retarded . . . ; the individual psychological evaluation, consultation, and referral of school children showing evidence of impaired mental health . . . ; the individual evaluation and subsequent consultation with educators, physicians, parents, and others concerned with all physically handicapped children provided for in special programs and child care centers in the public schools. . . .[6]

DEFINITION BY STATE DEPARTMENTS OF EDUCATION

State departments of education must also be recognized for their role in defining the profession. They view the school psychologist as one among many specialists in educational work. By 1967, forty-one states certified school psychologists. Two purposes, legalistic and administrative, underlie definitions formulated by state departments of education. Concerned with up-grading school psychology, they emphasize traditional regulatory and standard-setting responsibilities: 1) to facilitate their program of certification of the specialist; and 2) to facilitate the administration of a school finance reimbursement program. Several state departments have led the way by formulating definitions and clarifying roles for which they would certificate a specialist and share the cost to the local school district.

[6] CASPP Newsletter, 13 (March, 1966), 11–13.

An Indiana bulletin defines two levels of school psychology in terms of the personnel involved: the school psychometrist and the school psychologist. The pattern in each case defines the specialist in terms of the duties to be performed and the training required. The services of the psychometrist in Indiana are defined as:

> . . . administration of individual and group tests and interpretation of the findings of them; administration or supervision of group-testing programs and interpretation and analysis of test results; supervision of work of testing technicians and receipt of their reports; examination of children for un-graded classes, for classes of mentally retarded or gifted children, or for special classes whenever mental ability of the pupil is a considered factor; study of learning difficulties of children and suggestions for remedial treatment; and consultation with parents, correlating the work of home and school in meeting the personal needs of children.[7]

The definition of the services of the school psychologist is:

> . . . discharge of any and all of the duties of testing technicians and psychometrists as needed; direction and supervision of the work of testing technicians and psychometrists; investigation of personality and social maladjustment of school children; acceptance of responsibility of locating and reporting to proper school officials aspects of the total educational program found to be psychologically damaging; service as consultant to recommend or set up procedures for the development of psychologically constructive learning experience and relationships; initiation and execution of programs of psychological services with children, parents, and staff members; consultation with staff regarding diagnostic and remedial procedures used by teachers and supervisors to overcome learning difficulties or social maladjustments of pupils, and giving advice and assisting teachers and supervisors in the application of such measures; service as consultant in coordinating the work of such other counseling services in the school system as those of guidance workers, deans of girls, deans of boys, vice principals (with deans' functions), visiting teachers, testing technicians and psychometrists.[8]

A statement from the Ohio brochure on certification which defines school psychologists in terms of the scope of service is as follows:

A. Scope of Service
   The primary function of the school psychologist is:
   1. The intensive, individual, psychological study of children. He uses the resulting information and understandings about children in consultation and follow-up services with children, parents, teachers, and other professional workers in the school and in the community.
   As a result of such study and because of his special training he functions as:
   2. A consultant to supervisors and administrators in problems relating to

---

[7] Handbook on Teacher Education, Division of Teacher Training and Licensing of the Indiana Department of Public Instruction, Bulletin 129 (Indianapolis, Indiana: Department of Public Instruction), 65–68.
   [8] *Ibid.*

special education, curriculum, and instruction, group testing, counseling and guidance, pupil personnel policies, and other matters
relating to the adjustment of the individual child in the school setting.
3. A resource person to the school staff and community in developing
better understanding and applications of the principles of child
development, learning, mental health, and the implications of individual differences in an attempt to assure continuing, coordinated,
community planning for the needs of children and youth.[9]

DEFINITION BY LOCAL BOARDS OF EDUCATION

A third contributor to the definition of school psychological services is
local boards of education. They are, of course, limited to fixing programs
locally; however grass roots definitions and job descriptions are more operational than those of either professional organizations or state departments for
they constitute a description of actual programs. There is a reciprocal give-
and-take process through which definitions of the local boards and those of
broader influence serve the same purpose of clarifying the profession. Local
programs are regularly altered on the basis of newer concepts formulated at
the state and national levels. State and national agencies in turn look to the
local district for exploration and experiments implied above upon which to
reorganize their role definitions.

Locally formulated statements of definition and scope of service are
important to practicing school psychologists for they establish their duties and
relationships with other staff members, and set the limits of their responsibility. For the neophyte psychologist, it is important to investigate the definition given to services in the school district in which he is contemplating
employment, because a great variety exists in local definitions. Some view
their specialist as a limited contributor, assigning him only psychometric tasks
for screening and recommendation concerning placement of exceptional
children. On the other extreme are districts which consider the school psychologist an important contributor to school policy in the area of mental
health and assign him considerable responsibility, often having him report
directly to the superintendent. A more comprehensive view of the way programs are defined in local districts occurs in other chapters of this book
where services in different kinds and sizes of school districts are discussed.

DEFINITION BY TRAINING INSTITUTIONS

The fourth and final group contributing to definition are the training
institutions whose responsibility it is to prepare specialists for employment.
Universities, like the three agencies already discussed, have certain biases
and a particular frame of reference from which they approach the question.

---

[9] *Rules and Regulations Governing the Certification of School Employees in
Pupil Personnel Service* (Columbus, Ohio: Department of Education, 1962).

As a group, universities respond to a variety of professional, state, and field pressures that affect their perceptions of school psychology. An interesting question occurs with regard to university training programs: do they follow or lead in the task of defining the profession? Investigation reveals that they do both. On one hand they lead, giving direction to certification change and to developments in the field. Conversely, some institutions tailor their programs to existing state certification patterns and respond largely to field perceptions of role. Although not aligned strictly on a degree basis there is a relationship between leadership shown and the offering of a doctorate degree. Very few states require the doctorate degree for certification. Many more states have universities which prepare school psychologists at the doctoral level where the state statutes do not require this training. In those states where training at the doctoral level is mentioned in certification, the universities seem to have taken a leadership role in formulating certification patterns.[10]

By far the largest number of institutions training school psychologists are doing so at the masters or entry level of preparation. In these programs there is an element of realism emphasizing what will be required of a school psychologist for employment and certification. In these programs, definitions of school psychology tend to be more like those of the field and state departments and are operational. Doctoral programs, on the other hand, tend to deal with emerging roles. An example of the latter is George Peabody College for Teachers and Rutgers University which describe the purposes of their programs as the preparation of generic psychologists to apply their skills to the educational, social, and personal problems of school systems and individual children. The Peabody view of the school psychologist and the curriculum to train him

> ". . . is based on the belief that the psychologist best qualified to help his school system meet its educational and social problems is one who has well-developed research attitudes and skills along with a thorough grounding in the basic areas of psychology. The psychologist's problem solving orientation is seen as enabling him to approach school and community problems in an empirical, data oriented way which will help provide the evidence upon which school officials can base sound decisions." [11]

Singleness of definition has not characterized school psychology to date and it is unlikely in the foreseeable future. Variety and emergence will prevail as in most areas of educational and psychological specialization.

[10] Arthur J. Bindman, "University Training of School Psychologists and Certification Standards," *Journal of School Psychology*, 2, No. 1 (1964), 43–48, and also D. G. Ferguson, "Training Programs in School Psychology," in Gottsegen and Gottsegen, *op. cit.*, pp. 287–305.

[11] Jack I. Bardon, ed., "Problems and Issues in School Psychology–1964: Proceedings of a Conference on 'New Directions in School Psychology.' Sponsored by the National Institute of Mental Health, June 22–24, 1964," *Journal of School Psychology*, 3, No. 2 (1965). This issue lists the training programs in the U. S. and describes many of them.

Major Influences in the Advent and
Development of School Psychology

In the next several pages, attention is given to influences affecting the evolution of school psychology. Some of these stem directly from theories and practices in education; others derive from aspects of society outside of education. Several major influences have been selected to give the reader perspective and direct him to sources where he may find a more detailed analysis.

Before the twentieth century, the need for service was felt. This growing need plus the development and refinement of the testing movement, the growth of the field of psychology and the behavioral sciences, the mental health movement and special education, and the influence of professional organizations all helped develop a new school specialist—the school psychologist.

EARLY NEED FOR PSYCHOLOGICAL SERVICE IN SCHOOL

Two events, the work of Lightner Witmer at the University of Pennsylvania and the development of a child study center in connection with the Chicago public schools, are generally credited with beginning school psychology in America.

First recommendations for psychological service in schools. Lightner Witmer, who was head of the psychological laboratory at the University of Pennsylvania, undertook to apply psychological techniques to school problems when he worked with a boy who was deficient in English.[12] Although Witmer was not entirely satisfied that his experiment was successful, the boy later entered the university. Witmer's second attempt had as its subject a fourteen-year-old boy whose problem was reported by his teacher as an inability to spell. A diagnostic study determined that the primary cause of the child's difficulty was visual, and following the correction of this deficiency, the child soon learned to spell. Additional cases of retardation in school learning were then referred to the laboratory. In December, 1896, recognizing the value of diagnostic and treatment centers and believing himself to be equipped with sufficient experience to offer practical programs for laboratory work in the field, Witmer recommended a program of action to the American Psychological Association. Furthermore, as a result of his experiences, he foresaw a

---

[12] R. A. Brotemarkle, ed., *Clinical Psychology: Studies in Honor of Lightner Witmer to Commemorate the Thirty-fifth Anniversary of the Founding of the First Psychological Clinic* (Philadelphia: University of Pennsylvania Press, 1931), as reported in Cutts, *School Psychologists at Mid-Century*, pp. 17–19.

need for the cooperation of education and psychology to produce a new brand of psychologist possessing the special knowledge and resourcefulness to deal successfully with problems of mental and moral retardation in school children. He believed that the training necessary for this specialist was not possessed by either clinical psychologists, educators, or social workers. "In fact, we must look forward," he said, "to the training of men to a new profession which will be exercised more particularly in connection with educational problems but for which the training of the psychologist will be a prerequisite." [13]

Early Chicago efforts. On September 6, 1899, the public schools of Chicago established through the efforts of Walter S. Christopher the "Department of Child Study and Pedagogic Investigation" (now known as the Bureau of Child Study). Its establishment was also the result of the recommendations of two committees for the establishment of a department for the "scientific study of the physical and mental development of children," especially by the methods of "physiological psychology."

The primary functions of this pioneering development in the American public school system, that served as a prototype of latter developments elsewhere, were: 1) the collection of anthropometric and physical measurements for the establishment of age norms on height, weight, endurance, strength, motor control, and visual and auditory acuity; 2) the application of scientific methods to the study of many specific educational problems suggested by the school staff; 3) the examination of individual problem children (the acoustically and visually handicapped, subnormals, delinquents, etc.;) and 4) the instruction of teachers and principals. A "psycho-physical laboratory" was added to the department on April 4, 1900, for individual examinations on Saturdays. When the program of clinical examinations began is unclear, but during the first three years emphasis of the department was placed on the scientific study of the "laws of growth and mental development and on the establishment of age norms of physical development."

Unfortunately, no mental norms were ever published comparable with the extensive anthropometric data.[14] No exact information can be obtained about the nature of the psychological tests used in the Chicago laboratory during its pioneer days. Based on a statement made by MacMillan,[15] however, they were simple, disparate tests of "perception, memory, association, attention, imagination, and judgment," which were described as "perfectly workable for prediction purposes." To a large extent they probably consisted of

[13] Cutts, *op. cit.,* p. 18.

[14] Daniel P. MacMillan, "The Physical and Mental Examination of Public School Pupils in Chicago," *Charities and the Commons,* 17 (December 22, 1906), pp. 529–535; Fred W. Smedley, "Report of the Department of Child Study and Pedagogic Investigation," in the *Annual Reports* of the Board of Education in Chicago for 1899–1900 and 1900–1901.

[15] *Ibid.*

sensory tests employed in the Frank G. Bruner study of primitive people at the Louisiana Purchase Exposition in St. Louis in 1904, that had been enlarged upon as time went on.

THE INFLUENCE OF THE TESTING MOVEMENT

Although the scope of modern school psychology is much broader than psychometrics, testing constitutes a major contribution that the psychologist makes to the school's program. Psychologists must keep informed of new developments in testing, for they are often called upon as "test experts." Also there is a close cause-and-effect relationship between developments in the testing movement and those in school psychology. This close relationship and the importance of its influence are seen in a historical review.

The demand for scientific measurement techniques in the schools was based on many factors: studies of school retardation which heightened the demand for sectioning classes; the insistent demand for a more exact determination of the nature, extent, and causes of individual differences and deviations among pupils; the need for the development of more effective psychological and educational adjustment procedures to meet the conditions found; and the growing demand for the introduction of scientific methods in the study of psycho-educational problems. The cumulative effect of all these diverse pressures gradually produced a veritable revolution in school procedures and practices.

The beginning of psychological testing in modern times. From its very modest beginning in Germany in the psychophysics laboratories of Ernst H. Weber in 1834, Gustav T. Fechner in 1860, and Wilhelm Wundt in 1879, psychological testing rapidly spread into areas of practical usefulness.

In the sixties of the nineteenth century, Francis Galton, a distinguished British anthropologist and eugenicist and a pioneer student of mental measurement and of individual differences and their distribution, conducted various studies in mental imagery, weight discrimination, sensitivity to high pitches, association, and reaction time.[16] Emil Kraepelin, a German psychiatrist, used association tests as early as 1883 for making differential diagnoses between normal and psychotic persons. In 1887, an American physician, E. S. Chaille, used a few simple tests for estimating the intelligence level of youngsters to age three, which apparently never came into use, while J. Jacobs employed a graded series of letters and digits for measuring auditory memory span.

James McKeen Cattell, perhaps the first psychologist to employ the term "mental tests," in various articles appearing between 1885 and 1900,

---

[16] Condensed from J. E. Wallace Wallin, *Clinical and Abnormal Psychology, a Textbook for Educators, Psychologists, and Mental Hygiene Workers* (Boston: Houghton Mifflin Company, 1927), pp. 94–98.

emphasized the importance of studying individual differences with the aid of standardized tests. In 1896, he published the results of the tests given to Columbia College freshmen that measured strength of grip, reaction time, pain, memory, imagery, and various simple sensory processes. In 1893, J. A. Gilbert compared teachers' estimates of general ability of 1,200 pupils with scores made in tests of sensory discrimination, rapidity of tapping, simple choice reactions, memory, and various other measurements. In 1895, Hermann Ebbinghaus made his significant experimental study of memory, which was followed two years later by his celebrated "completion test" (involving the supplying of missing syllables and words in a mutilated text), conceived as a test of general intelligence, still a constituent of many such tests.

Of major significance during this pioneering period for the development of practical tests of general ability or intelligence were the trenchant criticisms of Alfred Binet and Victor Henri in 1894 and 1895. They emphasized the importance of study of more complex intellectual functions such as memory, creative imagination, attention, judgment, comprehension, synthesis, etc., rather than the study of simpler sensory processes. This shift of emphasis is reflected in their emerging scale of intelligence.

Up to the beginning of the twentieth century, little attempt had been made to standardize testing techniques, to establish age norms of performance, to combine discrete tests into unified or composite batteries of tests, or to utilize test results for the purpose of individual diagnosis or for practical life adjustment. These became the major goals of the next decade or two. The significant developments in these areas helped pave the way for the development of school psychology and the birth of the school psychologist. In this highly ramified movement, the invention of the individual or clinical scales of general intelligence occupies the lead position.

The individual or clinical scales of intelligence.   The first of these measuring scales were those devised in 1895 by Sante de Sanctis, professor of psychiatry at the University of Rome and director of a day school for mental deficients; by Alfred Binet, distinguished psychologist at the Sorbonne; and by Theodore Simon, Parisian psychiatrist. The de Sanctis scale consists of six simple tests arranged in ascending order of difficulty.[17] It was used to a limited extent at the Training School * at Vineland, New Jersey by Henry Goddard and in J. E. Wallace Wallin's early clinics, but acquired little vogue in this country because of the appearance of the 1905 Binet-Simon Scale. This Binet

[17] Henry H. Goddard, "The Grading of Backward Children, The de Sanctis Tests and the Binet and Simon Tests of Intellectual Capacity," *Training School*, 5 (November and December, 1908); Sante de Sanctis, "Mental Development and the Measurement of the Level of Intelligence," *Journal of Educational Psychology*, 2 (1911), 498–507.

* In 1965, the Training School was renamed American Institute for Mental Studies.

scale, far more elaborate, consisted of thirty simple tests in graded steps, including tests of memory span, attention, ability to form associations, adaptability, judgment, reasoning, and the like.[18] This scale was displaced by the 1908 scale in which fifty-nine similar tests were arranged in chronological age steps from three to thirteen.[19] The age arrangement made it possible to assign mental age (or more properly intelligence age) equivalents for the scores and later intelligence quotients. The intelligence quotient concept (IQ) was popularized by Lewis M. Terman in 1916.[20] The 1911 revision consisted merely of eliminations of some tests, transpositions of others, and some additions.[21]

The first American version and adaptation of the Binet based on the performance of school children in the United States was made by Henry H. Goddard in 1911. The Goddard standardization spread rapidly, over 30,000 copies being distributed in about fifteen years.[22]

Standardized group tests of intelligence. The hectic demands of World War I for a quick objective means of classifying masses of military recruits according to general ability led to the development in 1917 of the first standardized group intelligence tests, the Army Alpha, consisting of eight verbal tests, and the Army Beta, consisting of a half-dozen pictorial performance tests intended particularly for illiterates and soldiers deficient in the understanding of English.[23] These tests, equipped with readily scorable stencils and total or pooled scores, served as models for later test construction.

In 1918, Arthur S. Otis published the first group battery of intelligence tests standardized on pupils in American schools from fourth grade to college level.[24]

Individual performance or psychometer tests. So far as can be ascertained, the first individual performance tests used for clinical purposes were the form boards, the prototype of which was the Séguin form board devised by Edward Séguin for the training of mental deficients, particularly of the lower grades.

[18] Goddard, *ibid.*; Frank S. Freeman, *Theory and Practice of Psychological Testing* (New York: Holt, Rinehart & Winston, Inc., 1950), pp. 103–106; Guy M. Whipple, *Manual of Mental and Physical Tests* (Baltimore: Warwick and York, 1910), pp. 473–492.

[19] Freeman, *ibid.*, pp. 106–110; Whipple, *ibid.*, pp. 493–517; H. H. Goddard, "A Measuring Scale for Intelligence," *The Training School*, 6 (1910), 146–154.

[20] Lewis M. Terman, *The Measurement of Intelligence* (Boston: Houghton Mifflin Company, 1916).

[21] Freeman, *op. cit.*, pp. 110–112.

[22] H. H. Goddard, "A Revision of the Binet Scale," *The Training School Bulletin*, 8 (1911), 56–62.

[23] Clarence S. Yoakum and Robert M. Merkes, *Army Mental Tests* (New York: Rinehart & Winston, Inc., 1920), p. 303.

[24] Arthur S. Otis, *Group Intelligence Scale, Forms A and B* (New York: Harcourt, Brace & World, Inc., 1918).

The 10-block form board, used by Naomi Norsworthy about 1906 in the examination of mental retardates, presumably was an adaptation of the Séguin. Goddard utilized an adaptation of the Norsworthy board in the Training School; however, he did not publish anything on his modification until 1912.[25]

It has not been possible to learn how long before 1912 the board had been used at Vineland, but it certainly was in use in the summer school of 1910 when Wallin was connected with the institution. It remained for years the most frequently employed form board of those which appeared in rapid succession during the next decade or two, due in part to the availability of adequate norms that had been supplied by Goddard,[26] Reuel H. Sylvester,[27] and Wallin.[28] Moreover, it proved to be one of the best devices available for observing the reaction characteristics of the respondent.

The earliest performance test specifically designed for very young children was the peg board first used in 1914 for the selection of the prize winners in a better-babies contest in St. Louis.[29]

Trade and aptitude tests. The distinction usually drawn between a trade and an aptitude test is that the former reveals the amount of proficiency that an applicant already possesses in a given trade or occupation, while the aptitude test shows the degree of underlying ability or potential that he possesses for acquiring proficiency in a given vocation as a result of training. As early as 1918, army psychologists devised trade tests (eventually in eighty-four occupations) designed to show whether the candidates for work assignment possessed the proficiency they claimed. The tests consisted of a series of questions designed to reveal whether they possessed intimate knowledge of a given trade, the naming of the pictures of tools and explaining their uses, and the actual performance of specific jobs. The army psychologists also devised some aptitude tests.[30] In civilian life as early at 1912 or 1913, Hugo Münsterberg, then professor of psychology at Harvard, developed tests for the selection of street car motormen and telephone operators.[31] But the first attempt to develop definite aptitude tests administered under conditions of

[25] Henry H. Goddard, "The Form Board as a Measure of Intellectual Development in Children," *The Training School,* 9 (1912), 49–52.

[26] *Ibid.*

[27] Reuel H. Sylvester, "The Form Board Test," Psychological Monographs, 14 (1913), 56.

[28] J. E. Wallace Wallin, "Psycho-motor Norms for Practical Diagnosis," Psychological Monographs, 22, No. 94 (1916), 102; "Age Norms of Psycho-motor Capacity," *The Journal of Educational Psychology,* 7 (January, 1916), 17–25.

[29] J. E. Wallace Wallin, "The Peg Board Forms," *Psychological Clinic,* 12 (April, 1916), 40–53.

[30] J. Crosby Chapman, *Trade Tests* (New York: Holt, Rinehart & Winston, Inc., 1921), p. 435.

[31] Hugo Münsterberg, *Psychology and Industrial Efficiency* (Boston: Houghton Mifflin Company, 1912), Chapter VIII.

control seems to have been made by Louis L. Thurstone for prospective telegraphers, office clerks, and engineering students.[32]

The first individual test of general mechanical ability was constructed in 1923 by John L. Stenquist, founder of the Bureau of Educational Research in the Baltimore public schools. The client was required to assemble various disassembled objects, such as a mousetrap, a door lock, a bicycle bell, a push button, or a sash fastener.[33] Aptitude tests are now available by the hundreds in many areas.

Character and personality tests. The first attempt to measure personality characteristics objectively and quantitatively seems to have been made by Edward C. Elliott in 1910 by means of a weighted rating scale that involved the rating of one hundred traits. However, no definite information is available on the scale.[34] Better known is the man-to-man officers' Rating Scale devised in 1917 or 1918 by the Committee on Classification of Personnel in the United States Army. In rating an officer with respect to each of five traits, the rater calls to mind five officers well-known to him who occupy five positions on the scale of a given trait. The ratee is assigned a position on each of the five traits.[35]

The personal data sheet made by Robert S. Woodworth, published in 1919,[36] was a psychoneurotic questionnaire or self-rating inventory designed to screen out unreliable or neurotic soldiers on the basis of the neurotic symptoms revealed by the answers to such questions as: did you ever stutter? have you ever lost your memory? are you bothered with nightmares? do you blush frequently? and are you treated right by your teachers? That same year the Pressey Cross-Out Tests of emotional characteristics appeared.[37] From these modest beginnings have sprung hundreds of tests, many highly complicated and subtle and of varying degrees of reliability, which are designed to give information on personality attributes.

The most prolific development of standardized tests has occurred in the area of educational achievement. According to one estimate, over 2,600 achievement tests of all kinds had been produced up to 1940.[38]

[32] Louis L. Thurstone, "Mental Tests for Prospective Telegraphers," *Journal of Applied Psychology*, 3 (1919), 110–117; "A Standardized Test for Office Clerks," *ibid.*, pp. 248–251; "Mental Tests for Engineering Students," *Proceedings of the Society for Promotion of Engineering Education*, 27 (1919), 113–119.

[33] John L. Stenquist, *Measurement of Mechanical Ability* (New York: Teachers' College Contributions to Education, No. 130, 1923), p. 101.

[34] Wallin, *Clinical and Abnormal Psychology*, *op. cit.*, p. 562.

[35] Walter D. Scott, "The Official Method of Rating Army Officers," *Psychological Bulletin*, 16 (1919), 52–53.

[36] Personal Data Sheet, C. H. Stoelting Co. (n.d.).

[37] Sidney L. Pressey and Luella C. Pressey, " 'Cross-Out' Tests, with Suggestions as to a Group Scale of the Emotions," *Journal of Applied Psychology*, 3 (1919), 138–150.

[38] *Encyclopedia of Educational Research* (1950), p. 1461.

Standarized group achievement tests. The first achievement scale seems to have been the "scale of instruction" devised in France by V. Varney and Alfred Binet at an undetermined date. The scale, without evidence of objective standarization, embraced five stages of accomplishment in reading, spelling, and arithmetic from the preparatory stage (age six and seven) to the intermediate second stage (ages ten to eleven).[39]

The first scientifically established American achievement tests with grade norms were the arithmetic tests by Clarence W. Stone and by Stuart A. Courtis which appeared in 1910. Stone's tests measured the proficiency of sixth graders in the four fundamental operations and in problem solving.[40] The "Courtis Arithmetic Tests," the first such tests to become widely used throughout the country, were often used as survey tests and ranged from third grade through high school.[41] In Thorndike's handwriting scale, samples of handwriting are arranged on a chart in the order of merit. Each submitted specimen is placed on the scale and assigned a statistically determined numerical value.[42] This pioneer scale served as a pattern for later qualitative scales.

The first unified battery of achievement tests in different branches of instruction yielding pooled or total score seems to have been the attainment scale devised in 1920 by Sidney L. Pressey for use in the second grade. It included tests in spelling, arithmetic, reading, vocabulary, and sentence meaning.[43] Similar scales were provided the next year for the second and eighth grades. Such batteries eventually achieved great popularity for survey and placement purposes.

Diagnostic achievement tests. All educational tests are diagnostic to a certain extent. But some tests have been designed specifically to reveal the particular weaknesses or strengths of a pupil in different aspects of a given field. Most such tests are diagnostic only in the sense that they reveal the nature of the child's particular difficulties. They do not necessarily reveal the cause of the difficulties found. Nevertheless, diagnostic tests are of the greatest value to the school psychologist and teacher in supplying cues for remedial or diagnostic treatment.

[39] Alfred Binet and Theodore Simon, *Mentally Defective Children,* trans. W. B. Drummond (London: Edward Arnold, Ltd., 1914), pp. 54–64.

[40] Clarence W. Stone, *Arithmetical Abilities and Some Factors Determining Them* (New York: Teachers' College Contributions to Education, 1908).

[41] Stuart A. Courtis, "Measurement of Growth and Efficiency in Arithmetic," *Elementary School Teacher,* 10 (1909), 58–74, 177–199; 15 (1910), 171–178, 360–370, 528–539.

[42] Edward L. Thorndike, "Handwriting," *Teachers College Record,* 11 (1910), 1–81.

[43] Sidney L. Pressey, "Scale of Attainment No. 1: An Examination of Achievement in the Second Grade," *Journal of Educational Research,* 1 (September, 1920), 572–581.

Diagnostic tests or scales appeared in the field of motor activity near the beginning of the testing movement. Thorndike's "general merit scale" in handwriting has already been mentioned. Next to appear was Ayres' "legibility scale," in 1912, in which the specimens of handwriting are matched with eight standardized samples of varying degrees of slant, backhand, and mixed patterns.[44] In the Frank N. Freeman chart for diagnosing faults in handwriting, 1914, the specimens were rated in uniformity of slant, uniformity of alignment, and quality of line, letter formation, and spacing.[45]

In the field of literary academics, the first diagnostic test was Walter S. Monroe's "Diagnostic Tests in Arithmetic, Part I," that appeared in 1917 (however, the test blank itself is undated.) It consisted of six simple, timed tests in addition, subtraction, multiplication, and division.[46] By modern standards it can scarcely be classified as a diagnostic test.

Summarizing the testing movement, it is impossible to determine the exact number of standardized tests now available, but school psychologists have at their disposal far more tests of varying degrees of standardization and validity than they will ever be able to use. The latest volume of the *Mental Measurements Yearbook*,[47] lists 160 group intelligence tests of all kinds, 46 individual intelligence tests, and 195 character and personality tests. One must intelligently select a limited number of tests with adequate validity, reliability, and diagnostic penetration for specific evaluations, such as the evaluation of intelligence, performance, and achievement levels, specific aptitudes and disabilities, and personality assessments. In Chapter 7, the reader will be introduced to the role of the school psychologist in the school group testing program. This chapter will present some of the group tests used in today's schools.

THE INFLUENCE OF DEVELOPMENTS IN PSYCHOLOGY AND OTHER BEHAVIORAL SCIENCES

Scientific and applied psychology owe debts to several nineteenth century physiologists: Ernst Heinrich Weber, Johannes Müller, Gustav Theodor Fechner, Hermann von Helmholtz, and especially to Wilhelm Wundt. The work of these men led to the founding of the science of psychology. Wundt, who established the first psychological laboratory at Leipzig in 1879, is generally credited with providing unity to the work of his prede-

---

[44] Leonard P. Ayres, *A Scale for the Measurement of the Quality of Handwriting of School Children*, Bulletin No. 113 (New York: Russell Sage Foundation, 1912).

[45] Frank N. Freeman, *The Teaching of Handwriting* (Boston: Houghton Mifflin Company, 1914).

[46] Walter S. Monroe, *Diagnostic Tests in Arithmetic* (Bloomington, Illinois: Public School Publishing Co., 1917).

[47] Oscar Krisen Buros, ed., *The Sixth Mental Measurements Yearbook* (Highland Park, New Jersey: The Gryphon Press, 1965).

cessors and contemporaries which brought into being this new science. His book, *Physiological Psychology*, according to Heidbreder, ". . . is generally considered more than any other single book to draft the first constitution for psychology as an independent science." [48]

Acknowledging the above, authorities generally recognize that school psychology and other areas of applied psychology bear an even closer kinship with the pioneer work of Charles Darwin, Francis Galton, and others from the area of evolutionary biology. These were men whose concentrations were less on man as a physiological mechanism and more upon the observation, analysis, and prediction of human behavior.

In France and Italy, as well as Germany and England, late in the nineteenth century contributions were being made to the traditions which underlie modern school psychology, clinical psychology, abnormal psychology, educational psychology, and the child-study movement. In France, Phillippe Pinel and Jean-Martin Charcot were laying the groundwork for the modern fields of abnormal psychology and psychiatry. Alfred Binet was deeply engrossed in problems of measuring human intelligence and the development of an instrument for this purpose. Also in Italy men were expressing an interest in the diagnosis and treatment of abnormal human behavior. At the turn of the century Sante de Sanctis initiated the clinical procedure commonly known today as the team approach. Wall states:

> . . . as early as 1899, Sante de Sanctis, recognizing that psychiatry was not the only, or even the most important, discipline involved in the guidance of abnormal children, initiated a cross-disciplinary approach. In his *Asili Scuola per Anormali Psichici* he instituted a consultation based upon a team which included, as well as the psychiatrist, a specialized teacher, a psychologist, and a social worker.[49]

In America as well as abroad, during the latter part of the nineteenth century, the beginning of a new science of psychology was becoming apparent. Here, as in the several European countries mentioned, the most prominent pioneer of the new science, William James, was trained in physiology and biology and was a physician rather than a psychologist. Although James himself never founded or even adhered to any particular school in psychology, he left a permanent endowment to the traditions marking the beginning of the science; and he authored one of the earliest American texts in psychology, *The Principles of Psychology*. James had a profound effect on both American psychology and education; and, although his contribution could not be regarded as direct to the field of school psychology, his influence in its evolution is profound.

[48] E. Heidbreder, *Seven Psychologies* (New York: Appleton-Century-Crofts, 1933), p. 93.
[49] Wall, *op. cit.*, pp. 18–19.

American contributions to the development of psychology have been numerous and varied. Two areas of particular significance in relation to school psychology stand out: First, the field of learning theory and the work of experimental psychologists; and second, the field of personality theory and its application in clinical psychology.

Of the many individuals who have been dominant in American learning theory, several are distinguished for their contributions to education and school psychology: Edward Lee Thorndike, John Broadus Watson, Burrhus Frederick Skinner, and Neil Elgar Miller.

Thorndike, prominent in experimental work in animal learning and the development of psychological tests, is generally credited with providing definition for the emerging field of educational psychology in this country. John Watson, founder of the school of behaviorism in psychology, influenced classroom procedures and child-raising methods throughout the nation. In many ways Watson, although not an educational theorist himself, had a profound influence on American educational theory. Watson was to psychology what Dewey was to American education. While Dewey became a pragmatist and concentrated on educational theory, Watson promoted child-raising and educational practices based on pragmatic theory concerning how learning and behavioral modifications occur. He made parents and teachers alike aware of the effect of controlled learning conditions as a means of behavioral modification.

Another prominent American psychologist who has contributed recently to educational practices through the application of learning theory to specific educational activities is B. F. Skinner, one of America's outspoken advocates of machine teaching. The teaching machine may not revolutionize education, but its effect will be important. The teaching machine is based on knowledge that instructional results in the past have been too slow to satisfy learning requirements based on stimulus-response theory. With machine teaching the student knows almost immediately whether his responses are correct or incorrect. In this controlled situation he cannot repeat mistakes, and is able to identify errors more quickly. A second principle claimed by the supporters of teaching machines is that they are adapted uniquely to the individual learner in a way not possible for a teacher if she is working with a number of youngsters.

Another example of the application of learning theory to school activities and to problems confronting school psychologists is the work of Neil Miller, a Yale psychologist and learning theorist. Through collaboration with John Dollard, Miller has worked toward the formulation of a rationale for social learning, blending learning theory and sociological theory.[50] Recently their work has encompassed some psychoanalytic theory into a view concerning the development of behavior and the treatment of abnormal be-

[50] N. E. Miller and J. Dollard, *Social Learning and Imitation* (New Haven: Yale University Press, 1941).

havior.[51] The activities of this "Yale Group" are having an increased effect on the thinking and practices of school psychologists.

A continuing problem for learning theorists is the attempt to delineate criteria by which human behavior can be evaluated, predicted, and be better understood. Within the school setting, the psychologist is regularly called upon to do this. He is drawn into curriculum committees, for example, as an expert in the field of human behavior, to aid these committees in the formulation of clear and measurable goals for instruction. Similarly, he aids in the construction or selection of evaluation and measurement devices. It is to the field of experimental psychology that the future school psychologist will turn in order to contribute more effectively in the school setting.

The second major contribution of psychology to the development of school psychology has been in the area of personality theory and clinical psychology. From the clinical aspect of this behavioral science school psychologists derive their primary skills and competencies. This fact makes for a very close tie between these branches of psychology.

A discussion of the nature of personality theory by Hall and Lindzey explains further the congruence between personality theory and clinical psychology and school psychology.[52] In analyzing the influence that brought about the modern field of personality theory, they cite the tradition of clinical observation, the gestalt tradition with its emphasis on carefully controlled empirical research and theory construction, and the psychometric tradition. Personality theorists, they claim, have assigned a great deal of importance to the motivational process and have always been functional in their orientation. They contrast personality theory with activities in other areas of psychology and state that ". . . personality theory has occupied a dissident role in the development of psychology." [53] While the experimentalists concentrated on the analysis of segments of human behavior such as motor skills, perception, or audition, the personality theorist was attending to the need for a theoretical framework to explain human behavior, emphasizing the need to study the whole person.

Like the personality theorist and clinician, the school psychologist is compelled to consider the whole person. He must relate his findings and investigations to practices in the school in an attempt to effect a better adjustment for the client. He observes and measures a variety of specific aspects of behavior, but in the final analysis must integrate his findings toward a course of action within the framework of what is feasible in the school setting. He is operationally oriented and compelled to deal with the total behavior of the human being.

---

[51] See N. E. Miller and J. Dollard, *Personality and Psychotherapy* (New York: McGraw-Hill Book Company, 1950).

[52] C. S. Hall and G. Lindzey, *Theories of Personality* (New York: John Wiley & Sons, Inc., 1957).

[53] *Ibid.*, p. 4.

Another of the behavioral sciences that has effected the development of school psychology is sociology, and in particular, educational sociology. As defined by Brown, "educational sociology is the study of the interaction of the individual and his cultural environment, which includes other individuals, social groups, and patterns of behavior." [54] Sociology, like psychology, is a relatively new science beginning in the middle 1800's. August Comte, credited by authorities as its founder, was the first to use the term sociology, but the field did not become clarified and extended until 1876 when Herbert Spencer published his *Principles of Sociology*.

Sociology was being shaped into a science along with psychology at a time when some philosophers were turning their attention to a social conception of man. As stated by Butts and Cremin, the social conception of man, a major orientation that appeared in America prior to World War I, proved to be very influential in shaping American education. They state:

> It centered upon a social conception of human nature, thinking and learning. Whereas idealism had found the distinctive element in man to be spiritual and objective, psychology had found it to be in man's biological action system, a whole series of philosophers and psychologists began to find the distinctive nature of man in his social relationships with other human beings.[55]

The social theory of the late 1800's, and in particular that formulated by George H. Mead, has significantly influenced American education. Prior to this period, dominant beliefs regarded man as a spiritual entity, paying little attention to his social relationships and experiences, acknowledging these only as qualities that separated man from lower animal forms. Psychology, being in a large measure an offshoot of physiology and evolutionary biology, viewed man as essentially an inherited biological organism, who, though modifiable, would proceed in the direction which was determined by his inherited structure, basic drives and motives. Mead and a few others of the period viewed man more as a product of social interaction. The child, they claimed, develops a self and mind through communication with others. The self, rather than existing at first, emerges as the individual learns to distinguish between himself and others and as he assimilates attitudes and outlooks of others.

THE INFLUENCE OF THE MENTAL HEALTH AND
CHILD-CENTERED EDUCATIONAL MOVEMENTS

American schools have been interested in mental health for as long as the concept has existed. Mental health is generally viewed as a community

54 F. J. Brown, *Educational Sociology* (Englewood Cliffs, N. J.: Prentice-Hall, Inc., 1947).

55 R. Butts and L. A. Cremin, *A History of Education in American Culture* (New York: Holt, Rinehart & Winston, Inc., 1953).

responsibility with the schools occupying an important leadership position. The school is the only agency in the community that has contact with all children during a large part of their formative and developmental years. It also has a unique opportunity to work with parents.

Evidence of the schools' increasing interest is formal instruction in mental health topics. Similarly through an increased emphasis on child-centered and problem-centered teaching, a greater awareness of mental health issues and desirable mental health practices has become manifest throughout most school activities. While identification and correction of mental health problems among school children has long concerned specialists, more recently their attention is being focused on the school's role in positive mental health and in primary prevention, that is " . . . the promotion of mental health and the lowering of the risk of mental disorder in a population of children by interfering with pathogenic forces within the children and in their biologic, psychologic, and social environment before the appearance of identifiable pathology." [56]

Contributors to the mental health movement. The beginning of scientific child study and subsequent mental hygiene concerns predates the advent of school psychology in this country. Its beginnings seem to have been in England, and its origins according to Wall ". . . are to be found in the work of the evolutionary biologists of the latter half of the nineteenth century." [57] Wall presents a rather detailed discussion of the impact that the child guidance movement has had on the development of school psychological services in this country and several European countries. He points out that ten years before Witmer established the psychological clinic at the University of Pennsylvania, Francis Galton established a Child Guidance Center at University College, London.

The beginnings of the mental hygiene movement in this country are generally credited to Clifford Beers and his publication, *A Mind That Found Itself.* [58] Beers had been a mental patient, and from this experience he turned his attention to the prevention and treatment of mental health problems. In 1917, the first issue of the *Mental Hygiene* magazine was published, beginning a tradition of reporting the mental health status and needs in the nation.

Concerning the impact of the mental hygiene movement on the schools and school psychological services, Cutts states:

> The mental-hygiene movement and the emphasis on the importance of the early years of life and the "whole child" served to focus attention on the

[56] Gerald Caplan, ed., *Prevention of Mental Disorders in Children: Initial Explorations* (New York: Basic Books, Inc., Publishers, 1961), p. 17.

[57] Wall, *op. cit.*, p. 14.

[58] C. W. Beers, *A Mind That Found Itself* (New York: Longmans, Green & Co., Inc., 1908).

school as the first institution where work in mental hygiene might be done and on the work which the school psychologists were already doing. As a result some mental-hygiene and family-welfare societies collaborated with school psychologists to secure psychiatric and social-work service for children.[59]

By the 1920s, child guidance clinics were being established throughout the nation. Initially they were sponsored by the Commonwealth Fund and were concerned primarily with the detection and prevention of juvenile delinquency. More recently, in addition to a great increase in the number of established clinics, their programs and emphasis have broadened to include community education and treatment programs in connection with a variety of mental health problems besides juvenile delinquency.[60]

A variety of school reforms were occuring during the closing years of the nineteenth century. In a discussion of the foundations of American education, Rugg points to four Americans as having had the greatest influence in bringing about changes in general educational philosophy to "an original philosophy of experience:" Peirce; James; Dewey; and Veblen. Along with a more comprehensive analysis concerning their contributions Rugg makes these short summary comments:

> Charles Sanders Peirce, mathematician and logician; the founder of the current operational psychology and the primitive form of the philosophy known variously as "pragmatism" or "experimentalism."
>
> William James, author of the first fully integrative psychology of experience.
>
> John Dewey, first to make a full statement of the organic, experimental and functional psychology and the first to found a laboratory elementary school on a consistent theory in psychology.
>
> Thorstein Veblen, America's first social psychologist and pioneer student of the economic system.[61]

Progressive education as a movement in America lasted a relatively short time, and as an organization only from 1919 to 1955. The Progressive Education Association never developed a large membership, but the effect of the movement extended far beyond the Association.

It revolted against the dominant contemporary theories of essentialism and perennialism. Handlin in discussing *John Dewey's Challenge to Education* points out that Dewey's ideas and the significance of progressive education become meaningful only when the shortcomings of the "good old system" against which they were in revolt are understood.[62]

---

[59] Cutts, *op. cit.*, p. 24.

[60] Wesley Allinsmith and George W. Geothals, *The Role of Schools in Mental Health* (New York: Basic Books, Inc., Publishers, 1962).

[61] Harold Rugg, *Foundations for American Education* (New York: Harcourt, Brace & World, Inc., 1947), pp. 74–75.

[62] Oscar Handlin, *John Dewey's Challenge to Education* (New York: Harper & Row, Publishers, 1959), p. 16.

Dewey and the progressives focused attention on the individual learner as being of central importance in the educational process. They emphasized the employment of methods of instruction that were consistent with principles of child development and with the proposition that learning must proceed out of the experiences of the learner. Dewey's own definition of education is interesting in light of its focus on the role of the learner's experiences in the learning process. He defined education as "that reconstruction or reorganization of experience which adds to the meaning of experience and which increases ability to direct the course of subsequent experience." [63] He and his followers believed that the curriculum should be built around the experiences of the learner rather than from fixed and absolute authority. They believed in and supported the "whole child" concept, emphasizing the viewpoint that the child is more nonclassroom-oriented than school-oriented.

Child-study movement. Among other developments occuring in education and influencing the evolution of school psychology, the child-study movement deserves attention. The concept of childstudy helped to spotlight the role of the classroom teacher as the key figure in child-centered education. Also, it accentuated the need for child-study specialists—school psychologists and others—to aid teachers in their dealings with students in the classroom and to provide specific help in identifying and providing for exceptional children.

Evidence that childstudy has become a very important aspect of the educational scene is the wealth of theoretical and practical material in the volumes and articles devoted to the topic. Training patterns for elementary teachers commonly require at least one course in childstudy. Several universities have developed elaborate in-service training programs that are offered to school staffs throughout the nation. An outstanding example is the program conducted by the University of Maryland formerly directed by Daniel A. Prescott and discussed in his book *The Child in the Educative Process.* [64]

The Maryland Child-Study Institute is essentially an in-service training program conducted by the professional staff of the Center and is taken to local school districts on an invitational basis. Its statement of purposes shows clearly the beliefs underlying the child-study concept and demonstrates its consonance with principles of child-centered education.

1. To communicate to participants a body of specific scientific knowledge from many of the disciplines that study human beings.
2. To aid participants as they organize this knowledge into an interpreted theory of human development, learning, and behavior.

[63] John Dewey, *Democracy and Education* (New York: The Macmillan Company, 1916), pp. 89–90.

[64] Daniel A. Prescott, *The Child in the Educative Process* (New York: McGraw-Hill Book Company, 1957).

3. To guide participants to discover the kinds of information about individual children that are necessary to understand them, and to develop skill in gathering and objectively recording this information.

4. To acquaint participants with the steps in reasoning that are necessary to arrive at scientifically sound judgments about the motivation, behavior, and needs of individual children; and, by group processes, to guide them in developing skill in this method of analyzing children and arriving at sound judgment about them.

5. To encourage and aid participants in working out, within the scope of the teacher's normal professional functions, specific plans for assisting individual children and groups of children to take their necessary next steps in development, learning, or adjustment; and to aid them in working out the implications of the insights gained through their study of children for planning and practice in the general educative process.

6. To assist participants to recognize children who need expert diagnosis, therapy, or remedial instruction, and to help them locate and refer the child to available agencies for diagnosis, therapy, or remedial instruction.

7. To stimulate participants to develop and to live by a strong code of professional ethics; to encourage them to recognize the worth of every individual and to respect the dignity of all human beings.[65]

Having participated in the program, teachers are made more aware of the child in the school environment and of the many complicated factors—including those which are non-school—that have influenced and will continue to affect him. Participants are encouraged to explore and rethink their attitudes, feelings, and biases concerning the behavior of children and the responsibility of schools to the child. Prescott points out how his thinking has been affected as a result of his experience in the program. He states that he has been forced ". . . to accept the fact that children learn and cannot be 'taught' in the usually accepted sense of that term." He has become impressed with "the tremendous complexity and interrelatedness of the factors which influence children's learning readinesses and perceptions and upon which the teacher's judgments must depend if they are to be sound judgments." [66]

The development of special education. Coincident with developments in the child-study movement have been provision for special education and special services for mentally retarded children and those who demonstrated behavioral problems. As schools attempted to implement the philosophy of an education for all children and to enforce compulsory school attendance statutes, the need for special facilities and arrangements became clear.

Special education is defined by Good as:

. . . the education of pupils (for example, the deaf, the blind and partially seeing, the mentally subnormal, the gifted) who deviate so far physically,

[65] Prescott, *op. cit.*, pp. 447–448.
[66] *Ibid.*, p. ix.

mentally, emotionally, or socially from the relative homogeneous groups of so-called "normal" people that the standard curriculum is not suitable for their educational needs; involves the modification of the standard curriculum in content, methods of instruction, and expected rate of progress to provide optimum educational opportunity for such pupils; carried on in special classes, in special curricula, or in special schools.[67]

Mackie and Dunn estimate that approximately 12.7 per cent of the nation's pupil population is composed of children who fall within this definition and therefore require special attention.[68] From such a definition, it can be seen clearly that in order to be effective, special educational services require the attention of personnel who can contribute to a diagnosis of the learning and educational potential of pupils involved and to their early identification. As special education has developed, increasing numbers of school psychologists have come into the schools to perform this role. It is logical that school psychology and programs for exceptional children have become closely related.

In a number of states, special education has been directly responsible for the development of school psychology. As these states made legal provisions to extend the school's program to exceptional children, they included in the laws provision for child-study or psychological services.

Several states make special financial reimbursement to local school districts for the employment of a qualified school psychologist to work with exceptional children. In Illinois, as an illustration, the following statement is found in a state department *Handbook for Qualified Psychological Examiners:*

> For several years the Illinois Department of Public Instruction has reimbursed certain school districts for at least a major part of the salary of Qualified Psychological Examiners employed full time by those districts. These projects have been initiated because of the importance of psychological services in state-approved programs for the educable mentally handicapped. We are now realizing the need for psychological assistance with children in other classes for exceptional children.[69]

As early as 1919 the regulations of the State Education Department of Missouri provided that candidates for special classes should be psychologically tested. In Delaware the Special Education Law of 1939 mandated the examination of referred cases by the State Board of Education "with the aid

[67] Carter V. Good, ed., *Dictionary of Education* (2nd Ed.) (New York: McGraw-Hill Book Company, 1959), p. 515.

[68] R. P. Mackie and L. M. Dunn, *College and University Programs for the Preparation of Teachers of Exceptional Children,* Bulletin No. 13 (Washington, D. C.: U. S. Office of Education, 1954), p. 3.

[69] Isaac Jolles, *A Handbook for the Qualified Psychological Examiner in the Illinois Plan for Special Education of Exceptional Children,* Supplement to Circular Series "B," No. 12 (Springfield, Illinois: Superintendent of Public Instruction, 1954), p. 8.

of cooperating agencies." It was also the first state to provide for individual psychological examination (1936) and audiometric examination (1936) on a statewide basis.

Special education, like school psychology, is a growing and increasingly active aspect of the American school scene. As services for exceptional children broaden in scope and increase in number, it becomes continually more apparent that they must be based on a sound program of psychological evaluation and services. The psychologist's skills and competencies are critically important for programming in several of the most recently developing areas of special education: for example, programs for emotionally and socially disturbed children and for children with neurological disorders.

THE INFLUENCE OF PROFESSIONAL ASSOCIATIONS AND ORGANIZATIONS

Much of the professional advancement that has occured in school psychology, particularly during the 1950's and 1960's, has resulted from the activities of professional associations. The organization of greatest influence on a nationwide basis has been the American Psychological Association, Division 16, the Division of School Psychology. It is the only association of national influence whose exclusive purpose is to attend to developments and problems in school psychology. Although less influential, several other organizations contribute to the development of school psychology: The Council of Exceptional Children, The American Personnel and Guidance Association, The American Association on Mental Deficiency, etc. These are agencies of national influence but they are not concerned exclusively with school psychology.

State and local organizations are also important contributors to developments in the field. Several states have psychological associations with divisions or sections in school psychology. Regional and local associations of school psychologists are fairly common in many states. New York, New Jersey, California, and Ohio, for example, have very strong statewide school psychology associations. From these have come developments in program organization and stimulation for local experimentation. Perhaps their greatest contributions have been clarification of roles within regions, providing professional identification for members, and their constant efforts toward upgrading practicing psychologists through inservice training activities.

The American Psychological Association. Founded in 1892, and with a membership of approximately 26,000 in 1967, the American Psychological Association includes twenty-six special divisions, many of which are pertinent to school psychology: Division 5—Evaluation and Measurements, Division 7—Developmental Psychology, Division 8—Personality and Social Psychology,

Division 12—Clinical Psychology, Division 15—Educational Psychology, Division 17—Counseling Psychology, and in particular, Division 16—School Psychology.

Repeated references in many publications [70] to the inadequacy of professional preparation of the large majority of the early psychological examiners in the public schools was the most important provocative for the establishment of the American Association of Clinical Psychologists, on December 28, 1917, which was transformed into the Clinical Section of the American Psychological Association on December 31, 1919.[71] This was the first section, later termed "division" to be organized within the framework of APA. Moreover, growing recognition of the great complexity of psychological diagnosis eventually led to the creation of the division of school psychology and to numerous official committees charged with the responsibility of formulating definite recommendations to meet the issues. Of these reports, the most complete are those of the Boulder and Thayer conferences.[72]

Division 16 began in 1947 with the approval by the membership committee of the American Psychological Association of 167 applications. A constitution was drafted stating the purposes of the Division and describing the requirements for membership. Its purposes are: 1) to provide opportunities for professional fellowship and for exchange of professional ideas among school psychologists; 2) to advance the professional status of school psychology; and 3) to promote and maintain high standards of professional service among its members. The Division has grown phenomenally since 1947. In 1966 the membership included 135 fellows, 677 members, and 160 associates. The numerous committee activities of the organization are varied, and are reported to the membership in the *Newsletter*. An annual meeting is held regularly in connection with the annual meeting of the American Psychological Association.

Perhaps the most influential project of Division 16 has been the 1954 conference on the training and functions of school psychology that has been referred to frequently in this chapter and documented in *The School Psychologist at Mid-Century*.[73] A more recent publication, also mentioned earlier, *The Psychologist on the School Staff*, discusses the contributions that

[70] J. E. Wallace Wallin, "Danger Signals in Clinical and Applied Psychology," *The Journal of Educational Psychology*, 3 (April, 1912), 224–226; "Current Misconceptions in Regard to the Functions of Binet Testing and of Amateur Psychological Testers," *Transactions of the Fourth International Congress of School Hygiene*, Buffalo, 5 (August, 1913), 678–688; *Problems of Subnormality* (New York: Harcourt, Brace & World, Inc., 1917), pp. 106f., 118, 191–195.

[71] "Historical Inaccuracies," *Journal of Clinical Psychology*, 11 (April, 1955), 197–200; *The Odyssey of a Psychologist* (The Author, Lyndalia, Wilmington, Delaware), p. 120ff.

[72] Victor C. Raimy, ed., *Training in Clinical Psychology* (Englewood Cliffs, N. J.: Prentice-Hall, Inc., 1950).

[73] Cutts, *op. cit.*

the psychologist can make to the school system and is intended primarily for school administrators and other members of the staff. Among other notable Division contributions to the profession is the series of professional institutes that have been conducted each year prior to the annual meeting. Chapter 22 describes these activities in greater detail.

The American Personnel and Guidance Association. A second major organization exerting a strong influence on the destiny of school psychology is the American Personnel and Guidance Association that was founded in 1952. APGA grew out of the activities of four organizations in personnel work: American College Personnel Association, Association for Counselor Education and Supervision (formerly National Association of Guidance Supervisors and Counselor's Trainers), National Vocational Guidance Association, and Student Personnel Association for Teacher Education. More recently it has been enlarged by three divisions: the American School Counselor Association, the American Rehabilitation Counseling Association, and the Association for Measurements and Evaluation in Guidance. APGA is a composite of personnel workers from industry, business, and the military, with the majority representing some aspect of personnel work in education. It includes many school psychologists in its ranks. Its main purpose is to:

> . . . unify all qualified workers in the field so that mutual acquaintance may be cultivated, so that principles, practices and professional standards may be advanced, and to further the development of personnel and guidance workers in educational institutions, community agencies, government organizations, business and industry.[74]

The American Personnel and Guidance Association and the American Psychological Association appear to be the only organizations to have recognized the need for greater clarification of the several personnel work specializations within education and the need to achieve a better integration of them in the schools. Where APA provides a voice for the school psychologist among psychologists, APGA offers an opportunity for the school psychologist to discuss common problems with other personnel workers from the schools. *The Personnel and Guidance Journal* regularly carries articles which deal directly or indirectly with problems of interrelationship among the various specialists in pupil personnel work. At times such articles are authored by psychologists, school counselors, school social workers, or specialists from school medical work.[75]

---

[74] American Personnel and Guidance Association, *Report to the Profession* (Washington, D. C.: American Personnel and Guidance Association, 1961).

[75] Refer to C. R. Rogers, "The Place of the Person in the New World of the Behavioral Sciences," *The Personnel and Guidance Journal*, 39, No. 6 (February, 1961), 442–451.

The National Education Association. Also worthy of attention in this discussion is the National Education Association although its influence has been indirect rather than direct. The closest tie between school psychology and the National Education Association is through the Council for Exceptional Children which, since 1941, has functioned as a department of the NEA. The Council for Exceptional Children is made up of a variety of educational specialists, including teachers, psychologists, school administrators and others who share a professional concern about the schools providing for exceptional children. Articles that bear a direct relationship to the work of the school psychologist occasionally appear in the official organ of the Council, *Exceptional Children.*[76] The NEA is the largest professional organization in the world with over 1,000,000 members of whom over 26,000 are members of the Council for Exceptional Children in 1967.

In the present chapter consideration has been given to the developmental influences which have been important in the evolution of school psychology. In Chapter 22 the reader will find a detailed discussion of the developments in the profession since 1960. Here is presented an extended summary of the federal role in facilitating the growth of school psychological services as well as commentary relating to the various role conceptualizations proposed for the school psychologist in the 1960's.

Selected Supplementary Readings

The readings for Chapters 1, 21, and 22 are grouped together at the end of Chapter 22. The topics covered are the development of school psychological services, varying role conceptualizations for school psychological service workers, federal assistance, and state-related issues in school psychological services. Articles, books, and research which the various authors of all chapters have used in documenting their chapters are generally not included in the Selected Supplementary Readings Sections. The references used in the footnotes combined with the Selected Supplementry Readings from the twenty-two chapters would provide the reader with the most extensive bibliography ever published on school psychology.

[76] Refer to F. A. Mullen, "Therapy—and the School Psychologist," *Exceptional Children,* 21, No. 7 (April, 1955), 257–259, 271.

FRANCES A. MULLEN

2

The Role of the School Psychologist in the Urban School System

The modern city is an incredibly exciting place in which to live, play, and work. In it, we feel the soaring curve of technological advance, the impulse of research, and the population upsurge. We thrill to the gleaming new schools, with advanced curricula, overflowing with more college-bound youngsters, studying harder than any generation that has ever gone through our schools. We sense the buoyant health of irrepressible young persons, a generation who have never known the insidious ravages of the epidemic children's diseases. We see the slums replaced by the glitter of steel and glass high-rise housing or the interesting arcs of clover-leafed highways. Dingy business districts are transformed into landscaped malls, forbidding factories replaced by functionally designed buildings of beauty. The resources of cultural institutions, art museums, and music halls are open to all. Medical facilities in a bewildering array of complex specialties abound. University experts in every field are at hand. Private and public welfare agencies are vigorously attacking almost every conceivable problem. Top men from industry and commerce are giving their time and ability to movements for the improvement of their city.

Equally the modern American city is a terrifying milieu, oppressing the professional person who works with youth with a sense of the urgency of his task, with the knowledge that tomorrow may be too late to prepare a generation to meet the problems that daily grow greater. Appalling are the floods of bewildered migrants who might almost be from other universes, the traffic slaughter and crime rates, the deaths in fire traps that city inspectors have ignored, the flight to the suburbs of those most competent to bear the burdens and solve the problems of the inner city, the schools, on double shift though hundreds of classrooms have been added in the last decade, with teachers struggling, in some neighborhoods, to meet the needs of under-privileged youngsters, bored, truant, and out for "kicks."

Most cities are growing. Whether or not the actual population within a city's limits is increasing, its people may be changing rapidly in language, cultural, religious, and racial backgrounds. Great numbers of migrants from other parts of the country and from around the world are arriving; other groups are emigrating to the suburbs or to more distant localities. Certain areas within each city appear continuously to attract each new wave of immigration. As each wave attains enough economic stability and cultural sophistication to move to better neighborhoods, its place is taken by new migrants of a different background. Social problems as well as housing problems arise from this mobility and from the sweeps of slum clearance, housing redevelopment, and highway construction.

Both the dynamic and the sordid picture are simultaneously true, in varying degrees, for almost every city of America. The psychologist must grasp the significance of the total picture for his work, know insightfully the problems and resources of the whole, and work intimately with the neighbor-hoods where he may be assigned.

The Urban School System

The school system in modern Metropolitania is a focus of many of the community problems. The mobility of people, for example, plays havoc with the school pattern, creating vacant rooms in one area, tripling the school population in another neighborhood almost overnight. As a result the physical face of the school system is changing rapidly. Most urban school systems are in the midst of building and rehabilitation programs. Low glass-walled build-ings are replacing the dingy old fortresses of the central city that are being demolished by slum clearance and highway projects or that are too expensive to bring up to modern standards of heating, lighting, toilet sanitation, and fire safety. The remaining older buildings are being modernized.

The new schools are being built in smaller units than the old, allowing children to remain closer to home, and the school principal to remain closer to his pupils, his teachers, and his community. Facilities for TV and other types of audiovisual education are built in; large classrooms with running water and flexible seating reflect a recognition that children learn by doing. Large and small spaces are made available for different purposes—or if the school is still built of rows of identical rectangles, at least the partitions are of easily moved cement blocks with the structural supports and the utilities so concentrated that a maximum number of partitions can be moved without major difficulty.

The psychologist applauds, and in some cases has contributed to the discussions and the planning of these new facilities, so much better adapted to the needs of children. He is particularly concerned about the provision of clinic facilities. The modern school with its variety of psychologists, social workers, nurses, speech therapists, itinerant teachers of lip reading or of the visually handicapped or the gifted, needs spaces for these people to work with one client or a small group. The number of such clinic facilities varies with the school organization and program but all indications are that clinic space needs will increase. It is tragic when this growing need is overlooked. In the buildings of a former generation the school psychologist could find a corner somewhere. The ends of spacious corridors could be partitioned off or generous storage space converted. The principal had probably moved from the cubby hole built for him over the stairs to a remodeled classroom office, leaving his original office available for the visiting specialists. But the modern building has no inch of waste space, minimal corridors and little storage space. If the clinic facilities are not in the plans they are next to impossible to improvise, except by moving partitions—and few building programs provide leeway that will permit classroom space to be converted into clinics. Portable classrooms and administration units have been effectively used to enlarge existing schools or to establish new schools quickly in new subdivisions. Clinic facilities can sometimes be included in these facilities.

The only constant thing about an urban school system is change; it is equally true that area-wise the chief invariant is the variation between schools and school areas. Within the city, individual schools often differ from each other more than in the community schools of rural, small-town, or even suburban communities, which perforce must reach a cross section of the total population. The tendency of people to live near people of their own language, religion, or cultural background is reinforced by the location of churches and synagogues, business and cultural centers adapted to the language and customs of special groups. The housing pressures, economic and social, which restrict newcomers to certain areas, the building restrictions which limit another neighborhood to homes of the highest cost bracket, are reflected directly in the school population. Meanwhile, the conscientious efforts of school people to develop programs of education appropriate to the needs of the children before them are labeled as discriminatory by vociferous pressure groups, and recommendations to promote integration by transporting children to schools at a distance from their homes meet with little enthusiasm from the parents of the "under-privileged" and usually with concealed or open antagonism from others.

COMMUNITY EXPECTATIONS OF THE SCHOOLS

Urban schools, in common with all the schools of the nation, are under scrutiny from the American people. They face in intensified form the philosophical and practical dilemmas of all American education. They are responding to many current trends, some of them seemingly contradictory. School administrators, teachers, and curriculum experts, in full sympathy with the demand of the community for higher standards, are also aware of the tremendous needs of great blocs of their clients for slow patient indoctrination into the ways of living in the confusing whirl of city pressures. Curricula are revised to incorporate the newest thinking in science, to meet the American need for people fluent in a foreign tongue, to make mathematics an effective tool of thinking and a foundation for its actual present uses in technology and science. Simultaneously, the schools are faced with demands for more driver education, more consumer education, more human relations courses, more specific instruction in ethics, or in economics, or in plastering, or child care, or sex education. They are expected to teach all these things to a variegated school population, to the thousands who will become technicians, professionals, executives, or creative research men in the physical, biological and social sciences, and to the other thousands, who, unless some solutions are found quickly, will leave our schools early, meagerly prepared, to look for low-level jobs that are rapidly disappearing.

Each of these diverse goals is largely valid and important for American society, but the strategy and tactics the schools are urged to adopt to enable them to reach specific goals are sometimes in violent and basic contradiction. The urban school perhaps is particularly the center of conflict between those who want to raise standards for the college-bound and those who sense that the very survival of our cities may depend on how rapidly we can find ways to reach and meet the needs of the reluctant learners of the inner city, how well we can help children assimilate the elements of our culture. It is under cross fire from those who want to protect the school as they have known it for their part of the community, those who think it needs drastic revision, and those who want immediately an equal education for a different group of children. It gets urgent advice and bitter criticism from those whose own children go to suburban schools and want the city taxes on their businesses cut. It gets vocal demands from those who want the schools to serve the entire population around the clock and around the year with expanded summer and evening, recreational and vocational, cultural and athletic programs, and from those who want the schools to "return to their real function." Pressure groups demand expanded services for exceptional children: the emotionally disturbed, the trainable mentally handicapped, the involved cerebral palsied child, the totally blind, the pregnant girls, the school-resistant teenager, or whatever other group the particular city has previously relegated to the responsibility of state institutions, or to the streets. Some argue that most educational problems will be solved if the size of class can be reduced by five pupils per teacher whether this brings the ratio down to 30, or 25, or 20, while others adduce evidence that no matter how small the class, the skills of a variety of specialists will enrich the work of the teacher, and that expansion of the specialities, including psychology, guidance, social work, should go hand in hand with reduction of class size.

No one of these currents and pressures on the urban school system is remote from the school psychologist. Each affects the work he does; each has psychological implications. The profession of psychology should have insights and skills to contribute to the total school team as the see-saw struggle for balance between conflicting theories continues. The need for prompt solutions becomes ever more imperative.

URBAN SCHOOL ORGANIZATION

To meet these two-fold tasks of building a physical school plant to fit the changing needs of the city, and to create a diversified educational program adequate to the demands of the times, the urban school system must find ways to change and adapt and act rapidly. In doing so it has some very specific problems of its own. Many factors contribute toward inflexibility in an urban school system. Parents, pressure groups, and even teachers argue vociferously for the retention of the curriculum they knew a generation ago. Buildings built for uniform class sizes impede adoption of a more flexible organization. Teacher certification rules cemented in city and state regulations are bound with emotional as well as legal strictures. Promotion policies, tenure, merit rating are embalmed in slogans, crystalized into fighting words. Organized groups already man the fortress, readying themselves to charge to the attack at the faintest hint of a change in the status quo. Decision-making is complicated by the many people who are involved, the distance the ultimate authority is from the problem at hand. Bigness which can make possible experimentation and flexibility, can equally stultify progress. Urban school superintendents, much aware of this problem, are experimenting with decentralization, plans designed to return to the neighborhood school the values of small units intimately administered by persons close to the problems, while preserving the assets that size brings to the city schools. Many patterns of adaptation to the problems of urban public school education have been developed; many changes are in the making.

The Growth of Modern Psychology
as a Science and a Profession

To meet the demands of the urban school system, the school psychologist must keep abreast of the exciting developments in the psychological profession.

School psychology is but one, and in its present renascence one of the newest, of the applied fields of psychology. It operates in the currents established by the advances in the basic science of psychology and by the breakthroughs which professional psychologists in many fields of applied work have achieved. School psychology cannot afford to work in a vacuum; it must continuously evaluate these new ideas, skills, techniques, and theories to determine which can and should be translated to the school situation.

Much work has been done on the organic bases of behavior. We begin to know today more about the central nervous system, about retraining the brain injured, about the effect of drugs as energizers and tranquilizers in conjunction with therapy and treatment.

Social psychology has studied the activities of groups, the structure of interrelationships, the leadership phenomena in the industrial field and in the free flow of the gang situation. Industrial managers and political practitioners are eagerly seeking ways to extend psychological knowledge to the group processes that affect the people with whom they deal.

Learning theory, a focus of laboratory research in current psychology, has developed a body of fact and theory which in spite of its volume and its originality has not yet tackled situations as complex as the school classroom. Some of its most productive workers have disclaimed responsibility for the translation of their findings into practices useful in the classroom, but the school psychologist cannot ignore the translation process. The teaching machine may well revolutionize parts of the teaching process, releasing teacher energy for more creative instructional tasks. The need for a whole new profession of skilled programmers for machines is beginning to be felt.

Clinical psychology is perhaps the field of applied psychology most familiar to many school psychologists. Although since World War II it has neglected its original orientation toward children in its concern for the treatment of the disturbed veteran, it has contributed much that can be adapted to children in the uses of psychodrama, group therapy, and drug therapy. Reading the literature of clinical psychology, the school psychologist is interested and pleased to note the increasing emphasis on prevention rather than treatment. The Stanford Conference of 1955 on Clinical and Counseling Psychology was sponsored by the National Institute of Mental Health to review the findings of the Boulder Conference that had set the course of clinical psychology for the previous decade.[1] One of its conclusions was that clinical treatment could never catch up with the demands upon it, until the American people, through their schools and community organizations, developed real programs of prevention of mental illness. Clinical psychologists were urged to turn their attention to these fields. The National Institute of Mental Health in 1966 focused public and governmental attention on the problem of suicide, the third most common cause of death in the adolescent group. NIMH predicts that the rate can be reduced by 25 per cent in the next few years if current knowledge about the identification and treatment of the suicidally inclined teenager can be put to work on a national scale.[*] Obviously the schools of America with their teachers and psychologists must play a tremendous role, if this next big public health push is to be successful in saving lives and reducing mental illness.

In the rehabilitation agencies, public and private, and in the universities training workers for these agencies, the psychology of disability, the therapy of work values, the motivation of the handicapped, the satisfactions of illness or disability have come in for intense study. School psychologists need to follow these results carefully in order that their own work with handicapped children may be strengthened, and that findings of significance to the operation of special education and general education programs be brought to the attention of the educators concerned.

Motivational research for advertising and sales is demonstrating the manipulative power inherent in some of our basic psychological knowledge It calls our attention to the results of the repetition of subliminal stimuli, to the ways in which ideas become attached to value systems. Where have we equally large scale and sophisticated research on how to instill arithmetical skill, how to make Shakespeare sought after, or how to set the ideals of the American constitution at the core of the child's loyalties and personal values? The psychologist may well meditate on whether his school has made optimal use of the findings of business psychologists that might help to pass a local bond issue or state tax legislation.

THE ORGANIZATION AND PRACTICE OF SCHOOL
PSYCHOLOGY IN THE URBAN SETTING

It is understandable that the school psychology program in the modern city, subject to the pressures of the changing milieu of the urban school system, under the impact of the growth of psychological knowledge, is itself in

[1] C. R. Strother, ed., *Psychology in Mental Health*. Report of the Stanford Conference on Clinical and Counseling Psychology (Washington, D. C.: American Psychological Association, 1956).

[*] Stanley F. Yolles, Statement of the National Institute of Mental Health before the Ad Hoc Subcommittee on the Handicapped, Committee on Education and Labor, House of Representatives, Congress of the U.S., June 20, 1966 (Washington, D.C.: Government Printing Office, 1966).

flux. The varied ways in which psychological services operate in American cities reflect the historical evolution of the service in a given city, and the current pressures within that city and that school system.

Extent of service. It is the rare city school system today that does not employ school psychologists or psychological workers, under some one of a variety of titles. A recent survey by the author and editor brought responses from forty-two of the fifty largest cities. In that sample of cities the number of psychological workers (including psychometrists and psychologists) increased from 217 to 615 in the ten years between 1950 and 1960. Two of the reporting cities employed no psychologists in 1960, but one of these used area psychological services furnished by the state. No city showed a decrease in psychological service in the decade, and only three showed no change. The forty cities reporting some psychological staff represented twenty-five states from Massachusetts to California, Florida to Washington. Table 1 outlines in abbreviated fashion the 1960 survey and its 1966 follow-up. The reader will find much additional information in this table.

The number of psychologists per city school system reported in this 1960 survey ranged from 0 to 154 with a median at 9. Ten years previously the number ranged from 0 to 66, with a median at 3, in these same cities. The pupil-psychologist ratios in 1966 ranged from 1 psychologist per 2,000 pupils to 1 per 24,300, with a median at 9,000. In 1950 the range had been from 1 psychologist per 2,200 pupils to 1 psychologist for 68,000 with a median at 18,500 (see accompanying table).

In 1960 the cities surveyed employed from 0 to 62 school social workers per city, with a median at 11. There were twenty-two cities reporting more social workers than psychologists, sixteen cities reporting more psychologists, and only one city where the same number were employed.

As David Salten, Superintendent of Schools of Long Beach, Long Island, New York, has pointed out, there has been so little experience with really adequate psychological services that no one can say with certainty how many could be effectively employed.[2] Estimates of proper rates vary, according to Salten, from one school psychologist for 1000 pupils to one for every 3000.

In 1966, M. J. Keatley, Director of the Psychological and Testing Department of the Tulsa Public Schools conducted an unpublished survey of the role of the psychologist and psychometrist in 26 of our middle-sized cities with pupil enrollments ranging from 25,000 to 100,000, including Gary, San Jose, Salt Lake City and Tacoma. Twenty districts responded.

She found that the school psychological staff-pupil ratio varied from

[2] D. G. Salten *et al.*, "Public School Psychological Services: Recent Growth and Future Potential," *Educational Administration and Supervision,* XLII (1956), 100–107, 162–169.

Table 1

Urban Public School Psychological Services Survey
(School Year 1965–1966; Listed according to size, 1960 Census)

City and Name of Division	First Year for Psychologist or Psychometrist	No. of Psychologists and Psychometrists 1950	1966	Other PPSW in 1965–66	1965–66 Public School Enrollment
New York City Bureau of Child Guidance	1918	64	244	376 c, 222 sw	1,065,000
Chicago Bureau of Child Study	1899	61	117	12 rdg sps, 500 ec adj tchs, 8 sw, 200 sc	592,000
Los Angeles Guidance and Counseling	1920	23	268	224 scFT, 8 ec, 202 scPT	612,580
Philadelphia Psychological Services	1920	14	36	311 c	265,000
Detroit Department of Evaluative Services	1910	25	19	4 ec, 330 sc, 66 swPT, 15 swFT	300,000
Baltimore Div. of Special Services	1928	8	43	37 ec, 181 sc, 75 sw	191,000
Houston Dept. of Psych. Services	1929	2	11	56 ec, 112 sc	237,000
Cleveland Psychological Service	1917	9	15	5 sw, 115 c	150,000
Washington Pupil Personnel Services	1930	12	50	96 ec, 132 sc, 2 ps, 12 sw, 123 other PPSW	145,000
St. Louis Div. of Psych. Services and Research	1905	4	14	8 ec, 67 sc, 38 sw	103,000

TABLE 1—*Continued*

City and Name of Division	First Year for Psychologist or Psychometrist	No. of Psychologists and Psychometrists 1950	1966	Other PPSW in 1965–66	1965–66 Public School Enrollment
Milwaukee Dept. of Psych. Services and Research	1937	4	42	2 ec, 55 sc, 50 sw	124,500
San Francisco Child Guidance Services	1925	6	14	2 ec, 122 sc, 30 sw	94,000
Boston Dept. of Ed. Investigation and Measurement	—	0	38	18 ec, 32 sc	94,000
Dallas Research and Pupil Services	—	—	16	75 sc, 20 sw	155,000
New Orleans Div. of Pupil Personnel	1928 *	3	6	2 ec, 76 sc, 26 sw	106,000
Pittsburgh Div. of Pupil Services, Ofc. of ScP. Services	1931	2	11	11 ec, 80 sc, 64 sw, 1.5 ps, 17 other PPSW	78,000
San Antonio Special Education	1964	0	4	3 ec, 32 sc, 8 sw	78,000
San Diego Guidance Services	1918 *	6	27	103 sc, 56 vt, 9 sw, 2 psPT	116,057
Seattle Dept. of Guidance Services	1909	6	16	9 ec, 150 sc, 24 sw	95,900

TABLE 1—*Continued*

City and Name of Division	First Year for Psychologist or Psychometrist	No. of Psychologists and Psychometrists 1950	No. of Psychologists and Psychometrists 1966	Other PPSW in 1965–66	1965–66 Public School Enrollment
Buffalo Pupil Personnel Services	1935 *	3	7	41 c, 7 vt	42,000
Cincinnati Div. of Psych. Service	1911	10	14	71 sc, 39 sw, 5 I	88,000
Memphis Dept. of Pupil Services	—	—	2	85 sc	125,000
Denver Soc. Work and Psych. Services	1922	3	15	4 ec, 56 sc, 70 sw	90,000
Atlanta Dept. of Pupil Services	1921	—	12	4 ec, 65 sc, 25 sw	105,000
Minneapolis Child Study Dept.	1924 *	6	9	91 c, 70 sw	71,000
Indianapolis Pupil Personnel Services Division	1930 *	1	10	11 ec, 80 sc, 65 sw	105,000
Kansas City, Mo. Psychological Services	1920	1	9	26 vt, 8 psy ser wks, 3 sw	75,000
Columbus Dept. of Child Study and Student Counseling	1946	2	15	94 c, 36 sw	105,000
Phoenix Elementary Dist. #1 Child Study Service	1944	2	2.5	10 sw	11,800
Newark Child Guidance	1910	6	12	135 c, 30 sw	75,000

TABLE 1—*Continued*

City and Name of Division	First Year for Psychologist or Psychometrist	No. of Psychologists and Psychometrists 1950	1966	Other PPSW in 1965–66	1965–66 Public School Enrollment
Louisville Div. of Pupil Personnel	1914	0	3	19 ec, 32 sc, 19 sw	50,000
Portland Dept. of Child Services—Psych. Services	1940	0	11	90 sc, 38 sw	80,000
Oakland Research	1920 *	4	14	85 c, 10 sw, 2 ec	65,000
Fort Worth	1966	0	1	45 c, 15 cPT, 10 vt	78,000
Long Beach Counseling and Psych. Services	1929	4	10	39 ec, 80 sc, 6 sw	73,000
Birmingham Guidance Dept.	1924	4	8	15 ec, 22 sc, 17 sw	70,000
Oklahoma City Psych. Servs. Div.	1949	1	5	58 sc, 16 sw	118,635
Rochester Mental Health Clinical Services	1906	16	24	5 ec, 43 sc, 20 sw	45,000
Toledo Special Education Department	1920 *	3	4	6 ec, 29 sc, 14 sw	54,000
St. Paul Div. of Sp. Services	1924	2	5	43 sc, 25 sw	46,500

TABLE 1—*Continued*

City and Name of Division	First Year for Psychologist or Psychometrist	No. of Psychologists and Psychometrists		Other PPSW in 1965–66	1965–66 Public School Enrollment
		1950	1966		
Norfolk Dept. of Adjustive Services	1930	2	4	7 vt, 9 c	56,000
Omaha Psychological Servs.	1938	1	5	.5 p, 20 ptPT, 20 ec, 7 sw	60,000
Honolulu (All Hawaii)	1959	0	9	142 c, 14 sw	162,000
Miami (Dade County) Guidance Services	1947	2	12	2 ec, 350 sc, 46 sw	203,000
Akron	1941	2	10	52 c, 5 vt	59,000
El Paso Testing and Psych. Services	1936	1	2	10 ec, 39 sc	58,000
Jersey City Bureau of Special Services	1918	2	4	40 sc, 1 ps, 66 ec, 18 sw	35,000
Tampa	1951	0	4	53 c, 23 sw	91,000
Dayton Pupil Personnel Div. of Psych. Servs.	1944	2	9	7 ec, 50 sc, 10 sw	60,000
Tulsa Dept. of Psych. Testing	1930	1	12	71 c, 12 sw	77,000

LEGEND: *, *approximate*; ps, *psychiatrist*; c, *counselor*; ec, *elementary counselor*; sc, *secondary counselor*; vt, *visiting teacher*; sw, *social worker*; PPSW, *pupil personnel services workers*; PT, *part time*; FT, *full time*; I, *intern*.

NOTE: *James F. Magary collated this table. It was impossible to record idiosyncratic aspects of many programs.*

1:14,600 to 1:1,860. Her survey revealed that of the 180 psychologists and psychometrists employed by these twenty districts, 3 per cent had only a B.A. degree, 35 per cent had only the M.A., and 15 per cent had the doctorate; the remainder fell somewhere in between the M.A. and the doctorate. In setting the salary for the minimally trained psychologist, practices varied. The most common was to pay the same as master's level teachers or the teacher's scale plus a differential. Occasionally a district had a separate scale for psychologists, while others utilized the supervisory or administrative scales. For the school year 1965–66, the minimum salary for the minimally trained psychologist ranged from below $5,000 to over $7,000, while the maximum salary for the doctoral trained person ranged from below $7,000 to over $12,000 in Keatley's study.

Administrative Organization. Where do psychological staff members fit into the school organization? How are they organized and to whom are they responsible? Except as indicated by footnotes, the answers to these questions in the discussion below were obtained from the responses of these large city school systems to questionnaires distributed in 1960 and again in 1966. Table 1 lists the name of the division or the branch of the school system in which the school psychologist is employed.

Wherever several psychologists are employed, there is likely to be one person designated as Chief Psychologist, Director of Psychological Services or some other title implying responsibilities limited to the psychological staff. In other systems, however, the psychologists are apparently directly responsible to a director of pupil personnel, or other person who presumably has a variety of workers besides psychologists under his supervision.

Whether a chief psychologist is appointed or not, the psychological staff is seldom directly responsible to the general superintendent of schools, but finds itself attached to a department. These departments vary widely in title and in apparent function. The most frequent alignments are with a department of pupil personnel, or a department of special services, less frequently with a department of special education or of instruction.

The Director of Pupil Personnel (or similarly titled person) to whom some psychological staffs report may have responsibility also for the social work program, the guidance and counseling program, the attendance services, the group testing program, and similar pupil services. For example in Oklahoma City, the Director of the Department of Pupil Services supervises four divisions. Responsible to him are a Coordinator of Child Guidance and Research with three psychologists, a Coordinator of Testing and Evaluation, a Coordinator for the ten visiting counselors, and a Reading Consultant. In Buffalo, the Office of Pupil Personnel Services has seven sections, among which are guidance, attendance, employment certification, visiting teachers, and psychological services. In Seattle the Supervisor of Services to Individual

Children has just two responsibilities: the psychological services with twelve professionals, and the social work services with twenty-one.

In a somewhat different administrative alignment, the head of the psychological services reports to an Assistant Superintendent in charge of Special Services, as in Cincinnati, Newark, Providence, Milwaukee, and Portland, Oregon, or to a Director of Special Services as in St. Paul and Baltimore. The total responsibilities of the Special Services department vary widely, but may include not only the pupil personnel services (psychology, social work, attendance, psychiatry, counseling and guidance, etc.) but also special education, adult education, vocational education, curriculum consultants, and others. In San Francisco, the Department of Child Welfare shows a similar type of organization. It is directly under the general superintendent and has seven sections, including counseling and guidance, child guidance services, and special education, among others.

The Department of Special Education in 1960 still provided the administrative leadership for the psychological services in Toledo, Ohio, and Portland, Oregon, but the trend to remove psychological services from special education is illustrated in such cities as Chicago and Baltimore.

Origin of Psychological Services

The decade of the twenties was apparently the most prolific in establishing psychological services in large cities. Of thirty-six cities reporting data on this topic in 1960, thirteen organized their psychological services in the twenties, twelve before that time and eleven since then. The range of inaugural dates reported in 1966 ranged from 1899 in Chicago to 1966 in Ft. Worth with a median at 1923.

DEVELOPMENT OF PSYCHOLOGICAL SERVICES

Although in a dynamic changing organism like the modern American school system structure does not always reflect current function, it tends to follow it. A look at the original motives for bringing psychological services into a particular school system, and a history of the changing administrative structure of these services throw much light on its present functioning.

In Chicago, the Bureau of Child Study, the first public school psychological clinic in the nation, was established in 1899 to make city-wide studies of the characteristics and needs of pupils. It preceded the establishment of classes for the mentally handicapped and other forms of special education. The many types of special instruction for exceptional children which were introduced within the next twelve years (programs for the mentally handicapped, blind, partially seeing, physically handicapped, and speech correction) owed much of their impetus to the needs pointed up by the psychological surveys. As the special education programs expanded, and perhaps because leadership in the Bureau of Child Study failed to move out to new areas, the duties of the psychological staff, originally emphasizing research and survey and general study of all children, narrowed to the identification of children for special placement. The Director of the Bureau was made responsible to the Assistant Superintendent in charge of Special Education, where line authority remained for many years. Meanwhile, however, between 1935 and 1949 under the dynamic leadership of a new director, Dr. Grace Munson, the Bureau though still attached to the Department of Special Education broadened its services. It became active in training guidance personnel, in establishing remedial reading procedures and techniques, in organizing and supervising the city-wide group testing programs, in instituting cumulative folders and records to follow each child from kindergarten through twelfth grade. All these activities made it clear that the Bureau served all children, not just exceptional children, and belonged under a department concerned with all children. The change, however, was not made until 1949. In 1953 it was placed under a newly organized Department of Instruction.

In a number of other cities the psychological services were first organized within the Department of Special Education. For example in Baltimore, the Psycho-Educational Clinic was established in 1930 "to determine scientifically the capabilities of each child having special education needs and requirements, and to insure his proper placement," [3] and remained under the Director of Special Education as late as 1955. At that time it consisted of a supervisor, six psychologists, and two psychometrists. It has since been transferred to the Division of Special Services. Similarly in Detroit, a Psychological Clinic for the better identification of candidates for classes for the mentally retarded was organized in 1911 with one examiner and a doctor from the Board of Health to give accompanying physical examinations. Referrals were made to special classes for the subnormal, to the school for the deaf, and to classes for the partially seeing. From these beginnings the Clinic expanded to include every type of child deviating from the average in any way. Where 488 cases were studied individually in 1911–1912, 3,688 were studied in 1964–65.[4]

In Rochester the psychological program apparently developed out of an effort to reduce juvenile delinquency, dating back to the first years of the century. A special education teacher was assigned to this problem in 1903. Psychologists were added in 1908, and a school social worker in 1913. Coordination of these different services was delayed until 1938 when a

[3] B. B. Ogilvie and H. H. Whitenack, "Psychoeducational Clinic," *Baltimore Bulletin of Education* (April, 1955).

[4] H. L. Jarvis, *Psychological Clinic, Annual Report, 1959–1960* (Detroit Public Schools), Mimeographed.

Co-ordinator of Child Services was appointed to bring together the staffs concerned with Psychological Services, Home and School Counseling, Attendance, Child Accounting, and Vocational and Educational Counseling. In 1942 a Division of Child Guidance was established to include these services, plus special education, speech correction, and testing. In 1946 a Child Guidance Clinic was added.[5] Within the Division of Child Guidance, the progress of psychological services and of school social work were merged into a Mental Health Clinic Service in 1958.

In Cincinnati, psychological services have been identified with a Vocation Bureau, whose history suggests that though with a somewhat different focus, its origin, like Rochester's, was related to the juvenile delinquency problem. In 1910–1911 the Vocation Bureau was formed as a joint undertaking of the schools and the Council of Social Agencies. It included an Employment Certificate Office within the school, and a Psychological Laboratory to undertake an investigation of two groups of children, one leaving and one remaining in school. This study was the chief occupation of the Psychological Laboratory, within the Vocation Bureau, for the next four or five years. The later history of the Laboratory is instructive as indicating the way in which new functions are added to a school service, or developed within the unit, or reassigned as the function becomes well enough established for its administrative aspects to be transferred to other units of the school system. In 1916, the Psychological Laboratory took over the task of selecting children for placement in classes for defectives. Later services included the administration of a scholarship fund, the supervision of mental testing in the juvenile court, followed by addition of an adjustment officer to cooperate with the Juvenile Court and to handle school delinquencies not serious enough to necessitate court action. This adjustment officer represented the beginning of school social work in Cincinnati. Responsibility for a division of tests and measurements, an attendance department, and the school census were added in 1920 and 1921. The social work program became a separate division in 1926. The Laboratory began to publish occupational research data; this led to the establishment of a separate Division of Occupational Research and Counseling in 1927. By 1960 all these and other programs were subsumed under the Assistant Superintendent for Special Services, his colleague, the Assistant Superintendent for Administration having responsibility for elementary, secondary, and special education.

In California, school psychological services had an early start and have reached an outstanding level of development. For example, San Diego hired its first school psychologist in 1920 and added a school social worker in 1923, starting a program that by 1967 had expanded to include psychologists and

[5] H. C. Seymour, "Rochester's Coordinated School Services for Delinquency Prevention," *Journal of Educational Sociology*, 24 (1950), 30–35.

psychometrists, psychiatrists, and visiting teachers, plus speech therapists, lip reading teachers, teachers for the blind, home teachers and others. San Diego's psychiatric or child guidance clinic has two play therapy rooms. Throughout California progressive state laws have speeded the establishment of school services for all types of exceptional children and concomitant psychological services.

The relationships of school psychology and school social work vary from time to time and from city to city. For example, Milwaukee separated its psychological services from the Bureau of Pupil Personnel which included the social work services in 1957, but in Rochester, New York, the psychological and social work staffs were merged into one administrative unit, a Mental Health Service Clinic, in 1958.

Other school psychology programs appear to have originated within a formal child guidance clinic framework. These programs, from their beginnings, were influenced by the traditional concept of team work by psychiatrist, psychologist, and social worker. They concerned themselves with treatment of emotionally disturbed children, under psychiatric direction. For example Miami's program (the Dade County Public Schools) started with a County Child Guidance Clinic, jointly established by the public schools and a county public health unit. Later the entire staff of psychiatrists, psychologists and social workers was absorbed as a strictly community agency, and the school system developed a new psychological service with its own corps of school psychologists, expanding to an employment of eight psychologists in 1966. The duties of psychologists correspondingly moved from the diagnostic and therapy schedule of the clinic to the evaluative and consultative role of the school psychologists. Dade County school psychologists do, however, still carry a small number of children in continuing treatment.

In New York City, the present psychological services result from both the special education and the child guidance clinic approach. The Educational Clinic for the Mentally Retarded was formed in the special education department in 1929. The Child Guidance Clinics under psychiatric direction were established in 1938 to work with the emotionally disturbed. The two were merged in 1942, but the functions remain differentiated and the Child Guidance Clinics retain their emphasis on the emotionally disturbed child. They emphasize their role in helping the local school staff to work with these children and have deemphasized but not eliminated direct treatment of disturbed children. Additional psychologists are employed in a separate Bureau of Educational Research.

LOCALE OF SCHOOL PSYCHOLOGICAL SERVICES

Some school systems prefer to have their school psychologists carry out most of their service to children and families at a central clinic or at a few area clinic centers. Other systems, probably a majority, prefer to have the psychologist meet his clients in the school building of the child's residence. The clinics function under a wide range of titles, functions, and organizational patterns. The psychologist may be the organizing head and leader; he may be a team member cooperating on a par with the other disciplines; or he may play a relatively minor role in the clinic, depending on the needs of the situation and the way in which it is structured. The clinic operating in the public schools sometimes has affiliations outside the school system; sometimes it is completely supported and staffed within the school system. Urban school psychologists may be found attached to Child Guidance Clinics, chiefly concerned with emotional problems and behavior disorders, to reading clinics, educational clinics, eye clinics, hearing clinics, speech clinics, cleft palate clinics, orthopedic clinics, cerebral palsy clinics, epilepsy clinics, and many others. These clinics may operate in the school system's central administrative building or in separate headquarters of the special services department, or less frequently may be held on rotating schedules in schools in different sections of the city. In some cases the entire work of the psychological staff is seen as a clinic function, with children brought into a central office or to clinic headquarters for study.

More frequently modern school psychological services involve a psychologist bringing his talents to a school. He is not seen as operating a clinic there, but as an itinerant specialist either arriving on a regular schedule or on call, or more effectively as a full time member of one school staff. He fits his examinations and his conferences to the modes of operation and the needs and schedule of the school. Usually school psychologists, except the specialists who serve the entire city, are assigned a group of schools within a school administrative area, and effort is made to stabilize this relationship as much as possible, on the theory that the psychologist is most useful when he comes to know his particular group of schools well. It is helpful for him to know the personality and strong points of the staff, the community needs and resources, and the general characteristics of the pupil population. At least one director of a highly regarded psychological service, however, at a recent conference on the functions of school psychologists, stated that referrals of individual children were not assigned to psychologists on an area basis, but on a basis of the special competencies of the psychologists; and that requests of administrators for specific psychologists were somewhat deliberately ignored to avoid building up too close a relationship between the principal and the psychologist, apparently with some fear of pressure on the psychologist to see the child's problem as the principal saw it. All other communities represented at that particular conference expressed a preference for an opposite policy.

When school systems were more universally organized with elementary and secondary schools in separate departments, psychological assignments tended to follow this arrangement. Some psychologists served the elementary schools, others specialized on high school programs. However with the current trend to organize city school systems on an area basis, with a district superintendent responsible for all schools, elementary, secondary, special and vocational, in his area, there has been a similar trend in the assignment of schools to psychologists. This has advantages in keeping the psychologists aware of the entire developmental picture, both for the child and for the school program, but loses some of the values of specialization. Some psychologists are more adept at putting a first grader at ease and in evaluating his reactions and his parents, while others have special talents in relating to disturbed adolescents, having even acquired the vocabulary and an approximation to the language patterns that identify certain sub-groups in the teen age population of various communities.

It is not usual, but neither is it unknown, for a psychologist to be assigned full time to one public school. Chicago has found this necessary and desirable for certain of the social adjustment schools. Jeannette Vosk has reported on the values of a full-time assignment to one large Brooklyn elementary school.[6] She believes the value of her service to that school is increased immeasurably more than would be indicated by the mere additional hours. The crux of the matter is her availability at all times when children are in school. It becomes automatic for the school staff to think of referring pertinent problems at the time when a sense of urgency is felt. "Some help right away" is of far greater value, Vosk reports, than the promise of help in the future.

The number of schools assigned to a psychologist and the number of cases he is expected to complete vary widely. With the ratio of school psychologists to pupil population reported earlier in this chapter, it is clear that services must be restricted either in number of children served, or in thoroughness of individual study, or both. In Portland, Oregon, where the psychological testing is normally done in the schools, each examiner is expected to consult school personnel and school records and to evaluate approximately three youngsters per day. The statistics for the year suggest that the Portland psychologists come close to meeting this suggested rate. In Chicago the official standard has been two evaluations in the schools per day, with one day per week for writing reports and for special conferences concerning cases; but the yearly statistics show that the case studies cannot be completed at this rate, for the psychologists average considerably fewer cases.

RECRUITMENT AND TRAINING OF SCHOOL PSYCHOLOGISTS

As soon as a psychological staff enlarges to include more than two or three persons and acquires a supervising head, it must become involved in

[6] J. S. Vosk, "The Clinical Psychologist in a Difficult School," *American Journal of Orthopsychiatry,* 29 (1959), 157.

its own personnel problems. Questions concerning the recruitment and training of such staff members are not unique to the urban setting, but they become particularly apparent here, for urban school systems typically establish
their own hiring standards, making decisions which greatly affect the
character of their school psychology program. The tradition of requiring
teacher training or teaching experience was inherent in the development of
the profession in many cities, where formerly the teacher who took a few
courses in intelligence testing became the school psychologist. Since then the
profession of psychology itself has moved forward in a variety of areas of
knowledge of direct import to the teacher, and the profession of school psychology has become increasingly self-conscious. As a result the question of
whether the school psychologist is basically an educator or a psychologist has
come to the fore. The pronouncements of school psychologists through their
own organizations and of school psychology training programs tend to emphasize the latter with definitions beginning: "The school psychologist is a
psychologist who . . ." [7] However the school administrator tends to look
for the person who can identify himself as an educator as well as a psychologist. One article in a school administrators' journal affirms that the school
psychologist is "a specialist within the profession of education," who "must
be basically an educator who is highly trained in the techniques of educational and clinical psychology." [8]

Perkins, a former officer and a fellow of the Division of School Psychologists of the American Psychological Association, described the success of his
work in starting a program of school psychology in the complex of the Phoenix
school system,

> In this case, the psychologist had had training and experience as a teacher,
> principal, and school psychologist, an experience of value in establishing
> close relationship with school personnel. However, other psychologists with
> different backgrounds could have performed similarly, *provided* they were
> sufficiently interested and felt that school personnel and the center staff
> were *dependent on each other* and could be mutually helpful.[9]

Dr. C. Herman Gos, Deputy Superintendent of Public Instruction in
Pennsylvania, addressing the American Psychological Association in 1950 on
the topic, "What Does a School Superintendent Want in a School Psychologist?" said that he wanted a school psychologist who was first an educator.

The former Superintendent of Schools of Indianapolis in an influential
educational publication has warned that it is essential that the school psychologist not be too closely oriented toward a clinical approach but that he

[7] N. Cutts, ed., *The School Psychologist at Mid-Century* (Washington: American
Psychological Association, 1955).

[8] R. E. Barnhart and R. J. Baldave, "Role of the School Psychologist," *Nation's
Schools*, 61 (April, 1958), 49–51.

[9] K. J. Perkins, "Consultation Services to Public Schools by a Mental Health
Team," *Mental Hygiene*, 37 (1953), 585–595.

have an understanding of the influence of education and its aims.[10] This is not a mere semantic difference but an important difference in viewpoint. All agree that the good school psychologist must have deep understanding of and full sympathy with the aims and objectives of education in general and the local school system that employs him in particular.

The real question, of course, is where to find or how to produce the person who has the desired understandings and skills in the two fields of education and psychology. The trend in city schools has been to drop the requirements for teacher experience and to reduce the number of semester hours of education courses required; but this merely means that other ways must be found to insure that the psychologist has the necessary understandings and attitudes.

Internships as part of a well-structured training program are an obvious answer. Such training programs with their accompanying internships are developing steadily, in many parts of the country, but far too slowly for the needs of the field. Urban school systems have not yet accepted their full responsibilities for such internships, though they are not unknown. University professors and their students have a tendency to seek out internships in the more peaceful and less complicated setting of the suburban community; city systems have not been quick to cut their own red tape and provide the supervisory assistance that makes for a valid internship. The New York City schools have recognized the need.

Since the existing training programs in universities are still inadequate for training new school psychologists in the numbers the schools are currently seeking, schools are forced to accept psychologists with good clinical training, sometimes with VA hospital or other agency experience, but frequently with almost no orientation toward the schools, and in fact with attitudes of superiority toward school teachers and administrators, inherited at least in part from campus animosities between departments of education and psychology. Obviously in such circumstances an extensive program of retraining is necessary before the newcomer is useful in the schools.

Occasionally, also, schools are forced to fill psychological positions with educators with minimal psychological training. In California, with its rapidly expanding program of psychological services and with two levels of training and certification, this type of compromise has been sometimes used, as it has in other localities. In such situations extensive and intensive supervision and in-service training in psychology must be provided to the newcomer by the better trained and more experienced members of the city staff.

Urban school systems should be best equipped to provide, if they will, the closeness of supervision which will make it feasible for such a beginner

---

[10] H. L. Shibler, "Organization of Personnel Services," Chapter VII, *Personnel Services in Education*, 58th Yearbook, National Society for the Study of Education, Part II (Chicago: University of Chicago Press, 1959), 154.

to acquire experience. Some urban school systems have been reluctant to take on this task for they find themselves devoting much experienced staff time to the training of psychologists who, as soon as supervised experience is acquired, are lured away by smaller school systems not bound by rigid salary schedules. The task remains to be performed. The city must take what comfort it can in having performed a needed service to the profession and to the schools of the nation, and meanwhile endeavor to build up both the salary scale and the working conditions and professional service pattern that will hold its trainees.

Thus, indoctrination of new school psychologists becomes an important function of any school psychological service. The first year must give the embryo school psychologist practical acquaintance with the organization and day-by-day operation of a school and of a classroom, an acquaintance that will enable him to know what is and what is not feasible to plan or recommend for a child or for a school program. He must study the realities and the potentials of the school situation in general, and of his particular set of schools in particular. He must learn that a school of 750 pupils cannot revolve in 750 different orbits around each of its individual pupils. He must learn how vulnerable the school is to the pressures of public opinion and to the cries for punishment of the delinquent child. He must see the school as an institution of mass education that attempts to make group instruction effective and meaningful, a world in which his own knowledge of group dynamics should make him understand that plans must be gauged for their effects on the total class, the total school, the total community, as well as for their effect on the child. He must have some comprehension of the pressures of time alone on the administrator and the teacher.

Many people think they know schools because they went to school in the past. Actually few have thought through what they really think a school should do, or what the results of their pet cliché solutions of problems would be if ever applied widely. Psychologists not well-oriented can be as great offenders as any other group. The tyro school psychologist must acquire an appreciation of the magnitude and ramifications of the schools' task, a respect for the education profession and the individual teacher, insight into and interest in group as well as individual dynamics. Probably every alert chief psychologist plans specifically for the up-grading of his staff, including both formal and informal programs of professional growth.

Philadelphia reported a Professional Study Group for its psychological staff while Richmond, Virginia, reported that it added to the usual monthly half-day meetings of its seven psychologists, a series of afternoon meetings with psychologists from other community agencies. In Chicago, regular scheduled staff meetings and committees on a variety of topics have been augmented by special arrangements for groups of the psychological staff to earn university graduate credits through study groups specifically organized around needs of the group.

In New York City, supervision and administration of psychological services has become a profession in itself, with the department offering in-service training courses not merely for psychologists, but specifically for supervisors and administrators of psychological services. Every urban staff finds it necessary to assign staff time, usually not only from officially designated supervisors but from experienced staff members, to work with the newcomers to the program, and to specific student field work supervision, if students are accepted.

Whether in the student field work, or in the internship, or the beginning assignment of a trained psychologist without previous school orientation, there must be ample opportunity for observation of normal as well as deviant behavior. The psychologist who later works chiefly with the disturbed or the handicapped or the gifted needs a firm grasp of what is normal for a given age and community group. Some student psychologists and beginners show a tendency to overidentify with the child, against the parents or the teacher, visualizing all parents according to a stereotype of the rejecting mother, all teachers as the frustrated old maid taking out her aggressions on the child. The beginner must learn that his function has two foci: part of his work is child-centered, as he seeks for solutions for the individual child, but an important part of it is staff-centered, as he works as a psychological consultant to principals, teachers, and parents.

All this seems obvious to those who have worked in the schools; it is, however, not so obvious to some university professors responsible for the training of our new recruits in school psychology. Allen of the University of Miami for example deplores the separate concept of school versus clinical psychologists. He says, rightfully enough, "In the long run, both the school psychologist and his counterpart the clinical psychologist have to deal with the total child and not with the referral reason alone. . . . Emphases vary, but service functions generally cover diagnosis, therapeutics or remediation, and research." [11] Although true as far as it goes, this point of view ignores the importance of the school setting. Similarly the Miami Conference in 1959 on Graduate Training in Psychology [12] while acknowledging the importance of school psychology and other fields of applied psychology, held as its major theme the unity of all psychological training and the need within the doctoral degree program for a basic core of training in psychology as a science and a profession, with more emphasis on the common elements than on the specialty, whether the individual was eventually to teach in a university, work in an industrial plant, a school, or a mental hospital, specialize in animal behavior or psychoanalytical therapy.

[11] R. M. Allen, "Obfuscation of the School Psychologist," *Educational Administration and Supervision,* 44 (September, 1958), 290–296.

[12] A. Roe, ed., *Graduate Education in Psychology* (Washington, D. C.: American Psychological Association, 1959).

The schools continue to hope to find well-trained psychologists as recruits who do know and appreciate the educational scene with its problems and potentials. Urban schools will continue to plan ways to compensate for the deficiencies of the persons who come to them for employment in the psychological services.

Functions of the Urban School Psychologist

The functions of school psychologists have been outlined in Chapter 1 and each is discussed more fully in later chapters. The major focus of this section is to point out some of the ways in which the practice of school psychology in an urban school system affects those functions.

A composite of many job descriptions for urban school psychological services provides a roster of duties no one person could well undertake. The urban school psychologist as reported from one city:

A. Works with other school staff on problems of individual children.
   1. Accepts referrals from a variety of sources.
   2. Evaluates children individually using a wide range of sources of data from records, conferences, interviews, observations in the classroom and on the playground, as well as by his own instruments of evaluation in all aspects of personality.
   3. Synthesizes and interprets the evaluative data, either chiefly on his own, or more hopefully in a staffing where interchange of ideas and points of view may be brought into play.
   4. Confers with adults and children on ways of meeting the problems of the individuals he has studied.
   5. Carries on individual and group therapy, formal or informal.
B. Works with other school staff on positive mental health programs.
   1. Encourages thoughtful and careful utilization of group testing evaluation possibilities in a sound guidance program.
   2. Acts as consultant to a variety of school, parent, and community people, individually and in groups.
   3. Concerns himself with mental health aspects of the entire school program. A positive mental health program leads to concern with such topics as curriculum development, in-service training of teachers, staff personnel practices, and much more.
C. Works to improve the psychological services.
   1. Contributes to the training of new school psychologists or student psychologists.
   2. Re-evaluates the role of school psychology in the school program and his own performance.
D. Contributes to advancement of knowledge and understanding of the educational process.
   1. Initiates or cooperates in research or advises on research design.

2. Interprets research findings, especially those from other fields of pure and applied psychology, not otherwise promptly brought to the attention of educators.

Any summary loses the essence of the job, it lacks reality because it does not give us the frustrations the urban psychologist has in meeting the overwhelming load of routine or the unique and difficult tasks and challenges that are his. Neither does it hint at the wide range of opportunity for new and creative approaches that urban school psychologists have evolved, the possibilities that others see for future action.

REFERRALS

Legal demands as well as school history and tradition mean that a large proportion of the referrals in many cities will be for possible candidates for special education programs, including but not limited to the mentally retarded. Special education today includes the cerebral palsied and other physically handicapped, those with vision and hearing handicaps, the speech defective, the culturally deprived, the emotionally disturbed, the brain injured, the truant, the pregnant girls, and all types of maladjusted children. Psychological services are also needed in connection with programs for the gifted. Educational problems in reading and arithmetic lead into studies of aphasia and specific emotional blocks. The variety of cases is endless, the special skills needed are complex. In many systems, psychologists are proud that the value of their services is so widely recognized that both parents and pupils ask for help. Teachers bring up every type of problem that bothers them, including those of the children they expect to continue to serve in their own classrooms.

The processing of referrals can be very significant. The larger the school system, the more need there may be for uniform routines of screening these referrals. However, as the number of steps between the psychologist and the person who wants help increases, the dangers of impersonalization and loss of contact increase. Some cities have gone through a process of increasing complication of referral, and then reduced it by decentralizing the scheduling of psychological service to bring the decisions as to where service is most needed closer to the point of origin. A teacher's request for psychological service is always screened by the principal, sometimes it then goes to the district or area superintendent. The referral slips may then go directly to the psychologist serving the school, or they may be further screened in the central office. In some cities all cases having to do with emotionally disturbed children are first seen by a social worker, who decides whether a psychological evaluation is needed; in at least one city this has become such a pattern that all referrals are passed upon first by the supervisor of social work services. More fruitfully the screening of referrals becomes a learning experience shared by the psychologist and the local school administrator who jointly decide on the relative importance of requests. Routine needs for legally required examinations and re-examinations in certain educational programs may rule out other potentially more significant studies. The referral process, professionally handled, serves to point up the real needs of the school system and to suggest revisions in working procedures.

DIAGNOSIS

In the urban school system, psychologists develop specializations. Even a small staff encourages one member to become the expert on working with the cerebral palsied, or the hearing handicapped, the brain injured, the blind, or on other special diagnostic problems. Though there may be less than a full-time job in a special area, an individual carrying a general district assignment often has allowance made for his service to the entire city on certain types of cases. This specialization against a background of varied cases is a stimulating working arrangement, allowing the individual by formal and informal study, consultation with other clinics, and critical evaluation of his own experience, to grow in depth, wisdom, and skill in a selected and difficult field of evaluation.

The normal neighborhood specializations that arise because of housing and living patterns give the urban psychologist opportunity for interesting and challenging types of specialization. Areas of high delinquency rate bring the school psychologist squarely into the heart of this problem. He has to come to grips with the impact of population mobility, with the diverse cultures of his neighborhood, with the pressures out of which anti-social gangs develop. He learns to work with the community agencies interested in the prevention of delinquency, sorting out those content to end their contribution by passing resolutions deploring conditions and demanding law enforcement or punishment of parents, and learning to work closely with those carrying out action programs on a variety of fronts. He studies the attitudes, customs, and problems of the newcomers to his district and of the old timers of his district and finds that his psychological insights are much enriched. Assigned to a school in a gang-ridden neighborhood, he has opportunity to see at work the insidious forces of impersonality, anonymity, and boredom which drive the boys of the streets in their all-consuming search for status and for "kicks." He works with teachers and administrators to find ways to provide within the school, in spite of the pressures on the staff of such a school, the antidotes for these triple poisons.

The city environment provides the psychologist with rich opportunities for supplementing his own diagnostic skills, and all those of the school staff, with the skills of a variety of specialized clinics and agencies. The school psychologist sees that channels of communication are opened according to professional standards, and steers the parents with whom he works to appropriate sources of help. He does not attempt an inadequate work-up on an apparently brain injured child if there are specialists or clinics available to undertake the task or to supplement and check on his tentative findings.

The magnitude of urban problems, the sheer numbers of cases that are at least superficially similar, creates traps for the unwary psychologist. Under pressure for numbers of completed evaluations, he may yield to the temptation to superficial study, snap judgments, repetitions of diagnostic clichés and shop worn recommendations. Fortunately for the good of the program, if not for the peace of mind of the psychologist, only the most blasé individual could long function superficially if his work is in the schools. If the school psychologist presents a diagnosis that does not add to what the teacher already knew, or writes reports full of high-sounding phrases and fine recommendations which school people know are impracticable or inappropriate to this case, he has to return to that same school next week or next month to face the embarrassing questions and pointed comments of the teacher still struggling with a daily problem.

SYNTHESIS

Just as bits of diagnostic information come from many sources and many individuals, as well as from the psychologist's specific clinical instruments, so the interpretation, the process of arriving at an understanding and formulating recommendations, is a task that should represent the meeting of many minds. To those familiar with child guidance clinic procedures, this sounds elementary. We will call together the principal, teacher, school nurse, remedial reading specialist, school social worker, audiologist, music consultant who has noticed the child's sense of rhythm, or whoever else is involved, and we will all sit down and compare notes and come up with a diagnosis and a recommendation. To most school administrators and even to most school psychologists, such a suggestion comes as somebody's dream of a peaceful utopia bearing no relationship to the realities of school life. Actually there are schools doing it regularly for a majority of the psychologist's cases of any import; there are many more school psychologists finding time for formal staff conferences for their most important cases, after school, before school, at noon or recess, perhaps with inadequate time but still helpful. Still more frequently, the psychologist finds time to talk over the case individually or in small groups with each of the people concerned, at odd moments in the busy day, adjusting himself to their schedules, not expecting them to adjust to his, and still gets a great deal of interaction. In some cities a parent is almost routinely included in the staffing, in others the conference with the parent follows a staff conference at which decision is taken as to how much to share with the parent and what line of approach to use.

TREATMENT

In many cities, the psychologist is not expected to undertake continuing therapeutic relationships with pupils. The replies to a questionnaire sent in 1960 and 1966 to cities with over 100,000 population strongly suggested in many cases the psychologist was still chiefly concerned with diagnosis. A number of city statements if taken literally imply that the psychologist is limited to assessment as a function. More typical of the replies are those which place the diagnostic responsibility in a frame work of consultative and co-operative treatment. The Division of Special Services of the St. Paul schools submitted the following statement:

FUNCTIONS OF THE SCHOOL PSYCHOLOGIST

The school psychologist should serve in the capacity of a consultant and co-worker with all teachers and educational services in the public school system.

The school psychologist's major interest should be the mental health of all children. With this in mind his responsibilities lie generally in the following areas:

1. He deals with psychological problems involved in the (a) diagnosis, (b) treatment, and (c) prevention of learning and behavior problems and personality disorders.
2. He conducts psychological examinations which include extraction of case history data by personal interview and utilization of psychological testing devices.
3. He recommends a corrective program following analysis of facts revealed in examinations, including prescription of various corrective techniques and educational adjustment.
4. He collaborates with parents, teachers, visiting teachers, and other school personnel in study and treatment of pupils who are maladjusted.
5. He participates in an active program of research on psychological problems as they are manifested in a school setting.

From Seattle, the Department of Guidance Services wrote:

Up until about 1950 the Services to Individual Children was pretty routine relative to testing for classification and routine home visiting mainly to check on a chronic attendance case. In recent years our philosophy and effort has broadened considerably and the psychological and social work staff operate somewhat like a clinical team and with a more dynamic approach to personality growth and development.

A few school systems make specific mention of a continued counseling relationship or treatment. This topic is discussed in more depth in Chapter 6 by Donald C. Smith. Barnhart, in a job analysis of the Cedar Rapids, Iowa, school psychologist position, lists "intensive counseling with child" as one of the four forms of treatment, the others being environmental manipulation, remedial instruction, and referral to outside agencies.[13]

In San Francisco, school psychologists are considered clinical psychologists and carry a small number of children in treatment, psychiatric consultation service being available to them.

A Long Beach, California publication stated that extended therapy for the individual case sometimes falls to the school psychologist, depending on the needs of the case and the responsibility for it carried by other school workers. This psychologist concludes: "It is one of the rewarding and inspiring experiences to see how the child's normal growth urges can be realigned and started toward productivity by the relatively simple but fundamental therapy: establishing a warm, supporting dependable relationship between worker and child." [14]

Outstanding for treatment services among the large cities are the Child Guidance Clinics of New York City. Through these widely dispersed units (nine serve various areas in Brooklyn alone), a team of psychiatrists, psychologists and social workers engage cooperatively in the total process of diagnosis, consultation, and treatment.

A number of experiments in bringing child guidance clinic principles and practices into the schools are reported in a volume edited by a school psychologist.[15] Most of the reports are written by psychiatrists or social workers. The experiments are largely peripheral to the school, representing a service brought in by an outside agency. In these accounts, there appears relatively little participation by psychologists, and in many cases apparently little real involvement of the school administration and staff. It would be interesting, to know the later history of these experiments, and particularly whether the schools where the experiments were conducted were motivated to continue and expand the group therapy sessions or the psychiatric consultation described, after outside support was withdrawn.

The urban school psychologist with an assigned schedule of schools to serve probably is less likely to find time, or at least no more likely to, for a continuing counseling relationship in any formal psychotherapeutic sense with individual children than is the psychologist in another school setting.

The offering of treatment services by school psychologists is limited not merely by lack of time and personnel. Serious question as to the advisa-

---

[13] R. E. Barnhart and R. J. Baldave, "Role of the School Psychologist," *Nation's Schools,* 61 (April, 1958), 49–51.

[14] J. M. Haskell, "School Psychologists Counsels," *California Journal of Secondary Education,* 21 (1946) 88–91.

[15] M. Krugman, ed., *Orthopsychiatry and the Schools* (New York: American Orthopsychiatric Association, 1958).

bility of using clinical therapy or psychotherapy within the school framework has been raised. A psychiatric child guidance team, reporting their evaluation of an experiment in the therapeutic use of a school club conclude that

> group therapy, at least with seriously disturbed youngsters, should *not* be carried on in connection with or in a school setting. Despite some prevailing ideas to the contrary, the inherent value of school groups is educational rather than therapeutic. A teacher cannot be a teacher and a therapist at one and the same time. . . . The therapeutic failure may be attributed at least in part to the peculiar nature of the influence of the total whole environment on the therapeutic regimen. The requisite permissiveness in the group unavoidably carried over into the classroom—. . . added burden and confusion for teacher and child.[16]

From El Paso, Texas, comes a similar warning from the school psychologist:

> But the school psychologist unlike the psychologist in a clinic, rarely has time for more than three or four hours with each child and must not encourage a close personal relationship. The parents and the teacher cannot transfer any of their responsibilities to the psychologist. On the contrary the child's problem is handed back to them with trimmings, but with a practical plan of action. They, and not the psychologist, do the work and earn the rewards.[17]

The debate over psychotherapy as a function of the school psychologist will very likely continue. The factors involved are for the most part not unique to the urban setting. It is to be noted, however, that psychotherapy of many degrees of intensity is practiced by some urban school psychologists. It ranges from scheduled appointments in a clinic or on the weekly visits of a school psychologist through brief but planned friendly contacts at regular intervals, to the most informal of continuing interest relationships, in which the child knows that the pyschologist makes a point of greeting him and inquiring after his welfare and progress on each visit. Beyond the informal, supportive relationships, however, the evidence is that therapy is not the accepted responsibility of the psychologist in a majority of city school systems.

The problem is not limited to the United States. An Expert Committee of the United Nations Education, Scientific and Cultural Organization prepared a report on Psychological Services for Schools and Other Educational Institutions in 1954, listed minimal functions which emphasized diagnosis and collaboration with teachers and others to improve educational method and the climate of the classroom, and to plan remedial or other treatment from

16 M. L. Falik, B. Rubenstein and M. Levitt, "A Critical Evaluation of the Therapeutic Use of a Club in School," *Mental Hygiene*, 39 (1955), 63–78.

17 A. A. Larkin, "From the Files of the School Psychologist," *National Elementary Principal*, 34 (September, 1954), 117–130.

whatever quarter seems appropriate. This UNESCO report nowhere mentions direct therapy as a function of the school psychologist.[18]

GROUP TESTING

Responsibility for group testing has not disappeared from the list of school psychological services and will be discussed in depth by Stanley Marzolf in Chapter 7. It is mentioned, for example, among the duties of the psychological services in Milwaukee, Providence, New Orleans, and Houston. The psychological staff may organize and supervise group testing, select tests, train teachers to give tests, check test results, and assist in interpretation of tests. Some psychological departments, as in Milwaukee, have a separate section, headed by a test coordinator with a considerable staff of clerical and professional workers concerned with the group testing program.

In most cities, however, it would appear that as the group testing programs have expanded and become regular features of the school system, the administration of the program, even if it had been initiated by the psychological staff, has moved over to the general administration, and is increasingly decentralized. The enlarged testing programs stimulated by federal support through NDEA and the Elementary and Secondary School Acts of 1965 have apparently been largely administered by secondary school guidance departments that traditionally have only loose connection with the psychological services of the school system.

CURRICULUM CONSULTATION

Consultation on curriculum problems and membership on curriculum committees was mentioned in the list of duties of psychologists reported from many cities. Philadelphia in an annual report for 1959 indicated that its 24 psychologists served on 13 school committees. Louisville, Kentucky, Chicago, and Minneapolis are among other cities specifically mentioning the service of school psychologists on curriculum and other school committees. Minneapolis psychologists, for example, serve on committees concerned with the gifted child, reading, health staff, city-wide evaluation and testing, and on various curriculum committees. They participated in the development of the Social Studies Guide, Mental Health Guide, and the Health Education Curriculum Guide. However, a report from Toledo, Ohio, frankly starred this item and the group testing item on their own list of psychologists' functions and noted that these duties were not usually performed because of lack of time and the fact that psychologists were not always qualified or interested in curriculum development.

[18] F. W. Parkyn, "The Role of School Psychologists," *UNESCO*, XI (1954), 95–101.

IN-SERVICE TRAINING OF TEACHERS

School psychologists contribute to the formal in-service training of teachers on request of the school administration, usually as a part of a series of programs. However, the psychological staff not infrequently take the initiative in suggesting single sessions, institutes, or continuing programs on topics they are particularly interested in discussing with teachers. In Chicago where the elementary guidance program was an outgrowth in the thirties of the psychological bureau, that bureau has conducted regular one- or two-week training courses for all new persons assigned as "adjustment teachers" in the elementary schools. In Minneapolis the chief psychologist and her assistants give much time to specific teacher training programs, providing seminars and talks on mental health and related topics. They have lectured on classroom management and discipline, intelligence test interpretation, the gifted child in the classroom, and the handicapped child.

Invitations to talk to teachers and administrators' meetings are probably an inevitable concomitant of any successful program of school psychology. Where the psychologist's work is respected and understood, there will be a continuing demand for help that will afford teachers and administrators deeper insight into the psychodynamics of the classroom. A recent annual report from Richmond, Virginia, indicated that seven psychologists talked to eleven school faculty groups, to twenty-four PTA and other community groups, to six classes or other student groups, and presented a radio program. Philadelphia's psychological workers reported fifty-one talks given in one school year.

One school psychologist from New York City has described the use of recordings of the responses of delinquent boys in a series of workshops for teachers. Recordings of group discussions of delinquent and pre-delinquent boys were used as source materials.[19]

In addition to such formal contributions of a school psychologist to the in-service training of teachers, the importance of his daily work relationships with teachers should not be forgotten. As he and the teacher struggle together to understand Johnny and to find a solution to his problems, the teacher may well develop insights that will carry over to many other children.

STAFF PERSONNEL PROGRAMS

When the possible contributions of modern psychology to the personnel problems of teacher selection, promotion, rating, and morale are mentioned, most school psychologists draw back in alarm. They do not usually want their

[19] E. Mann, "What are They Saying?" *Pathways in Child Guidance*, 3 (October, 1960).

work to become associated with such topics. Yet the relationship does exist. In Minneapolis, every applicant for a teaching or promotion post is given the Minnesota Multiphasic Personality Inventory and these are interpreted by a psychological staff member. Psychologists have served from time to time on a committee for selecting teachers, assistant principals, and principals and on Personnel Department promotion committees.

From Indianapolis, a tentative job description of a psychologist, submitted in response to a recent questionnaire, listed two teacher personnel functions: 1) limited confidential counseling of teachers and other school personnel, at their request, and 2) assisting Staff of the Personnel Service Division upon request in evaluation of prospective school personnel. In Detroit, examination of teacher candidates is a function of the Psychological Clinic.

In Chicago the medical and psychiatric examinations of teachers, both for entrance into the system and for possible release from duty, were for many years carried out by physicians assigned to the Bureau of Child Study. In 1956 these functions and personnel were transferred to the Bureau of Health Services. Fortunately the medical examiners, even when attached to the Bureau of Child Study, were not seen by school staff as related to the work of the psychologist in the schools. The mere attachment of the psychiatrists who examined teachers to the Bureau did not appear to raise any unfavorable repercussions in the schools.

School administration could well call upon the best knowledge in the psychological profession for assistance in re-evaluating their personnel policies for the selection, evaluation, up-grading and separation of teachers and other staff members. The school psychologist with appropriate background might be a valuable consultant on a committee that was scrutinizing existing personnel practices and considering newer approaches. However, the psychologist who as an individual is to carry on continuing team work with the school staff on the problems of children should for the sake of his warm and intimate working relationship with the staff in the schools avoid any semblance of direct participation in the operation of staff-personnel programs.

Research is another function of the school psychologist given lip service in the meetings of the profession but seldom provided for in the budgets of schools systems. This function of the school psychologist is discussed by Professor Itkin in Chapter 19. Federal funds made available through the Cooperative Research Program, the National Defense Education Act, Vocational Rehabilitation, Vocational Education, and the Elementary and Secondary Education Act of 1965 have given school psychologists opportunity to organize or to participate in research programs in many school systems, on a scale not previously possible. School psychologists in Milwaukee are heavily involved in demonstration and research projects stemming from rehabilitation grants to a community agency there, but involving close relationship with the school.

New York, Chicago, and Detroit are among the city school systems which received Cooperative Research Funds from the U. S. Office of Education for research on the mentally handicapped while every large district has received funds partially for research through the 1965 federal acts. Philadelphia reported research by its school psychologists on a vocabulary test for deaf pupils and on characteristics of retarded trainable pupils. Richmond, Virginia reported that its seven psychologists in 1958–1959 were engaged in the following research activities:

> Service on committee of Virginia Council on Family Relations study of sex education
>
> Assistance in initiation of a child-study project for elementary school teachers on the withdrawn child
>
> New scoring technique for Bender-Gestalt
>
> Diagnostic value of Kahn Test of Symbol Arrangement
>
> Two research papers read at professional meetings.

Though definite data is not easy to produce, school psychologists' research activities have undoubtedly increased since a survey made in 1953, prior to the Thayer Conference when psychologists from communities of many sizes reported the average ranking of their duties. Of eleven categories of actual duties, research was ranked in eleventh place by psychologists from the large and small school systems. Only in the middle sized systems, with average daily attendance of 5,000 to 9,999, did research rise to tenth place in the list.[20]

The school psychologist feels a deep responsibility for keeping up to date in his field and for interpreting to the schools the results of research relevant to general behavior theories. The task is very great. He may for example be interested in the effect of learned socialization and personality patterns on problem solving and other mental functions, as studied by Davis and Eels. He may follow Bettelheim's work on the emotional or general personality concomitants of learning difficulties in disturbed children; he may note Havighurst's studies of the relation of developmental tasks and other socialization factors to the educative process and Getsel's conclusions concerning the effect of social role and role conflicts on the effectiveness of classroom teaching and learning, to make reference only to a part of the output of one university department of educational psychology in one year. He has perhaps an even greater responsibility to keep alert for developments in fields of psychology that school people are less likely to read, but that may

[20] B. Lantz, *Survey of School Psychologists, 1953–1954*, mimeographed report to the Thayer Conference (August, 1954).

produce findings raising exciting questions as to their school implications. The task of synthesis, of deciding what can be used and how the psychologist can promote its use, is an overwhelming one. No school psychologist can do it alone, but the psychological services of an urban school system are alert to the need and continue a search for the mechanisms that will translate new knowledge into action.

Schools have not always been hospitable to the research plans of psychologists or others from outside the system, whether from neighboring universities, hospitals, clinics or community agencies. Too often the would-be researcher develops his research design without consultation with the schools, on topics of little interest to them, or unknown to them, and demands time, space, and other facilities without any return that is at all clear to the school people concerned. School psychologists can be helpful in liason, initiating in some cases cooperative relationships with the agencies that can provide the manpower and material for needed studies, or at least helping the researcher at the point of planning to take the schools' needs into account, and to work in ways that will leave the faculty more enlightened, or at least with curiosities heightened, and the pupils unharmed by their participation.

There is good school-based psychological research coming out of Detroit, New York, Chicago, and elsewhere. The success in attracting Ph.D. level workers to the field of school psychology will be reflected in an acceleration of this trend. The cities with their plethora of subjects, their complex of cooperating agencies, medical or social, their increasing flexibility and decentralization should lead in this trend.

Selected Supplementary Readings

Abrahamson, David, Emanuel Hammer, Irving Jacks, and Sydney Connell, "Status of Mental Hygiene and Child Guidance Facilities in Public Schools in the United States," *Journal of Pediatrics*, XLVI (1955), 107–118.

American Psychological Association, *The Challenge of a New Decade in School Psychology*. Report of the Fifth Professional Institute for School Psychologists, Division of School Psychologists of the American Psychological Association, 1960, mimeographed.

Baltimore Bulletin of Education, XLI, 1964. Entire issue devoted to "Education and the Inner City Child."

Besag, Frank, "Deviant Student Behavior and the Role of the School," *Urban Education*, II (1966), 27–34.

Boskoff, Alvin, *The Sociology of Urban Regions*. New York: Meredith, 1962.

Brain, G. B., "Schools for Cities: The Problems of Urban Education," *College of Education Record*, 32 (January, 1966), 1–38.

Campbell, R. F., "Public Decisions for Urban Education," *Elementary School Journal,* 66 (January, 1966), 169–173.

Chapin, F. Stuart, and Shirley F. Weiss, eds., *Urban Growth Dynamics in a Regional Cluster of Cities.* New York: John Wiley & Sons, Inc., 1962.

Davis, Kingsley, "Urbanization-Changing Patterns of Living," in *The Changing American Population,* ed., H. S. Simpson. New York: Institute of Life Insurance, 1962.

Dukelow, D. A., "Mental Health Services in Large City Schools," *Journal of School Health,* XXXI (March, 1961), 75–82.

Dyckman, John, "The Changing Uses of the City," *The Future Metropolis, Daedalus.* Proceedings of the American Academy of Arts and Sciences, XC (Winter, 1961), 111–131.

Ernatt, Raymond, "The School in a Racially Changing Community," *National Elementary Principal,* XLV (Feb. 1966), 16–21.

Frisch, Paul, "A Program in School Psychology," *Mental Hygiene,* XL (1956), 258–266.

Fusco, G. C., "Preparing the City Child for His School," *School Life,* XLVI (1964).

Gottlieb, David, and Jon Reeves, *Adolescent Behavior in Urban Areas: A Bibliographic Review and Discussion of the Literature.* New York: Free Press of Glencoe, Inc., 1963.

Havighurst, R. J., "Metropolitan Development and the Educational System," *The School Review,* LXIX (Autumn, 1961), 251–267.

Herriott, R. E., and N. H. St. John, *Social Class and the Urban School.* New York: John Wiley & Sons, Inc., 1966.

Kelly, Earl C., *In Defense of Youth.* Englewood Cliffs, N.J.: Prentice-Hall, Inc., 1963.

Levine, Louis S., *et al.,* "The Use of the Child Development Specialist in the Elementary Schools," *Psychology in the Schools,* II (July, 1965), 255–262.

Levine, Murray, *et al.,* "Pupil Turnover and Academic Performance in an Inner City Elementary School," *Psychology in the Schools,* III (April, 1966), 153–158.

Mercer, Blaine E., "Rural Migration to Urban Settings; Educational and Welfare Problems," *Social Studies,* LV (February, 1964), 59–64.

Mullen, Frances A., "Middle-Class Urban Schools," *Professional School Psychology,* Vol. I, ed. M. G. Gottsegen and G. B. Gottsegen. New York: Grune & Stratton, Inc., 1960.

National School Public Relations Association, "Problems of the Big City Schools," in *Shape of Education For 1963.* Washington, D.C.: National Education Association, 1963.

New York Youth Board, *Reaching the Fighting Gang*. New York: New York City Youth Board, 1960.

Office of Education, U.S. Dept. of Health, Education, and Welfare, *Education of Handicapped Children and Youth: Title I, Elementary and Secondary Education of 1965*. Washington: U.S. Govt. Printing Office, 1965.

Pasamanick, Benjamin, Dean W. Roberts, Paul Lemkau, and Dean B. Krueger, "A Survey of Mental Disease in an Urban Population: Prevalence by Race and Income," *Epidemology of Mental Disorder*. Washington, D.C.: American Association for the Advancement of Science, No. 60, 1959.

Peddy, Lester, "Intensive Clinic Services in the School Setting," *Reaching the Unreached*. New York: New York City Youth Board, 1952.

Schuttler-Janikulla, K., "Schulpsychologische Tatigkeit in einem Groszstadtbezirk" ("School Psychology in Big Cities"), *Praxis der Kinderpsychologie und Kinderpsychiatrie*, 14 (1965), 264–271.

Sessions, John, "A New Approach to Urban Education," *Changing Education*, 27 (Spring, 1966), 6–11.

Seymour, H. C., "Rochester's Co-ordinated School Services for Delinquency Prevention," *Journal of Educational Sociology*, XXIV (1950), 30–35.

Shaw, Clifford, *Delinquency Areas*. Chicago: University of Chicago Press, 1929.

Srole, Leo, Thomas S. Lagner, Stanley T. Michael, Marvin K. Opler, and Thomas A. C. Rennie, *Mental Health in the Metropolis: The Midtown Manhattan Study*, Vol. I. New York: McGraw-Hill Book Company, 1962.

Stewart, Charles E., "Racial Issues Confronting Large City School Administrators," *Urban Education*, I (1965), 202–206.

Strang, Ruth, "Many Sided Aspects of Mental Health," in *Mental Health in Modern Education*, Fifty-fourth Yearbook of the National Society for the Study of Education, Part II. Chicago: University of Chicago Press, 1955.

Urban Education and *Integrated Education*, two recent journals, have many relevant articles.

Vernon, Raymond, *Metropolis 1958: An Interpretation of the Findings of the New York Metropolitan Region Study*. New York: Doubleday & Company, Inc., 1963.

Weaver, Robert C., *The Urban Complex*. New York: Doubleday & Company, Inc., 1964.

MERLE L. MEACHAM

VERDUN TRIONE

3

The Role of the School Psychologist in the Community School

The profession of school psychology has grown remarkably since its inception in the Chicago system in 1899.[1] In part this has been the natural growth one would expect with the increasing school population. The major population growth has been in the urban and suburban areas and consequently school systems in the metropolitan areas have expanded at a tremendous pace. Many rural and suburban school systems have developed extensive programs of special education and thus have provided employment for many school psychologists principally as diagnosticians for exceptional children.

However, as school population has increased, the total number of local school districts has decreased. In the years from 1945 to 1967 the number of local school districts decreased from approximately 103,000 to 26,000 [2] and the decline continues with further consolidation. The President's Committee on National Goals recommends

[1] J. E. W. Wallin, "The School Psychologist in Retrospect," *Journal of Consulting Psychology,* 6 (1942), 309–312.
[2] C. O. Fitzwater, "Trends in School District Reorganization," *School Life,* 39 (April, 1957), 5–7 and 15.

68

that "The approximately 30,000 school districts existing today should be reduced to about 10,000 by 1970." [3] Community and rural school districts that have combined to form more efficient units are entering a phase where they are able to offer special educational opportunities for many types of handicapped children who previously were not served in the schools.

It is difficult to write about the community or rural school for the reason that wide diversity exists within the rural pattern. As Miller has indicated,

> The ways of life of the cotton plantation owner, the sharecropper, the migrant worker in the citrus belt or in the sugar beet area, and the members of the family on a family farm in the Midwest are vastly different; yet all are rural. . . . According to U.S. Census practice, communities of 2500 population or less are classified as rural, but that is a frankly arbitrary procedure. . . . All of this means, of course, that the educator or psychologist who seeks to understand the rural-urban elements influencing students in his school must seek such understandings in the context of his own community, and in the experiences of students in this community, or in the communities from which they come.[4]

In 1960, Magary and Meacham [5] made a study of the growth of school psychology in the United States. A questionnaire was submitted to the fifty state departments of education and to the District of Columbia. The questions were designed to discover the rate of growth in school psychological services during the past decade and to find some of the factors affecting this rate of growth. The survey contained the following questions:

1. How many public school psychologists were there in your state ten years ago?
2. How many are employed in the public schools now?
3. Are there special requirements for certification?
4. How are children in the rural areas served by school psychologists?
5. Are there training programs for school psychologists?
6. Does the state office contribute in any special way to the salaries of the school psychologist other than the ordinary aid given to a classroom teacher?
7. Do you have any special publications regarding the role and functions of the school psychologist?

Table 1 summarizes the data obtained from the various state department of education offices. If their correspondents indicated that certain

---

[3] C. G. Wrenn, *The Counselor in a Changing World* (Washington, D. C.: American Personnel and Guidance Association, 1962), p. 84.

[4] C. H. Miller, *Principles of Guidance* (New York: Harper and Row, Publishers, 1961), pp. 40–41.

[5] J. F. Magary and M. L. Meacham, "The Growth of School Psychology in the Last Decade," *Journal of School Psychology*, 1 (January, 1963), 5–13.

TABLE 1

National Survey of the Development of School Psychology

(1) State	(2) No. in 1950	(3) No. in 1960	(4) Special Requirements for Certification (by January 1, 1967)	(5) Services in Rural Areas	(6) Special Financial Support	(7) Publications
Alabama	0	8	In process	Very limited	none	none
Alaska	0	2	MA + 2 yrs. teaching	State Health Dept.	none	none
Arizona	2	14	MA	none	none	none
Arkansas	0	1	none	none	none	none
California	75	600	2 yrs. grad. work	yes	for handicapped children; excess cost	yes
Colorado	4	50	MA and teaching experience	very little	for handicapped children	none
Connecticut	?	18 (42 Psych. examiners)	Ph.D. equiv. MA + for Psych. examiners	Child Guidance Clinics; private practitioners	none	yes
Delaware	6	17	Courses & minimum hrs.	All schools	yes	yes
District of Columbia	14		MA		none	none
Florida	4		60 hrs. grad. & teaching cert.	Child Guidance Clinics	none	none
Georgia	0	11	none	State purchases private services	none	none
Hawaii	0	1 + 4 Psych. Ex.	yes	very limited	none	none

State						
Idaho	0	1		none	none	none
Illinois	60	125	MA + Ph.D., Ed.D., MA	16 psychologists in 4 base areas	$3,000	yes
Indiana	?	6		?	?	none
Iowa	5	45	Ph.D., Ed.D. MA	Through County Superintendent yes	$4,000 + $200 increments	yes
Kansas	0	15	MA +	yes	$1,500–$3,000 travel	yes
Kentucky	0	2	MA + 24 hrs.	no	no	none
Louisiana	0	15	none	yes	In special Ed. centers	none
Maine	0	3	Guidance Cert. 60 Grad. hrs. Supervisor Cert.—	none	none	none
Maryland	2	44		State Health Dept	none	none
Massachusetts	12	200	MA and teaching certificate	Mental Health Clinics	share	none
Michigan	?	20 + 200 diagnosticians	Ph.D.–Psychologist MA–Diagnostician	Cooperative programs	up to $5,125 when serving 5,000 children	none
Minnesota	11	67	MA + examination	Cooperative programs	⅔ of salary not more than $3,600	none
Mississippi	0	0	none	none	none	none
Missouri	0	25	MA	none	no	none
Montana	0	0	none	Mental Hygiene Clinics	no	none
Nebraska	2	3	none	State Dept. & University	no	none
Nevada	0	2	none	Where employed	no	none

TABLE 1—Continued

(1) State	(2) No. in 1950	(3) No. in 1960	(4) Special Requirements for Certification (by January 1, 1967)	(5) Services in Rural Areas	(6) Special Financial Support	(7) Publications
New Hampshire	0	1	none	State Clinics	no	none
New Jersey	60	155	60 hrs.	Part time or per case service	some	none
New Mexico	0	0	Bach. + 15 hrs.	none	no	none
New York	200	573	MA	yes	up to ½ salary	yes
North Carolina	0	4	yes	Welfare Dept.	no	none
North Dakota	0	2 (visiting counselors)	Grad. work in psych. or Soc. work	Other state agencies	up to $1,500	yes
Ohio	42	146	MA	County offices	$2,000–8,690	yes
Oklahoma	2	25	Ph.D.–psychologist MA–psychometrist	Health Dept.	no	none
Oregon	3	5	MA	Some diagnostic work	50%	yes
Pennsylvania	?	282	Psychologist 66 hrs.	County Programs	for county supervisors	in process
Rhode Island	?	20	MA	Cooperative serv. & state agencies	no	none
South Carolina (effective 7/66)	1	3	Class I-MA + special courses Class II-Ph.D.	Mental Health Clin.–Private services	no	none
South Dakota	0	1	MA + special courses	on special request	no	none

72

State						
Tennessee	0	10	MA + special courses	State contracts services from local clinicians	no	in process
Texas	0	16	none	very limited	some (when listed as counselors)	none
Utah	4	12	MA + teaching cert. yes, by 1967	state agencies	no	yes
Vermont	0	0		Some state level staff in sp. ed.	no	none
Virginia	10	20	yes	?	no	none
Washington	?	56	MA + special courses	cooperative programs	"excess costs" special units	yes
West Virginia	1	4	in process	Health Dept. State Dept. of special ed.	no	none
Wisconsin	?	30 + 115 Psychometrists	MA +	Itinerant services	up to 15% in area of retardation	none
Wyoming	0	3	MA (psychometrist)	by referral	no	none
TOTALS	519	2836				

changes were in the offering the table indicates this by the words "in process." Some of the figures are obviously estimates but the trends are evident.

Twenty-two states reported no school psychologists in 1950. Only four indicated this in 1960 (Mississippi, Montana, New Mexico, Vermont). Exclusive of the categories—psychological examiner, psychological diagnostician and psychometrist—there is a reported growth in the number of persons with the title of school psychologist from 519 in 1950 to 2,836 in 1960, and interestingly enough 2,081 of these are concentrated in the seven states of California, Illinois, Massachusetts, New Jersey, New York, Ohio, and Pennsylvania. While these are very populous states, they would still seem to have a disproportionate number of the total population of school psychologists. It would seem there is considerable room for expansion in the other forty-three states. In 1967 California had well over 1,000 school psychologists and psychometrists.

Newland,[6] Hodges,[7] and more recently Nelson [8] have reported extensively on the state requirements for certification. We will not be concerned in detail with this here. However, it is significant for the growth of the profession that six states, Alaska, Minnesota, North Dakota, South Carolina, Utah, and Washington have recently completed certification requirements. Officials from two states, i.e., Alabama and West Virginia, report that they are in the process. In 1967 Georgia, Mississippi, and Nevada reported certification. This brings the total number of states with specific state credentials to forty including the District of Columbia. While there is wide variation in the requirements, their adoption is an indication of the acceptance of the profession and bodes well for its continued expansion.

In this chapter we are particularly interested in the services in the rural and community schools, and the above survey supplies some interesting information. Only seven states indicated that there were no school psychological services available in the rural areas. While there is considerable range in quantity and kinds of services offered, there does seem to be an effort toward expansion of these services in schools at a distance from urban cities. State agencies in addition to the schools or the state departments of education are involved. Perhaps, as school districts consolidation continues and more local special education programs are developed, we will see a much more rapid expansion of school psychological services in the rural areas.

Well-articulated training programs under qualified supervision are necessary for the physical and professional growth of school psychology. It is

[6] T. E. Newland, "Formalized Psychological Services in State Educational Programs," *American Psychologist,* 11 (1956), 136–200.

[7] W. L. Hodges, "State Certification of School Psychologist," *American Psychologist,* 15 (1960), 346–349.

[8] W. H. Nelson, "Variations in Patterns of Certification for School Psychologists," *Journal of School Psychology,* 2 (Winter, 1964), 17–33.

likely that these vary as do the certification requirements, but these training programs are an indication of community interest in the field and suggest marked expansion in the future.[9, 10]

A careful examination of Table 1 under the sixth question reveals a major reason for the growth of school psychological services. Only nineteen states in 1960 gave financial aid to the local districts for psychologists. However, these nineteen states employ 2,519 of those 2,836 reported in this survey. There seems to be no consistent method for alloting funds, as some states give specific amounts while others share only within limits. Other states limit disbursements for services to specific types of handicapped children only, while others cover a somewhat broader field. At any rate, it is evident that the growth of special education and psychological services depends to a large extent on available funds. This is particularly true in the rural areas that often lack a large school tax base. Probably the most efficient way to help these schools to expand their special programs is through state aid. No one can deny that the children in these areas are just as important as those in the more heavily populated districts. The question then becomes how to bring children in rural, especially depressed areas, psychological services. Federal and State financial aid seems to be at least part of the answer.

It seems obvious by now that the profession is growing rapidly in all areas, but is it being integrated into the schools or is it something of an appendage? There is some reason to believe that publications delineating role and functions are a reasonable indication of integration of a service. Twelve states in 1960 had such publications and two were preparing them. These fourteen states employ 1,848 of the psychologists reported here, or about sixty-two per cent. The publications spell out the role of the school psychologist in great detail and the student would do well to examine as many as he can find. These publications, especially those of his state, also indicate that much thought and energy has gone into the formulation of programs. More local, state, and federal publications will appear in the next few years as the profession inevitably expands to meet the needs of the schools. For, implicit in all of this growth is the value of psychological services in the schools. Undoubtedly, one of the greatest areas of expansion will be in community and rural schools. Another survey at the end of this decade will most certainly reinforce this view.

Community School Concept

The rural or community schools are no longer the step-children of the educational system. While population growth has not been as spectacular in

[9] M. A. White, "Graduate Training in School Psychology," *Journal of School Psychology*, 2 (Winter, 1964), 34–42.

[10] A. J. Bindman, "University Training of School Psychologists and Certification Standards," *Journal of School Psychology*, 2 (Winter, 1964), 43–48.

the rural areas as in and near the large cities, the process of consolidation has made it possible to improve curriculum and expand services. Children are transported rapidly from remote areas. In many instances, the newer buildings rival those found in the more densely populated areas. People in the smaller communities have long felt close to their schools and they are frequently eager to finance improvements. The day of the remote one-room school is not ended but that time is approaching. While some educators view this passing with nostalgia, most feel that there can be better educational opportunities for all children with the consolidated schools.

The addition of a school psychologist to a staff at a local or county level is usually the first move toward a special education program. A community must assess its needs in this area and it is largely the task of the school psychologist to do the kind of diagnostic case finding necessary before a comprehensive program can begin. It would be useless, for example, for a school system to undertake an educational program for the mentally retarded without specific information as to the number, age and educability of these children. Educability is determined through diagnostic evaluations by a competently trained person who has understanding of the educational needs of these children and awareness of the limits of the school system where he functions. Thus, the psychologist in the community school is not just a transplanted clinician or diagnostician, for he makes his diagnosis in relation to an educational problem. He is a person oriented to and trained in both psychology and education. It is his task to increase the educational opportunities of every child he sees.

Types of School Psychological Services

There are several methods of bringing psychological services to the rural and community schools currently in use in this country. These have developed to meet local needs and vary from area to area as demand and availability of personnel permit. There are highly developed programs in such states as California, New York, and Washington, and there are some states where there are no programs (see Table 1). In many instances, psychological services are provided to the schools by other agencies such as health departments or mental hygiene clinics. Although this type of service is useful and particularly valuable in those areas where there are no school psychologists, there is frequently some difficulty in translating clinic findings into a school program for a particular child. School personnel are very prone to ask, and with justification, what a particular diagnosis means in terms of curriculum adaptations for a particular child. How should this child be taught? What effect does the diagnostic category have on the learning process? A person without knowledge of the classroom is at a disadvantage. The ideal type of therapy or environmental manipulation may not be the practical one. What would work in one school may not work in another because of a different educational philosophy, different personnel, or different environmental conditions. Thus when an agency does an evaluation, much that is potentially of benefit to the child is lost in translation unless there is good communication. For example, Trione [11] found, in an unpublished study, that the school psychologist is frequently in a good position to help translate clinic findings to teachers. Clinic reports rarely distinguished between "family centered" problems and "school centered" problems. Yet this is an important distinction for the school staff and will have a real bearing on how they proceed. He also found that school systems in the rural areas may frequently have a large number of teachers on emergency credentials. In Trione's study thirteen per cent of the primary teachers and forty-five per cent of the eighth grade teachers were on sub-standard certificates. This would create a further problem of communication and possibly would necessitate some in-service training on the part of the psychologist.

Many state colleges and universities provide special psychological services to rural school districts. These units are frequently in conjunction with training programs and require that the child be brought to campus for testing and evaluation. However, Rosebrook [12] reports an instance in Ohio when itinerant psychological services were provided by the university with the school districts merely sharing transportation costs.

Although the college and university clinics are excellently staffed and frequently provide very fine service, they have their limitations. One is that they will often accept only certain types of children and those in limited numbers. For example, research and training needs may limit the case load to the very young mentally retarded. Or a psychiatric clinic will tend to accept, or more likely place on a waiting list, children with certain diagnostic labels. Another limitation is the necessity for travel. Often it is not feasible to transport a child long distances for an evaluation. This is particularly true if there is little likelihood of follow-up in the local community. It is also true if such a trip would prove threatening to the child his reaction would obscure the clinic findings.

Generally, then, the college and university resources are limited to a relatively small number of specific types of handicapped children. The more usual difficulties must be handled on the local level, with whatever resources are available. And this is as it should be. How much better for a community to organize a Community Council for Children or to provide special services

[11] V. Trione, "A Proposed Study of the Duties of California's School Psychologists and Psychometrists," *California Journal of Educational Research*, 8 (May, 1957).
[12] W. Rosebrook, "Psychological Services for School on a Regional Basis," *Journal of Consulting Psychology*, 6 (1942), 196–200.

locally. The more experience the local groups have in developing services to meet the needs of their children the better they will be able to meet future needs.

PATTERNS OF ORGANIZATION OF RURAL SCHOOL
PSYCHOLOGICAL SERVICES

Exclusive of the district that can hire its own full-time person or can obtain services as needed from other areas, psychological services in the community schools have generally followed two or three patterns or organization. The first pattern is an itinerant service brought in from outside the immediate area to be served. These are frequently supported by state departments of education or health as a means of bringing help to handicapped children in the more remote areas. A person or team will travel on a more or less regular schedule, examine children, and make oral and written recommendations. Baller and Worcester [13] described the functions of such a field clinic in Nebraska; they were met with an increasing demand for services.

A distinct advantage that this method has over the various agency services is the possibility for better communication between the travelling team and the local staff. If the professional team is hired by people in education they tend to have this orientation and the basic educational responsibility to the learning process. Their full time is devoted to school problems. Such a person or team can develop experience with many different types of children in a variety of settings and they have some opportunity to follow-up and re-evaluate. Thus there can be some continuity in the program. While there is still some distance from the local staff in the sense that responsibility is to a state rather than a local office, all are a part of the educational team and share at least some common training.

The most usual problem facing these travelling teams is that their services become spread too thinly. Travel over a large area requires time and subtracts from the amount of professional time in any one area. Furthermore, as such a service becomes accepted the demand for it increases and there is need for more staff. It is not always easy to find professional people who wish to travel so much of the time.

It is frequently at this point that a second type of itinerant service develops. The psychologist is based in a rural area and serves a small number of districts fairly close together. The actual mechanics of this may vary from state to state. Myer [14] indicates that in Pennsylvania each county has a school

    [13] W. R. Baller and D. A. Worcester, "The Field Clinic as a Means of Supplying Psychological Services to the Small School in Nebraska," *Journal of Exceptional Children*, 6 (1940), 163–166.
    [14] L. N. Myer, "Problems of a School Psychologist," *Education*, 75 (February, 1955), 412–416.

psychologist as a supervisor of special education. In New Jersey each county has a child study supervisor. There are also other psychologists in the local districts. The county psychologists are paid by the state department of education. In some states such as Washington, school districts within a reasonable geographic proximity will combine to hire psychological services. One district will assume the bookkeeping task and the state contributes the excess costs of such a program (mileage, supplies, salary) over and above the amount the district would receive from a certificated teacher. Thus, though the psychologist is hired by one district he is responsible to several. He is not a "county psychologist" although his area may frequently be limited to one county. In the December, 1965 issue of the *Minnesota Journal of Education,* A. W. Hepburn describes a Minnesota plan whereby the psychologists are based in a Mental Health Center and their services are contracted for by several small school districts.

In California, Trione, in an unpublished study, reports an interesting and practical means for the rural school psychologist to extend his usefulness. He borrowed ten graduate students, five from a state college and five from a university, and used money from his budget to house and feed these people and pay them a small stipend. Transportation was provided locally by the P.T.A. groups. Ninety children were examined in three days. Trione found the cost was less than half that for the psychologist in the area, if he alone had done the screening for mentally retarded and bright children. Also, it would have taken the psychologist six weeks to do the job. The graduate students received an excellent experience under field conditions. This was the type of situation where everyone benefited.

In Kern County, California, Conway [15] reported a method of subcontracting school psychological services for sparsely populated areas. School psychologists sign contracts with the county superintendent of schools office. Districts throughout the county contract with the county office for the amount of the psychologist's time desired. This varies according to the services needed, however, the amount of time varied from one-half day per week to two days per week. The services rendered also varied but in general included: assessment, mental hygiene consultation, special education, diagnosis, research, community public relations and in-service training.

One area where the itinerant school psychologist was of great assistance to the local school districts was in the operation of diagnostic clinics or on staffings of complex cases. On a regularly scheduled basis, the psychologist met one-half day per week at one of the schools served, for diagnostic consideration of a case referred from the school. Data was sent to the participating psychologist in advance, and school administrators and teachers were usually present at the diagnostic case conference. A report of the proceedings

---

[15] D. Conway, "Subcontracting Clinical Services for Rural School," California Association of School Psychologists and Psychometrists Conference Proceedings (1961).

and recommendations made during this conference were filed in the county office.

This method of providing psychological services for rural areas had great value for Kern County as it provided a unified organization of psychological services on the county level and yet provided for a greater amount and more personalized service to rural areas. Approximately one half of the districts in Kern County participated during 1961–62 in the subcontracting of clinical services. Fourteen times as many psychologists were employed by the county in 1961 as were employed in 1956 with only a twofold increase in cost to the county office. The local rural school districts have thus demonstrated the need for psychological services and have been able to bear the cost when allowed the opportunity to contract for only a part-time person.

The method, where a psychologist is centrally located and serves several schools, has definite merit in the rural communities. It may not be as satisfactory as having a professional person in each district but it is a realistic and flexible approximation of this ideal. The psychologist is directly attached to local staffs and directly responsible to them. There is an opportunity for communication, although we certainly understand that proximity is not the only requisite for this. There is much more opportunity for "feed-back" of information and the development of continuing evaluations of children. In this way curricular changes can be made when needed. The school psychologist and the local staffs have a chance to measure each other. Experience teaches how each might best function to help individual children. Referrals become more clearly stated and the psychologist's recommendations become more related to local resources. These include not only the staff but the other community resources as well. There are many avenues for helping children even in rather remote rural areas. We will discuss these in detail below. What the beginning psychologist in the community schools should remember is that the more professional contacts he has in the community and the more he utilizes local resources the more valuable he becomes. Hence he creates more opportunities for helping children locally.

Functions of the Community School Psychologist

Over the past several years much has been written to define the specific role of the psychologist in the public schools. Barker [16] writing in 1938 lists: group testing, individual testing, remedial reading, instructing teachers in remedial reading, diagnosis and treatment of personality and behavior problems, aid in the home-school relationship, participating in record keeping and supervising records, coordinating of the school with the community, participation in extra curricular activities, participation in curriculum reconstruction,

[16] M. Barker, "The Duties of a School Psychologist," *Journal of Consulting Psychology*, 2 (1938), 180–183.

and participation in formulation of policies. This is certainly a varied list but is not unrealistic for the community school where the psychologist cannot become limited to one aspect of his profession.

More recently the UNESCO Report of 1956 [17] delineates the school psychologist's function as remedial, advisory, and coordinative. This summary statement perhaps best expresses the role of the psychologist in the community or rural school since it subsumes a wide variety of specific activities. Emphasis and specificity will vary from community to community as the psychologist assumes a variety of roles based partly on administrative demands but primarily on his perception of local needs. The beginning psychologist in the community has an excellent opportunity to take an active part in delineating his functions to the administration. He can set up a program of services that satisfy both the local needs and his professional responsibility. However, if he finds that the pressures are such that he cannot function as his profession demands then he would do better to specialize in a larger school system with an established program of psychological services.

Tables 2, 3, and 4 illustrate how one of the authors, Trione,[18] was able to assume a variety of professionally sound roles in the community schools. In Table 2 can be seen how the emphasis on certain functions

TABLE 2

Log of a Rural School Psychologist,
1951–52 and 1953–54

	Time Devoted to Each Activity				
	1951–52		1953–54		Per
		Per		Per	Cent
	Hours	Cent	Hours	Cent	Change	Comments
1. Case Studies (Testing, interviewing, scoring) (School, district, and special education class)	248	30.0	348	32.0	+2.0	Addition of a Psychometrist to staff permitted more time with cases in field.
2. Supervisorial Duties	133	16.0	267	24.5	+8.5	See #1 above.
3. Dictation (Disposition of #1)	29	3.5	83	7.0	+3.5	Improved method of reporting despite heavier case load.
4. Inservice training with teachers	62	7.0	29	2.5	−4.5	See #1. Some functions delegated.

[17] W. Wall, ed., *Psychological Services in Schools* (New York: UNESCO Institute for Education, New York University Press, 1956).

[18] V. Trione, *et al.*, Address: "Report of the Research Committee Chairman," California Association of School Psychologists and Psychometrists (Santa Barbara: March, 1959, Mimeographed).

TABLE 2—*Continued*

	Time Devoted to Each Activity				
	1951–52		1953–54		Per
		Per		Per	Cent
	Hours	Cent	Hours	Cent	Change	Comments
5. Individual teacher conferences	26	3.0	34	3.0	0.0	
6. General Staff meetings (Curric.)	64	7.5	41	4.0	−3.5	Superintendent's policy
7. Individual staff conferences	114	14.0	41	4.0	−10.0	Change in reporting procedure, i.e. written reports more comprehensive.
8. Public Relations (PTA, service clubs, professional talks, etc.)	25	3.0	41	4.0	+1.0	Growing community interest.
9. Research (Normative data)	11	1.0	6	0.5	−0.5	Lack of time: work delegated.
10. Group Testing	41	5.0	30	2.5	−2.5	See #1.
11. Inter-agency conferences Social Service, Probation, Mental Hygiene Clinics, Public Health)	16	2.0	53	5.0	+3.0	Case load increase and where several agencies know case.
12. Institutes and Conferences	60	7.0	94	10.0	+3.0	Superintendent's policy.
13. Curriculum Material and Films (reviews) with staff	7	1.0	9	1.0	+3.0	
Totals	835	100.0	1076	100.0	+28.7	

Note: Travel time of 15 hours per month was not included in the table.
a—1951–52 Psychologist and secretary were only staff members.
b—1953–54 Psychologist, 2 psychometrists, secretary, and part-time clerical help constituted staff.

changed over a period of time with the addition of staff and some modifications in procedures. However, there is no compromise with professional standards. In Table 3 there is a detailed analysis of how the community school psychologist spent 600 hours of his time and in Table 4, a still later analysis. Certainly we see here, the diversity of activities that become a regular

TABLE 3

Log of Working Hours, October 1,
1956 to January 10, 1957

Activity	Time Spent Hours	Per Cent
Individual psychological examinations (This generally constitutes a complete case study of the child).	46.0	8
Consultations:		
(a) Individual (These are generally consultations with parent and/or school persons).	46.0	8
(b) Group Consultations, Guidance Committee (This refers to the technique of utilizing other specialists on the county staff and/or other professional personnel within the school system in working out the disposition of a case).	101.0	16
Reports (This means the scoring, analysis and dictation of reports that were done for Items 1 and 2).	40.0	7
Group Tests (This refers to either administering group tests for purposes of some pilot studies or training a teacher or administrator on how these tests can be used, and frequently this is done by means of a demonstration when they are first introduced into a school or district).	40.0	7
Correspondence (This refers to office correspondence).	31.5	5
Conference with Agencies (Agencies such as Public Health Dept., Probation Dept., Welfare Dept. frequently use this psychologist for consultation on individual cases that are known to any one or all of them. Part of the services rendered to the Probation Dept. would fall under Item 1).	15.0	3
Conferences with County Staff. (These refer to staff meetings or individual consultations on various problems where staff members must consult.)	21.5	4
Professional conferences (either educator or psychologist meetings elsewhere in the state).	17.0	3
Making use of state consultants from the State Dept. of Education or, occasionally, consultants from a University or a publishing company.	19.0	3
Research, statistical computation	46.0	8
In-service education with other staff members. (This is normally a joint effort with a general supervisor or secondary coordinator or Child Welfare and Attendance Officer).	31.5	5
Travel	159.5	26
Total	600.0	100

TABLE 4

*Average Daily Attendance 6000 K-12
Community: Industrial and Isolated—
Population 19,000*

Analysis of Professional Duties

RE: Supervisor of Psychological Services
    September 1, 1960 to December 16, 1960—Total of 71 days or 568 hours.

Activity	Hours	Per Cent
School Visitations	236	41
Consultation with staffs (163 hrs.—69%)		
Conferences with parent at school (12 hrs.—5%)		
Psychological exams at school (18 hrs.—7.5%)		
Counseling with pupils (20 hrs.—9%)		
Conferences with agency and school staff at school (5 hrs.—2%)		
Travel within district (18 hrs.—7.5%)		
(Note: Above categories represent 100% of School Visitation only)		
In-Service Training Sessions with Counselors and Administrative Assistants	22.5	4
Guidance Committee Meetings	7	1
Routine Office, i.e. filing, typing, telephone	42	8
Office: professional preparation of forms, work shop items	37	7
Dictation: Reports of exams and consultations	83	15
Conferences with MR Teacher Staff Placement Committee	21	4
Conferences with parents in Office	19	3
Agency Liaison: Consultation and inquiry	31	5.5
Psychological Exams in Office	15	2
Professional Conferences in office with District Staff	33	6
Professional Meetings: PTA, etc. (does not include evening meetings)	3.5	.5
Home Visits (MR Children)	12	2
Public Relations: (Speaking to Service Clubs, Nursery groups, PTA)	6	1
Total	568	100

part of the functions of the psychologist in the rural schools. He has a multiplicity of tasks but they are all aimed at his central function of improving the educational opportunities of the children in his district. Perhaps the reader is surprised that only a small percentage of the time is spent in direct contact with children. This leads us to the consideration of the best method for the community school psychologist to follow and some of the controversy that has developed around the general functioning of psychologists in the public schools.

There seem to be two points of view regarding the role of the psychologist in the schools. These have direct relevance to his training. Should the training be in psychology only with the emphasis on clinical techniques and child growth and development, or should there also be a concentration in education with classroom experience in particular? Should the school psychologist be qualified for a teaching certificate? Allen [19] states the case for the former point of view. He feels that the teaching certificate should not be required.

While not quarreling with the need for broad training in psychology, Barnhart and Baldauf [20] see an expanded role for the school psychologist. He has both child-centered functions and staff-centered functions. He is no longer a mental tester or even a clinician but a general consultant in learning and behavior. Coladarci [21] states the role of the school psychologist as follows:

> The apparent inclination of the school psychologists to think of themselves primarily as clinicians constitutes more of a disservice than a service to the educative process. Or, stated in positive terms, the task of confronting the schools is such that the school psychologist would fill a greater need in the role of the general educational psychologist.

Our experience in the community schools indicates that the school psychologist needs both the clinical skills and the educational orientation. Both the broad background in psychological theory and an understanding of how this theory is put to practice in the classroom. For in actual practice it is usually impossible to separate the one from the other. Even in a task as clinical as projective testing there are always the educational goals to be considered. It might reasonably be assumed that large urban school systems would hire psychologists who would function almost entirely in the clinical role. Yet even in this setting the enhancement of the child's education is the primary concern of the psychologist and some knowledge of the processes and goals of education is imperative.

[19] R. M. Allen, "Obfuscation of the School Psychologist," *Educational Administration and Supervision,* **44** (September, 1958), 290–296.

[20] R. E. Barnhart and R. J. Baldauf, "Role of the School Psychologist," *Nation's Schools,* **61** (April, 1958), 49–51.

[21] A. P. Coladarci, "A Note on the Role of the School Psychologist," *California Journal of Secondary Education,* **27** (November, 1952), 445–446.

Trione, in his 1965 doctoral dissertation (University of California, Berkeley), finally tested the point of view whether the school psychologist could effectively function as a consultant to teachers, administrators, and the community. Direct contact with children was held to a minimum.

Through the use of systematic interviews with teachers and principals for a year, Trione found that the solution of classroom problems became a mutual responsibility. The teacher learned to use the psychologist's training and skills. Thus, she developed insight and implemented her own efforts with her class.

The result was a gain in achievement by children of an experimental group of teachers, plus a significant change in teacher attitude related to guidance and reading principles. As an inservice consultant (Educational psychologist) he exerted a significant influence on a group of teachers and their respective classes.

Keeping a careful log, Trione also identified four areas of greatest concern to teachers (Tables 5 and 6). Not only did he provide heavily in coordinative and advisory services, but his counsel was focused most heavily in the areas of learning and curriculum, as well as the teacher's expressed interest with her role in the classroom.

In substance, Trione's experimental study revealed that a school psychologist could effectively aid a teacher by:

a. Working within her competence.
b. Developing an understanding of the makeup of her class.
c. Acting as a validator for her thinking.
d. Offering alternative methods, tools, and techniques to help her resolve her classroom problems.

TABLE 5

Total of Psychologist Functions With Experimental Teachers

Advisory		Remedial		Coordinative		Total	%
N	%	N	%	N	%	Total	%
17		15		22		54	
19		13		19		51	
14		12		18		44	
16		22		23		61	
11		10		11		32	
21		18		28		67	
14		10		20		44	
21		13		28		62	
18		14		30		62	
151	(31%)	129	(27%)	199	(42%)	479	(100%)

TABLE 6

Descriptive Tabulation of Psychologist Functions With Experimental Teachers in the Areas of Educational Psychology

Number of Conferences Per Teacher	Tests and Measures			Learning and Curriculum			Growth and Development			Personal Adjustment			Total
	Advi-sory	Reme-dial	Coordi-nation	Advi-sory	Reme-dial	Coordi-nation	Advi-sory	Reme-dial	Coordi-nation	Advi-sory	Reme-dial	Coordi-nation	
A 19	4	4	5	3	4	4	3	3	5	7	4	8	54
B 16	3	2	4	5	3	4	4	3	7	7	5	4	51
C 15	1	1	1	6	7	10	3	2	2	4	4	5	46
D 16	4	3	4	4	4	10	4	4	7	4	11	2	61
E 10	1	1	1	6	6	5	4	3	3	—	—	2	32
F 19	4	3	4	8	6	9	6	3	7	3	6	8	67
G 13	3	1	2	3	2	5	3	2	7	5	5	6	44
H 16	3	2	5	7	3	8	6	3	6	5	5	9	62
I 15	4	2	7	5	2	6	5	4	7	4	6	10	62
139	27	19	33	47	37	61	38	25	51	39	46	54	479
Sub-Category Per Cent	34%	24%	42%	32%	26%	42%	33%	22%	45%	28%	33%	39%	100%
Area Total	79			145			116			139			479
Area Per Cent	17%			30%			24%			29%			100%

87

In the rural areas it is not economically efficient for a psychologist to engage in just the clinical activities of diagnostic testing and treatment even if we could agree that this was his primary function. He would radically limit his case load and, while his effectiveness might be great for a small number of children, he would not be as effective to the total school program as he might with an expanded role. The authors of this chapter see the role as that of the consultant who brings to the task both the psychological training and the educational orientation.

The task of the consultant is highly complex. It requires the psychologist to focus the activities of several people on the problem of one child. He deals with parents, teachers, school administrators, and representatives of community agencies. Working through other people is a variable and intricate process. There is no room for a rigid approach. However, accepting this role, the school psychologist multiplies the possibilities of achievement even though the task is complex. For by utilizing the skills and knowledge of others he increases the probability of success and expands his usefulness to the community. The following two chapters deal with this communication process.

In consultation the problem of communication becomes paramount. The psychological terminology carefully learned in graduate school is usually not effective and may have negative results in this setting. It is much more meaningful for the teacher to discuss a particular behavior problem in terms of learning and re-learning, a language with which she is familiar, than to use obscure psychological "jargon." One's theoretical position may emphasize early infantile traumas as a basis of personality disorder. However, the teacher is dealing with a problem in the here and now. And as a consultant, it is here that the psychologist can be most effective. This role is frequently rewarding, sometimes frustrating, but always interesting. For as the school psychologist becomes more experienced and better acquainted with the schools, including the subtle differences between buildings in one school system, the more he is able to realize the potential of his professional training.

THE PROFESSIONAL AND TECHNICAL PRACTICES
OF THE COMMUNITY PSYCHOLOGIST

We have seen that the first task of the community school psychologist is to meet the needs of the community within the framework of sound professional practice. It is his responsibility to define this to the superintendent and board who hires him and then to establish a program that is most effective locally.

The next step is to bring some order to his services by establishing a referral system. If the psychologist is prudent, he will use the administrator of each building as his immediate source of contact. Cubberly's remark that ". . . as the administrator, so goes the school" is well taken in this instance.

The referral system helps screen and forces personnel to be discriminating in their choices of children. The specific form used is optional since it should be a cooperative enterprise with the teachers, counselors, and principals. The psychologist can suggest several alternatives with the option that the form can always be modified.

Then the psychologist sets a schedule of visitation to the schools. Nothing upsets a staff more than to have the psychologist "drop in." People may be in the midst of some special activity and the psychologist is the last person they desire to see. For example, secondary schools rarely want the psychologist on Fridays because of student activities. Also they usually prefer that he visit in the afternoons rather than the mornings. This allows for consultation with counselors after students are dismissed for the day. A tremendous amount of in-service training can be accomplished with this type of schedule.

Elementary schools, on the other hand, prefer to see the psychologist in the morning, as a rule. The youngsters are less fatigued at this time and one does not run into the problem of early primary dismissal so common in many school systems. Appointments with teachers can be made prior to the start of the class or for after dismissal. It is important that the psychologist not become so bound to a schedule that he cannot be flexible in making these appointments or that he cannot be available when urgently needed. Sometimes he can be quite effective in a broadly structured and fluid situation where important decisions are being made rapidly. If he is inflexible in scheduling he may not be available in a crisis and he will lose some of his effectiveness. A compromise between a rigid schedule on the one hand and random visitation on the other is an appointment system within the framework of the general schedule. The itinerant community school psychologist will have a definite day for visiting each school district in his territory. However, he will have a variable appointment schedule for each school within the district depending on local needs at the time.

Traditionally a school psychologist has been expected to be an expert in testing. The pressures from other members of the school staff are persistent for "IQ's." The psychologist must be alert to this trap. However, he can convert it into an excellent vehicle to expand his function. His approach should be that of a specialist in diagnostic casework on a teamwork basis and as such he procures the cooperation of other educational personnel. This in turn creates shared professional responsibility. The "high-priest" role is easy to assume but difficult to shake once the psychologist finds how unrealistic the demands may become.

Although testing, in the beginning, will constitute a major role it must not become so dominant that there is no time for "feed-back" of information to the staff. This is best done through case-conferences where all the personnel who are involved with a particular child are present. If this is not feasible, a carefully worded report with as many individual conferences as possible is a reasonable substitute. The task is essentially that of communication and it is the job of the psychologist to facilitate this in any way he can. He must be alert to the fact that he is receiving as well as disseminating information.

Trione, in a pilot study, studied the efficacy of the itinerant school psychologist's report to schools. Three years after the initial child study, where the report was found to be used, children demonstrated significant improvement. Where a report was not found to be used, the cases showed no improvement, or regressed. His study concluded that the school psychologist's report, if appropriately geared for use by teacher and/or principal, was an effective tool.

The beginning psychologist is frequently disturbed by the conditions under which he must test children in the rural areas. The schools, even the newer ones, do not have special facilities for this. Testing is done in the library, perhaps, or in the hall on a card table or even in a latrine on a rainy day. The psychologist is usually much more disturbed by this than his young client who prefers the familiarity of his own school to being transported to some clinic or office far from home.

It is important, however, that the child be informed prior to his appointment. The writers have yet to encounter a child who was not aware that he had a problem. Usually, if it is couched on the premise that he is not doing well in his school work (which is often the case) or he is having a difficult time getting along with his friends in and about school, this is accepted. Then, if the psychologist is offered as a specialist to help him out, this offer is rarely rejected. The prior cooperation of the youngster is particularly important in the secondary schools, since these boys and girls have some previous feelings about the role of psychologists. Being sent to the psychologist can be very threatening to them. Nothing is more exasperating than to have a child creep fearfully or stride belligerently into a room because he was not given adequate preparation. Parents should also be informed and no psychological study should be made without their knowledge and consent. The psychologist has the persistent task of educating the staff to the feelings of both the child and his parents.

The school psychologist must have a variety of tests at his command. He should be familiar with both the group and individually administered tests of intelligence, perception, and personality. However, he should not become so "test bound" as to rely entirely on scores and ignore the functions they purport to measure. It is also important that he choose the tests and that he not accept referrals for particular tests. The various instruments, particularly some of the projective techniques, have great charm for some school people. However, if the psychologist from the beginning insists on the right to decide procedures, there will be no problems.

In the State of California, the Bureau of Special Education has assisted school psychologists in small districts and in rural areas by providing a lending library of special clinical tests which are used infrequently in evaluating special groups of children. Thus the school psychologist in Dinuba or Visalia can borrow for a month's use such instruments as the Columbia Mental Maturity Scale, Nebraska-Hiskey, or the Leiter Scale.

There is some question as to just how valuable a tool the projective techniques are for the community school psychologist. They are time-consuming and thus costly in terms of total service to an area. It has been our experience and that of many of our colleagues that we tend to do less of this type of testing as we gain experience. There is the tendency at first to do a great deal since this is a well developed skill and the psychologist feels fairly secure with it. However, the insights one gains from these techniques can frequently be gained from a skillful interview. The interview is less costly in time and thus a more efficient use of the psychologist's skills. What seems to happen is that the psychologist comes to rely more on himself than any particular instrument. Instead of the testing tools dominating his behavior they become an adjunct to it. They are used, as they should be, to seek answers to specific questions rather than as a routine procedure without too much reference to a particular problem.

TYPES OF RECOMMENDATIONS IN THE COMMUNITY SCHOOLS

An integral part of any evaluative procedure is the recommendation for "treatment" or the specific types of things that may be done to help a particular child. There are two general considerations here. First, no school psychologist should feel that he has all the answers. Nor should he feel disturbed that others with less training, perhaps, but with excellent insight into behavior may frequently make the most cogent recommendations. If his unique contribution has helped a teacher to understand her pupil better and to reach her own solution to the child's problem, this is sufficient. Second, recommendations must be made within the context of what is reasonably available in the community. This is particularly true in the rural areas where such specialized services as psychiatry and neurology are difficult or almost impossible to obtain. For a psychologist to recommend psychiatric treatment where this is not feasible can only lead to frustration and certainly does nothing to alleviate the situation. But to seek solutions to problems in the local context strengthens the community to handle problems, increases awareness of needs, and may eventually lead to the acquisition of new resources. L. J. Peter in his 1965 book *Prescriptive Teaching* provides a schematic diagram for determining reasonable modifications in any one setting.

Frequently the school psychologist must decide whether to enter into a direct counseling relationship with a child or to maintain his consultant position and work through others. We feel that the latter role is generally more efficient but there are times when this direct relationship is necessary. If he enters into a counseling situation the psychologist must commit himself to continue until he has been effective or until he is certain that he cannot be.

The pressure from the school staff in the community is usually rather persistent for counseling services, and there are many children, especially at the elementary level, who will show real gains from a relatively brief number of sessions. The question for the school psychologist is how much time to devote to this activity without taking too much from his general consultative function. There can be no strict answer to this but here are some considerations. Experience will indicate what type of problem with which one can be most effective. Selecting children for counseling where the prognosis is best helps to keep the load from becoming too great. The age of the child and the severity of the problem will contribute to the decision. Psychological counseling can be very involved with a disturbed adolescent and he might better be referred to another agency, if possible. On the other hand, a few sessions with a first grader may have very positive results. A further consideration is the remoteness of some of the smaller school districts. This may preclude counseling altogether or it may mean devoting a disproportionate amount of time to this area. The needs of the children will determine what is done. Chapter 6 discusses other considerations in regard to counseling and psychotherapy in the schools.

As a consultant the school psychologist is constantly being asked to recommend changes in the child's school or home environment. These are as varied as the children he sees. They may include such things as placing a child in a classroom so that he is influenced positively by one of his peers; finding a job for the student in the school in order to give him a greater feeling of competency; changing teachers so as to better meet personality needs; or changing a teacher's perception of a child so that her behavior toward him is modified and he in turn reacts differently; helping parents to define limits, and any of hundreds of curricular changes that are significant in terms of the child's needs. Most schools that have articulated a philosophy of education insist on the maximum development of each child within the context of his abilities. The school psychologist feels very much at home in this "child-centered" philosophy. It encourages a creative approach to helping children and the concomitant development of skills and resources.

Once recommendations have been made, one of the most difficult problems for the psychologist in the community schools is to find time for adequate follow-up. Trione [22] has indicated the value of this not only for the child but also as a means of checking on the effectiveness of the service.

---

[22] V. Trione, "One Hundred Eighty Cases: A follow-up by a Rural School Psychologist," *California Journal of Educational Research,* 9 (1958), 86–90.

He notes that in some instances his recommendations did not reach the teacher so that he worked to no end. While it may not always be feasible it is desirable to have personal contact with the teacher both during the evaluation and after recommendations have been made. This tends to reinforce whatever program has been started and provides valuable "feed-back" to the psychologist. The most conscientiously devised program may not work as new factors enter to alter the picture. Re-evaluation may become necessary.

The school psychologist should have some method of consistent communication after he has made the initial recommendations. Just how he does this depends on local circumstances. Some psychologists use a form which is mailed out or left with the teacher to be used if she wants further help. Others try to keep a running log of the children seen in the various districts and make it a practice to check with the teachers from time to time. Whatever the method, it is the contact that is important.

Another concern of the community school psychologist is what should he consider as a reasonable case load in a given time. There are many variables involved in this and it is not possible to arrive at a definite figure. One major factor would be the time he allots to various functions. If he is involved in an intensive counseling program he will not see a large number of children, but he will see the same ones many times. If his primary function is diagnostic he will see many more. In Illinois [23] it was recommended that a qualified psychological examiner see about twenty-five children a month on the average. This could be difficult in rural areas if much travel is involved between schools. The following statement from the Illinois handbook [23] is an excellent rule to follow at all times:

> . . . at no time should a diagnosis be based upon an incomplete study in order to accommodate a large number of cases. A child with problems is better off living with his problems than to have his life modified by a diagnosis which does not have a sound basis.

COORDINATION OF COMMUNITY RESOURCES

One of the most important functions of the school psychologist in the rural areas is to act as the person who coordinates the school program with that of other agencies in the community and keeps the channels of communication open between the various staffs. This is a very personalized job in the small communities. There is no large central clearing house for the exchange of information and people generally seem to avoid too formalized procedures. The important resources for helping children in the small communities are the people, and it is the task of the school psychologist to try to maximize their effectiveness. This means some assessment of the functions of

---

[23] I. Jolles, "The Illinois Plan: A Handbook for the Qualified Psychological Examiner" (Springfield, Illinois: Superintendent of Public Instruction, 1954).

the various agencies but more importantly knowledge of the effectiveness of the individuals within these agencies.

Communication between agencies is usually person to person with a minimum of written reports. Requests for information flow back and forth with gratifying speed. Frequently several agencies will be involved with one child. It is not unusual, for example, to have the department of public assistance (foster home placement), the juvenile court (dependent child), the health department (nursing visits), and the schools actively at work on the same problem. On occasion it may become necessary to call a formal interagency staff meeting. Usually, however, the coordination of all these activities can be handled informally and quite effectively. The rural community is not the place for the person who is too dependent on formalized procedures. A certain amount of channelized communication is necessary for the sake of records but it is one of the joys of working in a small community that so much can be done with a personal touch rather than a form letter.

The particular agencies with which the psychologist must work will vary in name from area to area. However, there are several which are fairly universal in title and function, and the school psychologist starting in a rural area would be well advised to seek them out at once. Chapter 5 discusses in detail the synergistic relationship that the school psychologist must establish with these agencies; however the present discussion concerns those aspects of agency cooperation that are unique to rural areas.

The health department frequently provides the school nurse in the rural areas. A school nurse can be a great help to the psychologist. She gives hearing and vision tests on request and is intimately acquainted with the child's health history. She is frequently the only person who has ready access to the child's home. From her contact with the parents she can quickly obtain information, such as a developmental history, which is very important in many diagnoses and which might take the psychologist much longer to complete. Some nurses have received training in social work evaluations and this information is useful. The rural school psychologist soon learns to rely heavily on her.

The department of public assistance, more frequently called the "welfare department," is closely involved with a large number of children in the community. This is not just on a basis of providing for their physical needs but frequently includes counseling by members of the staff. This is the agency that often handles foster home placements, and a significant number of children referred to the school psychologist will live in foster homes. The social workers of this agency will be concerned with such problems as proper educational opportunities for young people about to leave school and with planning for environments (in and out of school) which will help a child to reach his greatest potential usefulness to himself and the community. Thus there is usually close liaison between the agency and the school. This is very beneficial to the school psychologist for there are many occasions when he is assisted by the staff and records of the department of public assistance.

In most communities there is a juvenile court or some representative of it. Here cases involving delinquency and dependency are heard and decided. Since the school psychologist may be the only trained person in the field of psychology in the area and since he is frequently involved with the children who come to the attention of the court by reason of his school contacts, he is often the person to advise the court. This usually takes the form of suggestions as to some possible dispositions which could best help the child. Here again is an opportunity to combine an intimate knowledge of the resources of the community with psychological understanding of a particular child. The psychologist does not make the decisions but is in a position to influence them; this is a heavy responsibility.

There is another important consideration here. When the psychologist considers the resources of the community he frequently overlooks the expanded community or the state resources, the institutions. So often people consider these as a kind of final disposition of a case rather than one more avenue of help. Part of the problem is the difficulty of communication between a local school system and a state institution. This need not be insurmountable.

When a child is returned to the community he has undoubtedly come from a very significant experience. He has been observed over a long period of time and should be well known to the professional staff of the institution. It follows then that these people should be able to make firm recommendations as to how this child might be helped in the home community. If the school staff, and the psychologist in particular, will develop the attitude that the institutions for the mentally ill, mentally retarded, and delinquents are merely extensions of the local efforts in these fields and will consistently seek to work with them, closer relationships will develop. Thus, this will add more resources to the community which is very important to the rural area.

SCHOOL RELATED FUNCTIONS

There are several ways in which the school psychologist can function in the smaller communities that, while not directly concerned with the problems of children, are indirectly concerned. In the long view these may be some of his most significant contributions.

The psychologist's background and attitude contribute most to this. In the more remote areas he is frequently the only person with the behavioral scientist's orientation. He comes to his position with the concern for the science of psychology and its application in the technology of education.[24] His training in psychology theory and research techniques are very important in helping a district plan a curriculum change in such a way that the value of the change can be measured. It is probably a widespread phenomenon in education that we take radical departures from traditional methods without carefully establishing controls or any reasonably accurate method of assessing our results. This is not intended as an indictment. But it is hoped that students of school psychology who eventually specialize in the community schools will take with them an enthusiasm for research and scientific methodology.

An interesting way this may be applied with benefit both to the district and to the staff is to give technical assistance to teachers who are seeking the masters degree through the research route. This does not imply that the school psychologist set up the project or gather the data. However, he can help with design and statistics and act as a consultant in research to various staff members who are interested. This has the double value of getting needed research done and helping others to see that this kind of activity is important. William Itkin discusses this in greater detail in Chapter 19.

Another way is for the psychologist to be ready to undertake a bit of research at an appropriate time. Meacham, for example, in 1961 carried out a research study that, although it will not be published, has already proven of value to the school and illustrates how little problems can be solved locally when there is some chance of using appropriate techniques.

The problem was to predict first grade achievement from an evaluation toward the end of the kindergarten year. The importance for the district was two-fold. It would aid in a new grouping situation, and there was a chance of identifying exceptional children. Two tests and a teacher evaluation were equated and predications on a five-point scale were made. The criterion was actual first grade achievement in reading. What we discovered was that the teacher evaluation was as good as any of the tests or combination of scores. Perhaps more important, we found that all our instruments underrated the children. This has led to a policy of checking through individual testing all children who are expected to be exceptional and to a rather healthy respect for the maturational processes in this age group. While we may find similar results in the literature there seems to be nothing so compelling as demonstrating these phenomena locally.

Another important function for the school psychologist is that of in-service training with the staff. This may be quite direct in the form of classes or study groups around such topics as child development or mental health. It may also be an indirect but very pertinent part of every conference the psychologist has with the teacher or administrator. A constant aim is to increase

[24] K. W. Spence, A. W. Melton, and B. J. Underwood, "Can the Laws of Learning be Applied in the Classroom?", *Harvard Educational Review*, 29, No. 2 (1959), 83–117.

each person's effectiveness in dealing with children. If he can help a teacher to a broader understanding of developmental principles and specific insights into the behavior of a particular child, the psychologist will have helped her to understand all her children a little better. It is true that the teacher is the most important staff member with whom the psychologist works. Anything that increases her ability to do a good job upgrades the curriculum. We might also observe here that a school psychologist can learn very much from effective teachers. A few hours in the classroom, with the teacher's permission, will teach one much about the children and various class climates and have a positive influence on staff relationships.

Finally the school psychologist may enter into the broader role of the educational psychologist with responsibilities in curriculum development, not only for the exceptional child but for the entire school program. We feel that there may be more opportunity for this in the community schools than in the urban areas. Not as a full time occupation of course, but as one of the several functions of the school psychologist. The itinerant psychologist is in contact with many schools and he has an opportunity to carry curriculum ideas from one district to another. It may be a new method of teaching arithmetic to the mentally retarded. But if it works here why not for other children? It may be a new set of texts that are proving useful with the gifted or it may be the result of a bit of research that has broad relevance. Whatever the idea, the school psychologist who is committed to more than just specific problems, will relate it to the broader goals of education. To achieve this broader perspective he must commit himself to both psychology and education. He then has two professional obligations. His identification may be more with one group than the other, but if he can create a synthesis of theory, practice, science, and technology he can perform a unique function for both.

Selected Supplementary Readings

Anderson, Frank A., "Some Ideas for Small Schools," *National Education Association Journal*, Vol. **52**, No. 21 (January, 1963).

Burchinal, Lee G., "Characteristics of Rural Youth," *The American Child*, **44** (January, 1962), 5–8.

Doll, E. A., "The Role of the Consulting Psychologist," *Educational Executive's Overview*, **3** (August, 1964), 47–49.

Feldhusen, John F., John R. Thurston, and Elvira Ager, "Delinquency Proneness of Urban and Rural Youth," *Journal of Research in Crime and Delinquency*, **2** (January, 1965), 32–44.

Fliegel, F. C., and E. J. Brown, "Low Income Farm People," *Journal of Cooperative Extension*, **8** (Spring, 1966), 44–50.

Franseth, Jane, *Supervision in Rural Schools: A Report on Beliefs and Practices.* Washington, D.C.: U.S. Office of Education, 1965.

Haney, G. E., *A School Transfer Record System for Farm Migrant Children.* Washington, D.C.: U.S. Office of Education, 1965.

Harding, J., E. C. Devereux, and U. Bronfenbrenner, "Leadership and Participation in a Changing Rural Community," *The Journal of Social Issues,* Vol. 16 (1960).

Hepburn, A. W., "South Central Meets Small School Needs," *Minnesota Journal of Education,* 46 (December, 1965), 26–28.

Hughes, R. B., and K. Lessler, "A Comparison of WISC and Peabody Scores of Negro and White Rural School Children," *American Journal of Mental Deficiency,* 69 (May, 1965), 877–880.

Isenberg, Robert M., "The Rural Disadvantaged," *National Education Association, Journal,* Vol. 52, No. 27 (April, 1963).

Ketcherside, W. J., and P. M. Allen, "Providing Specialists for Small School Districts," *Arizona Teacher,* 54 (November, 1965), 10–11.

McDaniel, L. J., "Psychological Services under State and Local Departments of Special Education," *Psychology in the Schools,* 2 (January, 1965), 85–88.

Minger, Paul F., "Guidance for Rural Schools," *Education,* 80 (April, 1960), 488–490.

Nash, R. C., *Rural Youth in a Changing Environment.* Washington, D.C.: National Commission for Children and Youth, 1965.

Rural Education News. Department of Rural Education of the NEA.

Rusch, R. R., "A Program for Gifted Students in Rural Areas," *National Education Association Journal,* Vol. 51, No. 12 (January, 1962).

Smith, P. M., Jr., "Problems of Rural and Urban Southern Negro Children," *The Personnel and Guidance Journal,* 39 (March, 1961), 599–600.

U.S. Office of Education, *Rural Youth in Crisis: Facts, Myths, and Social Change,* JD-3001, 1965.

RUDOLPH J. CAPOBIANCO

4

The Psychologist Collaborates with Other School Staff

Recently the author had occasion to serve on an examination committee for one of the newly graduated students of the "two-year specialist" program in school psychology. Members of the graduate committee, including the major adviser, were all professionally trained psychologists in school psychology and/or allied fields. The candidate for the degree appeared well trained and sufficiently professionally competent to succeed in his chosen area of school psychology. Questions and answers regarding responsibilities toward the children, relationships with professional colleagues and community interrelationships proceeded at a brisk pace, pleasing both the candidate and his examination committee in the probability that this would indeed be a relatively brief encounter. The verbal interchange proceeded smoothly until one well-meaning member of the committee asked the candidate, "What do you feel is your responsibility in the school setting with regard to therapy? More specifically, if your diagnosis of an individual student provided sufficient information to warrant the conclusion that the child was psychotic, what would you consider to be your responsibility?" The candidate responded, "To the best of my ability I would select and administer the most appropriate technique. I feel it is the responsibility of the school system through the services of its psychologist to do all within its power to provide a cure or at least to alleviate as far as possible such a problem." The prospect of the brief session disappeared. The members of the committee, not all in agreement, and the candidate proceeded to argue in review of the nature and scope of the responsibilities of school psychologists.

Although the pros and cons of therapy *per se* in the school setting are discussed in more detail in other chapters of this volume, it is apparent that the reader must be informed of the nature of the author's position before delving further into his particular views in relation to the complex problem of professional collaboration in the school setting.

The aforementioned candidate for the two-year specialist degree may or may not have been competent to administer the needed form of therapy to the child in question. The importance of the situation, however, is not this particular school psychologist's competence but the nature of his responsibility in relation to other professional workers in the school. When does the psychologist provide treatment and when does he resort to referral? Does the school system assume the responsibility for the removal of the infected appendix following such a diagnosis by the school physician? The competence of the medical doctor is not questioned. Nevertheless, referral is expected. The addition of "deep" therapy to the responsibilities of the school psychologist who is already overburdened with the responsibilities for diagnosis, preventive mental health programs, consultation with teachers, principals, and other school personnel, research, individual counseling with parents, and innumerable other duties, is demanding that "the jack of all trades" be master of all.

At a recent conference of the California Association of School Psychologists and Psychometrists held in Bakersfield, some specific recommendations for the future of school psychology were stressed. One of the recommendations dealt specifically with the responsibility for therapy, stating ". . . The function of therapy should not be assumed by the school itself. Rather, the school psychologist should act to refer cases to other agencies. If no appropriate agency exists in the community, it is the responsibility of the school psychologist to work with the community in setting one up."[1] The role of the school itself must be defined more clearly, its primary function is to instruct and inform. When a child is so emotionally disturbed that he re-

---

[1] California Association of School Psychologists and Psychometrists, *Newsletter*, 2, No. 3 (May, 1956), 3.

quires a disproportionate amount of time of professional personnel and/or disrupts normal classroom procedures, it is time for the school to acknowledge it cannot help this particular youngster and refer him to the appropriate resource. When all avenues of referral are exhausted, exclusion from school is the remaining recourse. Perhaps the suggestion of Krugman [2] should be followed to prevent these conditions from occurring. He suggests that the school psychologist be responsible for first grade or even pre-school surveys that would discover those youngsters needing special aids in education while they are young and before their problems become unduly aggravated.

In effecting a workable team approach toward the resolution of the universal problems confronting school-aged children, the services of other personnel representing allied professions are needed. These professionals include administrators, regular class teachers, special education personnel, school medical staff, social work staff, guidance personnel and, frequently, consultants from other professions. According to Harrower and Goldstein [3] the larger the city, the more adequate the services are apt to be. Often the community cannot afford so complete a team of professional workers. The services of a full contingent of specialists in the area of exceptional children are extremely rare at best. Oftentimes the school system may have the services of a part-time speech correctionist and/or a teacher for a special class of mentally retarded children, without the corresponding services for other types of exceptional children. All too frequently no special education personnel are available, leaving the problems posed by all exceptional children in the hands of the teacher of the regular classroom. In school settings such as the latter, the school psychologist earns yet another responsibility, that of serving as consultant to the regular class teachers as a specialist in the education of these children.

Another consequence of the inability to employ professional workers to represent the full team may result in other combinations of specialties. Many schools utilize the services of social workers as visiting teachers or guidance personnel in preventive mental health programs. In such situations the primary function of the school psychologist would become diagnostic rather than preventive. In recent years, however, there has been a notable shift in interest of school psychologists from diagnosis to the area of preventive mental health or personal adjustment.

In the quest for knowledge and understandings that may be applied to help children learn more effectively according to their capabilities, educators enlist the aid of allied professions. Considering the diagnostic and preventive

[2] M. Krugman, "The Psychologist's Role in Pupil Classification," *Journal of Consulting Psychology*, 6 (1942), 205–211.

[3] M. Harrower, and L. Goldstein, "New School Team in Mental Health," *Child Study*, 36, No. 2 (Spring, 1959), 19–24.

aspects in the school psychologist's role, a close working relationship with the classroom teacher is requisite. The Thayer Conference on the functions, qualifications, and training of school psychologists

> . . . had no doubt that the school psychologist needs an intimate and thorough understanding of the processes of education . . . there was general agreement that sometime, somewhere, the school psychologist should acquire: (a) Basic knowledge of education, including its history and philosophy, curriculum construction, methods and materials, remedial methods, test construction, exceptional children; (b) Skill in educational diagnosis along with his other assessment skills; (c) Practical knowledge of the classroom and the school, the roles and responsibilities of the teachers, principals, supervisors, and other specialized services, the necessary rules and courtesies for work in the schools, including a respect for what other school workers do, the practical limitations of the school situation, the school hierarchy, and the relations of the school to the various forces in the community.[4]

With the tools of his trade, the school psychologist serves as an indispensable aid to the classroom teacher. Interpreting the results of intelligence, aptitude, and achievement tests, interest and personality scales, in addition to direct interviews and observations, the psychologist serving as adviser to the classroom teacher can well effect modifications of teaching methods and techniques or suggest changes in curriculum and programming resulting from the complete assessment of individual children. Since there is no doubt but that teachers exert, perhaps, the greatest influence on children, the success of the school psychologist in his work depends upon his aptitude in working with the classroom teacher. In attempting to provide the most effective learning situation in the classroom the psychologist must be aware of the handicaps under which the teacher is working. It is not particularly unusual that a specific classroom may be composed of children with more than the average amount of hyperactivity and lack of self control which demand a great deal of the teacher's time. The teacher may also be faced with a range of achievement within her class that is too great for effective management. These situations demand not only understanding on the part of the psychologist in his cooperation with the classroom teacher but also the additional responsibility of serving as counsel to the principal in ways to effect a more adequately functioning school system. The psychologist must have a working knowledge of methodologies and techniques for the handling of hyperactive children. He must be familiar with the results of research and demonstration projects related to these disturbed children. He should benefit from the experiences of other school systems in their attempts to establish special classes for the emotionally disturbed and/or "special learning disabilities." Within his

---

[4] Norma E. Cutts, ed., *School Psychologists at Mid-Century. A Report of the Thayer Conference on the Functions, Qualifications, and Training of School Psychologists* (Washington, D. C.: American Psychological Association, Inc., 1955), p. 129.

background of information should be firsthand knowledge of the pitfalls of groupings of children with too wide a discrepancy in achievement and performance. On the other hand, he must realize that homogeneous groupings are, in fact, an idealistic fantasy—homogeneity in terms of what criterion? A realistic compromise on this issue is a necessity.

Recently the author administered a brief questionnaire to students enrolled in one of his classes. Since this questionnaire was administered during a summer session, it was felt that the respondents would represent a fairly adequate sampling of professional educators employed throughout the state. It was also felt that the sampling would represent rural as well as urban areas. The questionnaire in its entirety is presented below:

> With the greater availability of specialized psychological services to the teacher it becomes increasingly necessary to define the role of the school psychologists within the school setting. Due to the lack of recent data in this area we would appreciate your brief comments on the following items to give us an indication of any change in the last ten years:
>
> 1. Grade you teach ——————— (also specify normal class or otherwise).
> 2. General geographical area in which you teach.
> 3. What type of specialized services are available to you?
> 4. How often in the past year have you consulted with a school psychologist?
> 5. What do you think is the primary function of the school psychologist? And how well do you think this is met?
> 6. If you have more than one specialist available to you, e.g., school social worker, counselor, etc., are you sometimes puzzled as to which one to consult? (On what basis do you make this decision?)
> 7. What do you think the ideal team of specialists would consist of and how do you think they would work together?
> 8. In working with a school psychologist concerning a child in your class, what do you think are the desirable and undesirable aspects of such interaction and how do you think they could be improved?
> 9. What should the school psychologist's function be in relation to the:
>   a. principal
>   b. other administrators and/or specialists
>   c. classroom teacher

The respondents consisted of thirty-five teachers of regular classes, six special class teachers, three school administrators (superintendents or principals), two school psychologists or counselors, two college instructors, and one student who did not indicate his occupation. Twenty-nine of the respondents were from a metropolitan area and twenty represented rural areas. Item 3 of the questionnaire dealt with specialized services available to the respondents. Table 1 presents the responses to this item in terms of the number of specialized services available to the respondents.

TABLE 1

Availability of Specialized School Services
(Results of Questionnaire)

	None	Share One Resource	Have One Resource	Have More Than One	Have School Psychologist	Don't Know
Rural	2	3	2	9	7	1
Metropolitan			2	22	12	2

Note: Since the above categories are not mutually exclusive, the total number of responses exceeds the N of 49.

Since some of the respondents checked more than one specialty available in addition to having the services of a school psychologist, the totals for rural and metropolitan areas do not coincide with the original numbers presented. It may be seen from Table 1, however, that a substantial number of both rural and metropolitan school districts have the services of more than one specialist.

Item 4 of the questionnaire asked for the frequency of consultation with a school psychologist over the past year. Table 2 shows that these services were used sparingly if at all, this, in spite of the fact that approximately forty per cent of the school districts represented did have these services available to them.

TABLE 2

Reported Frequency of Consultation
With School Psychologists
(Results of Questionnaire)

Number of Consultations	0	1	2	3	4	10 or more
Number of Respondents	14	5	6	1	3	4

Note: Some of the respondents answered this item with the school counselor (or guidance worker) in mind rather than the school psychologist. Hence, a discrepancy exists between the reported number of school psychologists available (Table 1) and the frequency of consultation (Table 2).

The following generalizations were drawn from responses to the remaining portion of the questionnaire:

1. The true role of the school psychologist is vague in the minds of these respondents.

2. In spite of lack of initiative in enlisting the aid of specialists, the respondents conclude that school needs are not met.

3. Inter-personal contacts between the school psychologist and the child (or teacher) were seen predominately as negative, e.g., the child will fear the setting, the teacher will be concerned with her personal problems.

It is apparent from a review of the results of this questionnaire that the role of the school psychologist within the school setting is still vague to other school professionals. This does not reflect a lack of feeling for such direct services, for, as reported by Newland,[5] only a small number of responding state departments felt no need for such services. Although there is an apparent consensus regarding the need for a school psychologist's services, the nature of his duties, responsibilities, and the relationships which result seem difficult to define or describe. It should be borne in mind, in reviewing the figures stated above in response to this questionnaire, that the total frequencies are not always in keeping with the original number of respondents. These discrepancies are due to the fact that 1) In response to certain questions more than one answer was given by some of these students, and 2) Some of the respondents did not respond to all items. Nevertheless, in spite of the deficiencies of opinion polling with such instruments it may be seen that the professionals engaged in a school setting are unaware, or at best confused, as to the role of the school psychologist. Whether this unfamiliarity is the result of the lack of concern on the part of the school psychologist, the novelty of placing a school psychologist on the staff, or dereliction of duty on the part of many administrators with regard to informing his co-workers remains a question for further consideration.

It has been demonstrated that the teacher and other specialists within the schools are pathetically uninformed with regard to the role and functions of the school psychologist. A source of blame for these uninformed professionals may be the school psychologist himself. It has been well stated by Roberts [6] that all too often the school psychologist perceives his position as a one-to-one relationship with the child. Certainly this is partially a result of his training. But, unfortunately, this situation isolates both the psychological services and the school psychologist from the teachers and administrators within the school. As a result, the administrator may underestimate or fail to see the benefits of the services of the school psychologist.

A second possibility for the lack of close interrelationship and understanding between school psychologists and teaching personnel is the attitude of the teacher herself. Barker [7] speculates that teaching is a profession that

[5] T. Ernest Newland, "Formalized Psychological Services in State Education Programs," *American Psychologist,* 11 (1956), 136–140.

[6] A. D. Roberts, "The Cooperative Personnel Approach for the School Psychologist," *Occupations,* 30 (1952), 599–600.

[7] Roger G. Barker, "Difficulties of Communication Between Educators and Psychologist: Some Speculations," *Journal of Educational Psychology,* 33 (1942), 416–426.

attracts people who value social achievement and that teachers represent a social mobile class. As a result the teacher brings to the classroom ideas that are somewhat resistant to facts in the area of child psychology, e.g., intelligence is partially determined by heredity. This view is contrary to their concept of individual progress, attainment, etc. Barker indicates that one must also review the individual needs that brought about the selection of teaching as a profession: substitute parenthood, easy domination, etc. He states further that, as a group, teachers are highly religious and that these factors must be considered with respect to the degree to which the teacher accepts various concepts of child psychology: oedipus, egocentricity, etc. It may be inferred that the nature of the professional field of psychology would necessarily attract individuals with backgrounds that are indeed different from those stated, and the specific needs would also be unique.

Obviously the education and training with regard to the aforementioned concepts of child psychology would make for attitudes that are different if not contradictory to those held by the classroom teacher. However, there are probably several schools of psychology that have practical usefulness for educators, if followed consistently. It is not within the scope of this chapter to argue the relative merits and deficiencies of each. It is pertinent, however, to emphasize that the jumble of superficial viewpoints oftentimes presented to the teachers under the banner of eclecticism is likely to be of limited value.

Interdisciplinary School Conference

Before attempting to isolate specific interrelationships between the school psychologist and individual members of the staff, it is pertinent here to stress the overwhelming need for interdisciplinary school conferences. Many of the misconceptions emanating from ignorance regarding separate professional roles in our complex school systems might be easily disspelled by conferences geared specifically to define individual roles. Available resources must be spelled out in detail to allay the fears of the new teacher and to reassure the veteran. Procedures for referral, interviews, and staff meetings will insure knowledgeable methods for disposition of individual cases, alterations in instructional system and/or dissemination of information. Emphasis on the team approach will not only provide for maximum utilization of professional competencies for the student's welfare but will also assure better working relationships and bolster mutual respect among the school's professional staff.

THE SCHOOL PSYCHOLOGIST AND THE TEACHER

The school psychologist may be perceived as either help or threat by the teacher. As has already been pointed out, perhaps the basic criticism of teachers towards school psychologists is the teacher's feeling that the psychologist is "talking down" to them. To build a professionally profitable relationship, the psychologist must be aware that he may unintentionally injure a teacher's ego or status. Roberts [8] points out that the psychologist should consult fully with all school personnel and make practical recommendations. This will tend to reduce tensions of the school personnel and promote greater cooperation and positive action. It is the psychologist's responsibility to encourage a feeling of confidence on the part of the teacher for psychological consultation. Oftentimes in referring a child to the school psychologist the teacher may misjudge the problem. Undetected minor physical defects may be responsible for inattention and low performance rather than mental retardation. An emotional disturbance may hamper his performance in arithmetic rather than a lack of preparation. On the other hand, low intellectual capacity may be responsible for the child's inability to grasp educational concepts rather than his bullying, aggressive acts, or other misbehaviors in the classroom. The task presented to the teacher and psychologist in studying the psychological environment of children requires roles that are quite different but equally important on the part of both professionals. According to Driscoll,

> The teacher is well aware of the behavior of the children being studied. The school psychologist must contribute information regarding motivation of the behavior. At this point all the knowledge the psychologist possesses must be brought to use plus a large ingredient of common sense. It is on this service that educators lose their evaluation of psychological services. A report that describes the child's behavior is an insult to teachers as indeed is a report that cites such general conditions as insecurity or hostility as basic causes of the child's behavior. A psychologist who is able to suggest an effective method for developing constructive behavior from a child gains the respect of the teacher. An elaborate diagnosis may be heart-warming to a psychologist, but let him keep this in his files and give a brief explanation to the teacher. Action, not theory, is the need of the moment.[9]

With the constant demand for shifting of roles on the part of teachers from friend and confidant to target for hostility feelings, from referee to detective, from a source of knowledge to the object of affection, it is no wonder that the teacher may misdiagnose the source of the immediate school problem.

In his role as collaborator with the school teacher the school psychologist should serve as adviser to the teacher to help him understand why and how he is to act each role in a comfortable and effective manner. In some instances even the teacher relationship with the specific student may require a change

---

[8] Roberts, *op. cit.*

[9] Gertrude P. Driscoll, "The School Psychologist Looks to the Future," *Presidential Address Division 16* (American Psychological Association Convention, New York City, August–September, 1957), 4–5.

from time to time. Guidance is required in the establishment of the most opportune time for the security of authority and the most optimum time for readiness for freedom. Within each classroom there are children who are ready for democratic participation and others who need and demand decisions of an authoritarian. Teachers, like their students, also vary in their needs. Teacher A may need and demand fully prepared outlines or cookbooks describing specific behaviors for unique classroom situations, B may not.

On the other hand, the school psychologist must be willing to play a supporting role only, in consultations with other teachers. In dispelling the notion of mysticism commonly attributed to the assessments made by school psychologists, the myth is more readily destroyed by enlisting the aid of the teacher in cooperative efforts to diagnose and prognose. Bower states that,

> When the psychologist (1) involves the teacher in collection of pertinent information about a referred pupil; (2) removes a pupil from the teacher for the briefest time necessary for interviewing and testing; (3) enlists the help of the teacher in analyzing the facts and planning the follow-up program, and (4) recognizes the potentials for guidance in the curriculum and in the pupil-teacher relationship, he helps both the pupil and the teacher.[10]

Cooperative efforts of this nature are especially important when the pupil's problem is serious and complex or when the teacher is inexperienced. When the problem involves elements of the home situation, the school psychologist may participate and share in the parent conference with the teacher. The mutual learnings resulting from such cooperative endeavors by both teacher and psychologist will serve not only as a binding for the partnership but also as inestimable help to the teacher and her students in time to come.

ADMINISTRATION

Seeing that his schools have available services and facilities for exceptional children is a prime duty of the school psychologist. When special classes are financially prohibitive to his system he should see that specialized services from the various experts representing different areas of exceptionality are made available to these respective children while they remain in the regular classroom.

> The integration of exceptional children in a regular classroom is an an individual matter in all cases, and can be accomplished successfully only after a careful diagnosis and consideration of:
>
> 1. The extent to which the integrated placement can provide for the intellectual, social, emotional, and physical needs of the child under consideration.

[10] Eli M. Bower, "The School Psychologist," *Bulletin of the California State Department of Education*, 24, No. 12 (November, 1955), 81.

2. The degree to which the exceptional child can become a contributing member of the group and compete on a fairly equal basis with the group.

3. The extent to which the physical facilities of the school plant provide accessibility to the areas of the building to which he must go to the routine of his program.

4. The degree to which the teacher with whom the child is to be placed accepts and understands him.[11]

Heeding these criteria, the youngster who is competent to deal adequately with the activities of the regular classroom situation can make a satisfactory adjustment in the regular grades.

Individual consultation with the regular classroom teacher becomes a prime function of the school psychologist particularly when specialists representing the various areas of exceptionality are not available to his school system. As a supplement to individual interviewing, many communities have established a program of child study for teachers, administrators, and supervisors in which outside consultants are invited to participate. Adding to the fund of information of his colleagues regarding his specialties, the school psychologist may select for topics of consideration the latest and most complete information regarding the administration, scoring, and interpretation of various test results, limitations of IQ's, statistics and projective techniques, in addition to the appraisal of case histories and studies. Techniques to be utilized in efficient parent-teacher conferences may also be discussed. Collaborating with other specialized personnel and consultants, the school psychologist should participate in and/or organize in-service workshops, consult with staff groups, and organize study courses in relevant psychological areas. In topics of particular interest to the administration, teachers and other school personnel, he would serve as group discussion leader in areas of his own specific competence.

Committee participation is also within the realm of cooperative relationships with other school staff in such areas as human relations, mental health, and teacher personnel. Oftentimes the school psychologist is called upon to consult with fellow employees on their own personal problems (on request) but with the prime purpose of referral to appropriate resources for further assistance. Training of new teacher personnel in the administration, scoring and interpretation of group tests, as well as demonstrating the type of reports and interpretations they will receive from him, is a yearly function. To the administrator, the psychologist serves as adviser in the selection of appropriate tests and test programs to meet the particular needs of the school system, a specific school or an individual class. Clerical assistance should be

[11] Norris G. Haring, George G. Stern, and William Cruickshank, *Attitudes of Educators Towards Exceptional Children*, Syracuse University Special Education and Rehabilitation Monograph Series, 3 (Syracuse: Syracuse University Press, 1958), p. 4.

made available to the school psychologist, and under his supervision they should maintain a complete test file, type reports, score group tests, order and distribute a continuous inventory of test booklets, samples, manuals, and scoring keys.

Another method of professional collaboration within a school system was described by Prescott.[12, 13] Through the utilization of the study of one child, Prescott and his colleagues discovered that increased understanding of behavior, in general, resulted. After eleven years of experience, the following pattern was prescribed. Each participating professional selected one child for a study. The procedure included a complete study of school records, conferences with teachers who were familiar with the child, conferences with parents, home visits, visits and interviews with the child, a collection and analysis of the child's art work, writings, etc., and direct observation of the child in the classroom and on the playground, recorded as anecdotal records. The group activity served to objectify, validate, and solidify the information which had been gathered. Upon completion of this phase of the group activity, future assignments for the participants included the establishment of some framework of principles based upon the information already collected and analyzed on individual children and finally resulted in the encouragement of a gradual program of modification of attitudes and insights into the general area of child behavior.

These and other organized approaches to resolve the multifaceted problem of dissemination of information regarding methods and techniques of child study should provide additional resources to the psychologist interested in a cooperative, well-informed team of professionals. The many approaches designed to educate and train school personnel in the understanding of psychological principles underlying child growth and development could not become a reality without the cooperation of the school administration and the school psychologist. Administrators have expressed their need for a school psychologist in their respective school systems. One superintendent even went so far to state that he would want a school psychologist on his staff in preference to an assistant superintendent.[14]

The role of the psychologist on the school staff, however, places him in a unique position with regard to the administrative line. Does he have a specific rating with regard to other professional employees? And if this is the case, where is he placed—between the principal and other staff, between the superintendent and the principals—or is the placement flexible, based upon the size of the school system? The question has never been answered to the satis-

---

[12] Daniel A. Prescott, "Emotion and the Educative Process," *Report of the Committee on the Relation of Emotion to the Educative Process*, American Council on Education (Washington: American Council on Education, 1938).

[13] ————, "Is Child Study a New Fad?", *National Education Association Journal*, 39 (October, 1950), 507–508.

[14] Cutts, *op. cit.*

faction of all concerned; in fact, there are many authorities who feel that the psychologist should *not* be included within the administrative line but should serve in the capacity of consultant. Nevertheless, the problem of specific responsibilities would remain, even with the attempt to sidestep it by conferring the title of "consultant." Does the school psychologist need the permission of the principal to enter the latter's school? Should he arrange, well in advance, the schedule of children whom he intends to assess? What of emergency cases or breaks in the proposed schedules? These and other questions, in all probability, will not be resolved by a simple directive but will demand a concerted effort on the part of both professions concerned to satisfy or compromise the preferential positions held by administrators and school psychologists. Perhaps there is need for more frequent interaction between the two professions on the local, state, and national levels in the form of conventions, conferences, and workshops.

The relationships between principals and psychologists are not limited to the question of relegation of powers and responsibilities. In addition to the close cooperation necessary toward the establishment of in-service training and workshops within the school building, the matter of frequency and amount of consultation necessary on the part of the school psychologists in such matters as curriculum development and placement also needs to be examined. Although not necessarily rigorously trained in areas such as curriculum development, the school psychologist is (or should be) well versed in principles of learning. Such technical aspects of programming dealing with the most opportune time for reading readiness, developmental reading, and the corresponding elements of the arithmetic program lend themselves readily to the organized principles of learning at the disposal of the psychologist. The nature of mental age and its relationship to these components of the learning process should become an integral part of the consulting responsibility of the school psychologist in his cooperation with principal and teacher alike. Adapting learning principles to the school curriculum is considered a more important responsibility than the strictly psychometric function. State laws, in many states, have resolved the issue of placement of pupils in special classes by delegating the school psychologist's responsibility in this matter as *recommending* only; the decision for *placement*, or rather, the legal responsibility, rests in the hands of the superintendent. Slowly, some of the inconsistencies of opinion held by administrators and school psychologists are being resolved. Considering the fact that school psychology is, relatively, still in its infancy stage, the amount of cooperation already obtained is pleasantly surprising.

THE SCHOOL PSYCHOLOGIST AND SPECIAL EDUCATION

The school psychologist can make an essential contribution to various phases of the special education program. Historically, the special education program in the public schools dealt primarily with special classes for mentally retarded children. Of late, the special education programs deal with the gamut of educational disabilities underlying exceptionality. Joining special classes for the mental retardate are special programs for the gifted, blind, deaf, crippled, speech defective, socially and emotionally maladjusted, neurologically impaired, in addition to some less prevalent types of exceptional children. Oftentimes the academically retarded child is subsumed under the general title of special education.

Although he usually does not have the authority to place or transfer a child to a specific special program, the school psychologist has the responsibility for studying such children referred to him, making recommendations for their treatment and/or placement. With his unique tools for testing, observation, and consultation, he may give leadership to programs aimed at the identification of the various types of exceptionalities, oftentimes coordinating the efforts of school administrators toward the establishment and maintenance of special education programs. In addition to his capacity as adviser to the school team regarding the most efficient method for handling these children, the school psychologist has the additional responsibilities of interpreting data to the childrens' parents and serving as coordinator between school and non-school agencies. Even though the duties implicit within the framework of special education programs are many and time-consuming, the school psychologist must not be considered solely as an adviser to such programs. His first and foremost function is the mental health of all school children, not only those children who represent the narrow field of exceptionality.

Those psychologists employed in the smaller and rural school districts are oftentimes assigned much more responsibility with respect to the selection and placement of exceptional children. Cooperative boards of services are fast expanding throughout the country particularly in areas sparsely populated. Such cooperation eliminates the necessity for the establishment of full special educational facilities for all types of exceptional children by any one school district; rather, they provide for an apportionment of specific special education facilities among the various districts represented. Hence, school district "A" may have a program for the blind and the partially sighted, whereas school district "B" has facilities for the hard-of-hearing and the deaf. School district "C" may provide for the mentally retarded and gifted, whereas school district "D" may provide the services of speech correction and home-bound teaching. With all of these specialized services available, a free interchange of students provides for optimal educational facilities for most of the exceptional children involved with minimal expense. The school psychologist, whether representing only one or all of the cooperating school districts, thereby has the opportunity to participate as a member of the larger professional team.

Medical Services

His special knowledge in the areas of psychology and education provide the school psychologist with an advisory capacity that overlaps the unique responsibilities held by other professional workers on the school team.

PHYSICIAN

The school physician may well serve as a strong ally to the psychologist in the total assessment program. Since a medical examination is a necessity in the diagnosis of individual children with problems, the relationship between these two professionals becomes a co-advisory partnership. The indispensable contributions of the physician and psychologist often serve as a basis upon which the school program is geared toward the resolution of specific problems. In many cases, it is the findings of the physician which pinpoint the etiology of a specific reading problem. For others it is the remedial program established by the psychologist that overcomes minor physical deviations that were assumed to be the cause of the problem. In areas that demand a mutual contribution to assessment, collaboration from the beginning stages of the referral are mandatory. Such is the case in the area of brain injury.

With the initial referral by the classroom teacher the usual complaint is sometimes accompanied by behavioral descriptions of the child which may be indicative of possible brain damage. Although the typical school physician may not be adequately equipped to administer a complete neurological examination, he may cooperate with the school psychologist in the establishment of a tentative diagnosis. The psychological tests at the disposal of the latter specialist may confirm or reject the suspicions of the classroom teacher. Needless to say, all the referred children who demonstrate some overt behavioral symptoms of brain damage are not immediately dispatched to the nearest neurologist for complete examination. It is therefore imperative that the physician and the psychologist screen those cases that are referred with tentative diagnoses based upon the collective interpretation of both specialists. In one case, the physician's interpretation may conclude that the "inattention" or "lack of attention span" that was considered indicative of brain injury is apparently the result of a muscular imbalance in the eyes of his referred patient. In another case, the psychologist may discover through his battery of tests that the "impulsive behavior" exhibited by the child in the classroom is the aftermath of an emotional upheaval in the home situation rather than the result of a lesion to the brain. Incompatibility between referral information and ultimate assessment is not uncommon. The referral may have been based upon the child's "impossible" behavior—constantly disrupting the teacher, other children, and the general atmosphere of the classroom. The classroom teacher may have suspected emotional instability whereas the joint efforts of the physician and the psychologist may lead to a diagnosis of brain injury.

In cases of minor brain damage—not readily discernible on the basis of direct observation of physical disability, such as cerebral palsy, etc.—the tools for diagnosis of both the physician and psychologist are admittedly inadequate. It is, therefore, imperative that joint decisions become the rule rather than the exception in such cases. These joint decisions often include the services of an outside specialist such as a neurologist and/or pediatrician in addition to the opinions tendered by the school physician and psychologist. The partnership must not be dissolved upon the completed diagnosis. In addition to the medical prescription for specific drug treatment for the child, the behavioral treatment in the classroom setting also demands cooperative efforts on the part of both specialists. It is not inconceivable that drug treatment prescribed for a specific individual in good faith by the school physician be incompatible with the recommended classroom procedure for the teacher prescribed by the psychologist. Such incompatibility, however, is most often the result of independent behavior on the part of the two specialists rather than cooperative endeavors. The physician and the psychologist are cooperating—not competitive personnel—in rendering their important services to children. A free interchange of cases, ideas, and information leads to a cooperating unit which establishes a program of optimal child care which is of utmost importance to the individual child concerned, his teacher, and the other students.

NURSE

The influence of the school nurse should not be underestimated. She is likely to know as much, if not more, about individual children than any other person in the school. In addition to serving as an additional resource to the physician-psychologist team in particularly problematic areas such as brain injury, she may well serve as an indispensable aid for the school psychologist in identifying exceptional children, noting gross changes in overt behavior on the part of some children, and her knowledge of extra-school resources may contribute to the well-being of the child. In school systems that do not provide the services of a full-time school physician the nurse is in an even more strategic position; the school psychologist must rely on her cooperative services. When a child is referred to the psychologist, the nurse will review with him the previous medical record, hearing, and vison test results obtained on the student. She serves as an invaluable ally to the psychologist particularly in conferences with parents, often making home visits. She may also stimulate the teacher with suggestions regarding the keeping of anecdotal records. When there is a need for medical referral, she may help the psychologist formulate a letter to the family physician. In the establishment of cooperative learning endeavors within a school system described above, such as in-service training, workshops, lectures, consultation, etc., the school nurse would make a valuable contribution.

PSYCHIATRIST

Some school systems, usually those of larger populations, have available to the children the part-time services of a psychiatrist serving in the capacity of consultant. Although the number of consulting psychiatrists for school systems is yet relatively small, the expressed need for these services has been steadily increasing. Abrahamson et al.[15] report the relative expressed need for psychiatrist services in school systems to be second only to psychological social workers on the basis of one survey. The assumed responsibilities of the school system for total program planning for all children has been on the upswing in recent years. More and more these responsibilities include many of the traditional non-school functions.

With the service of a psychiatrist in a school system, the task of the psychologist becomes less overwhelming. The tools at the disposal of the psychologist may be valuable assets to the psychiatrist toward the goal of total assessment of the behavior problems. The typical testing techniques serve as excellent screening devices, identifying those youngsters who demonstrate potential emotional disorders. When recognized early the problem presented is not the all but hopeless task characteristic of emotional disturbances that have had sufficient time to mature into fully developed psychoses. Beyond the screening devices, the psychologist may choose to administer one, or a series, of projective techniques which may lead to the isolation or specificity of the problem, often providing the necessary clues for the treatment of the youngster. But with the resources of a psychiatrist on the school team, the therapeutic function formerly assumed by the school psychologist now, more appropriately, is the responsibility of the former. Together, the two professionals may arrive at a joint diagnosis and recommendation for those youngsters who present severe emotional problems which interfere with their learning process as well as serving to disrupt the classroom organization. Eliminating the costly hours of individual therapy by transfering this duty to the psychiatrist, the school psychologist may then spend more time in preventive work and devote more hours to the important problem of curriculum advisement.

SOCIAL WORKER

With the school psychologist and the school social worker as collaborators, the home and school environments become essentially one. The social

[15] David Abrahamson, Emanuel Hammer, Irving Jacks, and Sydney Connel, "Status of Mental Hygiene and Child Guidance Facilities in Public Schools in U.S.," *Journal on Pediatrics*, 46 (1955), 107–118.

worker assumes the responsibility for diagnoses, and remediation of factors which are adversely affecting the child, emanating from the home situation. The psychologist becomes responsible for the diagnosis and recommendations from the standpoint of the school's effect upon the child. The problems jointly confronting the school psychologist and social worker usually are of such a nature that the school adjustment problem also involves overtones of social maladjustment. Fortified with the clinical diagnosis of the child supplied by the school psychologist, the social worker concerns himself with the social adjustment of the child starting usually with the home environment.

Oftentimes other community agencies are enlisted in an attempt to solve successfully the child's problem, particularly when active cooperation from the parents is lacking. The social worker, in accepting the child's problem as his immediate task, is often confronted with additional, and sometimes more serious, emotional difficulties on the part of the parents and other individuals who comprise the home contingent. Needless to say, with the overpowering demands for individual therapy with the child and the other members of his immediate environment, the social worker cannot accept too big a case load without subsequent loss of efficiency.

Close and frequent cooperation is demanded of the psychologist and social worker to insure positive results. Perhaps as a result of the social worker's analysis of the social environment, the psychologist may recommend some changes in the curriculum or in teaching methodology for the child to best contribute a positive influence to the organized plans set up for his home life. The psychologist's clinical assessment of the child often helps to prescribe actions necessary for his adequate social adjustment. Operating as a closely knit unit, the school psychologist and school social worker provide for a total school-home plan for the child. Collaboration between these professionals is often facilitated by the similarity of their backgrounds; the jargon used is mutually understandable; the various methods of therapy are known to both; and there is a common awareness regarding the difficulties presented by the problem at hand. In case conferences the social worker and the psychologist can together enlighten the remaining school staff members of the nature of the problem and suggest techniques and methodologies to utilize in remedying the situation.

COUNSELOR

Up to this point in the chapter the major emphasis as seen by the author has been on the functioning of school psychologists in an elementary school setting. This is not, in any way, intended to restrict the functioning of school psychologists to elementary school levels; certainly, there is an equivalent need for his services at the secondary levels. In fact, there is a need for a permanent psychological bureau to continue educational, personal, and vocational guidance throughout the child's whole school career. As suggested by Miller,[16] a psychologist should direct such a bureau.

With the consideration of the counselor, the secondary school now becomes the scene. Counselors, in the past, have wielded many titles, including descriptions such as vocational, occupational, school, adjustment, psychological and many more. Of immediate concern to the vocational counselor is vocational planning. In a one-to-one relationship with the individual student, he is involved not only with problems of immediate concern but with planning techniques for the meeting of future problems as they involve vocations. The counselor is not concerned with psychotherapy or reconstructing personality; rather, he functions in a problem solving relationship, interacting with the student to plan for his vocational future.

The duties and responsibilities of the school psychologist and the vocational counselor supplement one another. The psychologist has a wealth of information on hand with which the task of the counselor is facilitated. Previous intelligence and achievement tests, personality, interest, and aptitude inventories, in addition to total individual assessment in particular cases, are available to the psychologist from the cumulative record and his own files. The obtained scores plus the psychological assessment of the student become a valuable tool to the counselor in helping to select that vocational goal most appropriate for the youngster. Consulting with the counselor, the school psychologist can add further valuable material regarding clinical impressions and prognosis for future success in various areas of vocational promise. Once serving in this advising function to the counselor, the school psychologist's task is completed—the vocational counselor then proceeds to work with the student.

Hence the relationship with these two professionals is almost the direct opposite of the relationship between school psychologist and social worker. Whereas the cooperation between the psychologist and social worker becomes more intense as the therapy is in progress, the initial precounseling phase of the relationship between school psychologist and vocational counselor is most cooperative, decreasing in intensity as the counseling progresses. Further, as the technical aspects of the counseling situation become more involved, such as the introduction to the student of many and varied occupational choices, occupational information, etc., the school psychologist would be at a loss to comprehend these technicalities as would the counselor to understand clinical educational diagnosis. The relationship between counselor and psychologist is one of mutual advisement and consultation rather than direct cooperative effort.

In recent years the guidance worker or counselor has concerned himself

---

[16] J. Miller, "Program of a Psychologist in a High School," *School and Society*, 26 (1927), 367–368.

with problems other than those directly affecting vocations. As guidance workers received additional training, their responsibilities correspondingly increased to encompass interests more typically characteristic of school psychologists. Since guidance includes within its scope the entire life span of the child, movement by the guidance worker into the early formative years of school-aged children becomes a logical consequence of their newly formulated interests. But guidance, particularly as it relates to occupational information and subsequent choice, is fundamentally for secondary level pupils. Hence the guidance worker does not have the available time to delve deeply into special problems confronting the individual student on all educational levels. Perhaps here lies the line of demarcation between guidance worker and school psychologist. Certainly there is sufficient need for the contributions of both workers in the school setting. The question of limits of responsibilities might better be imposed on the basis of previous training and experience rather than on the specific title identifying the professional worker. "There is more than enough demand for the services of both psychologists and guidance workers in the schools. It seems necessary for their respective professional organizations to explore the problems in overlapping functions and training and to clarify issues so that competitive situations will be minimized and collaborative relationships increased." [17]

Selected Supplementary Readings

As We Do It: A Handbook for School Psychologists. Oakland, California: Alameda County Schools, 1953.

Backus, O. L., "Collaboration among Psychologists, Pediatricians, Clinical Psychologists, and Speech Therapists," *Nervous Child,* IX, No. 3 (1952), 242–256.

Benincasa, B. D., "Toward a Better Understanding Between Psychologist and Teacher," *New York State Education,* 52 (November, 1964), 8–10.

Bower, Eli M., "The Psychologist in the School," California State Dept. of Education, Bulletin 27, VIII (1958), 43.

Byrne, R. H., *The School Counselor.* Boston: Houghton Mifflin Company, 1963.

Buhler, C. *et al., Childhood Problems and the Teacher.* New York: Holt, Rinehart & Winston, Inc., 1958.

Cohen, W. J., "The Parent-Teacher Conference As a Collaborative Effort," *Devereux Schools Forum,* 3 (Spring, 1966), 10–30.

[17] Cutts, *op. cit.,* p. 83.

Detjen, Ervin Winfred, and Mary Ford Detjen, *Elementary School Guidance,* 2nd ed. New York: McGraw-Hill Book Company, 1963.

Eiserer, P. E., "Consultant Roles," Washington, D. C.: *The School Psychologist.* The Center for Applied Research in Education, 1963.

Farwell, G. F., and H. J. Peters, *Guidance Readings for Counselors.* Skokie, Ill.: Rand McNally & Co., 1960.

Fisher, J. K, "Role Perceptions and Characteristics of Attendance Coordinators, Psychologists and Social Workers," *Journal of the International Association of Pupil Personnel Workers,* 10 (March, 1966), 55–62.

Garry, Ralph, *Guidance Techniques for Elementary Teachers.* Columbus, Ohio: Charles E. Merrill Books, Inc., 1963.

Gray, Susan W., "Working With and Through Others: III, The Psychologist as Social Inventor," in *The Psychologist in the Schools.* New York: Holt, Rinehart & Winston, Inc., 1963.

Hildreth, Gertrude, "Services of the School Psychologist," *Handbook of Applied Psychology,* ed. D. H. Fyer and E. H. Henry. New York: Farrar, Straus & Giroux, Inc., 1950.

Hill, H. J., "The Visiting Teacher: The School Troubleshooter," *Journal of the International Association of Pupil Personnel Workers,* 10 (June, 1966), 72–76.

Hirst, Wilma E., "Services to the School," Part III, *Know Your School Psychologist.* New York: Grune & Stratton, Inc., 1963.

Jacques, A., "Effective Communication in Pupil Personnel Services," *Journal of the International Association of Pupil Personnel Workers,* 10 (June, 1966), 83–87.

Johnson, W. F., B. Stefflre, and R. A. Edelfelt, "Pupil Personnel Roles," in *Pupil Personnel and Guidance Services,* Part III. New York: McGraw-Hill Book Company, 1961.

Kamin, E., "Cooperative Approach to Child Study," *Education Leadership,* VII (1950), 563–567.

Kimmitt, Y. G., W. G. Klopfer, and M. R. Reed, "The Decision-Making Process As It Relates to Dominance in Children," *Journal of School Psychology,* 4 (Autumn, 1965), 37–44.

Mackey, R. A., and F. R. Fassler, "Group Consultation With School Personnel," *Mental Hygiene,* 50 (July, 1966), 416–421.

Magary, J. F., "The Psychologist Views School Language Activities," *Elementary School Journal,* 60 (1959), 27–31.

Mahoney, Stanley C., "Preparing The Child for Psychological Referral," *NEA Journal,* 47 (1958), 49–50.

Mathewson, Robert Hendry, *Guidance Policy and Practice,* 3rd ed. New York: Harper & Row, Publishers, 1962.

Newland, T. Ernest, "Psychological Assessment of Exceptional Children and Youth," in *Psychology of Exceptional Children and Youth*, ed. William M. Cruickshank. Englewood Cliffs, N.J.: Prentice-Hall, Inc., 1963.

Patterson, C. H., "Relationships with other School Personnel," *Counseling and Guidance in Schools: A First Course*. New York: Harper & Row, Publishers, 1962.

Pearman, Jean R., and A. H. Burrows, *Social Services in the Schools*. New York: Public Affairs Press, 1955.

Peters, Herman J., and Gail F. Farwell, "Using School Resources for Guidance Purposes," in *Guidance: A Developmental Approach*. Chicago: Rand McNally & Co., 1959.

Porter, L. W., "Properties of Organizational Structure in Relation to Job Attitudes," *Psychological Bulletin*, 64 (July, 1965), 23–51.

Rich, Jeanne, and Jack I. Bardon, "The Teacher and the School Psychologist," *Elementary School Education*, LXIV (March, 1964), 318–323.

Shertzer, Bruce, and S. C. Stone, "The School Counselor and His Public: A Problem in Role Definition," *The Personnel and Guidance Journal*, XLI (April, 1963), 687–693.

Valett, Robert E., "Relationships with Professional Educators," in *The Practice of School Psychology*. New York: John Wiley & Sons, Inc., 1963.

Wallin, J. E., "The School Psychologist in Retrospect," *Journal of Consulting Psychology*, VI (1942), 309–312.

White, Mary Alice, and Myron W. Harris, "Referrals from the Classroom Teacher," and "The School Psychologist and Pupil Personnel Services," in *The School Psychologist*. New York: Harper & Row, Publishers, 1961.

WHO, UN, UNESCO Joint Expert Committee, *Psychological Services for Schools*. Hamburg, Germany: UNESCO Institute for Education, 1955.

Wolf, D., "Teacher and School Social Worker: Strategic Team for Mental Health," *Journal of Education*, CXLVI (1964), 35–42.

Wylie, Howard Lee, and Malcolm Sills, "Psychodynamically Oriented Procedures in School Consultation," in *Professional School Psychology*, ed. M. G. Gottsegen and G. B. Gottsegen. New York: Grune & Stratton, Inc., 1960.

WILLIAM J. RUZICKA

5

Working with Parents and Community Agencies

One of the most rewarding and enriching responsibilities of the school psychologist is his contacts with people and agencies within the larger social environment of students. Although his duties are primarily concerned with the "school environment" of students, the school psychologist's interaction with other than school personnel in his study of and working with students is a logical extension of his consultant's role.[1] In this chapter we will be concerned with ways in which the school psychologist helps students through his contacts with people not directly connected with the school. A brief outline of some of these functions can be found in the recent report of the A.P.A. committee on recommendations of the functions of the school psychologist.[2]

Certainly the most important social unit in determining the personality development of students is the family. Therefore, the largest part of this chapter will be concerned with discussing ways in which the school psychologist can work with parents and other significant

[1] "The School Psychologist, A Consultant to School and Community" (Mimeo.) (Columbus, Ohio: Bureau of Special and Adult Education, Ohio State Univ., 1955).

[2] American Psychological Association, Committee of Reconsideration of the Functions of the School Psychologist, Division 16. *The Psychologist on the School Staff* (Washington, D.C.: A.P.A., 1959).

members in the family. "Community agencies" may also help to fulfill the school psychologist's role. Some of these agencies are: the mental health clinics, juvenile court, private practitioners, and other social welfare groups. A proportionately smaller part of the chapter will deal with the school psychologist's role in working with these persons and agencies.

Working with Parents

The school psychologist can ideally occupy a most advantageous position—that of being a liaison between two groups of people, interested, according to their competence, in the individual child in school. One of the groups, that has been called the "clinical team," is composed of those specialists whose job it is to study and help the child in the area known as "mental health." The composition of the clinical team varies, but the school psychologist is always a participant. Its function will be described more in detail later. The other group, which we will call the "educational team," is composed of those persons directly concerned with the education, broadly defined, of the child. The composition of the educational team also varies, but for our purposes, we will include parents, teacher, principal, and school psychologist. Others may be included, such as the remedial teacher, but certainly the four mentioned above constitute a minimum. The school psychologist's role as a member of the educational team [3] is our immediate concern.

THE EDUCATIONAL TEAM APPROACH [4]

As Kanner has said in a recent institute: "Parents are no longer dealt with merely as passive recipients of authoritatively presented wisdom, but as deeply concerned persons who can, and should, be prepared for the task of becoming understanding and active participants." [5] The school psychologist, therefore, should know how to work with parents, as well as teachers, in their common endeavor of the education of school children.

As early as 1942, Zehrer, in speaking of the school psychologist as a mental health specialist noted: "Since we now recognize the importance of the preschool years upon the emotional and social development of children, it is essential that some assistance be offered parents if a valid mental hygiene program is to be effective." [6]

[3] Mr. Harrower and L. Goldstein, "The New School Team in Mental Health," *Child Study*, 36 (1959), 19–24.

[4] Some of the material in this section was taken from the writer's article on counseling parents, W. J. Ruzicka, "A Proposed Role for the School Psychologist: Counseling Parents of Mentally Retarded Children," *American Journal of Mental Deficiency*, 62 (1958), 897–904.

[5] *The Evaluation and Treatment of the Retarded Child in Clinics* (New York: National Association for Retarded Children, 1956).

[6] F. A. Zehrer, "The School Psychologist as a Mental Health Specialist," *Journal of Consulting Psychology*, 6 (1942), 218–222.

At the present time, because of his consultant role, the school psychologist assumes the responsibility, in the eyes of the parents, for the various professions involved in a case study. Thus, in his conferences with parents he may at times inform them of the medical diagnosis, advise them about available social services, suggest educational procedures, discuss vocational possibilities, and talk over their own emotional reactions to the stressful situation. He is, therefore, the coordinator of the clinical team's findings and the one who helps both parents and teachers in their application of these findings and recommendations.

Sarason's concise formulation of the purposes of interviews with parents is applicable not only to parents of the mentally retarded, but also to parents of all children studied by the school psychologist. He states: "Thus far we have attempted to do four things: 1) engender in the parents a particular attitude toward the interview, 2) identify the nature of the parents' problems, 3) utilize the diagnostic findings in order to help the parents to adopt a realistic conception of their child's condition; and 4) formulate and discuss with the parents a specific attack on their child's and their own problems." [7]

"Too much emphasis cannot be placed on the importance of 1) facilitating parental verbalization about their attitudes to the recommendation; 2) avoiding any display of impatience or hostility when parents ask questions or disagree with the recommendation; and 3) reiterating the recommendation always in terms of the considerations which give rise to it." [8]

The school psychologist's interviewing skills are nowhere put to better use than in his contacts with parents. It is necessary for him to be able to understand and to some extent control the interpersonal dynamics that take place. It is for this reason that the following counseling techniques are described.

1. The biggest obstacle in working with parents seems to be *initiating* their cooperation rather than *developing* and *maintaining* it. "Selling your services" before beneficial results can be seen is as necessary in motivating parental behavior as the inner motivation that arises from the parents' own needs and desires. The school psychologist acts with discretion so as not to push parents into a relationship before they see the need and the purpose of it; he should, however, take advantage of his position as a member of the educational team to guide and direct the parents' decisions through recommendations that are based on facts and have practical advantages.

2. The school psychologist should help both parents exercise their responsibilities in contributing to the establishment of educational goals for their children, whenever this is possible. Too often it is only the mother who accepts this responsibility and not the father. Too often, the mother exercises an over-dominant influence. The school psychologist can not only better

[7] S. B. Sarason, *Psychological Problems in Mental Deficiency* (New York: Harper & Row, Publishers, 1959), p. 344.
[8] *Ibid.*, p. 357.

understand the dynamics of power and control in a family by working with *both* parents, but he can then suggest ways of alleviating the stressful situation.

3. The interpretation of the findings of a case conference to parents presents difficulties not only in verbal communication, but also in the personal-social relationship itself. The role that the school psychologist should adopt in an interview with the parents for this purpose has been described very well by Rheingold:

> This interview differs in some respects from the typical therapeutic interview. The psychologist possesses information which the parent needs. This means that the parent's questions cannot be turned back upon himself at every point, although at many points they need to be. The psychologist's role is therefore, the more active one. Throughout the interview he should help the parent to clarify his own feelings about his problem but if asked a question concerning test findings, private schools, and so forth, he should give a direct answer. The attitude of the psychologist should be that of any psychotherapeutic worker—interested, sympathetic, understanding.[9]

4. Although the phenomena exist in a more weakened form than in psychoanalysis or psychotherapy, it is still appropriate to speak of the "transferences" of the parents and the "counter-transferences" of the school psychologist as both facilitating and inhibiting factors in the working relationship. On the part of the parents, transference of attitudes of over-idealization or hostility, for example, may have to be recognized by the school psychologist as neurotically determined and not reality-oriented. Much more difficult to recognize are the attitudes of condescension or fear, for example, that the school psychologist may have toward the parents—again not reality-oriented, but neurotically determined.

5. The school psychologist should sense when and when not to interpret parental resistances. If he is going to see the parents in short-term counseling, techniques for the handling of resistance in the parents should be studied. Symonds' (*Dynamics of Psychotherapy, Vol. I*) discussion of the handling of the uncooperative client, the argumentative client, and the passive-aggressive client should be very helpful to the school psychologist in developing skills in understanding and combating these defensive maneuvers when they are used by parents. Symonds' (Vol. 2) also mentions the use of bibliotherapy as an adjunctive technique in breaking through specific resistances.[10] This particular technique will be discussed later in the chapter.

6. The school psychologist should be especially attuned to the "psy-

[9] H. Rheingold, "Interpreting Mental Retardation to Parents," *Journal of Consulting Psychology*, 9 (1945), 143.

[10] P. M. Symonds, *Dynamics of Psychotherapy*, Vols. II and III (New York: Grune & Stratton, Inc., 1957).

chological messages" being transmitted by the parents during the interview. As White and Harris state:

> Throughout the interview, which is aimed both at getting the parents' co-operation and at developing information, the psychologist uses the techniques that any good interviewer would use. He is alert to the interplay between the parents, to who leads in presenting the information, to contradictions and where they occur, to the different explanations offered by either parent. The amount of understanding that he obtains of the parents' personalities and of the family interaction is dependent upon his clinical skills, upon his ability to recognize what is not actually stated, and upon the feeling that lies behind the words used.[11]

7. The school psychologist cannot hope to change chronic intrafamilial conflicts in a few interviews. When serious conflicts remain unresolved, he should recommend other facilities, such as individual psychotherapy or group therapy. Vigilance against the development of the "God-complex," an occupational hazard, should be maintained not only in this area but in any function in which the school psychologist is not qualified.[12] The school psychologist, however, should be able to pick out psychopathological reactions in the parents' verbal and nonverbal behavior so that he can make the proper referral for extended treatment if necessary.

8. The discussion of test results should be at the parents' level of comprehension. Quoting IQ, standard scores or percentile ranks is usually less advisable than translating these scores into meaningful *descriptions* and *predictions* of the child's performance. By doing this the school psychologist will avoid the pitfall of giving some parents more grist for their mill of rationalization. Since scores are sometimes used carelessly or even unethically by parents, it is most important for the school psychologist to explain their meanings adequately.

9. Much information about parental attitudes can be gained by using "general lead" questions and listening for comments that give hints about existing attitudes. Listening for "metaphors," slips of the tongue and cues as to the style of speech the parents use are very valuable bits of information to be judiciously used in inferring pre-conscious patterns of personality functioning. Rheingold has emphasized the importance of this skill when she noted:

> The importance of encouraging the parent to express his feelings of responsibility can scarcely be overestimated, for the success of the interview may depend upon it. A parent does not parade these feelings; in fact, he struggles to repress them and hesitates to admit them, even to himself. But until he can obtain relief for feelings of guilt, inadequacy, or humiliation, he cannot

---

[11] M. A. White and M. W. Harris, *The School Psychologist* (New York: Harper & Row, Publishers, 1961), pp. 312–313.

[12] E. M. Bower, *The School Psychologist.* California State Department of Education, **24**, No. 12 (1955).

view reality with sufficient objectivity to develop emotional acceptance of his child.[13]

10. The school psychologist should be alert not only to *what* the parents say and *how* it is said, but also to the many, often informative, *non-verbal cues.* Thus, self-attitudes, role-concepts, and unverbalized motivations can be hypothesized from the parents' physical appearance and movements, their clothing, posture, and flexibility in adapting themselves to a new surrounding. Wallen has summarized the importance of observing both verbal and non-verbal behavior during the interview in the following way:

> The practical implications of our discussion for the clinician are evident. Realizing that consistenecy and unity of personal expression may be present without being obvious, he tries to be alert to them. But he knows, too, that he should not assume consistency too quickly. He must test his hunches as he investigates the specific conditions in his client's life. He will seek the consistencies that were defined by the conditions of the client's social living, not consistencies as he thinks they ought to be. Approaching the data this way, the clinician is not likely to depend on pat formula such as "people who talk too much are showing their hostility toward others." Rather, he will recognize that this may not be a misguided effort to pacify others, to avoid self-insight, to drain off tension, or even all of these at once.[14]

11. The school psychologist should guard against identifying (consciously or unconsciously) with one group or person against another. These biases eventually become apparent to others and jeopardize his position of objectivity. Thus, if the school psychologist always is on the side of the student and takes great pains to blame one of the parents or a teacher regardless of the circumstances, he will undoubtedly lose the rapport necessary for a working relationship with parents. Ideally, the school psychologist should not "represent" either parents or teachers in working out the child's problems in school. Nevertheless, because of the emotional involvement of both parents and teachers, a certain amount of perceptual distortion is likely to occur when the various "sides" of a story are told. In situations where discrepancies are particularly flagrant and adherents of the "sides" are looking for justification of their position, it is most necessary for the school psychologist to refrain from joining one side against the other and making a public issue of the incident. He may either a) work with the parties separately until he can ascertain fact from fiction; b) bring unconscious feelings, the "unspoken thoughts," into the open in joint conferences for both parties to reconsider; or c) enlist the help of other noncommitted personnel in mental health to resolve the conflicts judiciously.

[13] H. Rheingold, *op. cit.,* p. 147.
[14] R. W. Wallen, *Clinical Psychology* (New York: McGraw-Hill Book Company, 1956), p. 131.

12. Finally, the school psychologist should not lose sight of the purpose for his contacts with parents, i.e., growth in the mutual understanding of the child's assets and problems, recognition of past parental influences or lack of influences upon the child's present behavior, and the application of mutually-arrived-at plans of action in the interest of helping the child and the parents to overcome obstacles to education and to resolve blocks to mental health.

These suggestions have been described to aid the school psychologist in developing his skill as counselor of parents. Each individual, of course, has to apply his knowledge and skill to the concrete situation at hand.

The following discussion is an adjunct to the basic person-to-person interview relationship based on the writer's own experiences. Several other writers have described their use of this technique, for example Karpman.[15]

BIBLIOTHERAPY

Bibliotherapy is a diagnostic-therapeutic directed-reading technique designed to help parents express thoughts and feelings about themselves and their children according to acceptable mental health practices. It can be used very effectively by the school psychologist in his contacts with parents when he does not have the time for a prolonged person-to-person relationship. To be most effective, the reading material should be selected according to the problem areas being experienced by the parents and/or their children, their level of reading ability and interest, and the opportunities available for discussion of the material with the school psychologist.

It has been very helpful to have printed materials in the forms of pamphlets, books, and magazine articles available for parents to peruse when they find it difficult to talk openly about their problems. The use of printed material thus becomes an avenue of communication less threatening to parents and eventually enables them to become more involved in the counseling process. One disadvantage, however, in using bibliotherapy is the tendency of some parents to use the printed materials as the sole means of contact with the school psychologist. The pamphlets and books are not an end in themselves, but are supposed to be one of the ways to enrich the personal contacts with the school psychologist. In other words, the reading should lead to better verbal communication, more expression of ideas and feelings, and a more enlightened discussion of what may need to be changed.

The following list of published materials is provided for the purpose of illustrating what materials can be used. Judicious use of the listed materials is of course preferred to a barrage of literature.

[15] B. Karpman, "Objective Psychotherapy," *Clinical Psychology Monograph,* No. 6, 1948.

Materials Useful
to School Psychological Services Personnel
in the Counseling of Parents

I. *For Parents of the Mentally Retarded Child*

Abraham, W., *Barbara, A Prologue*. New York: Holt, Rinehart & Winston, Inc., 1958.

Buck, P., *The Child Who Never Grew*. New York: The John Day Company, Inc., 1950.

Egg, Maria, *When a Child is Different*. New York: The John Day Company, Inc., 1964.

French, E. L., and Scott, C., *Child in the Shadows*. Philadelphia: J. B. Lippincott Co., 1960.

Junker, K. S., *The Child in the Glass Ball*. New York: Abingdon Press, 1964.

Kirk, S. A., *You and Your Retarded Child*. New York: The Macmillan Company, 1958.

Levinson, A., *The Mentally Retarded Child: A Guide for Parents*. New York: The John Day Company, Inc., 1952.

National Association for Retarded Children Pamphlets: "The Three R's for the Retarded," and "The Mentally Retarded Child at Home, a Manual for Parents."

Public Affairs Committee Pamphlets: No. 210 "The Retarded Child" and No. 219, "How to Help Your Handicapped Child."

Slaughter, S. S., *The Mentally Retarded Child and His Parent*. New York: Harper & Row, Publishers, 1963.

II. *For Parents of the Neurologically Impaired and Physically Handicapped Child*

Anderson, Camilla M., *Jan, My Braindamaged Daughter*. Portland, Ore.: The Durham Press, 1963.

Avery, Marie, and Alice Higgins, *Help Your Child Learn How to Learn*. Englewood Cliffs, New Jersey: Prentice-Hall, Inc., 1962.

Bindt, J. A., *A Handbook for the Blind*. New York: The Macmillan Company, 1953.

Bottke, Eleanor, Clari Bare, and Neva Waggoner, *Self-Help Clothing for Handicapped Children*. Chicago: The National Society for Crippled Children and Adults, 1962.

Graham, R., and Gloria Colovini, *Guide for Parents Requesting Home*

Instruction for Physically Handicapped Children. Springfield, Ill.: State Department of Public Instruction, 1961.

Hutton, Daniel A., *Understanding Cerebral Palsy: A Handbook for Parents.* Erie, Penn.: The Erie County Crippled Children Society, 1962.

Lewis, R. A., and L. Lehtinen, *The Other Child.* New York: Grune and Stratton, Inc., 1959.

McDonald, Eugene T., *Understanding Those Feelings: A Guide for Parents and Everyone Who Counsels Them.* Pittsburgh: Stanwix House, Inc., 1962.

Miers, E. S., *Why Did This Have to Happen, An Open Letter to Parents.* Chicago: The National Society for Crippled Children and Adults, 1957.

Myklebust, H., *Your Deaf Child: A Guide for Parents.* Springfield, Ill.: Charles C Thomas, Publisher, 1950.

Neville, Joan, *So Briefly My Son.* London: Hutchinson & Co. (Publishers), Ltd., 1962.

Public Affairs Committee Pamphlets: No. 197, "Doing Something for the Disabled" and No. 212, "Gains for the Handicapped Child."

Spock, Benjamin, and Marian O. Lerrigo, *Caring for Your Disabled Child.* New York: The Macmillan Company, 1964.

Stern, E., and E. Castendyck, *The Handicapped Child: A Guide for Parents.* New York: A. A. Wyn, Inc., Publishers, 1950.

III. *For Parents of the Emotionally and Socially Disturbed Child*

American Institute of Family Relations Pamphlet, "Home Study Course in Social Hygiene Guidance and Sex Education."

American Social Health Association Pamphlet, "Emotional Problems of Growing Up."

Bruch, H., *Don't Be Afraid of Your Child: A Guide to Perplexed Parents.* New York: Farrar, Straus & Giroux, Inc., 1952.

Canadian Mental Health Association, *How to Know Your Child.* New York: Human Relations Aid, 1954.

Child Study Association of America Pamphlets: "Aggressiveness in Children" and "When Children Ask About Sex."

Child Study Association of America, *Parent's Questions.* New York: Harper & Row, Publishers, 1947.

Mayer, Greta, and Mary Hoover, *When Children Need Special Help with Emotional Problems.* New York: Child Study Association of America, 1961.

National Association for Mental Health Pamphlets: "Being a Good Parrent" and "Keystones in Psychological Thinking About Young Children."

Science Research Associates Pamphlets: "How to Live With Parents"; "Self-Understanding—A First Step to Understanding Children"; "How to Live With Children"; "Understanding Hostility in Children"; "Fears in Children."

Spock, B., *The Common Sense Book of Baby and Child Care.* New York: Duell, Sloan and Pearce, 1946.

Stern, Edith M., *Mental Illness: A Guide for the Family,* 4th ed. New York: Harper & Row, Publishers, 1962.

Symonds, P., *The Dynamics of Parent-Child Relationships.* New York: Columbia University Press, 1949.

U. S. Children's Bureau Pamphlets: "Your Child 1 to 6"; "Your Child 6 to 12"; "The Adolescent in Your Family."

Van Riper, C., *Teaching Your Child to Talk.* New York: Harper & Row, Publishers, 1950.

Wolf, A., and S. Szasz, *Helping Your Child's Emotional Growth.* New York: Doubleday & Company, Inc., 1954.

Note: The following directory is a very useful publication for the school psychologist who is called upon to make recommendations for educational and therapeutic placement of emotionally disturbed children.

Directory of Resources for Mentally Ill Children in the United States, 1964, lists and describes 147 residential and day facilities that provide service to seriously disturbed children in separate units, distinct and apart from adult care. Both public and private resources are listed. The 96-page directory, published jointly by the National Association for Mental Health and the National Institute of Mental Health, is available for $2 from the NAMH, 10 Columbus Circle, New York, N.Y., 10019.

IV. *For Parents of the Gifted Child*

Abraham, W., *Common Sense About Gifted Children.* New York: Harper & Row, Publishers, 1958.

Brumbaugh, Florence N., and Bernard Roshco, *Your Gifted Child: A Guide for Parents.* New York: Holt, Rinehart & Winston, Inc., 1959.

Cutts, N. and N. Moseley, *Bright Children: A Guide for Parents.* New York: G. P. Putnam's Sons, 1953.

Freehill, M., *Gifted Children: Their Psychology and Education.* New York: The Macmillan Company, 1961.

Strang, Ruth, *Helping Your Gifted Child.* New York: Sutton and Co., 1960.

V. *To Parents of the Deaf and the Hard of Hearing Child*

Bloom, Freddy, *Our Deaf Children*. Washington, D.C.: Volta Bureau, 1963.

Fuller, Carl W., *Your Child, Maturity, and You: A Talk With Parents*. Washington, D.C.: Gallaudet Press, 1962.

Radcliffe, Margaret W., *A Letter To Parents*. *Hearing News*, (March, 1953).

The following periodicals can be obtained from the Volta Bureau, 1937 35th Street Northwest, Washington, D.C.
Volta Bureau, *If Your Child is Deaf*.
Montague, H., *Letters to the Mother of a Deaf Born Child*.
Fellendorf, G., *What Parents Can Do for Their Deaf Child*.
Fellendorf, G., *Factors Affecting Parents' Decisions*.

VI. *Special Parental Counseling Problems*

Blaine, Graham P., *Patience and Fortitude: The Parents' Guide to Adolescence*. Boston: Little, Brown and Company, 1962.

Jones, Eve, *Raising Your Child in a Fatherless Home: A Guidebook for all Mothers without Partners*. New York: Free Press of Glencoe, Inc., 1963.

Mok, Paul P., *Pushbutton Parents and the Schools*. Philadelphia: Macrae Smith Co., 1964. Book is divided into two sections: "Helping Your Child to Learn" and "Helping Your School to Help Your Child."

To help the school psychologist develop his own library of materials, a list of names and addresses of institutions which can be used as sources for reading lists, pamphlets and other inexpensive materials is located at the end of this chapter.

One further method of working with parents will now be considered— the use of discussion groups for group counseling and group therapy.

GROUP APPROACH

It is mainly through the use of group approaches that the school psychologist can deal with the attitudes and feelings of parents not only with reference to their children's problems, but also with reference to their own difficulty in dealing with their children. Indeed, it is often necessary to help parents resolve some of their own conflicts before they are capable of helping their children.

The close interaction between parents and children and the influence each has on the other's mental health makes it necessary for the school psychologist to do all he can to understand and help modify, if need be, the attitudes and feelings of parents. Sebold arrived at a similar conclusion when he said:

> It is generally agreed by psychologists that children reflect the social and emotional adjustment of their parents. This is true particularly of severely handicapped children who are of necessity bound closely to their parents emotionally and are dependent upon them for the simplest and most primal satisfactions. It is true, as well, of the gifted child whose deviation is so marked that it sets him apart from his peers, and who must seek stability and security from his parents to a greater extent than the normal child. The mental health of the parents thus becomes of paramount importance in the emotional and physical well-being of the child and hence should be the first and most important goal in parent education.[16]

Several writers [17] have discussed the problems of starting and continuing discussion groups, counseling groups, and therapy groups with parents. In this regard, it is very important to realize what goals we hope to attain in working with parent groups. The following explanation should help to clarify this point.

If our purpose is mainly an educational one, such as communicating with parents about instructional procedures, and understanding test results, with the personal involvement of parents being secondary, then group discussion techniques would seem to be advisable. A book such as that written by Barnlund and Harman [18] could be used most effectively by the school psychologist in understanding his role in discussion groups as well as the methods of motivation, handling group resistance and conflict, organizing individual and group "thinking through" procedures, etc. In general, the school psychologist's activities would approximate the "consultant's role" which has been described by many authorities. One of the benefits of group discussion is the mutual learning that takes place among the members, primarily in regard to educational techniques that have been used successfully by its members.

[16] D. Sebold, "The Importance of Education for the Parents of the Exceptional Children," in *Special Education for the Exceptional,* Vol. I, ed. M. Frampton and E. Gall (Boston: Porter Sargent, Publisher, 1955).

[17] A. D. Buchmueller, *et al.,* "A Group Therapy Project with Parents of Behavior Problem Children in Public Schools," *Nervous Children,* 10 (1954), 415–424; W. Hulse, "Helping the Parent of the Disturbed Child in School," in *Professional School Psychology,* ed. M. Gottsegen and G. Gottsegen (New York: Grune and Stratton, Inc., 1960); J. H. Levy, "A Study of Parent Groups for Handicapped Children," *Journal of Exceptional Children,* 19 (1952–53), 19–26; C. Popp, V. Ingram and P. Jordan, "Helping Parents Understand Their Mentally Handicapped Child," *American Journal of Mental Deficiencies,* 58 (1953–54), 530–534; and J. T. Weingold, "Parents' Groups and the Problems of Mental Retardation," *American Journal of Mental Deficiencies,* 56 (1952), 484–492.

[18] D. C. Barnlund and F. S. Harman, *The Dynamics of Discussion* (Boston: Houghton Mifflin Company, 1960).

If our purpose is both an educational and a therapeutic one, that is, being as concerned with long-standing parental attitudes and behavior toward children as well as with the problems of the children themselves, then group counseling techniques would be appropriate. The following articles and books are very helpful in understanding the process of group counseling: Kutkov [19]; Popp, Ingram, and Jordan [20]; and Slavson.[21] In so far as unresolved conflicts, such as differences in discipline techniques, have some influence on the children's behavior in school, whether academic, social or emotional, they are legitimate areas of concern for the school psychologist. Of course, only the school psychologist qualified in counseling procedures should use this group approach in trying to resolve some of the common parental conflicts.

Finally, if the purpose is mainly a therapeutic one, with the children's problems being just one aspect of the entire process with the parents, then group therapy would seem to be called for. It is still an unresolved question as to whether the school psychologist *should* participate in a group therapy process with parents even if he were qualified. Perhaps the community mental health clinic or child guidance clinic would be the more appropriate place for this kind of group work. The practical answer to the question would probably depend upon the interest and competence of the school psychologist and the specific way the school system has delineated his functions. In either case, participation by him or referral to another agency, an understanding of the procedures, psycho-dynamics, and advantages of group therapy is necessary for the school psychologist. For this general purpose, Corsini's book is very helpful.[22] As to the practical results of one kind of group treatment, the study by Buchmueller et al.[23] found that the majority of the children whose mothers attended groups showed clear-cut improvement in their behavior in school.

Working with the Community Mental Health Clinic

In this section we will discuss the school psychologist's role as member of the "clinical team." In this role the school psychologist uses his skills in psycho-educational-vocational diagnosis and treatment to fullest advantage.

[19] B. Kutkov, "Techniques and Explanatory Concepts of Short-Term Group Psychotherapy," *Journal of Psychology*, 28 (1949), 369–381.

[20] C. Popp, V. Ingram and P. Jordan, *op. cit.*

[21] S. R. Slavson, *Child-Centered Group Guidance of Parents* (New York: International Universities Press, Inc., 1958).

[22] R. Corsini, *Methods of Group Psychotherapy* (New York: McGraw-Hill Book Company, 1959).

[23] Buchmueller, *et al., op. cit.*

As long ago as 1940, a trend had been noted *in practice* toward an integrated clinical team approach in the treatment of a child and his parents. As Phyllis Blanchard remarked at that time:

> In the last ten years of child guidance clinic work, the trend has been away from case study and report and toward a very different approach to the problems of parents and children, namely the coordination of psychological therapy for the child and case work with the child's parents. This usually means that there are regular appointments for the child with a therapist and for the parents with a social worker, once or twice a week, for a period of several months. The actual length of time required for treatment of the child and case work with the parents varies with the individual case, but three or four months would usually be a minimum time for any case with once a week appointments.[24]

We shall endeavor to project this type of integrated approach into the context of the rather special kind of problems with which the school psychologist is concerned—the psycho-educational-vocational problems of children in school.

The school psychologist is certainly the appropriate person for making referrals to the mental health clinic or child guidance clinic in the community. One of the first problems he is likely to encounter in referral is active resistance or lack of cooperation by the parents. Bower summarized the job-at-hand when he stated:

> A school psychologist may find it necessary to have several contacts with parents before he suggests that the child be referred for psychiatric help. Some parents have problems and disturbances they have learned to cope with in a way that is acceptable to them. Others may have disturbances that are alien to their own concepts of themselves and hence cause them anxiety. Individuals who have problems that are not perceived as *problems* cannot be induced to accept therapy before they have some measure of understanding of what is involved. The school psychologist must endeavor to recognize those persons who can be helped by psychiatric therapy and those persons who are not as yet ready to profit from such treatment.[25]

Actually, treatment of a child is unduly handicapped if he is not accompanied by his parents. The situation is not so pessimistic when the patient is an adolescent, but even in these cases it is certainly more desirable for both parents and the child to be seen by the personnel of the mental health clinic.

The school psychologist's job is not over, however, once he has referred a student and his parents to a mental health clinic. He should participate as much as possible in the evaluation and treatment program. He participates in the evaluation by presenting his psycho-educational-vocational report at the case conference, along with reports and information gathered by the psy-

24 Phyllis Blanchard, "Interpreting Psychological Data to Parents," *Journal of Consulting Psychology*, 4 (1940), 120–123.

25 E. M. Bower and H. Mann, "Problems of Referral of Children and Adults to Psychiatrists and Mental Health Clinics," *The Psychologist in the School*. California State Department of Education, 27, No. 9 (1958).

chiatrist, social worker, and clinical psychologist. In some cases other consultants may also participate. It is in this type of case conference that the school psychologist should be able to contribute valuable information to be used in rounding out a complete psycho-diagnostic study of the child. He should also learn much more about the child, and as a result of his participation, be in an advantageous position to apply his findings in the school setting.

The school psychologist may participate in the treatment program by working with the child himself, his parents, teachers, and the principal. Frequently in cases of this kind, the child and the parents will be treated by personnel of the mental health clinic. Most of the school psychologist's contacts from here on, therefore, will be with the teachers and the principal. The school psychologist should be able to translate the recommendations given at the conclusion of the case conference into specifically psycho-educational terms, and most important, he should be able to help the teachers and the principal to carry out the recommendations so far as they are involved. This is a big order, to be sure, and the problems involved in implementing recommendations by working with teachers and principals will not be taken up at this time because this topic has already been discussed in another chapter. It should suffice to say now that in carrying through his consultant's role to completion, the school psychologist should end where he started—in the classroom, with recommendations to be applied to the alleviation of the problem.

Working with Other Agencies

Outside of the school system, the most frequent professional contacts of the school psychologist are with parents of school children and the community mental health clinics or child guidance centers. In addition to these contacts, however, the school psychologist can be involved in working with other agencies in the community. The range of his contacts is in part determined by his own interests and competencies, the time available for such contacts, and the recognized needs and desires of the various agencies in the community for consultation by a school psychologist. We will briefly consider some possible working relationships that could exist with the following agencies: the juvenile court, private practitioners (physicians, clinical psychologists, psychiatrists, ministers, and tutors), parent-teacher organizations, vocational rehabilitation agencies, various child-serving agencies, civic groups concerned with child welfare, and the university.

The school psychologist occasionally has contacts with the juvenile court, especially in regard to adolescents or pre-adolescents who have gotten into trouble with the police. His services in this consulting role may include psychological testing and interviewing, recommendations to the authorities regarding disposition of cases, and participation in treatment programs for the offenders.

The writer's experiences in working with juvenile offenders through the probate court will be published shortly in an article concerned with group counseling of socially maladjusted teen-agers. In this particular study, the service for which the writer was consulted was mainly group counseling. In other instances all that was required was a psychological test report or an evaluation interview. Working in collaboration with a social worker assigned to the court was still another example of a combined effort or "team-approach" in which the school psychologist can function effectively as a desirable new member of the team.

The school psychologist also occasionally refers students to "private practitioners" for more specialized examinations or treatment programs. Whatever the nature of the problem, be it severe emotional disturbances, organic dysfunctions, religious doubts, or reading disabilities, there are at least two parts to the school psychologist's job in referral: supplying the person who accepts the referral with all relevant information pertaining to the problem, and writing a follow-up report (with the cooperation of the professional personnel involved) when the examination has been completed or the treatment terminated. The school psychologist's initial referral report is certainly helpful to the private practitioner when he formulates his diagnosis or decides upon a treatment procedure. The follow-up report is desirable for two reasons: it provides the school psychologist with important feed-back information regarding the efficiency of his referrals, and it is very useful for a more complete understanding of the individual should he be seen by the school psychologist at a later date.

Several times a year the school psychologist is usually called upon to speak to parent-teacher organizations. The school psychologist can use this opportunity to great advantage if he can avoid the pitfalls inherent in his consultant's role to this organization. Theoretically, the school psychologist should not have to adhere to the "party-line" of an established school system; nor should he necessarily be the innovator of educational schemes supported by some parents. In practice, however, the school psychologist is usually paid (at least partially) by the school system, and therefore, owes some *professional* allegiance to his employers; he also probably lives in the community, and therefore, has experiences with parents as people he knows *socially*. In this kind of situation it is all too easy for the school psychologist to become the tool or pawn for one group. These maneuvers may exist at an unconscious level of awareness, by either or both parties, but they are manifestly evident to any one who studies the interaction process through a series of meetings. It has become apparent that one way in which the school psychologist can start to redefine and elaborate on *his role* in *his particular community* is to use P.T.A. meetings for airing grievances of existing conditions and discussing any ideas about his functions with regard to the grievances and proposals. Only when the school psychologist *is* relatively free to propose that certain conditions be altered and when both parents and educators *perceive* him in this light can be begin to make a significant contribution. It is suggested that the opportunity of using P.T.A. meetings be taken advantage of by the school psychologist for this purpose.

Let me hasten to add that the writer is not advocating that the school psychologist be "a law unto himself." This was one of the most frequently voiced criticisms of the school psychologist by superintendents [26]; but the fact that this criticism and another, "poor human relations," accounted for a large portion of the superintendent's criticisms should justify the action required to help alleviate this state of affairs. Perhaps the threat that the school psychologist poses to educational and parental authorities, as well as the tendency to perceive himself as "the solver of problems," cannot be resolved fully at this time, but one way to begin is to make people more aware of these problems through direct interaction in P.T.A. meetings.

The vocational rehabilitation agency is one of the social-welfare agencies that sometimes contracts for the school psychologist's services. In this setting the school psychologist functions mainly as diagnostician. He may be called upon to administer specific aptitude tests, general intelligence tests, tests of vocational interest, and "personality" tests. He is also likely to be asked to make recommendations regarding further schooling, change of vocational programs, advisability of institutionalization, and so forth. Since most of the referrals will be adults, the school psychologist should be as competent in testing adults as well as children.

There are many child-serving agencies at both local and national levels to which the school psychologist can refer certain children for specific help. For example, the parents of a child with gross physical handicaps could be referred to the local chapter of the National Society for Crippled Children for possible physical therapy for their child; the parents of a child with speech and reading problems could be helped to seek remedial training for him at a speech and reading clinic (sometimes connected with a university); or parents of a child with visual or auditory impairments could find some valuable assistance in guidance and training techniques from correspondence courses offered by the National Society for the Prevention of Blindness or The Volta Bureau. In general, the school psychologist should make it a point to familiarize himself with every possible source of assistance so that he can make the necessary referrals when the occasion arises.

Finally, there are certain civic groups interested in child welfare that call upon the school psychologist to give talks, conduct discussion groups, or just offer professional advice about projects. His associations with these groups

[26] N. Cutts, ed., *School Psychologists at Mid-Century* (Washington, D.C.: American Psychological Association, 1955).

can be very beneficial both for him and the groups in terms of disseminating practical information about mental health, promoting a "grass roots" community attitude of appreciation and respect for the services of the school psychologist, and fostering a cooperative working arrangement that will feed back information about the implementation and application of mental health practices.

The "community agency" that will be considered last is the university which trains school psychologists. In one respect, it is the most important contact that the school psychologist could develop since it deals with the education of students of school psychology in their practicum program. The role that the school psychologist can develop in this setting is of being a field supervisor for the practicum training of graduate students in school psychology programs at the university. It would be quite feasible to use the experience of the practicing school psychologist in a supervisory capacity in conjunction with the practicum courses offered at the graduate level. Thus, the school psychologist could supervise such training as the psycho-educational-vocational testing of students in both elementary and high school, writing reports and recommendations to teachers, interviewing parents of children being studied, counseling students with less serious difficulties, and working with teachers in a professionally consulting way. In this way it is hoped that a mutually benefiting relationship can be established between the practicing school psychologist and the training institution.

This chapter is concerned with a logical extension of the school psychologist's consultant's role within the larger social environment of students. It emphasizes the school psychologist's role as a member of an "educational team," broadly defined. It deals primarily with his working relationships with parents, and secondarily with interested professional and civic groups in the community.

Several practical suggestions about developing a working relationship with parents are given. Typical problems encountered by the school psychologist in this area are discussed. Specific mention is made also of the use of bibliotherapy (including a listing of materials useful in counseling) and the use of group techniques—discussion groups, group counseling, and group therapy.

The school psychologist's contacts with the community mental health clinic are discussed with a view toward understanding what contributions he can make and the information he can gain from this association. His role as liaison between the "educational team" and the "clinical team" is explained.

The school psychologist's contacts with the juvenile court, private practitioners, parent-teacher organizations, vocational rehabilitation agencies, various child-serving agencies, civic groups concerned with child welfare, and the university, are briefly explored.

Selected Supplementary Readings

American Journal of Psychiatry, entire issue, community mental health services, **122** (March, 1966).

Brockbank, Reed, and D. Westby-Gibson, *Mental Heatlh in a Changing Community.* New York: Grune & Stratton, Inc., 1966.

Canada's Mental Health, entire issue, **14** (August, 1966).

Condell, J. F., and R. D. Ebinger, "Providing School Psychological Services Through a Community Mental Health Center," *Community Mental Health Journal,* **2** (January, 1966), 82–85.

Frank, G. H., "The Role of the Family in the Development of Psychopathology," *Psychological Bulletin,* **64** (September, 1965), 191–205.

Ginnott, H. G., *Between Parent and Child.* New York: The Macmillan Company, 1966.

Gordon, H. L., *Casework Services for Children.* Boston: Houghton Mifflin Company, 1956.

Grams, A. and J. G. Chantiny, "Parent Education," *Journal of Cooperative Extension,* **4** (Summer, 1966), 75–84.

Gulo, E. V., "Attitudes of Rural School Children Toward Their Parents," *Journal of Educational Research,* **59** (August, 1966), 450–453.

Halpern, H. M., *A Parent's Guide to Child Psychotherapy,* New York: A. S. Barnes & Co., Inc., 1963.

Handel, G., "Psychological Study of Whole Families," *Psychological Bulletin,* **63** (January, 1965), 19–41.

Hermann, Robert O., "Families in Bankruptcy—A Survey of Recent Studies," *Journal of Marriage and Family,* **8** (August, 1966), 37–43.

Ilg, Frances and Louise Bates Ames, *Parents Ask.* New York: Dell Publishing Co., 1965.

Kastenbaum, Robert, ed., *Psychotherapy for the Whole Family.* New York: Springer Publishing Co. Inc., 1966.

Kelly, J. G., "Ecological Constraints on Mental Health Services," *American Psychologist,* **21** (June, 1966), 535–539.

Liberman, Robert, "Personal Influence on the Use of Mental Health Resources," *Human Organization,* **24** (Fall, 1965), 231–235.

Hunter, Starley, *et al., Families in an Urban Enclave.* Columbia, Mo.: University of Missouri Press, 1965.

Roberts, L. M., S. L. Halleck, and M. B. Loeb, *Community Psychiatry.* Madison: University of Wisconsin Press, 1966.

Sarason, S. B., M. Levine, I. I. Goldenberg, D. L. Cherlin and E. M.

Bennett, *Psychology in Community Settings: Clinical. Educational Vocational, Social Aspects.* New York: John Wiley & Sons, Inc., 1967.

Shertzer, B., and S. C. Stone, *Fundamentals of Guidance.* Boston: Houghton Mifflin Company, 1966.

Sources of
Inexpensive Reading Materials

The American Institute of Family Relations
5287 Sunset Boulevard
Los Angeles 27, California

American Social Health Association
1790 Broadway
New York 19, New York

American Association for Gifted Children
15 West Sixteenth Street
New York 11, New York

American Foundation for the Blind
15 West Sixteenth Street
New York 11, New York

American Hearing Society
817 Fourteenth Street N.W.
Washington, D.C.

Child Study Association
9 E. 89th Street
New York 28, New York

Council for Exceptional Children
1201 Sixteenth Street N.W.
Washington 6, D.C.

National Association for Mental Health
10 Columbus Circle
New York, New York

National Association for Retarded Children
420 Lexington Avenue
New York, N.Y.

National Council on Family Relations
1219 University Avenue S.E.
Minneapolis, Minn. 55414

National Society for Crippled Children and Adults
2023 West Ogden Avenue
Chicago 12, Illinois

National Society for the Prevention of Blindness
16 E 40th St.
New York, New York

Public Affairs Pamphlets
381 Park Avenue, South
New York, New York

U.S. Children's Bureau
Government Printing Office
Washington, D.C.

Metropolitan Life Insurance Company
One Madison Avenue
New York 10, New York

Volta Bureau
1537 Thirty-fifth Street
Washington 7, D.C.

DONALD C. SMITH

6

Counseling and Psychotherapy in the School Setting

Professional interest in psychotherapy has been contagious over the past two or three decades. It has spread rapidly from psychiatry, clinical psychology, and social work to the ministry, industry and education. As a result people of varied professional background currently spend a large portion of their time in some type of therapeutic activity in efforts to bring about constructive changes in attitudes and an improved adjustment on the part of their clientele. This interest in psychotherapy has been accompanied by controversy. Arguments among the mental health professions center around such issues as standards for training, certification or licensure, and the necessity for medical supervision. Psychotherapy itself is not always the real basis for controversy. Arguments often appear to represent a displacement of other concerns, such as the struggle of particular disciplines for greater prestige and status or economic competition among disciplines engaged in private practice. Nevertheless, the ego-involvements are powerful and the right to practice psychotherapy has become the focal point for disputes.

The school psychologist has not been immune to this contagion of interest and controversy over psychotherapy. A lively discussion and a sharp division of opinion in regard to the role of the school psychologist in psychotherapy was evident in the Thayer Conference report.[1] Extreme viewpoints tend to prevail. Some school psychologists appear to set no limits on their role as psychotherapists and are willing to apply wholesale the specialized psychotherapeutic techniques developed in the clinic or hospital. Others are just as strongly convinced that psychotherapy is an entirely inappropriate function in the school setting. It is much easier for us to temporize on the issue. After all, in the years to come, the roles of professions engaged in mental health activities are likely to remain in a stage of dynamic change and redefinition. As new techniques are discovered and refined, new specializations are likely to occur within and among the various disciplines. At the present time, it is impossible to find sound research evidence concerning desirable role differentials among pupil-personnel workers, or the relative effectiveness of different therapeutic services in the schools. Therefore, a rigid concept of the role of the school psychologist in psychotherapy would seem inadvisable. On the other hand, the psychologist working in the schools needs some tentative guidelines to follow. He should understand the realistic limitations of the schools as a setting for psychotherapy and he should become familiar with the experiences of other school psychologists in this area. To these ends this chapter applies itself. Its purposes are two-fold: 1) To develop a perspective in regard to psychotherapy in the school setting, and 2) To survey research and written accounts of experiences relevant to the therapeutic activities of the psychologist in the schools. The section which follows deals with a definition of terms. Factors in the school situation that help to shape the role of the school psychologist as a psychotherapist are then discussed. Next, a frame of reference is offered for therapeutic planning in the school setting. Finally, four broad approaches to therapy in the schools are discussed separately: psychotherapy with individuals, group psychotherapy, educational therapy, and environmental therapy. Throughout an effort has been made to emphasize those methods which seem most realistic in the school setting and to include accounts of actual experiences and research in the schools.

At least two problems are involved in an enterprise of this kind, one semantic and the other, a matter of personal bias. The literature on psychotherapy is rife with semantic difficulties. It is not uncommon to find different names used for processes or techniques which are very similar at the functional level. In a brief summary of this kind of information, we run the risk of misinterpretation because of unfortunate choices of words or the failure to

---

[1] Norma E. Cutts, ed., *School Psychologists at Mid-Century* (Washington, D. C.: American Psychological Association, 1955), p. 48.

elaborate on nuances of meaning. Furthermore, it is difficult to prevent personal biases and oversights from intruding in the selection and interpretation of reference material. The chapter, at best, serves as a point for departure for a more searching exploration of the subject. A special effort has been made to document statements and the original sources of ideas as a guide for further reading. Additional books and articles on the topic are found in the Selected Supplementary Readings at the end of the chapter.

Explanation of Terms

No single definition of psychotherapy will satisfy all psychologists. Almost as many definitions exist as there are writers on the subject. Wolberg,[2] for example, cites thirteen separate descriptions of psychotherapy. One definition arrived at by a committee of clinical psychologists is representative. It reads as follows:

> Psychotherapy is a process involving interpersonal relationships between a therapist and one or more . . . clients by which the former employs psychological methods based on systematic knowledge of the human personality in attempting to improve the mental health of the latter.[3]

A number of attempts have been made to distinguish between counseling and psychotherapy.[4] However, precise dichotomies concerning basic principles, assumptions, goals, clientele, and techniques are difficult to make. Some counselors indicate that they limit their concern to particular role-areas such as marital, vocational, or educational adjustment without reference to the total personality structure of the client. In contrast, other counselors focus on the internal conflicts that invade all the social roles of the client and describe this process as *personal* or *therapeutic counseling*.[5] No attempt will be made here to differentiate this latter type of counseling from psychotherapy.

[2] Lewis R. Wolberg, *The Technique of Psychotherapy* (New York: Grune and Stratton, Inc., 1954), p. 5.

[3] "Recommended Graduate Training Program in Clinical Psychology," American Psychological Association, Committee on Training in Clinical Psychology, *American Psychologist* (1947), 539–558.

[4] For example, see: William G. Perry, "The Findings of the Commission in Counseling and Guidance on the Relationship of Psychotherapy to Counseling," *Annals of the New York Academy of Science*, 63 (1955), 396–407. Also: American Psychological Association, Division of Counseling Psychology, Committee on Definition, "Counseling Psychology as a Specialty," *American Psychologist*, 11 (1956), 282–285; Institute for Human Adjustment, *Training of Psychological Counselors* (Ann Arbor: University of Michigan Press, 1950); O. H. Mohrer, "Anxiety Theory as a Basis for Distinguishing Between Counseling and Psychotherapy," in *Concepts and Programs of Counseling*, ed. R. E. Berdie, Minnesota Studies in Student Personnel Work, No. 1 (Minneapolis: University of Minnesota Press, 1951), pp. 7–26.

[5] E. H. Porter, *An Introduction to Therapeutic Counseling* (Boston: Houghton Mifflin Company, 1950).

In the remainder of this chapter the terms counseling and psychotherapy are used interchangeably. From a practical standpoint it might be preferable for the school psychologist to use the terms *counseling* or *re-education* to describe his activities in the school setting. The word *therapy* is associated with psychiatry and the clinical psychologist in private practice. Counseling therefore may be a more tactful word-choice and leave the school psychologist less open to misunderstanding and criticism by other professions. Similarly, the term *client* may be preferable to *patient* in reference to clientele.

Individual psychotherapy, group psychotherapy, and *play therapy* are the principal methods of therapeutic help through direct personal relationship. Group therapy offers the client the opportunity to interact with other people as well as with the therapist. Play activity serves as a means of communication in play therapy rather than exclusive reliance on language. *Educational therapy* refers to therapeutic efforts centered around a specific tutorial or remedial educational problem. Other activities having a therapeutic effect on the child are included under the heading of *environmental therapy*. For example, the therapeutic objectives of the school psychologist are also made effective through recommendations to others on the school staff, through referral of the child and family for medical, psychiatric or social work services, through arranging appropriate school placements or change of teacher, grade or school program, and through the propagation of mental health concepts within the school system.

Factors Determining the School Psychologist's Role in Psychotherapy

A number of factors help to determine for a school psychologist his particular role in psychotherapy: 1) his personal qualifications; 2) the availability of community mental health services; 3) the length of time the psychological service program has been in operation; 4) the availability of other counselors on the school staff; 5) the availability of time and physical facilities and; 6) the school's philosophy concerning its responsibility for the severely disturbed child and intensive psychotherapy.

PERSONAL QUALIFICATIONS OF THE SCHOOL PSYCHOLOGIST

There are two schools of thought concerning the training of psychologists in psychotherapy. Some advocate an extended training period including a Ph.D. in psychology and post-doctoral supervision. They stress the need for a fundamental background in academic psychology. Others minimize the importance of specific course requirements or academic degrees and place the emphasis upon the personality of the therapist and "experiential" rather than "cognitive learning." [6] They point out that competent therapists are found with varied professional backgrounds. A broad liberal education is recommended in literature, philosophy, sociology, and psychology. According to Rogers, the student in the course of his training should acquire: "A broad knowledge of the human being in the cultural setting, the ability to achieve empathy with others, the possession of a philosophy of life, and a knowledge of the dynamics of personality." [7]

Psychotherapy remains more of an art than a science and learning its art is a continuing process which extends far beyond the formal University training period. College courses usually provide the student with an orientation to a particular system of psychotherapy. Gradually, he should acquaint himself with the theory and technique of other approaches to therapy. Supervised experience should be sought beyond that provided in college practicums. Training opportunities are often available through apprenticeships in clinic or hospital settings or through professional institutes. Experience should be gained with both children and adolescents exhibiting a variety of symptomatic disorders. The psychologist should seek to develop a conscious awareness of the process of psychotherapy and a cautious regard for his own limitations. Without detracting from the value of a broad liberal education, the fact remains that the therapist-school psychologist would often be "whistling in the dark" without a firm foundation in academic psychology. The school psychologist must be selective in his choice of clients. In the initial phases of his contact with youngsters he needs to decide whether or not he can help them personally or whether a referral should be made. Psychodiagnosis and therapeutic planning require a thorough knowledge of personality development and personality theory, psychodynamics and psychopathology. The beginning school psychologist would do well to attend to the training standards set by professional groups of clinical and counseling psychologists before becoming too venturesome in offering counseling services. It is all too easy to underrate the skills involved and to be insensitive to one's personal limitations.

AVAILABILITY OF COMMUNITY TREATMENT FACILITIES

School psychologists frequently complain of the lack of community treatment facilities, particularly in some of the sparsely populated and economically poor areas of the United States. In smaller cities and in many rural

[6] Carl R. Rogers, "Training Individuals to Engage in the Therapeutic Process," in *Psychology and Mental Health,* ed. C. R. Strother (Washington, D. C.: American Psychological Association, 1956); John Kinzer, "The Education Counselor," *Journal of Counseling Psychology* (Summer, 1961); C. H. Patterson, *Counseling and Psychotherapy: Theory and Practice* (New York: Harper & Row, Publishers, 1959).

[7] Carl R. Rogers, *Client-Centered Therapy* (Boston: Houghton Mifflin Company, 1951), p. 429.

areas of the country, the school psychologist may represent the only professional person with training in psychotherapy. Near the larger Eastern cities
where there is a tradition of progressive psychiatry and social work, treatment
services are more readily available in the community. Yet, even when community clinics are more plentiful, school personnel often express dissatisfaction with the scope of their services. A survey was recently conducted in a
suburban area near New York City, in which seven community centers were
established for the out-patient treatment of emotionally disturbed children.
School counselors and psychologists without exception stated that community
agencies were inadequate to handle the number of problem children in the
schools. Every school administrator maintained that it was virtually impossible
to have a child admitted immediately for long-term therapy in community
agencies.[8]

For this reason, a considerable number of school psychologists participating in the Thayer Conference perceived intensive psychotherapy as a
legitimate function, even with the severely disturbed child.[9] They argued that
when treatment facilities were nominally available in the community, the
quality of the service rendered often was no better than that which could
be provided by the school psychologist. Furthermore, they felt that the offering of psychotherapy by the school psychologist could be an effective way to
demonstrate the need for more adequate community services. Another group
maintained that the school psychologist could make a more fundamental
contribution to the school and community by helping to promote community
mental health clinics than by trying to provide intensive psychotherapy to
a necessarily small number of cases.[10] A school psychologist engaged in psychotherapy with severely disturbed children would find it difficult to demonstrate the effectiveness of such services even in a two or three-year period. If
therapy were unsuccessful, certainly a likelihood with some cases, it *could*
prove a deterrent to the growth of community facilities. Promoting the interest of service organizations and parent groups is a much more constructive way
of stimulating the development of new services.

Other plans for increasing treatment resources for the schools deserve
mention. Decentralization of community facilities would be helpful in
sparsely populated areas. The mobile clinic, which sends a team of clinicians
into the school itself, would solve the problems of parents who otherwise need
to travel long distances outside the immediate community for service. Child
guidance clinics are sponsored by the schools in many of the larger city systems. Local school boards in New Jersey are authorized by law to establish

[8] *Survey of Exceptional Children, Part II: Emotionally Disturbed Children*
(First Supervisory District, Northern Westchester County and the School District of
Pleasantville, New York, 1955).
[9] Norma E. Cutts, *op. cit.*, p. 48.
[10] *Ibid.*, p. 49.

Children's Bureaus, which provide, among other things, individual and group counseling services for children and their parents.[11] Such arrangements also offer the opportunity for the properly trained school psychologist to engage more intensively in psychotherapy as part of a clinical team.

OTHER FACTORS

Whether or not the school psychologist engages in psychotherapy is contingent upon other realities in the local school-community situation. The climate of opinion regarding psychotherapy fluctuates from community to community and state to state. In certain areas, the standards of state departments of education obstruct the school psychologist's role in psychotherapy. The withdrawal of supporting state funds often can incite school administrators to suppressive action. The stage of development of psychological services is another important factor. In the beginning stages of program development the school psychologist is usually absorbed with organizational matters and pressing duties such as the screening of children for special class placement. Because of the broad range of service activities, time simply will not permit him to carry a caseload in psychotherapy. In contrast, larger, well-established programs with a smoothly-functioning team of school psychologists, often subdivide responsibilities, and certain members of the staff specialize in psychotherapy. The school psychologist's role also varies according to his position in the school system. If he is a member of a clinical team, there is a trend toward a more active role in therapy.[12] In other situations, a staff of school counselors or school social workers may handle the bulk of referrals for counseling. The availability of space and physical facilities is another crucial determining factor. Psychotherapy is simply out of the question, for example, by the itinerant school psychologist temporarily assigned to the cafeteria or a screened-off portion of the principal's office as a work-space.

The Responsibility of the Schools for
the Severely Disturbed Child

THE ISSUE OF INTENSIVE PSYCHOTHERAPY

Historically, the public schools have never assumed responsibility for illness. Severely disturbed children are "sick" children and in most cases they require long-term psychiatric treatment. The school is not a medical

---

[11] A summary of the Beadleston Act providing for special educational services for emotionally and socially maladjusted pupils in New Jersey may be found in *The Exchange*, 5 (1960), Division of Curriculum and Instruction, Office of Special Education, New Jersey State Department of Education, Trenton 25, New Jersey.

[12] M. Harrower and L. Goldstein, "New School Team in Mental Health," *Child Study*, 36 (1959), 19–24.

treatment agency and should not undertake the responsibility for prolonged, intensive therapy. It *is* responsible for the education of all handicapped children, including the emotionally and socially handicapped, as well as children with sensory, physical or mental handicaps. However, it cannot be all things to all children. Emotional and social disturbances originate in the home, the peer group or the neighborhood. Schools do not have the opportunity or the specialized staff for working with the whole family unit or with the larger social environment of the child. The child guidance clinic, the family casework agency, the psychiatric hospital and other community treatment agencies can best provide intensive diagnostic and treatment services for the severely disturbed child. So follows the argument of authorities concerning the responsibilities of the schools for severely disturbed children and intensive psychotherapy.[13-16]

School psychologists were sharply divided on these issues at the time of the Thayer Conference. Recently, a committee of Division 16 of the American Psychological Association arrived at a consensus in regard to the functions of the school psychologist.[17] This committee saw *short-term* individual and group counseling of children and parents as a legitimate function, by implication ruling out the desirability of *long-term* psychotherapy. Thumbnail sketches of eleven school psychologists employed in a variety of school settings were presented. Significantly, only one school psychologist reported he was involved in intensive therapy. In this situation, two psychologists were assigned to a school system having a student population of 3,500. They indicated the need for a third school psychologist on the staff so that the number of therapy contacts with children could be increased. Obviously, services that require a psychologist to pupil ratio of 3/3,500 are time-consuming and expensive.

The role of the school psychologist in psychotherapy is circumscribed by the fact that he is employed by the school. This limits the opportunity for personal involvement in prolonged and intensive therapy with the severely disturbed child. However, the question is not so much that of relieving the school psychologist of all responsibility as of redefining his therapeutic functions within the context of the schools. A broad range of therapeutic activities remains compatible with public school responsibilities:

[13] William M. Cruickshank and G. Orville Johnson, eds., *Education of Exceptional Children and Youth* (Englewood Cliffs, N. J.: Prentice-Hall, Inc., 1958), p. 48.

[14] *The Emotionally Handicapped Child and the School: A Research Program in the Prevention of Personality and Behavior Disorders in Children* (Sacramento: California State Department of Education, 1959), p. 34.

[15] Frances A. Mullen, "Therapy and the School Psychologist," *Exceptional Children,* 21 (1955), 257–259, 271.

[16] W. C. Kvaraceus, W. E. Ulrich, *et al., Delinquent Behavior: Principles and Practices* (Washington, D. C.: National Education Association, 1959), p. 26.

[17] *The Psychologist on the School Staff,* Report of the Committee on Reconsideration of the Functions of the School Psychologist (Division 16, American Psychological Association, 1957).

1. Identification and diagnosis of the emotionally and socially disturbed child. The school psychologist plays an important role in the selective placement of children in various types of educational programs.

2. Referral to community clinics for intensive treatment of those children who are not responding to educational help. Short-term counseling is not precluded, but for the most part, children with entrenched emotional difficulties which involve the family and the larger social environment are referred to community treatment centers. The school psychologist plays an important role in mobilizing parents toward seeking help for themselves and their children and acting as a liaison person between the community agency and the school.

3. Promotion of educational programs and services leading to the prevention of emotional and social disturbance in children.

4. Leadership in the development of special educational programs for the emotionally and socially maladjusted and participation in programs of mental health education for teachers and school staff.

A Frame of Reference for Therapeutic Planning in the School Setting

From the previous discussion it follows that the school psychologist must be able to assess the severity of disturbance in children and decide whether they should be referred to a community treatment center or whether they might benefit from therapeutic services in the school. The basis for therapeutic planning is differential diagnosis, one of the foremost practical problems of the school psychologist. The traditional approach to child study by the school psychologist is through the administration and interpretation of tests. A comprehensive battery of tests includes measures of intelligence and educational achievement, special clinical tests to evaluate perceptual and cognitive processes, and projective techniques to explore personality structure and ego defense mechanisms. Additional background for the case study is obtained through the perusal of cumulative school records, classroom observations and interviews with the child, parent, and teacher. Factors that are important in differential diagnosis and therapeutic planning are: the age of the child, the duration of the problem, the nature and severity of symptoms, past referrals for professional help and the outcome, the current home situation and the quality of parent-child relationships, and the school, family, developmental and medical history. An elaborate case-study however does not always insure security of diagnosis. Diagnosis frequently is a continuing process. Treatment plans sometimes must be initiated on a trial basis with the school psychologist constantly alert to positive or negative signs of progress. When short-term counseling appears feasible from the beginning contacts with the child, the school psychologist may decide to avoid lengthy probing and testing sessions which can hamper the counseling relationship. Certainly there is room for improvement of our diagnostic and predictive tools in school psychology and the process must remain flexible and oriented to the needs of particular children.[18]

The school psychologist needs to relate diagnostic information about the child to realistic therapeutic services in and outside the school setting. Recently, the St. Louis County Health Department published some guidelines for determining what types of disturbed children are rightfully the responsibility of the schools.[19] An attempt has been made to elaborate this material as a frame of reference for therapeutic planning. Four classifications of symptoms and environmental conditions are made, based on the following questions: How severe is the emotional or social disturbance of the child and what is the potential threat of the child's symptoms to himself, to the school or to the community? How intact or disrupted is the child's relationship with the school? How intact or disrupted are parent-child relationships? For each of the four groups, therapeutic services are identified which are likely to be the most realistic and effective. A classification system such as this is difficult to use in relation to individuals. Yet, it may serve as a useful guide for determining the feasibility of various therapeutic endeavors in the school setting.

Group I

Symptoms and Environmental Conditions. This group included children whose problems are essentially those of normal growth and development (normal mood swings and transitory disturbances associated with environmental, physiological, and developmental changes). The symptoms constitute no serious threat to the child, school or community. School attendance is not disrupted and the family is together as a unit.

Therapeutic Services. These children usually are able to remain in the regular classroom and special placement is not required. Short-term individual counseling could be provided, although the school guidance counselor would most likely provide this service rather than the school psychologist. Modifications of the curriculum (*human-relations classes,* etc.) could be helpful to members of this group in finding solutions to their personal problems.

Group II (approximately 25–30 percent of the school population)

Symptoms and Environmental Conditions. This group includes children with more persistent emotional, social, or learning problems. The symptoms are not so clearly associated with current situational factors as with children in Group I. Disturbances however are of a moderate degree, the family is together as a unit and school attendance is not disrupted.

---

[18] For further discussion of diagnosis and psychotherapy see: George A. Muench, "The Application of Diagnostic Psychological Methods to Counseling and Psychotherapy," in *Recent Advances in Diagnostic Psychological Testing,* ed. Molly Harrower (Springfield, Ill.: Charles C. Thomas, Publisher, 1950); also, Nathan Ackerman and P. B. Neubauer, "Failures in the Psychotherapy of Children," in *Failures in Psychiatric Treatment,* ed. Paul H. Hoch (New York: Grune and Stratton, Inc., 1958).

[19] For a summary of this material see: Cruickshank and Johnson, *Education of Exceptional Children and Youth,* pp. 48–50.

Therapeutic Services. School-centered services are appropriate for many of these children. Referral can be made to the school psychologist for individual diagnostic study. Short-term individual or group counseling with the child and/or his parents may be advisable. The school psychologist can assist in the coordination of special services and support the efforts of the teacher in the regular classroom. Changes in teacher, class, program, or school, referral to a remedial specialist, or assignment to extra-curricular play groups are among the possible therapeutic activities.

Group III (approximately 4–5 percent of the school population)

Symptoms and Environmental Conditions. This group includes children with recurring symptoms which constitute a threat to self, school, or the community. Symptoms may be internalized as with the psychoneurotic disorders (phobias, anxiety-states, compulsiveness, excessive withdrawal, fearfulness, or compliance) or externalized as in the behavior disorders (extreme aggression, rebellion, and erratic impulse control). Services provided for Group II children have been tried unsuccessfully. Although the family is together as a unit, the child frequently disrupts classroom activities and his school attendance is irregular.

Therapeutic Services. Usually these children should be referred for treatment to the community child guidance clinic or to a clinical team operating within the schools. There is often an emotional entanglement of parent and child, which requires coordinated treatment by a clinical team. Counseling by a lone therapist may be feasible with some adolescents, but ordinarily individuals in this group require prolonged and intensive psychotherapy. The teaching staff and the school psychologist continue to play a supportive role, maintaining close contact with the community clinic and implementing their recommendations in the schools. The school psychologist may need to help mobilize ambivalent parents to seek help at the clinic. If the child drastically reduces the teacher's effectiveness, or if he fails to benefit from regular classroom attendance, placement in a special class or a day-school program for disturbed children may be advisable.

Group IV (approximately 1 percent of the school population)

Symptoms and Environmental Conditions. Children in this group display fixed and entrenched social and emotional problems. In terms of standard nosology, one might include the severe psychoneurotic disorders, borderline or frank psychoses, and the sociopath or "unsocialized delinquent." In many cases there is a broken home or the parents are irresponsible insofar as cooperating with the outpatient clinic. School attendance is irregular, classroom behavior uncontrollable, and the child's symptoms a distinct threat to himself or others.

Therapeutic Services. With these children, the school psychologist can seldom do more than support the efforts of community-based treatment centers. Ordinarily, the child cannot be contained in the special-class or day-school program and the family situation precludes the possibility of outpatient clinic services. Placement usually is made in a residential treatment center or psychiatric hospital, where there is a total rehabilitation program, including educational services. The child may be carried on the school rolls until released from the treatment center and the school psychologist may need to assume the responsibility for helping the child make transitions to and from the institution.

APPROACHES TO THERAPY IN THE SCHOOL SETTING

In the previous section we discussed guidelines for the selection of clientele for therapy in the school setting. Two other questions now suggest themselves: What broad approaches to therapy are appropriate in the schools? What should be the ultimate objectives of therapy in the schools? In order to develop a rationale for school practice, we will differentiate three broad approaches to therapy: *supportive, re-educational,* and *reconstructive.* Table 1 summarizes the general objectives of these three approaches to therapy. Specific techniques of therapy are cited within each general category.[20]

TABLE 1

Classification of Approaches to Therapy

Approaches to Therapy	Ultimate Objectives
SUPPORTIVE APPROACHES Individual psychotherapy: directive techniques such as information-giving, persuasion, suggestion, reassurance, and coercion. Activity Group therapy (permissive play groups). Environmental therapy. Educational therapy (tutorial therapy and bibliotherapy).	Ventilation and catharsis. Reducing the secondary effects of symptoms by dealing with them directly. Helping the client to gain better impulse control through sublimation, suppression, or repression, the strengthening of ego defenses, and the externalization of interests.
RE-EDUCATIVE APPROACHES *Client-centered* and *relationship* approaches to individual psychotherapy, play therapy, and interview group therapy.	Insight into the more conscious conflicts with the objective of modifying the client's goals, self-concept, or symptoms and helping deal with current adjustment problems.
RECONSTRUCTIVE APPROACHES Psychoanalytically-oriented individual psychotherapy, play therapy and group therapy. Freudian or neo-Freudian analysis.	Insight into unconscious as well as conscious conflicts with the ultimate goal of removing the inner conflicts underlying the symptoms and a major structural change in personality.

[20] Table 1 is a modification of a table entitled "Varieties of Psychotherapy," found in Wolberg, *The Techniques of Psychotherapy,* p. 8.

"Directive" counseling, activity group therapy, environmental and educational therapy are classified as supportive approaches. Supportive therapies do not seek to produce major changes in personality structure, nor is it generally anticipated that the client will, by virtue of therapy, learn to cope with all subsequent difficulties. The emphasis is upon the release of emotional tension, the buttressing of existing defenses, and the relief of symptoms. The goal is that of inducing behavioral change rather than the internal reorganization of personality. Individual psychotherapy, play therapy, and interview group therapy based on *client-centered* or *relationship* techniques are classified as re-educative approaches. Re-educative therapies aim at developing insight into conscious or near-conscious conflicts and the constructive modification of ego mechanisms, goals, self-concepts, and symptomatic behavior. The objective, as with supportive therapies, is social recovery and adjustment to current life or situational difficulties. In contrast, the reconstructive therapies seek to effect a major structural change in personality. Such changes presumably are the consequence of insights deriving from the understanding of deeply rooted conflicts.[21]

Reconstructive therapy is usually an intensive and time-consuming process and these approaches are considered inappropriate in the school setting. Textbooks on counseling and psychotherapy geared for school counselors and psychologists deal exclusively with supportive and re-educational therapy.[22] These approaches are most useful with the normal or moderately disturbed individual of relatively sound personality structure. They are more readily learned and less dangerous in the hands of the relatively inexperienced psychologist. The section which follows surveys various applications of supportive and re-educative therapy in the school setting.

PSYCHOTHERAPY WITH THE INDIVIDUAL

Orientations to Psychotherapy. The *Client-Centered* orientation is often cited as a useful approach in student counseling. It is predicated on the philosophy that the client is responsible for his own destiny and has the right to choose solutions to his own problems. Each individual is regarded as possessing a drive toward growth and self-realization and the goal of therapy is to release this potential. The role of the therapist is to act as a catalytic agent, encouraging free expression of feeling. The therapist accepts the feelings of the client in a tolerant, nonjudgmental way and reflects, clarifies or rephrases

21 Frieda Fromm-Reichmann, *Principles of Intensive Psychotherapy* (Chicago: University of Chicago Press, 1950).
22 Stanley S. Marzolf, *Psychological Diagnosis and Counseling in the Schools* (New York: Holt, Rinehart & Winston, Inc., 1956); Francis P. Robinson, *Principles and Procedures of Student Counseling* (New York: Harper & Row, Publishers, 1950).

expressions to help him gain insight. Diagnosis and evaluation are thought to hamper the process of therapy by introducing an authoritative element.[23]

Relationship therapy was the name originally given by John Levy [24] to the process in which the client-therapist relationship is the focus of treatment. The therapist is particularly alert to the immediate feelings of the client toward the therapist, using the relationship as a vehicle for developing insight into general interpersonal modes of behavior. As with client-centered therapy, the emphasis is upon the present rather than the past. The important thing is how the client *uses* the therapist, what the client is doing or feeling *now*.[25] The theory of Alfred Adler and Otto Rank, as well as the concepts of Rogers, Allen, and Taft are fundamental in relationship therapy.[26] The technique has most often been used in child psychotherapy.

In *directive counseling,* the counselor is usually more active in offering interpretations, using diagnostic information, giving advice, persuading, reassuring, or asking direct questions. However, the arbitrary distinctions often made between nondirective and directive psychotherapy are useful mainly for the purposes of exposition. In the extreme, the directive counselor assumes an authoritative role, evaluates the client's problems, and defines specific courses of action. Not many counselors would adhere to this type of relationship with all clients referred to them for help. Instead they are likely to utilize a variety of techniques, even though their theoretical bases may differ.[27] It is probably unreasonable to suppose that one, and only one, form

[23] For a more detailed account of the philosophy and technique of client-centered therapy see Carl R. Rogers, *Client-Centered Therapy* (Boston: Houghton Mifflin Company, 1951); Carl R. Rogers, *Counseling and Psychotherapy, Newer Concepts in Practice* (Boston: Houghton Mifflin Company, 1942); C. H. Patterson, *Counseling and Psychotherapy: Theory and Practice;* W. U. Snyder, *Casebook of Non-Directive Therapy* (Boston: Houghton Mifflin Company, 1947).

[24] John Levy, "Relationship Therapy," *American Journal of Orthopsychiatry,* 8 (1938), 64–69.

[25] Frederick H. Allen, *Psychotherapy with Children* (New York: W. W. Norton & Company, Inc., 1942).

[26] An understanding of the rationale and technique of relationship therapy can be gained by reading: Frederick H. Allen, *Psychotherapy with Children;* Jessie Taft, *The Dynamics of Therapy in a Controlled Relationship* (New York: The Macmillan Company, 1933); Clark Moustakas, *Psychotherapy with Children, The Living Relationship* (New York: Harper & Row, Publishers, 1959); Otto Rank, *Truth and Reality and Will Therapy* (New York: Alfred A. Knopf, Inc., 1936); Heinz Ansbacher and Rowena Ansbacher, *The Individual Psychology of Alfred Adler* (New York: Basic Books, Inc., Publishers, 1956); Fay B. Karpf, *The Psychology and Psychotherapy of Otto Rank* (New York: Philosophical Library, 1953).

[27] Among the sources on directive counseling are: Frederick Thore, *Principles of Psychological Counseling* (Brandon, Vermont: Journal of Clinical Psychology, 1950); Ruth Strang, *Education Guidance: Its Principles and Practices* (New York: The Macmillan Company, 1947); Fred McKinney, *Counseling for Personal Adjustment in Schools and Colleges* (Boston: Houghton Mifflin Company, 1958); E. G. Williamson, *Counseling Adolescents* (New York: McGraw-Hill Book Company, 1950). For a more complete description of the eclectic counselor see: Marzolf, *Psychological Diagnosis and Counseling in the Schools.*

of counseling will suffice for all children and adolescents. Even the mildly disturbed student exhibits a variety of symptoms, based on disparate psychodynamic and etiological factors. Whatever systematic orientation he learns while in training, the counselor, as he gains experience, should learn to alter his techniques in order to adjust flexibly to the varying needs of different clients.

Common Elements of Psychotherapy. It is impossible here to discuss in detail the conscious, theoretical moves in psychotherapy. Excellent expositions of the technique of psychotherapy are found in a number of places.[28] Radical divergencies in the techniques of the various systems of psychotherapy are more apparent than real. Many distinctions vanish as soon as semantic difficulties are resolved.[29] Numerous efforts have been made to identify common elements in psychotherapy.[30] The major similarities are summarized below:

1. A common starting point for psychotherapy is an individual seeking help. Individuals vary in terms of their personal dissatisfaction and motivation for change, but their decision to seek help is the first and perhaps most significant step in psychotherapy.

2. All psychotherapy is organized around a unique relationship involving communication between a therapist and a client. A common element in this relationship is confidentiality and respect for the client's integrity. The therapist's personality—his warmth, sensitivity, understanding, spontaneity, empathy, etc.—may be a crucial element in all types of successful psychotherapy.

3. Some structure is involved in all psychotherapy. At the very least, appointments are regularly scheduled and there is a time limit on interviews.

4. Catharsis or release of feeling and emotional tension represents another important general feature of psychotherapy. Free expression of feelings occurs to some extent in all therapy experiences.

5. All psychotherapy is purposeful and goal-oriented. Conscious awareness of technique may be an important element of successful psycho-

---

[28] See, for example: Wolberg, *The Technique of Psychotherapy* and Percival Symonds, *Dynamics of Psychotherapy, Vol. III: Techniques* (New York: Grune and Stratton, Inc., 1958).

[29] Wolberg, *The Technique of Psychotherapy*, p. 9.

[30] See Emory L. Cohen, "Psychotherapy and Play Techniques with the Exceptional Child and Youth," in *Psychology of Exceptional Children and Youth*, ed. William Cruickshank (Englewood Cliffs, N. J.: Prentice-Hall, Inc., 1963), pp. 520–575; R. I. Watson, *The Clinical Method in Psychology* (New York: Harper & Row, Publishers, 1951), pp. 543–576; G. Watson, "Areas of Agreement in Psychotherapy," *American Journal of Orthopsychiatry*, 10 (1940), 698–709; Fred E. Fiedler, "Factor Analyses of Psychoanalytic, Non-Directive and Adlerian Therapeutic Relationships," *Journal of Consulting Psychology*, 15 (1951), 32–38.

therapy. Successful therapy may also depend to some extent upon the confidence of the therapist in his particular technique or method.

6. Successful therapy is characterized by the achievement of some degree of *insight*. Insight refers broadly to an increase in self-awareness or understanding of relationships with others. The degree of insight achieved is relevant to the goals of therapy. It may be a modest achievement, such as a realization of self-limitations, or it may be wider in scope, such as a major change in perception of self or others.

7. In successful therapy, insight is followed by actual alteration in modes of interpersonal response or other behavioral changes.

Play Therapy. Interview techniques are usually employed in counseling with adolescents. Children of elementary school age however are less facile in putting their feelings and emotions into words. For them play activity constitutes a more natural and spontaneous medium of communication. Much of the current therapy with children in the hospital or clinic is built around play. In the school setting, the objectives of play therapy are catharsis, sublimation, or the achievement of modest insights into problems of interpersonal relations. Play serves as a medium for the relationship between the child and therapist rather than a source of material for interpretation of unconscious motivation as in analytically oriented play therapy. The therapeutic relationship is the basic dynamic in play therapy. It is characterized by a warm, friendly, accepting, nonjudgmental attitude on the part of the therapist and a willingness to permit the child to experience his feelings fully and intensely. The major channels of communication are the play activity itself and the facial expressions, body movements and other nonverbal expressions of the child and therapist. The essential element of play therapy is the opportunity it provides the child to "play out" his difficulties and to resolve conflicts and unacceptable feelings at the symbolic level. Techniques of play therapy are often based on the principles of client-centered or relationship therapy.[31]

Although successful play therapy can take place in an office setting by careful selection of materials to suit the individual child, a well-equipped play room permits freer expression in diverse problem areas. A room ideally suited for play therapy is privately located and sound-proofed so that loud noises do not disrupt other school activities. Floors and walls should be wash-

---

[31] For a more detailed description of the principles and techniques of play therapy see: Virginia Axline, *Play Therapy* (Boston: Houghton Mifflin Company, 1947); Virginia Axline, "Play Therapy Procedures and Results," *American Journal of Orthopsychiatry*, 25 (1955), 618–625; Lydia Jackson and Kathleen M. Todd, *Child Treatment and the Therapy of Play* (London: Methuen & Co., Ltd., 1946); Clark E. Moustakas, *Children in Play Therapy* (New York: McGraw-Hill Book Company, 1953); Adolf G. Woltmann, "Concepts of Play Therapy Techniques," *American Journal of Orthopsychiatry*, 25 (1955), 771–783; Frederick Allen, *Psychotherapy with Children;* Emory L. Cohen, "Psychotherapy and Play Techniques with the Exceptional Child and Youth"; Helen Witmer, *Psychiatric Interviews with Children* (New York: Commonwealth Fund, 1946).

able, window-glass protected, and other facilities arranged to permit complete freedom of play. A large variety of equipment and play material is desirable, including the following:

> *Playroom facilities:* Running water, sand-box, stage for psychodrama, low tables with matching chairs, a workbench, child's rocker, building blocks, large cardboard shipping cartons, slides and other gymnastic equipment. *Materials for aggressive and regressive play:* Punching bags, rubber knives, toy guns, soldiers and military equipment, planes, vehicles, balloons, dartboard, come-back toys, rocking horse, nursing bottles, rattles, diaper doll, baby carriage, bathinette, etc. *Dollplay equipment:* A doll house fully equipped with furniture, rubber and plastic dolls representing various family members, puppets and masks, doll clothes, doctor and nurses' sets, household items such as brooms, mops, rags, telephone, utensils, dishes, etc. *Expressive media:* Combination easel and blackboard with chalk, brushes and water colors, fingerpaints, paper, crayons, scissors, modelling clay, etc. *Commercial games:* Games that involve competitive play.[32]

A search for personal accounts of play therapy in the school setting is unproductive. Murphy[33] suggests the usefulness of play therapy as a counseling technique at the elementary school level. Reports of experience and research, however, issue primarily from the clinic setting.

GROUP COUNSELING

Group counseling, according to Hadley[34] includes "any group brought together for the purpose of improving interpersonal or intrapersonal relations." In the public schools, however, a distinction is ordinarily made between the methods of *group guidance or instruction* and *group therapy*.[35] The two methods differ in terms of the kinds of on-going activity, the composition of the groups, and the quality of the relationship existing between the leader and the group participants.

Group guidance or instruction: Group guidance activities in the schools are designed for the normal functioning student who is facing certain developmental or life adjustment problems. Courses such as *psychology of personal adjustment* or *human relations* are sometimes added to the senior or junior-high school curriculum, or techniques such as role-playing incorporated in regular class discussions of adjustment problems. Bower[36] describes the

---

[32] For other suggestions see: D. Lebo, "A Formula for Selecting Toys for Non-Directive Play Therapy," *Journal of Genetic Psychology*, 92 (1958), 23–34.

[33] George W. Murphy, "Play as a Counselor's Tool," *The School Counselor*, 8 (1960), 53–58.

[34] John M. Hadley, *Clinical and Counseling Psychology* (New York: Alfred A. Knopf, Inc., 1958), p. 227.

[35] Stanley Marzolf, *Psychological Diagnosis and Counseling in the Schools*, p. 366.

[36] Eli M. Bower, "The Emotionally Handicapped Child and the School: Present Research Plans and Directions," *Exceptional Children*, 26 (1960), 232–242. Also see: *The Emotionally Handicapped Child and the School*, pp. 56–59.

rationale of classes in *human relations*, that were established as part of an experimental program in California. The classes are included in the regular curriculum for all children and the focus is on prevention of maladjustment. One of the primary objectives of the class is to demonstrate to students that their personal problems are not unique but shared by others. Formal didactic methods are employed to promote discussion of human relationship problems. In recent years many educators have experimented with the use of role-playing techniques to dramatize social relationship problems in the regular classroom.[37] *Sociodrama*, the type of role-playing recommended for instructional purposes, attempts to avoid personal confessions of problems by students; it is oriented toward the spontaneous dramatization of *group* ideas and experiences. *Psychodrama*, the spontaneous dramatization of *personal* ideas or experiences, is designed as a technique of psychotherapy. Role-playing however inevitably becomes a fusion of personal and group elements and psychodrama and sociodrama never can be truly separated.[38] There is always a danger of turning the classroom into a group therapy situation. It is unfair to students to urge them to uncover intense personal problems in the classroom when confidentiality cannot be assured.

The school psychologist often serves in an advisory capacity to the teacher or the school counselor who are directly involved in classroom instruction. Through individual and group conferences, he can help to clarify the basic differences between an instructional and therapeutic group. The similarities and differences of psychotherapy and education are discussed in detail elsewhere.[39] A school psychologist should be able to interpret these distinctions clearly to others on the school staff.

[37] Robert B. Haas, *Psychodrama and Sociodrama in American Education* (New York: Beacon Press, 1949); Howard Lane and Mary Beauchamp, *Human Relations in Teaching: The Dynamics of Helping Children Grow* (Englewood Cliffs, N. J.: Prentice-Hall, Inc., 1955), pp. 274–279; Helen H. Jennings, "Sociodrama as Educative Process," in *Fostering Mental Health in our Schools*, 1950 Yearbook, Association for Supervision and Curriculum Development (Washington, D. C.: National Educational Association); Charles E. Hendry, Ronald Lippitt, and Alvin Zander, "Reality Practice as Educational Method: Some Principles and Applications," *Psychodrama Monographs*, No. 9 (1944); George Shaftel and Fannie R. Shaftel, *Role Playing the Problem Story* (New York: National Conference of Christians and Jews, 1952); Hildred Nichols, "Role-Playing in Primary Grades," *Group Psychotherapy*, 7 (1954), 238–241.

[38] Abraham E. Knepler, "Role Playing in Education: Some Problems in Its Use," *Group Psychotherapy*, 12 (1959), 32–41.

[39] P. M. Symonds, "Education and Psychotherapy," *Journal of Educational Psychology*, 40 (1949), 1–32; Adele Franklin, "Teachers, Not Therapists," *Nervous Child*, 10 (1954), 368–377; H. S. Maas, "Applying Group Therapy to Classroom Practice," *Mental Hygiene*, 35 (1951), 250–259; Samuel Baron, "Limitations of the Teacher in Guidance," *American Journal of Psychotherapy*, 6 (1952), 104–111; K. F. Herrold, "Applications of Group Principles to Education," *International Journal of Group Psychotherapy*, 4 (1954), 177–182; Dorothy W. Baruch, "Some Principles of Group Psychotherapy Adaptable to Classroom Procedures," in *Professional School Psychology*, ed. M. G. and G. B. Gottsegan (New York: Grune and Stratton, Inc., 1960); Arthur J. Brodbeck, "Education as Psychotherapy," *Confluence*, 6 (1957), 26–39.

Group therapy. Many school psychologists are enthusiastic about the possibilities of group therapy in the school setting. Among the special values which have been associated with group therapy are:

1. The time-saving advantage. Group therapy could provide help for a greater number of students with less investment of time on the part of the professional school staff.

2. The effectiveness of group therapy with moderately disturbed individuals. Group therapy addresses itself most effectively to individuals with mild neuroses and behavior disorders. As pointed out before, the schools are most concerned with therapeutic services for the less seriously disturbed youngster.

3. The advantages of a miniature and controlled social gathering as a place for learning how to solve problems in social relations. Group therapy presents the opportunity for discovery of new and more satisfying ways of dealing with people. The individual can experiment with new modes of interaction in a permissive and accepting atmosphere before using them in a larger and personally more threatening social situation.

4. The catalytic effect of the group itself. The cumulative effect of others endeavoring to change their behavior patterns has been observed to produce a strong incentive toward change in individual members of the group. Furthermore, students with personal problems are prone to believe they are unique. When they find their problems are shared by others their own age, this may stimulate a change in self-concept.[40]

Despite its apparent advantages, there are several issues and special problems involved in the use of group therapy in the schools. For the most part, group therapy has been conducted with patients in a hospital or medical agency setting. Patients frequently are committed for treatment on the application of their family or physicians. The patient in the medical clinic or hospital often surrenders the right to withdraw from treatment. According to democratic tradition however, a student is autonomous and retains the right to make his own decisions. The student-client in therapy always may voluntarily withdraw from the therapeutic relationship. Also, in clinical practice group therapy is often employed as an adjunctive aid with clients already assigned for individual psychotherapy. If group therapy is found to be ineffective without personal counseling, this voids the possibility of extended service

[40] For further elaboration see: J. W. Klapman, *Group Psychotherapy: Theory and Practice* (2nd. Ed.) (New York: Grune and Stratton, Inc., 1959); Samuel R. Slavson, *An Introduction to Group Therapy* (New York: International Universities Press, 1954); Nicholas Hobbs, "Group Centered Psychotherapy," in *Client-Centered Therapy*, ed. Carl R. Rogers (Boston: Houghton Mifflin Company, 1951); Samuel R. Slavson, "Criteria for Selection and Rejection of Patients for Various Types of Group Psychotherapy," *International Journal of Group Psychotherapy*, 5 (1955), 3–30; Marzolf, *Psychological Diagnosis and Counseling in the Schools*, pp. 366–381; John Hadley, *Clinical and Counseling Psychology*, pp. 227–248.

and savings in time. There are few reports on group therapy in the school setting and certainly no research evidence that it is more effective than other therapeutic activities in the schools. Requisite training for the group therapist is another delicate issue. Experienced practitioners tend to be more cognizant of the need for careful training and supervision in group therapy. Other complications have been pointed out by Marzolf.[41] If all members of the group attend the same school, social contact will certainly occur in the school and community. Group members may be tempted to reveal what is said during group sessions and such gossip could pervade the school and reach the parents in an exaggerated and distorted form. These possibilities suggest the need for obtaining the permission of parents before a student joins the group. Group members should also be carefully screened and a pact should be formed not to discuss elsewhere what is said during therapy hours.

Group therapy with adolescents in the school setting. Interview and discussion techniques are usually employed in group therapy with adolescents. Systematic approaches to group therapy which seem to hold the most promise for the schools are the *activity-interview* and *interview* techniques of Slavson [42] and the *client-centered* techniques described by Hobbs.[43] Slavson views group therapy as a sheltered workshop for the development of social skills. The group leader is an active participant in group conversations and activities, at times carefully shielding group members from responsibilities for which they are not yet ready or helping to ward off impulses which they are unable to handle. The focus of therapy is upon the interpretation of therapist-client relationships. In client-centered group therapy the therapist is less active. The basic assumption is that the client has within himself the ability to solve his own problems and a growth impulse that makes mature behavior more satisfying than immature behavior. The therapist is accepting and permissive, limiting his remarks to the clarification of feelings or ideas expressed and the giving of support. Diagnosis and the interpretation of client-therapist relationships are avoided. Theoretically, group members themselves learn to act as therapists, gradually becoming more accepting, permissive and empathetic toward others in the group.

Bower [44] describes two types of group counseling efforts in the schools. With one group, called a *social living class,* educational methods are used to impart information about personal problems. About twelve adolescents meet one hour per day with a school psychologist or school social worker in the school's counseling office. A problem check list is administered anonymously

[41] Marzolf, *Psychological Diagnosis and Counseling in the Schools,* p. 367.
[42] Slavson, *An Introduction to Group Therapy.*
[43] Hobbs, "Group Centered Psychotherapy."
[44] Eli M. Bower, "The Emotionally Handicapped Child and the School." Also, *The Emotionally Handicapped Child and the School: A Research Program in the Prevention of Personality and Behavior Disorders in Children,* pp. 51–53.

to obtain a consensus of the main concerns of the students. Role-playing, movies, and a variety of other techniques are used to stimulate discussion. Conversations center around boy-girl relations, teacher-pupil and parent-child relations, peer acceptance, jobs, future plans, how to study, etc. Students are carefully selected for group membership on the basis of a review of school history and psychological study. A balance is sought so that the group is not overloaded with hostile and nonanxious, or withdrawn and nonverbal adolescents. A second group counseling plan is similar in design to the social-living class, except that more severely disturbed adolescents are included in the group, often those who are only one short step away from suspension or exclusion from school. Approximately eight students meet for two or three hours per week with a group leader. Some individuals are also seen for individual psychotherapy. The therapist is permissive and encourages "feeling" relationships among members of the group in an effort to help them gain insight into patterns of interpersonal relationships. The goals are more ambitious than mere catharsis and some efforts are made to interpret transference.

Other research studies on school-centered group therapy programs are extremely scarce. Schneer, et al.[45] report on an activity-interview group therapy program for delinquent boys attending a special day school for the emotionally disturbed. Group therapy appeared to facilitate their return to the regular schools. Caplan[46] reported on the effectiveness of group counseling with socially-maladjusted boys at the junior-high school level. Techniques were patterned after the "multiple counseling" approach described by Driver.[47] Aided by a consultant, regular school staff counselors met for ten weekly sessions with groups of boys who had been in long-term conflict with school authority and regulations. A control group of noncounseled maladjusted students was identified. Following counseling, the counseled group made significant gains over the noncounseled group in terms of better self-concept and improvement in school grades. More research of this nature is needed in order to establish a place for group therapy methods in the special service program of the schools.

Group therapy with children and parents. Slavson[48] originally developed the rationale for activity group therapy, a form of group counseling for children six to eleven years of age. Adaptations of this method in the schools

[45] H. Schneer, H. Gottesfeld, and A. Sales, "Group Therapy as an Aid with Delinquent Pubescents in a Special School," *Psychiatric Quarterly Supplement,* 31 (1957), pp. 246–260.

[46] S. W. Caplan, "The Effect of Group Counseling on Junior High School Boys' Concept of Themselves," *Journal of Counseling Psychology,* 4 (1957), 124–128.

[47] H. I. Driver, *Multiple Counseling: A Small Group Counseling Method for Personal Growth* (Madison, Wisconsin: Monoma Publications, 1954).

[48] Slavson, *op. cit.* Also: S. R. Slavson, *The Practice of Group Therapy* (New York: International Universities Press, 1947); S. R. Slavson, *Analytic Group Therapy with Children, Adolescents, and Adults* (New York: Columbia University Press, 1950).

are described by Schiffer [49] and Bower.[50] Adlerblum [51] reported on a group therapy program, patterned after nondirective methods, with kindergarten and first-grade pupils in the New York City Schools. Group therapy also was found to be effective with parents of behavior problem children in the schools.[52] A more detailed description of activity-group therapy and group counseling with parents is given by Bower in Chapter 15.

The relationship of the school psychologist to group therapy ventures in the schools varies according to the many conditions previously discussed. In some cases he assumes the role of group leader, but more frequently he serves as a special consultant to school counselors, teachers, social workers, or others on the school staff who act as therapists. The school psychologist can be of particular assistance in the selection of children for group counseling.

EDUCATIONAL THERAPY

Retardation in reading and other school subjects often is associated with emotional disturbance and family relationship problems.[53] Strictly pedagogical methods are likely to be ineffective in the tutoring situation, unless the teacher has intuitively met the emotional needs of the child. There is a noticeable trend towards perceiving remedial education as therapy.[54] According to this orientation, the remedial teacher remains focussed on the basic goals of instruction, but an attempt is made through the teacher-pupil relationship to relieve anxiety and negative feelings about learning. Seldom are direct remedial education services offered by the school psychologist. More often he serves as an advisor to the remedial or helping teacher concerning diagnostic and counseling problems.

The application of group therapy techniques in remedial tutoring is

[49] Mortimer Schiffer, "The Therapeutic Group in the Public Elementary School," in *Orthopsychiatry and the Schools,* ed. Morris Krugman (New York: American Orthopsychiatric Association, 1958), pp. 70–81.

[50] Bower, *op. cit.* Also, Bower, *The Emotionally Handicapped Child and the School,* pp. 55–57.

[51] See: Evelyn D. Adlerblum, "Mental Health Begins School," *Mental Hygiene,* 31 (1947), 541–555; Evelyn D. Adlerblum, "Beginning School Guidance Early," *Mental Hygiene,* 34 (1950), 600–610.

[52] A. D. Buchmueller, Frances F. Porter, and Margaret C. L. Gildea, "A Group Therapy Project with Parents of Behavior Problem Children in Public Schools," *Nervous Child,* 10 (1954), 415–424.

[53] See: Beulah H. Ephron, *Emotional Difficulties in Reading* (New York: Julian Press, 1953); Ben O. Rubenstein, M. L. Falick, Morton Levitt, and Rudolph Ekstein, "Learning Problems: II. Learning Impotence, A Suggested Diagnostic Category," *American Journal of Orthopsychiatry,* 29 (1959), 315–323.

[54] Grace Arthur, *Tutoring as Therapy* (New York: Commonwealth Fund, 1946); Hertha Riese, "Educational Therapy, A New Approach in Child Guidance," *Psychiatry,* 13 (1950), 465–488; Frances S. Sobel, "Remedial Teaching as Therapy," *American Journal of Psychotherapy,* 2 (1948), 615–623; Charlotte E. Grave, "The Psychotherapeutic Value of a Remedial Education Program," *Nervous Child,* 3 (1944), 343–349.

illustrated in studies by Heimbach [55] and Roman.[56] Heimbach employed role playing to advantage as an adjunctive aid in remedial reading with adolescents. Roman compared the effectiveness of three types of group activities with adolescents manifesting marked reading retardation in conjunction with severe emotional disturbance and antisocial behavior. Traditional didactic methods were employed in the *Remedial Reading Group*. The *Interview Therapy Group* was handled along formal therapeutic lines with no instruction in reading. In the *Tutorial Therapy Group*, the leader dealt primarily with the emotional concomitants of learning. Subjects were told they had been referred to the group because of reading difficulties. However, the therapist-tutor indicated that he was not going to teach them to read; instead, he would try to help them discover what could have interfered with their ability to read. Group members were encouraged to express freely their feelings about reading, early school experiences, teachers and the therapist-tutor. They could use the meetings as they wished, to talk, or to read materials which were easily accessible in the therapy room. When the activity chosen was reading, remedial help was offered. The reading process itself was used to stimulate group discussions about feelings associated with reading problems. Of the three approaches, this last method resulted in the greatest positive change in psycho-social adjustment and the greatest improvement in reading skills. It appeared to have the advantages of 1) anchoring therapy in concrete problems; 2) contributing to ego-strength through improvement of reading skill; 3) serving as a medium for promoting group discussions and releasing emotional tension.

A similar type of therapeutic reading group is described by Bower.[57] Students selected for the group by the homeroom teacher and school psychologist were of normal "measured" intelligence but exhibited a high degree of emotional disturbance as well as marked reading disabilities. A remedial reading specialist spent one to two hours a day with eight children in group and individual instruction. Attention was given to the reduction of anxiety about reading, on the premise that restoration of self-confidence and feelings of self-worth would be of positive value in changing the child's attitude about learning and authority figures in the school.

Bibliotherapy is a method of aiding the adjustment of individuals through the assigned reading of articles, pamphlets or books. It could represent an integral part of the regular language arts curriculum, a technique employed in classes on psychology or human relations, or an adjunctive aid for individual, group or educational therapy. The technique may be of

[55] Sylvia R. Heimbach, "Role Playing as an Aid in Improving Reading Ability and Empathy," *Group Psychotherapy*, 12 (1959), 42–51.

[56] Melvin Roman, *Reaching Delinquents Through Reading* (Springfield, Ill.: Charles C. Thomas, Publisher, 1957).

[57] Bower, *op. cit.* Also see: *The Emotionally Handicapped Child and the School*, pp. 53–55.

value to those not yet motivated to seek help for themselves in personal counseling or as a means of correcting misconceptions about psychotherapy, psychiatry, or psychology. Inspirational slogans or self-help formulas contained in various books may serve to bolster repressions and strengthen ego defenses. A large number of references on bibliotherapy are cited by Russell and Shrodes.[58]

ENVIRONMENTAL THERAPY

By natural inclination, school psychologists are eager to help youngsters achieve a better personal and social adjustment. Too often, however, according to Frances Mullen [59] they see this help as coming directly from themselves through direct psychotherapy and fail to sense the larger opportunity for service through support of the therapeutic activities of others on the school staff.

Dissenting voices [60] in regard to the role of the school psychologist as a psychotherapist are being heard more frequently in the middle sixties. Reger [61] questions on the basis of the research evidence whether psychotherapy is an effective means for the school psychologist to help children and whether psychotherapy is an appropriate way for the school psychologist to work toward the achievement of educational goals. Leavitt [62] reviewed twenty-two reports regarding the effectiveness of psychotherapy with children and pessimistically summarizes: "the inescapable conclusion is that available evaluation studies do not furnish a reasonable basis for the hypothesis that psychotherapy facilitates recovery from emotional illness in children." Thus, one might argue that the school psychologist can contribute more to the amelioration of school maladjustment through indirect or environmental therapy than through his personal counseling efforts.

Watson [63] has differentiated two types of environmental therapy: *environmental modification,* and *environmental manipulation.* In the school setting, modification refers to changes or alterations in the school environment as it exists in the present. Manipulation refers to the removal of the child to a different school or social environment. The objectives of environmental therapy in the schools are to modify or manipulate those conditions that contribute or are causally related to the child's maladjustment.

One approach to modification of the school environment is through

---

[58] D. H. Russell and Caroline Shrodes, "Contributions of Research in Bibliotherapy to the Language Arts Program, I," *School Review,* 58 (1959), 335–342.

[59] Frances Mullen, "Therapy and the School Psychologist."

[60] F. F. Lighthall, "School Psychology: An Alien Guild," *Elementary School Journal,* 63 (April 1963), 361–364.

[61] Roger Reger, *School Psychology* (Springfield, Ill.: Charles C Thomas, 1965), pp. 54–63.

[62] E. E. Leavitt, "Psychotherapy with Children: A Further Evaluation," *Behavioral Research and Theory,* 1 (1963), 45–51.

[63] Robert I. Watson, *The Clinical Method in Psychology,* p. 736.

improvement of the mental hygiene of teachers. The primary and central relationship in the school is the relationship between the child and his teacher. When a teacher displays deep prejudice or projects his own personality problems upon the child, he may actually contribute to pupil maladjustment. The APA Committee on Reconsideration of the Role of the School Psychologist suggests that the school psychologist may be of service to the schools as a consultant to teachers concerning personal mental health problems.[64] Bower, in another chapter of this book, maintains that the schools might better employ a mental-hygiene specialist from outside the school system for this type of consultation. Whatever discipline engages in this activity, it requires the utmost in tact and respect for the integrity of teachers. Holding a staff rather than a line position in the administrative hierarchy of the schools may result in a more intimate and spontaneous relationship with teachers. Teachers understandably might be reluctant to discuss personal limitations with someone to whom they are administratively responsible. In any case, the consultant would do well to let the teacher assume the initiative in asking for help. Nass[65] describes a group counseling plan for beginning teachers. Suggestions as to modes of operation in this area are also found in the psychiatric and social work literature on consultation techniques in mental hygiene.

Another approach to environmental modification is through an improvement of the mental hygiene climate of the classroom. Again, the school psychologist is of service primarily as a consultant and advisor. Conferences with individual teachers, wherein the school psychologist interprets psychological findings on children referred to him for diagnostic study, may promote better understanding of mental hygiene concepts. Spivak[66] studied the effects of telling teachers about the kinds of problems checked by their pupils on the SRA Inventory. There was no change in the number of problems of the control group upon retesting, whereas an experimental group whose teachers had been informed about their problems showed a significant reduction in problems. This study, although simple in method and design, suggests interesting possibilities for research on the effectiveness of more sophisticated teacher-consultation techniques. There are also vast possibilities for developing inservice education programs for teachers focussing on the better understanding of problem behavior and the application of mental hygiene principles in the classroom. Among the techniques used for inservice training are: informal group discussions of case material, individual case studies by teachers, role-playing of problem situations in the classroom, laboratory explora-

[64] The Psychologist on the School Staff.
[65] Martin L. Nass, "Characteristics of a Psychotherapeutically Oriented Group for Beginning Teachers," Mental Hygiene, 43 (1959), 562–567.
[66] M. L. Spivak, "It Pays to Tell the Teacher," Personnel Guidance Journal, 35 (1957), 452–453.

tions of mental health teaching aids, and teacher observation of children in psychotherapy.[67]

What about the possibilities of "milieu treatment" methods in the school setting? Fritz Redl [68] has stimulated interest in the use of the *life space* or *marginal* interview by the classroom teacher. The concept refers to the use of interview techniques for handling problems of disturbed children at the time and place where they occur, in order to offer "ego support on the spot" and to exploit a child's life experience for some specific therapeutic gain. Clarke [69] reports on an interesting attempt by school psychologists to adapt milieu-treatment techniques in the Seattle Public Schools. On the premise that consistency of teacher attitudes is a paramount factor in effective classroom guidance, school psychologists studied a group of disturbed junior-high school students and prescribed a hygienic attitude for each child. This *attitude prescription* was later transmitted to classroom teachers through case conference discussion of the children. The therapeutic attitudes were designed to meet the unconscious needs of the particular child. They were categorized in a special handbook for teachers [70] as *unsolicited friendliness, active friendliness, passive friendliness, firm kindness,* and *matter-of-factness.* The handbook describes the overt behavior and personality dynamics of children demanding each type of attitude and suggests specific ways teachers can manifest the attitude. A preliminary research study revealed no improvement or actual psychological change in an experimental group of children following one year in this modified school environment. Significant changes were noted in teacher's evaluations of children, however, after one year's experience with the *attitude consistency* technique. The author felt the method resulted in an improvement of teacher-child relationships and an increase in the effectiveness of teachers as guidance persons. One might question whether it is possible to arrive at valid prescriptions of attitudes for individual children, and if so, whether teachers without more intensive training in therapy could apply them hygienically. Such prescriptions are geared for closed institutions, with a specially-trained, closely-knit staff, dedicated to a

[67] See A. B. Abramowitz and Elaine Burnham, "Exploring Potentials for Mental Health in the Classroom," *Mental Hygiene,* 43 (1959), 253–259; Paul Frisch, "A Program in School Psychology," *Mental Hygiene,* 40 (1956), 258–266; E. F. Hammer, "Functions of a Psychological Consultant at a High School," *High Points,* 36 (1954), 5–15; H. A. Delp, "Training Teachers and other School Personnel to Understand Clinical Problems," *Elementary School Journal,* 51 (1951), 491–498.

[68] Fritz Redl, "The Life-Space Interview, I. Strategy and Techniques of the Life-Space Interview," *American Journal of Orthopsychiatry,* 29 (1959), 1–18. A workshop at the American Orthopsychiatric Association convention in March, 1961, was devoted to the training of regular classroom teachers in this technique.

[69] David L. Clarke, "Attitude Consistency: A New Approach to Classroom Guidance," *College of Education Record,* The Univeristy of Washington, 24 (1958), 25–29.

[70] *Attitude Consistency Handbook* (Department of Guidance Services, Seattle Public Schools, Administrative and Service Center, Seattle 9, Washington, 1958).

total treatment program.[71] Interestingly enough, though, the program apparently did produce an increase in teacher sensitivity to the emotional needs of children and to their own interpersonal effect upon pupils. Possibly this can be attributed as much to the initial case-study conferences with teachers as to indoctrination in the *attitude consistency* technique. Regardless, such programs of inservice education deserve more attention and more thorough evaluation since this is an area of service which could be particularly rewarding to the schools.

Lawrence J. Peter [72] in his 1965 book, *Prescriptive Teaching* expands these attitude consistency techniques and presents a rationale for the coordination of psychological test findings and case history data regarding children referred for therapy or other special services. He states that, "prescriptive teaching is based upon an interdisciplinary approach which accomplishes therapeutic aims by educational means."

The school psychologist also plays an instrumental role in the *manipulation* of the school environment to meet the needs of individual children. Through his diagnostic study, he can often recommend changes of school environment that will have a therapeutic effect on the child. For example, when there are unreasonable pressures on a child in a particular school, transfer to another school setting may be helpful. The same is true of changes in class, changes in teacher, changes in grade or program of studies, or placement of the child in a special class or public day school for the emotionally and socially maladjusted. The school psychologist also cooperates with various casework agencies in the community in efforts to improve the home environment of the child. Despite the brief space devoted here to these services, they are among the most important therapeutic activities of the school psychologist.

Selected Supplementary Readings

Axline, Virginia, *DIBS, In Seach of Self: Personality Development in Play Therapy*. Boston: Houghton Mifflin Company, 1964.

Baruch, Dorothy W., "Some Principles of Group Psychotherapy Adaptable to Classroom Procedures," in *Professional School Psychology*, ed. M. G. Gottsegen and G. B. Gottsegen. New York: Grune & Stratton, Inc., 1960.

Belenky, Robert, "Behavior Change Innovation by the School Psychologist," *Journal of School Psychology*, 3 (Autumn, 1965), 6–12.

Bellak, L., and Leonard Small, *Emergency Psychotherapy and Brief Psychotherapy*. New York: Grune & Stratton, Inc., 1965.

[71] Concerning milieu treatment methods see: William C. Menninger, "Psychiatric Hospital Therapy Designed to meet Unconscious Needs," *American Journal of Psychiatry*, 93 (1936), 347–360; Bruno Bettelheim and Emmy Sylvester, "Milieu Therapy: Indications and Illustrations," *Psychoanalytic Review*, 36 (1959), 54–68.

[72] Lawrence J. Peter, *Prescriptive Teaching* (New York: McGraw-Hill Book Company, 1965).

Blocher, D. H., *Developmental Counseling*. New York: The Ronald Press Company, 1966.

Brammer, Lawrence M., and Everett L. Shostrom, *Therapeutic Psychology: Fundamentals of Counseling and Psychotherapy*. Englewood Cliffs, N.J.: Prentice-Hall, Inc., 1960.

Breger, L., and J. L. McGaugh, "Learning Theory and Behavior Therapy: A Reply to Rachman and Eysenck," *Psychological Bulletin*, 65 (March, 1966), 170–174.

Colm, Hanna, *The Existential Approach to Psychotherapy with Children and Adults*. New York: Grune & Stratton, Inc., 1966.

Dreikurs, Rudolf, "Coping With the Child's Problems in the Classroom," in *Professional School Psychology*, Vol. 1, ed. M. G. Gottsegen and G. B. Gottsegen. New York: Grune & Stratton, Inc., 1960, pp. 162–176.

Farnham, Marynia F., "Psychotherapy With the Adolescent," in *Professional School Psychology*, Vol. I, ed. M. G. Gottsegen and G. B. Gottsegen. New York: Grune & Stratton, Inc., 1960, pp. 126–136.

Ferster, C. B., and J. Simons, "Behavior Therapy with Children," *The Psychological Record*, 16 (January, 1966), 65–72.

Ford, Donald H., and Hugh B. Urban, *Systems of Psychotherapy: A Comparative Study*. New York: John Wiley & Sons, Inc., 1963.

Freeman, Ruth, *Counseling: A Bibliography*. New York: Scarecrow Press, 1964.

Ginott, Haim G., *Group Psychotherapy With Children*. New York: McGraw-Hill Book Company, 1961.

Golden, Boris Schulman, "An In-Service Psychotherapy Training Program for School Psychologists," *Professional School Psychology*, Vol. II, ed. M. G. Gottsegen and G. B. Gottsegen. New York: Grune & Stratton, Inc., 1963, pp. 249–265.

Gray, Susan W., "Working With and Through Others: I. Counseling and Consultation," in *The Psychologist in the Schools*. New York: Holt, Rinehart, & Winston, Inc., 1963, pp. 107–140.

Harms, Ernest, and Paul Schrieber, eds., *Handbook of Counseling Techniques*. New York: The Macmillan Company, 1964.

Haworth, Mary R., ed., *Child Psychotherapy: Practice and Theory*. Basic Books, Inc., Publishers, 1964.

Jersild, Arthur T., and Eve A. Lazar, *The Meaning of Psychotherapy in the Teacher's Life and Work*. New York: Teachers College, Columbia University, 1962.

Kell, B. L., and William J. Mueller, *Impact and Change: A Study of Counseling Relationships*. New York: Appleton-Century-Crofts, 1966.

Kelleher, Daniel, and Carlah Lytle, "The Relationships Between Therapists and Educators," *Psychology in the Schools*, I, No. 3 (July, 1964), 288–296.

Kemp, C. Gratton, *Perspectives on the Group Process: A Foundation for Counseling in Groups*. Boston: Houghton Mifflin Company, 1964.

Klapman, J. W., *Group Psychotherapy: Theory and Practice,* 2nd Ed., New York: Grune & Stratton, Inc., 1959.

Lifton, Walter M., *Working With Groups: Group Process and Individual Growth.* New York: John Wiley & Sons, Inc., 1966.

Lubin, B., and A. W. Lubin, *Group Psychotherapy: A Bibliography of the Literature.* East Lansing: Michigan State University Press, 1966.

Millan, Hugh, and Max Rosenbaum, *Group Psychotherapy: Theory and Practice.* New York: Free Press of Glencoe, Inc., 1962.

McGowan, John F., and Lyle D. Schmidt, *Counseling: Readings in Theory and Practice.* New York: Holt, Rinehart & Winston, Inc., 1962.

Moustakas, Clark E., *Psychotherapy with Children, the Living Relationship.* New York: Harper & Row, Publishers, 1959.

————, *Existential Child Therapy.* New York: Basic Book, Inc., Publishers, 1966.

Newbauer, Peter B., "Current Advances and Problems in Child Therapy," in *Professional School Psychology,* Vol. II, ed. M. G. Gottsegen and G. B. Gottsegen. New York: Grune & Stratton, Inc., 1963, pp. 36–55.

Patterson, C. H.. *Theories of Counseling and Psychotherapy.* New York: Harper & Row, Publishers, 1966.

Perez, J. F., *Counseling: Theory and Practice.* Reading, Mass.: Addison-Wesley Co., 1966.

Shore, M. F., and J. L. Massimo, "Comprehensive Vocationally Oriented Psychotherapy for Boys," *American Journal of Orthopsychiatry,* **36** (July, 1966), 609–614.

Speers, R. W., and C. Lansing, *Group Therapy in Childhood Psychosis.* Chapel Hill: University of North Carolina Press, 1965.

Slavson, S. R., and Haim G. Ginott, "Groups in Guidance and Treatment of Adolescents in a School Setting," in *Professional School Psychology,* Vol. II, ed. M. G. Gottsegen and G. B. Gottsegen. New York: Grune & Stratton, Inc., 1963, pp. 56–75.

Starkman, S. S., "Psychotherapy in Schools: A Rationale for More Useful Application," *Psychology in the Schools,* **3** (July, 1966), 236–241.

Tyler, Leona E., *The Work of the Counselor,* 2nd Ed. New York: Appleton-Century-Crofts, 1961.

Valett, Robert E., "Problems in Psychological Counseling," Chapter 11, *The Practice of School Psychology.* New York: John Wiley & Sons, Inc., 1963, pp. 226–250.

Wagner, Rudolph F., "Short-Term Counseling in the School Setting: A Diagnostic-Therapeutic Approach," *Journal of School Psychology,* I, No. 1 (January, 1963), 42.

White, Mary Alice, and Myron W. Harris, "Psychological Therapy with Pupils," Chapter 13, "Psychological Therapy and Parents," Chapter 14, *The School Psychologist.* New York: Harper & Row, Publishers, 1961.

Wolber, Lewis R., *Short-Term Psychotherapy.* New York: Grune & Stratton, Inc., 1965.

STANLEY S. MARZOLF

7

Group Appraisal
of School Children

Group appraisal refers to inferences made from results of tests or inventories given to an entire group at once in order to save time. In schools intelligence and achievement tests are the most frequently used group appraisal devices, but interest and personality inventories are also utilized. Tests for special aptitudes are also given, particularly in the upper grades and in high school.

A number of states have state-wide testing programs at the high school level, and in 1967 we are now confronted with the possibility of a large scale achievement testing program coordinated by the United States Office of Education. Educational aptitude and achievement tests are given to juniors or seniors and results are made available to the schools. Under the impetus of the National Defense Education Act of 1958—recently extended to 1968—the extent of such testing increased at both the high school and elementary levels.

Appraisal of the individuals in the group is the major purpose for which group measures are used. However, the results may be used to compare one group with another. Usually the comparison is made between the performance of a particular school class and that of a norm group to see how the former compares with the latter. For example, the teacher of the sixth grade in the Lone Wolf Elementary School may find that the median of her class on a reading achievement test is higher than that of the appropriate norm group but that her class median for arithmetic is not as high as that of the norm group.

How the results of city-wide achievement testing compare with the norm group or more properly, the *reference sample*, should be a matter of concern to all school personnel. Investigation of factors responsible for divergence, either superiority or inferiority, should be studied regularly. The school psychologist should be able to make sound contributions to the planning and conduct of such investigations.

Among the factors to be considered in accounting for divergences from the reference sample are: 1) the intelligence or educational aptitude distribution of the pupils; 2) the appropriateness of the achievement test for the educational objectives of the school; 3) the effectiveness of procedures for early detection and analysis of educational disability; 4) the extent and effectiveness of remedial provisions; 5) socio-economic and cultural factors; and 6) teaching methods. The school psychologist's work relates particularly to the first, third, and fourth of the factors, but he should be able to assist in planning investigations of other factors as well.

Where there are interschool differences, the psychologist may be helpful to a particular teacher seeking reasons why the pupils of a class either excel or are relatively deficient in reading, arithmetic, spelling, or another subject.

It always should be remembered that "surpassing the norm" in achievement, even when one may be fairly confident that superior teaching has been a factor, does not necessarily mean that the best possible teaching has been done, and that search for better methods can be abandoned.

Intergroup comparisons are usually limited to comparisons between means or medians, so that the presence of differences in variability and the possible significance of such differences are neglected. For example, a wide range of scores in a particular class *might* result from teaching that benefits the better pupils, while a narrow range of scores *might* result from teaching that emphasizes helping the slower pupils only. There are many other possible reasons for differences in range of scores.

The School Psychologist and Group Appraisal

MAJOR FUNCTION OF THE SCHOOL PSYCHOLOGIST

Since the work of the school psychologist is primarily with the individual school child or youth, group appraisal procedures are not usually his major responsibility. There has been a disposition on the part of some school administrators to consider the person responsible for the school testing program as the school psychologist. Such a person may well be a psychologist, but historically and basically the essential characteristic of the school psychologist is, and must continue to be, work with the individual learner, helping him to achieve optimum self-realization.

USING GROUP RESULTS IN INDIVIDUAL DIAGNOSIS

Though group methods of appraisal are not his major responsibility, there are many ways in which the school psychologist is concerned with them. In the first place, study of the individual pupil must make use of the results of group tests that have already been given. Such results will probably be available in the child's cumulative record. As a child progresses through the school system, the extent of the cumulative record will increase, so that a longitudinal view of the child's personal and educational progress will be possible. Failure to obtain such a record for consideration, along with other data, as a part of a diagnostic study would be a serious lapse on the psychologist's part. Chapter 8 discusses how to extract material from school records in order to develop a meaningful case study or case history.

Even though the psychologist collects all available group appraisal data for a youngster who has been referred to him, he may yet fail to demonstrate desired competence if he does not know how to draw valid inferences from the data. He must also know when to reserve judgment because the data are insufficient, and what additional information is desirable to clarify the uncertainties raised by the cumulative record and the present behavior of the child. There are many ways in which the uninformed or careless worker may be misled by group appraisal data, so that it is necessary to be well informed about the whole process of group appraisal.

ASSISTANCE TO TEACHERS

Not only will the psychologist make use of group test data himself, but he will also be called upon to help teachers draw conclusions from such data. This help may be requested regarding the meaning of the class distribution of scores, or it may be given in a conference with the teacher about a particular child whose educational progress is in some way a problem.

The school psychologist should not allow himself to be maneuvered into the position of being the one who deals only with "problem children." It should be the aim of every school to help all children achieve the fullest possible self-actualization. The psychologist can be of considerable assistance, directly or indirectly, in helping all pupils establish a realistic integration of needs and abilities.

In addition to help in understanding existing group tests and their results, the psychologist may help the teacher construct tests for class use.[1] Help given to the teacher will lessen the amount of work with individual pupils that the psychologist will need to do, so that the time devoted to teacher conferences may be time saved.

CONFERRING WITH PARENTS

Because much of the school psychologist's work will be with parents, interpretation of the school's appraisal methods and the results for particular children will often engage his time. To explain measurement concepts to the layman requires a knowledge of such concepts that goes beyond mere repetition of technical jargon. Since most parents have gone to school, they can all speak on the subject of education from experience, and some believe that this experience qualifies them as experts on educational matters. One needs to be thoroughly informed in order to meet the challenges of questions from such persons. In 1965 the Public Affairs Committee published a pamphlet by J. McV. Hunt entitled *What You Should Know About Educational Testing*. This booklet is well written and will answer some of the questions raised by parents as well as provide a buttress against some of the more extreme popular books criticizing testing which have been published recently.

The school psychologist will have opportunity, in conferring with teachers and parents about individual pupils, to alter common misconceptions about the causes of poor school performance. Teachers and parents are frequently heard to say, "Tommy could do better if he would just try." Implicit in this statement is the belief that all that Tommy needs is to encounter sterner consequences for continued poor work. Teachers particularly need help in understanding that Tommy may not be trying simply because he does not know what to try. They may need help in analyzing Tommy's learning errors and in instituting measures to correct these errors. If the teacher does not know the precise nature of Tommy's misunderstandings how can *he* be expected to know them? If he doesn't know what he is doing wrong, what shall he try? Not knowing what to try eventually results in an attitude of hopelessness or rebellion.

[1] See Harold G. Seashore and John E. Dobbin, "How Can the Results of a Testing Program Be Used Most Effectively?", *Bulletin of the National Association of Secondary School Principals*, 42 (April, 1958), 64–68; William Coleman, "Assisting Teachers in Using Test Results," *The Personnel and Guidance Journal*, 36 (September, 1957), 38–40; Robert L. Ebel, "Writing the Test Item," in *Educational Measurement*, ed. E. F. Lindquist (Washington, D.C.: American Council on Education, 1951); John M. Stalnaker, "The Essay Type of Examination," in *Educational Measurement*; Dorothy A. Wood, *Test Construction: Development and Interpretation of Achievement Tests* (Columbus: Charles E. Merrill Books, Inc., 1960); H. H. Remmers, N. L. Gage, and J. Francis Rummel, *A Practical Introduction to Measurement and Evaluation* (New York: Harper & Row, Publishers, 1960), Chaps. 7, 8, and 9.

PLANNING GROUP APPRAISAL

The school administration should, and doubtless will, consult the psychologist about the school's program of group appraisal. Here the psychologist's technical knowledge of testing should be adequate for constructive assistance. Furthermore, the psychologist's experience with existing records, or lack of them, should provide specific evidence of need for certain kinds of group appraisal.

RESEARCH PLANNING

Finally, the school psychologist who is adequately trained should have something to offer the school on the subject of research involving data obtained through group appraisal. This topic will be discussed in depth in Chapter 19. The complaint that there is not time for research is often but an excuse for lack of ideas about what kind of research should or could be done. Even though one may not be able to conceive of any clever research designs relevant to pressing educational problems, there are certain continuing needs for evaluating the school's general program. Any schedule of group appraisal provides data which can be tabulated in ways which will not only reveal interesting information but will also arouse interest on the part of the staff in getting further information. If someone will take the initiative, volunteer assistance will be forthcoming. Exercising such initiative may well be a function of the school psychologist.[2]

Thus, if the school psychologist is to make full use of group test results in his own diagnostic endeavors, and if he is to assist teachers, the school as a whole, parents, and the community to gain optimal benefit from such results, he must be thoroughly informed about group appraisal instruments.

General Characteristics of Measuring Devices

TESTS

The principal devices used for measuring behavior are tests, inventories, and rating scales. A test is a sample of stimuli (test items) presented under standard conditions. A test in addition skill does not include all possible ad-

---

[2] Some of the research activities in which the psychologist may become involved are known as *action* research. See William H. Lucio, "Evaluation of the Educational Program," *Review of Educational Research,* 29 (April, 1959), 165–176, 168f, and Martin Kohn and Jerome Beker, "Special Methodological Considerations in Conducting Field Research in a School Setting," *Psychology in the Schools,* I (1964), 31–46.

dition problems, but only a sample of such problems. If valid inferences are to be drawn from the results obtained by the test, great care must be exercised so that the sample of items covers the kinds of problems on which the pupils tested have had instruction and practice. Standard conditions include the nature of the instructions, the time allotted for doing the tasks, and the general environmental conditions.

INVENTORIES

An inventory is a sample of items requiring responses indicating how the person usually behaves or feels. Standard instructions must be adhered to, but as a rule time limits are not of special importance. Examples are lists of statements describing situations that may or may not cause difficulty, to which the respondent may indicate whether or not the situation usually causes him difficulty.

RATING SCALES

A rating scale is a description of a personal characteristic together with a way of indicating the degree to which this characteristic applies to an individual. Usually a rating on more than one trait is called for. The rating may be done by someone who knows the person well or it may be done by the person himself.

Not all available measuring devices may be subsumed under the above headings, but those in common use, particularly in the school, can be so classified.

WAYS IN WHICH MEASURING DEVICES DIFFER

Measuring instruments used for evaluating behavior differ from one another in many ways. Some measuring instruments call for *maximum performance* and the results are intended to reflect the degree to which a particular characteristic is present. In evaluating results from such instruments the first question is whether anything prevented some or all of the individuals from responding at their maximum.

Sometimes it is information about the usual or *typical behavior* of the individuals that is sought. The various inventories (interest and adjustment, for example) call for this kind of response. Here the important question is whether the respondents answered honestly. Deviations from the truth may be deliberate and conscious or possibly unconscious.

The *degree of structure* of the test situation is an important characteristic. Items which call for one and only one acceptable response, such as "What is two plus nine?" are highly structured. Presenting a picture and asking the person to make up a story about the picture is a relatively unstructured situation. The majority of tests involved in group appraisal are highly structured, although more projective instruments are administered in groups today than formerly.

The manner of making the response may be *objective* or it may not. The degree of objectivity of response may vary to some degree. True-false and multiple-choice responses are definitely objective, and a completion item may be somewhat less so. The totally free response, usually called the essay response, is least objective.

Objective items avoid the influence of scorer bias, but they may still be poor items. The item may be one that tricks the respondent. Instructors who gleefully construct these kinds of items would probably have just as much fun deducting for irrelevancies encountered in essay responses.

Good objective test items require more than mere recognition of that which has been memorized. They should call for a weighing of alternatives, each of which may have some plausibility, but only one of which represents a sound judgment regarding the problem situation.

It may be true, as claimed,[3] that objective items cannot measure ability to do creative thinking, but this does not mean such items can evaluate only factual recognition, nor that the use of them will stultify creativity.

There are indeed abilities which cannot be evaluated by objective items. A student's ability to write a good paragraph can be evaluated only by having him write paragraphs. Free response items should be used where necessary.

Whenever free response items are used, care should be taken to minimize scorer bias. Pooling of judgments is one of the best ways of doing so, but this is a method that is not likely to be used. Reliability of scoring can be improved if *a*) papers are scored anonymously; *b*) the teacher prepares a "perfect" answer for each question before scoring; *c*) one question is scored at a time; and *d*) papers are scored a second time after an interval, without knowledge of the scores assigned the first time.

Tests may be either *verbal* or *nonverbal*, depending simply on whether the item is presented in words or in nonverbal form, such as in numbers, pictures, or geometric designs. Under the general heading of nonverbal may be classified the various performance tests that call for the manipulation of

[3] Joy P. Guilford, "The Structure of Intellect," *Psychological Bulletin*, 53 (July, 1956), 267–293, or, by the same author, "Three Faces of Intellect," *American Psychologist*, 14 (August, 1959), 469–479. See also Quinn McNemar, "Lost: Our Intelligence? Why?" *American Psychologist*, 19 (1964), 871–882; R. de Mille and P. R. Merrifield, "Review of *Creativity and Intelligence; Explorations with Gifted Students* by J. W. Getzels and P. W. Jackson," *Educational and Psychological Measurement*, 22 (1962), 803–808; Jim C. Nunnally, Jr., Tests and Measurements (New York: McGraw-Hill Book Company, 1965), Chap. 14; Calvin W. Taylor and John L. Holland, "Development and Application of Tests of Creativity," *Review of Educational Research*, 32 (February, 1962), 91–102.

objects. Performance tests usually are individual and are for the purpose of measuring intelligence, but there are job placement tests and others that are sometimes referred to as performance tests.

Finally, measuring instruments may be given either *individually or to groups*. Some must be given individually and all designed for group use may be used individually. The individual test is time-consuming but the opportunity provided the examiner to observe the individual, as well as the characteristics of the tests themselves, make the results of such examination worth the time required. The individual test does not necessarily yield a true measure, but the skilled examiner is likely to know when marked deviations from maximum or characteristic performance have occurred.

These are not all the ways in which measuring devices may differ. Consult references in the Selected Supplementary Readings at the end of this chapter for sources of more detailed information, especially Buros: *Sixth Mental Measurement Yearbook*, released in 1965.

Validity

Whether or not a test result tells us what we want it to is the major question in appraisal of any kind and at any time. Implicit in the problem is the existence of a purpose. Whether the purpose, whatever it is, has been achieved is never answered categorically; the answer is always in terms of degree. We cannot say that conclusions drawn from test scores are valid or invalid but only that they have such and such a degree of validity. The topic of validity is an intricate and extensive one and only a few of the more important aspects of it can be noted here.

There are different kinds of situations in which the question of validity arises.[4] The school psychologist will be especially concerned with content, concurrent, and predictive validity.

Evaluation of scores on achievement tests involves a consideration of *content* validity. If a pupil's arithmetic achievement score is to be interpreted as an indication of how much he has learned about what he has been taught, we must be sure that the test items are an adequate representation of what he has been taught. If the results for a group as a whole, such as a particular

---

[4] See *Technical Recommendations for Psychological Tests and Diagnostic Techniques* (Washington, D.C.: American Psychological Association, 1954); *Technical Recommendations for Achievement Tests* (Washington, D.C.: National Education Association, 1955); and Donald T. Campbell, "Recommendations for APA Test Standards Regarding Construct, Trait, or Discriminant Validity," *American Psychologist,* 15 (August, 1960), 546–553. The first two of the above citations include essential information on the topic of selecting tests and all include clear and concise treatments of the kinds of validity. See also Roger T. Lennon, "Assumptions Underlying the Use of Content Validity," *Educational and Psychological Measurement,* 16 (Autumn, 1956), 294–304, and Henry Moughamian, "General Overview of Trends in Testing," *Review of Educational Research, 35* (February, 1965), 11–12.

fifth grade, are to be properly evaluated, we must also be concerned with whether the test is representative of the instructional objectives.

Adjustment inventories call for knowledge of *concurrent* validity. We need to know whether adjustment inventory scores really indicate the pupils' relative levels of adjustment.

If we are to use any scores for the purpose of educational or vocational planning we must know the extent to which the scores have *predictive* validity. For example, how well do scores on an algebra aptitude test predict later success in algebra? The first problem in establishing predictive validity is that of getting an adequate measure of the criterion, the performance we wish to predict. If course grades in algebra are to be used as the criterion we should question how well the course grades represent the relative algebra knowledge of the pupils.

When validity quotients are low it means that factors other than what is measured by the predictor test are involved. Prediction can only be improved by taking these factors into account.

One important factor very frequently overlooked in the interpretation of validity coefficients is the effect of range of talent. A test used to predict success in algebra of a random sample of eighth graders may correlate quite highly with subsequent beginning algebra grades, but this same test used to predict the algebra success of only the top ten per cent of the eighth grade class might yield a low validity coefficient. When all the students are good to begin with, algebra aptitude will vary less and subsequent differences in performance, to the extent that they exist, will depend to a greater degree on other factors.

Reliability

The reliability of a distribution of scores is the proportion of the variance in scores which is attributable to true scores; the remaining variance is error variance. Less technically, reliability is the degree to which a set of scores represents the true relative standing of those measured. Reliability cannot be determined directly, but it can be estimated in several ways.[5] The reliability estimated by any of the available methods is usually expressed as a correlation coefficient.

Some principles of score reliability important for selection of tests and interpretation of results are:

1. A high degree of validity cannot be achieved for a test yielding measurements having a low degree of reliability, but a high degree of re-

[5] On the meaning of reliability and ways of estimating it see Guilford, *Fundamental Statistics in Psychology and Education* (4th ed.) (New York: McGraw-Hill Book Company, 1965), Chap. 17. Also Jum C. Nunnally, Jr., *op. cit.*, Chap. 4; and Samuel T. Mayo, "Statistical Trends Relevant to Measurement," *Review of Educational Research*, 35 (February, 1965), 86–87.

liability does not necessarily assure high validity of any kind. For validity of measurement, high reliability is a necessary but not sufficient condition.

2. Small differences between scores, either between individuals or between tests for a single individual, should not be taken seriously, even for the more reliable tests. Recording IQ's to one or more decimal points is unthinkable. It is ridiculous to state with assurance that since an individual's centile score on a mechanical aptitude test is 68 and his score on an art aptitude test is only 65, his mechanical aptitude is greater than his art aptitude.

3. Other things being equal, the longer a test the greater the reliability of the scores it will yield. Very short tests are almost certain to be quite unreliable. Consequently, judgments about characteristics based upon short subtests must be very tentative.

4. Just as with validity, the reliability of a set of measures depends upon the range of talent of the sample from which the scores are obtained. For example, a reliability coefficient for a test of musical knowledge, estimated from a sample of students majoring in music, would doubtless be quite low. Such a reliability coefficient would be considerably higher were it obtained from a random sample of students, since the *range* in amount of musical knowledge of the random sample would be much higher than that of the music students. It is because of this limitation of the reliability coefficient as an indicator of reliability that test publishers should, and often do, report the *standard error of a score* rather than simply the estimated reliability coefficient.

Kinds of Scores

Most measuring devices can be scored so as to yield numbers, usually the number of items responded to in a particular way. However, if on a test of stupidity a person makes a score of 27 we cannot tell whether this person is extremely stupid or is slightly tainted, like most of us. The score must be expressed in some other way.

One of the oldest ways of expressing such a score, known as a raw score, was to convert it to a percentage. If the stupidity test had 100 items then this score would become 27 per cent. Does this mean the person is 27 per cent stupid? Is 100 per cent complete stupidity? Obviously converting scores to a per cent of the total possible items is useful only to the extent we know what 100 per cent means.

Several kinds of scores are in common use. Achievement test results are most often expressed as grade equivalents and intelligence tests as ratio or deviation IQ's. Other test results may be converted to centiles (more commonly though less precisely known as percentiles), stanines, or other converted standard scores. In fact any of these forms may be used for any test from which numerical raw scores are obtained. The school psychologist must understand the rationale underlying each procedure so that misinterpretation may be avoided.[6]

It sometimes happens that youngsters are given two different intelligence tests with the result that the obtained scores, either IQ's or centiles, may differ even though the interval between testing is short and there is no obvious difference in the circumstances of testing. This sort of discrepancy may occur with other kinds of tests, and when it does, teachers are often quite mystified. There are a number of reasons growing out of the process of test construction which may readily explain such differences.

In the first place no two tests of intelligence, or of anything else for that matter, will contain the same sample of possible items; there will be some difference in content. It may be that an individual might do as well on one sample as on the other, but it would not be too surprising if he did not.

Secondly, the sample used for standardization (for providing the distribution from which the mental ages, centile equivalents, or standard scores are derived) will not be the same for both tests.

In the third place, not only will the kinds of items differ in the two tests, but it is likely that the difficulty distribution of the items in each test will be different. This can effect the shape of the sample distribution and the size of the standard deviation. It is an empirical fact that no two intelligence tests yield distributions of IQ's having the same standard deviation.

Norms

Group appraisal devices are often referred to as standardized tests. This refers to the fact that the raw scores obtained may be interpreted by comparing them with the distribution of scores which have been obtained by the "norm" group. Norm basically means a standard in the sense of an ideal. *However when used in psychology*, particularly with respect to tests, the norm is simply the central tendency of the distribution of scores obtained from a particular sample without any necessary implication of ideal performance.

It would be better to speak of the standardization sample as a *reference sample*. Any other sample distribution may be compared with the reference sample with respect to the central tendency, variance, or shape of the distribution. What the results of such comparison mean must be interpreted in terms of what you are trying to find out. Test manuals sometimes include more than one reference distribution so that there is a choice of which to use.

[6] See Guilford, Chap. 19.

Here again, which distribution shall be used must depend upon what you seek to learn by the comparison.

What kind of reference sample shall now be used for evaluating achievement test results? The composition of the fourth grade, or any other grade, varies as to age and intelligence. We could use either factor as a basis for the reference sample. In fact, it would be best to use both. Comparing a youngster with a sample of those of like ability would evaluate him in terms of his ability, but would neglect the fact that future vocational demands are determined by the vocation and by society.

Different reference samples may be available for special aptitude tests. For some purposes we wish to compare a score with a sample of the general population, but for other reasons it may be desirable to compare the score with beginning students in a specialized educational program. Art ability may be judged in terms of students in general or in terms of beginning students in an art school.[7]

Group Appraisal in Education

INTELLIGENCE TESTS

Group intelligence tests are available for use at all levels of the school population. Their content may be either verbal or nonverbal. The results are important for predicting learning accomplishment.

Such tests have been criticized on the grounds that they do not reveal the original and creative thinker. This possibility needs careful attention. Careful attention to and evaluation of all behavior of pupils may compensate for this deficiency to some extent.[8]

It has been argued that most of the tests in use are not fair to all cultural levels within our society. Tests have been devised for the purpose of correcting this deficiency. However, research does not seem to support the existence of cultural unfairness to any notable extent. Nevertheless, the influence of cultural deprivation should be seriously considered in evaluating individual scores.[9] This topic is discussed more fully in Chapter 16.

---

[7] On the subject of norms see William M. Shanner, "New Concepts in Norms," *The Positive Values in the American Educational System* (Washington, D.C.: American Council on Education, 1959); also Samuel T. Mayo, *op. cit.*, pp. 87–88.

[8] With respect to the adequacy of intelligence tests see Willard G. Warrington and Joe L. Saupe, "Development and Applications of Tests of General Mental Ability," *Review of Educational Research*, 29 (February, 1959), 15–25, and Norman E. Wallen, "Development and Application of Tests of General Mental Ability," *Review of Educational Research*, 32 (February, 1962), 15–24.

[9] For a report on research regarding culture-fairness see Warrington and Saupe, *ibid.*

APTITUDE TESTS

Tests used to predict probable learning rate designed for use at the high school and college levels are often called educational aptitude tests, thus avoiding the issue of the extent to which prior schooling may determine the results and taking into account the fact that the reference sample, taken from upper educational levels, is not a random sample of the general population, since the most retarded children are not likely to be included in the sample.

Aptitude and intelligence test scores always may be affected by differences in opportunity to learn. Differences in scores can be used as a basis for inferring differences in intelligence only to the extent that we may assume that opportunities for development in those being tested is comparable to those of the reference sample. For intelligence tests it is usually only very marked departure from usual opportunities for development that need be taken into account, but with educational and other aptitude tests more attention to this possibility is justified. In addition to general education aptitude tests there are special educational aptitude tests such as those for algebra and foreign language.

A number of multifactor tests are available. These are groups of tests each of which is supposed to measure a particular ability that indicates aptitude for special kinds of educational or vocational learning. Verbal reasoning, abstract reasoning, numerical ability, ability to handle space relations, and mechanical reasoning are examples of the kinds of tests included. The value of such tests will depend upon the differential predictive validities that research establishes.

A bright youngster who wishes to be an engineer may, in the eighth grade, earn a low score on an algebra aptitude test, or later on this youngster may make a relatively low score on an engineering aptitude test. This does indeed mean that his likelihood of success in this field is less than desired. However, tests of this kind usually have several parts, and one of them is likely to be a speeded test in arithmetic computation. It may be that the low score on the test as a whole is due primarily to a very low score on this part. Such a deficiency can perhaps be corrected by appropriate drill. An aptitude score does not need to be the final verdict.

In contrast there is the case of a boy who makes a very high score on an engineering aptitude test and who therefore was "counseled" to enter an engineering school. However, this particular boy, because of illness, finished high school by the aid of a bedside teacher and never had either physics or chemistry. As a result he failed at the end of the first semester. The counselor in this actual case was unbelievably incompetent. After all, no tests can compensate for the deficiencies of those who may interpret the results.

ACHIEVEMENT TESTS

Achievement tests are available for most curriculum areas. For the elementary school, tests may be arranged in batteries, that is, collections of separate tests in each of the school subjects, such as reading, arithmetic, language, social science, and the like. A particular battery is intended for use at more than one grade level. For example there may be a primary battery for grades one and two, an elementary battery for grades three and four, an intermediate for grades five and six, and an advanced battery for grades seven, eight, and nine. For the high school, achievement tests are more likely to be devised for individual subjects, but there are "basic content" batteries available.

Typically, the results of an achievement battery are converted to grade equivalent scores and these scores are plotted graphically on the test booklet, yielding a profile for each pupil showing his strengths and weaknesses.

Unfortunately, most published batteries encourage determining the median of these tests. A pupil having grade equivalent scores on the several subjects of 4.6, 5.9, 6.3, 6.6, and 7.1 would have a "battery median" of 6.3. However there are many patterns of subtest scores that could yield a median of 6.3. We need to know how much variation there is in subtest scores and the specific subjects in which any great variations exist if we are to gain much value from the administration of the achievement battery. Often it is only the battery median that is recorded in the cumulative record or given to the psychologist when a youngster is referred. If the test booklets are still available, the psychologist can make use of them, but one may well wonder whether the youngster's present difficulty may not be a result of past educational planning that has considered only the battery median and not the significance of subtest deviations.

INTEREST INVENTORIES

Interest inventories are available for use from the fourth grade upward. The majority are oriented toward vocational planning or occuptional choice, but educational planning less directly related to occupations is the principal use of some.

Roughly there are two kinds, those which sort out likes and dislikes and order them in categories of interests such as mechanical, scientific, literary, or musical and those which compare likes and dislikes, or degrees of preference for activities, with the likes and dislikes of those in specific occupations.

Those which sort interests into categories have broad utility, especially for educational planning, but interpretations from them with respect to occupational choice is sometimes hazardous. The teacher's or psychologist's judgment that a person with high interest in a certain area would like such and such an occupation may be erroneous. However, data indicating interest patterns differentiating various occupations are becoming available.

Those which relate interests to specific occupations are most dependable, so far as the available list of occupations goes, but it is not possible to obtain scores indicating the degree of interest in all occupations. Large scale use of such an inventory seems inadvisable, for a youngster may find that his interests are in accord with an occupation which requires academic preparation beyond his ability. Reinforced with knowledge of his interest in the occupation, he may try to enter the necessary educational preparation and meet with failure. Such an inventory had best be used only for those students having the ability, at least the general intelligence, necessary for any of the occupations in which interests might be shown.

Students, parents, and sometimes teachers will believe that interest in an activity implies ability to learn or perform that activity. Interest and ability often are associated but many times they are not. Listening to radio or television ought to convince anyone that there are many interested in singing who have little talent.

There are two main reasons that an interest inventory is necessary. We have so many likes and dislikes that it is necessary, by means of an inventory, to take stock and see where most are to be found and how the interests in each category compare with sortings made by other people. Secondly, we may be mistaken in thinking we would like an occupation simply because we know little about it. The safest way to decide is on the basis of how our likes and dislikes compare with those in the occupation.

PERSONALITY INVENTORIES

Personality inventories can be classified under two headings. There are those which give scores indicating degree of dominance, introversion, or of other traits. Scores are not necessarily desirable or undesirable but indicate only trait differences. If for example a high score indicates dominance, a low score may indicate submissiveness. It is possible that either extremely high or low scores indicate the presence of an adjustive problem, but this supposition should always be considered as a tentative hypothesis to be supported or rejected on the basis of further information.

Adjustment inventories, which seek to determine the extent to which many common, everyday situations cause difficulty or disturbance, are the second variety. A high score may indicate considerable maladjustment and a low score, good adjustment.

Both kinds of inventories may be useful in vocational planning. Adjustment inventories are useful in discovering those pupils having marked adjustment problems that are not manifested in overt behavior. For those with overt behavior disturbance, the inventory may help locate the particular area of disturbance.

It is claimed that inventories, either adjustment or personality, can be faked so that the scores will come out the way the person wants them to. Research has shown that such faking is possible.[10] That faking can be done is no cause for assuming that it will be done. Experience shows that scores indicating poor adjustment are made and that trait and interest scores maintain considerable stability over periods of time.

Rating scales are sometimes a part of the appraisal system. At the close of each year the teacher rates each youngster on the traits comprising the scale. Examples of the traits on which such ratings are made are responsibility, initiative, industry, and cooperativeness. Such a device, if constructed so as to minimize the sources of error common to rating scales, may be quite useful. Year to year comparisons are especially informative.

Other kinds of tests and inventories are available. For information on these consult the books listed in the Selected Supplementary Readings and in publishers' catalogs.

Interpreting Results

ACCURACY OF SCORES

When interpreting the results of group appraisal devices, the first thing to be investigated is the accuracy of the scores. It may seem that this is a matter too trivial to deserve mention. Perhaps it should be so, but experience with tabulations of group test results and with cumulative records has shown that errors and inaccuracies are exceedingly common. The raw score may be wrong, scores for one individual may be recorded for another, conversion of raw scores to grade equivalents, centiles, or IQ's, usually done by reference to a table, may be in error. Because of the possibility of these and other errors, spot checks of group testing should be made routinely, and in any individual case referred to the psychologist, a check on the accuracy of the basic data should be made. Of course, tact needs to be shown in the way such checking is carried out. Don't forget to verify the birthdate and check the calculation of the chronological age.[11]

---

[10] See William Coleman and Dorothy M. Collett, "Development and Applications of Structure Tests of Personality," *Review of Educational Research*, 29 (February, 1959), 57–72, and Eugene L. Gaier and William F. White, "Trends in the Measurement of Personality," *Review of Educational Research*, 35 (February, 1965), 63–81.

[11] See Beeman N. Phillips and Garrett Weathers, "Analysis of Errors Made in Scoring Standard Tests," *Educational and Psychological Measurement*, 18 (Autumn, 1958), 563–567.

GENERAL CONSIDERATIONS

Use of group test data usually involves making comparisons. When we make a comparison between one group and another, statistical methodology involves a comparison between central tendencies, best represented for comparison purposes, by the mean. By use of the appropriate statistic, e.g. Fisher's *t* test, we determine whether the difference between the means of the two groups is statistically significant.[12] Proper interpretation enables us to say what the chances are that the difference we find could have occurred by chance. Regardless of how unlikely it is that a chance difference could have occurred, it is always possible that the difference is due to chance. If we may be quite confident that the difference is not due to chance we are still left with the problem of accounting for the difference. The snares we encounter in the course of solving this problem belong to the province of the statistics textbooks and shall not be treated here.

A difference between two means may be statistically significant at a very high level of confidence, but this does not mean that the difference has educational significance, or that, if it has, we are going to do anything about it. For the curious, any reliable difference is a challenge for explanation. From the practical point of view, what is done about a small but reliable difference depends not only on whether we know what causes it, but how much it would cost. Costs may not necessarily be monetary, but whatever the cost, we must believe that the gains will be worth the expenditure. Simply stated, we probably could not justify the expense of changing a textbook because we found a reliable difference of but one month in mean reading achievement associated with the use of the book.

For research purposes comparisons are usually between means, but in dealing with test score distributions the median is frequently the preferred measure of central tendency, since it is least affected by extreme scores. What has been said about the significance of differences between means applies to differences between medians, though the formulas by which such significance is determined are somewhat different.

With respect to correlations, there is a common fallacy that correlations of the order of .10, .15, or .20 are worthless. Whether or not they are depends first on whether we may be confident that they are not chance correlations. If it is unlikely that such a correlation is a chance one, then what it is worth depends on how we wish to use it. If it is a validity coefficient, then it probably will have little utility. If, however, it is the correlation between some hitherto unrecognized variable and reading ability, it is worth

[12] On the statistical significance of differences between measures of central tendency see Guilford, *op. cit.*, pp. 173–185.

looking into since it might turn out to be a very important finding.[13]

These are some general ideas about interpretation of data that will have many applications in the school group appraisal situation. It is hoped that they will be understood and used and that curiosity about additional statistical understanding will be awakened.

STUDY OF GROUPS

After group tests have been administered and scored it is always interesting to see what the distribution of scores looks like. We wonder, "How did the group do?" Usually we first want to know how our distribution compares with some norm group.

To make the question concrete and specific, consider the data shown in Table 1, noting first the distributions of I.Q.'s. One distribution is that of I.Q.'s obtained from a group intelligence test calling for responses to tasks presented in picture form, while the other I.Q. distribution represents the results obtained by means of a verbal test. The median content I.Q. is four points higher than that of the reading content I.Q. Data were not available for determining the statistical significance of this difference.[14]

How shall we explain the fact that the median in each case is greater than 100, the defined median for the general population? This is always an important question. Sometimes such a discrepancy results from faulty test administration. There have been cases where a newly published test, for some reason inadequately standardized, yielded I.Q. distributions markedly different from what one would expect. The question cannot be answered from the data as here presented, but must be sought by testing various hypotheses. In this particular instance, it is known that the school system has a good program of special education for mentally retarded and by the third grade many retarded children have already been placed in such rooms. This fact alone would account for at least some of the observed difference. Then too there are differences between communities associated with the major occupational levels that comprise them. While it may not be possible to check all the possibilities in a definitive way, as much checking as possible should be done.

Confining ourselves to a comparison of central tendencies, be they means or medians, is far too limited an evaluation of results. The distributions must be compared with respect to their ranges, represented in this case by Q.[15] The difference between Q's of 7.87 and 10.45 reflects the greater spread of the reading-content I.Q.'s. Inspection of the latter distribution in-

---

[13] On the meaning of the correlation coefficient see Guilford, *op. cit.*, pp. 103–107.

[14] The significance of the differences between medians could not properly be obtained from the data here presented since the correlations between tests were not available.

[15] Q is the semi-interquartile range. See Guilford, *op. cit.*, p. 69.

Table 1

Distributions of Intelligence and Achievement Test Results
for Third-Grade Classes in One City *

I.Q.	Intelligence			Achievement	
	Picture Content	Reading Content	Grade Equivalent	Paragraph Meaning	Arithmetic Problems
145–149		1	7.4–7.7	1	
140–144	3	3	7.0–7.3	5	
135–139	8	3	6.6–6.9	1	
130–134	15	7	6.2–6.5	11	
125–129	22	15	5.8–6.1	12	
120–124	34	30	5.4–5.7	1	
115–119	46	41	5.0–5.3	25	
110–114	53	46	4.6–4.9	38	
105–109	69	45	4.2–4.5	31	
100–104	45	41	3.8–4.1	50	2
95– 99	18	34	3.4–3.7	62	22
90– 94	15	25	3.0–3.3	37	101
85– 89	5	27	2.6–2.9	26	202
80– 84	5	10	2.2–2.5	28	18
75– 79	7	13	1.8–2.1	19	3
70– 74		2	1.4–1.7	2	
65– 69	3	3	1.0–1.3		1
60– 64	1	2			
Total	349	348 **		349	349
Median	110	106		3.8	2.9
Q	7.87	10.45		.77	.27

* Grade placement at time of achievement testing was 3.2.
** One pupil did not take the reading content portion of the intelligence test.

dicates slight skewness toward the lower end. Is it not possible that a sizeable number of children with severe reading disability have been responsible, not only for this skewness, but also for the lower median reading-content I.Q.? These data do not tell us, but they do raise a question that should be investigated in the local school situation. Comparison of distributions affords opportunity to note the usual marked overlap between distributions, a fact too often forgotten.

Comparison of subject matter distributions is always interesting, if not for what is really learned, at least for the strange things that schools sometimes think they show. Perhaps it is questions to be answered rather than answers that should come from such comparisons. How this may be so is illustrated by the achievement test distributions shown in Table 1.

Since the actual grade placement of these pupils at the time of testing was 3.2 the "expected achievement" for the "average" third-grader would be 3.2. On paragraph meaning the 349 third-graders in this school system have a median grade placement of 3.8. This looks very good as long as you forget the median I.Q.'s for the same group. What should we expect of the 349 youngsters producing the picture-content I.Q. distribution? Even if we could say that the median to be expected was 3.8 and that therefore this group "reached the norm" we should never forget that this "norm" is not an ideal. It is only the central tendency of a reference sample.

What can we make of the distribution of arithmetic problems scores? In the first place, the median of 2.9 does not "reach the norm," especially if the intelligence distributions are considered. Does this mean that in this school system the curriculum differs with respect to arithmetic instruction from that of the schools contributing to the reference sample? If so, is this departure justified and is the final outcome at, say, the eighth grade in computational skill satisfactory? Do these findings mean that instruction in arithmetic computation is poor? No, the available data do not answer these questions, but the questions certainly should be investigated and answered with as much assurance as possible.

The two achievement distributions in Table 1 show with marked clarity the importance of viewing whole distributions, not just central tendencies. How can we account for the great difference in the ranges of the two distributions, represented by Q values of .77 and .27? Such a difference could be inherent in the standardization of the two achievement tests, in that the arithmetic problems test items are of such a range of difficulty as to make a wide range unlikely or even impossible. It is possible that minimal or poor instruction may be at fault. It may be that, for his age group in this community, there is marked difference in the out-of-school experiences which contribute to reading and those which contribute to an understanding of numbers. At any rate, here is another question that urgently needs answering.

All of the data in Table 1 demonstrate forcibly the existence of individual differences and the need for taking these differences into account. At the beginning of the third grade some children are reading at the seventh-grade level while others are barely able to read at all.

Space is not available for investigating correlations. How do the picture- and reading-content scores correlate? What is the correlation between achievement measures and each of the intelligence measures? How can we account for low correlations that should be higher?

How may questions raised by distributions of group appraisal data be answered? Only by further investigations. For example, from the 349 pupils constituting the third-grade distribution, the top and bottom 25 or 50 pupils on each achievement test could be selected. These low- and high-achievement groups could then be studied intensively beginning with intelligence test scores, achievement in other subjects, previous school experience, health factors, schools in which they are enrolled, and so on. Such intensive study should do much to explain why there are differences or why expected large differences are small or absent. Increased understanding of the educational task will certainly result from studies such as these.

The arithmetic problems test distribution shown in Table 1 certainly suggests the need for an item analysis of the responses to this test. What items are most frequently missed by good pupils, poor ones, and by all pupils? Are these items that get little attention, or are some of them items representing arithmetic topics that supposedly were intensively taught? There is no sense arguing about the meaning of a distribution; it is better to spend the time finding additional information. Item analyses are tedious but fortunately data processing equipment is now available for doing, or assisting in, the task.

It is profitable and interesting to compare the results obtained in the several schools that comprise a school system. Such a comparison is shown in Table 2 where the medians on each of the two parts of an intelligence

TABLE 2

Median Intelligence Quotients, Paragraph Meaning and
Arithmetic Problems Grade Equivalents for the
Third-Grade Classes of One City *

School	Median I.Q.		Median Grade Equivalent		N
	Picture Content	Reading Content	Paragraph Meaning	Arithmetic Problems	
A	108	101	3.6	2.8	21
B	112	113	4.9	2.9	33
C	108	105	3.9	2.8	25
D	109	108	4.2	2.9	33
E	115	113	4.2	2.8	29
F	108	96	3.2	2.9	25
G	106	102	3.7	2.8	25
H	113	106	3.6	2.8	30
I	110	109	3.9	2.8	12
J	110	116	4.3	2.9	24
K	110	101	3.8	2.8	27
L	106	100	3.3	2.8	32
M	116	112	3.6	3.0	33
Total	110	106	3.8	2.9	349

* *The actual grade placement of these pupils was 3.2.*

test and on each of two achievement tests are shown. There are interschool differences shown, but the table does not contain Q, the indication of the extent the scores vary about the medians, and thus considerable desirable information is kept from us. It is, nevertheless, just the kind of table that school systems present in annual reports.

An emphatic indication of what kind of data are left out of Table 2 is given by Table 3 where the class distributions of each of the two schools

TABLE 3

*Distribution of Intelligence Test Results for
the Third-Grade Classes Having the Lowest
and the Highest Median I.Q.'s in one City* *

I.Q.	Picture Content		Reading Content	
	Lowest	Highest	Lowest	Highest
135–9		3		1
130–4	1	2		1
125–9	1	4	1	2
120–4	1	2		6
115–9	3	8	2	3
110–4	4	2	3	6
105–9	6	1	2	2
100–4	3	8	3	5
95–9	3		2	2
90–4		2	3	1
85–9	1		2	3
80–4			3	1
75–9	1	1	4	
70–4				
65–9	1			
Total	25	33	25	33
Median	108	116	96	112

* *Highest and lowest classes determined by taking into account both the Picture Content
and the Reading Content medians.*

having the lowest and highest medians on the intelligence tests are shown. Doubtless the most impressive feature of the comparisons afforded in Table 3 is the amount of overlap between the distributions from the two schools. (Note however that we cannot assume that the amount of overlap is in any way proportional to the difference between medians.) This is the kind of situation that will be found generally in distributions of test data.

The distributions of achievement test scores for the same "high" and "low" schools are shown in Table 4. Here again the amount of overlap is

TABLE 4

Distribution of Achievement Test Results for the
Third-Grade Classes Having the Highest and
Lowest Median I.Q.'s in One City *

Grade Equivalent	Achievement			
	Paragraph Meaning		Arithmetic Problems	
	Lowest	Highest	Lowest	Highest
7.4–7.7		1		
7.0–7.3				
6.6–6.9		1		
6.2–6.5				
5.8–6.1	1	1		
5.4–5.7		1		
5.0–5.3	2	4		
4.6–4.9	3	1		
4.2–4.5	1	2		
3.8–4.1	2	1		1
3.4–3.7	2	11	4	4
3.0–3.3	4	2	8	12
2.6–2.9	3	3	10	15
2.2–2.5	6	2	3	1
1.8–2.1	1	3		
Total	25	33	25	33
Median	3.2	3.6	2.9	3.0

**The same two schools providing data for Table 3.*

the most distinctive characteristic of the table. Differences between central tendencies are worth noting but they do not tell us everything we should know.

STUDY OF INDIVIDUALS

Whatever use is made of group data for intergroup comparisons, their major use should be in helping teachers understand and evaluate individual pupils. Here again it may turn out that the results raise more questions than they answer, but it is better to have questions unanswered than unasked.

In Table 5 we have intelligence and achievement test results for five pupils from one of the schools represented in Table 2. Facts and hypotheses that may be gained from inspection of an individual's scores will be illustrated by giving attention to the scores made by each of these fifth-grade pupils.

TABLE 5

Intelligence and Achievement Test Scores for Five
Pupils from a Fifth-Grade Class

	Amos	Hilda	Pupils Rosie	Jerry	Fred
Chronological Age	11–6	10–10	10–3	10–11	10–1
Grade Placement	5.2	5.2	5.2	5.2	5.2
Intelligence Quotient					
Picture Content	86	113	90	122	93
Reading Content	58	82	120	125	92
Grade Equivalents					
Paragraph Meaning	2.8	3.9	7.1	9.0	4.1
Word Meaning	2.4	4.8	6.5	8.0	3.9
Spelling	2.3	5.5	7.5	7.0	3.7
Language	1.3	3.8	8.9	6.2	5.1
Arithmetic Reasoning	2.2	4.6	5.5	7.1	4.9
Arithmetic Problems	3.6	3.7	5.3	6.0	4.5
Social Studies	4.0	4.7	5.1	6.5	4.4
Science	1.2	2.0	8.0	7.2	2.9
Study Skills	2.5	5.1	6.9	6.8	6.5

Amos, the oldest, is from one to four years retarded educationally. There is a marked discrepancy between the intelligence quotient based on picture content and that based on reading content so that it is very likely that he has marked deficiency in reading. In view of his age, and the fact that he was born in April, it is likely that he has repeated one grade. He may very well enter any test situation with an expectation of doing poorly so that it is possible that the performance represented by the reading-content quotient was not optimal. Note too that he did relatively well on arithmetic computation, a performance inconsistent with a quotient of only 58. His low reading and language test scores are consistent with the low reading content quotient however. The relatively high score in social studies is not readily explained, but it might be that the teacher gives greater emphasis to these topics, or that they are taught in ways that permit Amos to learn without doing much reading. His very low score on the science test may also be a reflection of the teacher's emphasis or methods.

Hilda's intelligence quotients show the same kind of discrepancy as do those of Amos and the discrepancy is even greater. However, there is every indication that she is brighter than Amos since she earned a picture-content quotient of 113. She is indeed retarded in reading but her retardation is greater in paragraph meaning than in word meaning. In view of her spelling score, it is possible that she is quite good in word recognition. She too made a markedly low score on the science test. It is likely that she would explain this by saying that she is not interested in science, which may well be true, but this does not explain how she came to be disinterested.

Rosie is clearly a bright girl, as indicated by the reading-content quotient. Here there is a quotient discrepancy that may be difficult to explain. Her achievement is good but it does not appear to be commensurate with her ability, at least in some subjects. She does relatively poorly in arithmetic and social studies.

Jerry is clearly a bright youngster. The fact that he has not scored as high on some of the subtests as on others may be due in part to a limited range of difficulty in the subtests. (This may be a factor responsible for some of Rosie's relatively lower scores.)

Fred appears to be of low-average ability and he is educationally retarded.

By no means all of the cues and questions latent in the scores of these five youngsters have been noted but a start has been made. In actual practice it would be possible to supplement these test results with information obtained from the teacher, the cumulative record, and additional testing. Personality factors and the existence of emotional disturbance must be considered as possibly associated with school achievement at any level.

The earlier in the child's school life such irregularities in achievement as have just been noted are investigated the more likely it is that the child's potentialities will be realized. Such investigations may well constitute a major part of the psychologist's work. Let us turn now to some generally desirable practices in making use of group test results.

When we have a pupil's score on a group intelligence test, or tests, we should first ask whether anything entered into the production of the score that kept it from being higher than it is. This question should not only be asked for those scoring low, but for those scoring at any level.[16]

When considering the results of a group intelligence test the accuracy

[16] High-scoring pupils are usually assumed to have manifested maximum performance. However, many tests, both intelligence and achievement, do not reveal the highest degrees nor diverse kinds of performance possible for some youngsters. (See C. E. Meyers, "The Role of Educational Measurement in Stimulating or Discouraging Attention to Creative Thinking in the Curriculum," APA Symposium, Chicago, 1960, mimeo.) Furthermore, feelings of defeat, frustration, and inadequacy that hamper optimum performance are often present among the gifted.

of scoring, correctness of the chronological age computation, and proper conversion of the raw score to a mental age or deviation I.Q. should be checked first. The possible influence of reading disability or of sensory or motor disabilities must be considered. Test anxiety or deeper and more persistent and pervasive anxiety can cause a reduction of tests scores, either intelligence or achievement.[17] All material in the school record and information from teachers and other observers about nontest behavior must be considered. Certainly any previous group intelligence test results that may be found in the teacher's cumulative record deserve special attention.

An achievement test result must first be evaluated in relation to intelligence. In some cases the group intelligence score will need to be supplemented by an individual intelligence examination, but in any case the question is whether the achievement score is in line with expectation. When the achievement score is higher than one would expect, it may be that there are exceptional and special reasons for superior achievement in a restricted area or that for some special reason the intelligence test results are too low. Sometimes extraordinary effort may be the major factor. When the achievement score is lower than expectation, the pupil's attitude toward the particular subject, his prior educational experiences, or some special disability affecting this subject particularly are more likely possibilities.

Achievement in any area must not only be evaluated in relation to intelligence, but also in relation to achievement in other areas. A child with a low reading score who is not intellectually slow will often show a notably superior score in arithmetic computation. With older youth a defeatist attitude toward various subjects, typically mathematics, English, or physical science, may be chiefly responsible for low achievement. The source of these attitudes is sometimes difficult to discover, having developed gradually over many years.

The poor student in mathematics may have developed a defeatist attitude toward the subject as a result of lack of skill in simple computation. He does not recognize that it is simply his inability to respond quickly to addition or multiplication combinations that is causing him to be "poor in math." Once such a source of difficulty is recognized, drill sessions can produce marked improvement.

Any poor achievement calls for an analysis of erroneous responses. This may be begun by making an analysis of the errors found in the group test results. Sometimes a low score on a subtest may be due to failure on all of a particular type of item. In computation it may be found that all items involving percentage are missed. Attention to spelling words missed may indicate special kinds of difficulty. Such findings from an achievement test should not be viewed conclusively, but they should suggest the direction in

[17] See Seymour B. Sarason et al., *Anxiety in Elementary School Children* (New York: John Wiley & Sons, Inc., 1960), especially Chap. 10.

which further investigation should go. In some subjects there are analytical tests, especially designed for precise identification of kinds of errors.[18]

Interest inventory results must be interpreted in relation to intelligence, achievement, and personality traits and, what is most difficult of all to determine, basic needs. In connection with the latter the nature of the youngster's personal identification is important. The boy who has strongly identified with a person who is a mechanic may be influenced in his personal preferences as revealed on interest inventories. Whether this has happened in a particular case and whether inventory results have been influenced will be difficult to ascertain, but this and similar possibilities must not be overlooked. Apparent inconsistencies between measured interests and subject matter or out-of-school interests should be noted. Further investigation may reveal that apparent inconsistencies are not real. Special care should be taken to avoid being too definitive in interpreting results. The special limitations of the particular interest inventory must be well understood and allowed for.

Conclusions drawn from personality inventories are probably the most tenuous of any that may be drawn from measuring devices. This applies both to the adjustment and trait inventories. Nevertheless, results may be highly useful in working with an individual. One of the major uses to be made of an adjustment inventory is not the score, though what the score indicates about relative standing is worth noting. Most can be gained by inspection of the items checked in the unfavorable way. Time spent in reflecting upon the possibilities suggested by these items may be very worthwhile. How worthwhile will depend upon the background of training and experience in the area of adjustment problems of the person doing the reflecting.

The psychologist may assist teachers in evaluating individual pupil results and thus help individual learners indirectly. Often such collaboration between the teacher and the psychologist will result in a decision that direct study of the child by the psychologist is necessary. Individual intelligence testing, projective testing, analysis of learning disabilities, and, in the case of younger children, interviewing parents are the principal procedures the psychologist will use for furthering diagnosis.

By diagnosis we mean an understanding of the factors responsible for the behavior that now concerns us. Affixing a label to the child may be using an abbreviated code for the diagnosis but the code word or phrase is not the diagnosis. Such code phrases as retarded, withdrawn, gifted, educationally advanced may be necessary for annual report tabulations, but their use elsewhere should be avoided. Use of such words and phrases encourages lazy

---

[18] Analytic tests are perhaps more commonly known as diagnostic tests and may be so listed in publisher's catalogs. However, diagnosis is done by the person who uses the test and may involve data obtained from any test. Analytic test items are such as to make possible the precise identification of pupils' errors.

and stereotyped thinking and acting about and toward youngsters. A diagnosis reveals rather than conceals individuality.[19]

The Program of Group Appraisal

"What kind of a testing program do you have?" is a question one school superintendent or principal may ask another. How sound an educator such a questioner is could be clarified to some extent by knowing what he means by the question. If all the question means is what tests are given and when, the administrator does not see the full significance of testing. If, however, he wants to know how group appraisal methods are used to evaluate educational objectives he sees group appraisal procedures in their proper prospective. There must be a clear recognition of why testing is done if such testing is not to become a burdensome routine.

EXTENT OF THE GROUP APPRAISAL PROGRAM

The first consideration in deciding how extensive a program of group appraisal shall be is how extensively the results will be used. The National Defense Education Act and the Elementary and Secondary Act of 1965 provided impetus for more extensive testing, and committees of professional organizations devoted time to question of what additional testing should be done. For schools in which little or no plan of evaluation of the program or of individuals existed this was a worthy issue. However, in most schools the important question is how can the test results we now have be used more fully? The school psychologist, in conferences with teachers and administrators, should be able to show how test results can be used most fully. The added insights gained from an understanding use of test results will make an extension of the program desired rather than dreaded.

Whatever the extent of the formal testing program, it should not be relied upon to provide all the evidence on which evaluation of the school's program is based. Anecdotal material and sociograms are but examples of additional evidence useful in appraisal. It is only out of this realization that a well-balanced program can be developed. Some educational objectives are more important than others, but limited attention to certain ones should not lead to situations that are inimical to the development of the less important ones.

MINIMAL GROUP TESTING

Group appraisal of intelligence and achievement constitutes a minimum for any school system. Appraisal of intelligence is necessary to permit

[19] See Stanley S. Marzolf, *Psychological Diagnosis and Counseling in the Schools* (New York: Holt, Rinehart & Winston, Inc., 1956), Chap. 7.

diffierential educational planning for individuals. Knowledge of intelligence level is also necessary for proper evaluation of learning progress. These two kinds of tests are used quite extensively but it is doubtful whether anywhere nearly full value from their use is gained in many schools.

Before a more extensive program of testing is undertaken there are certain practices that should be regularly carried on. The following uses should be routine:

1. Preparation of frequency distributions by grades for each school and for all schools combined, for each test.
2. Investigation of low scores on the intelligence test.
3. Investigation of all low scores on all achievement tests.
4. Make item analyses of achievement tests to determine what kinds of instructional tasks have been well or poorly done.
5. Arrange for remedial assistance for those found to be in need of it. Make referrals to the school psychologist of those for whom an explanation of test results is obscure.
6. Make provision for continued optimal educational opportunity for those of superior ability who are achieving well and make careful investigation of those with superior ability who show relatively inferior achievement.
7. Note significant findings that may have influenced the learning of all pupils, not just those who have been studied as a consequence of the above investigations.

Any school system that regularly carries out the above procedures, even to a minimal degree, will be doing more than is customary.

It is too much to expect that all of these recommendations should be carried out before any additional group appraisal is undertaken. Some of the recommendations can be carried out minimally or intensively, and it may be that not all of them need be carried out every year or in all schools in any one year. It is likely that once the recommended minimal investigations have been undertaken, the effect will be to cause teachers and administrators to want more extensive appraisal. Whenever such feeling of need arises is the time to begin.

Suggestions for a Group Appraisal Schedule

It is difficult to outline the ideal group appraisal program because there are local conditions, varieties of school organization, and variations in professional personnel that must be taken into account. The existence of considerable agreement about what should be the common learnings makes planning a program for the elementary grades easier than for the high school. Nevertheless, changes have taken place that make the problem of appraisal in the elementary school more complicated than formerly. Foreign language is being taught in many elementary schools today. Algebra is begun at an earlier age than was once thought possible, and the amount of physical and biological science taught in the elementary school is increasing. The new math has been introduced in many systems in the elementary school while at the high school level there are marked changes in the content of mathematics courses. All changes in the curriculum must be reflected in the nature of the appraisal of achievement.[20] Increased emphasis upon the importance of creativity has not only raised questions about existing evaluative instruments, but has also shown a need for new ones.[21] Metfessel discusses instruments for the appraisal of creativity in Chapter 20. Thus it is that the suggestions which follow must be viewed as provisional guides only.

READINESS TESTS

Learning readiness, as determined by readiness tests, should be given as early in the first grade as the children have become acclimated to the teacher and the group situation. When this will be will depend in part on whether the children have had prior nursery school or kindergarten experience. Existing readiness tests are closely related to general intelligence tests but are especially designed to predict success in reading and number work. The question of readiness and the use of tests for evaluating it will doubtless increase due to the impetus provided by Project Head Start, an outgrowth of the Economic Opportunities Act of 1964.

INTELLIGENCE TESTS

A group intelligence test should be given early in the second year, and may be given at the end of the first grade. The group intelligence tests available for this level naturally do not require reading but are rather of the "picture content" variety. There are a number from which to choose.

A second administration of a group intelligence test should be given in the fourth or fifth grade. One factor determining in which of the two grades the test should be given is whether there is a junior high school. In

---

[20] On the relation of measurement to the curriculum see D. C. Adkins, "Measurement in Relation to the Educational Process," *Educational and Psychological Measurement,* 18 (Autumn, 1958), 221–240; and Paul L. Dressel, "Measurement and Evaluation of Instructional Objectives," *The 17th Yearbook, National Council on Measurements Used in Education,* 1960 (Ames, Iowa: The Council, 1960); and Warren J. Findley, ed., *The Impact and Improvement of School Testing Programs* (Chicago: University of Chicago Press, 1963).

[21] For research relative to new and recent tests see J. P. Guilford, Benjamin Fructer, and H. Paul Kelley, "Development and Applications of Tests of Intellectual and Special Aptitudes," *Review of Educational Research,* 29 (February, 1959), 26–41.

case there is a junior high school it would be better to give the test in the fourth grade, preferably near the end of the first semester. If there is no junior high school the test can be given some time during the fifth grade. Tests suitable for this level usually involve reading, but it would be best to use a test that has a "picture content" or nonverbal part, yielding a separate score, as well as a verbal part.

If there is a junior high school, and a test has been given at about the middle of the fourth year, a group intelligence test may be given near the end of the sixth grade. These results can then be used in planning the youngster's educational program in junior high school. If there is no junior high school, the immediately prior test having been given in the fifth grade, a test may be given toward the end of the eighth grade, so that the results may be used for planning the high school program. Here again it is desirable to use a test having both a verbal and a nonverbal part. It may be desirable, if there is reason to believe proper use will be made of the results, to give a multifactor aptitude test.[22] Such a test may be especially helpful in educational planning, though caution against drawing definitive conclusions is very necessary.

Intelligence testing to be done during high school, or following junior high school, during the senior high school period, is more difficult to recommend. A state high school testing program in which juniors participate will suffice, but if there is no such program it may be best to repeat the multifactor test that may have been given earlier. Such results will reveal intraindividual differences in aptitudes and can be useful for further educational and vocational planning.

Recently the use of group intelligence tests was discontinued in New York City on the grounds that group test results are unreliable and that teachers, once they knew a child's I.Q., used it as a limiting definition of the child's potential.[23] These charges can no doubt be supported by some, and even in some instances, considerable evidence. However, there is no assurance that the errors associated with the use of group tests of intelligence will be avoided when group achievement tests are used, nor that teachers who formerly used the I.Q. as a limiting definition of potential will not now use achievement scores as indicators of intelligence. The only assurance of minimal error in any kind of assessment is maximal attention to, and avoidance of, sources of error in both the administration and interpretation of tests.

[22] For an evaluation of multifactor tests see American Personnel and Guidance Journal, *The Use of Multifactor Tests* (Washington, D.C.: The Association, 1957). This is a single-volume publication of a series of reviews which appeared in the journal—an invaluable reference on this topic.

[23] Joseph O. Loretan, "The Discontinuance of the Administration of Group IQ Tests," The Bulletin of the National Association of Secondary School Principals, **49** (January, 1965), 70 ff.

ACHIEVEMENT TESTS

An achievement test battery should be given at least once every year beginning with the end of the first grade. After the first grade there is a question of whether the battery should be given near the beginning of the school year, or near the end of the year, or at both times. If a real effort is made to use the results and if conditions creating undue anxiety in the pupils are avoided, it would be desirable to give the tests at both the beginning and the end of the year. If only one test is given each year the choice of time for giving it will probably depend upon whether the teachers make better use of knowledge about where pupils begin or about where they are at the end of the year.

At the junior and senior high school levels tests other than the usual achievement battery will be used. Single tests for each of the great variety of high school subjects are available, but special care is needed in selecting tests that appraise the objectives of a particular course. For example, a French test that evaluates achievement in written expression should not be used in a school where the major emphasis is upon conversational French.

High school tests of the basic skills are available and should be used with all high school students. How often such tests are given will depend upon what is done as a consequence of the results obtained on any one administration. If corrective steps are provided for needed special help, then annual use may be worthwhile.

PERSONALITY INVENTORIES

Adjustment inventories may be given even in the lower grades, but since reading ability is required, some provision must be made for those in a grade whose reading skill may not be sufficient for the inventory. However, where teachers more or less regularly do sociometric studies, the adjustment inventories will be less necessary. They may be used with particular pupils if care is taken to prevent the child from being made conspicuous by having to fill out the inventory.

Personality trait inventories may be used in the upper grades and in high school, chiefly for use in educational and vocational planning. The youngsters will want to know the results, and doubtless they should know them. However it is difficult to interpret the results of such inventories so that they will be correctly understood. A more serious objection to their use is their low validity; for many of those available it is not clear to anyone what they mean.

During recent years there has been considerable public criticism of tests and testing, especially personality assessment. Some of the criticisms have been extreme and unreasonable, but many have been justified. These latter criticisms are not really directed toward the tests and inventories, but rather are complaints about the use to which assessment techniques are put and the manner in which results are interpreted. Some instances of misuse are the result of ignorance of the limitations of evaluative instruments and of the cautions which must be exercised in interpretation of results. Other instances are clearly the result of thoughtless, or even intentional, disregard of human rights, notably the right of privacy. The school psychologist must ever be aware that any misuse of a psychological device is harmful to the individual child or youth involved and to the psychological profession as a whole.[24]

INTEREST INVENTORIES

Interest inventories are available for use from the fourth-grade level on up. Great care must be exercised in interpreting results, especially in making inferences about their vocational significance. Where the more precise occupational inventories are used, showing the individual's similarity to those in a particular occupation, school-wide use is inadvisable for reasons already discussed.

APTITUDE TESTS

Various kinds of vocational and educational aptitude tests should be available for use with specially selected groups of students in connection with educational and vocational planning.

SUPPLEMENTARY TESTS

When budgeting for the group appraisal program, funds for the purchase of analytical tests should be set aside so that when achievement test results indicate the need for such tests they will be available.

Selected Supplementary List of Educational Achievement Tests

The Ohio Inter-University Council on School Psychology Committee on Internship [25] suggest that the beginning school psychologist should gain familiarity with the following educational achievement tests. (With the passage of time, other tests will need to be added to this list.)

---

[24] See the *American Psychologist*, 20 (February, 1965), 20 (November, 1965), and 21 (May, 1966). These issues are devoted, entirely or in major part, to public inquiry into testing practices and to the associated professional and ethical responsibilities of psychologists.

[25] S. J. Bonham, H. Bradshaw, J. Horrocks, Alma W. Jones and D. C. Smith, *The Internship Program in School Psychology* (Columbus, Ohio: Ohio State University, 1962, mimeographed) p. 7.

Gray Oral Reading Paragraphs.
Wide Range Achievement Test.
Stanford, Metropolitan and California Achievement Tests.
Durrell Reading Capacity Test.
Gates Reading Survey.
Iowa Tests of Educational Development.
SRA Achievement Series.
Gates, Lee-Clark, Harrison-Stroud, and Metropolitan Reading Readiness Tests.
Murphy-Durrell Diagnostic Reading Readiness Test.
Gates Reading Diagnostic Tests.
Durrell Analysis of Reading Difficulty.
Monroe Diagnostic Reading Examination.
Woody-McCall Arithmetic Fundamentals Test.
Brueckner Arithmetic Diagnostic Tests.
Buswell-John Diagnostic Tests of Arithmetic.

Selected Principles of Testing
for School Psychological Services Workers *

1. Only persons with competencies in testing methods and procedures should be responsible for the local school district's testing program.

2. Tests are used primarily for instruction, counseling, and placement of students. Public relations and administrative evaluation of staff and school are less desirable uses.

3. School districts should develop operational criteria to meet local needs for the selection of tests to insure continuity over the years.

4. When tests have been formally selected and used, local normative data should be accumulated to supplement publisher norms whenever possible.

5. Test authors and publishers should be held responsible for presenting adequate and accurate data in test manuals regarding the construction validity, use of a test, and possible limitations.

6. The aims and purposes set out as a basis for the development of

* Edited from the list prepared by the California Association of School Psychologists and Psychometrists, 1962.

the scales should correspond with the aims and purposes of the particular school district.

7. Tests are only one of several psychological services tools. Overly precise interpretations should be avoided due to common technical errors in measurement, i. e.:

    a. The influence of the "probable error" of group tests (especially strong in achievement tests of spelling and mechanics of grammar).

    b. The influence of differences in chronological age of students within the same classroom or grade on "intelligence" and achievement test scores.

    c. The influence of intelligence differences among students within the same classroom or grade on achievement.

    d. Significant score differences associated with sex membership (primarily in spelling, mechanics of English and grammar, and mathematics).

    e. Differences between the standardizing population used by the test publishers and local students (to be handled with local norms).

    f. Influence of differences in cultural background within the same grade or classroom.

    g. Necessity to compare achievement with intelligence—"under-achievement," etc.

    h. Differences in physical maturity of students (vision, hearing, co-ordination, etc.).

8. The test selected must be sufficiently extensive and its component items well chosen to yield a trustworthy or stable total score.

9. Tests should be scheduled to permit longest valid use with students that is possible.

10. Favorable teacher attitudes should be administratively encouraged by:
    a. Inservice training readministration.
    b. Use of clerical help or machines to score tests.
    c. Supportive assistance in proper interpretation.
    d. Taking minimal time from class for testing.

11. Instruction for administering and scoring should be followed implicitly and precisely.

12. Test interpretation should be intelligible and useful to parents, students and teachers.

Selected Supplementary Readings

Adams, Georgia S., and Theodore L. Torgerson, *Measurement and Evaluation in Educational Psychology and Guidance*. New York: Holt, Rinehart & Winston, Inc., 1964.

American Psychological Association, *Standards for Educational and Psychological Tests and Manuals*. Washington, D.C.: 1966.

Anastasi, Anne, *Psychological Testing* (2nd ed.). New York: The Macmillan Company, 1961.

Baker, Harry J., "Group Intelligence Examinations," in *Professional School Psychology*, I, ed. M. G. and G. B. Gottsegen. New York: Grune & Stratton, Inc., 1960, pp. 90–99.

Barnette, W. Leslie, ed., *Readings in Psychological Tests and Measurements*. Homewood, Ill.: Dorsey Press, 1964.

Bauernfind, Robert H., *Building a School Testing Program*. Boston: Houghton Mifflin Company, 1963.

Berdie, Ralph F., Wilbur L. Layton, and O. Theda Haganah, *Testing in Guidance and Counseling*. New York: McGraw-Hill Book Company, 1963.

Buros, O. K., ed., *The Sixth Mental Measurements Yearbook*. Highland Park, N.J.: Gryphon Press, 1965.

Chase, C. I., and H. G. Ludlow, eds., *Readings in Educational and Psychological Measurement*. Boston: Houghton Mifflin Company, 1966.

Chauncey, Henry, and John E. Dobbin, *Testing: Its Place in Education Today*. New York: Harper & Row, Publishers, 1963.

Cronbach, L. J., *Essentials of Psychological Testing* (2nd ed.). New York: Harper & Row, Publishers, 1960.

Davis, F. B., *Educational Measurements and Their Interpretations*. Belmont, Calif.: Wadsworth Publishing Co., 1964.

DuBois, Philip H., and Edward V. Hackett, eds., *The Measurement and Evaluation of Over-and Underachievement*. St. Louis: Washington University, 1963.

Ebel, Robert L., *Measuring Educational Achievement*. Englewood Cliffs, N.J.: Prentice-Hall, Inc., 1965.

————, *Proceedings of the 1965 Invitational Conference on Testing Problems*. Princeton, N.J.: Educational Testing Service, 1966.

Eiserer, Paul E., "Assessment Roles," in *The School Psychologist*. Washington, D.C.: The Center for Applied Research in Education, Inc., 1963, pp. 20–41.

Freeman, Frank S., *Theory and Practice of Psychological Testing* (3rd ed.). New York: Holt, Rinehart & Winston, Inc., 1962.

Gerberich, J. R., A. N. Jorgensen, and H. A. Greene, *Measurement and Evaluation in the Modern School*. New York: David McKay Co., Inc., 1962.

Ghiselli, Edwin, *Theory of Psychological Measurements*. New York: McGraw-Hill Book Company, 1964.

Gronlund, N. E., *Measurement and Evaluation in Teaching*. New York: The Macmillan Company, 1965.

Hawes, G. R., *Educational Testing for the Millions*. New York: McGraw-Hill Book Company, 1964.

Horst, P., *Psychological Measurement and Prediction*. Belmont, Calif.: Wadsworth Publishing Co., 1966.

Loretan, J. O., "The Decline and Fall of Group Intelligence Testing," *Teachers College Record*, 67 (October, 1965), 10–17.

Lyman, Howard B., *Test Scores and What They Mean*. Englewood Cliffs, N.J.: Prentice-Hall, Inc., 1963.

Mowers, G. E., "Using Tape-recorded Instructions to Administer Standardized Tests," *Journal of School Psychology*, 23 (Spring, 1965), 62–65.

Review of Educational Research, entire issue, educational and psychological testing, 35 (February, 1965).

Stanley, J. S., *Measurement in Today's Schools*. Englewood Cliffs, N.J.: Prentice-Hall, Inc., 1964.

Thorndike, R. L., and E. Hagen, *Measurement and Evaluation in Psychology and Education* (2nd ed.). New York: John Wiley & Sons, Inc., 1961.

Tyler, R. W, "A Program of National Assessment," *Educational Forum*, 30 (May, 1966), 391–396.

Tyler, Leona, *Tests and Measurements*. Englewood Cliffs, N.J.: Prentice-Hall, Inc., 1963.

Valett, Robert E., "The Assessment of Educational Achievement," in *The Practice of School Psychology*. New York: John Wiley & Sons, Inc., 1963, pp. 153–172.

Womer, Frank B., and Willard B. Frick, *Personalizing Test Use: A Counselor's Casebook*. Ann Arbor: University of Michigan Press, 1962.

DONALD A. LETON

LOUIS G. SCHMIDT

8

Case Studies and the Case Conference

This chapter will discuss some of the theoretical and methodological problems that confront the school psychologist in conducting case studies. The case study is the major vehicle for the school psychologist's services and therefore it is often evaluated as his contribution to the schools' services. Unfortunately, many school psychologists have not been adequately trained to make psychological and educational diagnoses, and others have regarded the administration of an individual intelligence test as the sum and the substance of the case study. Both of these situations have led to a general devaluation of the psychologist's role in education.

In conducting a case study, the psychologist is faced with several responsibilities that he shares with the teacher and other guidance staff members who work with the pupil. First, he must attempt to understand, and to conceptualize the pupil's problem in a meaningful way; secondly, he must communicate his findings to extend the teacher's and the pupil's understanding of the problem; and finally, he should aid the teacher and the pupil toward the resolution of the problems so they are able to carry out the necessary transactions of teaching and learning. In spite of the recent advances in automated instruction, and refinements in the field of tests and measurement, there is no single comprehensive instrument that can assess the complexities of the learner as he functions, and as he perhaps struggles, in the school setting. This is the task of the case study.

Case Study and Case History

The terms "case study" and "case history" are frequently used interchangeably, although in fact they signify two distinct and separate approaches.[1] The case history is a chronological presentation of life experiences of the individual up to the present time. No attempt is made to interpret the data nor to identify the highlights and symptoms usually brought into focus. Criteria for the content of life history records have been presented by Dollard.[2] If the school maintains a complete cumulative record system, the school psychologist has this basis for a continuous and up-to-date history for each pupil. The case history, then, is limited to the collection of as much data from as extensive a number of sources as possible about the individual under study. Although much of the case history is clinical in nature, a good case history forms the basis for the development of the case study.

The case study is a report of an intensive investigation of all of the important aspects of a student's behavior and functioning. Selected life history data is incorporated in the case study to the extent that it contributes to an understanding of the present problem or adjustment. Unlike the case history, the case study provides a synthesis and interpretation of the information about the student, his relationship to his environment, his social relationships, and emotional interactions. The case study is not a tool or technique in counseling, but rather a vehicle for the utilization and interpretation of the tools and techniques used by the school counselor or psychologist. Through case study procedures, a personality picture of the counselee is developed that becomes clearer and more life-like as each new bit of information is added.

Preliminary Conditions

The emphasis in this chapter will be on the procedures involved in case studies rather than on their content. Since the case study is itself an interaction between procedures and a problem, the content of the study

[1] Jane Warters, *Techniques of Counseling*, 2nd ed. (New York: McGraw-Hill Book Company, 1964).

[2] John Dollard, *Criteria for the Life History* (New Haven: Yale University Press, 1935), pp. 13–36.

becomes evident in the interaction. There are three conditions that are essential to carrying out a case study. The first of these is a common recognition of a problem; the second is a knowledge about the areas in which the problem exists; and the third is the establishment of tentative hypotheses about the causes and the correlates of the problem.

The first of these conditions is just as important as the others, since the successful completion of a study requires an agreement about what constitutes a problem. If the psychologist does not recognize or acknowledge the problem as it is referred, then he may not make the kind of analysis appropriate for the case. It is not only important that the school psychologist recognize the problem as it is presented, but also that he has an appreciation of the manifestation of the problem in the school setting. In this common recognition it is essential that the school psychologist perceive the problem as the teacher perceives it, and that he also identify with the pupil in his experiences with the problem. If the psychologist is professionally identified with the goals of the school and with the aims of the teacher, then his recognition of pupil problems is somewhat assured.

The problems referred to the school psychologist can be generally categorized as developmental or behavioral, with specific types of learning and adjustment difficulties. In order to be discriminating in the analysis of these problems, the school psychologist must have some knowledge and experience in relation to them. An understanding of classroom procedures and teaching variables is an important prerequisite to the analysis of pupil problems. Beyond this, however, the psychologist proceeds on the basis of his professional skills in psychometry, and with logical deductions about cause and effect relationships. It is obvious then that the professional identification and knowledge about education will not suffice for psychological case studies. In order to satisfy this second condition, the psychologist must have acquired scientific knowledge about learning, behavior, and development from his study of psychology.[3] The adequacy with which he can satisfy this second condition determines the degree of success he will achieve in dealing with school problems.

The third condition, that of tentative hypotheses about the causes and correlates of the problem, also represents a preliminary step toward its solution. The hypotheses that underlie case studies actually serve as a guide for case procedures. At the outset of a case study, the hypotheses would certainly be tentative and only vaguely formulated, but without them the psychologist would be unable to proceed. Case study hypotheses should not be implicit in the procedures, but should rather be explicit to determine the procedures to be followed in conducting the study. The ability of the school

[3] Norma Cutts, *School Psychologists at Mid-Century* (Washington, D.C.: American Psychological Association, 1955), pp. 113–118.

psychologist to establish hypotheses is obviously dependent on the previous conditions. The formulation of case study hypotheses should be regarded both as a preliminary condition and as a continuous procedure.

There may be a methodological difference between the preliminary and the procedural hypotheses; however, the same principles apply to both. First, these hypotheses should be rooted in the child's problem; secondly, they should require factual and relevant information for proof or disproof. All the data that are gathered in a case study should be directed toward the confirmation or refutation of case hypotheses. The data that are not derived for the formulation of hypotheses, or for their resolution, have little or no value for understanding the child's problem.

Case Procedures

The product of the case study and the nature of the psychological report has sometimes assumed a preliminary importance to the student or to the beginning psychologist. Some psychologists have also presumed that they have a special responsibility to produce a diagnostic classification of a child to meet the expectancy of the educator, psychiatrist, teacher or parent. The psychologists who approach case studies with this view soon become guilty of "slot thinking," and tend to fit all of the case data into preconceived pigeonholes. Their repertoire of diagnostic categories may even be limited to a few classical terms such as mentally retarded, anxiety-neurotic, compulsive, and so forth. Others will bring a few stereotyped procedures and phrases from their clinical training to suit their case studies.[4]

In the school psychology situation, the use of such classifications as learning "block," adolescent personality, reading disability, emotionally disturbed, and slow learner provides little or no help to the teacher or parent. A school psychologist may actually resort to such terms as a facade to cover his lack of understanding of the causes and the dynamics of the problem. The psychologist who views the psychological report as the important product of his case study tends to place the end before the means. He will usually conclude a case study far short of the responsibility which he should assume.

The procedures of a case study can be formulated into a number of steps. These steps are referral and pre-study inquiry, case study hypotheses, selection of tests and other approaches, administration of tests, observations and interviews, report of interpretations, conclusions, recommendations, and assistance to the pupil, teacher, or parents to effect a solution to the problem. In the remainder of the discussion on case studies, these steps will be analyzed in detail.

[4] Frederick C. Thorne, *Errors in Clinical Judgment* (Brandon, Vermont: Journal of Clinical Psychology, 1961).

Referral and Pre-study Inquiry

The referral action varies a great deal from one school to another. In some situations, the referral action is merely the addition of the pupil's name to a waiting list for an individual intelligence examination. In other situations, the teacher or counselor may actually carry out a preliminary study as part of the referral process. The child study procedures evolved by Prescott [5] are highly recommended for this purpose. In most school systems, the assemblage of background information by the teacher, principal, or counselor is part of the referral process. The referral and the pre-study inquiry together comprise the first step in the case study because they represent the initial collection of data. In addition to the referral information, the psychologist may also consult the cumulative records, and confer with the teacher, counselor, school nurse, or other personnel to obtain further background information.

The major purpose of the pre-study inquiry is that the school psychologist will be sufficiently informed about the manifestation of the child's problem before proceeding with the analysis. This information is necessary for two reasons: first, to formulate the hypotheses from which the study will proceed; and second, to direct the observations and the choice of tests so that the study can be carried out efficiently.

The referral problem as described by the teacher, parent, or other referent may actually represent the psychological problem. On the other hand, the teacher or parent may be describing symptomatic behavior, and the psychologist should deliberate various possible causes in the pre-study. In the pre-study the psychologist attempts to identify the factors which will require study and to associate a tentative significance to certain referral information.

Case Study Hypotheses

Although a number of writers [6, 7, 8, 9, 10] refer to the use of hypotheses in case studies, the crucial role which hypotheses assume in the success of a

[5] Daniel A. Prescott, The Child in the Educative Process (McGraw-Hill Book Company, 1957).

[6] Frederick C. Thorne, Principles of Psychological Examining (Brandon, Vermont: Journal of Clinical Psychology, 1955), p. 31.

[7] Norman D. Sundberg and Leona E. Tyler, Clinical Psychology (New York: Appleton-Century-Crofts, Meridith Publishing Co., 1962), p. 84.

[8] Edward S. Bordin, Psychological Counseling (New York: Appleton-Century-Crofts, 1955), p. 125.

[9] Milton Hahn and Malcolm S. MacLean, Counseling Psychology (New York: McGraw-Hill Book Company, 1955), p. 26.

[10] Paul Pigors and Faith Pigors, Case Method in Human Relations: The Incident Process (New York, 1961).

study is generally not recognized. The validity of findings in any case study, however, is always a function of the hypotheses on which they are based. In formulating hypotheses, it is first necessary to have some perception of the personal and the social significance of the problem. Secondly, it is important to consider which of the child's specific traits or behaviors may actually be causing or contributing to the problem. Thirdly, it is necessary to have a systematic understanding of how and why the traits have developed in the child's personality, and what their influence or expression may be in school behavior. Finally, it is necessary to relate the possible etiological factors to the problem as it is presently observed.

In order to formulate meaningful hypotheses, it is vital that the psychologist have a systematic knowledge of the types of factors or experiences which could be antecedent to the problem. The pivotal decision on the part of the psychologist is in discriminating what questions are important to investigate. Insofar as possible, the case hypotheses require objectivity by focussing on overt problems and relating these to specific antecedent causes or conditions. One of the difficulties in the analysis of pupils' problems is that information about antecedent conditions is not always available to the school psychologist. This should not, however, prevent his possible hypotheses, although it may certainly limit the confidence of findings or conclusions. Inferences based on unavailable data are not appropriate for case studies.

Selection of Tests and Other Approaches

The scientific value of the case study depends upon the reliability, validity, and the selectivity of all empirical data upon which it is based. When observational data, test findings, and interview information show consistencies and tend to corroborate each other, the conclusions and interpretations in the case study tend to be reliable. In order for case data to be valid, they must bear a direct relationship to the problem and its causes; they must reflect these accurately in the present situation; and finally, they should make possible certain predictions about future behavior.

In pointing out that observational data is an important type of case data, one should not presume that the school psychologist must make first-hand observations of the problem. There are several disadvantages which occur when the school psychologist assumes that responsibility. The first of these is in the expenditure of time. It would be both expensive and inefficient for the school psychologist to observe all the pupils referred, in the variety of situations in which their problems may be manifested. The teacher, who is skilled as a professional observer, will have the most opportunity to view the child's problem. Learning problems in particular will appear in various aspects of the curricula and in recurrent classroom situations from day to day. Since the pupil's problem may express itself in a variety of school situations there are other school personnel who may also have opportunity to observe it. Principals, counselors, school social workers, librarians, and supervisors all may observe certain aspects of the pupil's problem. It would not be economical, therefore, for the psychologist to conduct similar observations in these same settings.

One of the errors in conducting case studies is the assumption that a large sample of data must be gathered. A case study is not simply a collection of related and unrelated material about a pupil. The analysis of the child's problem requires an efficient search in background and developmental history and selectivity in the choice of tests for trait study.

The purpose of psychological tests in a case study is to give systematic and valid data in a concise form. Test data are always reported in relation to the norms established for other similar pupils. Data obtained from tests as well as through other approaches have no meaning until they are interpreted in the light of other information about the individual pupil and about the school group in which he performs. There has been an important theoretical issue in regard to the relative importance of test score data and life history data in the clinical study of personality. Allport's monograph [11] on the use of personal documents first brought the "idiographic versus nomothetic" controversy to the popular attention of behavioral scientists. Studies of individuals based on normative data, e.g. test norms, and seeking to predict behavior which is common to a group of individuals are illustrative of the nomothetic approach. Studies based on biographies and case histories, and that stress the uniqueness of the person, are defined as idiographic. Psychological case studies can also be viewed as containing both idiographic and nomothetic information. Psychologists in general are interested in the regularities in human behavior, formulating general principles for the prediction of behavior, and exploring interrelationships among variables in the light of developmental norms. In order to establish norms for the comparison of children, psychologists have generally followed a nomothetic approach. Major progress in psychology and in education has been concurrent with the nomothetic method. Advances in educational and vocational guidance, clinical and child psychology, have been contingent upon educational and psychological measurement. Nevertheless, Allport and other clinical theorists feel that this approach is not adequate for the understanding of the unique organization of experience in an individual personality. The value of personal documents, autobiographies, and diaries for the clinical analysis of personality is pointed out by Allport. For readers who are not familiar with this issue, the comprehensive review by Phillips [12] is recommended.

[11] Gordon W. Allport, *The Use of Personal Documents in Psychological Science* (New York: Social Science Research Council, 1951).

[12] E. Lakin Phillips, *Psychotherapy: A Modern Theory and Practice* (Englewood Cliffs, N. J.: Prentice-Hall, Inc., 1956), pp. 52–90.

In psychological case studies, the data obtained through idiographic and phenomenological approaches may have value for establishing the presence of certain traits or characteristics, for example pathological conditions or emotional states. The degree or intensity of any trait such as intelligence, interest, and achievement should be established through a nomothetic approach. The theoretical issue is primarily an academic question, and should not present any methodological problem in case studies for school psychology.

Phillips [13] points out that the dichotomy merely represents a procedural difference in the study of an individual rather than a methodological difference in scientific inference. The nomothetic and idiographic approaches are complementary, and both are utilized in the development of a case study.

An individual psychometric test is a partial model for the case study. The control of the environmental situation, the observation and the objective regard for behavior elicited by structured and unstructured stimuli are common elements in tests and in case studies. Whether psychologists use objective or projective tests, interviews, or observations, the validity of their information is the most important criterion. Concurrent validity is obtained within the case study when the findings correlate with independent findings in another area. Thus, the validity of certain intelligence test findings can be confirmed by the level of achievement which the child has attained. The validity of certain observations on the emotional adjustment of a child can be supported by independent information from his social adjustment or his emotional history.

Administration of Tests, Observations, and Interviews

Many teachers and parents conceive the school psychologist as a person with certain esoteric knowledge and with a mysterious set of tests that enable him to unravel the complexities of learning and adjustment problems. Some school psychologists may have fostered these impressions by making extensive interpretations from limited test evidence.

Other teachers and educators have conceived the function of school psychology as one of intelligence testing. A rather narrow conception of case studies in school psychology has evolved from this concept. The case studies in school psychology that are based on one, or even several intelligence tests, may never come to actual grips with problems in social and emotional adjustment. Because of his professional responsibility, the school psychologist should give first attention to the psychological variables that bear relevance to the problem. Regard for the physical, social, and emotional variables which may contribute to a learning or school behavior problem cannot be precluded because of a narrow definition of the school's educational purpose.

[13] *Ibid.*, p. 67.

An outline or guide to the areas that should receive investigation in a school case study is given below. A guide such as this should not be followed blindly or routinely for all cases. In conducting a case study, the psychologist selects the pertinent characteristics in the child, and the data from the entire school and social environments that confront the child. Because this is a selective operation for which no precise formulae are available, the guide for case studies can only present a number of topics and cues. The psychologist's work with a younger child may be guided more by the preliminary items in each area, whereas his study of older children and adolescents would be directed toward later aspects of development. Not all of the concepts or cues could pertain to a single case; and most psychologists would also elaborate in certain areas by considering further details.

OUTLINE FOR CASE STUDIES IN SCHOOL PSYCHOLOGY

I. Intelligence and Mental Development
   A. Performance
   B. Verbal
   C. Abstract

   1. Sensory-motor capacities: receptive abilities, coordination
   2. Perception: visual, auditory, kinaesthetic
   3. Memory: visual, auditory, kinaesthetic
   4. Association, meaning
   5. Comprehension
   6. Judgment, reasoning
   7. Abstraction, symbolization
   8. Ideation, intellectual creativity

II. Educational Development and Pupil Characteristics
   A. Reading: Oral and silent
      1. Word recognition
         Sight vocabulary
         Phonetic analyses and blending
         Context clues
      2. Sentence reading
         Fluency and inflection
         Rate
      3. Paragraph reading
         Comprehension
         Retention and recall
   B. Arithmetic
      1. Rote counting
      2. Enumeration
      3. Addition and subtraction
         Number combinations
         Column groupings
         Arithmetic processes
      4. Multiplication and division
         Number combinations
         Accuracy
         Arithmetic processes

     5. Fractions, decimals, percentages
       Conceptual knowledge of systems
       Converting between systems
       Procedures

C. Writing
    1. Manner of holding pencil
    2. Finger-hand control
    3. Manuscript: printing name
       Size and proportion
       Legibility, tremor, precision
       Grouping and spacing
    4. Cursive writing
       Rate, rhythm
       Legibility
    5. Writing from dictation

D. Spelling
    1. Grade level accuracy
    2. Rate
    3. Analysis of errors
       Vowel confusions, substitutions, omissions
       Consonant characteristics
       Phonetic approximation

E. Pupil Characteristics
    1. Attentional control
       Visual attention
       Listening attention
    2. Behavioral control
       Activity level
    3. Work span
    4. Achievement-motive
    5. Study habits

III. Physical Development

A. Birth: pre-natal and perinatal circumstances
B. Infancy
    1. Motor development: crawling, standing, walking, handedness
    2. Speech development: words, sentences, immaturity, impediments
    3. Feeding, weaning, eating behavior
    4. Toilet training and control
C. History of illnesses, injuries, and physical treatments
D. Sensory acuities: vision, hearing
E. Physique and present physical capacities

IV. Social Adjustment

Family background, parents, siblings, matrix of family relationships
Basic social skills: communication, dressing
Level of play development: solitary, parallel, cooperative, competitive
Relationships with siblings, peers friendships, nature of friendships
Sociometric choices and status, social distance or alienation
Relationship with teacher, relationship with authority figures
Social interests, social satisfactions

V. Emotional adjustment

Expression of pleasure and concern, mood state

Attitudinal state, cooperative or negativistic
Reaction to frustration, tolerance for frustration
Behavioral motivation: emotional needs
Ego-strength, ego-investment
Modes of defense
Level of anxiety or apathy
Contact with social reality
Conversational ideas and stream of thought

In the above outline, socio-economic and cultural data such as social class, religion, national descent, type of home, divorces, and so forth are not included. This does not infer that the psychologist should be unaware of these factors. Generally they have varying amounts of influence in the personality and adjustment of the child. A feature such as race or national descent may be of major significance in the development of a child's problem, or it may have no discernible importance. The school psychologist should not presume that these social and cultural factors have any implicit significance. He should rather determine whether they have any influence on the social, emotional, or intellectual functioning of the child.

In constructing this outline, an attempt was made to provide a developmental framework in the first four areas. Stages and sequence are not as well defined in the social and emotional areas, however, and the developmental lags or retardations are not as easily determined as in mental and educational development. Because of the focus on school learning problems, the academic skills in educational development are outlined in greater detail. Some school psychologists might regard this as educational diagnosis and presume it to be the responsibility of the teacher. On the other hand, most teachers do not have the longitudinal view of achievement necessary for a differential diagnosis of achievement difficulties. The school psychologist may not appreciate the influence that mental, physical, social, and emotional deviations have on achievement until he has observed their interrelationships in the pupil's problem.

Some school psychologists may object that the comprehensive study suggested in the guide would not be practicable in the school setting. Others routinely investigate each of the areas suggested in a superficial manner. There are no general rules, however, to indicate how intensively and extensively one should study a pupil's problem.

When a child is referred for a learning difficulty, the case study should not be limited to the testing of intelligence and achievement levels. A diagnostic study of the various subject areas should also be carried out. Thus, if a child is referred for a reading disability, analysis of his skills in oral and in silent reading should be made. Comparison of his achievement in reading should be made with the level which would be expected on the basis of his mental abilities. In addition to determining the achievement level, an analysis of errors or deficiencies should also be made. The detailed analysis of errors can be very informative as a guide for remedial instruction. A school psychologist should recognize and assume this responsibility to analyze learning difficulties in specific details rather than making a superficial approach by merely testing the child's intelligence. For school psychologists who have not received adequate training in educational diagnosis, a reference on the diagnosis and treatment of school learning difficulties is recommended.[14]

When a pupil is referred because of a problem of social behavior a detailed analysis of his social and emotional adjustment should be made. There is some question as to whether school psychologists should do comprehensive personality studies in the school situation. If the child's deviation and maladjustment is obviously severe, the detailed personality study may eventually be duplicated by other psychologists. When a child is referred to a treatment agency, for example a child guidance clinic, the staff in the clinic undertakes a personality study previous to their treatment. More commonly, however, psychiatric and psychological treatment services are not sufficiently available for all of the disturbed and maladjusted pupils, and the school continues to assume responsibility for its educational treatments of these children. In such situations, a personality study may be of value to parents and teachers.

In the performance of the case study, the psychologist makes moment-to-moment decisions regarding the type of data that has accumulated and the kind of information necessary for further understanding. Procedural hypotheses are developed and tentative conclusions are reached. In evaluating the data, it is important for the psychologist to distinguish between the sources of the information and the objectivity of the persons rendering it. For example, two parents, or a parent and a teacher may hold contradictory opinions about a child's intelligence and his achievement skills. Both may lack an objective basis for their appraisal. A teacher may judge a child's intelligence on the basis of his achievement, or may judge his achievement on the basis of his behavior as a pupil. In both cases, these judgments may be faulty. The parents may be inclined to judge a child's intellect on the basis of their experiences and their communication with him. They may presume that a child has certain aptitudes for school work without the comparison with other school children. In cases such as these, it is not only important that the psychologist present valid and objective data, but also that these data serve toward reconciling the conflicting opinions about the child.

There are a variety of interview skills necessary for psychological case studies. The interview can be used as a means of obtaining and reporting diagnostic information, and also as a means of treating the problem. The techniques of interviewing children, teachers, and parents vary markedly. There are perhaps certain common principles, for example communications

---

[14] Leo W. Brueckner and Guy L. Bond, *The Diagnosis and Treatment of Learning Difficulties* (New York: Appleton-Century-Crofts, 1955) or H. R. Myklebust and D. Johnson, *Learning Disabilities in Children: Educational Principles and Practices* (New York: Grune and Stratton, 1967).

and rapport, that apply to all interviewing. Because there are different purposes for the interviews, however, and because of the interviewee's special relationships to the problem, there are many differences. Variables such as the child's awareness of his problem, the parents' concept of a psychologist, and the teacher's regard for the pupil are just a few examples of the variables that may affect the course of an interview.

The interviewing skill of the psychologist may provide him access to a wealth of personal and social information, or the lack of skill could actually prevent its communication. Insomuch as his primary responsibility is to the child, his ability to relate and communicate with the child are of first importance. His interviews with others are either to gain further information about the child or to help them understand and resolve the difficulties that they experience in their relationships with the child. The school psychologist should not delegate the task of collecting interview information to other personnel. Although information from parent-teacher conferences and social work interviews maybe of value they may also omit the information most pertinent for the psychological study. In any interview the foci and purposes should be understood and accepted by the interviewee.

There are several points of view in regard to the nature and type of psychological studies appropriate for the school setting. The view presented in this chapter is that diagnosis is the central purpose for case studies in school psychology, and that all successful casework requires an accurate diagnosis. Many psychologists and educators view diagnosis as a process of clinical classification, not within the province of school psychology. However, a literal translation of the word *diagnosis* from its Greek origin is the "art-of-knowing."

In the earliest history of personality diagnosis Hippocrates applied trait theory in his classification of temperaments as sanguine, phlegmatic, choleric, and melancholy. He assumed that the temperamental differences between persons were due to an overbalance of certain "body humors." On the basis of overt appearance and behavior many other pseudo-scientific classifications of personality and behavior have been proposed through subsequent time. Often these have been inferences based on notions that seemed to be valid. Speculations about mind-states of individuals on the basis of their overt physical behavior have also frequently appeared in psychology as a mental science. The application of diagnosis in the field of medicine has eventually come to imply the establishment of a specific physical or mental illness. It has also led to convenience in the classification and treatment of illnesses.

Thorne [15] identifies the goal of psychological diagnosis as one of attempting to explain all behavior in terms of broad psycho-biological principles derived from the basic sciences. According to Thorne the principles of psy-

15 Thorne, *op. cit.*, p. 5.

chological diagnoses are essentially identical with the basic laws of diagnosis in other clinical fields such as medicine. The diagnostic processes consist of: a) collection of pertinent evidence; b) integration and interpretation of data in terms of the basic sciences; c) the formulation of hypotheses; d) the consideration of possible alternatives by differential diagnosis; and e) the positive identification of the disorder.[16] The identification of etiological factors is an essential aspect of differential diagnosis beginning with the initial collection of data.

Sundberg and Tyler point out that the evaluative study of an individual necessarily includes a study of the positive and constructive forces in the person.[17] They therefore suggest the term clinical assessment in lieu of psychodiagnosis for psychological case studies. They chart the sequential steps in assessment, and include mechanical and statistical procedures in conjunction with the clinician's cognitive processes, judgments, hypotheses, and interpretations as part of clinical assessment.

The sequence of diagnosis in child psychiatry described by Kanner [18] includes: 1) the symptom; 2) the initial contact; 3) the case history; 4) a physical examination; 5) psychometry; and 6) personality testing. He discusses the significance of the symptom as an admission ticket for psychiatric diagnosis.

In describing the essential steps in diagnosis in a child development clinic Beller [19] includes observation, description, a delineation of causation or etiology, classification, prediction or prognosis, and control, modification or treatment plan. Beller's study of the function and values of clinical procedures helps to establish a guide for recording data and evaluating records in a child guidance clinic. The procedures of child psychiatrists, child psychologists, nursery teachers and psychiatric social workers were included in the evaluation. Similar studies on the functions and values of various aspects of pupil personnel services are now being conducted by the Interprofessional Research Commission on Pupil Personnel Services at the University of Maryland.

School personnel are continuously involved in the screening of children for possible physical, mental, and emotional disorders; for example, visual and auditory acuity, intelligence capacities, and adjustment. Although the school is unavoidably involved in screening procedures, nevertheless the purpose of the screening pertains to the educability of the child rather than to the clinical identification of a physical, mental, or an emotional disorder. The

---

[16] *Ibid.,* p. 63.

[17] Sundberg, *op. cit.,* p. 81.

[18] Leo Kanner, *Child Psychiatry* (Springfield, Ill., Charles C. Thomas, Publisher, 1948).

[19] E. Kuno Beller, *Clinical Process* (New York: Free Press of Glencoe, Inc., 1962), p. 89.

latter function is not within the province of the school. In school psychology, it should be clearly understood that diagnosis does not imply a psychiatric, neurological, or pediatric classification. It is not only preferable to avoid any terms that may stereotype or stigmatize a child, but the school also does not have the prerogative to conduct diagnostic studies of this type.

The point of view expressed in this chapter is that educational and psychological diagnoses are essential to guide the learning and development of children. Diagnosis, in its broad literal meaning, is a responsibility for all persons working with a child. The diagnostic aspect of the case study is a descriptive formulation of the factors that have contributed to the pupil's personal and social problems.

Report of Interpretations, Conclusions, and Recommendations

Barbe [20] describes the case study as a "means of making certain that all pertinent facts about a given case are systematically included and considered." Much has been written about types of case data and the content for reports, but there is little information as to how case data should be analyzed. The integration of observational data, test data and interview information is a central methodological problem. If the data have met the criteria previously mentioned, then the integration can be readily accomplished.

In integrating case data, there are two kinds of relationships to be established. The first of these is for concurrent validity. This involves relating the traits or characteristics as they are presently observable in the pupil, to the problem under study. The relationships between intelligence, achievement, aptitudes, interests, and social behavior illustrate this integration. The isolated facts and test information are assembled into a meaningful mosaic of the child.

The second kind of relationship necessary for integration is across time. The present problem must be related to its antecedent conditions and also to future predictions. This integration provides depth and mobility to the mosaic. At this point, one might question whether the technique of case study is really an art or a science. The assurance remains, however, that the value of the case study lies in its scientific procedures rather than in artful techniques.

A strong theoretical position on the part of the school psychologist may introduce what is called perceptual errors, or a bias toward viewing and recognizing certain types of data. The various theoretical systems that attempt to explain behavior and adjustment are helpful in that they provide

[20] Walter Barbe, "Preparation of Case Study Reports," *Education*, 79, No. 9 (May, 1957), 570–574.

a framework for analysis. As much as possible, however, the school psychologist should be aware of biasing factors and take precautions against invalid conclusions.

Types of Reports

Tallent [21] defines the scientific report as one in which there is empirical evidence for the conclusions, predictions and recommendations.

Klopfer [22] analyzes and discusses reports on the basis of their focus and orientation. The *test-oriented* report is one that emphasizes the sources of information, and discusses how the test interpretations were derived. The test-oriented report seems to have value in the training and supervision of psychologists, but it may not serve the best purposes for field situations. Several authors criticize reports which focus entirely on tests. Hammond and Allen [23] state that reporting psychological data "test-by-test" in conformity with the examination procedure seems insulting to the reader. They describe the usual psychometric report as being too stereotyped, and criticize its quantitative nature.

Foster [24] feels also that a test-by-test discussion in the report is unnecessary and does not serve the functional purpose of the case study. Most authors agree, however, that case study conclusions should be based on objective evidence. The limitations of test-oriented case studies can be partly attributed to the psychologist's own perceptions of his function. If he has overlearned or is overidentified with the psychometric function, then he may be unable to undertake the appraisal of social and emotional adjustment and the analysis of achievement difficulties as necessary in a school study. He is inclined to describe the child in terms of test scores and test profiles. He may even interpret weighted subtest scores as if they had some intrinsic validity.

The school psychologist should keep in mind that the test is merely an implement for sampling the behavior that he wishes to analyze. The numbers which accrue to these tests, for example grade placement scores, sociometric ratings, deviation scores, quotients and percentiles, are not in themselves adequate to explain the child's problem.

In contrast to this, there are school psychologists who are unconstrained in their conclusions and recommendations. Because of psychologists' predilection for test evidence, however, they are in a minority. These school psy-

---

[21] Norman Tallent, "An Approach to the Improvement of Clinical Psychological Reports," *Journal of Clinical Psychology*, No. 12 (1956), 103–109.

[22] Walter G. Klopfer, *The Psychological Report* (New York: Grune and Stratton, Inc., 1960), pp. 22–24.

[23] Kenneth R. Hammond and Jeremiah M. Allen, *Writing Clinical Reports* (Englewood Cliffs, N. J.: Prentice-Hall, Inc., 1953).

[24] Austin Foster, "Writing Psychological Reports," *Journal of Clinical Psychology*, 7 (1951), 195.

chologists are inclined to postulate certain previous conditions as causes for the problem and then, without evidence, proceed as if these had been verified. The teacher may regard disinterested parents, faulty home training, working mothers, broken homes, or the lack of educational values in the home as the cause of school adjustment difficulties. Psychologists may hypothesize such causes as oedipal conflicts, sibling rivalry, deficient superego, emotional insecurity, or irregularities in the self concept as the cause for adjustment difficulties. The errors are not in the hypotheses, but rather in accepting them as conclusions without sufficient supporting evidence.

Garfield, Heine, and Leventhal [25] criticize psychological reports for their lack of clarity and focus, poor organization, and a lack of behavioral reference. The problems encountered by teachers and educators in attempting to utilize psychological reports are often due to the lack of focus and reference. When case studies are regarded as an exercise in testing, or an exercise in theoretical logic, the purpose intended in the referral becomes obscured. Cognizant of this, Hammond and Allen [26] emphasize that the report must be adapted to meet the needs of the primary reader. Holzberg, Allessi and Wechsler [27] concur with others that the psychological report should meet the needs of the referent.

The school psychologist should not be restricted to a written report, but he should participate freely in the discussion of the uses and limitations of his findings. As a supplement to the written report, verbal communication has many important advantages. The teacher can ask questions in regard to the findings and interpretations which have not been clarified. He can also request an explanation of the factors underlying specific adjustment or behavior problems. The school psychologist should keep in mind that teachers and school administrators need to have specific information to help them in their administrative and teaching decisions.

In some school systems referrals for psychological studies may be initiated by parents, physicians, probation workers, and social workers in community agencies. Others may originate in preschool nurseries and in clinics for exceptional children. In these situations, the orientation of the case study and the communication of the findings may differ slightly from those which have been referred by the classroom teacher. The school psychologist should bear in mind, however, that his function is a school-related function and the implications of findings for educational development and classroom adjustment should be stated for school purposes.

The problem of technical language and the use of psychological terms

[25] Solomon L. Garfield, Ralph W. Heine, and Morton Leventhal, "An Evaluation of Psychological Reports in a Clinical Setting," Journal of Consulting Psychology, 18 (1954), 281–286.

[26] Hammond and Allen op. cit., p. 168.

[27] Jules D. Holzberg, Salvatore L. Allessi, and Murray Wechsler, "Psychological Case Reporting at Psychiatric Staff Conferences," Journal of Consulting Psychology, 5 (1951), 425–429.

in the case study report is discussed by several authors. Klopfer [28] discusses some of the motivations of the psychologist as they influence his language in the case report. The psychologist is primarily motivated to help the referent and the client by communicating his findings clearly. Beyond this, he may also be motivated by his desire for status and prestige and by his wishes to impress the reader with his verbal skill and acumen. If he has a rejecting attitude toward one or the other of the persons involved, he may be motivated to use the report as a vehicle for making deleterious inferences. He may also identify favorably with the subject to the point of inadvertently glossing over some deficiencies and emphasizing certain positive characteristics. He may seek to demonstrate the value of one psychological test at the expense of another, or he may "go off into literary flights to demonstrate verbal skill to a potentially vast audience of colleagues, students, or staff members in an agency." It seems unlikely that these needs could be expressed or satisfied in school psychology, but their interference with communication is fairly obvious.

Dailey [29] investigated the practical utility of psychological reports. Psychologists were asked to make treatment recommendations for a hypothetical case. These were then submitted to other psychologists for their judgments about appropriate decisions. Finally, the recommendations and decisions were submitted to a third psychologist who made a checklist for his recommendation. The recommendations and decisions were submitted to a third psychologist who made a checklist for his recommendation. The recommendations and decisions that were agreed upon by two clinicians were regarded as useful decisions. The split-half reliability for useful decisions was .59. The length of the psychological report and its technical content were positively correlated with the number of clear and useful decisions which could be made from it. The longer reports, and those which contained more technical terminology, yielded clearer information and were therefore more useful for treatment decisions. In reviewing this study, it should be pointed out that the utility and clarity of reports are indices of reliability rather than of validity. The validity of any recommendations on treatment would have to be based on an evaluation of the treatment outcomes. Although most authors feel that the use of technical terminology should be avoided, this study indicates that it may be conducive to clear and useful decisions.

If one regards the successful communication of case information as an important end product, then the ability of the teacher and other school personnel to read and interpret the information also becomes important. Cuadra [30] analyzed the report-reading behavior of persons from six differ-

[28] Klopfer, op. cit., pp. 4–5.

[29] Charles A. Dailey, "The Practical Utility of the Clinical Report," Journal of Consulting Psychology, 17, No. 4 (1953), 297–302.

[30] Carlos A. Cuadra and William P. Albaugh, "Sources of Ambiguity in Psychological Reports," Journal of Clinical Psychology, No. 12 (1956), 108–115.

ent professional groups who ordinarily have access to psychological reports. He found only a 53 per cent agreement between the writer's intended meaning and the interpretations made by the readers. Although there were no gross errors in regard to the content of the reports, nevertheless the professional groups varied markedly in their ratings on the *degrees* of the subjects' feelings or emotions, and the *amount* of some personality characteristic that was described by the psychologist in the report.

The adequacy of the case study report might also be judged by the scope of information included. Whenever possible, the school psychologist might seek to identify the single positive cause that would account for all of the expression of the pupil's problem. Simple and direct explanations for pupil problems are not as frequently applicable as one might wish, and the possibility of multiple causes and correlates must be investigated. Comprehensive case studies of pupils who are being considered for special classes for retarded, emotionally disturbed, or gifted require extensive study of interests, achievement skills, abilities, and emotional adjustment. To judge whether the scope of any case study is adequate, one might ask whether there are any aspects of the problem that have not been adequately investigated.

Application of Case Findings

In school psychology the psycho-educational treatment of pupils requires the enhancement of various kinds of development as well as the remediation of learning and adjustment problems. Assuming that all of the case findings are appropriate and the recommendations for educational treatments can be followed, then there should be an immediate and substantial gain on the problem. The recommendations for school placement, instructional procedures, and teaching relationships resulting from case studies should be immediately applicable. When special instruction or other school placement is not available for a child, the school psychologist should attempt to make suggestions for interim treatment. For those pupils who are to continue in their present school placement, the school psychologist should assist the teacher in carrying out his recommendations.

Under ideal situations, the school psychologist might also attempt individual remedial work with the child. This individual remedial treatment may take the form of tutoring, play therapy, or counseling interviews, depending on the skills and competencies which he brings to his job. He would not attempt any intensive or extensive forms of psychotherapy, since this is not an appropriate school function.

When the school psychologist merely makes recommendations for educational treatment, there is no assurance that the teacher or other school personnel will be able to carry these out in the manner intended. In addition to the recommendations for treatment, therefore, the psychologist should plan a course of action to help the teacher or other persons implement them.

Recommendations at the conclusion of a case study are based on certain kinds of predictions. In some cases, the school psychologist must formulate his conclusions and state his predictions on the basis of minimal findings. In order to verify his own understandings and improve the accuracy of his findings, it would be desirable for the school psychologist to attempt short-range predictions, and to assist the school personnel in treatment recommendations. If, however, at the end of the case study the school psychologist does not have sufficient information to draw conclusions and make recommendations, he should not hesitate to communicate this. Such case reports should be regarded as temporary or progress reports rather than as completed case studies.

Kitano [31] surveyed the perceptions that pupil personnel workers and school administrators hold of pupils' behavior problems. He found that there was a high agreement among school administrators and pupil personnel workers on the severity of the pupils' problems, but that this tended to decrease through various levels of consultative treatment. At the conclusion of the case studies, the child guidance workers tended to assign higher ratings of improvement than the school administrators. Kitano postulated that the child guidance workers were inclined to perceive more gain from their own treatment efforts than the school administrators could perceive. The significant finding is the lack of agreement between the child guidance workers and school administrators about the effects of certain treatments.

The ultimate evaluation of school psychology will be made on the degree to which its services have aided pupils and teachers with the resolution of their problems. The number of case studies completed in any school year, or the number of tests administered, serve as a poor guide to this evaluation. It may be revolutionary for the school psychologist to accept and to actively assume a role in the educational and psychological treatment of a school child. The real value of psychological services, however, may not be realized until this is regarded as an integral part of the service.

Case Conference Techniques

Case conference procedures have been discussed in detail by a number of authors [32, 33, 34] and is generally accepted as a valid guidance procedure.

---

[31] Harry L. Kitano, "Perceptual Changes in School Administrators Following Consultation About Problem Children," *Journal of Counseling Psychology*, 8, No. 2 (1961), 129–135.

[32] Ruth Strang, *The Role of the Teacher in Personnel Work* (New York: Bureau of Publications Teacher's College Columbia University, 1953), pp. 210–212.

[33] Warters, *op. cit.*, pp. 313–332.

[34] Henry B. McDaniel, *Guidance in the Modern School* (New York: Dryden Press, 1956).

The case conference is used in a variety of settings, and for a number of purposes. In medical clinics and hospitals it is used for the assembly of diagnostic findings and for decisions on treatments and discharge. In social agencies the case conference is used for the discussion of investigative and casework information, and for agency decisions on social services and referrals. The use of the case conference in the school setting will be discussed at length in this chapter.

The school personnel who may participate in case conferences include the child's teacher, or the component of his teachers if he is a secondary school student, the school psychologist, counselor, school social worker, school nurse, school physician, guidance and curriculum supervisors, and school administrators. Specialists from various fields of medicine, clinical psychology, and social welfare might also participate in consulting roles. These would include psychiatrists, pediatricians, opthamalogists, clinical psychologists, social workers, and other specialists. Resource persons from other community agencies, for example child welfare, family service, and probation workers, may also be invited to participate in certain types of school conferences.

There are several basic assumptions underlying the use of case conferences. The first is that the various specialists and professional persons working with the child each obtain a different kind of diagnostic information. The second is that this information can be pooled to evolve a comprehensive understanding of the individual under study.

There are formal procedures for conducting case conferences as follows. First, the conference is chaired by a person who holds the responsibility to direct the discussion. The presentation, reports, and discussion in the conference are recorded by a secretary. At the beginning of the conference, the chairman or other guidance worker presents the referral and background information about the child. This presentation may include both an oral and written description of the problem. The chairman then formally requests information, observations, and findings from each of the conference participants. This is usually done systematically, so that each of the persons who have studied or worked with the child will have an opportunity to present first-hand information about the case. Subsequent to this the opinions and reactions of consultants and resource persons are requested. This is followed by an informal discussion among the conference participants. Throughout the conference the diagnosis and treatment plans are gradually formulated. Finally, the chairman reviews the findings and conclusions reached in the case conference and summarizes the treatment plans.

In directing the conference, it is important that the chairman allow a modicum of time for each participant. Discussions of the pupil's problems and the complaints and negative reactions of his teachers should be elicited early in the conference. This should be followed by objective reports of physical, psychological, and clinical examinations. Informal reports and discussion should then center around the etiology and dynamics of the problem. Throughout the discussion, the recorder must be particularly alert to record the various viewpoints, recommendations, and decisions. Since school problems often cannot be completely corrected or eliminated, it is important to establish realistic and practical goals. At the close of the conference, the chairman should review the recommendations and decisions so that each of the participants understands what his future involvement and responsibilities may be.

Before adjourning the conference, it is also desirable to schedule a follow-up meeting. The purpose of the follow-up meetings is to evaluate the progress or improvements that have been attempted, to receive any additional diagnostic information that was previously unavailable, and to consider any new problems that may have arisen. Because of the need to evaluate the effects of instructional treatments and social changes in the pupil, an interval of at least six weeks to three months is recommended between conferences.

If a series of conferences are to be scheduled for the same child, it may be advisable to allow the first conference to disclose what details of information are needed for a comprehensive understanding of his problem. The preferred procedure, however, is to have a systematic schedule of tests and observations prior to the case conference to obtain all of the pertinent information on the problem. Although the case conference is an expensive procedure from the standpoint of time and personnel costs, the assemblage of information in a single conference may be more efficient than separate reports and person-to-person communication. The case conference is further justified when there are a number of persons who need to learn more about the physical, social, and emotional factors which may be motivating the child's behavior. It would be unreasonable to expect that the teacher, the social worker, the psychologist, or the pediatrician to have a complete knowledge about the child's physical and emotional health, personal needs, and educational requirements. When there is a team approach as employed in case conferences, it is necessary that each participant limit his observations and opinions to his particular professional field.

Conference participants generally recognize their responsibility to bring their information, observations, and "expert" opinions to the case conference. Unfortunately, they are not always as aware of their responsibility to receive information and to accept the observations and opinions of others. Failures of the case conference procedure can often be assigned to failures in meeting these responsibilities. Sometimes, case conferences are held without sufficient new information to attempt an understanding of the child's problem. At other times, the case workers may not be receptive to the information or opinions expressed by others, and they continue to function on the basis of their own conclusions.

It is the pooling of findings and judgments in case conferences that theoretically serves to increase the validity of interpretations and predictions. If an interpretation or prediction by one member is invalid, those made by other participants serve to reduce the effects of the error. The scope of consideration given to a child's problem is enhanced by the number of specialists who have previously examined him. Consultants who have not worked with the child may also add to the scope of the study; however, the validity of their judgments rests on the relationship of the case information to the knowledge in their professional fields.

The special abilities and the limitations of the school psychologist may often determine the potentialities or limitations of the conference. So too with other conferees; each participant brings his ignorance to pool with his understanding in the case conference. The main advantage of the case conference over the case study is in the range of diagnostic information available for consideration. The educational, psychological, social, and pediatric considerations given to the case may be greatly extended over those previously available in separate studies. Nevertheless, there is still a variety of internal and external factors, for example, constitutional factors, emotional history, and social background, that are not available for case conferences. Some of this information is lost through the course of time and some is just not procurable with present diagnostic tools. For some conferences, the teachers and the school personnel workers have not had sufficient time to make intensive studies prior to the case conference. Thus, although many pupils' problems can be discussed in case conferences, their difficulties may not always be sufficiently analyzed. A group discussion of the pupil's symptoms and his problem behavior does not assure that the causes will be recognized and treated.

One of the values assumed for case conferencing is that the teacher will subsequently develop more understanding and better teaching skills for the problem children in her classroom. In a recent evaluation of the case conference method by Thompson and Finley [35] these values did not appear. Teachers indicated that the case conference was usually helpful in providing information about the pupils' problems. They also felt that the information contributed to a better understanding of the child. The teachers generally responded, however, that the case conference was of little or no value in helping them to "cope with the child" in the classroom. It appears that teachers' effectiveness and competencies with problem children may be independent of case conference procedures. An individual conference may be of immediate help in determining the regard which a teacher should hold towards a child, and in reaching decisions as to the school's disposition of

[35] Jack Thompson and Carmen J. Finley, "An Evaluation of the Case Conference Method," *California Journal of Educational Research,* 11, No. 2 (March, 1960), 87.

the case; but its value for the conduct of teaching and for the classroom adjustment of a problem pupil is still in question.

Selected Supplementary Readings

Ahr, A. Edward, "The Psychological Referral: A Procedural Approach," *Psychology in the Schools,* 2 (July, 1965), 224–227.

Bettelheim, Bruno, *Truants from Life.* New York: Free Press of Glencoe, Inc., 1955.

Bolgar, Hedda, "The Case Study Method," in *Handbook of Clinical Psychology,* ed. B. B. Wolman. New York: McGraw-Hill Book Company, 1965.

Callis, Robert, *et al., A Case Book of Counseling.* New York: Appleton Century Crofts, 1955.

Crosby, Muriel, *et al.,* "Children on the Fringe," *Childhood Education,* 35 (October, 1952).

Dailey, C. A., "The Life History Approach to Assessment," *Personnel and Guidance Journal,* XXXVI, No. 7 (1958), 456–460.

Division of Special Education, Ohio Department of Education, and Research Committee, Ohio School Psychologists Association, *Individual Child-Study Case Load Analysis,* School Year 1964–65.

Devereux, George, *Therapeutic Education.* New York: Harper & Row, Publishers, 1956.

Dollard, John, *Criteria for the Life History.* New York: Peter Smith, 1949.

Drake, Francis C., and C. A. Drake, *Human Relations Casebook for Executives and Supervisors.* New York: McGraw-Hill Book Company, 1947.

Engel, Mary, "Time and the Reluctance to Diagnose," *Journal of School Psychology,* 4 (Winter, 1966), 1–8.

Erickson, Clifford E., *A Basic Text for Guidance Workers.* Englewood Cliffs, N.J.: Prentice-Hall, Inc., 1949.

Fenton, Norman, *The Counselor's Interview with the Student,* School Case Work Manual No. 2. Stanford, California: Stanford University Press, 1943.

Froehlich, Clifford P., and John G. Darley, *Studying Students.* Chicago: Science Research Associates, 1952.

Garfield, Sol L., *Introductory Clinical Psychology.* New York: The Macmillan Company, 1957.

Gaw, Esther Allen, "Case Study Techniques," *Journal of Higher Education,* 14 (January, 1943).

Gordon, I. J., *Studying the Child in School.* Boston: Houghton Mifflin Company, 1966.

Greenbaum, Marvin, "A Method of Improving Referral Practices in Schools," *Psychology in the Schools*, I, No. 3, (July, 1964), 273.

Hollingshead, August B., *Elmtown's Youth: The Impact of Social Classes on Adolescents*. New York: John Wiley & Sons, Inc., 1949.

Huber, Jack T., *Report Writing in Psychology and Psychiatry*. New York: Harper & Row, Publishers, 1961.

Hutton, Jerry B., "Inconsistent Data as a Placement Dilemma: A Case Study," *Psychology in the Schools*, I, No. 3 (July, 1964), 274–278.

Jarvie, L. L., "The Interpretation of Case Studies," *Occupations*, 18 (April, 1940).

Johnson, Wendell, *People in Quandries*. New York: Harper & Row, Publishers, 1946.

Kahn, R. C., and C. F. Cannell, *The Dynamics of Interviewing*. New York: John Wiley & Sons, Inc., 1957.

Kessler, Jane W., *Psychopathology in Childhood*. Englewood Cliffs, N. J.: Prentice-Hall, Inc., 1966, pp. 68–99.

Kicklighter, R. H., "Problems in Psychological Evaluation on Children," *Psychology in the Schools*, 3 (April, 1966), 164–166.

Lohnes, P. R., and T. O. Marshall, "Redundancy in Students' Records," *American Educational Research Journal*, 2 (January, 1965), 19–24.

Margolin, R. J., and A. C. Williamson, *Case Conferences in Education*. Boston: Humphries, 1961.

Meehl, Paul E., *Clinical Versus Statistical Prediction*. Minneapolis: University of Minnesota Press, 1954.

Millard, Cecil V., and John W. M. Rothney, *The Elementary School Child— A Book of Cases*. New York: Dryden Press, Inc., 1957.

Mussman, Milton C., "Teachers Evaluations of Psychological Reports," *Journal of School Psychology*, 4 (Autumn, 1964), 35–38.

Neubauer, P. B., and E. K. Beller, "Differential Contributions of the Educator and Clinician in Diagnosis," in *Orthopsychiatry and the School*, ed. M. Krugman. New York: American Orthopsychiatric Association, Inc., 1958.

Patterson, Allen D., "Essential Pupil-Personnel Records," *Educational Administration and Supervision*, 33, No. 4 (April, 1947).

Reger, Roger, *School Psychology*. Springfield, Ill.: Charles C Thomas, Publisher, 1964, pp. 47–54, 93–103.

Rothney, John W. M., *The High School Student: A Book of Cases*. New York: Dryden Press, Inc., 1949.

Sarbin, Theodore R., "The Case Record in Psychological Counseling," *Journal of Applied Psychology*, Vol. 24 (April, 1940).

Sechrest, Carolyn A., *New Dimensions in Counseling Students*. New York: Teachers College, Columbia University, 1958.

Sitkel, E. George, "An Analysis of the Referral Process for Psychological Studies in the Pomona Schools," *Exceptional Children,* 32 (December, 1965), 256–258.

Strang, Ruth M., and Debora Pansegrouw, "Studies of Individuals," *Review of Educational Research,* 18, No. 5 (December, 1948).

Symonds, Percival M., "The Case Study as a Research Method," *Review of Educational Research,* 18, No. 5 (December, 1948).

Tallent, N., and W. J. Reiss, "Multidisciplinary Views on the Preparation of Written Clinical Psychological Reports, II: Acceptability of Certain Common Content Variables and Styles of Expression," *Journal of Clinical Psychology,* No. 15 (1959), 273–274.

Thorne, F. C., "A New Outline for Psychological Report Writing," *Journal of Clinical Psychology,* No. 12 (1956), 115–122.

————, "Clinical Judgment," *Journal of Clinical Psychology,* 1961.

————, "Operational Psychological Report Writing," *Journal of Clinical Psychology,* 26, No. 3 (July, 1960), 343–349.

Valett, Robert E., "Psychological Reports," in *The Practice of School Psychology.* New York: John Wiley & Sons, Inc., 1963.

Walker, R. N., "A Study of Action Taken on Recommendation of Psychologists in the Akron Schools," Doctoral Dissertation, Western Reserve University, 1962.

Watson, Robert I., ed., *Readings in the Clinical Method in Psychology.* New York: Harper & Row, Publishers, 1949.

Wattenberg, William W., "Causes of Child Behavior," *Understanding the Child,* 25, No. 3 (June, 1956).

White, Mary Alice, and Myron W. Harris, "The Techniques of Referral," and "Communicating Through Reports," in *The School Psychologist.* New York: Harper & Row, Publishers, 1961.

Williamson, E. G., *Counseling Adolescents.* New York: McGraw-Hill Book Company, 1950.

Wright, H. F., *Recording and Analyzing Child Behavior.* New York: Harper & Row, Publishers, 1966.

MAURICE F. FREEHILL

9

The School Psychologist and the Mental Health Needs of Children

Modern man is marked by very great external and technological accomplishments, but he is frequently described as inwardly empty, anxious, and dissatisfied. Statistics on emotional failure, delinquency, and marital discord are widely dispersed and remedies are favored topics in the press, pulpit, and living room. These public concerns are reflected in the schools.

The popular contemporary view probably concurs with a writer in *School Life,* formerly the official journal of the U. S. Office of Education, "Our schools are our second line of defense against mental illness, second only to the home."[1] In the formative years of later childhood, adolescence, and youth, classrooms and playgrounds serve as arenas in which skills and powers are developed and

[1] Horace W. Lundberg, "The School Supervisor's Role in Mental Health," *School Life,* 43, No. 4 (December, 1960), 8–10.

organized. It is difficult to overestimate school influences on personal development and mental health.

A Disputed Role for the School

There are widely divergent opinions on the proper role that formal education should play in either the maintenance and promotion of mental health or in the correction of personality defects. A magazine report on education in several countries concluded with six recommendations. The second of these was that, "We can re-examine our schools in the light of the German teacher's avoidance of personality training and stop insisting that our educators 'be at once priest, physician, policeman, parent and more, as well as teacher'." [2] This view is countered by those who turn to the Second World War for evidence that academic training does not bulwark the possessor against committing acts of primitive force, horror, and self-degradation. The science involved in those acts only highlights the need for personal development. Lawrence K. Frank wrote, "In the interest of social welfare and human happiness, we could wisely sacrifice much of our present academic achievement for better personality integration and social adjustment, since only sane, cooperative personalities can deal with our present social disorder." [3]

At mid-century it was estimated that only ten per cent of schools gave any real priority to mental health concerns and sixty per cent were characterized by negative attitudes. William Menninger proposed it would be a blessing to America if teachers should resolve to promote mental health.[4] It has been charged that teachers are overconcerned with discipline and good order and that they give attention to aggressive and active children, but neglect withdrawn and passive ones. The Wickman studies, published in 1928, are cited to prove this point, although numerous subsequent studies show a much altered profile of teacher attitudes.[5] The teacher, long criticized for disinterest in mental health, is now beset by critics who charge that too much attention is given to mental health. The early critics were led by specialists in mental health, guidance workers, and parents of less successful children. The new criticism comes from a cohesive and articulate group who favor an aristocracy of the academic. They object to an "educational philosophy which stresses 'adjustment' and the 'whole child'." [6]

[2] George Gallup and Evan Hill, "Is European Education Better Than Ours?" *The Saturday Evening Post*, 233, No. 26–27 (December, 24–31, 1960), 76.

[3] Lawrence K. Frank, *Society as the Patient, Essays on Culture and Personality* (New Brunswick: Rutgers University Press, 1948), p. 242.

[4] W. C. Menninger, "Mental Health in Our Schools," *Educational Leadership*, 7, No. 8 (May, 1950), 510.

[5] E. K. Wickman, *Children's Behavior and Teacher's Attitudes* (New York: Commonwealth Fund, 1928), 247 pages.

[6] George C. Benson, "Citizenship," in *The Case for Basic Education, A Program of Aims for Public Schools*, ed. James D. Koerner (Boston: Little, Brown and Company, 1959), 17–26.

Some of the critics admit that personality problems are important and related to intellectual achievement, but they are perturbed when guidance workers deal with these matters. One writer says that minor normal problems are best handled by the teacher, that psychological counseling, if confined to friendly mature advising, is permissible, but guidance should remain on the level of advice about courses and should be given only by those who have a liberal education.[7] Apparently specialized training in mental health is considered unnecessary and even detrimental.

The criticism is part of a general attack on mental health movements. Extreme critics charge that child study and psychology have increased emotional disturbances and adolescent crime. Most of the writers seem dependent on each other. Their contentions are so similar that they may be summarized as a common point of view: [8]

1. Mental health is a political instrument—the professionals, especially those associated with the World Federation for Mental Health, intend to remake the nation in terms of an ideology that devalues national sovereignty, is Leftish and One-Worldish.

2. Mental health protects entrenched institutionalism—"careerists" indulge in "modern witchcraft" to deprive others of independence and their natural rights to deviate from the norm. Particularly dangerous is commitment by expert rather than by jury because the professionals will quiet all opposition, even separating families to achieve their purposes.

3. Mental health is immoral—it eradicates the concept of right and wrong, opposes inhibition of impulses, advocates sexual release, and interferes with the development of "inner iron."

4. Mental health promotes conformity—it is group-minded.

5. Mental health overemphasizes culture and environment—the experts ignore basic temperament and sell the erroneous belief that mental illness, in most cases, is not from injury, deterioration, or other physical causes.

6. Mental health practice is "quackery"—"brain pickers" use techniques

[7] Irving Adler, *What We Want of Our Schools, Plain Talk on Education from Theory to Budgets* (New York: The John Day Company, Inc., 1957), pp. 26–28.

[8] See G. Sumner Small, "The Failure of Child Psychology," *American Mercury,* 89, No. 428 (September, 1959), 92; David Calderwood, "The Bible's Approach to Mental Health," *American Mercury,* 88, No. 425 (June, 1959), 135–139; Jo Hindman, "The Fight for Your Child's Mind," *American Mercury,* 85, No. 406 (November, 1957), 7–11; Harold Lord Varney, "Mental Health, Fact and Fiction," *American Mercury,* 84, No. 399 (April, 1957), 7–16; Gene Birkeland, "Mental Health Molds the Mind," *American Mercury,* 84, No. 401 (June, 1957), 79–84; Shirley Benson, "IQ Tests Mean Nothing!", *American Mercury,* 34, No. 401 (June, 1957), 56–61; and Jo Hindman, "Social Engineering for 1984," *American Mercury,* 89, No. 429 (October, 1959), 48–55; *The Canadian Intelligence Service,* Supplementary 9, No. 11 (November, 1959), 1–8.

like sociometry and intelligence tests. Testing is out-of-hand and might best be confined to subject matter tests.

7. Mental health practices disturb children—specialists suggest previously unimagined problems and increase neuroticism.

8. Mental health invades privacy—the techniques involve "mental undressing" and "mind inoculation" of helpless persons without consent of either the subject or the guardian.

The arguments are extreme and poorly substantiated, but they interfere with school practice. Thus counselors sometimes retreat to "safe" discussions. In vocational counseling they avoid personality and deal with matters of convenience and economic opportunity. However, a successful life-work is permeated by the worker's personality and each child has some right to invest his efforts in work that matters. Vocational advisement which avoids values and personality is, at best, a venial service.

Experts in mental health are themselves becoming more concerned with problems of morals and values.[9] Psychotherapy and counseling are sometimes defined as "just technique" or as "applications of behavioral science" and therefore neutral and objective. Counselors and therapists do not simply relieve anguish; they work with clients who are developing systems of belief, behavior and value. The lay criticism is not adequately answered by the pretense that no values are implicit in mental health theories or practices. The mental health approach does make a difference in human behavior and human development.

Schools cannot avoid playing a part in the formation of personality and values. Children are influenced by who their teachers are and what they do, by beliefs and behavior of their classmates, and by the content and methods of instruction. Some writers think that personality is continuously modifiable and therefore considerably affected at every level in the schools. Other writers emphasize the early stabilization of personality and in some measure discount the probability of extensive change from school experience. Concerning this point, Symonds wrote,

> Schools may be listed as one of the precipitating factors in the determination of the direction that personality will take, but they must work with the basic personalities of the children who come to them—they cannot hope to modify these basic personalities.[10]

[9] See Perry London, *The Modes and Morals of Psychotherapy* (New York: Holt, Rinehart & Winston, Inc., 1964); Thomas S. Szasz, *The Myth of Mental Illness: Foundations of a Theory of Personal Conduct* (New York: Hoeber-Harper, 1961); Floyd W. Matson, *The Broken Image, Man, Science and Society* (New York: George Braziller, Inc., 1964); O. H. Mowrer, *The Crisis in Psychiatry and Religion* (Princeton, N. J.: D. Van Nostrand Co., Inc., 1961).

[10] Percival M. Symonds, "What Education Has to Learn from Psychology, IX Origins of Personality," *Teachers College Record*, 61, No. 6 (March, 1960), 317.

The Relationship Between Personal
and Academic Outcomes

Mental health or academic outcomes are not matters of alternate choice. Intellect and emotion are not simply separated forces counteracting or supporting each other. They are integral aspects of one thing, and the fullest development of either depends on the development of the other.

Learning is always, at the personal level, dependent on the integration and meaning given by the learner. Whether the content is affective or objective, poetic or scientific, learning involves personal meaning and it changes the decisions or the behavior of the person.

Knowing changes the learner, but the learner also alters the knowledge. Personality is a kind of co-director in learning, granting or refusing permission for the individual to respond in new ways. Knowledge is screened and changed by the viewer: especially changed are the interrelationships between objective data or facts. On the basis of the same information, what is known about history differs greatly from the congenial person to the isolated one or from the mature to the immature. The more creative and unique the learning, the more clearly it carries the impact of the individual. Complex work of truly inventive or original quality is most distinctively marked by the originator.

The world we see seems to be filtered and arranged by the mind. The effects of personality on vision have been explored in experiments using aniseikonic glasses which distort normal vision or by using the Ames technique (a room specially designed to distort observed figures). It has been found that recently married women do not accept distortion of husband figures as readily as other man-figures, that men reject distortion in "mutilated" figures or simulated amputees, that recruits resist distortion in officers, and girls more than boys refuse to distort mirrored self-images.[11] In relationships containing even mild elements of threat or insecurity, observers refuse to accept distortion as readily as in less anxious relationships. If such apparently small anxieties play a large part in determining comparatively objective visual reports, then surely emotional conditions must play some part in every psychological activity.

The problems of negative emotions are most commonly discussed. One school psychologist wrote, "The time has come when schools must recognize severe learning disabilities for what they really are: *symptoms of emotional disturbances or neurotic behavior.*"[12] Maladjustment seems to block or inhibit

11 Warren J. Wittreich, "Visual Perception and Personality," *Scientific American,* 200, No. 4 (April, 1959), 56–60.
12 Katherine E. D'Evelyn, *Meeting Children's Emotional Needs* (Englewood Cliffs, N. J.: Prentice-Hall, Inc., 1957), p. 91.

natural capacity, reducing both the learning level and the learning rate. Dollard and Miller suggest that regression produces a kind of selective stupidity impairing the individual's capacity to find solutions in the area of the emotional problem.[13]

Attention to maladjustment and negative effects may obscure the fact that personality, maladjusted or well adjusted, has a dynamic function in all learning. A response natural for one person is foreign and impossible for another. Differences persist even if data are commonly shared. However, responses are more alike for two equally informed people acting in a matter of limited personal concerns. We may assume that there is some unconscious distortion of facts in all learning, but the greater effect centers on matters of greater moment and more personal significance.

Anxiety alters the attack on learning. Even at low levels of arousal, emotions tend to narrow the range of cue utilization.[14] In initial learning or in a well defined task this narrowing may increase organization or effectiveness, but it reduces incidental or concomitant learning. Peripheral facts and latent knowledge are excluded with narrowing of the receptor-effector span and shrinking of the perceptual field. This results in failure in complex tasks where a large number of cues are essential to a good response. Perhaps there is an optimum range of cue response for each task and likewise an optimum level of emotional involvement. This view would be consistent with the well-known Yerkes-Dodson principle.[15] A mild degree of anxiety may focus attention and activity thus facilitating learning of simple objectives, but in more difficult tasks anxiety held at the same level retards learning.

The level of personal organization or development is related to the learner's thinking style. Children think differently than adults, and immature personalities think differently than mature personalities of the same chronological age. Childish thought is egoistic and subjective. Some maturity is essential to objective and logical thought.

It appears that selected personal qualities should have a positive effect on academic performances. One writer suggests that the child needs: curiosity, appropriate aggressiveness so that he will expend energy, positive identification so that the expenditure will be selective, appropriate scepticism, enough masochism to endure some discomfort, and ability to concentrate.[16]

[13] John Dollard and Neal E. Miller, *Personality and Psychotherapy, An Analysis in Terms of Learning, Thinking and Culture* (New York: McGraw-Hill Book Company, 1950).

[14] J. A. Easterbrook, "The Effect of Emotion on Cue Utilization and the Organization of Behavior," *Psychological Review*, 66, No. 3 (May, 1959), 183–201.

[15] R. M. Yerkes and J. D. Dodson, "The Relation of Strength of Stimulus to Rapidity of Habit Formation," *Journal of Comparative Neurology and Psychology*, 18 (1908), 459–582.

[16] Harold F. Borenz and Melvin E. Kaufman, "Intellectual and Emotional Factors as Related to School Performance," *Exceptional Child*, 26, No. 8 (April, 1960), 401–403, 408.

This concentration will not come from children with a large number of unmet basic needs, unresolved inner conflicts, or neurological damage.

The literature more frequently deals with defects in personality that interfere with school success.[17] Children who have had unsafe and unsatisfying experiences approach school in fearful fashion. They may withdraw from learning or exhaust themselves in self-protecting activities. They may avoid tension through restless excitement and incur the teacher's displeasure which results in increased tension. They may find the classroom so confining and the teacher's authority so threatening that they become truant. Some children turn from anxiety to academic pursuits, but they are likely to use knowledge as an aggressive or protective instrument. They accumulate evidence of power and superiority. The variety of effects seems almost endless.

Effective learning is a function of the well-organized and enthusiastic student. It has been found that academic progress may provide an index of mental health.[18] An Academic Progress Chart developed along the lines of the Wetzel Grid was used to depict individual progress against class progress and a "normal channel." In each instance of marked deviation (about 150 cases) there was either evidence of increasing difficulty in the child's life or an early academic recovery apparently the result of greater attention from an alerted parent. Changes in the graph were related to significant factors in the life situation and the device provided a useful screening for emotional problems.

Studies that correlate personality traits with degree of academic success have not provided neat conclusions and probably none should be expected. The learners are both complex and unique, the situations vary, the school requirements differ, the learning activities vary, and the measuring instruments for personality and achievement are short of perfection. A fairly typical study found five factors associated with achievement.[19] These were power, resentment, dependence, social acceptance, and aggression. Four factors were associated with low achievement: pleasure seeking, extraversion, denial of shortcomings, and need for power.

One study of nonintellectual factors in predicting college success for talented students indicates that colleges differ greatly in the qualities which are rewarded.[20] Achievers in one major institution scored high on scales of

[17] Louise E. Harper and Benjamin Wright, "Dealing with Emotional Problems in the Classroom," *Elementary School Journal*, 63, No. 6 (March, 1958), 316–325.

[18] Lorene A. Stringer, "Academic Progress as an Index of Mental Health," *Journal of Social Issues*, 15, No. 1 (1959), 16–29.

[19] George Middleton Jr. and George Guthrie, "Personality Syndromes and Academic Achievement," *Journal of Educational Psychology*, 50, No. 2 (April, 1959), 66–69.

[20] John L. Holland, "The Prediction of College Grades from Personality and Aptitude Variables," *Journal of Educational Psychology*, 51, No. 5 (October, 1960), 245–254.

emotionality and instability, in another the achievers were persistent and conscientious. The study included subjects in 277 colleges and found variables such as "superego," "persistence," and "deferred gratification" to be broadly useful predictors. Another study of college achievement indicates that test anxiety greatly alters the performance of the generally anxious student but has limited effect on those of median or low anxiety levels.[21]

A study of 100 college women related "goal-setting" to self-acceptance and rejection.[22] Self-rejecting underachievers were least motivated but performed on examinations above their own anticipated grades. Self-rejecting overachievers were nervous and unhappy, had a sense of unworthiness, and they most exceeded the anticipated grade. Self-accepting underachievers seemed to fill their ego needs elsewhere and grossly overestimated their probable grades. Self-accepting overachievers were noncompetitive, good students who tended to overestimate their grades. A perusal of many studies leads to the conclusion that there is now no very complete and systematic list of personality factors associated with general achievement or general failure.

There are many studies of personality traits in relation to success in selected subject matters.[23] Reading is vital to success, intellectually difficult and introduced at a time of great personal change. The content of reading is affective or emotionally loaded and considerable relationship between personality and reading difficulty should be anticipated. A number of studies support this hypothesis.[24] The emotional difficulties cannot be easily fixed as cause or consequence but appear in a constellation of observations which include reading problems. This topic is considered in greater detail in Chapter 17.

The findings are in themselves complex. A study of 42 superior readers and 41 inferior readers among sixth grade boys with the same mean IQs is fairly typical.[25] The superior readers had higher scores on all parts of the California Test of Personality but no distinctive profile. Nevertheless, five clusters of response seemed to characterize inferior readers, poor family interaction, rejection by others, frustration-aggression by others, conflict about other-dominance, and inferiority feelings.

[21] Robert R. Grooms and Norman S. Endler, "The Effect of Anxiety on Academic Achievement," *Journal of Educational Psychology*, 51, No. 5 (October, 1960), 229–304.

[22] James V. Mitchell Jr., "Goal-Setting Behavior as a Function of Self-Acceptance, Over- and Under-Achievement, and Related Personality Variables," *Journal of Educational Psychology*, 50, No. 3 (June, 1959), 93–105.

[23] Eli M. Bower and Jack A. Holmes, "Emotional Factors and Academic Achievement," *The Education of Exceptional Children, Review of Educational Research*, 29, No. 5 (December, 1959), 529–544.

[24] Nila B. Smith, "Research on Reading and the Emotions," *School and Society*, 81, No. 2050 (January 8, 1955), 8–10.

[25] Ralph D. Norman and Marvin F. Daley, "The Comparative Personality Adjustment of Superior and Inferior Readers," *Journal of Educational Psychology*, 50, No. 1 (February, 1959), 31–36.

Findings from such studies seem frequently to support the view that reading competence may be associated with family dominance, family discipline, parental expectations, self-concept, and social success. However, the lists vary greatly. Some of the variability arises from inadequate definition, some from the fact that many of the personality factors are unusually ambiguous as they are imbedded in social class factors. Undoubtedly, the major reason for confusion is the complexity of the question itself.

A San Francisco study shows that children in emotional adjustment classes make different type spelling errors.[26] While normal children make errors related to difficulty and language peculiarities, the maladjusted make proportionately larger errors through refusals and illegible writing. Greater anxiety and rigidity seems to produce a learning block resulting in total misses or errors through unrecognizable writing.

The role of personal values in academic learning needs investigation. Using a tachistoscopic technique one study investigated the possibility that orientation to selected values made a subject particularly sensitive to certain stimulus words.[27] It was found that the profile on the Allport Vernon Scale of Values was related to differential ease in perceiving words. The subjects made fewer errors and needed less exposure to words typical of the personally preferred "value." This differential threshold of recognition may result from greater familiarity as a result of interest or from a proportionately larger number of hypotheses in the area of interest or from greater enthusiasm for responses in the preferred category. In any case, value orientation produced "perceptual sensitization" and it may be guessed that values play a major part in both differential and total academic success.

Human response appears to be unitary or internally consistent if both the subject and the situation are well understood. In relating personality to competence and mastery there has been a tendency to emphasize the primitivization of response and defective logic which comes from distorted feelings. Little emphasis has been given to sound personality as a contributor to truthful understanding, imaginative hypothesizing, and generous performing.

Focus on Mental Health

Good mental health is usually considered a legitimate educational objective in its own right and not just a contributing or concomitant outcome. Some writers see a paradox in this view. They see the school as necessarily arbitrary and authoritarian as a consequence of its responsibilities and orga-

[26] Harry H. L. Kitans, "Refusals and Illegibilities in the Spelling Errors of Maladjusted Children," *Journal of Educational Sociology,* 50, No. 3 (June, 1959), 129–131.
[27] L. Postman, J. S. Bruner, and E. McGinnies, "Personal Values as Selective Factors in Perception," *Journal of Abnormal and Social Psychology,* 43, No. 2 (April, 1948), 142–154.

nizational style. In their view the school is achievement rather than person centered, dedicated to absolute rather than personal goals, and organized so that all strive but some fail. To solve this dilemma it is sometimes proposed that achievement goals must be compromised to assure an accepting environment with some success for all children. An alternate proposal is that mental health must be promoted externally of the school.

In any major undertaking but especially in undertakings dependent on public support it seems necessary to define goals carefully and establish standards for minimum achievement. In mental health there is no well defined point of arrival. The label "mentally healthy" is affixed to the "good," as good appears in cultural and philosophic terms. In some cases the term has a normative connotation, being like the expected or "ought" man. In other cases the meaning is normative in a statistical sense, not extreme in measurable attitudes or responses. The mental health models are divergent and ambiguous.[28] A number of the concepts may be roughly placed in five categories.

1. Absence of pathology or symptoms.

2. Resistance to threat and potentially dangerous feelings.

3. Current effectiveness, mastery of situations.

4. Statistical normality, adaptation to ordinary standards.

5. An ideal person with some universal attributes.

Recent years have brought vigorous objection to definitions that emphasize adjustment to society, other-directedness, vendible personality, averageness, congeniality at any price, success orientation, and self-value in terms of what others think.[29] It has been argued that the achievement of psychological health requires moving from tribalism and mass society to independence and autonomy.

Attention to self-direction, self-acceptance, and achievement of inner-directedness is characteristic of most criteria for mental health. One survey of the literature lists six major approaches to classifying the content of positive mental health: [30]

1. Attitudes toward the self—self-objectification, self-acceptance, sense of identity.

2. Development and self-actualization—differentiation and integration of the total person, extension of self.

[28] Donald C. Klein, "Some Concepts Concerning the Mental Health of the Individual," *Journal of Consulting Psychology*, 24, No. 4 (August, 1960), 288–293; and David Freides, "Toward the Elimination of the Concept of Normality," *Journal of Consulting Psychology*, 24, No. 2 (April, 1960), 128–133.

[29] A. H. Maslow, "Health as Transcendence of Environment," Eastern Psychological Association (April 15, 1960, ditto).

[30] Marie Jahoda, *Current Concepts of Positive Mental Health* (New York: Basic Books, Inc., Publishers, 1958).

3. Integration—flexible balance of psychic forces, unifying philosophy.
4. Independence from social influences—appropriate nonconformism, inner controls.
5. Evaluation of the world—empathy, freedom from need-distortion.
6. Environmental adequacy—ability to meet cultural demands, effective personal relations.

No single emphasis is found in the schools, but the views are, to some degree, culture bound. The nature of the institution makes it so. School efforts are likely to be directed toward effectiveness and social acceptability more than toward unique personal development and a degree of detachment from cultural concerns. Nevertheless, schools work toward increasing integration of personal forces and the development of home values. The school contribution is toward mental health, broadly and imperfectly defined.

When attention turns toward good conditions and wholesome psychological development mental health becomes a common concern and not just that of the specialist. The various roles differ but are closely interrelated through focus on the development of an individual. It is convenient to think of mental health services in five modes with the last two being more traditional or treatment categories. These categories are:

1. Positive promotion of mental health, development of learning experiences and a milieu with maximum potential for mental health.
2. Primary prevention, discovering and altering environmental conditions that are potentially noxious or hazardous.
3. Secondary prevention, early diagnosis and care of incipient or developing mental disorders. This may include counseling.
4. Therapy for disturbed but socially functioning clients. This frequently includes environmental adjustments with counseling involving a supporting relationship, increased insight, and development of attitudes.
5. Therapy for those who require hospitalization, prolonged treatment, or a major reconstruction of personality.

The school contribution is limited to the first four categories of attack and often to the first three. Some experts narrow the matter further, for they insist that positive mental health is a will-o'-the-wisp, impossible to define and so involved with social, religious, and personal factors that no common approach is possible. In fact, the term "positive mental health" often means absence of pathology and is equated with primary prevention and reduction of hazards. In any case, schools have concentrated on primary and secondary prevention and cooperated with agencies providing therapy.

A survey of services in large cities in 1948 found school psychologists in 79 per cent of these cities and 75 per cent of the psychologists engaged in some treatment.[31] Observation would indicate that the total number of children who receive major treatment services on an individual basis is small indeed. Nevertheless, a large percentage of superintendents participating in the Thayer Conference thought that school psychologists should work intensively with children.[32] Some administrators place these services on relatively low priority. Others are either not convinced of the propriety of offering such service through the school or the effectiveness of therapeutic counseling. Mental health workers are enthusiastic about treatment services, but they argue from cases and offer little large-scale evidence of major changes in personality and behavior.

Statistical evaluations of therapy effectiveness are not universally positive and most are only mildly reassuring. Evaluative studies of therapy with adults show gains that are dishearteningly small.[33] Child studies almost parallel the adult ones. One author summarized findings from eighteen studies evaluated at close of therapy, seventeen evaluated at follow-up, and two evaluated at both close and follow-up.[34] The subjects were pre-school to twenty-one years with few over seventeen and a median age of about ten. Improvement rates varied from 42.0 per cent to 97.1 per cent with a gross average of 73.98 per cent. The control or "untreated" group had an improvement rate of 72.5 per cent. Evidence of success or failure from treatment is not readily found or easily presented.

One of the better known studies used delinquency reduction as a criterion.[35] The service input was large and the returns comparatively small. There are, of course, contradictory data from studies also using a criterion of relatively circumscribed behavior.[36] Some of the negative results may come from inadequate measures of change. It is unlikely that a single behavior will be truly representative of broad personality changes, if these occur. In the case of delinquency, there is no one-to-one relation with adjustment and, in fact, a large portion of delinquency may itself be adjustive behavior.[37]

[31] W. J. Nolan, "Survey of Practices in Meeting Pupil Adjustment Needs," *Journal of Educational Research*, 42, No. 4 (December, 1948), 268–278.

[32] Norma E. Cutts, *School Psychologists at Mid-Century, A Report of the Thayer Conference on the Functions, Qualifications, and Training of School Psychologists* (Washington, D.C.: American Psychological Association, Inc., 1955), pp. 47–48.

[33] J. H. Eysenck, "The Effects of Psychotherapy: An Evaluation," *Journal of Consulting Psychology*, 16, No. 5 (October, 1952), 319–324.

[34] Eugene E. Levitt, "The Results of Psychotherapy with Children: An Evaluation," *Journal of Consulting Psychology*, 21, No. 3 (June, 1957), 189–196.

[35] Helen Witmer and Edith Tufts, *The Effectiveness of Delinquency Prevention Programs*, Childrens Bureau Publication No. 350 (Washington, D.C.: U. S. Department of Health, Education, and Welfare, 1954).

[36] Melvin Zax and Armin Klein, "Measurement of Personality and Behavior Changes Following Therapy," *Psychological Bulletin*, 57, No. 5 (September, 1960), 435–448.

[37] William Kvarceus, Walter B. Miller, et al., *Delinquent Behavior, Culture and the Individual* (Washington, D.C.: National Education Association of the United States, 1959), p. 7.

In some cases, comparatively narrow validating criteria have correlated positively with therapy. Fleming used decrease in psychosomatic symptoms as a criterion in a study of school children.[38] The results were striking with only 50 per cent of the control group improved and 96 per cent of the treated group improved. In this experiment each child was studied and the teachers were helped to avoid tension, help children "save face," listen attentively, and adapt to individual needs. This is not traditional therapy, but there is a growing conviction that effective therapy is therapy backed up by suitable environmental and educational supports.

Earlier views of therapy as a specific process possible only in a specialized setting are giving way to beliefs that therapeutic attitudes must be developed but practices are highly individualized. Some psychologists believe that there are no absolutely necessary conditions for personality growth.[39] Contemporary trends are probably toward milieu therapy and working out problems in a total life space.[40] Individual psychotherapy emphasizes mutual respect and conscious communion in solving the client's present problems with reduced emphasis on recovery of memories, regression, or transference as essential elements. The borders of the treatment community are extended. Parents and teachers become vital participants, and group activities, reading, play, and music become adjuncts of therapy. The specialist is becoming one of a team working toward here-and-now changes in behavior as steps toward constructive personality change.

Concurrent attempts to articulate learning and personality theory have reduced the gap between education and therapy. This mutuality is accelerated as school psychologists work more closely in the school system, maximizing the effect of teachers, group life, and educational activities. This is, in part, a return to an original role. Early clinical psychology was not confined to mental health but worked with all school problems, subject matter deficiencies, retardation, and the planning of suitable educational experiences.[41] In the interim there was a tendency to separate guidance into two types, one vocational and advising, the other personal and counseling.

The trend is to see coalescence in human problems, vocational, educational, social, or moral. The counselee is a unified being with every decision involving his personality. He lives not in a loose aggregate of others, but in a highly organized system of which he is the center. The contemporary psychologist is not convinced that each troubled child must be removed from the school for intensive therapy. The emphasis is on solving current problems in natural settings, on hygiology more than pathology. With proportionately

[38] Robert S. Fleming, "Psychosomatic Illness and Emotional Needs," *Educational Leadership*, 9, No. 2 (November, 1951), 119–123.

[39] Albert Ellis, "Requisite Conditions for Basic Personality Change," *Journal of Consulting Psychology*, 23, No. 6 (December, 1959), 538–540.

[40] William C. Morse, "Socially and Emotionally Disturbed Children," *American Association of Colleges for Teacher Education Yearbook* (1960), pp. 73–83.

[41] Cutts, *School Psychologists at Mid-Century*, pp. 17–20.

less dependence on abnormal psychology there is increased attention to sociology, developmental psychology, individual differences, and educational psychology.[42]

Services to Individuals

School brings a succession of new challenges and new authority figures with new threats and new possibilities for satisfaction. The child who solves a problem or is successful at a particular level goes on to the next step. The unsuccessful child frequently stalls or fixates at the point of failure. The one who fails to cope with life tends to both exaggerate and persist in the previously tried inappropriate responses. Each new effort results in failure, threatens positive feelings, and reinforces archaic and static views of the self and the world. The child needs special opportunities to discover and understand his potentials and relationships with others as well as to grow out of primitive and inadequate feelings. School psychological services have a special responsibility in providing this second chance to grow up.

The work of the school psychologist is not less professional but does differ from that of other psychologists. The client has a primary relationship more often with the teacher than with the psychologist. Relationship with the psychologist is briefer and less intense than in nonschool therapy. Contacts are in a nonmedical setting where over-all organization is for group activities and teaching, not for therapy. The relationship is frequently initiated by someone other than the client and is often undertaken with some resistance and resentment on the part of the client. School affiliation encourages an aura of authority, and in general the school psychologist has responsibilities that modify both his relationships and responsibilities toward individuals. The school psychologist works less with social workers, psychiatrists, juvenile officers, and community agencies, but more with teachers.

There are no formulae for the most appropriate apportionment of a school psychologist's energies. Personnel are so few that there is little experience to indicate an effective mode of deployment. The larger cities are generally more adequately staffed, but even there it has been estimated that the number reaches about one quarter of adequacy. As a result school psychologists have been assigned to emergencies and school catastrophes and have rarely worked in prolonged relationship with individuals or in services other than those which are corrective or remedial.

SCREENING AND DIAGNOSIS

Testing is the one service most common in assignments of school psychologists. Many of the children have skewed understanding of the world,

[42] Percival M. Symonds, "Mental Health in the Classroom: Historical Perspective," *Journal of Social Issues*, 15, No. 1 (1959), 1–7.

inadequate human relations, personal dissatisfactions, and behaviors that disguise feelings from themselves. In such cases the school psychologist is asked to contribute insight drawn from the specialized tools of psychology. The projective techniques have been found particularly useful. These are treated in Chapter 11 of this volume and need not be elaborated here.

Adequate diagnostic process requires information from many sources and careful examination of both behavior and environment. The diagnostician needs expertness in interviewing children, for some of the most important information assuredly comes through self-report. Words are an economical device for bringing the experience of one person into forms comprehensible to another. Serious listening to the child helps the psychologist understand the unique perception of the world and the impact and meaning of experience in the individual's life. Interview findings prove to have low reliability, but the choice is sometimes between accurate measures of the inconsequential and less accurate measurement of significant facts. The interview is probably in the latter class.

Behavior, including symptoms of disturbance, may not always be attributed to internal or psychic factors. These may arise from peculiarities in the environment or from restrictions or demands placed on the person because of his peculiarities. The school psychologist must interpret classroom behavior, but this has meaning in terms of the past as well as the present. The child may be growth-restricted by parents who have either gratified every wish and instilled in him an insatiable need for adulation or inhibited his participation through over-demands and lack of reassurance. Useful diagnostic work requires not only classification of behaviors, but integrated understanding of these behaviors in relation to the strains and disorganizations which exist or have existed for the particular child.

Diagnostic services sometimes stress emotional problems, sometimes intellectual factors. No easy distinction is possible. Lack of achievement is soon converted into emotional disturbance and the corollary is equally true. There is a particularly forceful argument for the careful evaluation of primary children and early learning achievements or failures. During this time the child discovers his potential, establishes attitudes toward scholarship, and revises rather than replaces his self-understanding. The relationship between academic and personal development is particularly vital in these early years.

For information on both environment and behavior the school psychologist is particularly dependent on teacher cooperation and teacher report. Social workers and others contribute to this information, but in all cases teachers have extended acquaintance with the child, and some have considerable insight through observing social behavior, discussing feelings found in literature, reading self-report themes, or evaluating day-to-day work.[43] To

[43] Dorothy E. Sonke, "Growth Experience in Theme-Writing," *English Journal*, 42, No. 5 (May, 1953), 246–250.

secure the best possible information it is often necessary to extend the teacher's written report by means of an interview. Personal contact supplements and may change the meaning of the first referral. One child may reject discipline because he is making a first attempt at independence. Another may reject discipline because he has been disciplined in a foolish and inconsistent fashion, leaving the belief that discipline makes no sense. The difference between these behaviors is more likely to be noted in conversation than in written report.

Personality assessment is an extremely complex task, and, it is generally found that the most effective work is done when many indices of adjustment are combined.[44] Unfortunately, rigid schedules for testing sometimes prohibit adequate gathering of information from school records, home visits, observations, and interviews. As school psychologists refine their techniques it is possible that they will draw more heavily on information concerning school behavior and learning patterns. These data are more readily and more reliably collected than most other data, and there is adequate evidence of relation between them and the child's adjustment.

Individual differences in reading seem particularly great since the range of any classroom is frequently as much as seven or eight grade levels.[45] Reading is a major challenge in the school, contributes to further learning, promotes social understanding, and develops personal identification. Reading failure blocks communication, interferes with understanding self and others, and increases the probability of isolation. Reading preferences and abilities as well as the emotional response to reading materials appear to be a fertile source of information concerning the child's feelings and adaptations to life. Much evidence on unique characteristics, personal resources, modes of adjustment, and personality difficulties may be extracted from the achievement and the behavior of children involved in reading tasks. To be effective the school psychologist needs to be well informed on the problems and the methods of various subjects, but particularly reading.

COUNSELING AND TREATMENT

It is rarely possible for a school psychologist to carry a sizeable counseling case load. Nevertheless, it is essential that some children learn a new and better relationship between themselves and the world. They have a special need to discover who they are and what their role may be. Children are sometimes unable to direct energy toward tasks of development appropriate to their ages. Among school personnel, the school psychologist is best equipped to be helpful.

[44] Ralph M. Tindall, "Relationships Among Indices of Adjustment Status," *Educational and Psychological Measurement,* 15, No. 2 (Summer, 1955), 152–162.

[45] F. O. Triggs, "Psychologist in a Reading Clinic," *Educational and Psychological Measurement,* 14, No. 1 (Spring, 1954), 215–231.

Children, like other clients, bring expectations to counseling. Some expect hostility and rejection, others expect reassurance and support. Most sense danger to their secrets and to the personal organizations of their lives. They may be protective and reticent about their troubles, they may be overwhelmed by the danger of the new experience, or they may come to test their power against one more of the authoritarians. The school psychologist, in a special setting, works with the problems found elsewhere in therapeutic counseling.

The repertoire of techniques and abilities necessary in school psychology is particularly broad. The psychologist often works alone with children from pre-school to senior high school age, with parents from every social group, and with problems of intellect, discipline, and emotions. All this, with short term and abbreviated relationships, increases the need for special adaptations in counseling techniques.

Most school psychologists concentrate on diagnosis, integrating services, and counseling with teachers.[46] Counseling may emphasize cognitive and evaluative discussion more than emotional transference. The counseling session provides for formulating and testing possible courses of action in forms that involve little risk and in a situation that encourages prudent but courageous evaluation of the self and the situation.

The contacts, limited in both frequency and number, are directed toward developing a more accurate picture of assets and liabilities, a clearer view of confronting problems, and a more adequate appraisal of comparative solutions. The aim is a shift in direction more than a reformation of personality.[47] Naturally, personality problems are crucial whether the declared intent is to alter behavior or alter personality.

Many child psychologists favor play therapy. This approach has some characteristics of free association with relaxed and unstructured situations eliciting natural or impulsive responses. Most advocates of the technique hold that natural wisdom will produce increasingly appropriate behavior. It seems a suitable approach for children who are unable to express feelings since it permits experiment and change without developing great dependency on the therapist. Play therapy has been tried in a number of schools. In Brooklyn, New York City schools, an experimental group of students was involved in small but regular sessions conducted by ten teachers who had intensive training as play leaders.[48] The results of this experiment were positive.

[46] F. A. Zehrer, "The School Psychologist as a Mental Hygiene Specialist," *Journal of Consulting Psychology*, 6, No. 4 (July–August, 1942), 218–222.

[47] Leona E. Tyler, "Minimum Charge Therapy," *Personnel and Guidance Journal*, 37, No. 6 (February, 1960), 475–479.

[48] Eli M. Bower, "The Emotionally Handicapped Child and the School, An Analysis of Programs and Trends," *Exceptional Children*, 26, No. 4 (December, 1959), 182–188.

Group approaches capitalize on the effects of personal interaction as the individual seeks to solve problems of feeling. The leader role is limited and tolerant but essential to the development of a therapeutic culture. Teachers sometimes serve in this capacity, but it is apparent that attributes of some successful teachers defeat permissiveness and expressions of tension.[49] The leader needs the help of a consultant to interpret progress and to arrange sessions. Group techniques are not universally good. They do not provide immediate remedy and are not appropriate for accurate environmental problems or for persons with very inadequate reality contacts. Placement of individuals in such a group is contra-indicated by extreme nonconforming behavior, very dominant or monopolist personality factors, inability to express feeling, or inability to tolerate aggression.

It would be economical and effective if the mental health worker could counsel in family groups. Dreikurs and his associates have been developing such techniques. Sessions using this technique were initiated in Eugene, Oregon by Raymond Lowe.[50] They emphasize goal-directed strategies developed within the family. The diagnostic aspects are minimized and attention turned toward a study of family interaction. In the Oregon group, several families are involved at the same time. This is a study approach and the results are attributed to education, not healing.

Counseling that involves only ventilation and reassurance may result in damage by reinforcing inadequate adjustments or by lulling child, parent, and teacher into the belief that something is being accomplished. School psychologists must undertake some counseling that approximates relationship therapy where changes come largely through the medium of relationship with the counselor. The atmosphere that will permit and encourage change is marked by empathy and respect between child and counselor and by a school situation which meets minimal needs for security and affection.

Counseling of this kind involves self-evaluation supported by reflection and interpretation on the part of the counselor. It is probably not so much a matter of uncovering memories as it is a matter of disturbing the view of life so that memory and present knowledge will be reintegrated into a sound contemporary decision. These goals are not achieved without feeling and encounter between personalities, and they frequently demand extended help. Extreme limitation in time or in acceptable forms of counseling have caused some school psychologists to abandon the therapeutic role.

It is generally assumed that children establish a sense of identity largely by analogy. They evaluate and relate themselves to parents, relatives,

[49] Mortimer Schiffer, "The Therapeutic Group in the Public Elementary School," in *Orthopsychiatry and the School,* ed. Morris Krugman (New York: American Orthopsychiatric Association, Inc., 1958), pp. 70–81.

[50] Kris Stokes, "Mommy's Mad," *Old Oregon* (August–September, 1959), pp. 5–6, 24.

friends, and peers. To understand deeply they must have deep and prolonged relationships with a few people. Modern society offers propinquity
without depth. Children know many people but know few people well. For
them, the counseling relationship can be a very new experience, either shock-
ing or gratifying. Some recoil from the intimacy, and some become avid con-
sumers of attention. In either case the psychologist-counselor must establish
a mode of relationship that assures the child a new and appropriate experience in life perceiving.

Valuable solutions are those understood and accepted by children and
families. Counseling helps to enlarge the temporal view, helps the child to
understand his background and project himself into the future. It helps the
child differentiate the specifics in his life, associate aspects that he has selectively eliminated, integrate specific wants into general goals, and arrange
these goals in orders of importance and immediacy.

INTERPRETATION

The purpose of diagnosis and consultation is to change parent and
teacher views in order to change the child's milieu. Some psychologists insist
that the main problem with emotionally disturbed children is an unhealthy
family situation.[51] All psychologists give high priority to the early and close
relationships, although some reserve considerable weight for later broad experiences in school and community. Most child clinics have come to the conclusion that the family must be treated as a unit.[52] A similar conclusion is
appropriate in the school. It may be assumed that the psychologist works extensively with parents and teachers to increase understanding of individual
child problems and modern cultural factors which impinge on particular
children.

Problems of expectation and achievement serve to illustrate the relationship between personal problems and community attitudes. It is frequently necessary to help parents and teachers realize that certain goals are
incompatible with the child's ability or value system. There seems to be a
long-standing relationship between underachievement and over-ambition. One
who has been urged too much may withdraw from the task or indulge in his
own depreciation. Some children, achieving below expectation, live in a
world of compensating dreams and others indulge in hostile pay-back behavior. All must find some way to inhibit the tension that flows from failure.
The psychologist works with social workers, teachers, and parents to interpret
both the general principle and the specific application.

51 John Whithall and A. Rittenhouse, "Child Therapy—A Frame of Reference,"
Exceptional Children, 21, No. 4 (January, 1955), 122–126; and Caroline B. Zachry,
"The Psychotherapist and the School," *Nervous Child*, 3, No. 4 (July, 1944), 249–257.
    52 Donald C. Klein, "The Prevention of Mental Illness," *Mental Hygiene*, 45, 1
(January, 1951), 101–109.

The contemporary school psychologist will have a particular concern with achievement motives since academic standards have recently become a matter of renewed and popular concern. Unfortunately, standards often mean "toughness" more than thoroughness. Toughness tends to concentrate in peripheral matters and the toughest part may be some trivial aspect of a task. Academic goals and standards are not simple or universally agreed. If schools are to foster a disposition to find and to use the maximum potentials of each child, then it is necessary to clarify these values.

Failure, even in a specific area, is frequently followed by reduction in potential in that area and in others. For example, failure in academic matters makes the child conspicuous and to some degree unacceptable. In the long run, it isolates the child from peers. Teachers and parents often assume that they should increase the motivation, but the fact is that increased motivation in difficult tasks produces a marked increase in avoidance and fear conflicts.[53] If one has avoided the appropriate response, a strengthened approach to that behavior may heighten the fear and conflict which directed the previous failure. Reduced motivation with reduced fear and avoidance would increase the approach toward suitable behavior. Sometimes success is more likely if teachers and parents reduce motivation rather than increase it.

Almost every case requires work with parents and teachers. This is true even in problems associated with developmental plateaus. There are points of conflict more or less common in the process of growing up. Hostility and aggression in mild forms are characteristic of children at certain periods and these can develop into serious problems. It has been proposed that conflict with adults is normal in the adolescent period and particularly pronounced in our culture.[54] The reasons given usually include that the child is trying to establish independence, the child's individual family values and behavior may differ from those prevailing in other families, and the child and parent represent two different culture patterns. The school psychologist will not always be the consultant in these matters, but he participates in bringing about an agreed and orderly pattern of arrangements for the child.

The child who has been studied by school personnel, including the school psychologist, and even the child who has received some specialized psychological counseling, is not returned to the classroom with all problems solved. The counselor may have helped him integrate and accept facts but mostly at a symbolic level. Now he needs teacher support and help so that he may take appropriate action. Through diagnosis and consultation with teachers and parents it is hoped to develop a milieu in school and home conducive to the development of the child.

[53] Dollard and Miller, *Personality and Psychotherapy,* pp. 355–365.
[54] Henry A. Murray and Clyde Kluckhohn, *Personality in Nature Society and Culture* (2nd ed.) (New York: Alfred A. Knopf, Inc., 1953), pp. 3–49.

In-Service Work with Teachers

Mental health goals must be integrated with other educational goals and achieved primarily by teachers who are experts in providing opportunities for growth and not experts in remediation or reconstruction of personality. To meet subject matter demands, the teacher must be able to deal with content in a variety of arrangements and at various levels so that individual students may participate and learn. To meet mental health demands, the teacher must have both knowledge and personal adequacy. Some of the earliest criteria for selecting teacher candidates included personal maturity and warmth essential to the nurture of developing children. More recently, William Menninger said, "The capacity to form warm interpersonal relationships, with ability to love and inspire, the quality of feeling and sympathizing with the student—these are the special abilities of the most successful teachers." [55]

Educational goals beyond specific learning or beyond the simple absence of emotional disorder and unsocial behavior are made difficult in an impersonal, secular, and urban society where there is division of labor and where community functions are handled by secondary groups. The school is no longer characterized by personal intimacy, common values and knowledge, prolonged intercommunication, and the local pride and loyalty that were common in rural society. Sound relationships between ideas, emotions, and actions are achieved, "not by 'patching-up,' adding a specialist or two, setting aside a guidance hour, or including a 'personality check list'." [56] These outcomes are not tied to a special service, a specific area of study, or a specialized technique.

CONSULTATION

The trend is to expect more from teachers and provide more supporting resources.[57] An increase in consultation services is encouraged by the economy involved and by the growing conviction that some problems are most effectively managed in the classroom. The "case consultation" has more natural dynamic than "periodic consultation." To work successfully "through" the teacher requires a joining of forces toward a common goal. The teacher is eager to understand the individual child and to direct emotional energy into classroom work and acceptable social behaviors. The psychologist with special knowledge of personality dynamics, special techniques

[55] Menninger, *Educational Leadership*, 7, No. 8 (May, 1950), 514.

[56] Caroline Tryon, "Fostering Mental Health in Our Schools," *Association for Supervision and Curriculum Development, National Education Association Yearbook* (1950), p. 11.

[57] William G. Hollister, "Current Trends in Mental Health Programming in the Classroom," *Journal of Social Issues*, 15, No. 1 (January, 1959), 50–58.

of observation and diagnosis, and special understanding of individuated teaching can be immediately useful, and in the long run, influential by helping with the case.

The consultant is in a collaborative role. Contacts are often made at times of emotional crisis when the teacher is tempted to either get out of the classroom or get the child out of the classroom. An effective relationship helps to resolve the problem and contributes also to the teacher's personal development.[58] The work may be impeded by teacher anxiety over acceptance by another profession, willingness to let the expert solve the problem, or apprehension concerning personal adequacies. The shortcomings of the consultant may include minimizing the work or the ideas of the teacher, insisting on inflexible theories concerning personality and growth, making recommendations that are impractical or have been previously tried, or assuming the "my case" position.

The teacher as a representative of the adult world is the recipient of feelings arising from both school and non-school experiences. This results in confusion and insecurity and either one interferes with the teacher's ability to recognize the child's unique perception of the world. Consultation should serve to support the teacher as well as explain the child's behavior, thus freeing the teacher to be understanding and compassionate. Such a teacher uses discipline and requirements, for growth purposes and not merely for the maintenance of order.

Simple recognition of the teacher's problem bolsters confidence and helps the teacher bear the normal failures associated with inability to meet either the child's needs or community demands for discipline. Increasing teacher security parallels the ability to provide the aura of security found so essential in special classes. In these groups it has been found best to provide minimum basic satisfactions in a small group where belonging is encouraged. The emphasis is on assets, pressure is reduced, remedial opportunities are available, and offerings are flexible allowing selection of experiences on an individual basis.[59]

Large increments in teacher growth have come from a well developed referral system. The necessity to reduce case loads where psychological services are understaffed may be turned into a minor advantage through developing a careful screening system at the classroom and school levels. The screening becomes a minor case study involving teacher, supervisor, and

[58] Eloise B. Cason, "Some Suggestions on the Interaction Between the School Psychologist and the Classroom Teacher," *Journal of Consulting Psychology*, 9, No. 3 (May–June, 1945), 132–137; Edmond F. Erwin, Dorothy Drisbach and Finetha Groves, "Promoting Effective Relationships between the Schools and the Child Guidance Clinic," *Mental Hygiene*, 41, No. 4 (October, 1957), 542–545; and Gerald Caplan, "Opportunities for School Psychologists in the Primary Prevention of Mental Disorders in Children," *Mental Hygiene*, 47, No. 4 (1963), 525–538.

[59] Helen Moak, *The Troubled Child* (New York: Holt, Rinehart & Winston, Inc., 1958), pp. 130–142.

principal. This approach leads to a careful statement of the problem, more thorough presentation of pertinent data and the suggestion of possible hypotheses. It results in more careful consideration of the teacher-pupil relationship and more examination of classroom conditions that intensify or reduce the problem. After such study the school makes more effective use of the specialist and the study itself has increased the insight of teacher and administrator.

When such services are available, teachers make increasingly frequent use of them.[60] This popularity is not without hazards. The Rochester Plan for Mental Health grew out of a need for educational services in a mental hospital in Rochester, Michigan. The original enthusiasm for clinical mental health views was modified by experience.[61] Some of the children sensed the atmospheric change and began to "act out" minimizing educational outcomes. Even the best teachers could not abandon all of the characteristic teacher-pupil relationships. Infantile and instinctive responses, tolerable and useful in therapy, jeopardized group welfare and interfered with classroom accomplishments. It was found that teachers must retain the role of educators; they may cease to be successful when they overdepend on therapeutic techniques or when very great permissiveness disrupts previously organized patterns of control.

The well prepared teacher will not confuse accepting the child with removing controls. Acceptance may mean either the increase of affection and encouragement or the establishment of more rigid limits and controls. In all cases acceptance means responding intelligently to the child's needs. The teacher must make practical decisions with important consequences for the child. A teacher aware of the significance of these decisions needs support as well as expert interpretation of the case. In offering either of these the psychologist may wisely bear in mind that the classroom is not a clinic.

In most cases there will be a need to examine the interpersonal relations between teacher and child, but it should not be assumed that either teacher-child relationships or child-child relationships are the central content of learning.[62] They are a medium for learning and their quality influences both the amount and the quality of achievement. The outcomes of learning are inseparable from the learning environment including degrees of affection or isolation that exist between child and teacher.

The teacher may well exceed the administrator in capacity to promote

[60] David G. Salten, Victor B. Elkin, and Gilbert M. Trachtman, "Public School Psychological Services: Recent Growth and Further Potential," *Educational Administration and Supervision*, 42, No. 1 (January, 1956), 100–107, 162–169.

[61] M. L. Falick, Mildred Peters, Morton Levitt and Ben Rubenstein, "Observations on the Psychological Education of Teachers in a School Based Mental Hygiene Program," *Mental Hygiene*, 38, No. 3 (July, 1954), 374–386.

[62] Barbara Biber, "Teacher Education in Mental Health (From the Point of View of the Educator)," in *Orthopsychiatry and the School*, ed. Krugman, p. 172.

mental health in the school. The consultant may enlarge frustration by proposing procedures unacceptable to supervisors and principals, or procedures inappropriate to working conditions. Conflict may be avoided by involving the principal in the case study and in whatever decisions are made. Conferences involving administrator, teacher, and mental health specialist benefit the child and assure that psychological principles become incorporated in school policy and practice.

INSTITUTES AND SEMINARS

Mental health workers frequently offer courses and seminars for teachers. The objection has been made that some of these are not tied closely enough to problems of the classroom and that others increase teacher anxiety without providing for any solution. Some of the more successful seminars try to establish a therapeutic atmosphere and deal with the natural teaching problems.[63] They seek to increase the teacher's self-awareness, capacity to understand dynamics of behavior, responsible attitudes, and sensitivity.

Field experience in other social agencies has been used as a special training opportunity. Teachers have participated in the work of mental hospitals and to a lesser extent in other treatment agencies.[64] These experiences have been more often offered to teachers in-training than to teachers in-service.

CHILD STUDY

The most popular in-service work has been the child study group. A small group of teachers meets regularly over a prolonged period, sometimes two or three years, in order to improve attitudes and understandings. The study groups are sometimes associated with others in an organized program such as that of the Institute for Child Study, University of Maryland.[65] This program, begun in 1939 and housed at the University of Maryland since 1947, involves three or four thousand teachers each year. Efforts are directed toward developing the clinically oriented teacher in the hope of improving teacher-child relationships and effectiveness.

Each teacher studies one child intensively, keeps careful case records, and through discussion with other teachers seeks to understand both individ-

[63] Clark Moustakas, "A Human Relations Seminar at the Merril-Palmer School," in *Basic Approaches to Mental Health*, ed. Joseph Sampler (Washington, D.C.: American Personnel and Guidance Association, 1960), pp. 30–37.

[64] Alfred E. Kuenzli, "A Field-Experience Program with Emotionally Disturbed Children," *Exceptional Children*, 25, No. 4 (December, 1958), 158–161.

[65] Bernard Peck and Daniel A. Prescott, "The Program at the Institute for Child Study, The University of Maryland," in *Basic Approaches to Mental Health*, ed. Sampler.

ual and larger mental health problems. Each group comprises eight to fifteen teachers with a leader trained either in a six-week course at Maryland or a two-week workshop conducted by consultants from Maryland. The program continues for three years with the groups meeting two hours every second week. They are visited by a consultant at least three times each year. Otherwise the responsibility is with the local coordinator.

Another extensive program with a different organization has influenced Canadian mental health. This is the Forest Hill Village Project, sponsored by the Canadian National Committee for Mental Hygiene.[66] It was begun in 1948 with the general purpose of promoting mental health through developing a guidance clinic with a pervasive community influence. As one aspect of the program, established teachers were chosen as trainees and exposed to clinical practice in mental hospitals, juvenile courts, and other community agencies. They were given a broad view of treatment to prepare them, not as specialized therapists, but as liaison officers skilled in utilizing and cooperating with clinical personnel and able to interpret mental health to educators and the public. It was anticipated that a year of academic preparation and special awareness of clinical work would enable them to supervise programs of adult education and be of assistance to schools.

The project also carried on human relations classes with normal children in grades six to twelve. These children were given a special experience in a nondirective, free discussion class with a visiting teacher. Reports on the program assume that free discussion and comparatively free emotional expression are unusual in the school but that is debatable. In any case, the leaders took a minor role on the assumption that elimination of external forces would cause the children to concentrate on psychodynamic content of real significance.

Observers indicate that the discussions were particularly complex and mature for children of school age and that there was a large degree of emotional engagement. If unusual anxiety was provoked an associated therapeutic team gave direct service. From pre- and post-tests with the experimental children and with an equated control group there is evidence of improvement in attitudes and personality. An associated result was a dramatic improvement in academic grades, especially in English, the subject from which the time was taken for the discussions. Later evidence also indicates that the ex-

[66] John R. Seeley, "The Forest Hill Village Human Relations Class," *Basic Approaches to Mental Health,* ed. Joseph Sampler (Washington, D.C.: American Personnel and Guidance Association, 1960), pp. 37–47; M. I. Morgan and R. H. Ojemann, "The Effect of Learning Program Designed to Assist Youth in the Understanding of Behavior and Its Development," *Child Development,* 13, No. 3 (September, 1942), 181–194; and Committee on Preventive Psychiatry of the Group for the Advancement of Psychiatry, *Promotion of Mental Health in the Primary and Secondary Schools: An Evaluation of Four Schools,* Report 18 (January, 1951), pp. 11–12.

perimental students were much more successful in securing university scholarships.

Child study groups often follow a fairly well established procedure and numerous guides are available.[67] The study emphasizes a search for evidence that is valid, reliable, and sufficient. This is followed by making hypotheses and testing them in the discussion group. A study of interpersonal relations plays a major part. There is an attempt to understand how the study group influences current learning in order to clarify the conditions that exist in a particular classroom.

One outcome of child study has been the development of devices for studying pupil-pupil and teacher-pupil relationships. It has been found that some groups center on one leader and some on more wide-spread leadership and that the learning outcomes differ for the two groups.

Learning differs too in relation to dominative or integrative teacher behavior. With a dominative teacher pupils tend to be distractible as well as alternately compliant and rejecting of teacher domination. With an integrative teacher, pupils show more spontaneity, initiative, voluntary contribution, and problem solving.

Flanders, at Minnesota, developed an interaction analysis specifically to analyze classroom relations and patterns of teaching.[68] He found that teachers used much more of the total talking time than did clinicians and a much larger percentage of the talk was directive or authoritarian. The clinician controls his own verbal behavior in the interest of client participation. In the classroom the socio-emotional aspects are probably more subordinate to intellectual aspects and dominative behavior may be more appropriate. It was found, however, that eighth grade teachers talked 62 per cent of the time leaving a little more than one per cent for each student. The teacher talk was 60 per cent giving information or ideas, 22 per cent asking questions, and 10 per cent giving directions. The study group member discusses studies of this kind and is encouraged to relate it to his own behavior and effectiveness.

Studies of classroom social structure show considerable and comparatively stable stratification in children's relationships. Both popularity and expertness play a part in setting this structure.[69] Children of lower classroom status respond with primitive defenses while higher status children choose

[67] Millie Almy, *Ways of Studying Children* (New York: Bureau of Publications, Teachers College, Columbia University, 1959), 226 pages; and Gertrude P. Driscoll, *How to Study the Behavior of Children* (New York: Bureau of Publications, Teachers College, Columbia University, 1950).

[68] Ned A. Flanders, "Teacher-Pupil Contacts and Mental Hygiene," *Journal of Social Issues*, 15, No. 1 (1959), 30–39.

[69] Ronald Lippitt and Martin Gold, "Classroom Social Structure as a Mental Health Problem," *Journal of Social Issues*, 15, No. 1 (1959), 40–49.

more mature defenses and less reality distortion. The less successful children respond with more aggressive-assertive or passive-hostile activities thereby disrupting interpersonal feelings and classroom activities. Each child tries to influence his peers, but those who fail become aggressive and hostile and further deteriorate their condition. Teachers respond to the low status boys with criticism and to low status girls with support. Clearly, socio-emotional status is a problem for the teacher. In solving problems of pupil socio-emotional status or problems of teacher-child relationship, the child study approach makes its greatest contribution.

Evaluation of child study programs show an increased interest in further work and gains in ability to: [70, 71]

1. Accept the disturbed child;
2. Deal with provocation;
3. See underlying causes of behavior;
4. Express developmental concepts;
5. Substantiate statements;
6. Consider all factors in a case;
7. Report effectively;
8. Refer more selectively.

The teacher does not become a clinician but does acquire increased capacity to teach effectively and use the group relation for good mental health.

CURRICULAR MODIFICATION

Curricular adjustments to improve mental health have been of two kinds: inclusion of mental health materials or units; and examination of personality dynamics in the study of ordinary materials.

Some schools include units on mental health and human relations in health, social studies, or other courses. The Bullis Classes in Human Relations are among the better known programs.[72] First offered in Delaware and then more broadly used, these classes begin with a specially designed story, move to discussion and then, students write on associated questions. The course is based on a greatly simplified motivational scheme of four drives: adventure, security, recognition, and sex. Lesson plans in two volumes outline a sequence of topics and present conclusions for each topic. The plan has been criticized

[70] Robert H. Anderson and Elizabeth Zimmerman, "Evaluating a Child Study Program," *Educational Leadership*, 7, No. 8 (May, 1950), 568–571.

[71] Hugh V. Perkins, Jr., "Teachers Grow in Understanding Children," *Educational Leadership*, 7, No. 8 (May, 1950), 549–555.

[72] Michael J. Cortale, "Counselors and Discipline," *Personnel and Guidance Journal*, 39, No. 5 (January, 1961), 349–351; and Committee on Preventive Psychiatry of the Group for the Advancement of Psychiatry, *Promotion of Mental Health in the Primary and Secondary Schools: An Evaluation of Four Schools*, Report #18 (January, 1951), pp. 3–6.

as overprescriptive and narrow in theoretical view. It has also been criticized on the grounds that there is too much moralizing, the content may be forgotten because the principles are not employed or practiced, and discussion may heighten anxiety in some children.

A program known as the Force Project offers two courses, the first in social behavior, the second in family relationships.[73] These offerings are built not on a particular psychodynamic theory but on the everyday problems of social or family contact. The topic is behavior but the discussion naturally turns toward the evaluation of attitudes.

A research oriented approach requiring major modification in the regular curriculum has been associated with Ralph H. Ojemann from the State University of Iowa.[74] Traditional content is presented in dynamic terms. Material from social studies, literature, home economics, and English normally deals with human behavior and under this plan is taught to enlarge understanding of personality and interpersonal relations. Materials, especially in the social sciences, are examined to discover dynamics rather than to learn surface facts.

The object is to teach psychodynamic principles and provide practice in their use. The presentations emphasize concepts of a) motivation, b) multiple causation, and c) a distribution of values rather than a dichotomy. Essentially this is not a course in human relations but a humanizing of all content.

The Ojemann project has the advantage of breadth and its techniques are primarily teaching not therapy, therefore, acceptable in the schools. There is no concerted effort to uncover conflict or provide catharsis. The approach appears to produce enthusiasm with the probable development of greater tolerance, plasticity, and perhaps better personal integration.

The most frequent attempt to modify content for mental health purposes comes through teacher selection of educational materials and learning activities. Some teachers use dramatics, art, music, and literature to develop sensitivities and examine feelings and values. Literature, deliberately selected, has proved most useful. The term "bibliotherapy" was coined and many bibliotherapeutic lists of readings are available grouped by age, by specific emotional problems, or common situational hazards.

Elements from curricular arrangements reported in the literature can be found in different combinations in many schools. Evaluation of these must consider the adequacy of the classroom and the teacher, especially if the orientation is toward group therapy and the reflection of feelings. Can these efforts help with complex problems? Are they effective with delinquent,

[73] Committee on Preventive Psychiatry of the Group for the Advancement of Psychiatry, *Promotion of Mental Health,* Report #18 (January, 1951), pp. 6–8.

[74] M. I. Morgan and R. H. Ojemann, *Child Development,* 13, No. 3 (September, 1942), 181–194; and Committee on Preventive Psychiatry of the Group for the Advancement of Psychiatry, *Promotion of Mental Health,* Report No. 18 (January, 1951), pp. 6–8.

withdrawn or hostile children? Will the learning transfer? It appears that the school psychologist should participate in evaluating and establishing program offerings.

Mental health is affected by curricular offerings, administrative practices and personnel selection. The effects of good teaching are minimized in a school that offers a narrow curriculum inappropriate for children of many kinds and levels of ability. School-home relationships, scheduling, and discipline practices may exemplify and support the teacher's efforts or may conflict and defeat them. The psychologist properly plays a part in determining curriculum and policy.

A PEER RELATIONSHIP

In the in-service undertaking the psychologist and teacher are collaborators, both professional, both expert, but professional and expert in different things. The assumption that teachers are ignorant and careless of mental health values is outmoded. Teachers have long been concerned with more than grades, discipline, and good order. There is a very large body of recent evidence which indicates that clinicians' and teachers' attitudes on mental health converge more and more. It should be noted that this is a convergence from both sides. Both professions have matured and it should be expected that growing knowledge and increasing professionalism will create new points of agreement. On the other hand, the difference in assigned tasks probably precludes completely identical views.

Relationship to Community Mental Health

A good mental health environment in the school cannot be grafted on inadequate community attitudes. The community mental health program and the school mental health program have essentially similar objectives. They seek healthy emotional ties in the home, adequate care for emotionally disturbed adults, adequate educational opportunities for exceptional children, suitable recreational opportunities, and other common goals. The community approach is like that of the school; both emphasize situational studies and not only personal dynamics, both emphasize mental health consultation more than prolonged individual treatment, both emphasize group methods in matters of prevention, and both emphasize environmental intervention. The school psychologist representing the broadest community organization may expect to take a large role in community mental health projects.

The Thayer Conference recommended that the school psychologist should be an essential person in a complete mental health program.[75] He

[75] Cutts, op. cit., pp. 66–74.

should probably collaborate with and encourage development of non-school programs and be a well informed user of available services. Through contact with officials and groups he can point out community needs and give leadership in developing services.

The school psychologist will find it necessary to limit out-of-school responsibilities but the educator among psychologists can be of particular value in community mental health education. PTA members and others are capable of understanding the characteristic conditions out of which anxiety comes. It is useful for a community to sense that emotional breakdown is related to the arrid emotional climate and little opportunity to react, or that breakdown frequently comes with the disintegration of human supports and deteriorating relationships in structured groups. A community that examines itself, not in morbid curiosity but purposeful frankness, may be expected to improve the mental health environment. The effective school psychologist can help parents to improve their parenthood or to anticipate problems and seek early and appropriate help.

Community or adult education may also contribute to family organization. For example, parents are frequently confused in establishing a balance of control and freedom. The psychologist may usefully clarify the demand for autonomy, the hazards of inadequate controls, or the need to modify one's own environment. Some districts have found it particularly useful to work with "crises groups," parents of children with like tasks or like problems—new enrollees, physical handicaps, shyness, or antisocial behavior.

Education has become a major criterion of personal and community worth. Intensified concerns over school accomplishment have enhanced the potential of school psychologists as private counselors. Parents who seek consultations about children's reading or achievement continue in counseling to solve marital, interpersonal, and other problems. Data are sparse, but there are frequent reports of "moonlighting" and occasional opinions that a few years in the school is a fine route to the private practice of psychology. Obviously a departure in this direction brings many problems, both community and intra-professional. These are not fully controlled by either legislation or professional tradition.

By far the most important influence is national intervention in education. Federal programs and funds are powerful in special education, vocational rehabilitation, elementary counseling, and probably in the education of child development specialists. Indeed, educational functions are spreading into several departments, for example, into Youth Opportunity Centers under the Department of Labor. The functions of these services and the training of the personnel have very broad overlap with school psychology and school counseling. The parameters of service and the relationships between personnel have already produced rumblings in national professional organizations. The development of working agreements, the establishment of standards, and the clarification of these roles for the public will surely challenge the school psychologist and others for a decade or more.

The attack on underpriviledge as part of the War on Poverty provides an illustration of the uncertain demarcation which exists between community and school. The American conscience has been stirred by the proportions and permanence of poverty. People newly sensitive to the waste and damage which follow defective experience have enlisted school help but they have not dumped the problem into the schools. Several professional and many lay groups are actively involved in Head Start and related activities. These undertakings call for new forms of cooperation and new techniques. Children raised outside the achiever's culture with sparsity of objects, monotony in color, and noisy backgrounds demonstrate different perceptual and auditory development. Neither parent nor child responds well to the "talk cure," long the change process used in psychotherapy. Effective work with underpriviledged families calls for updated school psychology.[76]

Research and Evaluation

The evaluation of counseling, therapy, and psychological services is a problem of continuing concern and constant irritation.[77] The underlying psychological theories are themselves divergent and speculative. Their value is argued on large human functions which are hard to examine and the nature of the work is so dramatic and critical that research cannot be allowed to interfere with the primary ends. Nevertheless, there is a continuing need to establish criteria that show that progress is being made.

Appropriate criteria are elusive. For example, the number of people using mental health services in a community might increase and this could be a sign either of increasing mental health due to increased sophistication, or it might be a sign of increasing incidence of problems. Much of the evidence of good mental health services is essentially negative related to tragedies that did not occur. Some evidence would have to be drawn from the small changes in behavior which accompany large changes in feelings and happiness.

Evaluation is not impossible. A typical case at one point in the school's history may be compared with a typical case at another point in order to assess decreased or increased adequacy of management. Evidences of improvement include: better teacher-clinic relationships, more adequate financial

[76] Frank Riessman, Jerome Cohen, and Arthur Pearl, eds., *Mental Health of the Poor* (New York: Free Press of Glencoe, Inc., 1964); and Donald C. Smith, ed., *Journal of School Psychology*, 4, No. 3 (Spring, 1966), entire issue.

[77] Paul L. Dressel, "A. Some Approaches to Evaluation," E. J. Shoben Jr., "B. Some Problems in Establishing Criteria of Effectiveness," Harold B. Pepinsky, "C. Some Proposals for Research," in "Research and Counseling: A Symposium," *Personnel and Guidance Journal*, 31, No. 6 (February, 1953), 284–294.

support for special services, more effective use of non-school agencies, curricular adjustments to meet individual needs, and above all, improved student behavior.

Text books on school psychology usually emphasize a research function. Federal legislation and particularly the *Elementary and Secondary Education Act of 1965* enlarge the possibilities for such work. A significant portion of educational research may now be controlled in the public schools instead of universities. Perhaps the school psychologist will expand the research and data gathering which should contribute to curriculum and policy making. The opportunities are greatly enlarged.

The psychologist continues to be responsible for the development of his own skills and knowledge and for the improvement of psychological services. At the present time, school psychologists commonly share a responsibility for adapting techniques and findings from clinical, social, experimental, and educational psychology to the peculiar and unique uses of the school.

Contemporary urban culture, with its requirements for specialization and abstraction, assigns the school a large part in child-rearing. Some parents propose that children (especially others' children) be conditioned to failure and danger and believe that creativity squeezes out of insecurity and morality grows from punishment. Others contend that anxious experiences promote anxiety, and that affiliation and happiness are natural partners of morality and achievement. What seems proper solicitude for one is pampering to another. Both are concerned about socio-emotional loadings in the school but the role for school psychology is most ambiguous when it focuses on personality or mental health.

It seems almost impossible to escape the conclusion that thought and performance are deeply marked by the personality of thinker and performer. So too, educational outcomes bear a valid relation to the learner and the process of learning. An advancing culture is likely to enlarge the expectation that, hand-in-hand with scholarship, schools will promote the development of purpose, confidence, and imagination.

Selected Supplementary Readings

Allinsmith, Wesley, and George W. Goethals, *The Role of Schools in Mental Health*. New York: Basic Books, 1962.

Ausubel, David P., "Some Misconceptions Regarding Mental Health Functions and Practices in the School," *Psychology in the Schools*, 2 (April, 1965), 99–105.

Bardon, Jack I., "Mental Health Education: A Framework for Psychological Services in the Schools," *Journal of School Psychology*, 1, No. 1 (January, 1963), 20–27.

————, ed., *Journal of School Psychology,* 3, No. 2 (Winter, 1964–65), whole issue.

Becker, Ernest, *The Revolution in Psychiatry: A New Understanding of Man.* New York: Free Press of Glencoe, Inc., 1964.

Bennett, Chester C., "Community Psychology: Impressions of the Boston Conference on the Education of Psychologists for Community Mental Health," *American Psychologist,* 20 (October, 1965), 832–835.

Bindman, Arthur J., ed., *Roles and Functions in School Mental Health,* all of *Journal of Education,* Vol. 146 (1964).

Bellak, L., ed., *Handbook of Community Psychiatry and Community Mental Health.* New York: Grune and Stratton, Inc., 1964.

Bonham, S. J., and T. M. Stephens, eds., *Mental Health Planning in Education,* Report of Invitational Work Conference, Division of Special Education, Ohio Department of Education: 1964.

Bower, E. M., "Mental Health and Education," *Education Leadership,* 21 (1963), 8–10.

————, "Mental Health in Education," *Review of Educational Research,* 32, No. 5 (1962), 441–454.

Caplan, Gerald, "Opportunities for School Psychologists in the Primary Prevention of Mental Disorders in Children," *Mental Hygiene,* 47 (1963), 525–538.

————, ed., *Prevention of Mental Disorders in Children* (especially Chapter XVI). New York: Basic Books, Inc., 1961.

Cutler, Richard L., Phillip E. Spieth, and Mary F. Wilkinson, "School and Community Mental Health Programs," *Review of Educational Research,* 32, No. 5 (1962), 476–483.

Freeman, Hugh, and James Farndale, eds., *Trends in the Mental Health Services: A Symposium of Original and Reprinted Papers.* New York: The Macmillan Company, 1963.

Gray, Susan W., "Psychology's Contribution to the School," in *The Psychologist in the Schools.* New York: Holt, Rinehart & Winston, Inc., 1963.

Henry, Nelson B., ed., *Mental Health in Modern Education,* 54th Yearbook, Part II, National Society for the Study of Education. Chicago: University of Chicago Press, 1955.

Hodges, Allen, "The Mental Health Profession in the Community: Some Generalizations for Effectiveness," *Mental Hygiene,* XLIII (July, 1964), 363–365.

Hubbard, J. I., and R. F. Peck, "Mental Health in the Schools," Conference Proceedings, *The School Psychologist* (Spring, 1966), pp. 43–45.

Knutson, Andie L., "New Perspectives Regarding Positive Mental Health," *American Psychologist,* XVIII (June, 1963), 300–306.

Krugman, Morris, ed., *Orthopsychiatry and the School.* New York: American Orthopsychiatric Association, Inc., 1958.

Lambert, Nadine M., *et al.*, *The Protection and Promotion of Mental Health in Schools.* Washington, D. C.: U. S. Department of Health, Education, and Welfare, Public Health Service, Mental Health Monograph 5, 1964.

Mental Health of Children. U. S. Public Health Service Publication No. 1396. Washington, D. C.: 1966.

Morse, W. C., "Perceptions of Classroom Mental Health, Group Process and Learning from Diverse Points of View," *Perceptual and Motor Skills,* XIV (1962).

Myers, E. S., ed., *Community Mental Health Advances.* Bethesda, Md.: U. S. Department of Health, Education and Welfare, Public Health Service, National Institute of Mental Health, 1964.

Osterweil, Jerry, "School Psychology and Comprehensive Mental Health Planning," *Community Mental Health Journal,* 2 (Summer, 1966), 142–145.

Rhule, Warren Allen, "Mental Health and the School in the Future," *Psychology in the Schools,* 2 (April, 1965), 167–168.

Seidman, Jerome M., *Educating for Mental Health; A Book of Readings.* New York: Thomas Y. Crowell Company, 1963.

Strother, Charles L., ed., *Psychology and Mental Health.* Washington, D. C.: American Psychological Association, 1957.

Szasz, Thomas S., *The Myth of Mental Illness: Foundations of a Theory of Personal Conduct.* New York: Hoeber-Harper, 1961.

Torrance, E. Paul, *Constructive Behavior: Stress, Personality, and Mental Health.* Belmont, California: Wadsworth Publishing Company, 1965.

Torrance, E. Paul, and R. D. Strom, *Mental Health and Achievement.* New York: John Wiley & Sons, Inc., 1965.

Waetjen, W., and R. Leeper, eds., *Learning and Mental Health in the School.* Washington, D. C.: NEA-ASCD, 1966.

White, Mary Alice, and Myron W. Harris, "Mental Illness in Relation to the Pupil Population," and "Surveys of Maladjustment in the Pupil Population," in *The School Psychologist.* New York: Harper & Row, Publishers, 1961.

Yamamoto, Kaoru, "The Healthy Person: A Review," *Personnel and Guidance Journal,* 44, No. 6 (February, 1966).

IRLA LEE ZIMMERMAN

HIRSCH LAZAAR SILVERMAN

10

Individual Intellectual Evaluation of School Children

Major Considerations in Individual Intellectual Testing

The intellectual assessment of school children was the original, and for years, the primary occupation of the school psychologist. Historically, such a role could be dated from the construction of the first Binet-Simon Scale [1] in 1905, as a tool to segregate subnormal children attending Paris schools.

With the increasing number of psychologists working in the schools, the individual assessment of intelligence is still a primary task.[2] Sometimes this testing is routine, to meet the requirements of a state law, such as placement in a special class. Sometimes the testing is ex-

---

[1] A. Binet and T. H. Simon, "Méthodes Nouvelles pour le Diagnostic du Niveau Intellectuel des Anormaux," *Année Psychologie,* 11 (1905), 191–244.

[2] E. M. Bower, *The School Psychologist* (Sacramento, Calif.: State Department of Education, 1955).

268

ploratory, when children rated at either extreme of the distribution on group tests are referred for individual testing to explore the meaning of the deviant group test score. The history of the development of intellectual assessment is presented in Chapter 1.

Another source of referral stems from the current emphasis in some schools on homogeneous or cluster grouping, and the selection of "gifted" children for special programs. However, often the most challenging referral is that of the child with classroom problems that may or may not be related to his intellectual functioning. Both learning and behavior difficulties can be involved. Adequate evaluation of such children can be crucial for their future development. For example, many remedial classes and child guidance clinics reject applicants with less than average intelligence.

Originally, the Binet-Simon Scale had been constructed to predict school success and the child's need for a special or limited curriculum. With the introduction of the concepts of mental age and IQ, the intelligence test data provided estimates of the level of maturation and the rate of development of the child as well. Currently, such tests are considered not only for an objective comparison of the child with others of his age, but also to provide a measure of his intellectual resources, the nature and extent of his strengths and weaknesses on cognitive tasks, his ability to deal with the here-and-now problem solving provided by the test, his characteristic response to challenge, authority, and school-like problems, and other aspects related to school adjustment. The examiner's skillful observations of a variety of behaviors elicited by the test leads to summaries of results that are far from simple numbers such as IQs.

In order to reach a proper evaluation of intelligence test results, the school psychologist must have considerable experience with tests. Intelligence tests have been based on a number of tacit assumptions that must at times be spelled out, to make results meaningful. For example, the inherent interest of test material to the child, and the motivation to solve the problems presented, are assumed to be relatively similar for each child. However, the anxious or emotionally disturbed child may have little interest in testing, and this reaction may be clearly evident to an observant examiner. The danger in not utilizing such information is clearly and tragically illustrated in a recent investigation [3] of individuals who had been institutionalized as mentally retarded, only to be released as within normal limits at a later date. A review of original testing indicated repeated evidence of disturbance that limited the child's ability to perform adequately on test material. For example, negativeness, peculiarity, or other unusual behavior was frequently reported, yet the influence of this on the test performance had been ignored.

[3] S. L. Garfield and D. C. Affleck, "A Study of Individuals Committed to a State Home for the Retarded Who Were Later Released as not Mentally Defective," *American Journal of Mental Deficiency*, 64 (1960), 907–915.

On the other hand, the Fels studies,[4] among others, reveal the tendency to increase test scores over the years as a function of a "problem solving set" which could be related to family goals and personality variables.

Intellectual testing also assumes that the child has been exposed to the culture in which the test was constructed. The exposure of children to relevant items in the environment (for example, money, pictures, or language itself) is often assumed without further question. Yet a physical handicap may limit the child's experiences with such material, thus penalizing him unduly on his test performance. Attempts to construct tests that minimize past experiences, and are thus "culture fair," have not proved too successful. Actually, such measures may be more influenced by cultural enrichment, which broadens a child's background, than was originally believed. For example, the Raven's Progressive Matrices Test, involving picture analogies problems, may penalize children from lower socio-economic levels,[5] perhaps because it represents the kind of problems most meaningful to children with wide exposure to picture puzzles.

Another assumption inherent in the use of intelligence tests is that the child to be tested is similar to those upon whom the test was standardized. If the standardization population consisted solely of urban, white children, the test cannot be assumed to measure adequately the intellectual functionings of rural, Negro children. This point will be discussed in greater detail in Chapter 16.

The meaning of test items at different ages has also been assumed to be constant, yet this too must be questioned on the basis of the careful factorial studies of major tests.[6, 7] Thus, a subtest labeled Comprehension may measure knowledge of solutions to social situations at one age, and judgment only at an age where the solution must be thought out, rather than dredged from memory.

When the above assumptions are kept in mind, test results can be interpreted in a meaningful way. By describing the child's present ability to cope with problems within the grasp of the average child, test results can give some estimate of the degree to which a child, even with specific problems or limitations (physical, emotional, or cultural), can compete with average children. For example, a child with mild cerebral palsy might be evaluated in terms of ability to fit in an average classroom. By the same

[4] J. Kagen, L. W. Sontag, C. T. Baker, and V. L. Nelson, "Personality and IQ Change," *Journal of Abnormal and Social Psychology*, 56 (1958), 261–266.

[5] C. Higgins and C. H. Sivers, "A Comparison of Stanford-Binet and Coloured Raven Progressive Matrices IQs for Children with Low Socio-economic Status," *Journal of Consulting Psychology*, 22 (1958), 465–468.

[6] Q. McNemar, *The Revision of the Stanford-Binet Scale* (New York: Houghton Mifflin Company, 1942).

[7] J. Cohen, "The Factorial Structure of the WISC at Ages 7½, 10½, and 13½," *Journal of Consulting Psychology*, 23 (1959), 285–299.

token, the test results may indicate the extent to which an emotionally handicapped child can function in the classroom, in spite of his disturbance.

Limitations of the IQ Concept

With all the qualifications inherent in the application of intelligence tests, and all the information to be sought from such a measure, the intelligence quotient, or IQ, has become progressively less significant to the school psychologist.

Terman noted the apparent constancy of the IQ upon retesting, pointing out, however, that large variations in relative test standing could occur.[8] The apparent simplicity of the ratio IQ led to its wide adoption in the field of testing. Like the concept of mental age, it could be readily understood by the public, and soon gained popular usage. As a result, the concept of the ratio IQ dominated intellectual testing for many years, attaining a reified status as an infallible measure of intelligence, in sharp contrast to Terman's early warning of possible instability.

However, longitudinal studies of mental development have led to a growing awareness of the limitations of the ratio IQ.

The ratio IQ had been assumed to represent a fixed rate of development, that not only indicated relative brightness, but also allowed for prediction of future mental age as the child progressed. Such constancy simply did not exist, except within broad limits. Clarke and Clarke [9] state:

> Indeed, if individual mental growth were a uniform mental process, then this would represent the one form of biological growth not characterized by "fits and starts."

A second limitation of the ratio IQ is based on problems relating to the technical characteristics of the scale used. The proper distribution of item difficulties from age to age was not always achieved, resulting in variable standard deviations. The relative position of a child at one age was not the same as that achieved at another age. While the differences were not always large, the variations in standard deviations on the 1937 Binet were significant enough to require the calculation of "corrected IQs." [10]

Another limitation of the IQ was inherent in its calculation directly from the mental age. For children of elementary school age, or for individuals who were severely retarded, mental age proved to be a meaningful concept, and a ratio based on it was useful. However, as testing was extended to older and further developed individuals, the mental age concept failed to maintain

[8] L. M. Terman, *The Measurement of Intelligence* (Boston: Houghton Mifflin Company, 1916).

[9] A. M. Clarke and A. D. B. Clarke, *Mental Deficiency: The Changing Outlook* (New York: The Free Press of Glencoe, Inc., 1958).

[10] McNemar, *op. cit.*

its usefulness. For example, by the age of fifteen, the mean mental age did not appear to continue to increase with increasing chronological age. This led to the use of fifteen as a standard top chronological age, and the extrapolations of mental ages up to twenty-two to allow for above average functioning. Thus, a college student of twenty-one might have a mental age of twenty-one, but an IQ of 140. Not only has the whole concept of mental ages above fifteen been questioned, since these must be extrapolations,[11] but recent studies indicate that the average mental age does improve significantly beyond the age of fifteen,[12] requiring new calculations to establish an IQ for older individuals.

The Deviation IQ

The limitations of the ratio IQ, briefly summarized above, led to the development of a standard score to replace the older intelligence "quotient." A standard score IQ expresses the subject's distance from the mean (of 100) in terms of the standard deviation of the distribution. Most deviation IQs on intelligence tests are calculated to conform to the average standard deviations from the original Stanford-Binet, and usually approximate that of the 1937 Stanford-Binet, or sixteen. Because of this, such test results can be interpreted and classified as were the 1937 Binets. Since the ratio IQ distributions had proved to be nearly normal, and the deviation IQs are based on the normal curve, the deviation IQ can be interpreted both as an indication of a child's position in his age group, and roughly equivalent to a ratio of mental age over chronological age. This means that those long familiar with the Binet classifications can accept the newer deviation IQs without the need for extensive "translations."

While the deviation IQs overcome a number of difficulties inherent in the ratio IQs, they too are limited by the test material administered. The validity and reliability of the test must be adequate, before any weight can be given to an IQ derived from it. A second point involves the standardization of the test. Technically, deviation IQs can be compared from one test to another. However, results must be restricted to the particular normative population on which each test was standardized. Thus, the absence of Negro children in the WISC standardization sample limits the use of this test. The standardization of the 1960 Binet on children from two to eighteen limits the use of this test with adults. Deviation IQs are susceptible to this point as are any such scores.

---

[11] D. Wechsler, *The Measurement of Adult Intelligence* (3rd. Ed.) (Baltimore: The Williams & Wilkins Co., 1944).

[12] Nancy Bayley, "On the Growth of Intelligence," *American Psychologist*, 10 (1955), 513–522.

General IQ Limitations

The statistical limitations of the IQ are important, but can be minimized by cautious interpretation. It is possible, for example, to describe a child as having such and such a score as compared to the test standardization sample, and then to add a cautionary note as to the meaningfulness of such results.

However, there are more general limitations to the use of the IQ, even when statistical artifacts are kept in mind. One is that intelligence *per se* is lacking in a vigorous theoretical foundation.[13] Especially at the extremes, it has too often been considered, "an infallible and crucially significant index (which would) ignore the importance of the many other characteristics which contribute to attainment." [14] The use of the IQ as an "explanation" (for example, that a child does not read well because he has a low IQ) rather than a descriptive concept has been criticized by Liverant.[15]

The IQ also fails to reflect *constant* ability to perform. Cronbach [16] differentiates between measures of what a person can do, and what he does. In an attempt to use test results differentially, the IQ is often labeled a measure of "present functioning," with an implied search for a "basic capacity" within the test scatter. Such an inference is certainly questionable.

Another limitation is inherent in the reliance on any single numerical score to describe complex behavior. The IQ concept results in "a grossly oversimplified picture of the organization of the mind." [17] It is calculated from a composite of a number of measures of different abilities, often "a muddled combination of predictive measures." [18] Especially when these are averaged together, ignoring differences, the resulting index can be meaningless.

Recognition of the limitations of the IQ concept is inescapable to those who test children and are able to follow their development and plan for their future education. The greater the knowledge of standard tests of intelligence used in the schools, the more the school psychologist can overcome such limitations and use his tools in a meaningful manner. The specific contribution of the intelligence test, then, is not the IQ, but the picture it gives of an individual performing in "situations in which he can

[13] J. M. Stalnaker, "Recognizing and Encouraging Talent," *American Psychologist*, 15 (1960), 513–522.

[14] *Ibid.*, p. 516.

[15] S. Liverant, "Intelligence: A Concept in Need of Re-examination," *Journal of Consulting Psychology*, 24 (1960), 101–110.

[16] L. J. Cronbach, *Essentials of Psychological Testing* (New York: Harper & Row, Publishers, 1960).

[17] Stalnaker, *op. cit.*

[18] Cronbach, *op. cit.*, p. 241.

rely extensively upon learned experiences, daily routines, and other familiar clues." [19]

In the following section, the major intelligence tests used in the schools will be reviewed in terms of their strengths and weaknesses and rationale for administration.

The 1960 Revision of the Stanford-Binet Scale (Stanford-Binet L-M)

With the 1960 revision of the Stanford-Binet,[20] the best known and most widely used test of individual intelligence has been brought up to date. In the process, a number of weaknesses of the 1937 form [21] have been overcome. Since the Stanford-Binet has been used as the standard criterion against which other measures of intelligence have been gauged, in some ways most of the major tests of intelligence can be viewed as revisions of the Binet. In view of the extensive research literature available, and its long term acceptance as the prototype of intelligence tests, the Stanford-Binet is assured a permanent place in school testing.

The revised Stanford-Binet retains the major characteristics of the older Binet-type tests. It continues to measure general ability rather than specific or related groups of abilities. The age scale format is retained, along with the assumption that general intelligence is a trait which develops with age, and the use of age standards of performance.

The 1960 Binet utilizes the best subtests of the L and M forms (1937), retaining the most discriminative items. Mental age scores range from two years to twenty-two years, eleven months, but deviation IQs replace the former ratio IQs for ages two through eighteen. Mental growth has been found to extend beyond age sixteen,[22] and this factor is controlled by the extended norms and deviation IQ tables. The deviation IQ assures that the IQ continues to indicate the same relative ability from age to age, representing "the same amount of change in relative standing regardless of the ability level." [23]

Along with the adoption of the deviation IQ, other structural changes are introduced. Long recognized structural inadequacies of the 1937 revision have been corrected. No longer do mean IQs rise above 100 at certain age

[19] M. M. Meyer, "The Case of El: Blind Analysis of the Tests of an Unknown Patient," *Journal of Projective Techniques*, 25 (1961), 4.

[20] L. M. Terman and M. A. Merrill, *The Stanford-Binet Intelligence Scale* (Boston: Houghton Mifflin Company, 1960).

[21] ————, *Measuring Intelligence* (Boston: Houghton Mifflin Company, 1937).

[22] Nancy Bayley, "Constancy and Variability in the Growth of Intelligence from Birth to Eighteen," *Journal of Genetic Psychology*, 75 (1949), 165–196.

[23] Terman and Merrill, *The Stanford-Binet Intelligence Scale*, p. 28.

levels, and the standard deviations do not vary from the standard of 16. As a result of the revision, while the new deviation IQs approximate the ratio IQs at most age levels, at some points there may be a change of as much as 8 points by adopting the deviation IQs. This suggests that cutoff scores used in the schools in screening for special classes may need reevaluation.

In context, the less satisfactory material, including out-of-date and duplicate items, have largely been eliminated, and some items relocated or rescored.

When item success and failure on the Binet is evaluated relative to other information available on the subject, such as school achievement and performance records, the test results become more powerful. The Stanford-Binet has always correlated highly with performances in academic courses, particularly those requiring verbal skills. It has been considered predominantly a predictor of scholastic aptitude, and the revision continues this emphasis.

However, a number of limitations of the Binet are not affected by the new revision. One is the problem of lengthy administration. In order to establish a "ceiling," or the ultimate success the child could reach, as many as eleven consecutive failures must be faced. Passing the first item at one age, the subject must be given the other five, plus all six at the next age level. Any unexpected or erratic success at the next level will mean another six tests to administer until the criterion of failing an entire age level is met. As Haworth [24] has pointed out, this can be too great a strain for too little information. Also, the cumulative effect on the child of such massed failure can be penalizing, so that the test results may not represent his best performance.[25]

Another problem is the shift of item content from age to age. Below age six, many nonverbal items are encountered. Retesting at the school age may result in a significant drop in rating if the child has a speech or language problem. By the same token, measuring "giftedness" on the Binet may penalize the highly verbal preschool child, who might perform significantly better by age eight. The changes in mental abilities measured at different ages can mean that an almost entirely different test may be administered upon retest from one age to another. Thus, judgment, discrimination, and attention are involved at the younger ages, while verbal reasoning is emphasized in items placed at an older age level.[26] In reporting results, the yearly shift in item content makes a qualitative summary of abilities essential, but largely dependent upon the age level covered and on the examiner's interpretation of item meaning. McNemar's [27] factorial study of the

[24] Mary R. Haworth, "The Stanford-Binet, 1937 Revision," in *The Fourth Mental Measurement Yearbook*, ed. O. K. Buros (New Brunswick, N.J.: Rutgers University Press, 1953).

[25] M. L. Hutt, "A Clinical Study of 'Consecutive' and 'Adaptive' Testing with the Revised Stanford-Binet," *Journal of Consulting Psychology*, 11 (1947), 93–103.

[26] Cronbach, *op. cit.*

[27] McNemar, *op. cit.*

1937 Binet indicated that 50 per cent of the item variance could be attributed to a general factor, while other variance could be attributed to specific items not repeated frequently enough for a reliable estimate of specific skills.

The all-or-none scoring of items, while simplifying and objectifying administration and scoring, results in a loss of potentially useful material that would have been incorporated into a point scale.

The revision of the Binet has led to some tendency for items to overlap, and thus cut down on the variety of material administered. For example, two rhyming items are given at the same age (LX, 4 and A). A number of items that have disturbing implications for some youngsters are grouped together (Verbal Absurdities: hangings and train wrecks; arms cut off and death from flu). The utilization of items from both L and M forms has led to a large number of items identified only by number (Opposite Analogies I, II, II; Comprehension II, III, IV; Verbal Absurdities I, II, IV) that can cause confusion in administration and entry of responses.

Personality variables and emotional habits influence Stanford-Binet scores to a decided extent. Shyness and a lack of self-confidence tend to lower scores,[28] as does passivity,[29] while a more aggressive orientation leads to problem solving successes and increasing IQ ratings.[30]

The Binet continues to underemphasize such factors as insight, foresight, originality, and organization of ideas. At the same time, the verbal emphasis penalizes the hard of hearing, the poor reader, and the bilingual child.[31]

While the improved standardization would appear to result in IQs more comparable to the WISC verbal IQs, since they are calculated the same way, the 1960 Stanford-Binet continues to produce higher IQs at the superior level.[32] Even so, the ceiling of the Binet has proved low for gifted teenagers.[33]

Nevertheless, the 1960 Stanford-Binet remains the test of choice for measuring extremes at the school age level, and for evaluating scholastic aptitude. The Binet gives sufficient floor and ceiling to evaluate children suspected of mental deficiency or screened for gifted programs. With the introduction of the deviation IQ, results are comparable from age to age, and results from other tests using the deviation IQ are now relatively comparable.

[28] Hutt, op. cit.
[29] L. M. Sontag, C. T. Baker, and V. L. Nelson, "Personality as a Determinant of Performance," American Journal of Orthopsychiatry, 25 (1955), 555–562.
[30] Ibid.
[31] Cronbach, op. cit.
[32] B. W. Estes, M. E. Curtin, R. A. DeBurger, and C. Denny, "Relationships Between 1960 Stanford-Binet, 1937 Stanford-Binet, WISC, Raven, and Draw-a-Man," Journal of Clinical Psychology, 25 (1961), 388–391.
[33] W. A. Kennedy, H. Moon, W. Nelson, K. Linder, and J. Turner, "The Ceiling of the New Stanford-Binet," Journal of Clinical Psychology, 17 (1961), 284–286.

The reader who wishes to review further research conducted with the 1960 Binet is referred to Philip Himelstein's "Research with the Stanford-Binet," in the *Psychological Bulletin,* 63 (March, 1966), 156–164. He concludes, "On the basis of the reputation of this scale, its past performance as a clinical instrument, a standardization more carefully performed than for almost any other individual test of intelligence, it can be expected to continue in its role as leader. There is still a need, however, for carefully designed studies with large samples from heterogeneous populations."

Binet Behavior Samplings and Guilford's Structure of the Intellect *

When Guilford (1956) suggested that there may be as many as 120 identifiable factors that make up the intellect, this was quite different from the way of thinking of Binet users who, at least quantitatively, dealt with a single, molar measure of "intelligence." When it was learned that one of the five processes identified was that of divergent thinking, and when it appeared that the Binet sampled this kind of intellectual behavior to what seemed to be a very limited extent, those who uncritically accepted Guilford's conceptualization tended to reduce the Binet and other good group tests of academic learning aptitude to a very low value level. The Binet and other good tests of "book learning" potential were denigrated both because they did reasonably well what they were properly constructed to do, and because it was "discovered" that they didn't do what they were not intended to do in the first place. Out of such a misperception, many lay and some professional persons have done some of their challenging of the use of even good tests of learning aptitude.

On the other hand, the school psychologist could, not without profit, continue to make effective use of the Binet (or the verbal part of the Wechsler) secured by the conviction that it did tap heavily, though inferentially, the capacities of individuals to acquire the symbols essential to existence, communication, and culture—the largest single commitment of the schools. He could with equal profit continue his sampling to ascertain the extent to which conventional responses have been acquired, since it is upon such that we depend for a modicum of social predictability. We still expect, for instance, the correct change from the quarter we give for the four-cent purchase.

The competent school psychologist long has sought to structure a youngster's behaviors observed while taking the Binet. His attempts along this line have resulted in observations regarding at least the child's vocabu-

* This section reprinted from *Journal of School Psychology,* II (Winter, 1964), 554–559, by permission of the editor.

lary level, his verbal fluency, his conceptualization level, his verbal and quantitative reasoning ability, his memory, and his visual perception.

On the other hand, the school psychologist might, in addition, ask himself the question, "To what extent does the Binet make behavior samples that are relevant to or which involve the kinds of behavior reflected in Guilford's 120 factors?" If the Binet [34] were found to sample in any significant way any of the 120 ways of behaving, then the Binet would be found more valuable than even its proponents had believed; it could have value not only in a molar manner—in reflecting a mass, undifferentiated learning potentiality—but also in such a way as to permit certain important differentiations in intellectual behaving.

It was in the latter direction that the curiosity of some school psychologists in the Los Angeles County schools moved. In a study nurtured by Marcella Bonsall, implemented by Mary Meeker, and assisted by others, outcomes resulted that should intrigue and challenge the practicing school psychologist. The goal was to make available to the practicing school psychologist a means whereby a child's performance on the Binet might be perceived in terms of the Guilford factors. Educationally, such an analysis can be of particular value insofar as it throws light upon different kinds of intellectual processes, and the extent to which such processes have been operative in performance on the Binet.

Total intellect, according to Guilford, can be perceived in terms of three dimensions: a) *Contents*—those stimuli to which the individual reacts when he "uses his intelligence"; b) *Operations*—the kinds of behavior the individual manifests or "employs" when he is behaving intellectively; and c) *Products*—the kinds of behavior that result after operations take place on the different kinds of content. In other words, when an individual behaves in a way called "using his intelligence," he reacts in certain ways to certain kinds of phenomena, which results in certain kinds of outcomes.

GUILFORD'S DIMENSIONS OF INTELLIGENCE

Operations	Contents	Products
C—Cognition	F—Figural	U—Units
M—Memory	S—Symbolic	C—Classes
D—Divergent Production	M—Semantic	R—Relations
N—Convergent Production	B—Behavioral	S—Systems
		T—Transformations
		I—Implications

For convenience and preciseness in communication, each type of operation, content, and product is represented by a capital letter, thereby enabling

[34] The "Binet" mentioned in this study is the 1960 revision.

one to designate each factor by a trigraph. Thus, CFU denotes visual (or auditory) cognition—as in identifying words in which a part of each letter has been blotted out. This kind of item constituted, for instance, one of the tests in the sixth edition of the Kuhlmann-Anderson group intelligence tests. In like manner, the vocabulary portion of the Binet would be understandable as involving the Guilford factor CMU—the ability to be aware of (cognition) the meaning of (semantic) single words (units).

In thinking of Binet test items,[35] as *kinds* of test items, in terms of the Guilford conceptualization, it is very important to be fully sensitive to the fact that certain items will involve seemingly entirely or predominantly one factor, as in the case of CMU—Vocabulary—but to recognize also that even here memory plays some role. In other cases, a single item may need to be characterized in terms of more than one factor. Item SA II, 2 (Finding Reasons, III) for instance, is presently described in terms of these five factors: a) CMI—Anticipates needs or consequences of a given situation; b) MMR—Remembers meaningful pairs of words; c) DMU—Calls up many ideas of a specified class; d) DMI—Specifies details that develop scheme or variation of ideas; and e) EMR—Uses logical relationships in testing correctness of a given situation.

CLASSIFICATION OF BINET ITEMS AT THE SIX-YEAR LEVEL ACCORDING TO GUILFORD FACTORS

Item	Name	Trigraph	Factor Characterization
1	Vocabulary	CMU	Is aware of words or ideas.
2	Differences	CMT	Sees several meanings to a word or expression.
		CFI	Explores visually ways to select most effective action.
		DMI	Specifies details that develop scheme or variation of idea.
		NMC	Forms correct groups from a large number of words or objects.
3	Mutilated Pictures	SFU	Visual and auditory recognition of familiar material.
		MSI	Memory for well-practiced number operations.
4	Number Concepts	MSI	Memory for well-practiced number operations.

[35] The term "item" is used here to denote, in addition to Vocabulary (a type of sampling that recurs at different age levels), the "clusters" of samples which occur at separate age levels, as in the case of IX, 4. In this latter case, there are four *elements* which constitute the *item* on rhyming, just as a number of words (or elements) constitute the *item* sampling vocabulary.

Item	Name	Trigraph	Factor Characterization
5	Opposite Analogies	CMR	Discovers relations in conceptual materials.
		EMR	Uses logical relationships in testing correctness of conclusion.
6	Maze Tracing	CFI	Explores visually ways to select most effective action.
	Alt. Response to Pictures (Level II)	EMR	Uses logical relationships in testing correctness of conclusion.
		CMC	Classifies and evaluates words and verbal concepts.

The accuracy with which each of these test items is characterized is not of primary concern here. The important point is the underlying idea of the possibility of describing the behavior sampled by Binet items in terms of the intellective functionings in the Guilford structure.

The implementation of this important and potentially fruitful idea makes necessary two kinds of research before any formal chart reflecting factor allocation can be used with confidence. The accuracy with which each item is characterized in terms of Guilford factors must be established. This requires, first, that persons who understand the kind or kinds of intellective process sampled by each item identify judgmentally those factors that properly describe it. This must be done with complete accuracy—essentially a problem of intra- or inter-judge reliability. Then, as a more rigorous check on the results of this operation, statistical verification should be obtained. Two possibilities suggest themselves here: a) either correlating performance on each item with performance on the tests initially used in the identification of the factors involved, or b) making a factor analysis of performance on Binet items to see if those factors emerge that were judgmentally determined to be involved. At any rate, there appears to be merit in inviting wider exploration of this idea by practicing school psychologists.

The Wechsler Intelligence Scale for Children (WISC)

Few will deny that the right arm of most school psychologists is the Binet box, while the left arm is the WISC kit. The literature on these tests is exceedingly large and the school psychologist in training should be very familiar with their strengths and limitations. Yet most writers on school psychology dispatch these instruments with one page of comment, while they discuss personality appraisal and projective techniques at great length.

The introduction of the Wechsler Intelligence Scale for Children

(WISC) [36] in 1949 represented an important milestone in the history of intelligence testing. Ten years earlier, the Wechsler Bellevue Intelligence Scale [37] had been published, allowing for the first time an adequately standardized measure of adult intelligence. The second form of the Wechsler Bellevue (WB II),[38] introduced in 1946 but never adequately standardized, was expanded to become the WISC, a test for children aged five to fifteen. The revised Wechsler Bellevue I became the WAIS,[39] a test for adults from age sixteen.

Just as the original Wechsler Bellevue answered many objections raised about the Stanford-Binet, 1937 revision, when used for ages ten to sixty, the WISC had a number of advantages for administration to school age children.

Among the advantages inherent in the WISC are the introduction of both verbal and performance scales standardized on the same population. Even though the Binet could be paired with a performance scale, such as the Grace Arthur Scale of Performance Tests,[40] results cannot be in any sense directly comparable, since different standardization samples were involved.

The verbal-performance scale dichotomy is helpful when the WISC is administered to physically limited individuals, such as the blind, deaf, or orthopedically handicapped, for whom only a part of the test is applicable. For example, when a hard-of-hearing child is given the WISC, the performance score can be compared with the verbal score, allowing for an estimate of the extent of limitation in verbal areas.[41] The Wechsler scales are also appropriate for testing blind children, by administering only the verbal scale.[42] More information relative to specific adaptations for exceptional children and youth will be found in Chapter 18.

The grouping of items of similar content into subtests on the WISC offers the advantage of serial testing. In this way, the child need not be given item after item beyond his ability, with resulting feelings of frustration. This has been pointed out as a chronic problem on tests calling for the

[36] D. Wechsler, *Wechsler Intelligence Scale for Children: Manual* (New York: Psychological Corporation, 1949).

[37] ――――, *The Measurement of Adult Intelligence* (3rd ed.) (Baltimore: The Williams & Wilkins Co., 1944).

[38] ――――, *Wechsler Bellevue II: Manual* (New York: Psychological Corporation, 1945).

[39] ――――, *Manual for the Wechsler Adult Intelligence Scale* (New York: Psychological Corporation, 1955).

[40] Grace Arthur, *A Point Scale of Performance Tests,* Volumes I & II (New York: The Commonwealth Fund, 1933).

[41] H. R. Myklebust, *The Psychology of Deafness* (New York: Grune & Stratton, Inc., 1960).

[42] M. K. Bauman and S. P. Hayes, *A Manual for the Psychological Examination of the Adult Blind* (New York: Psychological Corporation, 1951).

establishment of a ceiling year, such as the Binet. Hutt [43] has studied the penalizing effect for some children in meeting repeated failure in this manner. By the same token, the WISC can be given in a more standard time interval, since a set number of subtests are administered, while on the Binet, the amount of testing will be determined by the speed of establishing the basal and the ceiling. Also, the grouping of items into subtests allows for the calculation of an IQ on the basis of only a portion of the total tests ("brief testing"), an important time saver, permitting a meaningful interpretation of results when testing must be interrupted before completion.

Another advantage of the WISC is the use of twelve subtests, so that a broad range of tasks may be evaluated. The wide sample of behavior and thought processes present at every age level is in contrast to the Binet, where progressively greater emphasis is placed on abstract verbal tasks at the eight year level and beyond. As in the Binet tests, the subtests are of interest to children, and motivation remains high. If the child shows evidence of fatigue as testing progresses, the effect can be assessed by a comparison of weighted scores on the subtests according to their position in the battery. On the Binet, the easier items are administered first, and as the examination proceeds, the child faces the progressively more difficult items. Fatigue, failure, and discouragement interact in a manner difficult to assess.

The use of subtests has led to considerable analysis of pattern of subtests and of scatter of successes within each subtest. The search for clear diagnostic signs has been uniformly disappointing.[44] In a recent study,[45] the WISC profiles of children in a child guidance clinic were analyzed to find what relationship existed between the diagnostic categories in which each child was placed, and the high and low scores on the profile. No relationship of any kind could be detected. However, as Schafer [46] has pointed out, the nature of the errors and successes, rather than the numerical treatment, can give a qualitative picture of personality that is more than mere diagnostic significance. Children identified as emotionally disturbed by the schools and matched with children considered well adjusted could be identified on the basis of their WISC protocol at a statistically significant level.[47] Discriminating signs were the child's reaction to the test situation: brashness, impulsivity, *non sequiturs* in response to test questions, and the flooding of emotional material at presumably innocuous questions. (Example: what to do when you cut your finger: "Go to the hospital! Be cut off!")

[43] Hutt, *op. cit.*

[44] Cronbach, *op. cit.*

[45] B. P. Frost, "An Application of the Method of Extreme Deviations to the WISC," *Journal of Clinical Psychology,* 16 (1960), 420.

[46] R. Schafer, *The Clinical Application of Psychological Tests* (New York: International Universities Press, 1948).

[47] Irla Lee Zimmerman and Nadine Lambert, "The Relationship Between Individual Psychological Tests and School Screening Procedures for the Identification of Emotionally Disturbed Children," *American Psychologist,* 16 (1961), 370.

The basic analysis of the WISC indicated that the norms used in the standardization are excellent for the average range, and consist of a representative sample of the United States.[48] Various studies show the validity and reliability of the WISC to be at least comparable to the Binet.[49] The advantages of a deviation IQ are clearly indicated in the adoption of it in the 1960 revision of the Binet.

Experience with the WISC since its introduction has led to the recognition of a number of limitations, a few of which will be summarized. One important limitation involves the extent of standardization. The WISC was standardized on white children only, with excessive emphasis on individuals at the upper or middle levels of the socio-economic scale. The very children most often referred for evaluation, such as non-white or socio-economically impoverished, may be unduly penalized because of this narrow standardization.

The standardization is also limited at both extremes of the intellectual range; for example, only half as many children with IQs over 130 were included in the standardization sample as were tested on the 1937 Binet. There is insufficient range for dependability at either end of the scale, so that the test is best applied to children in the middle age bracket (ten). It is not to be used by choice for children whose mental age runs below the standardization age of five, nor for children being screened for gifted programs. Neither extreme is as adequately measured as on the Binet. For example, the WISC does not give an IQ above 154 nor below 46 (although a recent study has presented extrapolated scores below this point).[50] The inadequate range of items at the younger ages was illustrated by Anderson's [51] calculations that a five year old could achieve an IQ of 52 by attaining a score of zero on each subtest. Only by age twelve is a raw score of zero on a subtest not given a weighted score bonus. For example, at age seven, a Block Design raw score of zero is given a weighted score of 3.

WISC results tend to be lower than the Binet for abilities in the middle and upper ranges, but higher in the lower ranges. Because of the lower range limitations it is not practical for the severely mentally retarded before the age (chonological) of ten or eleven.[52]

The WISC is a combination of tasks more than thirty years old, and in many ways, essentially a "revised Binet." Like the Binet, it is based on an assumption of a general mental ability, and while composed of separate sub-

[48] Anne Anastasi, *Psychological Testing* (New York: The Macmillan Company, 1961).

[49] *Ibid.*

[50] O. P. Ogdon, "WISC IQs for the Mentally Retarded," *Journal of Consulting Psychology*, 24 (1960), 187.

[51] J. M. Anderson, "Wechsler Intelligence Scale for Children" in *The Fourth Mental Measurement Yearbook*, ed. O. K. Buros (Highland Park, N.J.: Gryphon Press, 1953), 477–479.

[52] G. A. Holland, "A Comparison of WISC and Stanford-Binet IQs of Normal Children," *Journal of Consulting Psychology*, 17 (1953), 147–152.

tests, there is no adequate rationale for interpreting the subtest scores. Also, all subtests are given equal weight at all age levels, although factorial studies [53] indicate that the subtests are measuring different aspects of intellectual functioning at different age levels. Thus, Comprehension at age ten is more a measure of a child's general information, while at seven, it measures something closer to judgment. The WISC is not based on any clear theory of intelligence. There is no separation of mental ability from other aspects of adaptation.

At present, there is no alternate form of the WISC. Formerly, the Wechsler Bellevue could be used for retesting at age ten or over (although the comparability of the two tests has been questioned). However, with the introduction of the Wechsler Adult Intelligence Scale (WAIS) as a replacement for the Wechsler Bellevue I, there is no overlap possible, since the WAIS starts at age sixteen. While Wechsler Bellevue II has been recommended for retesting, the inadequate standardization, and the fact that the WISC is merely an extension of the Wechsler Bellevue II, limits its value.

Item difficulty and meaning on the WISC has been questioned by Ross.[54] While helpful personality description can be gained by an analysis of responses on the WISC (for example, Comprehension items may elicit important attitudes toward injury i.e., cut finger, or aggression [someone smaller starting to fight with you]), these items can be upsetting and unduly influence the child's performance. The need to "test the limits" on the WISC and to discover the meaning of failures has been developed by both Taylor and Volle.[55] For example, the question about "government examinations" (Comprehension) requires a vocabulary beyond the level of many children who might, however, understand the practical considerations involved.

Littel summarizes many of the disadvantages of the WISC by pointing out that 1) there is strong evidence that the WISC norms are not applicable to children of markedly different sub-groups such as southern Negro and bilingual children; 2) socioeconomic status appears to be a significant factor; 3) the WISC seems to be relatively insensitive to differences among mentally retarded children; 4) when the WISC is administered to children below five to six years of age, the scores can be expected to be unreliable due to a limited number of functional test items. The topic of intellectual evolution of culturally deprived children is discussed in greater detail in Chapter 16.

---

[53] J. Cohen, "Factorial Structure of the WISC at Ages 7½, 10½, 13½," *Journal of Consulting Psychology*, 23 (1959), 285–299.

[54] A. O. Ross, *The Practice of Clinical Child Psychology* (New York: Grune & Stratton, Inc., 1959).

[55] Edith M. Taylor, *Psychological Appraisal of Children with Cerebral Defects* (Cambridge, Mass.: Harvard University Press, 1959). F. O. Volle, "A Proposal for Testing the Limits with Mental Defectives for Purposes of Subtest Analysis of the WISC Verbal Scale," *Journal of Clinical Psychology*, 13 (1957), 64–67.

However, while the WISC can be criticized on a number of points, its usefulness as a flexible and adaptable individual test of intelligence for school age children is undeniable.

The Other Wechsler Scales

In 1955, the Wechsler Adult Intelligence Scale (WAIS) [56] replaced the Wechsler Bellevue Scale Form I, that since its introduction in 1939 had been the standard clinical instrument for the individual examination of adult intelligence. A revision and complete restandardization of the Form I of the Wechsler, the WAIS offers norms only from age sixteen. An introduction of easier items gives it a better "floor" for mentally retarded adolescents. However, norms were not calculated at levels that would allow it to be used as a retest for the WISC. The many changes introduced prevent the WAIS from being interpreted as identical to Wechsler Bellevue I. Nevertheless, the WAIS is acknowledged as the best measure of adult intelligence. In 1966 Wechsler released through his publisher, the Psychological Corporation, an experimental edition of the Wechsler Preschool and Primary School Scale of Intelligence, a downward extension of the WISC suitable for ages four to seven.

Individual Instruments in School Use

While the Stanford-Binet and the WISC are the most frequently used individual tests of intelligence in the school setting, other measures have proved valuable for specific purposes. Typically, these are based on non-language factors, and in some cases a motor response is not required. Such tests prove useful for individuals with language or speech problems, the deaf, and orthopedically handicapped children. A number are considered to be more "culture fair" than either the Stanford-Binet or the WISC, in that they call for less emphasis on factors related to socioeconomic status.

Columbia Mental Maturity Scale (1959 Revision)

The Columbia Mental Maturity Scale (CMMS) [57] was first introduced in 1953 as a test suitable for children with serious physical or verbal impairment, since it requires no speech and a minimum of motor responses. The test consists of 100 cards with a series of drawings on each. The child's task is to indicate the one drawing in each series that does not belong. Administra-

---

[56] D. Wechsler, *Wechsler Adult Intelligence Scale* (New York: Psychological Corporation, 1955).

[57] B. B. Burgemeister, L. H. Blum, and I. Lorge, *Columbia Mental Maturity Scale* (New York: Harcourt, Brace & World, Inc., 1959).

tion requires no longer than twenty minutes, and raw scores are converted into mental ages from which a ratio IQ can be calculated. Norms are available from a mental age of two-and-one-half to sixteen. Standardization is based on a population of 957 presumably normal children.

The Columbia appears to be a test of perceptual ability, with some items calling for a grasp of spatial relationships.[58] A number of studies suggested reliabilities near .90,[59] and correlations with the Binet at about .75.[60] However, the problem of item difficulty and of questionable item meaning (for example, too many number analogies), plus the tendency of the test to give IQs as much as 37 points above the Binet,[61] led the authors to withdraw it from circulation for restandardization. The 1959 edition [62] has overcome many of the earlier criticisms.

Current studies suggest that the Revised Columbia Mental Maturity Scale is useful in screening for mental retardation, in one study correlating with the Binet at .68.[63] It is also useful in testing children who have difficulty in verbal communication, correlating with the Binet at .88.[64] However, the CMMS has a low ceiling. The highest IQ for a child of twelve is 116, while for children of ten or under the maximum IQ is as high as 139.

In general, however, the Columbia Mental Maturity Scale appears to be a rapidly administered test of intelligence suitable for handicapped children and for screening for mental retardation.

Picture Vocabulary Tests

Among the methods used to test handicapped children are the picture vocabulary tests. Vocabulary has been repeatedly found to be one of the best single measures of intelligence,[65, 66] and the best individual item for predicting school success.[67]

---

[58] E. M. Bower, op. cit.

[59] Cronbach, op. cit.

[60] Burgemeister, et al., op. cit.

[61] E. S. Barratt, "The Relationship of the Progressive Matrices (1938) and the Columbia Mental Maturity Scale to the WISC," *Journal of Consulting Psychology*, 20 (1956), 294–296.

[62] Burgemeister, et al., op. cit.

[63] S. A. Warren and H. L. Collier, "Suitability of the Columbia Mental Maturity Scale for Mentally Retarded Institutionalized Females," *American Journal of Mental Deficiency*, 64 (1960), 916–991.

[64] S. Hirschenfang, "Further Studies on the Columbia Mental Maturity Scale (CMMS) and Revised Stanford Binet (L) in Children with Speech Disorders," *Journal of Clinical Psychology* (1962).

[65] Terman and Merrill, op. cit., 1937 ed.

[66] D. Wechsler, op. cit., 1949 ed.

[67] E. Dale and D. Reichert, *Bibliography of Vocabulary Studies* (Columbus, Ohio: Ohio State University Board of Educational Research, 1957).

By measuring auditory comprehension of word meaning, the Ammons Full Range Picture Vocabulary Scale [68] and the Peabody Picture Vocabulary Test [69] allow a rapid estimate of intelligence without the need for speech, sustained attention, or more than a simple pointing response. Children who are hesitant to talk because of shyness respond readily to the pictures, making it a good "ice breaker" in a test battery. Children without speech, with inadequate speech, or with physical handicaps, can indicate a response easily. Since each plate calls for only a brief response, the penalizing effects of a limited attention span can sometimes be bypassed. The Picture Vocabulary tests offer particular advantages in checking differences between word understanding and word usage, as for example, comparing the picture vocabulary score (recognition) with the Binet vocabulary score (recall).

The Ammons Full Range Picture Vocabulary Scale consists of sixteen plates with four cartoon-like drawings on each. A series of words of rapidly increasing difficulty are presented orally for each plate, and the child is asked which picture best represents the particular word. Response can be made by pointing or indicating yes or no as the examiner points to each drawing. Raw scores are converted into mental ages, from which a ratio IQ can be calculated. Norms are provided from a mental age of two to the superior adult level for the two available forms. The standardization is based on a population of 589 children and adults, representative of the general population in occupational level and in age-grade placement. Reliability is satisfactory, and the correlation with the Stanford-Binet vocabulary score is high.[70]

The test can be readily administered in ten minutes, and proves to be easy and interesting for most children. However, the drawings are not always clear, and the use of an uneven number of words of increasing difficulty for each plate often leads to a tendency to perseverate serially, with the child pointing from one picture to the next in a fixed pattern. Errors on the Ammons often are of value in understanding a child's view of his world. For example, on a plate that shows a picture of both a prize fight and a classroom, the word "competition" frequently is associated with the latter picture.

The Peabody Picture Vocabulary Test is an individual test of "the ability to associate a verbal symbol with its pictorial representation." [71] This wide range picture vocabulary test, using a graduated series of 150 plates,

[68] R. B. Ammons and H. S. Ammons, *Full-Range Picture Vocabulary Test* (Missoula, Montana: Psychological Test Specialists, 1954).

[69] L. M. Dunn, *Peabody Picture Vocabulary Test* (Minneapolis, Minnesota: American Guidance Service, 1959).

[70] Anne Anastasi, *Psychological Testing*, 2nd ed. (New York: The Macmillan Company, 1961).

[71] L. M. Dunn and J. V. Hottel, "Peabody Picture Vocabulary Test Performance of Trainable Mentally Retarded Children," *American Journal of Mental Deficiency*, 65 (1961), 452–488.

each containing four pictures, requires the subject to point to or otherwise indicate the picture which best illustrates the meaning of the stimulus word presented orally. Only one word is given for each plate. The plates are arranged in order of difficulty, so that testing need cover only the critical range for each subject, requiring about fifteen minutes to administer and score. Raw scores are converted to three types of derived scores: mental age, standard score IQs, and percentiles. Norms are provided from a mental age of twenty-one months to eighteen years and from an IQ of 55 to 45. Standardization data extend over the age range two and one-half through eighteen years, with the original standardization sample of 4,012. Reliability and validity seem comparable to the Ammons.[72]

The limitation of one response per card, and slowly increasing difficulty of the words offers several advantages. This tends to limit serial perseveration, although positional responses are sometimes adopted (for example, a perseverating child may continuously point to the bottom right hand corner). The simplified line drawings are clear, minimizing possible perceptual errors. However, the author notes that the test is weak at ages six and thirteen because insufficient words were retained at these levels. Since the Peabody is often used for screening children in the early grades, the weakness at age six is likely to be a problem. Another pictorial vocabulary test is the Van Alystyne Picture Vocabulary Test for children two to seven published by Harcourt, Brace. For critical reviews by Mary Haworth and Ellen V. Piers of the Van Alystyne, the reader is referred to the *Sixth Mental Measurements Yearbook*.

The Pictorial Test of Intelligence by Joseph L. French of Pennsylvania State University was published in 1964 by the Houghton Mifflin Company. This test can be administered to three- through eight-year-old children. The test yields seven scores: picture vocabulary; form discrimination; information and comprehension; similarities; size and number; immediate recall; and total score. Little research is available as yet on this scale, however it appears to hold promise for school psychologists.

In general, picture vocabulary tests are excellent rapid measures of intelligence, particularly suitable for the handicapped child. When combined with a nonverbal test such as the Raven, they provide a fair estimate of ability.

Draw a Man Test

A simple measure of intelligence long available to the psychologist is the Draw a Man Test (DAM). First standardized by Goodenough [73] in

[72] Dunn, *op. cit.*
[73] Florence L. Goodenough, *Measurement of Intelligence by Drawings* (New York: Harcourt, Brace & World, Inc., 1926).

1926, the DAM has been used extensively both to evaluate intelligence and as a source of hypotheses as to the child's view of significant others in his life. The newly developed norms by Harris [74] make this test even more useful as a rapidly administered addition to the examiner's test battery.

Leiter International Performance Scale

The need for a measure that could evaluate a wide range of functions similar to those found in verbal scales was met by the construction of The Leiter International Performance Scale.[75] Developed to serve as a non-language test that could be used as a substitute for the Stanford-Binet, the Leiter can be given almost without instructions. Directions are simple and can be either spoken or pantomimed. No language response is required, and since the child need only indicate the correct item, the Leiter is suitable for handicapped children. Items are novel and appealing to children, selected on the principle that general intelligence is indicated by the ability to cope with entirely new situations. Perceptual matching and analogies are among the items used, and many are remarkably similar to verbal tests. Techniques of administration and scoring resemble the Stanford-Binet in most respects, resulting in a mental age and a ratio IQ. Norms are available from mental age two through adult, and standardization appears adequate.

The Leiter has been used to screen mentally retarded children, correlating .80 with the performance scale on the WISC, but from .77 to .83 with the full scale and from .40 to .78 on the verbal scale.[76] The Binet correlated at the same level (.86) in one study,[77] but the IQs varied so widely from the Binet, that the Leiter has been questioned as to its adequacy to measure mental retardation.

Original norms seemed to be slightly too strict (by some five IQ points), but both Leiter and Arthur (in the Arthur revision of the Leiter) [78] have published tables where necessary corrections can be applied for this error.

In general, the Leiter International Performance Scale is a novel and useful performance test that can be given entirely without spoken directions, and responded to without speech and with minimal motor reactions. It is

---

[74] D. B. Harris, *Children's Drawings as Measures of Intellectual Maturity* (New York: Harcourt, Brace & World, Inc., 1963).

[75] R. B. Leiter, *Leiter International Performance Scale* (Chicago: C. H. Stoelting, 1948).

[76] A. E. Alper, "A Comparison of the Wechsler Intelligence Scale for Children and the Arthur Adaptation of the Leiter International Performance Scale with Mental Defectives," *American Journal of Mental Deficiency*, 63 (1958), 312–316.

[77] H. C. Sharp, "A Comparison of Slow Learners Scores on Three Individual Intelligence Scales," *Journal of Clinical Psychology*, 12 (1957), 372–377.

[78] Grace Arthur, "Arthur Adaptation of the Leiter International Performance Scale," *Journal of Clinical Psychology*, 5 (1949), 345–349.

particularly useful for the deaf, the handicapped, and children with speech handicaps of various sorts.

Alexander Performance Scale

Alexander [79] developed this scale for the purpose of providing a means of measuring performance skills so that educators could meet the problem of allocating children to different types of secondary schools in England. This problem arose after the passage of the Education Act of 1944 which required that a decision be made when the child reaches eleven years of age regarding his placement in secondary school programs. Alexander noted that existing performance tests did a poor job of predicting success in technical educational programs. In spite of this purpose, or perhaps because of it, the test is peculiarly valuable for testing the deaf and hard of hearing as well as appraising the intellectual potential of persons who perform low on tests such as the Stanford-Binet or the WISC because of cultural or other language deficiencies.

The scale consists of three subtests whose separate scores are combined to yield a practical ability ratio (PAR) which is interpreted as an IQ ratio. That is, practical age divided by chronological age multiplied by 100. The subtests are the Passalong test, the Block design test, and the Cube Construction test. The first is Alexander's test, and the last two are Alexander's adaptation of the Kohs Blocks and Cube Construction Tests which have appeared in other performance scales. The tests can be administered in pantomime and no verbal response is required. Separate norms for boys and girls are provided.

The advantages of this test over other non-verbal tests appear to be in the area of convenience in administration and the fact that it can be given relatively rapidly. Its major disadvantage would appear to be its relatively restricted sampling of behaviors which would be of value in making special education placements. This is more a function of a use which was not of paramount importance to the author.

Raven's Coloured Progressive Matrices Test

The Raven Coloured Progressive Matrices Test (RCPM) [80] is a non-verbal perceptual test that measures the ability to note relationships in

---

[79] W. P. Alexander, *A Performance Scale for the Measurement of Practical Ability* (London: Thomas Nelson and Sons, 1946).

[80] J. C. Raven, *Guide to Using the Coloured Progressive Matrices 1956* (London: H. K. Lewis, 1960). See also J. C. Raven, *Guide to Using Raven's Progressive Matrices Test 1938* (London: H. K. Lewis, 1952).

analogies problems. Raven himself describes it as a test of observation and clear thinking. The test is discussed also in Chapter 12.

The original Raven Progressive Matrices Tests (1938) had been widely used to screen recruits in the British Army, and was considered relatively "culture fair" in minimizing the effects of poor education on selection and military classification. However, an easier colored form was introduced in 1945 and revised in 1956 for use with children from five and one-half to eleven years. The Coloured Progressive Matrices consists of a series of 36 designs, each incomplete. The child is to indicate which of a series of possible inserts will complete the design. Raw scores, which consist of the sum of correct responses, can be converted into percentile points by use of age norm tables. Norms were developed for 608 Scottish children, aged five to eleven and one-half. Since the test does not call for a verbal response, and can be administered by having the child point to or otherwise indicate the correct pattern, it has proved suitable for handicapped children. Bilingual or deaf children can also be administered the RCPM, since the easier items serve as training experiences for the later patterns, minimizing the need for verbal instructions.

Raven reported the CPM to correlate highly with the Stanford-Binet, at .90.[81] In a study of nine-year-old American children, the correlation with the WISC was equally high (.91).[82] However, there has been controversy as to the adequacy of Raven's norms, based upon the examination of Scottish children, for Americans. Green and Ewert [83] suggest that for the six through twelve year levels, American children score consistently higher than the normative sample. By contrast, Tuddenham, *et al.*,[84] report that for grades three through six, the norms are close to Raven's, but that socioeconomic factors prove to be very significant, with scores higher at the upper socioeconomic levels. Sperrazzo and Wilkins [85] found similar results, and also discovered race and age to be important variables. In one study,[86] while the Binet did not differentiate between the low and high socioeconomic status of nine-year-old children, the Raven IQ tended to average ten points higher in those children of upper socioeconomic status. Current studies suggest that the correlations of the Raven with the WISC and the Binet are relatively low for

[81] Raven, *op. cit.*

[82] A. W. Martin and J. B. Wiechers, "Raven's Coloured Progressive Matrices and the Wechsler Intelligence Scale for Children," *Journal of Consulting Psychology,* 18 (1954), 143–144.

[83] M. W. Green and J. C. Ewert, "Normative Data on the Progressive Matrices, 1947," *Journal of Consulting Psychology,* 19 (1955), 139–142.

[84] R. D. Tuddenham, L. Davis, L. Davison, and R. Schindler, "An Experimental Group Version for School Children on the Progressive Matrices," *Journal of Consulting Psychology,* 22 (1958), 30.

[85] C. Sperrazzo and W. L. Wilkins, "Further Normative Data on the Progressive Matrices," *Journal of Consulting Psychology,* 22 (1958), 35–37.

[86] Higgins and Sivers, *op. cit.*

mentally retarded children (below .60 for the WISC,[87] and at .70 for the Binet [88]) indicating the need for supplemental tests with such a select population.

A specific criticism of the Raven is its minimal range. The maximum IQ for the nine and one-half year old is 111. On the other hand, at the lower age level the items do not discriminate adequately.[89]

In general, the Raven is a readily administered test of intelligence, particularly suitable for the handicapped or nonverbal child. It correlates equally well with verbal and nonverbal tests. However, the Raven does not seem to be measuring nonverbal reasoning, as originally assumed. Instead, it calls for fairly complex intellectual reasoning processes apparently related to socioeconomic factors. The limited range makes its use somewhat curtailed.

Grace Arthur Performance Scale, Forms I and II

The Point Scale of Performance Tests [90, 91, 92] has been described as one of the best collections of performance tests.[93] This instrument has been used successfully to measure the abilities of deaf children, non-English speaking or bilingual children, those with delayed or defective speech, children from educationally and culturally impoverished environments, and those with reading disabilities.[94] It can be given by pantomime directions, with one or two exceptions. A combination of the Binet and the Arthur serve as a rough parallel of the WISC verbal and performance scales when retesting is needed.

The Arthur consists of two forms, Form I, published in 1930, and Form II, introduced earlier, but revised in 1947. The raw scores are translated into a point score that can be converted into a mental age, from which a ratio IQ can be calculated. The tests were primarily drawn from the Pintner-

---

[87] L. F. Malpass, R. Brown, and D. Hake, "The Utility of the Progressive Matrices with Normal and Retarded Children," *Journal of Clinical Psychology,* 16 (1960), 321.

[88] C. L. Stacey and F. O. Carleton, "The Relationship Between Raven's Progressive Matrices and Two Tests of General Intelligence," *Journal of Clinical Psychology,* 11 (1955), 84–85.

[89] T. E. Jordon and C. M. Bennett, "An Item Analysis of the Coloured Progressive Matrices, 1947," *Journal of Consulting Psychology,* 21 (1957), 222.

[90] Grace Arthur, *A Point Scale of Performance Tests,* Vols. I & II (New York: The Commonwealth Fund, 1933).

[91] ————, "A Point Scale of Performance Tests," Manual for Administering and Scoring the Tests, Revised Form II (New York: Psychological Corporation, 1947).

[92] ————, "A Point Scale of Performance Tests," *Clinical Manual,* Volume I (2nd ed.) (New York: Commonwealth Fund, 1943).

[93] Cronbach, *op. cit.*

[94] A. W. Brown "Arthur Performance Scale," in *The 1940 Mental Measurements Year Book,* ed. O. K. Buros (Arlington, Virginia: Gryphon Press, 1945).

Paterson Scale of Performance Tests,[95] and restandardized on 1,000 public school children. Norms are available for mental ages six through sixteen, with extrapolated values above and below these ages. A particular advantage of the Arthur Point Scale is the weighting of the subtests according to their "discriminative value," with more credit given to subtests which most sharply discriminate one age group from another. The Arthur correlated with the Binet from .50 to .75,[96] which is similar to correlations of the WISC verbal and performance scales reported by Wechsler (.56 to .68).[97]

A limitation of the Arthur is its tendency to stress speed of performance on motor tasks at the older age levels, penalizing the slower child. Since both the Arthur and WISC have drawn items from a common pool, there is considerable overlap (Manikin, Feature Profile, Mazes, Kohs Blocks). Mental ages tend to be lower than the Binet, owing to defects in standardization.[98]

In general, the Arthur Point Scale of Performance Tests is useful as a measurement of intelligence when verbal skills should be bypassed. In combination with the Binet, it seems to be roughly equivalent to the WISC verbal and performance scales. Since much of the test can be given with pantomime instructions, the Arthur is suitable for administration to children who might be penalized by other tests.

Adaptation of Tests

The demand for appropriate testing instruments for special populations has led to the adaptations of existing tests to meet specific needs. Since it is easier to establish norms for such tests, and the item content is pretested and accepted, such adaptations offer obvious advantages.

Translations of the Binet and the WISC have been made into most standardized European languages, and norms are available for such populations as Spanish American [99] and Puerto Rican [100] children, to mention a few.

Tests have also been adapted for the handicapped. Blind children can be given the Interim Hayes-Binet,[101] which consists of all items that can be

[95] R. Pintner and D. G. Paterson, *Pintner-Paterson Scale of Performance Tests* (New York: Psychological Corporation, 1927).

[96] Brown, *op. cit.*

[97] D. Wechsler, *op. cit.*, 1949 ed.

[98] Cronbach, *op. cit.*

[99] M. Keston and C. Jimenez, "A Study of Performance on English and Spanish Editions of the Stanford Binet Intelligence Test by Spanish American Children," *Journal of Genetic Psychology*, 85 (1954), 263–269.

[100] P. Roca, "Problems of Adapting Intelligence Scales from One Culture to Another," *High School Journal*, 38 (1955), 124–131.

[101] S. P. Hayes, *The Interim Hayes-Binet Intelligence Tests for the Blind* (Watertown, Mass.: Perkins Institution and Massachusetts School for the Blind, 1942).

administered without the use of vision, from both the Stanford Binet L and M forms, plus a few additional tests for ages three through six. The verbal scales of the Wechsler tests have also been adapted for blind subjects.[102]

Children who are deaf can be examined with a number of standard tests by developing pantomime instructions. The Grace Arthur Revision, Form II,[103] has reduced verbal instruction to a minimum for this purpose, and the Leiter International Performance Scale [104] is also useful for deaf children,[105] since items can be self-coaching.

The WISC has been used for examining deaf children. In a study involving deaf and normal children,[106] the performance scale was given with pantomime instructions to both groups, and results compared to those of children tested under standard conditions. Results suggested that the pantomime instructions were only slightly penalizing to the normal and the deaf children.

The orthopedically handicapped child has often been a problem for the examiner when both physical and speech handicaps are involved to such a degree that standard tests are useless. The 1937 Stanford-Binet has been adapted for use with cerebral palsied children [107] in much the same way as for the blind, by pooling L and M items to utilize those where solutions can be indicated by pointing or other forms of identification, making this version suitable for the severely handicapped. The same approach has been used with the Leiter International Performance Scale, where the examiner places the pieces as indicated by the child.[108]

Testing emotionally disturbed children has led to concern for the effects of failure inherent in the Stanford-Binet when administered under standard conditions. Hutt [109] has reported the effects of adapting the Binet to minimize failure, by following each item that is failed with an easier item on which the child may experience success.

Another approach to adapting tests is to revise the administration so as

[102] M. K. Bauman and S. P. Hayes, *A Manual for the Psychological Examination of the Adult Blind* (New York: Psychological Corporation, 1951).

[103] Grace Arthur, *A Point Scale of Performance Tests: Manual for Administering and Scoring the Tests, Revised Form II* (New York: Psychological Corporation, 1947).

[104] R. G. Leiter, *Leiter International Performance Scale, Revised Manual* (Washington, D.C.: Psychological Service Center Press, 1948).

[105] J. Mathews and J. Birch, "The Leiter International Performance Scale—A Suggested Instrument for Psychological Testing of Speech and Hearing Cases," *Journal of Speech and Hearing Disorders*, 14 (1949), 318–321.

[106] E. E. Graham and E. Shapiro, "Use of the Performance Scale of the WISC with Deaf Children," *Journal of Consulting Psychology*, 17 (1953), 396–398.

[107] E. Katz, "Pointing Modification of the Stanford-Binet L and M," *American Journal of Mental Deficiency*, 62 (1958), 698–707.

[108] Gwen Arnold, "A Technique for Measuring the Mental Ability of the Cerebral Palsied," *Psychological Service Center Journal*, 3 (1951), 171–180.

[109] Hutt, *op. cit.*

to allow for a better understanding of the child's difficulty. Thus, Volle [110] has suggested "testing the limits" with the verbal WISC by altering the wording of items to see whether the child can solve the simplified problem. Taylor,[111] on the other hand, has combined similar items from a variety of tests, so that failures on a specific type of item can be explored by administering easier items. Thus, a child who fails the Comprehension subtest on the WISC may be administered the easier Comprehension items on the Binet.

The Brief Binet

Probably the most common adaptations of psychological tests are the development of brief forms. The Binet and the various Wechsler scales have been adapted in this manner, often for use as rapid screening devices, or when intellectual factors *per se* are not assumed to be in question. For example, a brief WISC might be given as part of a larger test battery. When either the Binet or the Wechsler is involved, the brief test has an advantage in that by administering further items or subtests, the standard test can be completed on the spot, if initial results warrant it. For example, those who score extremely low, or show considerable deviation on the administered section, can then be tested in full.

The standard Binet short forms consist of the administration of four of the six subtests at each age level,[112] with an alternative of administering all items at the basal and ceiling years.[113] Since the more useful and discriminating items are utilized, a rapid establishment of basal and ceiling can be achieved, while reducing the number of items administered within the body of the test. Results indicate that the brief Binet gives a reasonably accurate estimate of the full IQ, when the selected items are drawn from and compared with the full test given to a large sample of children.[114]

A different approach to the brief Binet consists of a selection of items that are able to screen selected populations. For example, a five-item Binet

110 F. O. Volle, "A Proposal for Testing the Limits with Mental Defectives for Purposes of Subtest Analysis of the WISC Verbal Scale," *Journal of Clinical Psychology*, 13 (1957), 64–67.

111 Edith M. Taylor, *Psychological Appraisal of Children with Cerebral Defects* (Cambridge, Mass.: Harvard University Press, 1959).

112 J. W. Birch, "The Utility of Short Forms of the Stanford-Binet Tests of Intelligence with Mentally Retarded Children," *American Journal of Mental Deficiency*, 59 (1955), 462–483.

113 Clare Wright, "A Modified Procedure for the Abbreviated Revised Stanford-Binet Scale in Determining the Intelligence of Mental Defectives," *American Journal of Mental Deficiency*, 47 (1942), 178–184.

114 A. B. Silverstein and G. M. Fisher, "An Evaluation of Two Short Forms of the Stanford-Binet Form L-M for Use with Mentally Retarded Adults," *American Journal of Mental Deficiency*, 65 (1961), 486–488.

has proved to be a relatively quick device for screening potential candidates for mentally retarded classes.[115] Using the same approach, Stroud [116] selected seven items capable of identifying gifted children between the ages of ten and twelve. Using cut-off scores, the number of children requiring the administration of the full test could be cut considerably.

The Brief WISC

While the brief form of the Binet has been predetermined by the authors, the WISC and other Wechsler scales offer the possibility of any number of brief forms, determined only by the particular combination of subtests administered. In some settings it is so common to omit one or more of the WISC subtests, that essentially nothing but brief WISCs may be administered. Unfortunately, the omitted subtests often vary from examiner to examiner, almost by whim, adding little to the value of brief testing.

A brief WISC has been defined, somewhat arbitrarily, as one in which no more than six subtests are used to calculate the full IQ, since the time saved by omitting less than four subtests seems insignificant.[117] All current studies of brief WISCs are based upon calculation of the correlation of the brief form with the total or full scale IQ, with the best form considered to be that with the highest correlation. This is apparently a carry-over from the Binet, where the omission of items is based primarily on their lesser discriminative value in predicting the total score, and seems to ignore the meaning of serial subtests. Actually, the composition of a brief WISC may be based on a number of criteria such as time requirements; ease of administration and scoring; and freedom from the need for test materials or stop watch. More important, perhaps, the evaluation of specific skills can be stressed, or subtests may be chosen for their ability to elicit material valuable for diagnostic or clinical interpretation. So far, such variables have barely been considered in published studies.

Brief tests have been evaluated for three specific groups of children: normals, suspected mentally retarded, and emotionally disturbed. Initial studies [118] indicated that the latter group was least likely to be reliably evalu-

115 J. E. Slutsky, J. Justman, and J. W. Wrightstone, "Screening Children for Placement in Special Classes for the Mentally Retarded: a Preliminary Report," *American Journal of Mental Deficiency*, 57 (1953), 687–690.

116 Bertha E. Stroud, "A Short Form Stanford-Binet for Identifying Gifted Children" (Western Reserve University, Unpublished Manuscript, 1960).

117 L. Schwartz and E. E. Levitt, "Short Forms of the WISC for Children in the Educable, Noninstitutionalized, Mentally Retarded," *Journal of Educational Psychology*, 51 (1960), 187–190.

118 J. M. Yalowitz and Renate G. Armstrong, "Validity of Short Forms of the WISC," *Journal of Clinical Psychology*, 11 (1955), 275–277.

ated by a brief form of the WISC. However, a current study [119] of combinations of 3, 4, and 5 subtests that can be used to calculate the intellectual functioning of children referred to a Child Guidance Clinic for emotional problems indicates that a sizable number of combinations meet the requirement for predicting the full IQ accurately. Schwartz and Levitt [120] note that a correlation of .90 or better between the brief form and the full scale would result in an estimated error of 8.6 scale score units, which is probably as much error as should be allowed in prediction. Since brief testing is of most value in screening children suspected of being retarded as opposed to emotionally disturbed, the following measures that proved to be most valid in a variety of studies might be recommended.

The triad Arithmetic, Vocabulary, and Block Design correlated with the full scale at .91 for a group of emotionally disturbed children,[121] at .82 for a group of suspected mentally retarded,[122] and was among the highest predictors of the full scale in a study of the Wechsler normative data, ranging from .88 to .94 for the seven and one-half, ten and one-half, and thirteen and one-half year olds listed.[123] When four tests are used, the combination Arithmetic, Vocabulary, Picture Arrangement, and Block Design correlated .89 for a group of suspected mentally retarded children [124] from .92 to .94 for the normative data,[125] and from .93 to .96 for a large sample of children, a few unreferred, and drawn from schools and clinics.[126] A combination of five tests consisting of Comprehension, Arithmetic, Similarities, Picture Arrangement, and Block Design correlated at .96 for a group of emotionally disturbed children,[127] and .90 for a group of suspected mentally retarded youngsters.[128] It has been noted that the four test combinations reported above tend to underestimate intellectual functioning somewhat, even though the validity is high, presumably because three of the four items involve timed tests, not characteristic of the test as a whole.

Reviewing current studies, Ross [129] has questioned the artificial method

[119] R. Enberg, V. N. Rowley, and B. Stone, "Short Forms of the WISC for Use with Emotionally Disturbed Children," *Journal of Clinical Psychology*, 17 (1961), 280–284.

[120] Schwartz and Levitt, *op. cit.*

[121] Enberg, *et al., op. cit.*

[122] Schwartz and Levitt, *op. cit.*

[123] Mary P. Geuting, "Validities of Abbreviated Scales of the WISC," unpublished master's thesis, 1959, Fordham University.

[124] Schwartz and Levitt, *op. cit.*

[125] Geuting, *op. cit.*

[126] D. M. Guyol, J. W. Byrd, and H. E. Russell, "A Short Form of the WISC," U.S. Army, unpublished manuscript, n.d.

[127] Enberg, *et al., op. cit.*

[128] Schwartz and Levitt, *op. cit.*

[129] A. O. Ross, *The Practice of Clinical Child Psychology* (New York: Grune & Stratton, Inc., 1959).

of selecting subtests from the total to determine the composition of a brief battery, since the entire test will not be administered once the subtests are selected. Instead, he suggests giving the verbal scale alone, since this correlates well with the total test (.90), and yet is an integral unit, with the IQ already calculated in the Wechsler manual. The verbal scale has the additional value of being useful for predicting school success, and can be considered a fair parallel for the Binet.

However, the advantage of using both verbal and performance subtests in a brief form is the chance to evaluate the child's intellectual functioning in a variety of areas. Erratic functioning on the subtests, while limiting prediction of the full IQ, may be an important signal to complete the entire battery.

In summary, the adaptations of standard tests allow for the use of well-accepted item content in new settings and with special standardizations. A study of current well-known tests reveals that most standard tests are actually adaptations of previous tests, so the idea of adaptation is far from novel, and has long since proved its worth.

Reporting Results

Intelligence test findings are of no value unless they can be reported to others in meaningful form. An IQ or other test score stuck away in a cumulative folder will be useless to a principal concerned about a youngster sent to the office, or to a teacher trying to help a nonreader. The presentation of test findings in simple, easy to understand terms, terms that actually illuminate the problem for which testing was initiated, is the goal of any examiner.

The initial problem in intellectual testing is to establish the reason for referral. Unless this is clearly formulated, the proper selection of questions to be answered by a test instrument is unlikely, the basis for hypothesis making on the part of the examiner becomes diffuse, and results may have no meaning to the referring teacher or administrator. The reason for referral may, when clearly stated, actually rule out the need for individual examination. Once the reason for referral is available in written form, it should be placed conspicuously in the body of the written report. Not only is this essential for the organization of the report itself, but the same test findings may be used at a later date in order to answer quite different problems. It is not unusual to refer back to a Binet administered to a child at five years of age. At that time, he might have been considered for possible retention because of immaturity in the classroom. At a later age, the same child may be referred for evaluation of emotional disturbance. The initial test can throw considerable light on the child's development in the following years, as well as indicate that at an earlier age, the "emotional" components were not prominent in his behavior.

The challenge to each school psychologist is to devise the best possible referral blank to enable him to function economically and effectively in his role of problem solver in the assessment of children. Once a good referral system is established, it carries itself—for a period of time at least—and does not need reworking anew with every child referred. This is one of the reasons why a referral blank optimal for a given situation will enable the school psychologist to make himself more broadly useful.

Following the reason for referral, a description of the child and his behavior in the test situation is essential. Studies have repeatedly demonstrated that careful attention to this aspect of the examination allows for the evaluation of the adequacy of the test results, and reveals a rich source of personality material. Check lists such as those on the Stanford-Binet booklet can orient the examiner as to points to observe.

In a comparison of children as "emotionally disturbed" and those evaluated by the school as having "good mental health," the description of behavior in the test situation proved to be remarkably effective in identifying the disturbed child. From the examiner's notes, such variables as lack of physical control while working (for example, standing up during the examination), failing to help the examiner by boxing material when requested, inappropriate friendliness ("brashness") in response to a strange adult, and considerable chatter about personal happenings was characteristic of the emotionally disturbed children.[130]

The third step in reporting results is to give the test findings. Huber [131] suggests that the following points be covered:

1. level of functioning and estimated level of "capacity"
2. functioning in various intellectual areas
3. relationship between intellectual and total functioning
4. relationship between intelligence findings and that of the class or peer group (normative evaluation)

Huber's first point involves the interpretation of the test scores, and an evaluation as to their representativeness of the child's ability. Here, the test behavior can serve as an aid in interpretation. For example, when many responses are limited to a flat "don't know!", testing may be a fair measure of anxiety or negativeness, but intellectual "capacity" has hardly been touched. The second step involves an analysis of the child's strengths and weak-

---

[130] Zimmerman and Lambert, *op. cit.*

[131] J. T. Huber, *Report Writing in Psychology and Psychiatry* (New York: Harper & Row, Publishers, 1961).

nesses as revealed by successes and failures on items and subtests. Various studies indicate the sources of error inherent in "pattern analysis," yet a cautious interpretation of responses and methods of approach to different materials can be rewarding.

The third step seeks to integrate intellectual and total functioning. This often involves an integration of findings with the referral problem. A child referred for consideration for special education but showing average ability on a standard test of intelligence, calls for some evaluation. What sort of behavior in the classroom led to the referral? How can this child be helped to function at his level of ability? Do specific limitations within the test suggest the reason for referral, even though he shows successes in other areas? What instructional level could be expected both at present and with functioning restored to "capacity"?

The final step suggested by Huber is the evaluation of the relationship between the subject's intelligence and that of the peer group. For example, a child of average ability may be under a considerable handicap in trying to function in a fast moving classroom.

In the summary of intellectual test findings, the examiner can evaluate some of the hypotheses introduced in the body of the report. Thus, specific test scatter may be discussed in a speculative way, but summarized as likely rather than sure. The test findings may be presented as representative or as at best only a minimal estimate of ability. Further testing with specific test instruments may be recommended. Specific socioeconomic factors may be indicated as influencing results. The summary should, of course, include as well a terse formulation of the salient abilities and disabilities evidenced by the tests given. In general, the summary gives someone reading the report rapidly a sure clue as to the adequacy of test findings and the confidence to be placed in the results, as well as specific recommendations based upon an integration of findings and the original referral problem.

Special Bibliography:
Recent Articles and Research Studies
on the WISC and Stanford-Binet *

Alimena, B., "Note on Norms for Scatter Analysis on the Wechsler Intelligence Scales," *Journal of Clinical Psychology*, 17 (January, 1961), 61.

Bligh, H. F., "Concurrent Validity on Two Intelligence Measures for Young Children," in The Sixteenth Yearbook of the National Council on Measurements Used in Education, ed. Edith M. Huddleston, pp. 56–60.

---

* For additional bibliographic sources for information on the utilization of the WISC and the Stanford-Binet with retarded subjects, the reader is directed to the special listing at the end of Chapter 13, p.

Bonsall, Marcella R., and Mary M. Meeker, *Structure-of-Intellect Components in Stanford-Binet Form L-M and WISC.* Los Angeles County Superintendent of Schools Division of Research and Guidance, Programs for the Gifted, 1964.

Bradway, K. P., and N. M. Robinson, "Significant IQ Changes in Twenty-Five Years: A Follow-Up," *Journal of Educational Psychology,* **52**, No. 2 (1952), 74–79.

―――, and Clare W. Thompson, "Intelligence at Adulthood: A Twenty-Five Year Follow-Up," *Journal of Educational Psychology,* **53** (1962), 1–14.

Bridges, C., "Nomographs for Computing the Validity of WISC or Wechsler-Bellevue Short Forms," *Journal of Consulting Psychology,* **23** (October, 1959), 453–454.

Burkhart, Ann, W. Findley, and G. H. Fort, "A Comparison of Determinations of Intelligence by Individual and Group Tests," The Sixteenth Yearbook of the National Council on Measurements Used in Education, ed. Edith M. Huddleston, pp. 184–187.

Cohen, Jacob, "The Factorial Structure of the WISC at Ages 7–6, 10–6, and 13–6," *Journal of Consulting Psychology,* **23** (August, 1959), 285–299.

Coleman, J. C., and B. Rasof, "Intellectual Factors in Learning Disorders," *Perceptual Motor Skills,* **16**, No. 1 (1963), 139–152.

Darbes, Alex, "A Comparison of Scores Achieved by 55 Subjects Administered the Wechsler and Binet Scales of Intelligence," *Proceedings of the West Virginia Academy of Science,* **33** (1961), 115–119.

Darley, Frederic L., and Harris Winitz, "Comparison of Male and Female Kindergarten Children on the WISC," *Journal of Genetic Psychology,* **99** (1961), 41–49.

Durkin, Dolores, "A Study of Children Who Learned to Read Prior to First Grade," *California Journal of Educational Research,* **10** (May, 1959), 109–113.

Edwards, A. J., "Using Vocabulary as a Measure of General Ability," *Personnel and Guidance Journal,* **42** (October, 1963), 153–154.

Estes, Betsy Worth, Mary Ellen Curtin, Robert A. DeBurger, and Charlotte Denny, "Relationships Between 1960 Stanford-Binet, 1937 Stanford-Binet, WISC, Raven, and Draw-a-Man," *Journal of Consulting Psychology,* **25**(5) (1961), 388–391.

Frost, B. P., "Application of the Method of Extreme Deviations to the Wechsler Intelligence Scale for Children," *Journal of Clinical Psychology,* **16** (October, 1960), 420.

Gallagher, James J., and Leonard J. Lucite, "Intellectual Patterns of Gifted Compared with Average and Retarded," *Exceptional Children,* **27** (1961), 478–482.

Giannell, A. S., and C. M. Freeburne, "Comparative Validity of the WAIS and the Stanford-Binet with College Freshmen," *Education and Psychological Measurement,* **23** (Autumn, 1963), 557–567.

Goulet, L. R., and A. Barclay, "Vineland Social Maturity Scale: Utility in Assessment of Binet M. A.," *American Journal of Mental Deficiency,* **67** (May, 1963), 916–921.

Hafner, A. J., *et al.,* "Relationship Between the CMAS and WISC Functioning," *Journal of Clinical Psychology,* **16** (July, 1960), 322–323.

Himelstein, P., "Research with the Stanford-Binet," *Psychological Bulletin,* **63** (March, 1966), 156–164.

Hirschenfang, S., "Further Studies on the Columbia Mental Maturity Scale (CMMS) and Revised Stanford-Binet (L) in Children with Speech Disorders," *Journal of Clinical Psychology,* **17** (April, 1961), 171.

Hirst, L. S., "Usefulness of a Two-way Analysis of WISC Subtests in the Diagnosis of Remedial Reading Problems," *Journal of Experimental Education,* **29** (December, 1960), 63–70.

Hopkins, K. D., and W. B. Michael, "The Diagnostic Use of WISC Subtest Patterns," *California Journal of Educational Research,* **12** (1961), 116–117, 130.

Jones, S., "Wechsler Intelligence Scale for Children Applied to a Sample of London Primary School Children," *British Journal of Educational Psychology,* **32** (June, 1962), 119–132.

Kallos, G. L., J. M. Grabow, and E. A. Guarino, "The WISC Profile of Disabled Readers," *Personnel Guidance Journal,* **39** (1939), 476–478.

Kennedy, Wallace A., Vernon Van DeRiet, and James C. White, Jr., "Use of the Terman-Merrill Abbreviated Scale on the 1960 Stanford-Binet Form L-M on Negro Elementary School Children of the Southeastern United States," *Journal of Consulting Psychology,* **27**(5) (1963), 456–457.

Koppitz, E. M., "Relationships Between the Bender-Gestalt and the WISC," *Journal of Clinical Psychology,* **14** (October, 1958), 413–416.

Lehmann, Irwin J., "Rural-Urban Differences in Intelligence," *Journal of Educational Research,* **53** (1959), 62–68.

Lessing, Elise Elkins, "A Note on the Significance of Discrepancies Between Goodenough and Binet IQ Scores," *Journal of Consulting Psychology,* **25** (1961), 456–457.

Levinson, B. M. "Binet Non-Verbal Preschool Scale," *Journal of Clinical Psychology,* **16** (January, 1960), 12–13.

Levinson, Boris M., "Reevaluation of the Revised Stanford-Binet Scale, Form L Vocabulary, as a Test of Intelligence for the Kindergarten and Primary School Child," *Journal of Genetic Psychology,* **93** (1958), 237–248.

————, "Subcultural Values and IQ Stability," *Journal of Genetic Psychology*, 98 (1961), 69–82.

————, "Subcultured Variations in Verbal and Performance Ability at the Elementary School Level," *Journal of Genetic Psychology*, 97 (1960), 149–160.

————, "The Intelligence of Applicants for Admission to Jewish Day Schools," *Jewish Social Studies*, 19 (1957), 129–140.

Lindholm, B. W., "Changes in Conventional and Deviation IQ's," *Journal of Educational Psychology*, 55 (April, 1964), 110–113.

Littell, William M., "The WISC: Review of a Decade of Research," *Psychological Bulletin*, 57 (March, 1960), 132–156.

Lucito, Leonard, and James Gallagher, "Intellectual Patterns of Highly Gifted Children on the WISC," *Peabody Journal of Education*, 38 (1960), 131–136.

Massey, J. O., *Scoring Supplement for the WISC*, 3rd ed. Palo Alto: Consulting Psychologists Press, 1965.

Maxwell, A. E., "Discrepancies Between the Pattern of Abilities for Normal and Neurotic Children," *Journal of Mental Science*, 107 (1961), 300–307.

————, "Tables to Facilitate the Comparison of Subtest Scores on the WISC," *Journal of Clinical Psychology*, 15 (1959), 293–295.

McCarthy, Dorothea, "Administration of the Digit Symbol and Coding Subtests of the WAIS and WISC to Left-Handed Subjects," *Psychological Reports*, 8 (1961), 407–408.

Moed, G., *et al.*, "Interest Correlations of the Wechsler Intelligence Scale for Children and Two Picture Vocabulary Tests," *Education and Psychological Measurement*, 23 (Summer, 1963), 259–263.

Mohan, T. W., Jr., "Diagnostic Consistency and Prediction: A Note on Graduate Student Skills," *Personnel and Guidance Journal*, 42 (December, 1963), 364–367.

Moyer, Robert W., "A Study of the STEP Reading, SCAT and WISC Tests, and School Grades," *Reading Teacher*, 12 (December, 1958), 117, 142–271.

Neville, D., "Comparison of the WISC Patterns of Male Retarded and Non-Retarded Readers," *Journal of Educational Research*, 54 (January, 1961), 195–197.

Ogdon, D. P., "WISC IQs for the Mentally Retarded," *Journal of Consulting Psychology*, 24 (April, 1960), 187–188.

Parsley, L. K. M., Jr., and M. Powell, "Relationships Between the Lee-Clark Reading Readiness Test and the 1937 Revision of the Stanford-Binet Intelligence Test, Form L," *Journal of Educational Research*, 54 (April, 1961), 304–307.

Pattera, M. E., "Study of Thirty-Three WISC Scattergrams of Retarded Readers," *Elementary English*, 40 (April, 1963), 394–405.

Robeck, Mildred C., "Subtest Patterning of Problem Readers on WISC," *California Journal of Educational Research*, 11 (1960), 110–115.

Roberts, Helen Erskine, "Comparison of Otis and Stanford-Binet IQs," *California Journal of Educational Research*, 12 (1961), 8–15.

Rushton, C. S., and A. E. Stockwin, "Changes in Terman-Merrill IQs of Educationally Sub-Normal Boys," *British Journal of Educational Psychology*, 33 (January, 1963), 132–142.

Rychlak, J. F., "Self-Confidence, Ability, and the Interest-Value of Tasks," *Journal of Genetic Psychology*, 94 (June, 1959), 153–159.

Schachter, Frances Fushs, and Virginia Apgar, "Comparison of Pre-School Stanford-Binet and School-Age WISC IQs," *Journal of Educational Psychology*, 49 (1958), 320–323.

Schereo, I. W., "Prediction of Academic Achievement in Brain Injured Children," *Exceptional Children*, 28 (October, 1961), 103–106.

Schneider, Jenny, and David Smillie, "The Use of Scatter on the Stanford-Binet," *Psychology Service Center Journal*, 11 (1959), 73–75.

Sheldon, M. Stephen, and Jeanette Garton, "A Note on 'A WISC Profile for Retarded Readers,'" *Alberta Journal of Educational Research*, 5 (1959), 264–267.

Shine, A., "Relationship Between Arithmetic Achievement and Item Performance on the Revised Stanford-Binet Scale," *Arithmetic Teacher*, 8 (February, 1961), 57–59.

Simpson, W. H., and C. C. Bridges, Jr., "Short Form of the Wechsler Intelligence Scale for Children," *Journal of Clinical Psychology*, 15 (October, 1959), 424.

Taylor, J. R., "Screening Intelligence," *Journal of Speech and Hearing Disorders*, 28 (February, 1963), 90–91.

Thompson, Jack M., and Carmen J. Finley, "The Relationship between the Goodenough Draw-a-Man Test and the Stanford-Binet Form L-M in Children Referred for School Guidance Services," *California Journal of Educational Research*, 14(1) (1963), 19–22.

———, "Abbreviated WISC for Use with Gifted Elementary School Children," *California Journal of Educational Research*, 14 (September, 1963), 167–177.

———, "Further Comparison of the Intellectual Patterns of Gifted and Mentally Retarded Children," *Exceptional Children*, 28 (March, 1962), 379–381.

———, "Validation of an Abbreviated Wechsler Intelligence Scale for Children for Use with the Educable Mentally Retarded," *Education and Psychological Measurement*, 22 (Autumn, 1962), 239–242.

Vallet, R., *A Clinical Profile for the Stanford-Binet*. Palo Alto: Consulting Psychologists Press, 1965.

————, "A Psychoeducational Profile of Basic Learning Abilities," *Journal of School Psychology*, 4 (1966), 9–24.

Weise, Phillip, "Current Use of Binet and Wechsler Tests by School Psychologists in California," *California Journal of Educational Research*, 11 (1960), 3–78.

Winitz, Harris, "Relationships Between Language and Nonlanguage Measures of Kindergarten Children," *Journal of Speech and Hearing Research*, 2 (1959), 387–391.

GLADYS L. ANDERSON *

11

Projective Techniques and the Illinois Test of Psycholinguistic Abilities

PART ONE: THE UTILIZATION OF
PROJECTIVE TECHNIQUES IN THE SCHOOLS

Projective techniques have emerged from a setting that
has come to be known as clinical psychology. They are
essentially clinical instruments. The school psychologist
who uses these techniques is, like the clinical psychologist, concerned with the total interacting of a changing
child in his changing environments. It will be the purpose
of this chapter to discuss projective techniques and the
ITPA but first to put these techniques in an orientation of
trends in psychological thinking as these trends bear upon
clinical psychology, school psychology, and upon education.

The history of any science is a record of process,
evolution, differentiation, and integration. It is a record
of struggle for new meanings and refinements of observations. It is also a record of abandoning old ways of perceiving and thinking. Looking back to the beginning of
this century, one can see emerging a vigorous systematic
effort to make a science of the study of human behavior.
In this growing expression of inquiry and experimenta-

* Dr. Anderson died in 1965. The editor of the volume did
the final editing and rewriting.

tion, one can now distinguish two early general trends of approach. These two approaches were each valid in their ways, but their contributions to the development of psychology as a science have been different.

(1) THE MEASUREMENT OF SINGLE VARIABLES

On the one hand, there was a trend that adapted to the study of behavior the methods of the physical sciences, a trend that had as its chief procedure the control of all variables except the one that the experimenter was trying to measure. That necessitated the measurement of very small fragments of human behavior. Examples were the determination of the threshold of the sense of touch, the threshold of discrimination of weights, and the decrement of energy output of the index finger in the repeated lifting of a known weight at equal intervals of time. That approach was exemplified in the work of Weber, Fechner, Wundt, and others, and is sometimes thought of as a German approach.

(2) THE STUDY OF COMPLEX BEHAVIOR

On the other hand, there were psychologists whose admitted objective was to study not isolated, simple variables but rather to observe and understand the more complex behavior of the whole person. Representatives of this approach were, for the most part, Frenchmen. Itard, who tried to educate the "Wild Boy of Aveyron," followed by his brilliant pupil, Seguin, and much later by Binet, were all interested in the more complex psychological processes found in the behavior of a person in day-to-day experiences.

Binet, to be sure, whose name is associated with IQ, and all too frequently with nothing else, made many studies of the so-called simpler functions, such as memory, sensation, reaction-time, and discrimination. From his own studies of these processes, he rejected the association theory of memory then current among psychologists and looked for more meaning in the experiences of the subject. But he initiated many other studies with methods and materials which have since been called "projective techniques." He experimented with sentence completion tests and with the interpretation of ink blots.

In one experiment, Binet asked children to write twenty words as fast as they could; then, by careful questioning, tried to discover from the children's own introspections what made them think of the individual words and groups of words, and what they were thinking about before and after they hesitated in the middle of the test. In another experiment, he asked children to describe objects and to tell stories about pictures, and used a question period afterward to discover more meaning in the children's private mental life out of which the details of the stories emerged.

Binet published books and articles on his findings as well as interpretations of the complexities of human behavior. He did all of these things before he was asked to develop the mental tests for which, unfortunately, he is so uniquely known to Americans. Of Binet's monograph, "L'étude expérimentale de l'intelligence," [1] reporting his elaborate experimental study of his two daughters, aged fourteen and one-half and thirteen, Goodenough said, "In my opinion it remains the best, as it almost certainly is the first, example of the projective approach to the study of personality differences." [2] Of this same monograph, Cronbach has written, "Binet described the application of the ink blot and imagery tests to his daughters, coming out with clinical qualitative descriptions of the way their intelligence functioned, which read as if taken from the most modern results of projective techniques." [3]

Herman Rorschach, the Swiss psychiatrist, published his "experiment" in symbolic expression of perception in 1921. At his untimely death in 1922, he left one paper in which he explained more fully the relation of his ideas to psychoanalysis. Oberholzer published this material jointly with Rorschach in German in 1923 and in English translation in 1924. The first American study using the Rorschach method was published by Beck,[4] who alone had eighteen publications on the Rorschach in the 1930's. During this time Beck [5] published his monograph manual, *Introduction to the Rorschach Method*. Meanwhile others had begun to use and to report on the Rorschach. The *Rorschach Research Exchange*, established in 1936, became the communication medium for the Rorschach Institute founded by Klopfer and his associates in 1939. As interest in projective techniques became more general the name of the Rorschach Institute was changed to the Society for Projective Techniques and Personality Assessment Inc., and their journal was renamed the *Journal of Projective Techniques and Personality Assessment*.

In the mid-1930's there was undertaken at the Harvard Psychological Clinic a daring experiment without parallel either before or since. A group of twenty-eight psychologists of various schools and persuasions among whom were three physicians and five psychoanalysts made a three-year study of fifty young men. The sustaining inspiration for this complicated program was Murray, who said in his preface to *Explorations in Personality*:

[1] A. Binet, *l'Étude expérimentale de l'intelligence* (Paris: Alfred Costes, 1902).

[2] F. Goodenough, *Mental Testing* (New York: Holt, Rinehart & Winston, Inc., 1949).

[3] L. J. Cronbach, *Essentials of Psychological Testing* (New York: Harper & Row, Publishers, 1949), p. 104.

[4] S. J. Beck, "Personality Diagnosis by Means of the Rorschach Test," *American Journal of Orthopsychiatry*, 1 (1930–31), 81–88.

[5] S. J. Beck, "Introduction to the Rorschach Method: A Manual of Personality Study," *Research Monograph American Orthopsychiatry Association*, No. 1, 1937.

Four years ago every investigator at the Harvard Psychological Clinic was a pioneer with his own chosen area of wilderness to map. Each area was an aspect of human personality—a virgin forest of peculiar problems. Here he lost and sometimes found himself. Though there were plenty of opportunities for communication, his obligations to other experimenters were minimal and he was free to follow the wilful drifts of his own elusive thought. He enjoyed, in other words, relative autonomy in a Jeffersonian democracy of researchers—an atmosphere that is breath to the nostrils of every seeker after hidden truth.

All we workers were bound by a common compulsion: to inquire into the nature of man; and by a common faith: that experiment would prove fruitful. We devoted ourselves, therefore, to the observation of human beings responding to a variety of controlled conditions, conditions which resembled as nearly as possible those of everyday life. Our emphasis was upon emotional and behavioral reactions, what previous experiences determined them, to what degree and in what manner. This preoccupation set our studies somewhat outside the university tradition. For it has been the custom in academic psychology to concentrate upon the perceptive and cognitive functions of the human mind or, more recently, upon the behaviour of animals.[6]

During this program of research at the Harvard Psychological Clinic Morgan and Murray [7] developed the Thematic Apperception Test, a test that has become so widely used and so well known that it is referred to as test that has become so widely used and so well known that it is referred to as the TAT. Other home-made devices such as sentence completion and word association lists were devised.

Other techniques began to appear. For example, Bender's *A Visual Motor Gestalt Test and Its Clinical Use*,[8] was published as a monograph by the American Orthopsychiatric Association. This instrument and its theoretical underpinning is discussed in greater detail in Chapter 12.

It was L. K. Frank [9] in 1939 who first used the term "Projective Methods" for the new non-normative techniques. Frank had been a field representative for the Laura Spelman Rockefeller Foundation during the period of their support of the Research Institutes of Child Welfare. He had had an opportunity to become familiar in detail with much of the then current research involving children. He was in fact a one-man interdisciplinary

---

[6] H. A. Murray, *Explorations in Personality* (New York: Oxford University Press, Inc., 1938).

[7] Christiana D. Morgan and H. A. Murray, "A Method for Investigating Fantasies: The Thematic Apperception Test," *Arch. Neurol. Psychiat.*, 34 (1935), 289–306.

[8] Lauretta Bender, *A Visual Motor Gestalt Test and Its Clinical Use*, Research Monograph No. 3 (New York: American Orthopsychiatric Association, 1938); see also her *Instructions for the use of the visual motor Gestalt test* (New York: Amer. Orthopsychiat. Ass., 1946).

[9] L. K. Frank, "Projective Methods for the Study of Personality," *J. Psychol.*, 8 (1939), 389–413. Reprinted in R. I. Watson, ed., *Readings in the Clinical Method in Psychology* (New York: Harper & Row, Publishers, 1949).

instigator, inciter, and critic of research in the child development field. He lived, thought, and wrote on the research frontiers. Frank (1939) gave critical and constructive consideration to the limitations of the normative, quantitative, objective tests then current. He also offered a rationale for viewing personality as involving the private, idiosyncratic, non-normative organization of personal perceptions.

Frank wrote:

> . . . we may approach the personality and induce the individual to reveal his way of organizing experience by giving him a field (objects, materials, experiences) with relatively little structure and cultural patterning so that the personality can project upon that plastic field his way of seeing life, his meanings, significances, patterns, and especially his feelings. Thus we elicit a projection of the individual personality's *private world* because he has to organize the field, interpret the material and react affectively to it. More specifically, a projection method for study of personality involves the presentation of a stimulus-situation designed or chosen because it will mean to the subject, not what the experimenter has arbitrarily decided it should mean (as in most psychological experiments using standardized stimuli in order to be "objective"), but rather whatever it must mean to the personality who gives it, or imposes upon it, his private, idiosyncratic meaning and organization.[10]

In the same paper Frank also explained that projective methods were not a substitute for the quantitatively scorable tests but offered something new, different, and important beyond the frontiers of the testing movement:

> It may be emphasized that projective methods are not offered as a substitute for the quantitative statistical procedures, but rather are designed to permit a study of the unique idiomatic individual which is conceived as a process of organizing experience and so must elude the investigator who relies upon methods that of necessity ignore or obscure the individual and the configural quality of his personality. Finally it should be noted that projective methods of personality study offer possibilities for utilizing the insights into human conduct and personality expression which the prevailing quantitative procedures seem deliberately to ignore.[11]

Other evidences of a changing thinking about personality dynamics appeared in print in this decade. The theme of non-normative studies was the basis of a monograph by G. W. Allport (1942), *Personal Documents in Psychological Science*.[12]

Rapaport, Gill, and Schafer [13] published two volumes on *Diagnostic*

---

[10] L. K. Frank, *Projective Methods* (Springfield, Ill.: Charles C Thomas, Publisher, 1948), p. 272.

[11] *Ibid.*, p. 68.

[12] G. W. Allport, *The Use of Personal Documents in Psychological Science* (New York: Social Science Research Council, 1942).

[13] D. Rapaport, M. Gill, and R. Schafer, *Diagnostic Psychological Testing*, Vol. I, 1945; Vol. II, 1946 (Chicago, Ill.: Year Book Publishers).

Psychological Testing. In the introduction, Rapaport again made a distinction, previously made by Frank and discussed by G. W. Allport, between the normative, statistical approach and a "projective hypothesis," which Rapaport had earlier advanced.

According to the "projective hypothesis"—

every reaction of a subject is a reflection, or projection, of his private world. This approach to testing contrasts sharply with that usually characterized as psychometric. The main aim was not to attribute to a person a percentile rank in the population or any other numerical measure allegedly representative of him. The aim was rather to understand the individual: to give him a chance to express himself in a sufficient number and variety of controlled situations, the nature of which has been well enough explored to enable the psychologist to infer, out of the subject's reactions, the gross outlines of his personality makeup. This expectancy, however, implies the "projective hypothesis"; it implies that every action and reaction of a human individual bears the characteristic features of his individual makeup. The choice of tests on the basis of this hypothesis would favor tests whose material is unconventional and not limited to eliciting habitual reactions. This hypothesis would find the Rorschach most satisfactory; the Thematic Apperception Test less satisfactory; and the standard intelligence tests least satisfactory, because the intelligence test questions themselves would appear, at first glance, aimed at eliciting highly conventional responses. We include in this battery not only clearly projective tests; but we attempted to demonstrate that the projective hypothesis, though in generalized form, can be applied even to intelligence tests. In fact, we approached all of these tests with this hypothesis.[14]

Rapaport's statement in 1942 was a milestone leading the way toward a further and more subtle and differentiated understanding of personality. The two volumes by Rapaport, Gill, and Schafer set a pattern for graduate training in psychological diagnostic testing in United States universities for the next decade. Their approach, however, was still in the traditions of psychiatric nosology, diagnosing the individual, making finer and more subtle analyses of the individual person and his private world. It can now be seen that they failed to give scope to the phenomenon of the *person in process of interacting with his environment* which was a creative innovation in the OSS assessment program [15] and had been emphasized by Follett,[16] Murray,[17] and Frank.[18]

[14] D. Rapaport, "Principles Underlying Projective Techniques," *Character & Personality*, 10 (1942), 214–219, 16.

[15] OSS Assessment Staff, *Assessment of Men: Selection of Personnel for the Office of Strategic Services* (New York: Holt, Rinehart & Winston, Inc., 1948).

[16] M. P. Follett, *Creative Experience* (New York: Longmans, Green & Co., Inc., 1924).

[17] H. A. Murray, *Explorations in Personality* (New York: Oxford University Press, Inc., 1938).

[18] Frank, *op. cit.*

Other publications had begun to appear. Sargent in 1945 [19] wrote a scholarly general review and summary on "Projective Methods: Their Origins, Theory, and Application in Personality Research." Frank in 1948 [20] published his little volume on *Projective Methods* which gave wide support to speculative thinking and has since become a classic. An unprecedented amount of scattered publications suddenly seemed to loom on the horizon. In a span of three years the authors of three books attempted to assemble, assess, and summarize these materials. Bell,[21] for example, classified 798 references on the Rorschach alone. Abt and Bellak,[22] as editors, and authors, expanded the theoretical bases and clinical uses of projective techniques. Anderson and Anderson,[23] also as editors and authors, presented all projective techniques on which there had been substantial research, and in addition two chapters on the qualitative or projective interpretations of standardized intelligence tests: the Wechsler-Bellevue Intelligence Scale and the Stanford-Binet. Although the early work on projective techniques began with the study of adults and for a long time continued with adults, there was by 1960 sufficient material for Rabin and Haworth [24] to edit a comprehensive review of *Projective Techniques with Children,* and for Henry [25] to review projective techniques in a handbook of research methods in child development. Lindzey [26] produced a book on *Projective Techniques and Cross-cultural Research.* Excellent critical reviews of projective techniques in relation to other psychological tests are found in Anastasi [27] and Cronbach,[28] in the 1965 *Handbook of Projective Techniques,*[29] and in the *Sixth Mental Measurements Yearbook.*[30]

[19] H. D. Sargent, "Projective Methods: Their Origin, Theory, and Application in Personality Research," *Psychol. Bull.,* 42 (1945), 257–293.

[20] L. K. Frank, *Projective Methods* (Springfield, Ill.: Charles C Thomas, Publisher, 1948).

[21] J. E. Bell, *Projective Techniques: A Dynamic Approach to the Study of the Personality* (New York: Longmans, Green & Co., Inc., 1948).

[22] L. E. Abt and Bellak, eds., *Projective Psychology: Clinical Approaches to the Total Personality* (New York: Alfred A. Knopf, Inc., 1950).

[23] H. H. Anderson and Gladys L. Anderson, eds., *An Introduction to Projective Techniques* (Englewood Cliffs, N.J.: Prentice-Hall, Inc., 1951).

[24] A. I. Rabin and M. R. Haworth, eds., *Projective Techniques with Children* (New York: Grune & Stratton, Inc., 1960).

[25] W. E. Henry, "Projective Techniques," in *Handbook of Research Methods in Child Development,* ed. P. H. Mussen (New York: John Wiley & Sons, Inc., 1960).

[26] G. Lindzey, *Projective Techniques and Cross-Cultural Research* (New York: Appleton Century Crofts, 1961).

[27] Anne Anastasi, *Psychological Testing,* 2nd ed. (New York: The Macmillan Company, 1961).

[28] L. J. Cronbach, *Essentials of Psychological Testing,* rev. ed. (New York: Harper & Row, Publishers, 1960).

[29] B. I. Murstein, *Handbook of Projective Techniques* (Don Mills, Ontario: General Publishing Co., 1965).

[30] O. K. Buros, ed., *Sixth Mental Measurement Yearbook* (Highland Park, N.J.: Griffin Press, 1965).

A Review of the Projective Techniques

We have just reviewed a swift evolution of perception, discovery, and thinking about the behavior of the individual person that has been taking place in the last half century and is still progressing. We have seen a tidal wave of quantitative "scientific" testing with standardized, normative mental and ability tests sweep the psychological and educational world, then subside, only to be followed by an inundation of more abstract, abstruse, unstructured stimulus materials, now known as projective techniques.

These waves have each been constructive, building up the shorelines of human understanding. But they have also been erosive, digging deep into biases, scientific traditions, cultural tabus, such as the stigma of mental illness and of the mentally handicapped, and misperceptions of the wise men and scientists of the past. There is no magic in the new things that in the past two decades have been washed ashore. The deep waters of enthusiasm have again somewhat subsided. A next wave, however, seems indeed on the horizon. As it breaks, a new generation of students will reexamine the wisdom of the past, reevaluate it for themselves, discard much in psychology that we are still revering and make their own constructions, hypotheses, and understandings.

In the last part of this chapter we shall try to examine both the horizon and the shoreline and try to discern some of the areas of our own perceptions where the next erosions will be most conspicuous.

Meanwhile, let us consider some of the more widely used projective techniques. This is not the place to attempt a manual of administration, scoring, and interpretation. The administration of most projective techniques is relatively simple. The scoring, however, is usually complicated; and the interpretation of some of the projective techniques has constituted a career for some clinicians. There are many special sources for detailed instructions and discussions on each of the projective techniques.

THE RORSCHACH INKBLOT EXPERIMENT

The interpretation of inkblots had been used by Binet and others long before the time of Hermann Rorschach. Rorschach, however, was the first to carry his observations and experimentations to the point where he could offer inkblots as stimulus materials for the study of the whole personality. As Rorschach explained, the inkblot cards were made by putting a blot of ink on a piece of paper, folding it and pressing it to make a symmetrical design. After much trial and error the ten designs finally selected were chosen with certain specific criteria and hypotheses in mind.

Five of the inkblots are gray in varying amounts of shading; two are gray with bright blotches of red; and three are made of a variety of colors. The cards are numbered and are administered to the subject one at a time in sequence.

There are several systems for administration, scoring and interpretation of the Rorschach. The two most widely used in the United States have been developed by Beck [31] and by Klopfer.[32] In the following discussion comments have chief reference to the Beck system. As the subject is given the card he is asked to tell what he sees—what the blot could represent. During the administration the examiner takes note of the time for each card, the position in which the subject holds the card, and of the subject's remarks and other behavior. After the subject has finished with the tenth card the examiner questions him as to the exact location and the aspect of the area which prompted each response. Separate records are made of the responses in this inquiry.

The responses are scored as to location, determinant, and content. Location is scored as to whether the whole card (W) was used, as for example a "Bat," or a major detail (D), or a fine detail (Dd). According to Rorschach the whole response (W) represents an abstracting or theoretical approach. The D responses represent a concrete, practical intelligence.

The determinants include Form (F), Color (C), and Movement (M). Usually the response depends upon the form of the blot or the part of it perceived. When accurately perceived the response is scored F+; when the percept is vague or inaccurate it is scored F—. Color scoring depends upon whether the response mentioned only color (C) or whether it was combined with form (F). For example, a "red bird" response would be scored FC, presumed to depend first on form and secondarily on color. Whereas form appears to relate more to intellectual functioning, color has been found to be a symbol of emotional or affective perception.

Movement is a response that the subject adds to his perception of the blot, for there is no movement on the blot. Movement responses, such as "two clowns dancing," are related to wishful living, fantasy, or creative imagination. Movement is more often found associated with Human (H) or Animal (A) percepts.

In addition to the above, each response is scored in terms of con-

[31] B. Beck, "Introduction to the Rorschach Method: A Manual of Personality Study," *Research Monograph American Orthopsychiatry Association*, No. 1, 1937; see also *Rorschach's Test*, Vol. 1, *Basic Processes* (New York: Grune & Stratton, Inc., 1944); Anne G. Beck, E. E. Levitt, and H. B. Molish, *Rorschach's Test I: Basic Processes*, 3rd rev. ed. (New York: Grune & Stratton, Inc., 1961).

[32] B. Klopfer and D. M. Kelley, *The Rorschach Technique* (New York: Harcourt, Brace & World, Inc., 1942); B. Klopfer, Mary D. Ainsworth, W. G. Klopfer, and R. R. Holt, *Developments in the Rorschach Technique*, Vol. I. *Technique and Theory* (New York: Harcourt, Brace & World, Inc., 1954), B. Klopfer, ed., *Developments in the Rorschach Technique*, Vol. II. *Fields of Application* (New York: Harcourt, Brace & World, Inc., 1956).

tent. Beck reported as the five most common categories: humans, parts of humans, animals, parts of animals, and anatomy. In addition there is a long list of content categories beginning with abstraction, alphabet, anthropology and ending with sex, travel and vocation. There are other scoring categories such as Popular responses (P), Original (O), white space, vista, shading, and texture perceptions. Beck has added an organization (Z) score. The response productivity of the subject is scored in the total number of percepts given for the ten cards, or total R.

Scoring includes also the numbers of responses in the various content categories, the computation of numbers of per cents and ratios: for example, the percent of F+ to total response, and the ratio of human movement to color. These numerical scores are summarized in a psychogram that forms the basis for the writing of a comprehensive personality description. For research purposes psychologists have made "blind diagnoses" from the Rorschach responses and psychogram, with no other information except perhaps age and sex. For clinical work, however, and especially with children, psychologists not only base their diagnoses on the interdependencies of the many scores on the Rorschach, but use all available additional information about the subject and his past experiences.

Over the years Rorschach tests with children have been accumulating. Attempts have been made to report these results in terms of normative and developmental data. Age and developmental comparisons have been made among others by Thetford, Molish, and Beck; [33] Rabin and Beck; [34] Meili-Dworetzki; [35] and Ames.[36] Perhaps the most comprehensive study of adolescents to date is reported by Ames, Métraux, and Walker.[37] Halpern [38] and Hertz [39] have excellent discussions of the use and limitations of norms in clinical work with children and adolescents.

[33] W. N. Thetford, H. B. Molish, and S. J. Beck, "Developmental Aspects of Personality Structure in Normal Children," *J. Proj. Tech.*, 15 (1951), 58–78.

[34] A. I. Rabin and S. J. Beck, "Genetic Aspects of Some Rorschach Factors," *American Journal of Orthopsychiatry*, 20 (1950), 595–599.

[35] G. Meili-Dworetzki, "The Development of Perception in the Rorschach," in *Developments in the Rorschach Technique*. Vol. II., ed. B. Klopfer (New York: Harcourt, Brace & World, Inc., 1956).

[36] Louise Bates Ames, "Longitudinal Survey of Child Rorschach Responses— Younger Subjects Aged 2 to 10 Years," *Genet. Psychol. Monogr.*, 61 (1960), 229–289; see also her "Longitudinal Survey of Child Rorschach Responses: Older Subjects Aged 10 to 16 Years," *Genet. Psychol. Monogr.*, 62 (1960), 185–229.

[37] Louise B. Ames, Rhoda W. Métraux, and R. N. Walker, *Adolescent Rorschach Responses* (New York: Hoeber, 1959).

[38] Florence Halpern, "The Rorschach Test with Children," in *Projective Techniques with Children*, ed. A. I. Rabin and Mary R. Haworth (New York: Grune & Stratton, Inc., 1960).

[39] Marguerite R. Hertz, "The Rorschach in Adolescence," in *Projective Techniques with Children*, ed. A. I. Rabin and Mary R. Haworth (New York: Grune & Stratton, Inc., 1960).

Rickers-Ovsiankina [40] has been the first one to plan a systematic effort to integrate the perceptual theories of clinical psychologists with those of experimental psychologists. Toomey and Rickers-Ovsiankina offered for the first time a comparative diagrammatic chart of six different scoring systems for the Rorschach.

The Rorschach offers possibilities for a more complete personality description than any one other method of personality study. It has nevertheless not satisfied the ordinary criteria of "science." The literature on the Rorschach is full of apologetics about the low reliability and low validity of the Rorschach. Perhaps the best summaries of these problems are those on reliability by Holzberg,[41] and on validity by Harris.[42]

A number of persons have produced other sets of inkblots, but these have been used chiefly in research. A set of 90 inkblots, the Holtzman Inkblot Technique,[43] in two parallel forms of 45 inkblots each, has been developed in an effort to make the scoring procedures more consistent with objective scoring and psychometric treatment. Some authorities on school psychology feel the Rorschach has limited utility in the schools because of its requirement of a large amount of time for administration and interpretation.

PICTORIAL TECHNIQUES

The interpretation of pictures has been used in the Stanford Revision of the Binet-Simon tests as a test of intelligence. The purpose was to elicit enumeration of objects or description at age three; the identification of cultural absurdities, such as sitting in the rain, at age seven; and shooting at the wrong Indian at age ten. In these pictures there are "correct" ways of responding which give little opportunity for uniqueness of the child's perception or of idiosyncratic meanings that a picture might have for a child. In fact, the farther the child's response might be from the culturally expected answer the more likely he was to fail.

The use of pictures as projective techniques has an entirely different purpose by comparison with the purposes above of the objective, behavioristic, stimulus-response, correct-incorrect, plus-minus, right-or-wrong, or half-credit for near miss, responses in the traditional, normative intelligence tests. It was

[40] Maria A. Rickers-Ovsiankina, ed., Rorschach Psychology (New York: John Wiley & Sons, Inc., 1960).
[41] D. Holzberg, "Reliability Re-examined," in Rorschach Psychology, ed. Maria A. Rickers-Ovsiankina (New York: John Wiley & Sons, Inc., 1960).
[42] J. G. Harris, Jr., "Validity: the Search for a Constant in a Universe of Variables," in Rorschach Psychology, ed. Maria A. Rickers-Ovsiankina (New York: John Wiley & Sons, Inc., 1960).
[43] W. H. Holtzman, J. S. Thorpe, J. D. Swartz, and E. W. Herron, Inkblot Perception and Personality: Holtzman Inkblot Technique (Austin, Texas: University of Texas Press, 1961).

Morgan and Murray [44] who introduced psychologists to the possibility of using imaginative responses to pictures as situations in which the subject could reveal his interpretations of individual motivations, intentions, frustrations, anxieties, fears, ecstasies, and delights.

Thematic Apperception Test. Next to the Rorschach in extent of clinical use is the Thematic Apperception Test, widely known as the TAT. The test materials consist of 30 pictures and a blank card. The pictures have been selected so that they constitute four separate tests of 20 cards each: one for boys, one for girls, one for men over fourteen, and one for women over fourteen. Cards that bear only numbers are used in each of the four sets; cards marked "BM" are used in the tests for boys and for men; cards marked "GF" are used in the sets for girls and for women. Examples of card descriptions given in the manual by Murray [45] for two cards are the following:

1. A young boy is contemplating a violin that rests on a table in front of him.

2. GF. A young woman is standing with downcast head, her face covered with her right hand. Her left arm is stretched forward against a wooden door.

The directions for administration appear relatively simple, but are really complicated, involving the examiner's experience, purpose, and attitudes in relation to the subject. The cards are usually administered to the subject in sets of ten in two sessions of one hour each. The subject is asked to make up a plot or story giving the relation of the individuals in the picture; what has happened to them; what are their present thoughts and feelings; and what will be the outcome. Depending upon the production of the subject the examiner may use some method of inquiry. Holt [46] listed and discussed nine "determinants" that bear upon the procedure of administration. The subject's story productions are recorded verbatim by the examiner. In addition the examiner makes note of the subject's behavior, posture, facial expressions, hesitations, or emotional blocking.

According to Murray's original proposals for content analysis a hero is identified for each card. Each story is analyzed and interpreted through a "need-press" system of needs of the hero and presses of the environment upon him. Murray's methods of interpretation are probably still the most widely used though a dozen or more scoring systems have been presented in

[44] Christiana D. Morgan and H. A. Murray, "A Method for Investigating Fantasies: The Thematic Apperception Test," *Arch. Neurol. Psychiat.,* **34** (1935), 289–306.

[45] H. Murray, *Thematic Apperception Test* (Cambridge, Mass.: Harvard University Press, 1943).

[46] R. R. Holt, "The Thematic Apperception Test," in *An Introduction to Projective Techniques,* ed. H. H. Anderson and Gladys L. Anderson (Englewood Cliffs, N.J.: Prentice-Hall, Inc., 1951).

books, chapters, and articles, for example: Bellak; [47] Tomkins; [48] Aron; [49] Fry; [50] Fine; [51] Stein; [52] Henry; [53] and Wyatt and Veroff.[54] Kagan [55] has given a theoretical discussion of the use of the thematic apperceptive techniques with children.

The examiner has not only the freedom but the responsibility of deciding which of these many scoring systems, combinations or variations of his own to use. Part of the general usefulness of the TAT is to offer corroboration of other clinical material as well as leads for further investigation.

The Rorschach test had been designed in the 1920's as a tool for diagnosing the personality structure in pathological conditions of adults. While the Rorschach findings today are interpreted along with all other information about the subject, a conspicuous limitation of the Rorschach today is that the interpretation is essentially in terms of internalized perceptions, structures, functions *within* the person. This same emphasis, and also limitation, is a basic part of classical psychoanalytic approaches to the understanding of human behavior. So entrenched have become the constructs which psychologists have made and so traditional now is this perspective of regarding the individual that a new pyschological frontier in the original TAT has almost been overlooked.

The TAT was designed to be interpreted in terms not only of *needs* of the individual, but also of *press, press from the environment* in the nature of *restriction,* and press in the nature of environmental *facilitation.* The addition of environmental *restrictors* and *facilitators* was not inconsistent with the constructs of Rorschach. But Murray's emphasis on the inseparability of the person and the environment in interacting went far beyond Rorschach interpretation even of today. That is, human beings interact in behaving, and they can more easily perceive and report interacting from viewing the TAT cards than they can from viewing inkblots.

[47] L. Bellak, *A Guide to the Interpretation of the Thematic Apperception Test* (New York: Psychological Corp., 1947).

[48] S. S. Tomkins, *The Thematic Apperception Test* (New York: Grune & Stratton, Inc., 1947).

[49] Betty Aron, *A Manual for Analysis of the Thematic Apperception Test* (Berkeley, Calif.: Berg, 1949).

[50] R. D. Fry, "Manual for Scoring the Thematic Apperception Test," *Journal of Psychology,* 35 (1953), 181–195.

[51] R. Fine, "A Scoring Scheme and Manual for the TAT and Other Verbal Projective Techniques," *J. Proj. Tech.,* 19 (1955), 306–309.

[52] M. I. Stein, *The Thematic Apperception Test: An Introductory Manual for Its Clinical Use with Adults,* rev. ed. (Cambridge, Mass.: Addison-Wesley, 1955).

[53] W. E. Henry, *The Analysis of Fantasy: The Thematic Apperception Technique in the Study of Personality* (New York: John Wiley & Sons, Inc., 1956).

[54] F. Wyatt and Joanne B. Veroff, "Thematic Apperception and Fantasy Tests," in *Progress in Clinical Psychology,* ed. D. Brower and L. E. Abt (New York: Grune & Stratton, Inc., 1956).

[55] J. Kagan, "Thematic Apperceptive Techniques with Children," in *Projective Techniques with Children,* ed. A. I. Rabin and Mary R. Haworth (New York: Grune & Stratton, Inc., 1960).

Though the concepts of interacting, of flow, two-way communication, interweaving of desires and of activities in practical affairs of human relating had been advanced by Follett (1924) in a book called *Creative Experience,* and can be found in scattered treatises of philosophers, *interaction* was as strange to behavioristic psychologists of the 1920's as was the concept of gravity to physicists in the days of Newton.

The psychological world in 1938 was not yet ready for Murray's Proposition No. 5, which reads in part:

> Since at every moment an organism is within an environment which largely determines its behavior, and since the environment changes— sometimes with radical abruptness—the conduct of an individual cannot be formulated without a characterization of each confronting situation, physical and social. . . . Finally, the assimilations and integrations that occur in an organism are determined to a large extent by the nature of its closely previous, as well as by its more distantly previous, environments. In other words, what an organism knows or believes is, in some measure, a product of formerly encountered situations. Thus much of what is now *inside* the organism was once *outside.* For these reasons, the organism and its milieu must be considered together, a single creature-environment interaction being a convenient short unit for psychology. . . .[56]

Following World War II a rash of projective techniques based on the TAT, and designed for use with children, appeared.

The Picture-Frustration Study: Form for Children. Work with the adult form of the P-F Study led to the development of a form for children.[57] A booklet of 24 cartoon-like drawings depicts two persons, one of whom is saying something of frustrating significance to the other. The subject is asked to write in a blank box the comment of the other person. Group administration is possible with children who can read and write with ease. Scoring is made on the basis of nine defined factors and interpreted on a triadic hypothesis of extrapunitive, intropunitive, or impunitive aggression in the subject.

Children's Apperception Test (CAT). The Children's Apperception Test was devised by Bellak and Bellak[58] for use within the age range of three to eleven years. It consists of 10 pictures of animal figures only, the not substantiated hypothesis (Budoff, 1960) being that children will identify more easily with animals in a picture than with humans. The themes of the

---

[56] H. Murray, *op. cit.,* p. 39.

[57] S. Rosenzweig, "The Rosenzweig Picture-Frustration Study, Children's Form," in *Projective Techniques with Children,* ed. A. I. Rabin and Mary R. Haworth (New York: Grune & Stratton, Inc., 1960); see also Helen Jane Clarke, "The Rosenzweig Picture-Frustration Study," in *An Introduction to Projective Techniques,* ed. H. H. Anderson & Gladys L. Anderson (Englewood Cliffs, N.J.: Prentice-Hall, Inc., 1951).

[58] L. Bellak and Sonya S. Bellak, *Children's Apperception Test* (New York: C.P.S. Co., 1949).

pictures relate to familiar problems of childhood, namely, feeding, toileting, sibling rivalry, and Oedipal problems. Bellak and Adelman [59] have given a detailed discussion of the theory and clinical application of this test and of its adaptation to children in different cultures.

The Blacky Pictures. This test is a set of 11 cartoon drawings that depict the adventures of a dog named "Blacky" in situations some of which involve "Papa," "Mama," and "Tippy." Blum [60] designed the test as a medium to study the psychoanalytic theory of psychosexual development of adults and children. The test is scored from four sources: the spontaneous story, inquiry, cartoon preferences, and related comments on other cartoons.

The Picture-Story Test. The Symonds Picture-Story Test [61] was designed for the study of the personality of adolescent boys and girls. The picture-story approach was patterned after the TAT as was also the scoring and interpretation. The set contains 20 pictures divided into Set A and Set B. It was the author's judgment that in the interpretation of the stories sex differences were relatively insignificant; the same set was therefore designed to be used with both boys and girls.

Make-a-Picture-Story (MAPS). Shneidman's MAPS test [62] is described as a projective method in which the subject chooses a background, populates it with figures and tells a story to account for his choices and arrangement, or uses the figures to act out his story dramatically. The materials include 22 pictorial backgrounds such as bedroom, bathroom, street, a grotto or cave-like opening. There are 67 cut-out figures of persons young, old, clothed, nude, wounded, etc., and animals. Not required, but offered separately is a miniature theatre which serves also as a carrying case for the materials.

Michigan Picture Test. Another variant of the TAT has been prepared under the auspices of the Michigan Department of Mental Health and re-

[59] L. Bellak and Crusa Adelman, "The Children's Apperception Test (CAT)," in *Projective Techniques with Children*, ed. A. I. Rabin and Mary R. Haworth (New York: Grune & Stratton, Inc., 1960).

[60] G. S. Blum, "A Study of the Psychoanalytic Theory of Psychosexual Development," *Genet. Psychol. Monogr.*, 39 (1949), 3–99; see also *The Blacky Pictures: Manual of Instructions* (New York: Psychological Corp., 1950).

[61] P. M. Symonds, *Symonds Picture Story Test: Manual* (New York: Teachers College, Columbia University, Bur. Publ., 1948); see also *Adolescent Fantasy: An Investigation of the Picture-Story Method of Personality Study* (New York: Teachers College, Columbia University, Bur. Publ., 1949).

[62] E. S. Shneidman, *Make a Picture Story (MAPS): Manual* (New York: Psychological Corp., 1952); see also "The MAPS Test with Children," in *Projective Techniques with Children*, ed. A. I. Rabin and Mary R. Haworth (New York: Grune & Stratton, Inc., 1960).

ported by Hartwell, Hutt, Andrew, and Walton.[63] The Michigan Picture Test was designed to study emotional adjustment of children from eight to fourteen years. Twenty pictures are used in two overlapping sets of 12. An analysis sheet has been prepared for scoring.

The School Apperception Method (SAM). In 1966, Solomon, Klein, and Starr [64] reported on the development of a TAT type instrument which served as a "technique for initiating and maintaining an interview with an elementary school child with the aim of revealing his attitudes toward school." The authors of the SAM point out that the apperceptive instruments discussed here have a paucity of school related stimuli. Malpass [65] in 1953 had devised an apperceptive test consisting of school scenes, however the authors of the SAM felt that her stimuli were "crude sketches and were used solely in terms of ascertaining some specific relationships between students' perceptions of school and their achievement."

The SAM technique consists of presenting to the pupil ten ambiguous school pictures and asking the child to make up a story about each one. In the past school psychologists have used observation to ascertain how the child perceived school or he assessed the child's school attitudes by interviewing either the teacher, the parent, or both. Two other methods of eliciting the child's attitudes toward school by the psychologist were directly interviewing the child about this area of his experience or through the use of the Rorschach or the TAT.

Underlying the ten pictures which depict ambiguous school situations are the following concepts: (a) interaction with peers in group play; (b) close contact with female teacher; (c) interaction of home and school; (d) expression of aggression; (e) formal interaction with teacher; (f) close interaction with adult male figure; (g) conformity and school action; (h) academic achievement; (i) one-to-one peer interaction; (j) daydreaming in formal class situations. The authors used an *a priori* method of choosing these constructs based upon their combined experience in school psychology.

The pictures used in the SAM are detailed drawings of typical school situations. The following are two examples: Picture 1, A group of children lining up in a school yard. Next to the group is one monitor; Picture 6, In front of the classroom two boys are fighting. In the foreground a boy is

---

[63] S. W. Hartwell, M. L. Hutt, Gwen Andrew, and R. E. Walton, "The Michigan Picture Test: Diagnostic and Therapeutic Possibilities of a New Projective Test in Child Guidance," *American Journal of Orthopsychiatry,* 21 (1951), 124–137; see also G. S. Andrew, W. Hartwell, M. L. Hutt, and R. E. Walton, *The Michigan Picture Test* (Chicago: Science Research Associates, Inc., 1953).

[64] I. L. Solomon, M. I. Klein, and B. D. Starr, "The School Apperceptive Method," *Journal of School Psychology,* 4 (Winter, 1966), 28–35.

[65] L. F. Malpass, "Some Relationships Between Students' Perceptions of School and Their Achievements," *Journal of Educational Psychology,* 44 (1953), 475–482.

getting up from his desk while off to the left a teacher is entering the room. The Winter 1966 *Journal of School Psychology* contains sample drawings from the SAM.

Regarding the instructions, the authors state, that the instructions are similar to the TAT, "except for the more liberal use of questions during the course of the child's narration. Initially, the children are asked to make up a story about the people in the picture to tell what they are doing, saying or feeling and to give the story a beginning, a middle and an end."

> Besides being a practical aid in the day to day work of the school psychologist, the SAM may be useful as a research instrument. Combined with the development of a scoring scheme and adequate normative data, it may lead to a more complete understanding of the dynamics of school phobia and other school related problems. It could prove useful as a pre-kindergarten screening device to ascertain those children who are socially not ready for kindergarten work. The SAM technique might also be used for the longitudinal study of attitude changes toward school. In summary, the SAM in conjunction with other techniques, is considered to be a promising aid for the understanding of the child's perception of school. . . . While the SAM appears to have content validity, concurrent, predictive, and construct validity and reliability have not been demonstrated.[66]

Another effort to develop a school projective test was reported at the 1959 annual convention of the American Psychological Association by Stephan Sheldon.[67] His test was a story-telling test which he had developed for high school students. The test was scored for interpersonal relations among friends, principal, teachers, counselors and students of the opposite sex.

In each of the above pictorial techniques a basic assumption is that it is easier with such devices to induce a child without threat to communicate his private perceptions, repressed motivations, and idiosyncratic concerns than it is for most clinicians to obtain such communication by direct interview as in obtaining the child's "Own Story" which Healy and Bronner featured in the 1920's. It is in fact important that the psychologist use both methods: a direct approach as might be employed by a sympathetic good-listener in an interview, and an indirect approach such as would be offered by projective methods. The psychologist can then relate the findings of both methods to each other and to all other available materials about the child's life at home and at school.

VERBAL COMPLETION

The word association method was used by Galton, Wundt, and others as an experimental tool before Jung [68] established a standardized method

---

[66] I. L. Solomon, M. I. Klein, and B. D. Starr, *op. cit.*, p. 35.

[67] *Journal of School Psychology*, 4 (Winter, 1966), p. 35.

[68] C. G. Jung, "The Association Method," *American Journal of Psychology*, 21 (1910), 219–269; see also *Studies in Word Association* (New York: Dodd, Mead & Co., 1918).

for his study of emotional *complexes* in 1910. Kent and Rosanoff [69] attempted to develop norms of frequency tables after the scientific fashion of the day but thereby lost the discriminating value for the understanding of the individual. Although other experiments have been made with the method it has not had extensive clinical use with children.

Sentence Completion. Payne [70] and Tendler [71] are credited with being the first to use complex phrases as stimulus materials to be completed as sentences. The incomplete sentence test has come to be used to elicit a subject's attitudes toward certain persons, relationships, or areas of experience, e.g., toward father, mother, work, play, school, authority, fears, joys. The phrases may have different degrees of structure as:

I feel ———

I feel that my father ———

I feel that my father seldom ———

The phrases may also be expressed in the first or third personal pronouns, or in a named third person, as:

My greatest mistake was ———

His greatest mistake was ———

John's greatest mistake was ———

My father's greatest mistake was ———

Numbers of sentence completion tests, with much borrowing and much overlapping in both content and form, have been published, e.g., Rohde,[72] Rotter,[73] Sacks, and Levy.[74] Forer [75] adapted his adult forms for use with boys and girls and has discussed their clinical use with children.

Story Completion. Story Completions offer again the contrast between the purposes of mental tests and of projective techniques. The Problem Situation

[69] Grace H. Kent and A. J. Rosanoff, "A Study of Association in Insanity," *American Journal of Insanity*, 67 (1910), 37–96, 317–390.

[70] A. F. Payne, *Sentence Completions* (New York: New York Guidance Clinic, 1928).

[71] A. D. Tendler, "A Preliminary Report on a Test for Emotional Insight," *Journal of Applied Psychology*, 14 (1930), 123–136.

[72] Amanda R. Rohde, "Explorations in Personality by the Sentence Completion Method," *Journal of Applied Psychology*, 30 (1946), 169–181; see also *Sentence Completion Method: Its Diagnostic and Clinical Application to Mental Disorders* (New York: The Ronald Press Company, 1957).

[73] J. B. Rotter, "Word Association and Sentence Completion Methods," in *An Introduction to Projective Techniques*, ed. H. H. Anderson and Gladys L. Anderson (Englewood Cliffs, N.J.: Prentice-Hall, Inc., 1951).

[74] J. M. Sacks and S. Levy, "The Sentence Completion Test," in *Projective Psychology: Clinical Approaches to the Total Personality*, ed. L. E. Abt and L. Bellak (New York: Alfred A. Knopf, Inc., 1950).

[75] B. R. Forer, *The Forer Structured Sentence Completion Tests* (Santa Monica, Calif.: Western Psychological Services, 1957); see also "Word Association and Sentence Completion Methods," in *Projective Techniques with Children*, ed. A. I. Rabin & Mary R. Haworth (New York: Grune & Stratton, Inc., 1960).

of Donald and the skunk at Year Eleven in the Stanford Revision of the Binet-Simon tests of intelligence has a defined correct answer which children must give in order to pass the test; the story, moreover, is located empirically at a specified age level. In the standardized tests the fixed answers are in the back of the book; the subject who passes is not permitted to wander outside the closed defined system from which the norms were devised. With Incomplete Sentences, or Incomplete Stories used as a projective technique any response of the child is accepted; there are no right answers or wrong answers; moreover, it is important that the psychologist record the child's verbatim responses.

Madeleine Thomas Stories. Madeleine Thomas [76] in Switzerland announced that in asking children to complete her short stories or to answer the question, "Why?", she was not devising a "test," but was using the stories as a method of clinical investigation. It is historically significant that the stories published by Madeleine Thomas came in the 1930's, at a time when clinical psychologists were groping for more than could be obtained through standardized procedures and norms on large numbers of subjects.

Würsten [77] translated the Madeleine Thomas Stories into English in 1947 and has discussed their use with children. The first two of the fifteen stories, quoted from Würsten, are as follows:

1. A boy (or girl) goes to school. During recess he does not play with the other children, he stays by himself in a corner. Why?

2. A boy fights with his brother. Mother comes. What is going to happen?

There seems to be no scoring system specifically adapted to these stories, but the interpretation of Thomas includes intellectual aspects, emotional aspects, the defense system and symbolism of the responses.

Fables. The Düss [78] Fables, also of Swiss origin, were translated by Despert,[79] and in this country have become associated with her name as the Despert Fables. They are reproduced by Würsten [80] in his own translation and with a brief discussion. Others who have reported on the use of fables with

---

[76] Madeleine Thomas, "Méthode des histoires à compléter pour le dépistage des complexes et des conflits affectifs enfantins," *Arch. Psychol., Genève,* 26 (1937), 209–284.

[77] H. Würsten, "Story Completions: Madeleine Thomas Stories and Similar Methods," in *Projective Techniques with Children,* ed. A. I. Rabin and Mary R. Haworth (New York: Grune & Stratton, Inc., 1960).

[78] Louisa Düss, "La Méthode des fables en psychanalyse," *Arch. Psychol., Genève,* 28 (1940), 1–51; see also *La Méthode des fables en psychanalyse infantile* (Paris: Editions de l'Arche, 1950).

[79] J. L. Despert, "Psychosomatic Study of Fifty Stuttering Children," *Amer. J. Orthopsychiat.,* 16 (1946), 100–113; see also "Dreams in Children of Preschool Age," *Psychoanal. Study Children* (1949), 141–180.

[80] H. Wurstein, *op. cit.*

children are Fine,[81] Mosse,[82] and Peixotto.[83] Friedman [84] wrote two fables for a study of castration anxiety in children between the ages of five and sixteen years.

Incomplete Stories. Miller and Stine [85] and Blum and Miller [86] have written incomplete stories related to psychoanalytic theories for research with children. Engel [87] adapted for children the Sargent [88] Insight Test for adults, retaining Sargent's elaborate scoring system for responses mainly to two questions about problem situations: "What did he do?" and "How did he feel?"

The Anderson Incomplete Stories, first used in Germany in 1952, consist of eleven short stories, Series A and Series B, depicting situations of interpersonal conflict in parent-child, teacher-child, and child-child relating. They have been administered as group tests to over 10,000 school children in the fourth and seventh grades in a cross-national research program in eight countries. The children's completions are analyzed according to coding manuals constructed for each story. Large and significant differences are interpreted according to hypotheses for the impact of the culture on children's social creativity in interpersonal relating. Research has been reported by Anderson and Anderson; [89] Métraux; [90] Geierhaas; [91] Heber; [92] Robinson; [93] and others.[94]

[81] R. Fine, "Use of the Despert Fables in Diagnosis Work with Children," *Rorschach Res. Exch. & J. Proj. Tech.,* 12 (1948), 106–118.

[82] H. L. Mosse, "The Duess Test," *American Journal of Psychotherapy,* 8 (1954), 251–264.

[83] H. E. Peixotto, "Reliability of the Despert Fables, a Story Completion Projective Test for Children," *Journal of Clinical Psychology,* 12 (1956), 75–78.

[84] S. M. Friedman, "An Empirical Study of the Castration and Oedipus Complexes," *Genet. Psychol. Monogr.,* 46 (1952), 61–130.

[85] D. R. Miller and Margaret E. Stine, "The Prediction of Social Acceptance by Means of Psychoanalytic Concepts," *J. Pers.,* 20 (1951), 162–174.

[86] G. S. Blum and D. R. Miller, "Exploring the Psychoanalytic Theory of the 'Oral Character,' " *J. Pers.,* 3 (1952), 287–304.

[87] Mary Engel, "The Development and Applications of the Children's Insight Test," *J. Proj. Tech.,* 22 (1958), 1.

[88] Helen D. Sargent, "An Experimental Application of Projective Principles to a Paper and Pencil Personality Test," *Psychol. Monogr.,* 57, No. 5 (1944); see also *The Insight Test: A Verbal Projective Test for Personality Study* (New York: Grune & Stratton, Inc., 1955).

[89] H. and G. Anderson, "Children's Perceptions of Social Conflict Situations: A Study of Adolescent Children in Germany," *American Journal of Orthopsychiatry,* 24, No. 2 (1954a), 246–257; see also, "On the Meaning of Creativity." Prepared for a Workshop on Creativity in Childhood and Adolescence, American Orthopsychiatric Association, Los Angeles, Calif., 22–23 March 1962, and "Image of the Teacher by Adolescent Children in Seven Countries," *American Journal of Orthopsychiatry,* 31, No. 3 (1961), 481–492.

[90] Rhoda Métraux, "The Consequences of Wrongdoing: An Analysis of Story Completions by German Children," in *Childhood in Contemporary Cultures,* ed. Margaret Mead and Martha Wolfenstein (Chicago, Illinois: University of Chicago Press, 1955).

DRAWING AND PAINTING

Given accessibility of materials, drawing and painting are activities in which children engage spontaneously. It is in part the universality of such experience among children of all ages that made drawing a suitable item to include in many tests of intelligence.[95]

The perception of the human figure, particularly of one's own figure took on other psychological and psychiatric implications in the 1920's and 1930's. Levy,[96] investigating body interest in children in a clinic setting, adapted the physical examination of children to an interview relationship in which he in effect asked the child to give himself his own evaluated physical examination: How tall are you? How tall do you think you should be? How much do you weigh? Do you weigh as much as other children your age? Levy sought larger meanings in the child's perception of his physical self. Schilder [97] speculated on the psychiatric meaning of the perception of the human body, the "body image." It was some time, however, before the drawing of the human body was used as a projective test.

Draw-a-Person Test. According to Machover the child is given standardized drawing materials and is asked to draw a person; when the draw-

---

[91] F. G. Geierhaas, "Problems of Reliability in Evaluating Story Completions about Social Conflicts by German Adolescent Children." Master's thesis, Michigan State University Library, East Lansing, 1955.

[92] R. E. Heber, "A Cross-Cultural Comparison of Children's Judgment of Parent-Child Conflict in Germany, England, Finland, United States and Mexico." Master's thesis, Michigan State University Library, East Lansing, 1955.

[93] Barbara M. Robinson, "A Further Cross-Cultural Comparison of Children's Judgment of Parent-Child Conflict in Germany, Finland, England and the United States." Master's thesis, Michigan State University Library, East Lansing, 1955.

[94] Edith Sylvia Levitov, " 'The Broken Bicycle,' a Comparative Study of Story Completions by Adolescents in United States and German Cities" (Master's thesis, George Washington University, 1960); D. J. Erickson, "A Comparison of Children's Social Values in Story Completions by Culture-Groups" (Master's thesis, Michigan State University, 1961); L. G. Terdal, "Consistency in Use of Themas in Story Completions: a Cross National Study in Seven Countries" (Master's thesis, Michigan State University Library, East Lansing, 1961); K. W. Terhune, "A Comparison of Two Methods of Content Analysis on Story Completions from Three Countries" (Master's thesis, Michigan State University Library, East Lansing, 1961); Ingeborg Lydia Erika Paulus, "Children's Fantasy Perceptions of Social Conflict Situations Involving Wrong-Doing, and How They Solve These Conflicts" (An essay for the degree of Bachelor of Arts in the Department of Anthropology & Sociology, The University of British Columbia, Vancouver, B.C., April, 1962).

[95] Florence L. Goodenough, *Measurement of Intelligence by Drawings* (Harcourt, Brace & World, Inc., 1926).

[96] D. Levy, "Body Interest in Children," *American Journal of Psychiatry*, 12 (1932), 295ff.

[97] P. Schilder, *The Image and Appearance of the Human Body*, Psyche Monograph No. 4 (London: Kegan, Paul, Trench, Trubner & Co., Ltd., 1935).

ing is completed he is asked to draw a person of the opposite sex. With young children the child is asked to "draw somebody." Careful notations are made of the child's behavior and verbal responses. Machover used an inquiry form at the conclusion of the drawing. Among the structural features that Machover considered in the interpretation were size of the figure, pressure of line, placement on the page, theme, stance of figure, background, exactness, degree of completion and detailing, symmetry, midline emphasis, perspective, proportions, shading, reinforcements, and erasures. In addition, the content of the drawing was interpreted: head, eyes, ears, nose, hair, mouth, other body features, clothing. Machover [98] has given descriptive accounts of sex and age differences of children from four to twelve years of age on the Draw-a-Person Test. This approach has been recently criticized by psychometrically oriented psychologists because few of Machover's hypotheses hold up when subjected to statistical analysis.

The House-Tree-Person Test. Buck [99] proposed the combining of the drawings of three objects: a house, a tree, and a person into one drawing test. His reasons for choosing these objects were that they were familiar to the child, willingly accepted by the child as objects to be drawn, and easily productive of verbalization in the Inquiry. Buck has written a manual of qualitative and quantitative scoring of the H-T-P Test.

Hammer [100] has also written a chapter on the application of the H-T-P in clinical work with children.

Finger Painting. Although finger painting dates from antiquity it was Ruth Faison Shaw [101] who reintroduced finger painting as an educational and psychological technique. Ruth Shaw solved a practical problem of developing colorful paints that were safe to use and that could be washed off hands and clothing with water. She was also a spontaneous, nonthreatening person, such that almost any timid, anxious child could in a few moments share her enthusiasm for anything. Miss Shaw could have achieved her therapeutic

[98] Karen Machover, *Personality Projection in the Drawing of the Human Figure* (Springfield, Ill.: Charles C Thomas, Publisher, 1948).

[99] J. N. Buck, "The H-T-P Test," *Journal of Clinical Psychology*, 4 (1948), 151–158; see also, "The H-T-P Technique: A Qualitative and Quantitative Scoring Manual," Part I, *Journal of Clinical Psychology*, 4 (1948), 397–405; "The H-T-P Technique: A Qualitative and Quantitative Scoring Manual," Part II, *Journal of Clinical Psychology*, 5 (1949), 37–76.

[100] E. E. Hammer, "The House-Tree-Person (H-T-P) Drawings as a Projective Technique with Children," in *Projective Techniques with Children*, ed. A. I. Rabin and Mary R. Haworth (New York: Grune & Stratton, Inc., 1960); see also "Guide for Qualitative Research with H-T-P," *Journal of Genetic Psychology*, 51 (1954), 41–60; *The H-T-P Clinical Research Manual* (Beverly Hills, Calif.: Western Psychological Services, 1955); *The Clinical Application of Projective Drawings* (Springfield, Ill.: Charles C Thomas, Publisher, 1958).

[101] Ruth F. Shaw, *Finger Painting* (Boston: Little Brown and Company, 1934).

objectives with mud pies. In fact, Shaw wrote, "Finger paintings are the direct descendants of mud pies—all I have done is to add the rainbow." Again it was some time before psychologists began to verbalize their observations of children's behavior with finger paints and to organize their concepts into hypotheses as to the meaning of the activity and the productions. A major contributor to work with this technique has been Napoli [102] who wrote a manual for interpretation of the finger painting process for personality diagnosis and elaborated on this manual in a chapter. Napoli has devised a record booklet for recording in detail three important aspects of finger painting: performance observation, the painting analysis, and the verbalization. Kadis [103] has also written a chapter on finger painting as a projective technique.

Free Art Expression. Other forms of drawing, painting, and modeling have been used in the personality assessment and treatment of children. In the Draw-a-Person Test and the H-T-P, the child has a structured content selected for him by the examiner. In the free art expression the child has a spontaneous choice of content, and sometimes of medium; the variety of processes and productions, however, makes the interpretation more complicated and subjective. Bell,[104] who presented an excellent summary of research on drawing, painting, and other arts, developed also a tabulation of methods of analysis of art and of their clinical significance. Elkisch [105] has also developed criteria for analysis of children's free art expression together with suggested symptomatology.

OTHER TECHNIQUES

Many other activities and techniques have been used for projective interpretation in research studies and in diagnostic and therapeutic work with children. Indeed a symposium on Custom-Built Projective Methods was held in 1960.[106] The title of this symposium was not so strange, for each existing

[102] P. J. Napoli, "Finger Painting and Personality Diagnosis," *Genet. Psychol. Monogr.*, 34 (1946), 129–231; "Interpretative Aspects of Finger Painting," *Journal of Psychology*, 23 (1947), 93–132; "Finger Painting," in *An Introduction to Projective Techniques*, ed. H. H. Anderson and Gladys L. Anderson (Englewood Cliffs, N.J.: Prentice-Hall, Inc., 1951).
[103] Asya L. Kadis, "Finger-painting as a Projective Technique," in *Projective Psychology: Clinical Approaches to the Total Personality*, ed. L. E. Abt and L. Bellak (New York: Alfred A. Knopf, Inc., 1950).
[104] Bell, *op. cit.*
[105] Paula Elkisch, "Fre Art Expression," in *Projective Technique with Children*, ed. A. I. Rabin & Mary R. Haworth (New York: Grune & Stratton, Inc., 1960).
[106] B. R. Forer, "Introduction." In "Custom-Built Projective Methods: A Symposium," *J. Proj. Tech.*, 25(1) (1961), 3–5; A. I. Rabin, "Devising Projective Methods for Personality Research." In "Custom-Built Projective Methods: A Symposium," *J. Proj. Tech.*, 25(1) (1961), 6–10; F. J. Goldstein, "Custom-Made or Store-Bought Projective Techniques? What do They Represent?" In "Custom-Built Projective Methods: A Symposium," *J. Proj. Tech.*, 25(1) (1961), 11–20; G. S. Lesser, "Custom-Making Projective

projective technique has been at its outset "custom-built," i.e., it was designed to suit the purposes or the hypotheses of its author. The symposium brought out the fact, among other things, that purposes vary from the study of the "total personality," as in the Rorschach and the TAT, to the more narrowly defined objectives of studying specific segments or dimensions of personality, as, for example, in the Blacky Test, an instrument for studying the Freudian hypotheses of psychosexual development. Others have used projective techniques to study "aggression," the approval motive, dependency, and need for achievement. In fact, it is possible as will be illustrated below to make projective, qualitative interpretations of responses to many objectively scored, normative tests.

Play, as a projective technique, has been discussed by Bell; [107] the therapeutic use of play by Solomon; [108] free play as a projective tool by Murphy and Krall; [109] psychodrama by Haas and Moreno. [110]

The family has also been an area for a variety of different approaches, e.g., The Test of Family Attitudes, Jackson; [111] family drawings, Hulse; [112] the Family Relations Test by Anthony and Bene. [113]

The use of puppetry both for diagnostic and therapeutic purposes has been developed by Woltmann, [114] who has also discussed spontaneous pup-

---

Tests for Research," in "Custom-Built Projective Methods: A Symposium." *J. Proj. Tech.,* 25(1) (1961), 21–31.

[107] J. E. Bell, *Projective Techniques: A Dynamic Approach to the Study of the Personality* (New York: Longmans, Green & Co., 1948).

[108] J. C. Solomon, "Therapeutic Use of Play," in *An Introduction to Projective Techniques,* ed. H. H. Anderson and Gladys L. Anderson (Englewood Cliffs, N.J.: Prentice-Hall, Inc., 1951), pp. 639–661.

[109] Lois B. Murphy and Vita Krall, "Free Play as a Projective Tool," in *Projective Techniques with Children,* ed. A. I. Rabin & Mary R. Haworth (New York: Grune & Stratton, Inc., 1960).

[110] R. B. Haas and J. L. Moreno, "Psychodrama as a Projective Technique," in *An Introduction to Projective Techniques,* ed. H. H. Anderson and Gladys L. Anderson (Englewood Cliffs, N.J.: Prentice-Hall, Inc., 1951).

[111] L. Jackson, "Emotional Attitudes towards the Family of Normal, Neurotic and Delinquent Children," Part I, *British Journal of Psychology,* 41 (1950), 35–51; see also "Emotional Attitudes towards the Family of Normal, Neurotic and Delinquent Children," Part II, *British Journal of Psychology,* 41 (1950), 173–185; *A Test of Family Attitudes* (London: Methuen & Co., Ltd., 1952); *Aggression and Its Interpretation* (London: Methuen & Co., Ltd., 1954).

[112] W. C. Hulse, "The Emotionally Disturbed Child Draws his Family," *Quarterly Journal of Child Behavior,* 3 (1951), 152–174; see also, "Childhood Conflict Expressed through Family Drawings," *J. Proj. Tech.,* 16 (1952), 66–79.

[113] J. Anthony and E. Bene, "A Technique for the Objective Assessment of the Child's Family Relationships," *Journal of Mental Science,* 103 (1957), 541–555; see also, E. Bene and J. Anthony, *Manual for the Family Relations Test* (London: National Foundation for Educational Research in England and Wales, 1957).

[114] A. G. Woltmann, "The Use of Puppetry as a Projective Method in Therapy," in *An Introduction to Projective Techniques,* ed. H. H. Anderson and Gladys L. Anderson (Englewood Cliffs, N.J.: Prentice-Hall, Inc., 1951); see also "Spontaneous Puppetry by Children as a Projective Method," in *Projective Techniques with Children,* ed. A. I. Rabin and Mary R. Haworth (New York: Grune & Stratton, Inc., 1960).

petry. Haworth [115] wrote a monograph on the use of a puppetry film as a group projective medium for young children.

The Bender Visual Motor Gestalt,[116] discussed in Chapter 12, is an important projective technique for the school psychologist. Another motor drawing test is the Myokinetic Psychodiagnostic Test by Mira y Lopez [117] with manuals in Portuguese, French, and English. Lowenfeld developed both the World Test (1939) and the Mosaic Test.[118]

Sources of these and other projective materials and their manuals for use with children are given by Rabin and Haworth in an Appendix.[119]

Projective Interpretation of Standardized Tests

The early regard for the importance of rapport in intelligence test administration was an admission that there were certain intangibles of motivation, certain inhibitions to action, certain fears, apprehensions, and anxieties that might either inhibit a response altogether, cause a lapse in attention, or otherwise effect a distortion in the perception of the problem of the test. Although these possibilities were probably known to Binet, they have at no time been very clearly stated.

Traditionally, scant qualitative interpretation has been offered, apart from a rating of the child's test behavior, an interpretation of the child's attitudes during the test, and the examiner's judgment as to whether the results represented the child's best performance. Supplementary scoring manuals by Pintner, Dragositz, and Kushner [120] and by Wrightstone [121] have clarified certain ambiguities but have drawn a clearer line between pass and fail responses.

Yet, for clinical psychologists, the qualitative interpretation of psychological examinations, including tests of general intelligence, is not new. In 1927, Bronner, Healy, Lowe, and Shimberg [122] wrote:

[115] Mary R. Haworth, "The Use of a Filmed Puppet Show as a Group Projective Technique for Children," *Genet. Psychol. Monogr.*, 56 (1957), 257–296.

[116] Florence Halpern, "The Bender Visual Motor Gestalt Test," in *An Introduction to Projective Techniques*, ed. H. H. Anderson and Gladys L. Anderson (Englewood Cliffs, N.J.: Prentice-Hall, Inc., 1951).

[117] E. Mira y Lopez, *M.K.P., Myokinetic Psychodiagnosis* (New York: Logan Press, 1958).

[118] Margaret Lowenfeld, "The World Pictures of Children," *British Journal of Medical Psychology*, 18 (1939), 65–101; see also *The Lowenfeld Mosaic Test* (London: Newman Neame, 1954).

[119] Rabin and Haworth, *op. cit.*

[120] R. Pintner, A. Dragositz, and R. Kushner, "Supplementary Guide for the Revised Stanford-Binet (form L)," *Appl. Psychol. Monogr.*, No. 3 (1944).

[121] J. W. Wrightstone, *A Supplementary Guide for Scoring the Revised Stanford-Binet Intelligence Scale, Form L* (New York: Board of Education, 1941).

[122] Augusta F. Bronner, W. Healy, Gladys M. Lowe, and Myra E. Shimberg, *A Manual of Individual Mental Tests and Testing* (Boston: Little Brown and Company, 1927), 14–15.

Emotional conditions are of exceedingly great importance in their influence on test results. Yet, in spite of this they are frequently overlooked, or, if noted, not taken into account. It is a matter of primary concern . . . to know the emotional attitude of the subject. Emotions may be inhibitory, "blocking" responses. Fear, anger, or indifference may play a very important role in the psychological examination. . . . Underlying or persisting emotional disturbance about one's situation in life may be, and in many cases is, a complicating factor in test results.

Twenty-one years later Carter and Bowles [123] wrote *A Manual on Qualitative Aspects of Psychological Examining*, summarizing the available literature, that is scanty indeed, and adding many provocative ideas from their own experience. There is nothing for the Stanford-Binet, for example, comparable to the extended consideration given to the detailed analysis of responses to individual test items on the Wechsler-Bellevue by Rapaport, Gill, and Schafer (1945), or by Mayman, Schafer, and Rapaport.[124]

QUALITATIVE INTERPRETATION OF THE STANFORD-BINET

Studies relating the interpretation of individual items of the Stanford-Binet test to emotional problems have been reported by Bühler,[125] and others. In a brief paper in 1948 Murphy [126] showed the possibility of qualitative use of content analysis, form analysis of drawings, and distribution of successes and failures.

Protocols by students in training. The studies cited above represent the work of trained and experienced examiners. Even so, the studies reporting the qualitative interpretation of performance on the Stanford-Binet have shown very meager relation to the motivational and emotional life of the subject. The writer has maintained that not only expert examiners, but also student examiners in training, can give attention to the details and subtleties of behavior of the child in the psychological test situation.

To test this hypothesis, a number of devices were used in training students to administer the Revised Stanford-Binet:

123 J. W. Carter and J. W. Bowles, "A Manual on Qualitative Aspects of Psychological Testing," Monograph Supplement, *J. Clin. Psychol.*, 4 (1948), 109–150.

124 D. Rapaport, M. Gill, and R. Schafer, *Diagnostic Psychological Testing*, Vol. I, 1945; Vol. II, 1946 (Chicago, Ill.: Year Book Publishers); M. Mayman, R. Schafer, and D. Rapaport, "Interpretation of the Wechsler-Bellevue Intelligence Scale in Personality Appraisal," in *An Introduction to Projective Techniques*, ed. H. H. Anderson and Gladys L. Anderson (Englewood Cliffs, N.J.: Prentice-Hall, Inc., 1951).

125 Charlotte Bühler, "The Ball and Field Test as a Help in the Diagnosis of Emotional Difficulties," *Char. & Pers.*, 6 (1938), 257–273; see also C. W. Young, "The Possible Use of the Memory Span for Indication of Complexes," *Journal of Abnormal Social Psychology*, 36 (1941), 115; W. M. Cruickshank, "Qualitative Analysis of Intelligence Test Responses," *J. Clin. Psychol.*, 3 (1947), 381–386.

126 Lois B. Murphy, "The Appraisal of Child Personality," *J. Consult. Psychol.*, 12 (1948), 16–19.

1. The student examiner wrote a description of the child.

2. The student examiner wrote a description of the child's behavior during the examination.

3. The examiner made a verbatim record of the responses to the test items and of spontaneous remarks of the child.

4. The examiners were provided with 5 by 8 inch mimeographed blanks on which they could report for test items so-called *unusual* responses. Most of the unusual responses were recorded under five categories:
   (a) doubtful scoring
   (b) double meaning in interpreting the test response
   (c) example of emotional blocking
   (d) subtle errors in test administration
   (e) other kinds of unusual response

The form provided space for the examiner to write the child's response and to record a description of relevant behavior. The accumulated reports of unusual responses were discussed at weekly meetings of the class.

At this stage of their training, the students had not had systematic training in the field of projective techniques. The testing was not part of a clinic study. Beyond the strict adherence to the standard test procedure of the Stanford-Binet, the students were expected to be alert for incidents in test behavior that *might* be related to the child's problem of getting along with the world in which he lived.

The following examples of test responses and test behavior have been reported by student examiners.

Connie. C.A. eight years, six months. At year ten the test item is Picture Absurdities—Frontier Days, a picture showing a white man shooting at a distant Indian when he is under immediate attack by two other Indians. The child is shown the picture and is asked, "What's foolish about that picture?"

Connie replied, "Four Indians and one cowboy. And the cowboy is shooting right at the Indians." Connie then said, "I don't see how they can fight in that lot, because somebody might own it."

On the previous Picture Absurdities test at year seven, where a man is sawing a log with the teeth of the saw turned up, Connie had given a correct response to which she added remarks about herself: "He's keeping his leg on the log . . . That isn't funny. No, he's got the saw on the wrong side. I guess I must be blind. That's what my mother calls me."

During the test, Connie made several references to her cousin. At year eight, Comprehension test: "What makes a sailboat move?" Connie replied, "I can't think what that thing is. I just can't say it. You know I'm not an artist like my cousin is. That thing right there. . . . No, the wind does." Here was a child who, in a standardized test situation, on almost every item in the test, had to work through the problem of her relationship to the outside world.

Examples of other remarks that Connie made are: "Shall I make it as wide as this?" "Shall I do it this way?" "I shouldn't have done that." "I promised not to forget, but I did." "I don't think I draw good at all."

Although no further work was done with the child, the examiner did learn from the teacher that Connie had recently enrolled in the same school as her cousin; Connie and her parents had been forced to move when their house was sold and were temporarily living with her cousin and the cousin's parents. It may be that for Connie, all the world belonged to somebody else and even the cowboys and Indians were trespassers.

Terry. C.A. eight years, nine months. At year thirteen, there is this situation: a purse with a lot of money in it has been lost in a big field. The child is told, "Take this pencil and start here at the gate and show me where you would go to hunt for the purse so as to be sure not to miss it." If the subject fails to understand that he is to mark the path, the examiner adds, "Mark it with the pencil to show me where you would go to hunt for the purse."

Terry, with an IQ of 120, responded to this thirteen-year-level test: "Here is how my father would do it." He then indicated the approved plan by moving his pencil above the paper in a perfect detailed spiral, saying as he did so, "He would go round, and round, and round." The student examiner then asked, "How would *you* do it?" Terry then marked the paper as shown in Figure 1.

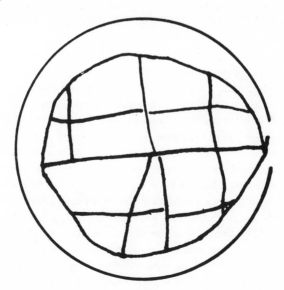

FIGURE 1. *Year XIII. Plan of Search.*

Terry understood the problem and showed that he had an intellectual awareness of how to cover the field, but for some reason, he was unable to give the popular, that is, the correct response. He had to be different from his father, even if he made his performance a failure in problem-solving.

Sam, a Negro boy. C.A. five years, zero months. Pictorial Likenesses and Differences occur at year four–six and year six. The examiner presents card (a) and says, "See these crosses that are just alike? Here's one (*pointing*) that is *not* like the others. Put your finger on the one that is *not* the same as the others." For each following card the child is asked to "put your finger on the one that is *not* the same as the others." When Sam was shown the card with the three white circles and one black one (Figure 2), and was asked to put his finger on the one that is *not* the same as the others, he replied: "None of 'em's different." He then looked up at the examiner, and back to

FIGURE 2. *Years IV–6 and VI. Pictorial Likenesses and Differences.*

the card, and very hesitatingly pointed to the black circle and said, "I guess, maybe, this one is a *little* different." All the other cards in the series were passed with no hesitation and no error.

Henry. C.A. six years, one month. The Maze-Tracing Test is presented at year six. The problem is, "This little boy lives here, and here is the school house. The little boy wants to go to school the shortest way, without getting off the sidewalk. Here is the sidewalk. Show me the shortest way. Mark it with your pencil, but don't go off the sidewalk. Start here and take the little boy to school the shortest way."

On Maze 1 (Figure 3), Henry, IQ 121, carefully stayed within the lines. But one can notice that he did not stop at the school house.

On Maze 2, Henry did not take the "shortest" way and he did not go all the way to school. And on Maze 3, he again went past the school house. Did this child comprehend the problem of taking the boy to school the shortest way? On two of the three trials he overshot the mark. The little boy did not "stay" at school, though he did take the shortest path. At this point in the examination, the examiner noted that the child was easily distractible and talked constantly about his younger brother at home. As has been said, Henry had an IQ of 121, and it was the failure on this maze-tracing test that placed his basal age at five years. The examiner seriously questioned whether Henry should have been credited with a failure on this item, which purported to test his intelligence. The examiner learned later that Henry's younger brother not only was not at school, but was at home having a birthday party.

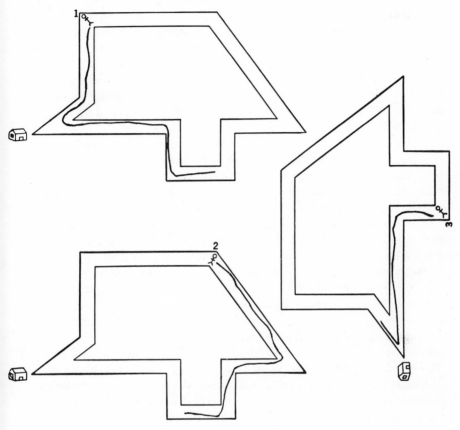

FIGURE 3. *Year VI. Maze Tracing.*

Bert. C.A. twelve years, nine months, IQ 73, filled his test responses with projections of his own personality problems. Asked to state in what way a snake, a cow, and a sparrow are alike, he replied, "If you get 'em mad, the cow sticks you, the snake wraps his tail around you, and the sparrow eats stuff out of your garden."

Bert failed at year ten to name 28 words in one minute. The student examiner noted that the words he did name related only to farming. The examiner discovered later that the father had recently lost his job. The father and the boy wanted to move to a farm, but the mother had a job in town and refused to move.

In the Verbal Absurdities Test, year eleven, item 2-a, the judge says to the prisoner, "You are to be hanged and I hope it will be a warning to you." Bert commented, "The judge shouldn't have told him that he was going to hang him. He will try to find some way to get away." In defining *obedience,*

Bert said "got enemies." Defining *courage,* Bert said "get somebody mad and get 'em all mixed up."

Both in his successes and in his failures, when Bert revealed himself as a person, he revealed an unhappy boy in conflict with the world in which he lived and greatly frustrated by powers beyond his control.

At year seven, Comprehension III has the question: "What's the thing for you to do when you have broken something which belongs to someone else?" Something more than failure and success is revealed in the two answers following:

1. "Go and tell them, cry, then you won't get in much trouble."
2. "Buy them a new one with your own money."

Naming 28 words in one minute, year ten, is often revealing of undisclosed conflict and tension if the words are written verbatim by the examiner and the contents studied. This was a method of free association used by Binet.

Definitions of abstract words provide another kind of almost free association, particularly when the words are at a level too difficult for the child. The content analysis of the child's failed responses often discloses important information concerning preoccupations and areas of misperception.

One other example of a test in which children frequently give a personal interpretation or a personal involvement in the answer is the Problem Situation at year eleven. This is a simple story about a boy who wanted a pet. The examiner says, "Listen, and see if you can understand what I read. Donald went walking in the woods. He saw a pretty little animal that he tried to take home for a pet. It got away from him, but when he got home, his family immediately burned all his clothes. Why?" The only persons mentioned in the story are Donald and his family. Terman and Merrill describe the test as another variation of the completion method, a method that permits unlimited elaboration. The following responses are examples of those offered by school children:

1. He probably ran away like I did—(told of running away from home) —I stayed at my grandma's for a week. My ma tried to get me to come home but I wouldn't.

2. He tried to catch a little birdie and pulled his feathers off. The little birdie told his mother and the mother took her little boy's clothes off to see how he would like it.

3. To punish him for trying to get something.

4. 'Cause he brought the animal back. 'Cause when they would give him a spanking his clothes would burn he would be so red—a red-hot whipping.

5. Because he was cruel for catching the little animal in the woods.

6. It was his step-mother who burned them—you know step-mothers are mean to kids.

In the Revised Stanford-Binet, the child's personal relations with the world are revealed in his reactions to many of the test items. The several drawing tests disclose the child's spontaneity or lack of it in his methods of work. In the reproduction of the circle, the square, and the diamond, in the Maze Drawing, the Memory for Designs test, and the Plan of Search for the lost purse, one can distinguish and deliberate from the impulsive method of putting an idea into action; one can find children who are careless and others who are meticulous perfectionists. Many of the hypotheses underlying the Bender Gestalt test are equally applicable to the drawing tests in the Stanford-Binet. In these tests are found frequent examples of retracing lines, erasing, exaggerated or open angles, distortion of proportion, inversion of design, omissions of detail, faint lines, and heavy lines.

In the Picture Completion: Man, year four and five, are some of the same scoring and interpretation problems found in the Draw-a-Person Test or in the H-T-P Test discussed above.

Personal content from the life experiences of the child is found more frequently in some test items than in others. The child's misperceptions and projective behavior are more easily elicited by the less structured test items that require abstract symbolic expression and tolerate a wide latitude of responses. Such test items involving verbal expression and abstract thinking are found at numbers of age levels. Open-ended questions, which admit anything the child cares to say, are found in the Picture Absurdities I, year seven; II, year ten; Verbal Absurdities I, year eight; II, years nine and twelve; III, year eleven; Comprehension III, year seven; and IV, year eight. The question about a statement or a picture: "What is funny (or foolish) about that?" permits a wide range of individual variation in response. It permits different kinds of expressions of exactness and of errors in perception. It reflects variations in attention with its ranges of intensity and its varieties of instantaneous or momentary diversions, and variations in logical arrangement of detail.

In a chapter on "Projective aspects of intelligence testing," Erika Fromm [127] has called for a reappraisal of the concept of intelligence in terms of dynamic aspects of personality and motivational functioning. Fromm reviewed research and presented a chart of forty-three personality variables found in their clinical work to bear upon success and failure on intelligence test items by children. Of the forty-three variables "three of them are expres-

[127] Erika Fromm, "Projective Aspects of Intelligence Testing," in *Projective Techniques with Children*, ed. A. I. Rabin & Mary R. Haworth (New York: Grune & Stratton, Inc., 1960), p. 235; see also E. Fromm and L. D. Hartman, *Intelligence—a Dynamic Approach* (New York: Random House, Inc., 1955); E. Fromm, L. D. Hartman, and M. Marschak, "A Contribution to a Dynamic Theory of Intelligence Testing," *Journal of Clinical and Experimental Psychopathology*, 15 (1954), 73–95; E. Fromm, L. D. Hartman, and M. Marschak, "Children's Intelligence Tests as a Measure of Dynamic Personality Functioning," *American Journal of Orthopsychiatry*, 27 (1957), 134–144.

sions of the id-ego; thirty-three tap the perceptual, reality-adaptive, integrative and defensive functions of the ego; one is related to the ego ideal; five represent superego functions; and one cultural influences."

Another plea for reexamining the concept of intelligence has been made by Liverant [128] who pointed out that it is a fallacy for psychologists to assume that by establishing rapport they can hold constant the nonintellective situational factors bearing upon test performance. "Perhaps most crucial," said Liverant, "is the failure of intelligence theory to specify systematically the effect of situational variables on the behaviors it is purported to predict."

Interpreting the Environment As Well As the Child—Dynamic Interacting

SITUATIONAL AND INTERPERSONAL ASPECTS OF INTERACTING

The concept of individual differences is a central one in American psychology and education and has been for the past forty or fifty years. This concept of the person as a detached, isolated individual that could be subdivided for study and analysis into parts, faculties, motives, instincts, traits became modified to include "responses" to an environment. A new concept of the whole child "responding" to the whole situation became in turn an unsatisfactory expression. There was next imputed in human relating interaction, transaction, mutual interweaving, integration of desires, purposes, activities, two-way communication.

Situational and interpersonal variables in the test productions, both projective and nonprojective, began to receive research attention. By the 1950's psychologists were becoming uneasy about these concepts of interacting. Numbers of studies were published; small adventures in research on factors in the clinical situation itself were made. In 1954 Sarason's book was entitled *The Clinical Interaction: With Special Reference to the Rorschach*,[129] while Schafer wrote on *Psychoanalytic Interpretation in Rorschach Testing*.[130] Both books discussed situational variables and the influence of the examiner on Rorschach responses.

Studies that have appeared in numbers in the late 1940's and the 1950's have been summarized in an excellent review by Masling [131] under four topics: influence of the method of administration; influence of the testing situation; influence of the examiner; and influence of the subject.

[128] S. Liverant, "Intelligence: a Concept in Need of Re-examination," *J. Consult. Psychol.*, 24(2) (1960), 101–110.

[129] S. B. Sarason, *The Clinical Interaction: with Special Reference to the Rorschach* (New York: Harper & Row, Publishers, 1954).

[130] R. Schafer, *Psychoanalytic Interpretation in Rorschach Testing* (New York: Grune & Stratton, Inc., 1954).

[131] J. Masling, "The Influence of Situational and Interpersonal Variables in Projective Testing," *Psychol. Bull.*, 57(1) (1960), 65–85.

To illustrate the nature of the interview, interacting in the test situation, and the effectiveness with which a child can interpret her own symbolism, and in her own words tell her "Own Story," the following small vignette from a part of a testing situation is presented. It also shows how penetrating and valid can be a child's perceptions of a cold and forbidding environment with which she was unable to communicate.

Carol, C.A. six years, six months, at Christmas time was unable to read and was failing the first grade. She was also truant and frequently tardy, arriving a half-hour late so often that the Public Health nurse called on the mother. The mother said she had to whip Carol to make her go to school. The teacher was distressed because, with all other children reading, Carol could not read. So Carol was referred to the school psychologist with a request for a report on Carol's intelligence.

On the Stanford-Binet Carol gave a consistent performance, achieving an IQ of 97. When she had finished, the psychologist asked if she would like to draw a picture. What Carol drew was a kind of wobbly circle at the bottom of the page.

"I suppose you know what that is," the psychologist remarked, "but I couldn't even guess."

Carol: "Why,—don't you know what that is? Why,—that's a snowball." The conversation continued.

Psychologist: "I suppose you know who made the snowball?"

C: "Oh, yes, a little boy made it." This seemed like a dead-end to the psychologist, even though the Public Health nurse had reported Carol hostile toward a three-year-old brother. But the psychologist continued.

P: "Well, what is going to happen now?"

C: "Why, a bad little girl is going to knock it over."

P: "I suppose *you* know who that bad little girl is?"

C: "Oh, yes, that bad little girl doesn't like her brother, and she won't go to school, and she won't empty the waste paper baskets, and she won't set the table."

P: Do you know why the bad little girl doesn't want to go to school?"

C: "Oh yes, it's because nobody knows my name. Nobody knows I'm there. . . ."

From the Public Health nurse it was learned that the mother, Carol, and baby brother had recently moved from a farm to the city and had taken a small apartment to be near the father who had just entered the County TB Hospital. They moved late in November and entered Carol in the first grade.

From the teacher it was later learned that all the regular seats in the school room were occupied, so Carol sat in a chair in the back of the room.

The teacher was spending considerable time preparing the first grade to sing for a Christmas program for the Parent-Teacher Association. Carol was the only child who had been asked not to participate, because "She didn't know the words and would look bad just standing there." The psychologist learned these details one morning before school when she went for a conference with the teacher. The teacher was concerned about Carol's rating on the intelligence tests; the above facts that she reported were for her almost irrelevant information.

When the psychologist informally discussed the test results, presented the picture of the snowball, and gave details of the child's "Own Story," the teacher remarked, "Oh, dear me, we ought to be able to do something about that." The teacher admitted that Carol was not a part of the group; said that she could find a "Big Sister" for her from the class; and that she *could* put her in the Christmas program. She remarked, "After all, what is Christmas for?" Before the conference ended the teacher had tears in her eyes and said, "Oh yes, we can help her." From the free, mutually nonthreatening interacting of the child, the psychologist, and the teacher a beginning was made in changing the school from a restricting to a facilitating environment.

Yarrow [132] has written with clarity, scope, and understanding on the difficult process of interviewing a child. Though the documentation which he presents is in the context of research, the principles and the techniques of interviewing are applicable to a clinical study of the child.

The Paradox of Projective Techniques and Scientific Method

THE DILEMMA OF THE SCIENTIST USING PROJECTIVE TECHNIQUES

In the 1940's the American Psychological Association, through its committees, took responsibility for setting minimum standards and for approving university programs of graduate training in clinical psychology. Since that time it has held to two objectives rarely required of other professions: 1) clinical psychology students were to be trained first as "scientists," i.e., to be knowledgeable in the history of psychology as a science, in the design of experiments, and in the use of statistical and other scientific methods in research; 2) they were to be trained "professionally," i.e., skilled in applying psychology in the service of their clients. These two objectives represented little fundamental change from the two historical approaches at the beginning of the century: the control and measurement of single variables; and the study of complex behavior.

[132] L. J. Yarrow, "Interviewing Children," in *Handbook of Research Methods in Child Development*, ed. P. H. Mussen (New York: John Wiley & Sons, Inc., 1960).

In the decades since the turn of the century, those psychologists attained and rather jealously guarded an academic respectability as "scientists," with an avowed insistence on control of variables and evidence of reliability, validity, repeatability, prediction, and proof. Those concerned with the complexities of human behavior were for decades found in smaller numbers; until recently they usually worked outside of academic settings. But for them, too, the tenets of science were a professional ideal.

When intelligence tests were first devised they were soon standardized in an effort to satisfy the tenets of science. Their reliability, validity, repeatability, and predictability, though often strained in the interpretation, were nevertheless deemed acceptable. At least these were goals in test making. Norms, central tendencies, and correlations are measures of similarities, ways in which one individual is *like* or *different* from others. The personal, original, unique, imaginative, idiosyncratic perceptions and communications were irrelevant to the purpose of the standardization and were, like the most common responses, scored "pass" or they were scored "fail." For many children problems still remained, as, for example, why a first-grade child with normal intelligence could not read and had to be whipped to be made to go to school. Psychologists interested in the larger interpretations of behavior ultimately discovered important limitations in the standardized tests.

When projective techniques appeared as open-ended escapes from the closed constrictures of norms, they, too, were christened in the name of science. Distinguished careers have been spent, almost with a single purpose of making the Rorschach test reliable, valid, and otherwise scientifically "respectable." But with thousands of publications, and now scores of projective techniques used by hundreds of newly trained clinical and school psychologists all trained and dedicated to scientific method, projective techniques are still low in reliability, low in validity, and admittedly not "scientifically respectable." Some psychologists [133] have pleaded that human behavior may be such that projective techniques record behavior that should perhaps be measured on dimensions other than those used for standardized tests. Such doubts, such scientific skepticism are a part of the trend of the times. In fact, they constitute a horizon currently being explored. Psychologists have found no solution to this dilemma.

In the past decade or so psychologists have shown research interest in the personal, unique, original, idiosyncratic, creative responses of individuals in an area that has come to be called creativity research. One can see again the two theoretical approaches, namely, the study of the individual person with controlled variables in the case of Guilford and his followers, and the

---

[133] L. E. Abt and L. Bellak, eds., *Projective Psychology: Clinical Approaches to the Total Personality* (New York: Alfred A. Knopf, Inc., 1950); see also Maria A. Rickers-Ovsiankina, ed., *Rorschach Psychology* (New York: John Wiley & Sons, Inc., 1960).

study of the dynamic interaction of complex interpersonal and intrapersonal variables, as illustrated in the work of Carl Rogers, H. H. Anderson and others. Out of these formulations and many other researches may come new perspectives on the paradox of projective techniques and scientific method. Not only have all researchers met an impasse in finding relevant criteria for validity of creativity, but new doubts arise regarding the logical consistency of external criteria for evaluating the unique responses of an individual and the alleged controls in the testing situation.

In Chapter 20, Newton Metfessel discusses the psychometric and projective approaches to creativity assessment. His chapter provides a scholarly review of the topic as well as thorough documentation and selected supplementary readings.

PART TWO: THE ILLINOIS TEST OF PSYCHOLINGUISTIC ABILITIES
AND THE SCHOOL PSYCHOLOGIST

The school psychologist needs instruments which will provide valid psychological correlates of specific areas of educational pathology and tests which will allow him to provide more specific assistance to the classroom teacher in implementing differential educational milieux for different children —in this way providing for individual differences in a way that was not possible formerly. The testing devices which appear to hold most promise for the school psychologist today are concerned with diagnosis, prediction, remediation, and research of specific definable, educationally relevant aspects of children's affective, cognitive, social and perceptual-motor development. Of all the experimental instruments, the one that seems most valuable as a differential diagnostic instrument in the area of the language development of disadvantaged and retarded children, and for children with specific learning disabilities, is the Illinois Test of Psycholinguistic Abilities (ITPA).

DEVELOPMENT OF THE ITPA

The ITPA shares with many of the projectives discussed in this chapter the presence of a theoretical model as the basis for its construction. For example, in the case of Blum's *Blackie Projective Test* the theoretical basis is rooted firmly in psychoanalytic theory regarding the psychosexual development of the child. In respect to the ITPA, the theoretical model had its origin in the work of Charles Osgood who, in 1952, produced a model for the communication process based upon an extension of Hull's learning theory.[134] Prior to the development of this battery, the only kind of linguistic assessment

---

[134] Charles E. Osgood, "Psycholinguistics: A Survey of Theory and Research Problems," *Journal of Abnormal and Social Psychology*, 49 (1954), 2–18. See also "A Behavioral Analysis," in *Contemporary Approaches to Cognition* (Cambridge: Harvard University Press, 1957).

was an isolated test or two of the picture identification and normative survey type.

Dunn and Smith stated the reasons for the interest in psycholinguistic theory as applied to education as follows:

> During the past decade, interest in the psycholinguistic processes of children with potential learning handicaps has increased rapidly. Much of the current research has been based on the efforts of such Soviet scientists as Pavlov, Vygotsky, and Luria who recognized the key role of language in human endeavor. The three central functions include: 1) a means of communication and social interaction, 2) an instrument for the higher thought processes of man, and 3) a method for regulating the individual's behavior through directions and cautions from others. While children with adequate intellectual and cultural backgrounds acquire efficiency in language informally and often incidentally, the disadvantaged and the intellectually slow (who are in less stimulating environments, or who are less able to assimilate from the culture around them) are not so fortunate. Therefore, it has become increasingly clear to American behavioral scientists that more systematic procedures need to be developed for measuring and stimulating the development of the psycholinguistic processes of children with potential learning handicaps.[135]

With Osgood's assistance, a listing and definition of essential psycholinguistic abilities was made and tests were designed to assess them by the staff of the University of Illinois Institute for Research on Exceptional Children under the direction of Samuel A. Kirk. The first test battery was constructed in 1955. These tests were administered to several hundred preschool children and the data were analyzed by Dorothy J. Sievers.[136] Subsequent work with the test has been carried out by Smith,[137] Mueller,[138] Bateman,[139] Kass,[140] and others.

[135] Lloyd M. Dunn and James O. Smith, *Peabody Language Development Kits Manual for Level #1* (Minneapolis, Minnesota: America Guidance Service, Inc., 1965), p. xv.

[136] Dorothy J. Sievers, *Development and Standardization of a Test of Psycholinguistic Growth in Preschool Children.* Unpublished Ph.D. Thesis. (Champaign: University of Illinois, 1955). See also Dorothy J. Sievers, J. J. McCarthy, J. L. Olson, Barbara D. Bateman, and Corrine E. Kass, *Selected Studies on the Illinois Test of Psycholinguistic Abilities* (Madison, Wis.: Photo-Press, 1963).

[137] J. O. Smith, "Language Development and the ITPA," *Training School Bulletin*, 62 (November, 1965), 97–107.

[138] Max W. Mueller, "Comparison of Psycholinguistic Patterns of Gifted and Retarded Children," *Journal of School Psychology*, 3 (Spring, 1965), 18–26. See also Max Mueller and J. Weaver, "Psycholinguistic Abilities of Institutionalized Trainable Mental Retardates," *American Journal of Mental Deficiency*, 68, No. 6 (1964), 775–783.

[139] B. Bateman and J. Wetherell, "Psycholinguistic Aspects of Mental Retardation," *Mental Retardation*, 3 (April, 1965), 8ff. See also B. Bateman, *The ITPA in Current Research: Summaries of Studies* (Urbana, Ill.: Institute for Research on Exceptional Children, 1964).

[140] C. E. Kass, "Psycholinguistic Disabilities of Children with Reading Problems," *Exceptional Children*, 32 (April, 1966), 533–539.

The present test battery—still called experimental—is the outgrowth of a decade of work, and the authors assume that further clinical and theoretical work will point up the need for revision. This battery was standardized in 1959 and 1960 on 700 children. The authors' plan was to obtain norms on a sufficiently large number of randomly selected, linguistically normal children between the ages of two and nine from a representative Illinois school district. The preschool sample was largely the siblings of the school age subjects. Only those children with IQ's on the 1937 Binet between 80 and 120 were included; children with serious sensory or physical handicaps were eliminated; no Negroes or parochial school children were used as subjects. An analysis of the fathers' occupations approximated the national picture of occupational and socio-economic status. Examiners of the standardization sample were carefully trained psychometricians.

In terms of the reliability and validity of this scale the interested reader is directed to the original research monographs on this test.[141] Reliability data at the time of the standardization suggested that the test was sufficiently reliable for experimental work and that further efforts to refine reliability could better be applied to the problems of remediation and validation. The ITPA shows internal consistency coefficients ranging from .50 to .89 for the subtests by age, and from .90 to .95 for the ages pooled by subtest. Test-retest stability coefficients for the subtests extend from .18 to .86 with the restricted range of subjects (the 6–0 to 6–6); estimates of reliability for the full range of subjects range from .73 to .95. Reliability by the split-half method ranges from .40 to .94 for the subtests by age grouping, and from .90 to .99 for the subtests pooling the age groups.[142]

McCarthy summarized the validity studies as follows:

> Generally the data suggest the concurrent, construct, and predictive validities to be adequate, followed by the content and diagnostic. The chief cautions to the test users would be these: 1) Our data suggest that the encoding subtests and especially the Auditory-Vocal Automatic subtest may deviate from the definition in the manual. It is particularly critical that, when a diagnosis or a prescription for remediation is based on the results of *ad hoc* tests, clinical observations be used to confirm performance on them. Of the three, the Vocal encoding subtest appears to be the most valid. 2) In the diagnosis of children with linguistic defects, particularly dyslexia, it is recommended that auxiliary tests accompany the use of the ITPA. A good interim array is suggested by Kass.[143]

[141] J. J. McCarthy and S. A. Kirk, *The Construction, Standardization and Statistical Characteristics of the ITPA* (Urbana: University of Illinois Press, 1964). See also J. J. McCarthy and J. L. Olson, *Validity Studies on the ITPA* (Urbana: University of Illinois Press, 1964).

[142] J. J. McCarthy, "Notes on the Validity of the ITPA," *Mental Retardation*, 3 (April, 1965), 26.

[143] C. E. Kass, *Some Psychological Correlates of Severe Reading Disability*, Unpublished Doctoral Dissertation. (Urbana: University of Illinois, 1962).

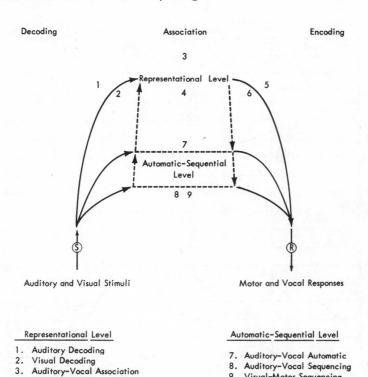

Decoding   Association   Encoding

Representational Level

1. Auditory Decoding
2. Visual Decoding
3. Auditory-Vocal Association
4. Visual-Motor Association
5. Vocal Encoding
6. Motor Encoding

Automatic-Sequential Level

7. Auditory-Vocal Automatic
8. Auditory-Vocal Sequencing
9. Visual-Motor Sequencing

FIGURE 4. *A model of psycholinguistic abilities.*

DESCRIPTION OF THE ITPA

The authors define a psycholinguistic ability as a given process at a given level via a given channel (see Figure 4). The test consists of nine subtests (see Figure 5) and yields nine standard subscores measuring: differential language abilities in two levels, representational and automatic sequential; five abilities: decoding, association, encoding, automatic, and sequencing; and four channels: visual, auditory, vocal, and motor related to communication skills. The test also yields a global language age.

The nine psycholinguistic abilities defined by McCarthy and Kirk,[144] and Olson are presented below. Each definition is accompanied by a brief explanation of how the ability is tested. The arabic numbers correspond to those in Figure 4.

[144] J. J. McCarthy and S. A. Kirk, *Examiners Manual*, 6–7.

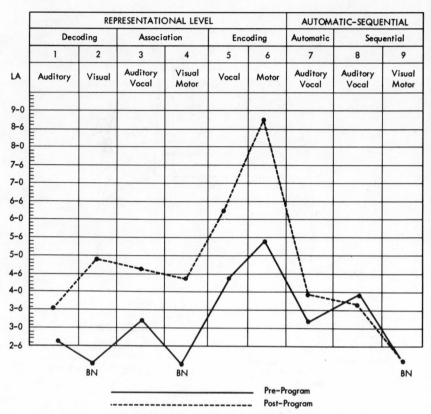

REPRESENTATIONAL LEVEL						AUTOMATIC-SEQUENTIAL		
Decoding		Association		Encoding		Automatic	Sequential	
1	2	3	4	5	6	7	8	9
Auditory	Visual	Auditory Vocal	Visual Motor	Vocal	Motor	Auditory Vocal	Auditory Vocal	Visual Motor

LA

Pre-Program

Post-Program

FIGURE 5. *Pre- and post-program psycholinguistic test results.*

I. TESTS AT THE REPRESENTATIONAL LEVEL

Tests at this level have one thing in common. They all assess some aspect of the subject's ability to deal with meaningful symbols—to understand the meaning of symbols (decoding), to express meaningful ideas in symbols (encoding), or to relate symbols on a meaningful basis (association).

A. *The Decoding Tests.* Decoding is the ability to comprehend auditory and visual symbols—that is, the ability to comprehend spoken words, written words, or pictures.

TEST 1. *Auditory decoding* is the ability to comprehend the spoken word. It is assessed by a controlled vocabulary test in which the subject is asked to answer yes or no by voice or gesture to a series of graded questions.

TEST 2. *Visual decoding* is the ability to comprehend pictures and written words. It is assessed by a picture identification technique in which the subject selects from among a set of pictures the one which is most nearly identical, on a meaningful basis, to a previously exposed stimulus picture.

B. *The Association Tests.* Association is the ability to relate visual or auditory symbols (which stand for ideas) in a meaningful way.

TEST 3. *Auditory-vocal association* is the ability to relate spoken words in a meaningful way. This ability is tested with the familiar analogies test in which the subject must complete a test statement by supplying an analogous word (e.g., the examiner says, "Soup is hot; ice cream is ———").

TEST 4. *Visual-motor association* is the ability to relate meaningful visual symbols. The present test requires the subject to select from among a set of pictures the one which most meaningfully relates to a given stimulus picture.

C. *The Encoding Tests.* Encoding is the ability to put ideas into words or gestures.

TEST 5. *Vocal encoding* is the ability to express one's ideas in spoken words. It is assessed by asking the subject to describe simple objects such as a block or ball.

TEST 6. *Motor encoding* is the ability to express one's ideas in gestures. The manual language of the deaf is an example of motor encoding. This ability is tested by showing the subject an object and asking him to supply the motion appropriate for manipulating it (e.g., drinking from a cup or strumming a guitar).

II. TESTS AT THE AUTOMATIC-SEQUENTIAL LEVEL

Tests at this level deal with the non-meaningful uses of symbols, principally their long term retention and the short term memory of symbol sequences.

Unlike the representational level tests, no attempt has been made to subdivide the automatic-sequential level tests into their decoding, association, and encoding aspects because of the lack of theoretical clarity at this level.

A. *The Automatic Tests.* Our frequent use of a language and the abundant redundancies of language lead to highly over-learned or automatic habits for handling its syntactical and inflectional aspects without conscious effort. So familiar are we with linguistic structure that we come to expect or predict the grammatical structure of what will be said or read from what has already been seen or heard. In speaking or writing, these automatic habits permit one to give conscious attention to the content of a message, while the words which express that message seem to come automatically.

TEST 7. *Auditory-vocal automatic* ability permits one to predict future linguistic events from past experience. It is called "automatic" because it is usually done without conscious effort. In listening to a speech, for example, we develop an expectation of what will be said which is based on what has already been said. In the present test, the subject must supply the last word to a test statement, invariably a word requiring inflection (e.g., the examiner says, "Father is opening the can. Now the can has been ———").

No suitable visual-motor counterpart to this test could be designed. The ability to read incomplete sentences and supply the correctly inflected word in writing would seem an appropriate task, but obviously it is not suited for two-and-a-half-year-old children. After many unsuccessful attempts to design a picture substitute for the visual-motor channel, the effort was abandoned.

B. *The Sequencing Tests*. Sequencing, as used here, is the ability to correctly reproduce a sequence of symbols; it is largely dependent upon visual and/or auditory memory.

TEST 8. *Auditory-vocal sequencing* is the ability to correctly reproduce a sequence of symbols previously seen. It is tested by requiring the subject to duplicate the order of a sequence of pictures or geometrical designs presented to the subject and then removed.

ADMINISTRATION AND UTILITY OF THE ITPA

This ITPA can be mastered by those persons who already have clinical finesse with the WISC; however, the test authors suggest that before utilizing the test for differential diagnosis, the psychologist should study the manual carefully, conduct a minimum of ten practice administrations, and continue to use the manual during each testing. Persons who have not had training as school psychometrists should not attempt to utilize this scale.

Administration time runs about 30 minutes or less. Although the test manual provides normative data for children from approximately two and a half to nine years of age, the test has some usefulness for retarded children up to a mental age of about ten years regardless of their chronological age. At the lower end, several investigators have found that a mental age of about four years is required before the scores fall consistently within the norms of the test.

According to McCarthy the utility of this instrument is limited to assessment of the following kinds of abilities. Does the subject: 1) Use the English language adequately (Auditory Vocal Automatic)? 2) Understand what he reads (Visual Decoding)? 3) Put his ideas into gestures well, such as in acting out a story (Motor Encoding)? 4) Think, reason, and solve problems in his head (Auditory Vocal Association)? 5) Put his ideas into words well (Vocal Encoding)? 6) Remember correctly symbol series that he sees, such as in written spelling tests (Visual Sequential)? 7) Remember correctly symbol series that he hears, for example, telephone and house numbers (Auditory Vocal Sequential)? 8) See relationships, for example, in assembling a picture puzzle (Visual Motor Association)? 9) Understand what he hears (Auditory Decoding)? [145]

McCarthy drew the following conclusions regarding the use of the ITPA: [146] 1) A significant improvement in either overall language ability or in a specific ability can be obtained over a treatment period of three months in the EMR and this gain will be maintained for from three to nine months following cessation of training. 2) The ITPA profile of various types of exceptional

[145] J. J. McCarthy, "The Use and Usefulness of the ITPA," in *Inspection and Introspection in Special Education* (Washington, D.C.: Council for Exceptional Children, 1965), 195–201.
[146] *Ibid.*, p. 200.

children has been compared without notable success. Trends have suggested that the gifted are more able in Auditory Vocal Ability while the mentally retarded are strongest in the Visual-Motor areas. 3) There appears to be a rather persistent correlation of about .65 between the ITPA Language Age and MA in handicapped and normal children. 4) In handicapped children, at least the cerebral palsied and mentally retarded, the language age is typically lower than the mental age. 5) Research and clinical observation seem to indicate that the ITPA confirms clinical impressions. The psychologist finds what he thought he would find. In addition, it has been suggested that the theoretical model be re-examined for factors which have not been included in the present ITPA battery. Kass found in working with severe reading problems or dyslexic children that some of the tests which best distinguished the dyslexic from the normal reader were not included in the ITPA battery, for example, perceptual speech, visual closure, and sound blending.[147] 6) There appear to be no real sex differences in ITPA profiles; children from a higher SES do better than children from a lower; there is some evidence to suggest that the first born child in a family does better than the other members of the family.

Bateman and Wetherell summarized the ITPA research regarding the language performance of the retarded as follows:

> There appears to be a "typical" profile for groups of retarded children whose IQs are near or below 75. The outstanding feature is a deficit in the entire automatic-sequential level as compared to the relative strength at the representational level. A prominent secondary feature frequently seen, especially in culturally deprived low IQ children, is a stronger performance on the visual-motor channel than on the auditory-vocal channel. Deficits in the association process (especially auditory-vocal) are also quite common. The "Strauss-syndrome" child characteristically deviates from the typical retardate in that he shows marked visual decoding and motor encoding disabilities, regardless of age or IQ. A relative weakness in motor encoding is seen in public school children but not in private residential school children. Mongoloid children show relative strength in motor encoding and a deficit in the automatic usage of grammatical structure. No differences are seen in the psycholinguistic patterns of urban and rural low IQ children.[148]

A general finding has been that the educable retarded and the disadvantaged have quite similar profiles of psycholinguistic processes. In most groups surveyed, language age on the ITPA has lagged significantly behind the mental age on the 1960 Binet. The interested reader will find in the Readings at the end of the chapter ITPA investigations of children with

[147] C. E. Kass, "Psycholinguistic Disabilities of Children with Reading Problems," *Exceptional Children*, 32 (April, 1966), 533–539.
[148] B. Bateman and J. Wetherell, "Psycholinguistic Aspects of Mental Retardation," *Mental Retardation*, 3 (April, 1965), 12.

functional defects of articulation, cerebral palsy, aphasia, deafness, and visual impairment, and of children from disadvantaged environments.

PLANNING A CHILD'S PROGRAM OF EDUCATIONAL DEVELOPMENT OR REMEDIATION FROM THE ITPA

The ITPA holds considerable promise for curricular prescriptive practices. Evidence from many Russian and American researchers indicates a direct relationship between intellectual growth and language development. Thus, an effective analysis of a child's language development could possibly serve as the basis for instruction in this most important curricular area.

Olson, Hahn and Hermann report on a summer eight-week special education program for educable mentally retarded children under the age of seven.[149] The level of language development of each of the children was analyzed in light of his ITPA strengths and weaknesses. Staff conferences led to the development of an individualized program for each child. Thus, psycholinguistic abilities were assessed, and curriculum was based upon the outcome of the assessment. The activities presented to the children focused upon each of the areas of the ITPA on a rotating basis so that at least three different language areas were emphasized each morning. In addition to this general exposure, each child was tutored for the remediation of his specific deficit. Examples of the types of activities are presented in an article by D. E. Wiseman.[150] The activities paralleled those included on the ITPA; however, none were duplicated from the test itself. The authors include case studies of success and failure. The very successful case of JH is reprinted here. The reader is directed to the reference for a provocative discussion of the relationship of the child's degree of success to the program variables, to the child's presenting problem, and to the psychometric assessments devices utilized.

JH entered the program at the age of 4-9 after a short period of nursery school attendance. Referral was initiated because of slow, erratic speech and motor development. His medical history relates a Caesarean delivery followed by a jaundiced condition. Aside from bronchitis at the age of six months, there are no other significant medical factors.

Performance during previous psychological evaluations has indicated that JH's language difficulties may be multiple in origin. In addition to possible mental retardation, there has been a question of organic interference, suggested because of his coordination problems, hyperactivity, speech difficulty, and extreme distractibility. Certain behavioral characteristics also suggest a possible emotional maladjustment.

149 J. L. Olson, H. Hahn, and A. L. Hermann, "Psycholinguistic Curriculum," *Mental Retardation*, 3 (April, 1965), 14–19.
150 D. E. Wiseman, "A Classroom Procedure for Identifying and Remediating Language Problems," *Mental Retardation*, 3 (April, 1965), 20ff.

A psychometric evaluation prior to the initiation of the language program indicated that JH was within the normal range of intellectual functioning on verbal tests.

The ITPA pre-remediation profile (Figure 5) clarifies his assets and deficits. JH's vocal and motor encoding performances illustrate his ability to express ideas in vocal and manual terms at levels commensurate with his mental age. Although subtests utilizing the auditory-vocal channel disclosed a general discrepancy between mental age and language age, the visual-motor channel presented the most marked discrepancy. JH scored below norms in visual decoding, visual-motor association, and visual-motor sequencing. He was unable to respond in these three areas.

Remediation: The remedial program for JH utilized his ability in auditory-vocal association and his motor encoding strength to improve functioning in the visual-motor channel. The prime emphasis was on his visual decoding and visual-motor association deficits at the representational level. Psychometric evaluation following the termination of remediation is presented in Table 1.

The post-training psycholinguistic profile (Figure 5) shows language age gains of more than two years in visual decoding and visual-motor association, the two areas of concentration in JH's remedial program. Motor encoding remains his major strength and constituted the area of greatest gain. Visual-motor and auditory-vocal sequencing represent the areas in which no gain was made. These tests require the short-range retention of visual and auditory symbols, and performance on them may be adversely affected by inattention and distractibility, both behavioral characteristics of JH.

Some examiners have felt that the range of abilities shown by JH suggests an overall intellectual potential which may be higher than that revealed in psychometric evaluations. This factor must be considered in conjunction with the possible existence of organicity and/or emotional maladjustment in evaluating his psycholinguistic gains.

TABLE 1

JH: Pre- and Post-Program Psychometric Data

	CA		MA		IQ	
	Pre	Post	Pre	Post	Pre	Post
S-B (1960)	4-9	4-11	4-1	4-3	85	85
PPVT	4-9	5-0	4-8	5-8	95	106

Samuel A. Kirk and others are presently working on further developments in an empirically based psycholinguistic curriculum to enhance the development and support remediation for children with special learning problems. Although the ITPA is still in an experimental form, it is important that all school psychologists in the 1960's and '70's become familiar and comfortable with its terms and its utility for the schools. At present, it should not be interpreted alone but rather always in relation to other test and case study data.

Selected Supplementary Readings

PART ONE: PROJECTIVE TECHNIQUES

Entwisle, D. R., *Word Associations of Young Children*. Baltimore, Md.: Johns Hopkins Press, 1966.

Evvard, Evelyn, "Results of the Bender-Gestalt Test in a Beginner's Class and in First and Second Grades," *Journal of American Indian Education*, 5 (May, 1966), 6–10.

Hammer, Max, and Arthur M. Kaplan, "The Reliability of Children's Human Figure Drawings," *Journal of Clinical Psychology*, 22 (1966), 316–319.

Harrower, Molly, *Psychodiagnostic Testing: An Empirical Approach*. Springfield, Ill.: Charles C Thomas, Publisher, 1965.

Haworth, Mary R., *The CAT: Facts about Fantasy*. New York: Grune & Stratton, Inc., 1966.

Jones, L. W., and C. B. Thomas, "Studies on Figure Drawings," *Psychiatric Quarterly Supplement*, 39 (1965), 241–267.

Kunce, Joseph T., and Bert Worley, "Projective Drawings of Brain-Injured Subjects," *Perceptual and Motor Skills*, 22 (1966), 163–168.

Lickorish, John R., "Evaluating the Child's View of His Parents," *Journal of Projective Techniques and Personality Assessment*, 30 (1966), 68–76.

McBeath, Marcia, "Behavioral Characteristics of Visually Perceptually Handicapped and Nonhandicapped Kindergarteners," *Psychology in the Schools*, 3 (July, 1966), 264–266.

Mundy, J. M., "Junior Children's Responses to the Murray Thematic Apperception Test and the Cattell Personality Questionnaire," *British Journal of Educational Psychology*, 36 (1966), 103–104.

Pati, G., "Personality Pathology of Delinquents," *Psychological Studies*, 11 (1966), 35–41.

Scarr, S., "The Adjective Check List as a Personality Assessment Technique with Children," *Journal of Counseling Psychology*, 30 (April, 1966), 122–129.

Skolnick, Arlene, "Stability and Interrelations of Thematic Test Imagery Over 20 Years," *Child Development*, 37 (1966), 389–396.

U.S. Public Health Service, *Evaluation of Psychological Measures Used in the Health Examination Survey of Children Ages 6–11*. Washington, D.C.: Government Printing Office, 1966.

Zimmerman, Irla Lee, Nadine M. Lambert, and Loretta Class, "A Comparison of Children's Perceptions of Rorschach Cards III, IV, and VII with Independent Ratings of Parental Adequacy, and Effectiveness of School Behavior," *Psychology in the Schools,* 3 (July, 1966), 258–263.

PART TWO: ITPA

Bateman, Barbara, "Reading and Psycholinguistic Processes of Partially Seeing Children," *Council on Exceptional Children Research Monographs,* 1963, Series A (5).

Bilovsky, D., and J. Share, "The ITPA and Down's Syndrome: An Exploratory Study," *American Journal of Mental Deficiency,* 70 (July, 1965), 78–82.

Bulletin of the Orton Society, 16 (1966). Entire issue contains articles by Katina deHirsch et al., "Early Prediction of Reading Failure" (1–14) and A. L. Benton, "The Problem of Cerebral Dominance" (38–55).

Exceptional Children (December, 1964). Entire issue devoted to Learning Disabilities: Diagnosis and Remediation.

Ferrier, E. E., "Investigations of the ITPA Performance of Children with Functional Defects of Articulation," *Exceptional Children,* 32 (May, 1966), 625–629.

Hart, N. W. M., "The Differential Diagnosis of the Psycholinguistic Abilities of the Cerebral Palsied Child and Effective Remedial Procedures," *Special Schools Bulletin,* 5 (1964).

Kirk, S. A., and Barbara Bateman, "Diagnosis and Remediation of Learning Difficulties," *Exceptional Children,* 29 (1962), 73–77.

Outridge, M., "Psycholinguistic Abilities of Five Children Attending a Brisbane Opportunity School," *The Slow Learning Child,* 2 (March, 1965), 165–176.

Rosenberg, Sheldon, ed., *Directions in Psycholinguistics.* New York: The Macmillan Company, 1965.

Schiefelbusch, R. L., "Discussion of Language Treatment Methods for Mentally Retarded Children," *Mental Retardation,* 3 (April, 1965), 4ff.

Semmel, M. I., and M. W. Mueller, *A Factor Analysis of the Illinois Test of Psycholinguistic Abilities with Mentally Retarded Children.* Unpublished Study. Nashville, Tennessee: George Peabody College for Teachers, 1962.

————, "Language Research in Relationship to the Mentally Retarded and the Culturally Deprived," in J. F. Magary and R. B. McIntyre, eds., *Fifth Annual Distinguished Lectures in Special Education.* Los Angeles: University of Southern California Press, 1967.

Shields, O. L., "Remediation of Learning Disabilities in a Public School System," *Mental Retardation,* 3 (December, 1965), 27–28.

Smith, J. O., "Effects of a Group Language Development Program upon the

Psycholinguistic Abilities of Educable Mental Retardates," *Peabody College Research Monograph Series in Special Education*. No. 1. Nashville, Tennessee: George Peabody College for Teachers, 1962.

Weaver, S. J., *Use of the ITPA with Exceptional Children*. Unpublished paper. Nashville, Tennessee: George Peabody College for Teachers, 1965.

ROBERT M. ALLEN

12

The Appraisal of Social and
Perceptual Competence
of School Children

The title and hence the subject matter of this chapter is, at best, an artifact stemming from the nature of psychological and educational tests and measurements. The manner in which the child organizes and reacts to the multiplicity of stimuli impinging upon him from his total environment is imbedded in every step of his development from conception to the moment of observation and beyond, since projection into the future in terms of hopes, goals, and aspirations is also part of the currently functioning individual. Thus, from a phenomenological point of view, the present reaction to test items must be considered as an abstraction in which the response is in focus against an experiential background. It is in these terms that inferences regarding the current efficiency need to be made. An ahistorical current view that limits the evaluation and inferential horizon to "how," to the exclusion of "why," the child behaves as he does is a static approach. If behavior is to be regarded as lawfully determined, then the school psychologist should be sensitive to the present picture in the context of the behavior's past, present, and future determiners. Otherwise process would refer to the *now*, to what is given, with little reference to the reasons for *becoming*. The foregoing is offered as an indication that the presentation and discussion of specific tests are made with the knowledge that they extract from the cross-sectional picture of the longitudinally functioning individual. As such, it becomes the examiner's responsibility to relate current test data to dynamic inferences evolving from historical events. Without this awareness testing remains a sterile number-finding technique rather than a dynamic, qualitative, and descriptive process.

What does this mean with specific reference to the appraisal of social and perceptual competence of the school child? In its simplest terms the implication is that these processes are closely interwoven into the total complex of living. Therefore, any attempts to evaluate or measure these processes focus on part of the total picture. This is the only reasonable approach available at this time. It is *as if* the examiner continually reminds himself that he is not viewing the whole organism at one time but he must deal with the extracted part-processes that are available for observation. This is not unlike any other sampling situation in which unattainable absolute certainty is compromised for feasible accuracy in dealing with human behavior.

The assessment of social competence is intimately tied in with the perceptual level of the child. Both are reflected in, and influenced by, the intellectual growth and status of the individual. For example, the social relationships of the youngster will be mirrored in the intelligence manifested in social situations. Furthermore, the extent to which the child can enjoy being with others will determine the breadth and variety of experiences he may have and the fund of information he will be able to assimilate into his apperceptive mass. How he organizes and perceives his world and the myriad of details within it and how this accords with, or is determined by, his needs will direct the nature of responsiveness at any given moment. It would not be fruitful to elaborate this point any further. More agree than question that a relationship exists among the psychological events of daily living. Furthermore, these persons regret the need for the artificial separation of the to-be-measured processes yet see no way out of this evaluation dilemma. In keeping with this attitude, the currently more widely used testing devices will be discussed under two categories: tests of social competence, and tests of perceptual competence.

Tests Of Social Competence

In evaluating the social growth of the child the purpose should revolve around the effort to relate social adjustment to the youngster's biological maturity as well as chronological and mental age. Very little attention is usually given to the former facet of the developing person. Criteria for social competence are based on behavioral manifestations expected of children at various chronological ages with little consideration to the wide variations in physical growth, defects and/or anomalies.

What is involved in the evaluation of social competence? The definitions and opinions are as varied as the points of view of those who have written on this subject. The core of these views would seem to center about the "goodness" of the individual's mode of coping with life situations whether academic, social, recreational, or vocational, taking into account the age, developmental status, intelligence, and the opportunities for learning. Since the whole organism is to be rated rather than physical growth, intelligence, or the developmental environment separately, these variables are lumped together and over-all behavior is noted. Each one or combination of these phases may so influence social responsiveness as to reflect an undue immaturity or insufficiency of social adjustment. This is an accepted feature of the appraisal process since it is the total person about whom the school psychologist, teacher, and parent are concerned.

Doll [1] seems to have distilled the meanings of social competence in his contention that a view of behavior must be holistic as it meets the individual's needs within the context of the social group. More formally, he writes: "In short, social competence may be defined as a functional composite of human traits which subserves social usefulness as reflected in self-sufficiency and in service to others." An analysis of this viewpoint gives the impression that social competence leans on personal, social, and biological anchors. Of these three we may dispose of the biological except when dealing with the evaluation of the infant and young child. These biological aspects are considered in the Gesell inventory, for example.

The personal and social components are evaluated through scales and variables of certain personality inventories, questionnaires, and schedules. The logic of this position stems from the assumption that behavior (actual, or presumed from responses to test items) is a reflection of the child's attitudes, hopes, anxieties, etc., in short, his personality. From the adequacy of behavior in situations (as measured by social expectancies within the culture and at the observed age level) inferences are made with regard to the behaver's social competence. Doll supports this position as does Gesell,[2] both of whom are authors of widely used scales for the appraisal of social competence anchored in behavioral manifestations but initially concerned with neurological and physical development as the foundations for early competencies. At no particular point, but certainly within the first two months of life, the

[1] E. A. Doll, *Measurement of Social Competence* (Minneapolis, Minnesota: Educational Test Bureau, 1953), p. 2.

[2] A. Gesell and C. S. Amatruda, *Developmental Diagnosis* (New York: Hoeber, 1954).

VINELAND SOCIAL MATURITY SCALE

EDGAR A. DOLL, *Director of Research*
The Training School at Vineland, New Jersey

Name_____Sex_____Grade_____Date_____
                                                              Year   Month   Day

Residence_____Descent_____Born_____
M.A. or   I.Q. or   Year   Month   Day
M.G.U._____P.A._____Test Used_____When_____Age_____
                                                              Years   Months   Days

Occupation_____Class_____Yrs. Exp._____Schooling_____

Father's Occupation_____Class_____Yrs. Exp._____Schooling_____

Mother's Occupation_____Class_____Yrs. Exp._____Schooling_____

Informant_____Relationship_____Recorder_____

Informant's est._____Basal Score*_____

Remarks: Additional pts._____

                                                          Total score_____

                                                          Age equivalent_____

                                                          Social quotient_____

V–VI
_____57. Uses skates, sled, wagon_____
_____58. Prints simple words_____
_____59. Plays simple table games_____
_____60. Is trusted with money_____
_____61. Goes to school unattended_____

VI–VII
_____62. Uses table knife for spreading_____
_____63. Uses pencil for writing_____
_____64. Bathes self assisted_____
_____65. Goes to bed unassisted_____

VII–VIII
_____66. Tells time to quarter hour_____
_____67. Uses table knife for cutting_____
_____68. Disavows literal Santa Claus_____
_____69. Participates in pre-adolescent play_____
_____70. Combs or brushes hair_____

FIGURE 1. *Vineland Social Maturity Scale, years V–VI
to XV–XVIII inclusive.*

VIII-IX

——————— 71. Uses tools or utensils ———————————————————
——————— 72. Does routine household tasks ———————————————
——————— 73. Reads on own initiative ———————————————————
——————— 74. Bathes self unaided ————————————————————

IX-X

——————— 75. Cares for self at table ————————————————————
——————— 76. Makes minor purchases ———————————————————
——————— 77. Goes about home town freely————————————————

X-XI

——————— 78. Writes occasional short letters ——————————————
——————— 79. Makes telephone calls ————————————————————
——————— 80. Does small remunerative work ————————————————
——————— 81. Answers ads; purchases by mail ———————————————

XI-XII

——————— 82. Does simple creative work————————————————————
——————— 83. Is left to care for self or others————————————————
——————— 84. Enjoys books, newspapers, magazines ————————————

XII-XV

——————— 85. Plays difficult games————————————————————————
——————— 86. Exercises complete care of dress————————————————
——————— 87. Buys own clothing accessories————————————————————
——————— 88. Engages in adolescent group activities————————————————
——————— 89. Performs responsible routine chores————————————————

XV-XVIII

——————— 90. Communicates by letter————————————————————
——————— 91. Follows current events————————————————————————
——————— 92. Goes to nearby places alone————————————————————
——————— 93. Goes out unsupervised daytime————————————————————
——————— 94. Has own spending money————————————————————————
——————— 95. Buys all own clothing————————————————————————

infant embarks on activities that lead gradually into the area of social behavior and adjustment. This is reflected in the scales that are more commonly used for the appraisal of pre- and early school adjustment of the young child. Intimately interwoven in personal-social development is the growth in perceptual abilities. For example, in the eighteen-months to three-years zone of the *Preliminary Behavior Inventory* [3] are located items involving motor coordination based on visual perception, e.g., imitating a pencil stroke at eighteen months, building a tower with cubes at two years, and reproducing a cross at three years. However, perceptual tests will be considered in the second section of this chapter.

There are only three scales that have been designed primarily to evaluate social growth and competence. Other instruments and procedures may be

[3] A. Gesell, *Developmental Schedules; Form 7: Preliminary Behavior Inventory* (New York: The Psychological Corporation, 1956).

employed to yield impressions of social competence, but these latter devices measure more directly personality dimensions from which inferences are made with regard to personal and social adjustment.

VINELAND SOCIAL MATURITY SCALE

This is by far the most frequently used instrument. Doll [4] based this behavioral scale on these premises:

1. Social competence may be defined as the functional ability of the human organism for exercising personal independence and social responsibility.

2. This competence may be measured progressively in terms of maturation by sampling its genetic stages by means of representative performances at successive life ages.

3. Such maturation may be taken as a practicable measure of the changing organism as a whole. . . .

4. Individual status in social competence may be expressed in terms of numerical and descriptive deviation from established maturational norms and evaluated in terms of related variables.

5. The Scale . . . affords a unique procedure for the measurement of individual social competence in its group and clinical ramifications.

The criteria for social adequacy include the youngster's movement ". . . 1) from dependence to independence; 2) from irresponsibility to responsibility; and 3) from incompetence to competence." The items in this scale go from Year 0 to One to Year Eighteen +. The school years range from Five for the kindergartner to Fifteen to Eighteen for the high school senior. The items in this range are presented in Figure 1.

This is not a test in the usual meaning of the term. It is a rating or check scale with information regarding each item obtained through observation *and* from an informant. The latter is presumed to be in a position to report creditable data regarding the child. Allen [5] reviewed this device as one that was designed to disclose

. . . the individual's level of competence in various areas of life that are important for establishing, maintaining, and developing personal and interpersonal relationships. These areas are self-help, general (the extent to which the child can take care of such personal needs as eating, dressing, cleanliness, and toileting); the individual's social locomotion (the ability to move about to fulfill social responsibilities); occupational activities (ranging from infant crawling to responsible vocational participation); communication (from baby babbling to symbolic formulations); self-direction or the degree

[4] Doll, *op. cit.*, p. 10.
[5] R. M. Allen, *Personality Assessment Procedures* (New York: Harper & Row, Publishers, 1958), 408–409.

of personal independence; and socialization or the extent and nature of the child's interpersonal ties.

This scale has a respectable research and applied history best summarized in Doll 's [6] *The Measurement of Social Competence* which also serves as a detailed manual for administration, scoring, and interpretation. This scale may be used with the newborn, children, and adults for appraising social adequacy through these developmental years. While outside information is essential, some of the items may be satisfactorily completed by direct observation, e.g., Year Five to Six, a child could be given a pencil and a sheet of paper by the psychologist who may note how he uses the pencil for writing; or Year Seven to Eight, the examiner could ask the child to read the time from a wall clock or wrist watch (to be scored plus, the reading would have to be accurate only to the quarter hour). Most of the necessary information, however, will call for a person other than the child as the source. Some pertinent and valid data may be gleaned from case history material and from tests previously administered that may be part of the youngster's school folder or diagnostic clinic file.

Insofar as possible the informant should be encouraged to describe the child in the areas assessed by the scale. Direct questions should be avoided since these may tend to discourage elaborations and the recital of minor details that could yield further insights into the child's activities. However, if the requisite information is not forthcoming from open ended questions, the psychologist may have to resort to direct query. At Year Five to Six the mother, for example, should be asked to elaborate regarding the child's activities prior to going to sleep rather than the direct question, "Does Johnny go to bed by himself?" or "Do you have to help Johnny get to bed?" A question such as "How does Johnny behave at his usual bed time?" or "How does Johnny get ready for bed?" might encourage the informant to speak more freely. Not only will the answers be relevant but it may elicit information that will be applicable to other items in the scale. More important, however, is the opportunity given the informant, especially if a parent, to reveal attitudes, problems, and anxieties toward the child. This will enable the psychologist to gain some insights into the family's feelings and possibly the youngster's reactions to these.

It is not sufficient to know that a child does or does not engage in the activity probed by the items. The *extent* and *quality* need to be noted. These serve as a check on the liberality of the informant's interpretation of the child's activity (usually overestimated by the mother especially if the youngster is mentally retarded and/or neurologically handicapped) and sheds more light on the behaving child. In Year Ten to Eleven the item—Writes occasional short letters—may be answered in the affirmative by the mother whose

[6] Doll, *op. cit.*

youngster adds "XXX" to the letter to grandmother. This does not meet the criteria for a plus score since the performance is not even minimally creditable at Year Five to Six: Prints simple words.

The scoring criteria should be adhered to rigidly for a representative picture of the child's social development. These responses are given in minute detail in the manual.[7] For more refined scoring and information regarding the variability of item performances over the pre- and school years the examiner should refer to Doll's 1953 volume, Chapter 6, *Item Specification*.

The scoring scheme is a bit complicated. In general:

Plus (+) is given the item performance which is habitual and clearly satisfies the scoring criteria.

Plus F (+ F) describes the performance that was previously present and observed in the child but is not currently accomplished because of a temporary interfering circumstance.

Plus NO (+NO) or (No Opportunity) is checked if the activity required by an item is not and has not been performed by the child ". . . because of environmental restraint or environmental lack of opportunity, such as parental solicitude, arbitrary adult domination . . . but which the subject presumably would perform habitually or could quickly learn to perform if such limitations to behavior were removed."

Plus-Minus (±) is ascribed to ". . . those items which are in transitional or emergent state, that is, which are occasionally but not ordinarily performed with full success." [8]

Minus (—) is given to those items clearly not performed up to the criterion.

The assigned scores are summed up to yield a social age value. Thus, a raw score based on items checked in the plus categories is translated into a Social Age (SA) score. From this and the child's chronological or life age (LA) a Social Quotient (SQ) is obtained: SQ = SA/LA × 100. This affords a rather crude method of comparing social competency with intellectual status. The raw and SA scores range from 1.0 at .06 years to 110 points at 30+ years of age.

Beyond the quantitative aspects is the classification of items and interpretation of responses into eight activities of daily living:

1. Self-help, general (SHG)—the extent to which the child can satisfy his "immediate personal wants." In the school years from ages six to sixteen there is only one such item, the ability to tell time. Most of the SHG activities are neurologically based and pertain to growth in the pre-school years.

2. Self-help, eating (SHE)—during the years usually dealt with by the school psychologist these items refer to table manners in contrast to

[7] E. A. Doll, *Vineland Social Maturity Scale* (Minneapolis, Minnesota: Educacational Test Bureau, 1947).

[8] Doll, *Vineland Social Maturity Scale*, 284–285.

the earlier eating-related items which emphasize the ability to use eating utensils and to differentiate edible foods, etc.

3. Self-help, dressing (SHD)—refers to personal cleanliness and grooming within the six to sixteen years range.

4. Self-help, direction (SHD)—these items come closer to the usual notion of growth of the child toward independence and responsibility in personal and social activities. They appear first at Year Five to Six and increase in number with the year levels to a total of three of the six items at Year Fifteen to Eighteen.

5. Occupation (O)—the kinds of activities ranging from play to gainful employment that are characteristic of the testee at the time of observation are significant in this area. They assume major importance in late adolescence and early adulthood.

6. Communication (C)—items reflect the child's growth in verbal ability and comprehension from infantile crowing to the expectation of letter writing and reading of current events at Year Fifteen to Eighteen.

7. Locomotion (L)—runs the gamut of motor activity from infantile crawling, to the school beginner's going to school unattended, to the adolescent's freedom to go places away from home, not necessarily by walking.

8. Socialization (S)—these items reflect the youngster's growth toward activities involving ties to, and ability to get along with, others in his peer age group.

An analysis of the Vineland Scale protocol yields a great deal of anecdotal and observational information useful for arriving at a fairly representative picture of the child. These data are desirable for the adjusted and the deviant child.

Ruth, a ten-year-old gifted child, was referred to the school diagnostic center for "maturity" evaluation. Her teacher had recommended advancement to the class one year ahead which would necessitate being with girls at least one year older. Intelligence test and academic achievements were approximately at the twelve- to thirteen-year levels. The principal wanted to be certain that the youngster "could take" the accelerated program on grounds other than intellectual and academic abilities that she already demonstrated satisfactorily.

The Vineland Scale was completed from the school records and from an interview with Ruth's father. She achieved a basal age at Year Eleven to Twelve (see Figure 1). Her work for the art teacher showed outstanding ability in that field, including an appreciation for composition and the use of color. She was class president and junior baby sitter at home; and she followed a definite reading program with books selected from the school and public libraries that she read and reported to her class. Because of her ad-

vanced intellectual ability she received (+) checks on several items in the
Year Fifteen to Eighteen level. Her raw score was 87, SA of thirteen years,
nine months, and SQ of 137, all in accord with her superior intelligence
(Stanford-Binet, Form L-M, IQ of 133). On the basis of these favorable
findings Ruth was permitted to enter the accelerated program. The school
psychologist saw in the youngster's manner of coping with life activities a
maturity and stability beyond her chronological age. Her style of life and the
attitudes reflected in her father's discussion on the child's activities gave every
assurance of Ruth's continued growth toward responsibility, independence,
and competence in a fairly secure environment.

On the other hand, there is Cathy, also a ten-year-old, who is intellectually retarded. She was referred to the school clinic because of typical
organic syndrome behavior—restless, hyperactive, irritable, short attention
span, outbursts, and pouting—all in quick succession and continuous. Testing
with the *Leiter* (*LIPS*) *Scale* [9] and the Ammons *Full-Range Picture Vocabulary Test* [10] indicated a mental age of six on the LIPS and eight on the picture
test. This is not an unusual discrepancy because the latter is a recognition
test more closely associated with objects and events of everyday living than
the LIPS items.

The personal-social competence evaluation on the Vineland Scale
yielded an uneven picture. In the area of SHG Cathy achieved at Year Four
to Five in that she could care for her toilet needs. She could not tell time at
Year Seven to Eight. With regard to eating, this child's performance was quite
irregular due, in some measure, to motor impairment and athetoid movements of her hands and arms. Her highest satisfactory performance with
regard to SHE items was at the Year One to Two level. The upper-age items
were not checked in view of her motor involvement rather than because of
an inability to learn these activities. For example, the child's mother simply
would not permit Cathy to handle a knife or fork because she felt that the
child might injure herself in the throes of an athetoid tremor. As for drinking,
she was helped with this activity in order to keep the table and her clothing
dry.

The lowered attainment, then, is also a function of a solicitous mother
who constantly deprives the child of opportunities for training in these
activities of daily living. Her dressing (SHD) accomplishments reach Year
Seven to Eight. Locomotion terminates at Year Five to Seven, if "goes to
school unattended" is liberally interpreted. Cathy's goings and comings are
closely supervised by her mother. This is a necessary precaution in view of
the heavy traffic in the vicinity of her home. Motor incoordination, short

        [9] R. G. Leiter, *Leiter International Performance Scale* (Chicago, Illinois: C. H.
Stoelting Company, 1948).
        [10] R. B. Ammons and H. S. Ammons, *Full-Range Picture Vocabulary Test*
(Missoula, Montana: R. B. Ammons, 1948).

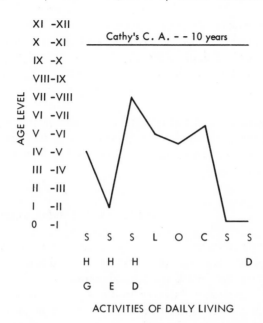

XI -XII

X -XI   Cathy's C. A. - - 10 years

IX -X

VIII-IX

AGE LEVEL

VII -VIII

VI -VII

V -VI

IV -V

III -IV

II -III

I -II

0 -I

S S S L O C S S

H H H   D

G E D

ACTIVITIES OF DAILY LIVING

FIGURE 2. *Profile of Cathy's Vineland Scale Attainments.*

attention span, and impatience are mirrored in spotty Occupation scale attainment. She can scribble with crayon and pencil (Year Four to Five) but is not a constructive member of the household in terms of helping her mother (Year Three to Four) with little tasks. Mother would rather do for herself and for Cathy than go through the usual difficulties, as she put it, of having to redo what she had assigned to Cathy. Communication skills are at Year Five to Six, if printing her name and a few simple words is loosely interpreted as meeting the criteria. Reading, writing, and communicating in other media except speaking on the telephone is unacceptable. The area of interpersonal relationships is a low point—Year Zero to One—because Cathy cannot play with other children cooperatively. Any group that she joins, according to the teacher and mother, becomes a target for her irritable, explosive, and hyperactive notice. Her "performance for others" is a self-centered and inordinate demand for attention. Cathy is unable to settle down, cannot love or be loved, and cannot seem to understand what is going on around her. She is struggling with the simplest kind of academic work in her ungraded class. As for self-direction, the very first item at Year Five to Six is beyond her intellectual ken.

Figure 2 depicts the struggles of ten-year old Cathy who is functioning well below her chronological age and is definitely at a disadvantage in comparison with her peers. The reasons for referring this child to the clinic for complete evaluation are quite obvious. Most significant among these is the need for future planning on a sound informational basis.

The most valuable source for references and reviews of the pertinent studies are contained in Doll's [11] *Measurement Of Social Competence,* Part V. Every possible field of application that holds interest for the school psychologist is discussed. For work with this scale since 1953, Buros' *Sixth Mental Measurements Yearbook* [12] (1965) will bring the user of this scale up to date.

In 1942 Maxfield and Fjeld [13] published an adaptation of the Vineland Scale for blind preschool children. A more recent revision by Maxfield and Buchholz contains 95 items standardized on 484 blind youngsters from one to six years of age.

Cain-Levine Social Competency Scale

The heightened interest in mental retardation is producing a real effort to evaluate children from every point of view so as to enhance planning and training for a better life. While intellectual attainments still remain the more important criteria, professional workers in this field have turned their attention to the social aspect as an equally significant criterion of mental retardation. In 1963, Cain, Levine, and Elzey [14] devised a standardized interview technique patterned after the Vineland Social Maturity Scale with one major difference—the standardization population consisted of 716 trainable mentally retarded children ranging in CA between 5 and 13 years, 11 months. The IQs and MAs were 25 to 59 and two through seven years respectively. The scale consists of four subscales:

1. Self-Help (SH) subscale has 14 items which focus on the child's ability "to do" for himself in the literal sense, i.e., his motor skills in dressing, undressing, washing self, etc.

2. Initiative (I) subscale utilizes 10 items to ascertain the extent to which the child can "self-direct" his activities. The point to this subscale is that initiative and self-direction are related to the dependence-independence continuum. The activities inquired into refer to dressing, keeping self and surroundings clean and play operations.

3. Social Skills (SS) subscale is a measure of the child's interpersonal relationships. These 10 items touch upon helpfulness in the home,

[11] Doll, *Measurement of Social Competence,* pp. 460–584.

[12] O. K. Buros, ed., *The Sixth Mental Measurements Yearbook* (Highland Park, New Jersey: Gryphon Press, 1965).

[13] K. E. Maxfield and S. Buchholz, *A Social Maturity Scale for Blind Preschool Children: A Guide To Its Use* (New York: American Foundation for the Blind, 1957); see also K. E. Maxfield and N. A. Fjeld, "The Social Maturity of the Visually Handicapped Preschool Child," *Child Development,* 13 (1942), 1–27.

[14] L. F. Cain, S. Levine, and F. F. Elzey, *Cain-Levine Social Competency Scale.* (Palo Alto: Consulting Psychologists Press, 1963).

getting along with other children and general regard for other persons in the social surroundings.

4. The Communication (C) subscale is self-explanatory—to what extent can the child make himself understood by others. Language usage is the core of the evaluation in this subscale. Not mere verbalization, but purposeful use of language is the basis for assessment.

For each of the subscales and total scale the authors have provided percentile equivalents for the raw scores earned. The recording booklet has four descriptive statements for each area inquired into and the raw score is the number of the alternative (1 to 4) checked by the psychologist as most accurately describing the child's status as indicated by the informant, usually a parent. The four alternatives progress, in each specific area, from absence of the function to complete ability to perform the task. The higher the raw score the more competent the child with regard to the particular area or dimension being evaluated.

Cain, Levine, and Elzey furnish specific details on interviewing procedure and criteria for scoring each item in the *Manual*. The test-retest reliability is satisfactory and varies from .88 to .98. The validity data are based on the opinions of expert judges as to the usefulness of the items and their alternatives as "describers" of the specific item in the realm of social competency. Percentile norms are furnished for children from 5 years to 13 years, 11 months for each subscale and the total scale raw score. Other statistical data aid the psychologist in understanding the background of the scale standardization population and as these may apply to the interpretation of the findings.

It is important that the psychologist be constantly aware that these results apply *only* to mentally retarded children in the CA range of 5 to 13 years, 11 months, in the IQ band of 25 to 59 (trainable mentally retarded), and for MAs two through seven years. In its present form it should *not* be used with children outside these limits.

GESELL DEVELOPMENTAL SCHEDULE

Occasionally the school psychologist may be called upon to evaluate a severely retarded and/or neurologically handicapped youngster of pre- or early school age. It is not likely that a normally developing young child will be referred to the school clinic. In the less frequent instance of a child six years of age or over who is eligible for attendance in the public school system and who gives overt indication of serious mental, social, and/or physical retardation, the *Gesell Developmental Schedule, Form 7: Preliminary Behavior Inventory*,[15] may be the appropriate appraisal device. This is especially

15 Gesell, *op. cit.*

FORM 7: Preliminary Behavior Inventory

GESELL DEVELOPMENTAL SCHEDULES

Name _____ Age _____ Date _____ Case No. _____

Age Zone	MOTOR	ADAPTIVE	LANGUAGE	PERSONAL-SOCIAL
4 wks.	Lacks head control	Brief eye following	Impassive face	Stares at surroundings
16 wks.	Asymmetric in supine	Drops toy immediately	Small throaty sounds	'Listens' to sound
	Head erect, slight bobbing	Incipient approach, rattle	Coos	Spontaneous social smile
28 wks.	Symmetric supine postures	Regards rattle in hand	Laughs aloud	Hand play
	Sits, leaning forward	Reaches & grasps toy	Squeals	Feet to mouth
40 wks.	Sits well, creeps	Transfers toy	m-m sound (crying)	Nursery tricks
	Pulls to feet at rail	Combines 2 toys	Dada-Mama	Feeds self cracker
52 wks.	Walks, one hand held	Picks pellet, thumb & index	One other 'word'	Cooperates in dressing
		Cube into cup	Two other 'words'	
15 mos.	Walks, alone, toddle	Tries tower 2 cubes	Responds "Give it to me"	Points & vocalizes wants
		Tower, two cubes	4–6 words	Casts toys
18 mos.	Walks well alone	Six cubes into cup	10 words	Toilet regulated, day
	Seats self small chair	Tower 3–4 cubes	Jargon	Carries, hugs doll
2 yrs.	Runs	Imitates a stroke	Joins 2–3 words	Asks for toilet, day
	Up, down stairs alone	Tower 6–7 cubes	Names 3–5 pictures	Puts doll to bed, etc.
3 yrs.	Rides tricycle	Imitates circular scribble	Sentences	Feeds self well
	Stands 1 foot, momentarily	Imitates 'house' of cubes	Gives full name, sex	Puts on sox, unbuttons
		Imitates cross +		

INSTRUCTIONS: (1) Check the most advanced behaviors in each field of behavior. (2) The checks will indicate an approximate maturity age zone. (3) NO DIAGNOSIS CAN BE MADE ON THE BASIS OF THIS INVENTORY. Gross deviation from actual age, or marked disparity between behavior fields indicates the need for a diagnostic behavior examination.

CHARACTERIZATION: (physical factors, social factors, posture, attention, rapport, emotion, speech, etc.)

FIGURE 3. Gesell Developmental Schedules, Form 7: Preliminary Behavior Inventory.

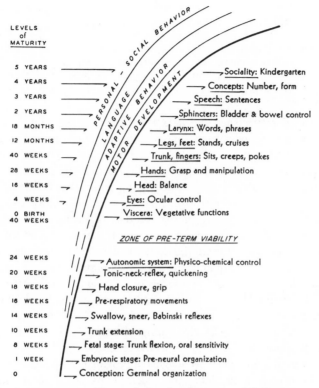

LEVELS
of
MATURITY

5 YEARS	Sociality: Kindergarten
4 YEARS	Concepts: Number, form
3 YEARS	Speech: Sentences
2 YEARS	Sphincters: Bladder & bowel control
18 MONTHS	Larynx: Words, phrases
12 MONTHS	Legs, feet: Stands, cruises
40 WEEKS	Trunk, fingers: Sits, creeps, pokes
28 WEEKS	Hands: Grasp and manipulation
16 WEEKS	Head: Balance
4 WEEKS	Eyes: Ocular control
0 BIRTH 40 WEEKS	Viscera: Vegetative functions

ZONE OF PRE-TERM VIABILITY

24 WEEKS	Autonomic system: Physico-chemical control
20 WEEKS	Tonic-neck-reflex, quickening
18 WEEKS	Hand closure, grip
16 WEEKS	Pre-respiratory movements
14 WEEKS	Swallow, sneer, Babinski reflexes
10 WEEKS	Trunk extension
8 WEEKS	Fetal stage: Trunk flexion, oral sensitivity
1 WEEK	Embryonic stage: Pre-neural organization
0	Conception: Germinal organization

FIGURE 4. *Chart of the development of behavior
in the four major fields.*

so if the school psychologist desires to make a more detailed assessment of the child's developmental history at the earlier chronological ages than afforded by the Vineland Scale.

Figure 3 discloses the four major areas evaluated by this interview procedure. Like the Vineland Scale most of the data is secured from a parent or other person close to the infant or young child. In addition, there is room for clinic observation, actual testing (adaptive items), and material garnered from case records. Gesell and Amatruda [16] based this inventory on the lawfulness of human development anchored in neurological and physical maturity. This is conceptualized in Figure 4 for the first five years after birth. Because of the close relationship between physical and neurological growth on the one hand and functional behavior on the other, this inventory serves as an excellent means for utilizing behavior as the appraisal referent. Gesell and Amatruda offer this rationale: [17]

[16] Gesell and Amatruda, *op. cit.*
[17] *Ibid.,* p. 6.

Behavior Grows. Behavior assumes characteristic patterns as it grows. The principles and practice of developmental diagnosis rest on these two simple but far reaching propositions. Developmental diagnosis is nothing more or less than a discriminating observation of patterns of behavior and their appraisal by comparison with normative patterns. . . .

It takes time to mature. We express the amount of time consumed by *age.* We express the actual maturity attained by equivalent behavior values.

In short, behavior furnished the data for inferences regarding competency.

The normative or average motor development proceeds from gross control of skeletal structure to finely coordinated movements. Social competence is involved in the youngster's ability to relate motorically to others, i.e., by being with, running with, and playing with other children. Adaptive behavior goes beyond motor adjustments to ". . . the ability to utilize the motor equipment appropriately in the solution of practical problems. . . ." How does the child enter into his environment? Language performance, the medium for exchange between the individual and his environment, starts early and continues throughout life. Most important for the school psychologist are the verbalizations and levels of language symbol usage exhibited by the child. Finally, "Personal-Social behavior comprises the child's personal relations to the social culture in which he lives." Many of the items in this area are related to Doll's self-help, eating; dressing; and general comments.

The examiner checks each item as the criteria for each are met. There is no final or over-all score. The psychologist approximates the age zone achieved by the child in each of the four areas assessed. As previously indicated, the normal three-year-old or under would most likely not come to the attention of the school psychologist. The more frequent use for this inventory would be with the school age child referred for appraisal because of physical, neurological, and intellectual retardation.

Here is Billy, last seen by the school psychologist when he was six years, one month of age. Previously he had been evaluated by the psychologist of the cerebral palsy center when he was twenty-five, thirty-two, and forty-eight months old. On the first evaluation, twenty-five months, he achieved at these developmental levels of the *PBI:* motor—irregular at the twelve to eighteen months zone; adaptive—twelve months zone; language was uneven at the ten to twelve months zone; and in personal-social behavior he attained the fifteen months zone. Approximately two years later, forty-eight months of age, Billy achieved as follows: motor—two years zone; adaptive— two years zone; language—two years zone; and personal social irregular at the eighteen months to two years zone. When tested by the school psychologist prior to formal admission to the special adjustment class at seventy-three months of age, Billy measured in the three years zone in motor development, i.e., he could mount and ride a tricycle but he could not stand on one foot, even momentarily. The adaptive test items were satisfactorily completed up to the three years zone. He failed the bridge building and cross imitation items which are at the three and three to six (alternative) levels of the *Revised Stanford-Binet Intelligence Scale,* Form LM. This should give an approximation of Billy's intellectual level. In keeping with the over-all retarded picture, the youngster attained the two years zone in both language development and in personal-social activities. He could repeat only those phrases "drilled into him" by his parents and he was unable to state his name in full. Feeding activities, personal cleanliness, and toileting were almost dependent on mother's assistance. The Ammons *Full-Range Picture Vocabulary Test* [18] and the *Cattell Infant Intelligence Scale* [19] gave results in accord with the Gesell findings.

Allen [20] describes this inventory as a behavior scale that lends itself easily to use in situations where testing procedures need to be, for any reason(s), less formal than usual. The manual, *Developmental Diagnosis,* offers excellent guides with regard to expectancies for the normal and the deviant child. These norms for development are well illustrated and detailed. The normative concepts are carried over into the discussions of such deviant conditions as: mental deficiency, endocrine and convulsive disorders, cerebral and sensory damage, pre-maturity, precocity, and others. Valuable insights into the interdependent roles of neurological, physical, social, personal, and intellectual development are a major advantage in the use of this behavioral inventory.

Two record forms derived from the Gesell and Amatruda approach have been devised by Blum and Fieldsteel: *Cumulative Record of Motor Behavior* [21] and *Cumulative Record of Functional Behavior.*[22] These are actually charts with age in months on the horizontal axis and lists of motor activities and adaptive behavior on the vertical axis of each form. A heavy line printed diagonally across each chart indicates the average rate or level of behavioral development for easy reference with regard to the acceleration or delay in progress toward social competence.

Another approach to the task of appraising social competence, as indicated earlier in this chapter, is to assess various aspects of personality and social living. The logic of this would be the assumption that personal stability and adequacy of social behavior are reflected in the nature of interpersonal relationships which, in turn, may yield bases for inferring the social competence of the individual. This opens the door to a variety of appraisal

[18] Ammons, *op. cit.*

[19] P. Cattell, *The Measurement of Intelligence of Infants and Young Children* (New York: The Psychological Corporation, 1950).

[20] Allen, *op. cit.*

[21] L. H. Blum and N. D. Fieldsteel, *Cumulative Record of Motor Behavior* (New York: The Psychological Corporation, 1952).

[22] L. H. Blum and N. D. Fieldsteel, *Cumulative Record of Functional Behavior* (New York: The Psychological Corporation, 1952).

instruments available to the school psychologist. Among these are the paper and pencil psychometric personality questionnaires, schedules, and inventories and the projective techniques. There are single and multiple dimension psychometric devices that incorporated many specific personality traits and their behavioral manifestations as the referents for evaluation. The school psychologist should experience little difficulty selecting an appropriate test or battery of tests to elicit a picture of those aspects of the functioning individual which may be considered important for appraising social competency. The more frequently used inventories are: the *Personality Inventory* (PI),[23] the *Adjustment Inventory*,[24] and the *Minnesota Multiphasic Personality Inventory* (MMPI).[25] However, these inventories are best used with high school students since the norms and the level of vocabulary do not reach into the elementary grades. These three devices, like most others of this type, consist of questions and items ranging from 125 in the *PI* to 565 in the *MMPI*. The "Yes" and "No" answers are scored and profiles depicting degrees of adjustment for each of the scales, e.g., sociability, dominance-submission in the *PI;* home and health adjustments in the *Adjustment Inventory;* or depression, psychopathic deviate scales in the *MMPI*. By selecting the more "social" oriented scales the psychologist may tease out inferential data for social competency. These may come from the social adjustment scale of the *Adjustment Inventory;* the psychopathic deviate and social introversion scales of the *MMPI;* and the dominance-submission and sociability scales of the *PI*. The examiner must understand, however, that the items, stemming from daily life experiences, are so interwoven,[26] that a score reflecting poor adjustment in one scale of an inventory usually will be reflected in the other scale scores. This is especially characteristic of the *PI* and the *MMPI* since each item is so scored that it contributes in varying degrees to more than one scale or personality dimension within a test.

Mary, a fifteen-year-old bright ninth grader, was referred to the school psychologist's office because of uncontrollable rages, inability to get along with classmates, and poor academic achievement. The teacher insisted on exclusion from the classroom because of her behavior. On the student form of the *Adjustment Inventory* she presented significantly high, and therefore poor, scores in the Home, Social, and Emotional scales. Interviews with the parents by the school social worker disclosed faulty child-parent and immature peer group relationships. As the mother summarized the situation, "It seems as if Mary is growing physically but that's all. She hasn't learned to get

23 R. G. Bernreuter, *The Personality Inventory* (Palo Alto, California: Consulting Psychologists Press, 1931–38).

24 H. M. Bell, *Manual for the Adjustment Inventory* (Stanford, California: Stanford University Press, 1934–38).

25 S. R. Hathaway and J. C. McKinley, *Manual and Booklet for the MMPI* (New York: The Psychological Corporation, 1943).

26 Allen, *op. cit.*

along with us and with children in the neighborhood." An analysis of the Social scale items, clearly coded in the inventory, revealed a dislike for other people, an inability to relate with them in a healthy manner, and a marked discomfort in being with other boys and girls. This emotionally disturbed girl was incapable of meeting the minimum of social amenities. Referral was made to the county child guidance clinic for individual and group therapy.

Another mode of evaluating the social competence of school youngsters is through an assessment of the nature and intensity of the problems affecting them. The SRA *Youth Inventory*, Form S [27] for the junior and senior high school student and the SRA *Junior Inventory*, Form S [28] for youngsters in grades 4 to 8, exemplify this approach. The *Youth Inventory* is a booklet with 296 items each to be checked if the statement constitutes a problem or source of difficulty for the testee. The student indicates the intensity of feeling about the problem statements by checking one of the following three for each item: seriously felt problem, moderately felt problem, small or occasional problem. If the item is not a source of difficulty for the student he X's the "0" box for that particular statement. This is an improvement over the previous form of the inventory since responding with intensity of feeling permits the school psychologist to learn about the student's specific problems *and* how important these are. The areas of students' concerns are subsumed under those having to do with school adjustment, 1. My School; problems of the future, 2. After High School; personal adjustment, 3. About Myself; social adjustment, 4. Getting Along With Others; familial, mostly parental, relationships, 5. My Home And Family; the difficulties in psychosexual role playing, 6. Boy Meets Girl; 7. Health; and 8. Things In General. The last covers a wide range of problems not readily classifiable under the other categories. Social competence may be implied from: 1. My School, 37 items; 2. After High School, 36 items; 4. Getting Along With Others, 43 items; and 6. Boy Meet Girl, 35 items. This inventory is helpful in eliciting the kind of personal-social data essential to a counseling program and for gaining insights into the maturity of the adolescent from the indicated nature of the difficulties assailing the youngster and how he copes with them. While a score may be obtained for comparison with the mean number of items checked by the sampling group as a whole, the real value is having available clues to the problems confronting the youngster. This is made more meaningful for the individual student because the *Manual* [29] contains tables showing the percentages of boys and girls in grades 9 through 12 who marked each of the 296 items as serious, moderate, occasional or no problem. This is especially

[27] H. H. Remmers and B. Shimberg *Manual, SRA Youth Inventory, Form S* (Chicago, Illinois: Science Research Associates, 1950).
[28] H. H. Remmers and R. H. Bauernfeind, *SRA Junior Inventory, Form S* (Chicago, Illinois: Science Research Associates, 1955–57).
[29] Remmers and Shimberg, *op. cit.*, 23–33.

helpful since adolescence is a trying period of life and problems take on varying degrees of significance as the student progresses from grade 9 to 12. In addition to this another helpful device is the Basic Difficulty Score which pinpoints one hundred items judged to be indicators of marked personality difficulties.[30]

From a phenomenological viewpoint, the score on the test is less meaningful than an item analysis and the information this can disclose about the manner in which the student perceives his role and how he fulfills this concept of self in a social milieu. Mary, the bright ninth grader, was also given the Youth Inventory, Form A. The items checked in 1. My School, revealed an inadequate knowledge of study methods and more significant disclosed a paranoid attitude toward her teachers. She felt that they did not understand her and rejected her. With regard to 3. About Myself, Mary admitted to a personal immaturity that sharply pointed up the dynamics behind her social incompetence—resentment, dependence-independence ambivalence beyond normal expectancy for the adolescent in our culture, feelings of insecurity, and an inability to define her role in society. These attitudes spilled over into 4. Getting Along With Others, and 6. Boy Meets Girl. The tragedy of her outbursts and aggressive behavior is quite evident in the latter area of inquiry—Boy Meet Girl. This situation was negatively enhanced by the over-privileged and under-controlled atmosphere in her home under the influence of parents who "had never had it so good" according to their own self descriptions. In short, the SRA Youth Inventory revealed a poor social adjustment and Mary's incompetent modes of dealing with life.

For youngsters in grades 4 through 9, mean age group from ten to fifteen years, the Personality Inventory For Children [31] is available. The five subcategories of the 80-item inventory are: Home, School, Physical Symptoms, Insecurity, and Instability. The child encircles "Yes," or "No," as the particular item applies to him. The final score consists of the number of items checked in the affirmative (with one exception). Normative data indicate the level of overall adjustment. Mean and standard deviation scores for each of the subcategories provide referents for appraising adjustment in each of the five areas. For more detailed analysis the Manual provides a list of the items in each of the five subcategories. This enables the examiner to appraise the social competency of the child in terms of his adaptation to the home and school situations and his personal-emotional adjustment. School children about a year younger, in grades 4 to 8, may indicate their problems in the SRA Junior Inventory, Form S, in the same areas as the senior inventory. Like its older age-level counterpart, this inventory permits the child to note intensity of feeling for each problem-statement.

[30] Ibid., 19–22.
[31] F. Brown, Personality Inventory for Children (New York: The Psychological Corporation, 1935).

The above inventories and questionnaires are self-evaluative. Another mode of appraisal for social competence is the rating scale in which the teacher assesses the child on several personal and social dimensions. The *Behavior Rating Schedules* [32] has two forms, Schedules A and B. In Schedule A, the *Behavior Problem Record,* the teacher checks from a list of fifteen undesirable behavior items any that she has observed in the child. As the teacher reviews her ideas there should emerge a picture of the child's social maturity and adjustment. This data, supplemented by the teacher's judgments on Schedule B, *Behavior Rating Scale,* should give the school psychologist a view of the behaving youngster. While scoring is feasible, of greater use are the individual ratings on the 35-item scale covering intellectual, physical, social, and emotional behavioral manifestations. Division III (Social Behavior) and Division IV (Emotional Adjustment) are the focus for social competence clues. Olson's *Problem Tendencies In Children* [33] should be used as a reference for the interpretation of this test.

The *Pupil Adjustment Inventory* [34] was developed by Group B of the Suburban School Study Council and the Educational Service Bureau of the University of Pennsylvania School of Education. There is a Long Form with 55 scales to be rated and a Short Form with 15 scales. It is used with school age boys and girls and is usually completed by the teacher. The Long Form has eleven social items for rating the student on such attributes as social participation, acceptance, skills, relationships, cooperation, leadership, etc. This scale plus the emotional characteristics items should yield a fairly good description of the youngster's social-emotional maturity and behavior. Since there is little published research as yet, the interested school psychologist may use this device experimentally to build a conceptual basis of the scale's value.

A second major method of appraising social competence is with the projective techniques which are discussed in greater detail in Chapter 11. To select, administer, score, and interpret a projective protocol requires specialized training. The use of projective tests with children is discussed in Allen's *Personality Assessment Procedures.*[35] For a more comprehensive view of this specialized field Rabin and Haworth's *Projective Techniques With Children* is recommended reading.[36]

Caution is desirable and pitfalls need to be pointed out in the use of

---

[32] M. E. Haggerty, W. C. Olson, and E. K. Wickman, *Haggerty-Olson-Wickman Behavior Rating Schedules: Manual* (New York: Harcourt, Brace & World Inc., 1930).

[33] W. C. Olson, *Problem Tendencies in Children* (Minneapolis, Minnesota: University of Minnesota Press, 1930).

[34] Educational Service Bureau, *Pupil Adjustment Inventory: Manual* (Philadelphia, Pennsylvania: University of Pennsylvania, School of Education, 1957), pp. 19–51.

[35] Allen, *op. cit.,* Chaps. 8–14.

[36] A. I. Rabin and M. Haworth, *Projective Techniques with Children* (New York: Grune & Stratton, Inc., 1960).

projective tests with children. Allen [37, 38, 39] calls attention to the inappropriateness of adult standards for the interpretation of children's Rorschach
protocols. Care must be used with all projective devices especially when
interpreting protocol contents within the psychoanalytic framework. "The
cornerstone of the rationale for the use of specially designed stimulus material
with children," writes Allen,[40]

> lies in the still unproved contention that children feel more comfortable
> when associating to animal characters than to humans and to peerage human
> figures than to pictures of adults. . . . A related issue is the suitability of
> using adult concepts in the interpretation of the child's story. This is a
> common practice among the less sophisticated psychologists and leads to
> an unsatisfactory perception of the child's dynamics as they apply to the
> child's behavior. The assumption that the child is a miniature adult is
> untenable both biologically and psychologically.

Used judiciously, the projective techniques do have a place in the school
psychologist's battery of tests.

A final word, the projective procedures should be employed only by
those with adequate supervised training. It is temptingly easy for the unwary
psychologist to go "off the deep end" in the interpretation of projective test
protocols. The tester's theoretical position will play an important role in the
interpretive process. This imposes on the psychologist the responsibility of
being knowledgeable of normative data, modes of adapting test procedures [41]
and the specific nature of the sampling populations discussed by the various
authors offering norms for children and adolescents. The need for caution is
especially encumbent upon those testers whose interpretations are made
within the psychoanalytic context.[42]

While social competence is an inferred attribute of the school youngster
its appraisal must derive from the manner in which the individual meets the
demands by the situations in which the child is immersed. The kinds of
situations that make these inferences possible and plausible vary from
answers to formal test items to real life behavior. Objective observations
yield less subjective evaluations of social competence. On the other hand,
no formal or objective test can equal the real life situation. It seems to be

[37] R. M. Allen, "A Longitudinal Study of Six Rorschach Protocols of a Three-
Year-Old Child," *Child Development*, 22 (1951), 61–70.
[38] ————, "Nine Quarterly Rorschach Records of a Young Girl," *Child Development*, 26 (1955), 63–69.
[39] ————, "An Analysis of Twelve Longitudinal Rorschach Records of One
Child," *Journal of Projection Techniques*, 19 (1955), 111–116.
[40] *Personality Assessment Procedures*, pp. 245–246.
[41] R. M. Allen, "Suggestions for the Adaptive Administration of Intelligence
Tests for Those With Cerebral Palsy," Part II, *Cerebral Palsy Review*, 19 (1958),
6–7. See also R. M. Allen "Cerebral Palsy," in *Psychological Practices with the
Physically Disabled*, ed. J. F. Garrett and E. Levine (New York: Columbia University
Press, 1962).
[42] Allen, "Nine Quarterly Rorschach Records of a Young Girl."

a difficult choice but the school psychologist would do best to confine most of his assessing to tests since real life situations are not readily available nor are valid norms usually at hand. In any event, it should be kept in mind that no test is better than the person using it.

Chapter 13, The School Psychologist's Role With The Mentally Retarded, and Chapter 18, The School Psychologist And Other Types Of Exceptional Children, are excellent sources for the discussion of some of the issues not elaborated in this chapter.

TESTS OF PERCEPTUAL COMPETENCE

The use of the term "perceptual competence" will be limited, for the purpose of this section, to the quality of the reproduction of stimuli under conditions of direct experience by the testee, as in the *Bender Visual Motor Gestalt Test,* or by recall of experience, as in the *Goodenough Draw-A-Person Test.* This narrow view is the specific reason for test administration; scoring the test is the appraisal of perceptual competence.

The more encompassing underlying theoretical assumption in the evaluation of perceptual adequacy is that the child's development involves physical growth as well as psychological maturation. Both are continuing and interrelated processes in which the latter, psychological growth, is dependent upon the intactness of the brain, nervous system, and the sensory-motor apparatus on the one hand, and on the extent of the person's life experiences on the other. The organization, assimilation, and availability of the phenomena in the person's perceptual experience are sampled by the various test procedures. The adequacy of the responses to these test tasks is the raw datum for competency description.

In its broadest meaning perceptual competence is assessed each time a child is given an intelligence test. While not particularly labeled as a measurement of perceptual competence, intelligence tests do tap functions associated with this process. For example, several items in the Adaptive area of the Gesell *Preliminary Behavior Inventory* [43] (see Figure 3) are perception tests— starting with the eighteen-month zone (imitates stroke, |), two-year zone (imitates circular scribble, ⟳), and three-year zone (imitates cross +). These same items are included in standard intelligence tests. Starr [44] reviews the history of the visual-perception-reproduction test as a means of appraising the development of the child. Norms disclose that the ability to copy a test figure is a function of the complexity of the model design *and* the total maturation of the child (as well as the intactness of the brain). As the child matures there is a concomitant increase in the ability to reproduce figures

---

[43] Gesell, *op. cit.,* 1956.
[44] A. S. Starr, "The Rutgers Drawing Test," *The Training School Bulletin,* 49 (1952), 45–64.

from a simple vertical line, at two years, to a diamond, at seven years of age. It is in these terms, reproducibility of figures presented visually or the recall of visual experiences, that the school psychologist will be concerned.

LEITER INTERNATIONAL PERFORMANCE SCALE (LIPS)

As discussed on pages 289 and 567, this is a scale for children of two to eighteen. The items require matching, completing, and reasoning activity dependent upon direct perception and recall of previous experiences. While quite useful with nonhandicapped children, this scale finds more frequent application with the mentally retarded, neurologically impaired, and physically handicapped youngster, especially if the child has difficulty in the use of his hands.[45, 46] This test is particularly useful with the mentally retarded school youngster since the items are more independent of formal schooling than many other intelligence (actually scholastic achievement) tests. LIPS tasks are more "culture fair" at the pre-school and school ages than the Revised Stanford-Binet Scales because understanding of verbal directions and giving verbal responses is eliminated. The population with whom the LIPS may be used also includes illiterates in English, the deaf, and the speech impaired. The unique value, then, is in not penalizing the testee who becomes emotionally disturbed when attempting to comprehend verbal test directions and give verbal replies to test items. It is obvious that this could introduce an artificial intellectual inefficiency that would confound the assessment picture.

Julia, nine years, five months of age, was referred to the school diagnostic center by the classroom teacher because of almost complete inability to read. On the Gates Primary Reading Tests,[47] for grades one and two, this girl was unable to match even one picture with an associated word. On the California Test Of Mental Maturity [48] she scored below the tenth percentile on the test factors and was in the retarded range for language factors (below the first grade). Her Revised Stanford-Binet Scale achievement disclosed three years retardation with a basal at six and terminal age at eight. She accomplished very poorly in the verbal concept items and was unable to reproduce the diamond at Year Seven. When administered the completely nonlanguage LIPS her over-all performance shifted upward into the backward to dull normal range with a basal at Year Seven and terminal at Year Ten. Her ability to deal with verbal and number concepts was her weakest

    45 Allen, "Suggestions for the Adaptive Administration," Part II.
    46 R. M. Allen and M. G. Collins, "Suggestions for the Adaptive Administration of Intelligence Tests for Those with Cerebral Palsy," Part I, Cerebral Palsy Review, 16 (1955), 11–14, 25.
    47 A. I. Gates, Gates Primary Reading Tests, Form 1 (New York: Bureau of Publications, Teachers College, Columbia University, 1934).
    48 E. T. Sullivan, W. W. Clark, and E. W. Tiegs, California Test of Mental Maturity, Primary Series (Los Angeles, California: California Test Bureau, 1946).

area but she could *recognize* and differentiate among various test forms. When asked to *reproduce* some of these forms she failed. Visual recognition, then, is excellent but visual reproduction, a more complex visual-perception process, is poor. On the basis of this information a remedial academic program was devised for Julia. By tapping the less culturally influenced aspects of perception and by making a distinction between visual recognition and visual-motor productivity a more appropriate sampling of ability became feasible and available for academic planning.

THE WECHSLER TESTS

The performance items of the *Wechsler Intelligence Scale For Children* (WISC) [49] are designed to contribute to the global concept of intelligence of which the organization of visually perceived events is an integral part. Children with average or better intelligence are expected to attain higher verbal than performance subtest scores. This is the case because the verbal items are influenced by school experiences. The performance items are less a function of schooling and more closely related to the ordinary expriences of daily living. The Block Design and perhaps the Mazes subtests come closest to appraising the perceptual maturation of the youngster. Each of these subtests can be prorated to yield an over-all score of perceptual competence that makes comparison with the other performance and verbal subtests possible. With the exception of the Mazes subtest the same rationale may be applied to the *Wechsler Adult Intelligence Scale* (WAIS).[50]

THE REVISED BINET SERIES

Perceptual test items have been included in the Binet Scales since the 1916 Terman revision. The latest in the series, Form L-M [51] continues this tradition with the Three-Hole Form Board, Block Building, Copying A Circle, Drawing A Vertical Line, Discrimination Of Animal Pictures, Discrimination Of Forms, Picture Completion: Man, and Copying A Square—items in the pre-school age levels. Starting with Year Six the occurrence of visual perception problems decreases but competency is sparsely appraised at Year Seven, Copying A Diamond; Years Ten and Eleven, Memory For Designs I; Year Twelve, Memory For Designs II; and Year Thirteen, Plan Of Search. These tasks cover the school years and offer the psychologist opportunities for making a brief survey of perceptual competence for school children.

[49] D. Wechsler, *W.I.S. for Children: Manual* (New York: The Psychological Corporation, 1949).

[50] D. Wechsler, *W.A.I.S. Manual* (New York: The Psychological Corporation, 1955).

[51] L. M. Terman and M. A. Merrill, *Stanford-Binet Intelligence Scale, Manual for third revision, Form L-M* (Boston: Houghton Mifflin Company, 1960).

GOODENOUGH DRAW-A-PERSON TEST

This is one of the older and still popular perceptual tests of the recall variety, i.e., the child has as model the life-long experience of his own body image perceived through many sense modalities. Despite the direct observation of an external model, the psychologist close by, it is remarkable how the child's perception of himself is reflected in his figure drawings and how these drawings are commensurate with this developmental level. Goodenough's [52] historical survey is highly recommended reading for its theoretical information. The descriptive norms by Goodenough are excellent insights into the developmental stages of concept formation ranging from the crude stick figure of the five-year-old to the detailed drawing of the twelve-year-old. The final raw score is translated into a mental age and intelligence quotient rating for an over-view of the youngster's perceptual level. Competence, then, is derived from a comparison of chronological age with mental age. Interestingly enough, artistic ability has a negligible affect on the quality of the drawings. A more recent refinement for administering and scoring the Goodenough Test has been written by Harris which will probably enhance the clinical usefulness of this test.

With the development of the projective method in psychological testing, the figure drawing is considered to be the product of the child's self perception, a reflection of such personal attributes as preoccupation, anxiety, degree of freedom to take in experiences, and to make them part of his self concept. This has resulted in a shift from intellectual evaluation to personality appraisal as the major focus of this type of test. Its more modern counterpart is Buck's *House-Tree-Person Test*.[53] Imbedded in the description of personality are inferences with regard to perceptual distortions and level of maturity. Goodenough's summary statement [54] tells the story adequately.

FIGURE COPYING TESTS

In the repertory of the school psychologist desirous of appraising the area of perceptual competence there should be figure copying tests such as Bender's [55] *Visual Motor Gestalt Test* (also known as the *Bender-Gestalt*) and the *Rutgers Drawing Test*.[56] The *Bender-Gestalt* has, by far, the most prolific research literature of the various figure copying tests. The test consists

52 F. L. Goodenough, *Measurement of Intelligence by Drawings* (New York: Harcourt, Brace & World, Inc., 1926), pp. 1–13.

53 Buck, *op. cit.*

54 Goodenough, *op. cit.*, 80.

55 L. Bender, *A Visual Motor Gestalt Test and Its Clinical Use* (American Orthopsychiatry Association Monograph, No. 3, 1938).

56 A. S. Starr, *Rutgers Drawing Test B* (Highland Park, New Jersey, 1959).

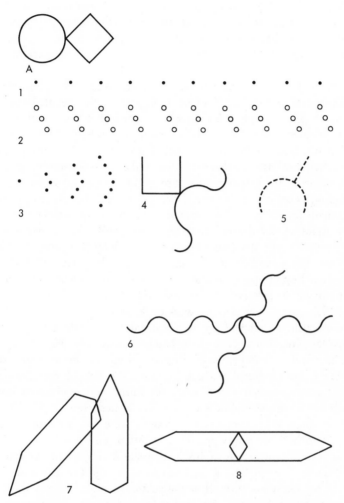

FIGURE 5. *The nine Visual Motor Gestalt figures.*

of nine figures, adapted by Bender from Wertheimer [57] shown in Figure 5. This figure copying test purports to assess visual-motor maturity of the child (and adult) and to be a means of exploring the effects of encephalopathy. Bender [58] defines the "gestalt function" as the manner in which the individual "responds to a given constellation of stimuli as a whole, the response itself being a constellation or pattern or gestalt." In other words, the manner

[57] M. Wertheimer, "Studies in the Theory of Gestalt Psychology," *Psychol Forsch*, 4 (1923), 301–350.
[58] L. Bender, *Instructions for the Use of the Visual Motor Gestalt Test* (Boston: American Orthopsychiatry Association, Inc., 1946), p. 3.

in which the model figures are reproduced by the testee reflects the maturational status of the child's perceptual processes. The scoring is qualitative, subjective, and includes a consideration of such elements as distortions, modifications, magnifications, elaborations, rotations, and organization of the figures on the sheet of paper used for copying them.

Perceptual competence, featured by regressive age-level performance, is amply illustrated in Bender's [59] monograph and in the detailed manual by Pascal and Suttell.[60] While it is generally accepted that this visual perceptual task may be used with the normally progressing school child, most of its application has been in the area of pathology. Within this area its greatest and most frequent use has been to detect the presence of brain damage. Bender's rationale for this particular use of her test emphasizes the notion that the child's copying of the model designs reflects differences in "maturation or growth levels" as well as organic or functional pathology.[61]

For those school psychologists concerned with the formal aspects of scoring the child's reproductions there are manuals by Billingslea,[62] Peek and Quast,[63] and Pascal and Suttell [64] that purport to help with this feature of the test while Koppitz provides the most recent scoring system for children. The latter book is profusely illustrated and is most helpful for objective scoring of the designs. See also the work of Addison and Lonstein.[65, 66]

Harold, thirteen years of age, was referred to the center staff psychologist by the special education teacher of the cerebral palsy class. He was an underachiever in reading despite his intelligence rating in the average category. The *Bender-Gestalt* protocol revealed the usual signs of the presence of brain pathology: gross *gestalten* (configurations) fairly well reproduced but with the details distorted; spaces where parts of the figures were supposed to touch; relationships between portions of the designs were so poorly perceived and executed as to indicate faulty spatial orientation; and finally, verbalizations disclosing Harold's awareness of his inadequate reproduction yet continuing with the same low quality of performance. A significant feature of the reproduced figures was a reversal of the spatial relation between the parts of the figures in plates A, 4, 6, 7, and 8 that have more than one element in the design. This perseveration strongly suggested one possible cause of Harold's

[59] Bender, *op. cit.*, 1938.
[60] G. R. Pascal and B. J. Suttell, *The Bender-Gestalt Test* (New York: Grune & Stratton, Inc., 1951).
[61] Bender, *op. cit.*, 1938.
[62] F. Y. Billingslea, "The Bender-Gestalt," *Journal of Clinical Psychology*, 4, No. 1 (1948), 1–27.
[63] R. M. Peek and W. C. Quast, *A Scoring Scheme for the Bender-Gestalt Test* (Hastings, Minnesota, 1951).
[64] Pascal and Suttell, *op. cit.*
[65] M. Addison, "A Note on the Pascal and Suttell Scoring System of the Bender-Gestalt Test," *Journal of Clinical Psychology*, 8 (1952), 312–313.
[66] M. Lonstein, "A Validation of the Bender-Gestalt Scoring Scheme," *Journal of Consulting Psychology*, 18 (1943), 377–379.

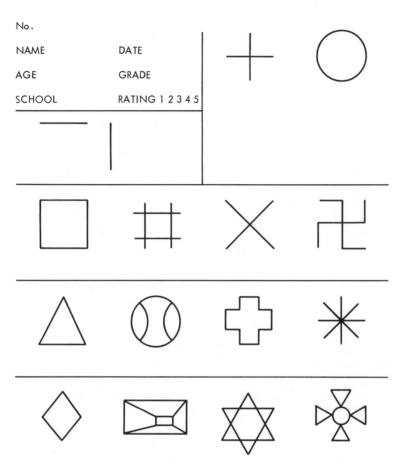

FIGURE 6. *Rutgers Drawing Test.*

reading problem—reversal of figure-parts could be similar to his reversal of parts of words, i.e., letters within words, as he read the printed page. While the disclosure of encephalopathy was not new data in Harold's case, it did yield information regarding an academic difficulty that resulted in adding a remedial reading hour to his schedule at the center's school.

A less widely known, but quite effective, perceptual test is Starr's [67] *Rutgers Drawing Test.* Like the *Bender-Gestalt* it consists of model designs to be copied by the child. Starr comments that this test elicits behavior expressive of the testee's ability (perceptual competence) as well as personality. The two practice lines of the test and the fourteen figures to be copied are shown in Figure 6. The child reproduces each figure in the blank spaces. These

[67] Starr, "Rutgers Drawing Test."

are scored in accordance with samples in the *Manual*.[68] Norms based on total raw scores range from Year Four to Zero to Six to Eleven. The spread is quite narrow but the increase in difficulty of the model designs is steep.

An experimental form, *Rutgers Drawing Test B*, was published by Starr in 1959.[69] It was devised so as to raise the ceiling through the nine year level. The lower age level form, as may be seen in Figure 6, consists of designs with simple straight line and curve combinations. The later form, B, extends the complexity of the figures in terms of their angularity, juncture of lines, intrafigure spatial relationships, and size. Since this form is still in the experimental stage there is no published research literature.

Starr suggests that this nonverbal test, like others of its kind, has the advantage of affording a view of the child that is not the consequence of a halo spread deriving from the child's verbal facility. This is not an uncommon problem with testing of children and adults. While verbal facility does require some intellectual ability, it may be unduly influenced by the flow of words rather than by the quality of the contents. Another testing medium such as this one could give a broader picture of the child.

PROGRESSIVE MATRICES

A more recent test on the American scene is Raven's (1947) *Progressive Matrices Test*,[70] booklet form. This technique was not designed primarily to assess intelligence but rather as a means of ascertaining ability to solve problems of spatial organization. In this process the testee selects one of several alternatives to fill a gap in a large design. Some of the matrices are simple completion tasks with lines or form as the major clue. These tasks are almost self-completing and requiring the ability to perceive and follow discontinued lines or recognize forms for satisfactory performance. Other design-completion tasks are much more complex than line or form matching. It is in these items that the perception goes beyond recognition to include reasoning of a more complex sort to solve the problem of selection. The level of perceptual competence beyond simple matching and recognition is derived from the latter items of each of the individual tests which are successfully completed. This test is especially applicable with children who are unable to verbalize or are motorically handicapped. Norms based on American elementary school children from six years to twelve years, five months of age are reported by Green and Ewert.[71] The majority of the published studies with this test has been with neurologically handicapped and mentally retarded

---

68 *Ibid.*
69 Starr, "Rutgers Drawing Test B."
70 J. C. Raven, *Progressive Matrices* (London: H. K. Lewis, 1947).
71 M. W. Green and J. C. Ewert, "Normative Data on Progressive Matrices," *Journal of Consulting Psychology*, 19 (1955), 139–142.

children.[72, 73, 74] The purposes of many of these studies may be categorized as: 1) to ascertain the nature of matrix-completion errors as possible indices to the perceptual distortions characteristic of psychologically and neurologically defined groups of children; and 2) attempts to utilize misperceptions as bases for differential diagnoses between neuropathological conditions and within a particular diagnostic category. Costello, for example, reported a unique selection error by a group of cerebral palsied children that distinguished them from a group of post-polio youngsters. Knehr's work with this instrument as a test of intelligence independent of formal school experiences led him to conclude that the *Progressive Matrices* may suggest the histopathology involved in intellectual impairment. An analysis of the performance of the encephalopathic group disclosed the usual perseverative and perceptual distortions associated with this condition. Hudson [75] was able to establish significant differences between athetoid and spastic cerebral palsied children with this test. The difficulties in perception mirror a lowered efficiency or level of competence. A significant issue involved in misperception is the accompanying and resultant dysfunctions that interfere with learning. It is this which should more directly concern the school psychologist and the nature of his report to the classroom teacher.

John, fourteen years of age and moderately cerebral palsied, was referred for pre-vocational evaluation and tryout prior to assignment to the work-sample unit of the local rehabilitation center. He achieved at the lowest five per cent level on the *PM* indicating a serious impairment in his perception of visually presented material. In addition he was markedly retarded intellectually. The decision of the center's guidance and vocational committee was strongly influenced by this information. John was assigned to the building maintenance (cleaning) work-sample class rather than to those pre-vocational tryout samples requiring the perception of space relationships such as assembling flashlight cases or fountain pens. The selected pre-vocational work-sample minimizes the effects of perceptual distortion that was characteristic of John's handling of visually presented material. Furthermore, ascertaining and focusing on the nature of John's difficulty led to the selection of a more realistic pre-vocational job sampling goal.

Frostig Developmental Test of Visual Perception. A test in this area was published in 1961 by Frostig in collaboration with Lefever and Whittlesey—

[72] C. G. Costello, "Aphasic Cerebral Palsied Children's Wrong Answers on Raven's 'Progressive Matrices,'" *Journal of Clinical Psychology*, 15 (1959), 76–77.

[73] C. A. Knehr, "Progressive Matrices Findings Associated with Cerebral Histopathology," *Perceptual Motor Skills*, 6 (1956), 249–254.

[74] V. S. Tracht, "Preliminary Findings on Testing the Cerebral Palsied with Raven's 'Progressive Matrices,'" *Journal of Exceptional Children*, 15 (1948), 77–79.

[75] A. Hudson, *A Comparative Study of the Test Response of Two Groups of Cerebral Palsied Children: Athetoid and Spastic*, Doctoral dissertation, University of Wisconsin, 1952.

Marianne Frostig Developmental Test of Visual Perception.[76] Norms are based on over 1800 nursery school and public school children between the ages of three and nine years, three months. Normative curves drawn from the standardization sample support Piaget's contention that maximum perceptual development occurs between the ages of four and six, with little growth after the age of approximately seven and one-half, when cognitive functions begin to predominate. The instructions for administering the test have now been translated into German, and norms are now being obtained in England, Austria, and Australia.

The test, designed to measure certain operationally defined perceptual functions, contains five subtests: eye-motor coordination, perception of figure-ground relationships, of constancy of shape, of position in space, and of spatial relationships. (See Figure 7). It it a paper-and-pencil test that may be easily administered either individually or to groups. The time required for group administration is less than one hour; individual administration takes approximately twenty-five minutes. Scoring is objective and requires from five to ten minutes. The child's raw score for each subtest is converted into a perceptual age equivalent (representing the age at which the average child achieves this score). A perceptual quotient (PQ) can then be derived in a manner similar to that used for determining an intelligence quotient (IQ).

The test has proven useful as a screening tool with groups of kindergarten and first grade children, since it permits identification of those children who need special perceptual training. By indicating the areas of visual perceptual disability, it also provides the basis for instituting remedial programs.*

The authors report a significant correlation between scores on the perceptual test for kindergarten and first grade children and ratings for classroom adjustment assigned by their teachers. (This rating may be conceptualized as a measure of school readiness.) For a sample of 373 kindergarten children, a two-by-two chi square correlation of 45.56 (significant beyond the .001 level) was found between scores below 90 on the perceptual test and ratings of maladjustment in the classroom; for 277 first grade children the chi square value was 12.82 (also significant beyond the .001 level); the correlation for 283 second grade children was insignificant.

---

[76] M. Frostig, *Developmental Test of Visual Perception* (3rd ed.) (Los Angeles, California: Marianne Frostig School for Educational Therapy). See also M. Frostig, D. W. Lefever, and J. R. B. Whittlesey, "A developmental Test for visual perception for evaluating normal and neurologically handicapped children," *Perceptual Motor Skills*, 12 (1961), 383–394; P. Maslow, *et al.*, The Marianne Frostig Developmental Test of Visual Perception, *Perceptual Motor Skills*, 19 (1964), 463–499; and M. Frostig, *et al.*, *Administration and Scoring Manual* (Palo Alto, California: Consulting Psychologists Press, 1964).

* Material especially designed to help children with disabilities in any of the areas sampled by the test has been developed by Frostig and published by Follett, and preliminary research has demonstrated that visual perceptual difficulties as measured by the test can be ameliorated by group training in a regular school situation.

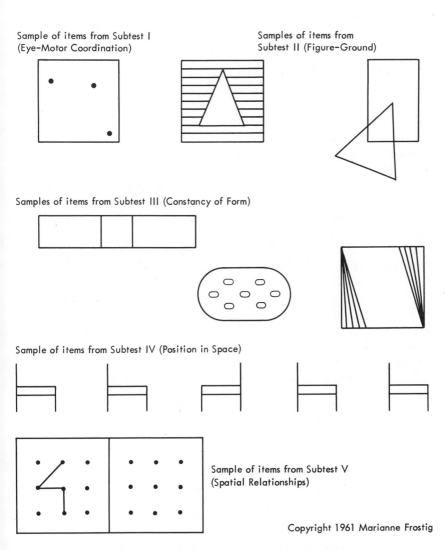

Sample of items from Subtest I
(Eye-Motor Coordination)

Samples of items from
Subtest II (Figure-Ground)

Samples of items from Subtest III (Constancy of Form)

Sample of items from Subtest IV (Position in Space)

Sample of items from Subtest V
(Spatial Relationships)

Copyright 1961 Marianne Frostig

FIGURE 7. *Marianne Frostig Developmental Test
of Visual Perception.*

A group of 71 neurologically handicapped children between three and
nine years of age have also been tested with the Frostig test. These children
performed significantly poorer on the test than the nursery and public school
sample. But the test constructors point out that lowered achievement on the
test items does not necessarily reflect organically based perceptual difficulties.

They write (see fn. 76), "Children who deviate from the norm can be identified and the range and severity of perceptual disabilities measured [by the test], regardless of the etiolɔgy, *be it brain injury, developmental lag, or emotional disturbance*" (authors' italics). The authors acknowledge that a test of perceptual ability *per se* cannot establish the causes of disturbances; etiology can only be assessed by a *battery* of tests, medical as well as psychological. Their test is intended only to assess perceptual difficulties and the level of perceptual maturation. They suggest, however, that further research with various clinically defined groups may establish its usefulness as a diagnostic screening tool for indicating etiology. Further research is especially important for determining the presence or absence of differential patterns of responses in the subtests and/or individual test items.

The test was basically designed as a tool to evaluate the perceptual readiness for school learning in kindergarten and first grade and to provide the basis for training and remediation in visual perceptual abilities. It can also be helpful in determining remedial reading programs. Schiffman [77] has mentioned it as one of the fundamental tests to be included in a battery for complete reading analysis. It is also useful as part of a battery for establishing the diagnosis of neurological dysfunctions.

The final test in this chapter is representative of techniques employed to ascertain the specific language handicap(s) of the neurologically impaired person. Accordingly, this test is seldom used with the non-neurologically involved child.

HALSTEAD-WEPMAN SCREENING TEST FOR APHASIA

This test [78] seeks to specify language dysfunctions which are encompassed by the generic term *aphasia*. These dysfunctions are traceable to perceptual distortions and disabilities attributable to pathologic brain tissue (except those conditions definitely the result of poor habits). The perceptual handicap(s) impairs learning processes with subsequent faulty response patterns.

The diagnostic nature of this test probes: 1) agnosia or extent of loss of the child's ability to recognize and comprehend stimuli received through the various sense modalities—these are the receptive functions; 2) apraxia or the degree of ability to perform various acts utilizing language and other symbols—these are the expressive or motor functions; 3) anomia or impaired ability to name objects, events, and other phenomena; 4) dysarthria or spoken language difficulties; and 5) paraphasia or receptive and expressive defects in

---

[77] Gilbert Schiffman, "Dyslexia as an Educational Phenomenon: Its Recognition and Treatment," in *Reading Disability: Progress and Research Needs in Dyslexia*, ed. John Money (Baltimore: The Johns Hopkins Press, 1962), p. 51.

[78] W. C. Halstead and J. M. Wepman, "The Halstead-Wepman Aphasia Screening Test," *Journal of Speech and Hearing Disorders*, 14 (1949), 9–15.

the proper use of the structure of language such as syntax and grammar. All of these are subsumed under the term *aphasia* or difficulty with language due to brain tissue lesion and not to mental deficiency or sensory-motor impairment alone.

The test wheel used in this examining procedure will hold the child's interest because it is so different from the usual testing experience. The results are not scored as to yield an over-all rating. Rather, each item is analyzed for its contribution to the picture of specific disabilities and handicaps in the five categories listed above.

John, discussed previously, was given the *Halstead-Wepman Screening Test*. On the twelve agnosia subtests he did well with those tasks dependent on auditory and tactual sense modalities. Visually presented materials resulted in extremely poor attainment. The latter level of performance characterized his ability to reproduce designs, to write words, and to draw figures exposed by the test wheel. He appeared to have receptive-expressive aphasia for handling language symbolization requiring the organization of visual stimuli.

The Eisenson [79] *Examining For Aphasia* is a briefer test for expressive and receptive aphasia.

In the space limitation of one chapter much that is relevant and significant for the appraisal of social and perceptual competence is either briefly mentioned or omitted entirely. Theoretical implications for practical application and interpretation are necessarily minimal. Details for the tests discussed and alluded to in this chapter will be found in the pertinent references below, as well as in the chapter's footnotes.

Selected Supplementary Readings

Allen, R. M., and G. H. Frank, "Experimental Variation of the Mode of Reproduction of the Bender Gestalt Stimuli," *Journal of Clinical Psychology*, 19 (1963), 212–214.

Allen, Robert M., and Thomas W. Jefferson, *Psychological Evaluation of the Cerebral Palsied Person: Intellectual, Personality, and Vocational Applications*. Springfield, Illinois: Charles C Thomas, Publisher, 1962.

Allen, R. M., and R. W. Jones, "Perceptual, Conceptual, and Psycholinguistic Evaluation of the Mentally Retarded Child," in *Mental Retardation*, ed. A. Baumeister. Chicago: Aldine, 1966.

————, and T. D. Haupt, "A Note of Caution for the Research Use of the Frostig Test with Mentally Retarded Children," *Perceptual Motor Skills*, 21 (1965), 237–238.

[79] J. Eisenson, *Examining for Aphasia* (New York: The Psychological Corporation, 1954).

————, "Visual Perceptual Abilities and Intelligence in Mental Retardates," *Journal of Clincial Psychology*, 21 (1965), 299–300.

Ayers, Jean, A *Study of Perceptual Problems*, Workshop Report at San Francisco State College, United Cerebral Association; San Francisco, 1963.

Bender, Lauretta, *Psychopathology of Children with Organic Brain Disorders*. Springfield, Illinois: Charles C Thomas, Publisher, 1956.

Birch, Herbert G., ed., *Brain Damage in Children: The Biological Social Aspects*. Baltimore: The Williams & Wilkins, Co., 1964.

Boydston, Eleanor H., ed., *Neurologically Handicapping Conditions in Children: Implications for Maternal and Child Health and Crippled Children's Programs*. Berkeley: University of California Press, 1961.

Chansky, Norman M., "Perceptual Training with Elementary School Under-Achievers," *Journal of School Psychology*, I, No. 1 (January, 1963), 33–41.

Clawson, Aileen, *The Bender Visual Motor Gestalt Test for Children: a Manual*. Beverly Hills, California: Western Psychological Services, Inc., 1962.

Cruickshank, William C., Frances A. Bentzen, Frederick H. Ratzeburg, and Miriam T. Tannhauser, A *Teaching Method for Brain-Injured and Hyperactive Children*. Syracuse: Syracuse University Press, 1961.

Daley, William T., ed., *Speech and Language Therapy with the Brain-Damaged Child*. Washington, D. C.: Catholic University of America Press, 1962.

Frostig, Marianne, "Visual Perception in the Brain-Injured Child," *American Journal of Orthopsychiatry*, XXXIII (1963), 665–671.

Fuller, G. B., and J. T. Laird, "Minnesota-Percepto Diagnostic Test," *Journal of Clinical Psychology*, Monograph Supplement No. 16 (1963), p. 1033.

Fullmer, B. G., "Perceptual Considerations in Children with a Reading Disability," *Psychology in the Schools*, I (July, 1964), 314–318.

Graham, F. K., and B. S. Kendall, *Memory-for-Designs Test*. Missoula, Montana: Psychological Test Specialists, 1960.

Herbert, M., "The Concept of Testing of Brain Damage in Children: A Review," *Journal of Child Psychiatry and Psychology*, 5 (1964), 197–216.

Ilg, Frances L., and Louise Bates Ames, *School Readiness, Behavior Tests Used at the Gesell Institute*. New York: Harper & Row, Publishers, 1964.

Kagan, Jerome, "Body Build and Conceptual Impulsity in Children," *Journal of Personality*, 34 (March, 1966), 118–128.

Keogh, B., "School Achievement Associated with Successful Performance on the Bender Gestalt Test," *Journal of School Psychologists*, 3 (1965), 37–40.

Koppitz, Elizabeth, *The Bender Gestalt Test for Young Children*. New York: Grune & Stratton, Inc., 1963.

————, *The Bender Gestalt Test With the Human Figure Drawing Test for Young School Children*. Columbus, Ohio: Ohio Department of Education, 1962.

————, Verdena Mardis, and Thomas Stephens, "A Note on Screening School Beginners with the Bender Gestalt Test," *Journal of Educational Psychology*, 52 (1961), 80–81.

Lambert, N., and H. Grossman, *Problems in Determining the Etiology of Learning and Behavior Handicaps*. Sacramento, Calif.: California Department of Education, 1964.

Lefkowitz, Monroe, M., "Aggression and Size of Human Figure Drawings," *Psychology in the Schools*, I, No. 3 (July, 1964), 312–313.

Light, Beulah, ed., *A Symposium: The Mentally Retarded Child With Accompanying Neurological Handicaps: Current Concepts in the Neurology of Learning*, especially, M. Frostig and D. Horne, "Assessment of Visual Perception and Its Importance in Education," *The A.A.A.D. Education Reporter*, II (April, 1962).

McBeath, M., "Behavioral Characteristics of Visually Perceptually Handicapped and Non-Handicapped Kindergartners," *Psychology in the Schools*, 3 (July, 1966), 264–266.

Mecham, M. J., *Verbal Language Development Scale*. Minneapolis, Minn.: American Guidance Service, 1958.

Reitan, Ralph M., "Psychological Deficit," *Annual Review of Psychology*, Vol. 13, ed. P. Farnsworth, O. McMemar, and Q. McMemar. Palo Alto, California: Annual Reviews, Inc., 1962.

Singh, Balwant, "The Bender Gestalt as a Group Test," *Ontario Journal of Educational Research*, 8 (Autumn, 1965), 35–45.

Spivak, George, "Perceptual Processes," Chapter 15, *Handbook of Mental Deficiency Research*, ed. N. Ellis. New York: McGraw-Hill Book Company, 1963.

Tolor, Alexander, and Herbert C. Schulberg, *An Evaluation of the Bender-Gestalt Test*. Springfield, Illinois: Charles C Thomas, Publisher, 1963.

Taylor, Edith Meyer, *Psychological Appraisal of Children with Cerebral Defects*. Cambridge, Mass.: Harvard University Press, 1959.

HENRY PLATT

JACK I. BARDON

13

The School Psychologist's Role with the Mentally Retarded

Public interest in the problems of mentally retarded children continues to grow. Spurred on by dedicated parent groups and by governmental and private grant-giving agencies, the broad spectrum of research and service has expanded to include all phases of concern for the retarded. Public interest has been sharpened by no less than the former president of the United States, John F. Kennedy, whose family interest in retardation brought national attention to this problem.

The literature during the past five years shows considerable interest in basic research related to the etiology of mental deficiency, in the identification and diagnosis of the mentally retarded child, and in his training, education, and rehabilitation. There is ever-increasing awareness that special provisions must be made in the schools for the education of intellectually retarded children and youth. Crowded state institutions, long waiting lists for admission to such institutions, and criticism of the schools' efforts to provide for exceptional children of all kinds have served to center attention on the role schools should play in educating and training retardates.

Many states have responded to these multiple problems by passing laws making public education mandatory for both severely and moderately retarded children and have assisted local schools in setting up special education facilities. Other states have provided permissive legislation calculated to assist school in the same ways.

It is interesting to note that the mentally handicapped child was included as a major topic for discussion at the 1960 White House Conference on Children and Youth for the first time since these conferences were held. In Forum XV—"The Young with Mental Handicaps"—such conditions as "convulsive seizures, psychoses, serious emotional disturbances, or severe learning problems" were included in addition to mental retardation.[1, 2]

BROADENING ROLE OF SCHOOL PSYCHOLOGIST
WITH THE RETARDED

Concern for the retarded pupil in the schools is deeply embedded in the historical antecedents of present-day school psychology. The original Binet-Simon Scale to measure intelligence, published in 1905, was constructed at the request of Paris school officials who were interested in distinguishing the genuinely dull from others in the schools so that a special, simplified curriculum could be planned for them.[3] Among the first assignments given to school psychologists was that of study of individual differences so that educational planning for the non-learner or slow-learner could take place.

It is not surprising, then, that school psychologists continue to serve as assessors of intellectual retardation. What is more important is the extent to which they have assumed responsibility for other phases of service to the retarded and a position of authority as experts in retardation. In at least 17 states, screening of children for admission to special classes for the retarded is based primarily on psychological evaluation.[4] As school psychology moved closer to the status of a professional specialty, and as both applied and academic psychology became more sophisticated and refined, the number of ways in which psychologists could serve the school multiplied. At the White House Conference, emphasis was placed on

[1] Project on Technical Planning in Mental Retardation of the American Association on Mental Deficiency, *Project News*, 4 (1960), 1–6.

[2] U. S. Government Printing Office, *Recommendations: Composite Report of Forum Findings—1960 White House Conference* (Washington, D. C., 1960).

[3] L. J. Cronbach, *Essentials of Psychological Testing*, 2nd ed. (New York: Harper & Row, Publishers, 1960).

[4] U. S. Office of Education, *Preparation of Mentally Retarded Youth for Gainful Employment*, Bull. No. 28 (Washington, D. C., 1959).

developing a greater awareness that the needs of the mentally handicapped child should be recognized as those encompassing all children, with additional needs, however, for special care arising from the nature of the handicap. In accordance with this philosophy, school psychologists work with many types of children irrespective of diagnostic nomenclature. The variety of tools and procedures available for assisting children, parents, and teachers in different ways have been adapted for use when concern is for the retarded.

The school psychologist's role with mentally retarded children and youth will, of course, vary with the academic setting and with the facilities that are available. As the need for various types of school psychological services increases it becomes difficult for him to keep up with demands for direct services to children. The psychologist seeks, and often finds, other methods for reaching both students and staff in practical ways.

By serving as a resource person or consultant to the teachers, administrative personnel, and special education services in the school, the psychologist can better integrate his work into a total educational plan while eventually reaching many more children. When children are referred to the psychologist for service, a mutual sharing of observations and findings with other school personnel may lead to a meaningful learning experience for them as well as for the child. The recognition that final responsibility for the welfare of the individual child rests with the classroom teacher, under the general authority of the school administrator, helps the psychologist to recognize the limitations of his responsibilities and to save him from the dangers of feeling or being placed in a position of omnipotence.

The school psychologist in his consultant role can help to establish and maintain a "psychological climate" for application of mental health concepts and dynamic educational techniques to the work with the child. The teaching process and the role of the teacher may be enhanced through greater insight into the behavior dynamics of children in general as well as of the child presenting problems of intellectual retardation. The school psychologist should be on the alert for ways and means of imparting psychological knowledge to school personnel so that he may help them to develop greater understanding of the educational, social, and personal needs of the retarded child referred for psychological services.

This framework for psychological service in the schools is in keeping with the "new look" in clinical psychology as well. Its applicability to work with the retarded will be pointed out where appropriate in the rest of this chapter.

Although the setting may vary, and the applicability of a broad consultative function may be more or less possible in different school settings as suggested in Chapter 3, the literature and experience show that the school psychologist's role with the mentally retarded generally encompasses the manifold areas of diagnosis of intellectual retardation and consultation on: curriculum planning, evaluation of vocational potential, and referral to community resources for specialized services. It is likely that diagnosis still remains the core activity for most school psychologists as they work with the retarded. However, more time is being given to psychological counseling and consultation with parents than was previously. There is also an increasing interest in research, usually of an applied nature, and in some instances this is considered an integral part of the psychological services provided to the school.

DEFINITION OF MENTAL RETARDATION NOT CLEAR

A major stumbling block encountered in understanding the role of the school psychologist working with the mentally retarded is the lack of a universally accepted definition of mental retardation. The mentally retarded do not constitute a homogeneous group any more than do many other groups identified by a single label. A recent manual on terminology and classification in mental retardation published by the American Association on Mental Deficiency incorporated under this rubric "all of the meanings that have been ascribed historically to such concepts as amentia, feeble-mindedness, mental deficiency, mental subnormality, idiocy, imbecility, moronity." [5]

The AAMD manual indicates that "mental retardation refers to subaverage general intellectual functioning that originates during the developmental period and is associated with impairment in one or more of the following: maturation, learning, and social adjustment." According to the manual, the choice of the term "mental retardation" was predicated on the basis that "it appears to be the most preferred term among professional personnel of all disciplines concerned."

The American Psychiatric Association has continued to use the term Mental Deficiency in its Manual of Mental Disorders and has included in this category only those cases "presenting primarily a defect of intelligence existing since birth, without demonstrated organic brain disease or known prenatal cause." They have further divided this group into three levels: mild, meaning "dull normal"; moderate, meaning I.Q.'s of approximately 50–70; and severe, meaning I.Q. below 50. [6]

Mental retardation, then, may be seen as a result of a disease process or as a behavioral description of intellectual and social functioning. The problem is further complicated for the school psychologist who must also be aware of how the definition fits the school curriculum. When a school

[5] R. Heber, *A Manual on Terminology and Classification in Mental Retardation,* Monograph Supplement to *Amer. J. Ment. Defic.,* **64,** No. 3 (1959).

[6] Diagnostic and Statistical Manual of Mental Disorders (Washington, D. C.: American Psychiatric Association, 1952).

psychologist classifies a child as mentally retarded, he must be cognizant of both general usage of the term and its particular relevance to the school.

In an attempt to untangle this complicating factor, a number of states have provided educationally oriented definitions intended to help schools classify children for special classes provided by law. These definitions also vary, but, in general, two categories have been established—the trainable and the educable retarded. Although each state has worded its definitions differently, there is enough consensus on major points to make the terms somewhat meaningful across state lines. For example, several definitions of "trainable" are given below.[7]

> Massachusetts—"children who receive a score of from 20 to 49 on an intelligence test approved by the Department of Mental Health and Education and administered by an examiner approved by said departments; and in exceptional cases other children who, in the opinion of the Superintendent of Schools, and subject to the approval of the Department of Education, are incapable of performing the school work of Grade 1."

> California—"minors who do not come within the provisions (for the educable mentally retarded) . . . who may be expected to benefit from special educational facilities designed to educate and train them to further their individual acceptance, social adjustment, and economic usefulness in their homes and within a sheltered environment."

> New Jersey—"those who are so severely retarded or socially immature that they cannot be classified as educable but are, notwithstanding, potentially capable of self-help, of communicating satisfactorily, of participating in groups, of directing their behavior so as not to be dangerous to themselves or others, and of achieving with training some degree of personal independence and social or economic usefulness within sheltered environments."

> Illinois—"trainable mentally handicapped children who are incapable of being educated properly and efficiently through ordinary classroom instruction, or special educational facilities for educable mentally handicapped children . . . but who may be expected to benefit from training in a group setting designed to further their social adjustment and economic usefulness in their homes or in a sheltered environment."

Differences will also be found in the definitions of the educable mentally retarded. In general, these definitions concern themselves with those children whose I.Q.'s are somewhere in the 50–75 I.Q. range. One acceptable definition of the educable retarded child is New Jersey's—"those who may be expected to succeed with a minimum of supervision in homes and schools and community life and are characterized particularly by reasonable expectation that at maturity they will be capable of vocational and social independence in competitive environment." [8]

[7] S. A. Kirk, *Public School Provisions for Severely Retarded Children; A Survey of Practices in the United States* (N. Y. State Interdepartmental Health Resources Board, July, 1957).

[8] New Jersey State Department of Education, *Mentally Retarded* (Trenton, N. J., 1960).

An examination of these few definitions indicates that the role of the school psychologist will differ, in terms of the various state educational codes in the educational classification of retardates. In some states, the criteria for classification are such that clinical judgment plays an important part in the classification procedure while in others, I.Q. is the major determining factor. It is of some interest to note here how the role of the school psychologist is in a very real measure determined by definitions and laws rather than by professional considerations.

School psychologists find themselves, for better or worse, tied to state classification criteria and definitions. Sometimes, such definitions serve as useful standards for organizing special classes. In other instances, the school psychologist must use all his clinical skill and knowledge of educational procedures to help provide adequate educational opportunities for the retarded despite the state definitions.

The term "mentally retarded" as employed in this chapter will apply to children who have been diagnosed by procedures that include an individual psychological evaluation as being intellectually retarded and are considered incapable of deriving maximum academic benefits from the regular classroom instruction.

Evaluation of Mental Retardation

As already indicated, the identification of mentally retarded children to determine special class eligibility and the subsequent classification and placement of these children constitute an important function of the school psychologist. The psychologist may be asked to judge whether a child is capable of going to school at all, whether he would better profit from a special program for the mentally retarded, or whether he can adapt successfully to a regular classroom.[9] The degree of responsibility he assumes in the initial screening of the child, in establishing a diagnosis of mental retardation, and in the evaluation of problems associated with the condition will vary with the school setting.

In a small school system, the psychologist may work independently and have the major responsibility for such activity. A larger school setting may utilize the combined skills of such disciplines as those represented by the psychiatrist, psychologist, social worker, and remedial and teaching personnel in an interdisciplinary team approach, to provide a more comprehensive evaluation and educational plan for the child. At the 1960 White House Conference a recommendation was made that all schools provide multidisciplinary services for identification of mental handicaps at the start of a child's school experience, with an on-going process of evaluation throughout his

[9] L. F. Cain, "Basic Assessment by the School Psychologist," *Training School Bulletin*, 52, No. 9 (1956), 218.

education. The multidisciplinary approach to assessment offers the opportunity for thoroughness not possible with the single diagnostician, but it also poses a problem for the school psychologist who may be relegated to the role of "I.Q. tester" unless he is prepared to see his examination procedures in broader scope.

Regardless of who is involved in the examination procedures, a comprehensive assessment should be made of the child's intellectual and emotional status, his social competence, his grade readiness and academic potential. These data should be evaluated in the light of considerable knowledge about the child's home conditions and the school situation in which he will be expected to function. It is this last factor, the school, which gives the school psychologist, or team, the opportunity to offer a unique contribution to the assessment procedure and which makes classification for school purposes different from the more usual, straightforward clinical approach.

The clinical examiner, in his office or clinic, can provide important basic information by which the classification of mental retardation and the level of retardation can be determined. But classification for placement in the school also involves the translation of such information to the context of the school. For example, what is known about the child's school, his classroom, the dynamics of the interaction among the children in that room? How can the examiner determine whether or not a child is incapable of being educated efficiently through ordinary classroom instruction unless he knows what the school is doing and how it is structured? How can one say a child can or cannot profit from group experience and instruction unless he knows something about the groups involved? [10] Considerations such as these, incorporated in the classification and assessment procedure, require a specialized knowledge of the school and give the school psychologist an approach to assessment which differs from the non-school oriented psychologist.

INITIAL PSYCHOLOGICAL EVALUATION

In preparing for the initial psychological evaluation interview, care must be taken to structure the scene to insure optimal test performance. The mentally retarded child usually reflects a short attention span and low frustration tolerance. His motivation may be erratic and he may not respond too well to the test materials. Whenever possible, short breaks should be taken during a testing session to allow the child some relaxation. It will also provide an opportunity for stimulating his curiosity in the testing situation.

In testing young children, it may be helpful to have the child's mother sit in the examination room during the evaluation as an aid to enlisting the child's best efforts during the session. She should remain in the background

---

[10] Jack I. Bardon and Stanley I. Alprin, "An Approach to the Educational Classification of Mentally Retarded Children," *Exceptional Children*, 27 (1961), 235–238.

and must not, of course, coach the child. Richey [11] points out that the child's mother may sometimes be able to help the examiner establish whether failure on a test item was actually due to the child's inability to handle it, allowing, of course, for some degree of subjectivity on her part. This procedure also serves as a way of helping the mother understand the evaluation and may provide the rapport which permits future counseling to take place.

The psychological evaluation should take a number of factors into consideration in order to obtain a more realistic picture of the retarded child's potentials and the school's responsibility for his educational program. For example, although the intelligence test is utilized as an important predictor of school performance, attention must be given to the child's physical status, self-help abilities, and social and emotional characteristics. If medical records are available, they should be reviewed to note whether there are any debilitating handicaps that might limit the use of particular test materials. Consideration should also be given to possible opportunities for non-academic functioning in the community.[12]

An all important goal in the diagnosis is to determine, insofar as possible, the etiology and extent of the mental retardation. Not only is this necessary for proper school classification where two or more levels of classes are available, but the educational procedures used will depend on what can be learned about cause and resultant effects. Psychologists are now paying more attention to the children who reflect pseudo-retardation. These children appear to be mentally limited when they actually may have greater intellectual potentials than their overt behavior reflects.

For example, there may be a background of delayed motor and speech development that may be attributed to anoxia at birth, or some other postnatal damage to the brain. It should be noted, however, that in many instances intact areas may take over the functions ordinarily carried out by the areas which are traumatized.[13] The intellectual potential may remain within an average or even higher range despite the delayed development, and this needs to be considered in evaluation and educational planning for the child.

Handicaps of vision and hearing may influence the diagnosis. A visual defect in fusion of images may not be apparent in the usual tests for vision. Hearing defects, if undetected, may result in the child not understanding commands or instructions, and he may appear retarded in his dealings with others. Childhood schizophrenia has been confused with feeblemindedness.

[11] Marjorie H. Richey, "Psychological Procedures in the Diagnosis of Mental Retardation," *Exceptional Children*, 27 (1960), 6–10.
[12] I. Lorge, "Planning Cooperative Utilization of Data on the Mentally Retarded," *American Journal of Mental Deficiencies*, 64 (1959), 269–277.
[13] H. Bakwin and Ruth M. Bakwin, *Clinical Management of Behavior Disorders in Children* (Philadelphia: W. B. Saunders Co., 1953), pp. 277–280.

Differential diagnosis is usually made on the basis of a history of normal development and then regression, as well as on the presence of other symptoms and signs of schizophrenia. Severe deprivation, emotional and cultural, may result in intellectual performance that places a child in a range usually considered retarded.

It is not sufficient to merely label the child as defective, slow, brain-injured, emotionally disturbed, etc. Wide variations in behavior occur among the mentally retarded as among normal children. In order to understand the child and constructively plan for his future, much more needs to be known about his actual functioning level and capacity for growth. The need is great for more readily accessible community facilities for diagnosis and identification of children suspected of a mental handicap.

Intelligence testing. While they may leave much to be desired, the currently available intelligence tests do represent objective, standardized procedures for measuring intelligence and serve as a useful basis for defining mental retardation.

Psychologists are usually expected to include an individually administered test of intelligence in the psychological evaluation. This topic is discussed in greater detail in Chapter 10. A bibliography at the end of the chapter provides the reader with many additional references on intellectual assessment of mentally retarded children. The tests mentioned in this chapter are available from the test publishers commonly known to school psychologists.

There are a number of individual tests of intelligence that have been used with good results in testing retarded children who do not have concomitant impairments. These include the Wechsler Intelligence Scale for Children and the Stanford-Binet Form LM. The WISC is not applicable to severely retarded children as a group. The use of the Binet is limited to children with mental ages of two or higher. The Kuhlmann Tests for Mental Development contain norms for children below a mental age of one.

There are other factors that the school psychologist must consider in choosing an intelligence test. Some children may come from an impoverished or nonstimulating environment and appear to be intellectually retarded. Since intelligence tests are standardized on a certain uniformity of environment, the cultural milieu of the child must be taken into consideration. For example, early deprivation of affection and acceptance by parental figures, growing up in an impoverished setting and lack of environmental stimuli for learning may reflect a low intellectual functioning level which takes on the appearance of pseudo-mental deficiency. The intellectual level of children with this syndrome may be far more developed than that reflected on psychological testing.

Some attempts have been made by investigators to construct a culture-free test; however, it has been noted that for the most part such tests do little more than the more conventional tests to minimize this environmental difference. Lorge [14] feels that although intelligence may be culturally biased, a culture-free test of intelligence can never be made. He calls attention to the fact that a person does not function independently of his culture. He further points out that intelligence, as estimated by observations of behavior, must consider functioning as it is influenced by "constraints, demands and opportunities that the culture affords." Havighurst [15] has gone so far as to suggest that, "A good rule to follow is to add ten points to the I.Q. of all children who come from underprivileged homes or homes where English is not spoken as the first language. For children from native American families of stable factory and clerical workers, it would be best to add five points to the measured I.Q." It is, of course, difficult to establish a definite set of standards in this regard and the problem still remains as a fruitful area of research for the school psychologist.

In many instances, the school psychologist may be pressed for time to examine a large number of referrals, especially prior to the beginning of a new school year. Because of the time element and lack of sufficient personnel to screen these referrals, shorter yet reliable and valid means of evaluation are constantly being sought in order that the children in need of special education may be rapidly evaluated. McNemar,[16] Herring,[17] and others, have published summaries of articles bearing on this topic. Studies related to the utilization of abbreviated forms of the Wechsler scales with retardates have more often been based upon institutional type populations than upon public school children.

Finley and Thompson,[18] using a group of educable mentally retarded children in the California public schools, employed an abbreviated Wechsler Intelligence Scale that included the subtests of Information, Picture Arrangement, Picture Completion, Coding, and Block Design. They reported that this short form of the WISC presented a valid predictor of full scale scores with educable mentally retarded children, the error of prediction being no greater than that of a test-retest situation.

Clinical tests of impairment.   In addition to tests of intellectual potential, a differential diagnosis should also include clinical tests for evaluating intellectual impairment suggestive of organic etiology. Descriptions of such tests

[14] I. Lorge, *op. cit.*

[15] R. J. Havighurst, "Using the I.Q. Wisely," *NEA Journal*, 15 (1951), 540–541.

[16] Q. McNemar, "On Abbreviated Wechsler-Bellevue Scales," *Journal of Consulting Psychologists*, 4 (1952), 79–81.

[17] F. H. Herring, "An Evaluation of Published Short Forms of the Wechsler-Bellevue Scale," *J. of Consult. Psychol.*, 16 (1952), 119–123.

[18] C. J. Finley and J. Thompson, "An Abbreviated Wechsler Intelligence Scale for Children for Use with Educable Mentally Retarded," *Amer. J. Ment. Defic.*, 63, No. 3.

and those described below, appear in Buros [19] and catalogues of test publishers.

The Benton Revised Visual Retention test, a standardized measure of visual memory, has been found useful by some psychologists in psychological evaluations of children suspected of intellectual retardation; the A-B-C Vision Test, a disguised visual-manipulative test, has been used for determining ocular dominance and may be used along with the Harris Tests of Lateral Dominance. Although the most effective use of several clinical tests are limited by lack of specific age norms, tests like the Goldstein-Scheerer Tests of Abstract and Concrete Thinking have been useful with individuals suspected of brain injuries. There are five tests in this series: a Cube Test; Color-Form Sorting Test; Stick Test; and an Object Sorting Test are used to measure, both quantitatively and qualitatively, impairment in brain functioning as related to abstract and concrete reasoning.

Tests of social competence. Some measurement of the social competency of the retarded child is helpful to the psychologist both in terms of assessment of the present level of social maturity and also for future planning. Social competence, at present, may be appraised in gross and often unreliable terms, and there is need for more objective definitive measures. Yet, it ranks with mental ability as one of the significant factors in assessing level of retardation. The Vineland Social Maturity Scale and the Cain-Levine Scale are used by many psychologists as measures of social competency.

The Vineland data along with other pertinent psychological test findings and the social history are useful as a record of developmental history, as a guide to establishing the child's readiness to adjust to school and social situations, and in assessing possible management problems. Successive Vineland testing may be utilized as a measure of social growth, improvement, or regression, as a guide for child training, and in social education. The Cain-Levine Scale has particular pertinence to the training goals in classes for trainable mentally retarded children. More on the topic of assessment of social and perceptual competence is found in Chapter 12.

Projective personality testing. The measurement of personality development in the mentally retarded child has not kept pace with the tests and techniques for evaluation of his intellectual potentials and social competency. There have been studies showing the importance of personality factors in predicting success in school and on the job out of school. In Gallagher's [20] paper on

[19] O. K. Buros, *The Sixth Mental Measurements Yearbook* (Highland Park, N.J.: Gryphon Press, 1965).

[20] J. J. Gallagher, "Measurement of Personality Development in Pre-Adolescent Mentally Retarded Children," *Amer. J. Ment. Defic.*, 64 (September, 1961), 296–301.

the measurement of personality development in the pre-adolescent mentally retarded child, it is pointed out that the lag is due primarily to the unavailability of a suitable instrument for such measurement which is easy to apply and interpret. Cronbach [21] has suggeted that in tests of intelligence the examiner is looking for optimum behavior, whereas in personality testing, he is looking for typical behavior trends.

Gallagher reports that use and interpretation of projective tests with the retarded child must be observed with care. He points out that the retarded child seems less likely verbally to give feeling tones that "represent the deepest core of personality" and is more likely to give the feeling tone of the movement, a feeling tone that might have been markedly influenced by the last experience he had prior to the testing situation. The assumption that the test behavior is typical is less justifiable with the mentally retarded than with the normal child of the same age.

Molish [22] has reported on the contribution of projective tests to problems of psychological diagnosis in mental deficiency. He calls attention to a current trend of regarding mental deficiency as a complex of symptoms in which personality factors exert an important influence. Molish feels that projective tests have contributed to an increased understanding of the dynamic relationships between a person's potential and his actual functioning. Sarason [23] feels that the value of the Rorschach as a diagnostic tool must be questioned. He feels Rorschach norms based on mental retardates are inadequate. However, in discussing the use of the Rorschach and the Thematic Apperception Test, he reports that projective techniques may be useful in evaluating personality characteristics.

Although questions have been raised concerning the adequacy of using projective tests in the diagnosis of mental retardation, the skilled psychologist may, nevertheless, obtain important information about the child by making a realistic interpretation of the examination findings. In addition the test situation and performance on intelligence tests also may be used "projectively" by the competent school psychologist. This point is discussed in some detail by Anderson and Magary in Chapter 11.

The need is evident for more information about what clearly diagnosed mental defectives of different types and normal children of the same mental power do with the projective techniques, particularly in measurement of cognitive abilities, an important consideration in diagnosis of mental deficiency.

[21] L. Cronbach, *op. cit.*
[22] H. B. Molish, "Contributions of Projective Tests to Problems of Psychological Diagnosis in Mental Deficiency," *Amer. J. Ment. Defic.*, 63 (1958), 282–293.
[23] S. Sarason, *Psychological Problems in Mental Deficiency*, 3rd ed. (New York: Harper & Row, Publishers, 1959).

EVALUATION IN A SCHOOL SETTING

The procedures and approach to the initial psychological evaluation just described are appropriate for both clinic and school. The necessity to consider the school and the class placement, however, offers fresh opportunity to extend the concept of evaluation in new ways. Although many different approaches are possible, here is one way in which cooperative classification might be arranged for a trainable-level class in a small school system.

When the child comes to the school's attention, the psychologist arranges an appointment with the parents and child in his office. He sets the child to play and talks with the parents, getting information about the child's medical, educational, and family history. He administers the Cain-Levine San Francisco Social Competency Scale, or another instrument of his preference, in order to assess social maturity. He observes the child at play and, if it seems appropriate at the time, attempts to do some testing. With the parents there, he is able to answer questions about the class and makes it clear that if the child is accepted for placement, such placement is on a trial basis and must be mutually satisfactory to the school and the parents.

He then takes the child and his parents for a short visit to a special class, pre-arranged with the teacher. He watches the child in the class, with the parents seated to one side. He makes notes on both office and classroom behavior. At this point, unless there is conclusive proof that the child is untrainable or is operating at too high a level for the group, he asks the parents to submit pertinent records and information and arranges with the teacher for trial placement in the class.

During the trial placement, the examiner observes the child in class, and the teacher records her impressions of the child as he functions in the group. Testing is done during this time if it is felt that testing will help to clarify the decision as to placement, and if rapport can be established. If proper conditions for adequate testing cannot be met, testing is delayed until later. The examiner may use the teacher as a test-partner; e.g., to interpret difficult speech, to administer test items if the child finds it difficult to respond to the examiner. If the child is then classified as trainable, he is placed on the register.[24]

This kind of long term evaluation does not negate the importance of clinical assessment. It does stress, however, the possible use of observation in the setting in which the child will be expected to perform. Here, tests are considered as of secondary importance. I.Q. scores are considered as less valuable than on-the-spot functioning behavior.

The same system of cooperative classification could be applied to educable level classes as well, with some modifications.

The psychologist would want to see the child in his regular class. The special class teacher would want to see him in this setting too. Placement

[24] Bardon and Alprin, *op. cit.*, p. 237.

would be temporary, even for just a few hours a day if this could be arranged. Determination of mental ability would be extremely important, but equally as important would be how this child learns in the two situations.[25]

Vocational Evaluation

The school psychologist can perform a very valuable service in working with teachers, curriculum planners, and community resources in the development of vocational evaluation and training programs for retarded youth. Delp [26] points out that it is necessary to consider many facets of personality in vocational training and placement besides that of the "minimum mental level" of a job.

Research on the occupational placement of the mentally retarded has ranged from descriptions of the types of jobs they have been able to hold to studies on why they lose their jobs.[27] Such studies have indicated that success on the job is influenced by many factors and depends not only on the individual's interests and abilities, but on his general personal adjustment. Goldstein [28] feels that studies of this type have contributed to our knowledge about the breadth of occupational possibilities for the mentally retarded and highlights the fact that "factors" other than intelligence are highly significant in their own right. Goldstein does not discuss just what these "factors" may be. There is, however, a growing trend toward consideration of more than the individual's intellectual level with greater emphasis placed on the total child in the selection, training, and placement process. Goldstein's findings offer the school psychologist many fruitful areas for investigation.

The school psychologist may be called upon to evaluate the vocational potential of the older retarded child or adolescent to determine whether he has basic occupational aptitudes, skills, and work attitudes which can be further developed in an occupational training program for retarded youth either in the school system or in the community through cooperating agencies and services. The psychologist, as time permits, is usually expected to evaluate the individual's interests, capacities, achievements and personal adjustment and to offer recommendations and prognosis as to the youth's potential for vocational training and placement. Although some vocational screening procedures have been developed in resident institutions serving the mentally

25 *Ibid.*, p. 237.

26 H. A. Delp, "Criteria for Vocational Training of the Mentally Retarded; a Revised Concept of the Necessary Mental Level," *Train. Sch. Bull.*, 54, No. 2 (1957), 14–20.

27 R. Peckham, "Problems in Job Adjustment of the Mentally Retarded," *Amer. J. Ment. Defic.* (October, 1951), 448–453.

28 H. Goldstein, "Methodological Problems in Research in the Educational Programs," in *Approaches to Research in Mental Retardation* (Langhorne, Pa.: Woods School, 1959), pp. 341–345.

retarded, these materials as well as other vocational evaluation techniques and procedures for use with retarded youth in a public school setting are still in an experimental stage and remain a challenge to the school psychologist.

There are few occupational interest inventories and tests of vocational aptitude suitable for use with retarded, and those that are used do not have adequate norms for this type of population. The Weingarten Picture Interest Inventory [29] has been used with older retarded children and adolescents with some degree of success. This is a nonverbal occupational interest inventory which employs a series of sketches of occupational significance as stimuli to which the subject responds, purportedly in terms of his own interests and needs. A feature of this type of interest inventory is that it can be handled by the person without depending on reading skills. His responses, therefore, are not influenced by his understanding of words or occupational terms. The ingenious psychologist might like to consider developing other nonverbal occupational interest material for use in the vocational evaluation process. A useful publication of the U. S. Department of Labor [30] that gives estimates of the worker trait requirements for a number of jobs may also be of help in the initial vocational assessment of the individual.

Aptitude tests have been found valuable in showing a person's ability to prepare for an occupation, but they cannot predict his success or satisfaction on the job. The qualitative clinical observations by the psychologist during psychodiagnostic examinations as well as the obtained qualitative and quantitative findings on the performance sections of such tests as the Wechsler Adult Intelligence Scale may be predictive as to work efficiency and may be studied by the psychologist for this purpose. However, the artificial climate of the examination session in relation to an actual on-the-job situation must be kept in mind.

Super [31] and other investigators feel that manipulative dexterity generally matures at an early age. Performance tests, like the Purdue Pegboard,[32] a test of manipulative dexterity such as may be required in assembly, packing, machine operation, and the like, may have their place in some school settings serving retarded adolescents. One must bear in mind, though, that the performance of the retarded youth under study is being compared, in this case, with a normative population of adult non-retardates rather than the school age population with which the psychologist is con-

[29] Catalog Standardized Tests, California Test Bureau (Monterey, Calif., 1967).
[30] U. S. Dept. of Labor, Bureau of Employment Security, Estimate of Worker Trait Requirements (Washington, D. C., 1956).
[31] I. Lorge, op. cit.
[32] Examiner Manual for the Purdue Pegboard, Science Research Associates (Chicago, 1948).

cerned. Siegel and Hirschon [33] have worked out norms for the Purdue Pegboard based on an adolescent population in the 12–18 year old age range of non-retardates at a vocational counseling center. The school psychologist should be familiar with resources on the local, state, and federal levels offering direct and indirect vocational and rehabilitation services to retarded youth. Informative professional materials are available [34, 35, 36] that present basic knowledge to workers in the field of mental retardation, including summaries of experimental and ongoing programs in schools and elsewhere together with suggestions for much needed research. The Research and Demonstration Grants Program of the U. S. Office of Vocational Rehabilitation sponsors a number of training facilities throughout the country which offer vocational rehabilitation to the mentally retarded. These are often under the auspices of such facilities as the local chapter of the National Association for Retarded Children, or a family service agency in the community.

Curriculum Planning

The educational goal for the retarded child is essentially the same as for other children—the fullest possible development of the individual. It is recognized, however, that the goal must be reached through somewhat different approaches and techniques. The growth in special education programs for the mentally retarded child has brought about an increased interest in the development of curricula and instructional methods geared to the needs, interests, and abilities of these children. The 1960 White House Conference on Children and Youth emphasized that the public schools' responsibilities include the provision of a program for all educable mentally handicapped children from kindergarten through secondary school. An increasing number of programs for trainable retarded children are also being developed.

The determination that the retarded child is educable or trainable and whether he can be helped through specially designed courses of study and methods of teaching are often important functions of the school psychologist. In the role of consultant, he is in a position to make specific recommendations to school personnel for placing the child in an educational program

---

[33] M. Siegel and B. Hirschhorn, "Adolescent Norms for the Purdue Pegboard Test," *Personnel Guid. J.* (1958), pp. 563–565.

[34] U. S. Office of Education, *The Retarded Child Goes to School* (Washington, D.C., 1960).

[35] U. S. Children's Bureau, *The Child Who Is Mentally Retarded* (Washington, D. C., 1956).

[36] S. G. Di Michael, ed., *Vocational Rehabilitation of the Mentally Retarded* (Washington, D. C.: U. S. Dept. of Health, Education and Welfare, Office of Vocational Rehabilitation, 1950).

best suited to his needs to insure maximum development of the child's potential. It is desirable that he have a good understanding of the problems of curriculum development for mentally retarded children and that he keep abreast of the research in this area so that he can share reported findings with the school personnel.

Goldberg[37] has pointed out the considerable body of research information relating to the education of the mentally handicapped that is often not accessible to the teacher. The school psychologist, however, working closely with the teacher is in a position to interpret up-to-date research findings that have bearing on the work with children. Goldberg feels that "the interpretation of the various research findings and their applications to the actual special classroom organization and curriculum may be one of the important functions of school psychologists."

Curriculum development for the intellectually retarded is still in the experimental stage. At a recent national meeting of the American Association of Mental Deficiency, Wrightstone and Lynch[38] presented preliminary findings on a study indicating that the two-track plan for education of the mentally retarded—placing children with I.Q.'s below 59–65 in one program and those with higher I.Q.'s in a different group—gave better results than the single track plan. Hudson[39] studied lesson areas for the trainable child and analyzed procedures for teaching such children to determine the frequency of use of types of lessons in classes. An analysis of her lesson plans for retarded children may prove helpful in curriculum planning. She reports in her study that the types of lessons taught should vary according to the age levels of the group and that major lesson areas can be adapted to wide age ranges in any class. Hudson feels that school programs should include new lessons to fit increased experience and physical growth.

The curricula for the retarded should emphasize planned preparation for living. The education of the retarded begins with very simple basic skills, and progresses to experiences he is most likely to meet in community living. Traditional school subjects, at the appropriate level, may be integrated in an over-all program of life situations that all individuals are likely to encounter in the world of work and must solve according to their own ability. Along with the trend toward helping the retarded child develop social attitudes and skills, there is added emphasis upon providing opportunities for

---

[37] I. I. Goldberg, *Advances in Educational Planning for the Educable Mentally Handicapped Child* (Paper presented at the 65th Annual Convention of the American Psychological Association, New York City, 1957).

[38] J. W. Wrightstone and Katherine D. Lynch, *A Comparison of Educational Outcomes under Single-Track and Two-Track Plans for Educable Mentally Retarded Children* (Paper presented at annual meeting of the American Association on Mental Deficiency, Cincinnati, 1961).

[39] Margaret Hudson, "Lesson Areas for the Trainable Child," *Except. Child.*, 27, No. 4 (1960), 224–229.

vocational exploration and preparation for realistic future employment and economic usefulness.

If the school psychologist is capable of assisting school personnel concerned with curriculum development to provide for a better school environment for the mentally retarded child, he will be able to perform much more effective service for the school system and for the children referred to him for psychological services.

Counseling Retarded Youth

The school psychologist has a challenging and creative opportunity to contribute to the knowledge and understanding of the dynamics of the counseling and psychotherapeutic process as related to the retarded child. However, there may be a tendency to avoid a formal psychotherapeutic relationship with a retardate because it is felt that his limited skills in communication and in verbal understanding on the interpretative level, make it difficult for him to gain insights concerning his impulses and feelings that might help him modify his attitudes and behavior.[40] Counseling and psychotherapeutic techniques are discussed by Donald C. Smith in Chapter 6.

The retarded child is subject to the same range and variety of emotional reactions as those of normal intelligence. Rejection by parents, the community, relatives, peers, and in many cases by the school will affect his emotional adjustment and development of a realistic self-concept. Yepsen[41] stresses that the mentally retarded individual is "fundamentally the same as the so-called normal child, only operating at a lower level of intelligence. As a result, the degree of self-sufficiency is at a much lower economic and social level, sometimes precariously so mainly because of the unenlightened attitude and behavior of society in general." The counselor must realize, however, that he is dealing with an intellectually limited individual and be prepared to have greater patience in working with him, possibly taking slower steps in fewer or in increased sessions, depending upon the individual child.

In vocational training and placement of retarded youth, it has been demonstrated that personal and social skills and attitudes are most important for vocational success, and the mentally retarded succeed more frequently when they have been specifically assisted through counseling and guidance. It has also been established that few retardates, if properly placed, lose their jobs because of inability to keep up with the requirements of the job. All too often, they quit or lose their jobs because of emotional difficulties, lack of

[40] Theodora Abel, "Resistances and Difficulties in Psychotherapeutic Counseling of Mental Retardates," *Journal of Clinical Psychology,* 9 (1953), 9–11.

[41] L. N. Yepsen, "Counseling the Mentally Retarded," in *Vocational Rehabilitation of the Mentally Retarded.*

social sophistication, limited initiative and responsibility, and faulty work habits.

Development of healthy attitudes and habits depends a great deal upon the effectiveness of early as well as later influences, both in and out of school. A primary objective of counseling the mentally retarded adolescent is to help him recognize his individual potentialities for accomplishment so that he may learn to develop reliance upon his capabilities and become more self-sufficient in his dealings with the world about him. The school psychologist in the typical school setting probably has limited time to devote to psychotherapy, *per se*, with retarded youth. Time permitting, he should consider the use of supportive counseling to help the retarded child become more realistic in making a vocational choice within his limitations. Supportive counseling may help the child develop responsibility and proper work habits to enable him to hold his own on the job and to make a place for himself in the community and in the world of work.

Group counseling in a warm, friendly and accepting atmosphere has been known to contribute to the modification of social attitudes, beliefs, and personal adjustment. The use of role playing in groups has particular value for retardates because of its approximation to real life. Reports of group psychotherapy carried on in institutional settings [42, 43] have indicated that it has contributed to the development of happier, better adjusted children, an increase in group morale, and in a lowering of uncontrolled emotional reactions. Heber [44] has stressed the need to change from emphasizing success experiences, to preparation of the retarded "to tolerate failure and go beyond it." Unlike the normal child who uses failure as a spur to greater effort, the retardate, Heber points out, is more likely to give up when faced with a threat of failure in a learning situation.

In vocational counseling of retarded adolescents, emphasis should be placed on understanding, in relation to each other, of all factors including personal, social, intellectual and vocational data, in determining a realistic vocational goal. Some school psychologists use vocational counseling sessions to interpret vocational test results at the counselee's level of understanding. In this way it is hoped the retarded adolescent will achieve some degree of insight into his limitations and potentials as they relate to job requirements in the world of work.

It is fairly obvious that many of the goals of counseling, both individual and group, are those toward which special class teachers, in particular, work.

[42] H. Michal-Smith, M. and G. Gottsegen, "A Group Technique for Mental Retardates," *Int. J. Group Psychother.* (1955), pp. 84–90.
[43] F. C. Thorne and Katherine M. Dolan, "The Role of Counseling in a Placement Program for Mentally Retarded Females," *J. Clin. Psychol.*, 9 (1953), 12–15.
[44] R. Huber, in *Mental Hygiene News*, 31, No. 8 (1960).

The busy school psychologist may serve many more students by using the teacher as a counseling resource. By offering supervision to the teacher in his attempts to help the retardate, the psychologist can extend his influence and knowledge in order to help more individual pupils at the same time that he helps the teacher make more effective use of the school day.

Working with Parents

During the past decade there has been increased attention to direct work with parents of retarded children. Much of this emphasis has stemmed from the efforts of parents themselves who have banded together to make their needs known through such organizations as the National Association for Retarded Children and its local chapters which have been established in many communities throughout the country.

An important function of the school psychologist is, very often, consultation with parents concerning problems related to their children. In some settings, such consultations may be handled by other disciplines, as for example, the school social worker, the guidance counselor, or other personnel designated for special services to the parents. Frequently, the school psychologist is faced with the responsibility for telling the parents that their child is retarded. Begab[45] points out that parents ". . . have to give up their unrealistic expectations for the child and must resolve the feelings aroused in them by the child's deficiency. To accomplish this objective, a great deal of effort must be directed toward the parents whose needs for emotional support, understanding and acceptance by their human environment is no less than that of their child." The school psychologist should be realistic in describing to them the retarded child's present level of functioning and estimated potential, the tentative prognosis for his future educational and vocational growth and development.

He should present this information in a professional, yet warm, sympathetic and tactful manner that stresses the child's potential abilities and yet does not minimize the limitations. Some psychologists are able to present such information in a manner suggesting a mutual sharing of knowledge about the child, drawing the parent into the current and future educational and vocational planning. This cooperative planning, whenever possible, is probably the most helpful course of action to follow. In working with parents and the general public there is need for a terminology that will focus more upon the child as a total individual and not merely as a clinical type of mental deficiency. As Sarason points out, "the failure to adequately commu-

[45] M. J. Begab, "Unmet Needs of the Mentally Retarded in the Community," *Amer. J. Ment. Defic.* (January, 1958), pp. 712–723.

nicate to parents the nature and implications of a diagnosis of mental deficiency probably causes more unnecessary problems and suffering than any other factor, with the obvious exceptions of those factors that originally produced the mental deficiency." [46]

The psychologist may be called upon to meet with parents seeking practical suggestions for handling the retarded child in the home and during the after school hours. Parental attitudes toward children who are mentally retarded have definite effects upon the mental health of the child. These attitudes may spring from their own guilt feelings based on mistaken concepts of heredity or on a feeling of being punished for some past experience or behavior. This situation can set up a barrier between the child and parent, lessening the opportunity for sound emotional development of the child, which in turn may bring about partial or even a greater rejection of the child.[47]

The parents need to be helped to examine their feelings toward their retarded child. The mentally retarded child should not be pushed beyond his intellectual capacities as this may inevitably lead to irritability, frustration, low self-concept and a feeling of rejection as he realizes he is unable to perform at the expected level. Social training and character development may be more significant than academic attainment for some retarded children who may have difficulty distinguishing proper standards of social behavior and are easily influenced by peers and adults.[48] The psychologist working with the parent can perform an important service by helping them to come to some resolution of such conflicting feelings as guilt, anger, hopelessness. It may often be too much to expect them to "accept objectively all their problems, especially the finality of the child's condition and the limitations of any assistance that may be offered." [49]

Group counseling has been effective, in many instances, with parents of retarded children in helping them to develop better insight into the dynamics of their own parent-child relationships and to provide the impetus for constructive and realistic thinking and planning for the child. By means of the group process, they may come to realize that their feelings concerning the child are also shared by other parents, thus helping to lessen their own feelings in this regard. In addition, the free and open discussion of the problems related to mental retardation often lead to more comprehensive understanding and care in handling of the child at home by the other members of the family. The role of the school psychologist as a group leader is an all-important one

---

46 S. Sarason, *op. cit.*

47 D. A. Davis, "Counseling the Mentally Retarded," *Vocational Guidance Quarterly* (1959), pp. 184–188.

48 *Ibid.*

49 A. Mendelbaum and M. E. Wheeler, "The Meaning of a Defective Child to Parents," *Soc. Casework*, 41 (1960), 360–367.

and the success of the group may depend to a large extent, especially in its initial stages, on his own personality, skill, and understanding.[50]

The problem of institutionalization does not arise routinely in a public school setting since the schools themselves serve as selective agents. However, potential educability or trainability are not always the all-important determiners of whether a child should remain in the community or be placed in a training school or residential treatment center. Perhaps the needs of the child cannot be adequately handled in the home; there may be other siblings who are being deprived emotionally because of the retarded child's over-dependence; the child may represent a severe medical or a discipline problem with which the parents cannot cope; financial problems may preclude specialized care, treatment and training. Responsible professional people such as the psychologist and the school counselor can be helpful in assisting the parents in selecting the proper residential setting to serve the needs of the child. They can also perform a valuable service in preparing the parents and the child for the placement.

It is often helpful for the school psychologist to have on hand resource material especially prepared for parents of retarded children. Inexpensive pamphlets and books are available from many sources. The publications of the National Association for Retarded Children, local agencies such as the Mental Health Association, state departments of education and of public health, and federal agencies such as the Children's Bureau and the Office of Education, often publish material of interest to parents. He should also be familiar with popular texts written especially for parents; for example, *Child in the Shadows*, by French and Scott.[51] In general such publications discuss the causes and signs of mental retardation, what parents can do to give the child proper care and training, sources of help to parents and placement away from home. The reader will find a listing of such materials in Chapter 5.

Research

It is unhappily true that most school psychologists have little time or inclination to engage in research activities. They tend to be "practitioners" in spirit as well as in practice. Nevertheless research investigations in mental retardation offer the school psychologist many challenging areas for exploration, especially in applied or service-oriented research related to the education,

[50] B. L. White, *Counseling Parents of Retarded Children* (Paper presented at the 66th Annual Convention of the American Psychological Association, Washington, D.C., 1958).

[51] E. L. French and J. C. Scott, *Child in the Shadows* (Philadelphia: J. B. Lippincott Co., 1960).

training and rehabilitation of the mentally retarded. Dunn and Capobianco summarize a number of research studies of interest. Hindman reports on a survey study of cooperative programs of training and research in mental retardation established between a number of residential facilities for the retarded and certain colleges and universities. A special issue of the *American Journal of Mental Deficiency* [52] was devoted to research design and methodology in mental retardation. The publications of the American Association on Mental Deficiency provide many helpful suggestions. Original abstracts of articles and publications relative to mental retardation are published regularly by the AAMD and the federal government.

Federal funds are available for research and program development in mental retardation. Psychological studies are supported by the National Institute of Mental Health and the National Institute of Neurological Diseases and Blindness. The U. S. Office of Vocational Rehabilitation supports research and demonstration programs related to rehabilitation of the retarded. The Cooperative Research Program of the U. S. Office of Education has stimulated a great deal of research in special education. Approximately 25 per cent of the Cooperative Research Programs [53] are concerned with education of the mentally retarded, as for example: assessment of changes in the behavior of severely retarded children after enrollment in special classes; comparative studies of speech responses and social quotients of educable mental retardates in regular and special classes; comparative studies of responses of bright, normal, and retarded children in different types of learning tasks; studies of development of mental, educational, and social skills of retarded children in special classes.

School psychologists will find creative opportunities in developing and experimenting with "teaching machines"—automated teaching devices—to supplement other instructional techniques in building up basic skills. Smith and Quackenbush [54] report on significant gains obtained in using automated devices in teaching arithmetic to exceptional children who were very difficult to reach through conventional teaching methods.

The opportunities for research and training related to mental retardation should challenge school psychologists into greater activity despite their busy daily schedule of applied psychological services. Stolurow [55] reports that research on learning in mental deficiency tends to be more oriented toward

[52] D. A. Hindman, *Cooperative Programs of Training and Research in Mental Retardation* (Yellow Springs, Ohio: Antioch Press, 1959).

[53] U. S. Office of Education, *Cooperative Research Projects,* fiscal year 1959 (Washington, D. C., 1960).

[54] E. A. Smith and J. Quackenbush, "Devereux Teaching Aids Employed in Presenting Elementary Mathematics in a Special Education Setting," *Psychological Reports,* 7 (1960), 333–336.

[55] L. Stolurow, "Requirements for Research on Learning in Mental Deficiency," *Amer. J. Ment. Defic.* (September, 1959), pp. 323–332.

learning theory than toward the more fundamental approach; i.e., "based upon psychological analysis of tasks which the retarded are required to learn." He feels both approaches are needed and should go on concurrently for maximum development of information. Both contribute to a better understanding of the learning problems of mental deficiency and the way in which the mentally retarded differ in learning ability from other children.

Goldstein [56] calls attention to the fact that researchers involved in studies related to selection for training and occupational placement of the mentally retarded all too often "fall back on the I.Q. as the major criterion." He feels that "other factors" are highly significant and that intelligence accounts for little of the predicted variance. He adds, "just what the other factors are is still a matter of conjecture."

Research on criteria for selection, training and placement of the mentally retarded remain promising areas of research for the school psychologist.

Selected Supplementary Readings

Allen, R. M., "Contributions of Psychology to Mental Retardation," *The Training School Bulletin*, LX (November, 1963), 105–113.

American Association on Mental Deficiency, *Residential Schools and Homes for the Mentally Deficient*. New York, 1954.

American Orthopsychiatric Association, "Mental Retardation in Urban Areas: A Symposium," *American Journal of Orthopsychiatry*, XXVII (1957), 484–507.

Begab, Michael J., *The Mentally Retarded Child: A Guide to Services of Social Agencies*. Washington, D. C.: U. S. Department of Health, Education and Welfare, Children's Bureau, 1963.

Bijou, Sidney W., "The Special Problem of Motivation in the Academic Learning of the Retarded Child," *Exceptional Children* (1952), pp. 103–104.

Borreca, Frank, et al., "A Workshop in Developing Lessons for Retarded Adolescents in a Program of Occupational Education," *American Journal of Mental Deficiency* (1950), 23–59.

Burghart, E., and G. Spivack, *Minimum Muscular Fitness and Endurance of Exceptional Children: A Pilot Project*. Unpublished manuscript, The Devereux Schools, 1960.

Butterfield, Earl C., and Edward Zigler, "The Effects of Success and Failure on the Discrimination Learning of Normal and Retarded Children," *Journal of Abnormal Social Psychology*, 70 (1965), 25–31.

[56] H. Goldstein, *op. cit.*

California Association of School Psychologists and Psychometrists, *Recommended Procedures for the Evaluation and Placement of the Mentally Retarded in California.* Special Education Committee Report, 1965.

Carriker, W. R., "Research Related to the Education of Mentally Retarded Children," *School Life,* XLII (1960), 26–28.

Charney, Leon, "The Trainable Mentally Retarded," in *Behavioral Research on Exceptional Children,* ed. S. A. Kirk and B. B. Weiner. Washington, D. C.: The Council for Exceptional Children, NEA, 1963.

Conner, Frances P., and Mabel E. Talbot, *TC Series in Special Education: An Experimental Curriculum for Young Mentally Retarded Children.* New York: Teachers College, Columbia University, 1964.

Di Michael, Salvatore, *Vocational Rehabilitation of the Mentally Retarded.* Washington, D. C.: Government Printing Office, 1950.

Earl, C. J. C., *Subnormal Personalities: Their Clinical Investigation and Assessment.* Baltimore: Williams and Wilkins Co., 1961.

Ellis, Norman R., ed., *Handbook of Mental Deficiency: Psychological Theory and Research.* New York: McGraw-Hill Book Company, 1963.

Farber, Bernard, and W. C. Jenne, *Family Organization and Parent Child Communication: Parents and Siblings of a Retarded Child.* Lafayette, Ind.: Child Development Publications, 1963.

Garrison, M., Jr., "Research Trends in Mental Deficiency," *Children,* VI (1959), 10–12.

Gibson, David, "Psychology in Mental Retardation: Past and Present," *American Psychologist,* XIX, No. 5 (May, 1964), 339–341.

Grebler, Anne, "Parental Attitudes Toward Mentally Retarded Children," *American Journal of Mental Deficiency* (1952), pp. 475–483.

Havighurst, Robert J., "Educationally Difficult Students, What the School Can Do," *National Association of Secondary School Principals Bulletin,* 49 (1965), 110–127.

Heber, Rick F., "The Educable Mentally Retarded," in *Behavioral Research on Exceptional Children,* ed. S. A. Kirk and B. B. Weiner.

————, "Promising Areas for Psychological Research in Mental Retardation," *American Journal of Mental Deficiency,* LXIII (1959), 1014–1019.

Hobbs, Nicholas, "Statement on Mental Illness and Retardation," *American Psychologist,* XVIII (June, 1963), 295–299.

Hutt, Max, and R. G. Gibby, *The Mentally Retarded Child,* 2nd ed. Boston: Allyn and Bacon, Inc., 1965.

Johnson, G. Orville, "A Study of the Social Position of Mentally Handicapped Children in the Regular Grades," *American Journal of Mental Deficiency,* LV (1950), 60–89.

Kirk, Samuel A., "What is Special about Special Education? The Child Who Is Mentally Handicapped," *Exceptional Children* (1953), pp. 138–142.

Kolb, Lawrence C., Richard L. Masland, and Robert E. Cooke, eds., *Mental Retardation*. Baltimore: The William and Wilkins Co., 1962.

McCoy, George F., "Some Ego Factors Associated with Academic Success and Failure of Educable Mentally Retarded Pupils," *Exceptional Children*, XXX (1963), 80–84.

Masland, R. L., "The Prevention of Mental Retardation," *Journal of Diseases of Children*, Part II (January, 1958).

Mayo, L., "Philosophy and Recommendations of the President's Panel on Mental Retardation Relating to Education, Vocational Rehabilitation and Training," *Exceptional Child*, 29 (1963), 425–430.

Michal-Smith, Harold, "The Mentally Retarded and the Slow-Learning Child," in *Professional School Psychology*, I, ed. M. G. Gottsegen and G. B. Gottsegen. New York: Grune & Stratton, Inc., 1960, pp. 190–205.

Miller, M. B., "Psychometric and Clinical Studies in Mental Deficiency, 1954–59: a Selective Review and Critique," *American Journal of Mental Deficiency*, LXV (1960), 182–193.

Mueller, M. W., "Mental Testing in Mental Retardation: A Review of Research," *The Training School Bulletin*, LX (February, 1964), 152–168.

Mullen, Frances A., "How Mentally Handicapped Children Learn," *Exceptional Children* (1958), pp. 224–226.

Patterson, C. H., "Methods of Assessing the Vocational Adjustment Potential of the Mentally Handicapped," *Training School Bulletin*, 61 (1964), 129–152.

Rothstein, Jerome H., *Mental Retardation: Readings and Resources*. New York: Holt, Rinehart & Winston, Inc., 1961.

Sarason, Seymour B., "Psychological and Cultural Problems in Mental Subnormality: A Review of Research," *Genetic Psychology Monogram* (1957), pp. 3–290.

Stacey, Chalmers, et al., *Counseling and Psychotherapy and the Mentally Retarded: Book of Readings*. New York: Free Press of Glencoe, Inc., 1957.

Stevens, Godfrey D., "An Analysis of the Objectives for the Education of Children with Retarded Mental Development," *American Journal of Mental Deficiency* (1958), pp. 225–235.

Strauss, A. A., and L. E. Lehtinen, *Psychopathology and Education of the Brain-Injured Child*. New York: Grune and Stratton, Inc., 1950.

Thorne, Frederick, "Tutorial Counseling with Mental Defectives," *Journal of Clinical Psychology*, XVI (January, 1960), 73–79.

Thurstone, John R., "Counseling the Parents of the Retarded," *The Training School Bulletin*, LX (November, 1963), 113–117.

Tizard, J., and J. C. Grad, *The Mentally Handicapped and Their Families: A Social Survey*. London: Oxford University Press, 1961.

Vergason, G. A., "Some Implications of Research for the Education of the Mentally Retarded," *High School Journal*, 48 (1964), 152–159.

Wallin, J. E. Wallace, *Education of Mentally Handicapped Children*. New York: Harper & Row, Publishers, 1955.

Washburn, Wilbur C., "Self Structure Theory as a Basis for Understanding Personality Problems in Child Retardation," *California Journal of Educational Research*, XV, No. 2 (March, 1964).

Wolk, Shirley M., "A Survey of the Literature on Curriculum Practices for the Mentally Retarded," *American Journal of Mental Deficiency*, LXII (1958), 826–839.

Annual Conference Reports. Langhorne, Pa.: Woods Schools, 1947–1967.

.

Special Bibliography:
Psychological Evaluation
of the Mentally Retarded *

Alper, A. E., "An Analysis of the Wechsler Intelligence Scale for Children with Institutionalized Mental Defectives." Unpublished doctoral dissertation, University of Florida, 1960.

Baroff, G. S., "WISC Patterning in Endogenous Mental Deficiency," *American Journal of Mental Deficiency*, 64 (1959), 482–485.

Baumeister, A. A., and C. S. Bartlett, "A Comparison of the Factor Structure of Normals and Retardates on the WISC," *American Journal of Mental Deficiency*, 67 (1962), 257–261.

————, "Further Factorial Investigations of WISC Performance of Mental Defectives," *American Journal of Mental Deficiency*, 67 (1962), 257–261.

Butler, R. L., "Responses of Institutionalized Mentally Retarded Children to Human and to Animal Pictures," *American Journal of Mental Deficiency*, 65 (1961), 620–622.

Clarke, A. D. B., and Ann M. Clarke, ed., *Mental Deficiency: The Changing Outlook*. New York: Free Press of Glencoe, Inc., 1958.

* This special bibliography is an adaptation of the bibliography prepared by Max W. Mueller which appeared in the *Training School Bulletin*, 60, No. 4 (February, 1964), 165–168.

Condell, J. F., "Note on the Use of the Ammons Full-Range Picture Vocabulary Test with Retarded Children," *Psychological Reports*, 5 (1959), 150.

Dentler, R. A., and B. Mackler, "The Porteus Maze Test as a Predictor of Functioning Abilities of Retarded Children," *Journal of Consulting Psychology*, 26 (1962), 50–55.

Dunn, L. M., and S. T. Brooks, "Peabody Picture Vocabulary Test Performance of Educable Mentally Retarded Children," *Training School Bulletin*, 57 (1960), 35–40.

————, and J. V. Hottel, "Peabody Picture Vocabulary Test Performance of Trainable Mentally Retarded Children," *American Journal of Mental Deficiency*, 65 (1961), 448–452.

Feldhusen, J. F., and H. J. Klausmeier, "Anxiety, Intelligence, and Achievement in Children of Low, Average, and High Intelligence," *Child Development*, 33 (1962), 403–409.

Fisher, G. M., "The Attitude Quotient as an Index of Intellectual Potential: WAIS Data for Familial and Undifferentiated Mental Retardates," *American Journal of Mental Deficiency*, 65 (1960), 252–255.

————, "A Cross-Validation of Baroff's WISC Patterning in Endogenous Mental Deficiency," *American Journal of Mental Deficiency*, 65 (1960), 349–350.

————, "Differences in WAIS Verbal and Performance IQ's in Various Diagnostic Groups of Mental Retardates," *American Journal of Mental Deficiency*, 65 (1960), 256–260.

————, "A Comparison of the Performance of Endogenous and Exogenous Mental Retardates on the Wechsler Adult Intelligence Scales," *Journal of Mental Deficiency Research*, 5 (1961), 111–114.

————, M. D. Dooley, and A. B. Silverstein, "Wechsler Adult Intelligence Scale Performance of Familial and Undifferentiated Mental Subnormals," *Psychological Reports*, 7 (1960), 268.

Gray, H., D. F. Votaw, and J. L. Rogers, *General Achievement Test*. Austin, Texas: Steck Co., 1948.

Hunt, Betty M., "Differential Responses of Mentally Retarded Children on the Leiter Scale," *Exceptional Children*, 28 (1961), 99–102.

Illingwerth, R. S., "The Predictive Value of Developmental Tests in the First Year, with Special Reference to the Diagnosis of Mental Subnormality," *Journal of Child Psychology and Psychiatry*, 2 (1961), 210–215.

Kimbrell, D. L., "Comparison of Peabody, WISC, and Academic Achievement Scores among Educable Mental Defectives," *Psychological Reports*, 7 (1960), 502.

Kirk, S. A., and J. J. McCarthy, "The Illinois Test of Psycholinguistic Abilities—an Approach to Differential Diagnosis," *American Journal of Mental Deficiency*, 66 (1961), 399–412.

Lawson, J. R., and D. Avile, "Comparison of Wide Range Achievement Test and Gray Oral Reading Paragraphs Reading Scores of Mentally Retarded Adults," *Perceptual and Motivational Skills,* 14 (1962), 474.

Malpass, L. F., R. Brown, and D. Hake, "The Utility of the Progressive Matrices (1956 Edition) with Normal and Retarded Children," *Journal of Clinical Psychology,* 16 (1960), 350.

————, Sylvia Mark, and D. S. Palermo, "Responses of Retarded Children to the Children's Manifest Anxiety Scale," *Journal of Educational Psychology,* 51 (1960), 305–308.

Matthews, G., and L. H. Levy, "Response Sets and Manifest Anxiety Scores in a Retarded Population," *Child Development,* 32 (1961), 577–584.

Mein, R., "Use of the Peabody Picture Vocabulary Test with Severely Subnormal Patients," *American Journal of Mental Deficiency,* 67 (1962), 269–273.

Miller, D. R., G. M. Fisher, and H. F. Dingman, "A Note on Differential Utility of WAIS Verbal and Performance IQ's," *American Journal of Mental Deficiency,* 65 (1960), 482–485.

Porteus, S. D., *Guide to Porteus Maze Test.* Vineland, New Jersey: The Training School, 1924.

Pryer, Margaret W., and R. H. Cassel, "The Children's Manifest Anxiety Scale: Reliability with Aments," *American Journal of Mental Deficiency,* 66 (1962), 860.

Rohns, F. W., and Mary R. Haworth, "The 1960 Stanford-Binet, WISC, and Goodenough Tests with Mentally Retarded Children," *American Journal of Mental Deficiency,* 66 (1962), 853–859.

Schiefelbusch, R. L., ed., "Language Studies of Mentally Retarded Children," *Journal of Speech and Hearing Disorders, Monograph Supplement,* No. 10 (1963).

Schwartz, L., and E. E. Levitt, "Short Forms of the Wechsler Intelligence Scale for Children in the Educable, Non-Institutionalized Mentally Retarded," *Journal of Educational Psychology,* 51 (1960), 187–190.

Share, J., A Webb, and R. Koch, "A Preliminary Investigation of the Early Developmental Status of Mongoloid Infants," *American Journal of Mental Deficiency,* 66 (1961), 238–241.

Shipe, Dorothy, "Discrepancies between the Peabody Picture Vocabulary Test (PPVT) and the Wechsler Intelligence Scale for Children (WISC) as Related to Emotional Disturbance in Children of Retarded and Normal Intelligence." Unpublished doctoral dissertation, Peabody College, 1962.

Silverstein, A. B., and G. M. Fisher, "An Evaluation of Two Short Forms of the Stanford-Binet, Form L-M, for Use with Mentally Retarded Adults," *American Journal of Mental Deficiency,* 65 (1961), 486–488.

————, and E. P. Owens, "The Altitude Quotient as an Index of Intellectual Potential: Three Studies of Predictive Validity," *American Journal of Mental Deficiency,* **67** (1963), 611–616.

Smith, J. O., "Efforts of a Group Language Development Program upon the Psycholinguistic Abilities of Educable Mental Retardates," *Peabody College of Special Educational Research Monograph Series,* No. 1 (1962).

Stott, D. H., "Observations on Retest Discrepancy in Mentally Subnormal Children," *British Journal of Educational Psychology,* **30** (1960), 211–219.

Throne, Frances M., J. L. Schulman, and J. C. Kaspar, "Reliability and Stability of the Wechsler Intelligence Scale for Children for Group of Mentally Retarded Boys," *American Journal of Mental Deficiency,* **65** (1962), 455–457.

Tobias, J., and J. Gorelick, "The Porteus Maze Test and the Appraisal of Retarded Adults," *American Journal of Mental Deficiency,* **66** (1962), 600–606.

Warren, Sue A., and H. L. Collier, "Suitability of the Columbia Mental Maturity Scale for Mentally Retarded Institutionalized Females," *American Journal of Mental Deficiency,* **64** (1960), 916–920.

Wolfensberger, Wolf, "Age Variation in Vineland SQ Scores for Four Levels of Adaptive Behavior of the 1959 AAMD Behavioral Classification," *American Journal of Mental Deficiency,* **67** (1962), 452–454.

————, "The Correlation between PPVT and Achievement Scores among Retardates: A Further Study," *American Journal of Mental Deficiency,* **67** (1962), 450–451.

HARRIET E. O'SHEA

14

The School Psychologist
and the Gifted Child

In many schools and school systems today, nothing is
being done to encourage action on behalf of the intellectually gifted child. If the school psychologist does not
initiate the activity, no one else will.

This unconcern for the child of superior mental
gifts is difficult to understand in a democracy such as ours.
For, under the impact of world conditions most citizens
have become acutely aware of the immediate need for
superior brain-power in the nation. No longer is the identification and nurture of the intellectually gifted child an
academic matter, no longer is it simply a question of good
educational practice. The school psychologist these days
is virtually under mandate to see to it that the intellectually gifted are found, and that everything possible is
done to provide them with appropriate experiences and
challenges, not alone for their own satisfaction but for
the welfare and very existence of society.

There are many different kinds of giftedness in the
human organism. Probably the least understood and the

least nurtured of all gifted persons are those with the power to think pene-
tratingly, effectively, brilliantly—the intellectually gifted.[1, 2, 3] Other facets
of giftedness—special ability in music or in athletics, for example—are generally recognized at once, and the schools are quick to provide special services
for them. But giftedness of intellect, if not shunned, is usually ignored. The
problem is of great concern to the school psychologist. This chapter, therefore, will examine the problem from the standpoint of the school psychologist,
to see what can and should be done with those children who have high
abstract thinking ability, as distinct from children with other forms of
giftedness.

General Considerations

IDENTIFICATION OF INTELLECTUALLY GIFTED CHILDREN

The responsibility for locating and identifying the children who possess
superior intellectual ability rests primarily with the school psychologist, by
the very nature of his work.

It should be remembered that children who are endowed with high
ability to do abstract thinking are typically high, also, in other kinds of
giftedness.[4] Consequently, it is to be expected that the search for highly
intelligent children will be closely allied with the search for those with other
special forms of giftedness.

At the outset the school psychologist will need to appraise existing
testing procedures so that he may ally himself with whatever efforts are
already being made to identify and provide for the intellectually gifted. In
South Bend, Indiana, all kindergarten children are given individual intelligence tests, not by the psychologist, but by specially-screened teachers
who have been given specific training by the school psychologist. In other
communities, inspection of available test records by the school psychologist
may identify a good many children of outstanding ability (in spite of errors
in test administration that might have been made by untrained persons).

Refinement of existing appraisal procedures and techniques will need to
be made if the school psychologist is to identify intellectually gifted children
who may not have been identified by traditional methods. The best of group
tests cannot be assumed always to be reliable locators of intellectual gifted-

[1] Joseph L. French, ed., *Educating the Gifted: A Book of Readings* (New York:
Holt, Rinehart & Winston, Inc., 1959, rev. ed., 1964).

[2] Robert J. Havighurst, "Community Factors in the Education of Gifted Children," *School Review*, 65 (September, 1955), 324–329.

[3] Robert J. Havighurst, "Conditions Favorable and Detrimental to the Development of Talent," *School Review*, 65 (March, 1957), 20–26.

[4] Frank T. Wilson, "Some Special-Ability Test Scores of Gifted Children,"
Journal of Genetic Psychology, 82 (March, 1953), 59–68.

ness,[5] and must be scrutinized and used judiciously by the school psychologist. Some schools and school systems never administer tests of intellectual ability. Such systems pose a challenge to the psychologist to utilize his professional skill and administrative wisdom to devise ways in which valid measures may be established.

A few schools are so fortunate as to have a fully trained staff psychologist to supervise or administer valid tests at regularly scheduled times. These schools are in a position to know at all times, as a matter of routine, who their intellectually gifted children are.

In some school situations, the psychologist may be able to foster a preschool testing program in order that admissions to the school system may be based on readiness to do school work and not rigidly on chronological age.[6, 7]

WHO SHALL BE CONSIDERED TO BE INTELLECTUALLY GIFTED?

Within branches of psychology concerned with development and intelligence testing, there are perhaps two major schools of thought concerning what constitutes intellectual giftedness. One maintains that a designated top percentage—possibly 10 percent—of any school population, regardless of its *absolute* status, shall be considered the population of gifted children. The other maintains that more value accrues to society by establishing an approximately "absolute" scale of giftedness (possibly sensing implications for the eventual adult accomplishments of intellectually gifted children). Those who lean toward this view tend to select some specified rate of mental growth —perhaps 1.4 mental years per calendar year—as a significant boundary at or above which the child will eventually arrive in the outstandingly productive region of adult mentality.

Perhaps the school psychologist's chief responsibility lies in understanding and nurturing and, in fact, protecting the intellectually gifted children, regardless of which standard of selection is used in locating them.

It appears highly probable that a given number of years of mental age between the mean of a group and the level of an individual at a higher mental age, precludes any real possibility of productive, stimulating, interesting, or friendly interactions between the two. Any child far removed from

[5] Ruth A. Martinson, *Educational Programs for Gifted Pupils* (Sacramento, California: California State Department of Education, 1961), 35–39.

[6] James R. Hobson, "Mental Age as a Workable Criterion for School Admission," *Elementary School Journal*, 48 (February, 1948), 312–321.

[7] James R. Hobson, "Scholastic Standing and Activity Participation of Underage High School Pupils Originally Admitted to Kindergarten on the Basis of Physical and Psychological Examinations," Presidential Address, American Psychological Association, Division 16, *Newsletter*, 11 (October, 1956).

the mean of his group must have special care in today's organization of education.

At the same time that the school psychologist is providing for the care of all children markedly above the mean mental age of their group, he must of necessity make additional effort on behalf of those children whose potential mental growth is such that they will be especially productive as adults. Both Terman's [8, 9, 10] and Hollingworth's [11] studies make clear the adult potentialities of children whose rates of mental growth during childhood are 1.4 mental years per year or higher. Such children require careful attention and support from the school psychologist to insure that they will have the kinds of experiences that will help them to develop and use their full intellectual potential.

TWO CRUCIAL ELEMENTS IN A CHILD'S HEALTHY MENTAL DEVELOPMENT

Two elements are of critical importance to the healthy development of the child's intellect: one concerns the child within himself, his own inner development; the other the child as he interacts with others in the social setting.

First, every child needs constantly and in liberal amount the stimulating, invigorating experience of doing battle with what are for him interesting, difficult, but solvable problems. He needs to experience the exquisite glow of having solved these problems. Problems that are too difficult for him to solve are disheartening and deflating. On the other hand, problems to which he knows the answer before he starts cannot engage his vigorous activity and can only leave him intellectually bored and personally limp.

In other words, every child has the right to challenging, interesting problems of such a level of difficulty that he must "stretch himself" to solve them, thereby establishing the important feeling that he is the person who *can* solve problems. Without this stimulus, it is difficult if not impossible to build habits of hard work. In a study many years ago, E. L. Thorndike [12] perceived that an individual operates best at his own mental age level. If he talks, he must talk at his own level and cannot operate at a simpler, less abstract level.

---

[8] L. M. Terman, *et al., The Gifted Child Grows Up*, Genetic Studies of Genius, IV (Stanford, Calif.: Stanford University Press, 1947).

[9] L. M. Terman, *et al., The Gifted Group at Mid-Life*, Genetic Studies of Genius, V (Stanford, Calif.: Stanford University Press, 1959).

[10] Douglas A. Thom and Nancy L. Newell, "Hazards of the High IQ," *Mental Hygiene*, XXIX (January, 1945), 61–67.

[11] Leta Hollingworth, *Children above 180 IQ, Stanford-Binet* (New York: Harcourt, Brace & World, Inc., 1942).

[12] Edward L. Thorndike, *et al., The Measurement of Intelligence* (New York: Bureau of Publications, Teachers College, Columbia University, [n.d.]).

The other constant and eternal need of the child is to be on a genuinely interacting basis with his fellowman, and to be liked by his associates when his behavior is pro-social. Like all children, the highly intelligent child has the need and the right to be liked and to feel secure in relationships with others. The goal of engineering the appropriate intellectual challenges for children of diverse mental ages within a single class group is seldom possible to accomplish in an ordinary classroom. The problem is seen in the daily interactions of children when a child with a nine-year-old mind is grouped with children with six-year-old minds, all of them being chronologically six. The gifted child confuses and alarms the rest of the group whenever he speaks. What can they do but automatically dislike him? Being in the majority, they easily psychologically push him out of the group. Various studies have reported the relief of the group when those of higher mental age have been removed.[13]

What apparently happens to the intellectually gifted child who is left with those of lower mental age through six elementary grades, through three more years in junior high school, and through the final three years of high school is that he arrives at the freshman year in college (if he arrives there at all) with a solid feeling that other people do not like him, because for twelve years they have not liked him. This child's right to satisfactory, satisfying relationships with his mental peers has been denied. He has never experienced the thrill of acceptance when he says interesting things. He has not been intrigued by what the others say because he has, in effect, been in intellectual "cold storage." Unlike his lesser-endowed classmates, he has suffered isolation tinged with hostility during all of his elementary school, junior high school, and senior high school years.

CURRENT ATTITUDES TOWARD THE GIFTED

Studies have been made [14, 15] and further studies are under way that endeavor to appraise the attitudes of schools, parents, and communities toward their intellectually gifted children. There is great distress at high government levels, evidenced in statements of the Manpower Commission,[16] that much of the highly gifted thinking power of the country is not being developed.

---

[13] Jackie Mallis, "A Seminar for Superior Students," *The Clearing House*, 31 (November, 1956), 175–178.

[14] Joseph Justman, "The Expressed Attitudes of Teachers Toward Special Classes for Intellectually Gifted Children," *Educational Administration and Supervision*, 42 (March, 1956), 141–148.

[15] Harold J. Reed, "Opinion Survey on Gifted Pupil Programs" (Guidance Committee, California School Supervisors Association, 1958, Mimeo.).

[16] Dael Wolfe, "Education and New Approaches to Manpower," *Teachers College Record*, 57 (February, 1956), 290–294.

One reason, possibly, is that attitudes of different groups, both within the profession and within the community, appear to be widely divergent in terms of the needs of gifted children and the kinds of programs that will meet these needs. A state-wide study in California [17] involving some 400 adults showed that psychologists feel it to be their special responsibility to identify intellectually gifted children, but that other groups—teachers, principals, guidance workers, lay groups—do not recognize the psychologists as having special knowledge and skills which qualify them for this task; they do not feel that the psychologist should have the major responsibility for identifying the intellectually gifted child. While laymen do not know that gifted pupils are generally underachieving, most professional workers (all but the principals) know that this is the case. Given three choices of ways of handling intellectually gifted children (segregation, acceleration, or enrichment), the principals strongly favor "enrichment" and teachers strongly oppose it. Superintendents, psychologists, and guidance workers are close to the high school teachers in feeling that other procedures are distinctly better than "enrichment."

Perhaps the chief implications for the school psychologists of the California study are 1) that a tremendous variety of attitudes toward the gifted, and toward programs for the gifted, exist in any school system; and 2) that the school psychologist must be cognizant of the attitudes of different adult groups in order to be able to assist all groups in learning about experimental findings, and in adjusting their points of view to harmonize with these findings.

With respect to the attitudes of teachers themselves toward programs for the gifted, an interesting New York study [18] has shown that teachers who have had experience with programs for the gifted are much more favorable to them than are those who have had no such experience. Younger teachers are more favorable toward programs for the gifted than are older teachers. (In a more recent California study,[19] it appeared to be not the youngest teachers but those between thirty and forty who were most interested in and most favorable toward programs for the gifted.) These findings would appear to encourage a school psychologist to begin programs, since it is not until programs have been in operation for some time that interest in them or approval of them can be expected to develop.

No definitive studies as yet have answered the question of why, in the midst of a general atmosphere of endeavoring to meet the individual needs of children, the education profession so frequently closes its eyes to the

[17] Reed, *op. cit.*
[18] Justman and Wrightstone, *op. cit.*
[19] Jean Wiener, *The Relationship Between Selected Variables and Attitudes of Teachers Toward Gifted Children*, Unpublished Doctoral dissertation, University of California, 1960).

needs of intellectually gifted children and either fails to meet those needs or actually opposes procedures aimed at giving gifted children at least the same educational chance given to all other children.

One is at a loss to explain the remarkable void regarding the gifted that exists in many branches of education. Certainly one would hesitate to suggest that a majority of the teaching staff of the public schools of the United States might tend to identify itself with mediocrity, or that, like their children, these teachers have reflected an uneasy, sibling-like, unconscious jealousy of anyone who seems to rise above the average.

There are informal evidences that this may be the case, as for instance when a fifth grade teacher states with real alarm that she does not know how she can deal with an intellectually gifted child of seven whom the school psychologist wishes her to take into fifth grade in September—even though the teacher, of course, has an adult mental age. Such unrealistic concern seems to be a revelation of the teacher's fear that she is inferior to intellectually gifted children, and that consequently she cannot deal with them.

If, indeed, such emotional blocks as these exist in teachers' thinking about intellectually gifted children and their needs, as seems quite likely, then ways must be found to increase the self-confidence and the self-estimate of the educational profession in order that teachers may feel confidence in dealing with intellectually gifted children.

The teaching profession is the one that must help to create a community-wide atmosphere of understanding and warmth toward meeting the needs of all children in the light of their individual characteristics. But before it can do this, it must somehow rid itself of its own hampering fears or antagonisms in order to do whatever may be needed to build the understanding and the friendliness of the community.

In many situations the school psychologist may be the chief motivating, encouraging, and educating force, first with the educational profession, then with the community, in building the desired attitudes.

LIMITATIONS ON EARLY ENTRANCE TO SCHOOL

A growing number of studies, some of them longitudinal studies following children over many years,[20, 21, 22, 23] demonstrate conclusively that starting a child in kindergarten or in first grade by mental age and by rate of mental growth is a highly successful procedure from every viewpoint (academic achievement, social adjustment, and so on). Yet, in spite of the estab-

[20] Jack W. Birch, "Early School Admission for Mentally Advanced Children," *Exceptional Children*, 21 (1954), 84–87.

[21] Hobson, "Mental Age as a Workable Criterion for School Admission."

[22] Hobson, "Scholastic Standings."

[23] Vera V. Miller, "The Superior Child Enterprise," *American School Board Journal*, 134 (April, 1957), 43–46.

lished experimental facts, many school boards still rule that no child may enter kindergarten or first grade unless he reaches a chronological age of five or six by some assigned date—such as the first of November or the fifteenth of December. In some states, there is even an act of the legislature establishing a chronological age below which a child may not be taken into the public school system.

In addition to community-wide and state-wide interpretation of the needs of the intellectually gifted children which the school psychologist may need to undertake, he may be able to do much within the school system itself to improve the conditions surrounding intellectually gifted children until such time as restrictive rules and restrictive legislation can be removed.

Long-range Plans for the Intellectually Gifted Child

The advisability of projecting a long-range or even a lifetime plan for the intellectually gifted child is seen in the findings of studies revealing the ages of maximum production of eminent people,[24] and in the findings of Terman's monumental study reporting the younger age of college graduation of his most successful intellectually gifted group [25] and their later tremendous productivity as recorded in the 25-year and 35-year follow-ups.[26, 27] An over-all plan outlining tentatively when the child needs to pass each school milestone will help immeasurably to clarify how fast he should move through each of the lower units of the school, whether it be by early entrance, by a "rapid track" system, by being skipped past grades, or by completing such a unit as the three-year junior high school in two years. An over-all life schedule plan should especially take into account the possible damage to the gifted child when time is lost through delays in the early grades.

Two recent studies [28, 29] have shown strikingly that individuals of high ability, contrary to findings reported in earlier horizontal studies, increase their intelligence test scores for from twenty to thirty-five years beyond the first testing. These findings underscore the need for more appropriate handling of individuals of high intelligence through childhood and adolescence, in line with the expectation that they will keep contributing at increasingly higher intellectual levels throughout their adult years.

[24] Harvey C. Lehman, *Age and Achievement,* American Philosophical Society Memoirs, Vol. 33 (Princeton, N.J.: Princeton University Press, 1953).

[25] Terman and Oden, *op. cit.*

[26] *Ibid.*

[27] Terman, *The Gifted Group at Mid-Life.*

[28] Nancy Bayley and Melita H. Oden, "The Maintenance of Intellectual Ability in Gifted Adults," *Journal of Gerontology,* 10 (1955), 91–107.

[29] W. A. Owens, "Age and Mental Abilities: A Longitudinal Study," *Genetic Psychology Monographs,* 48 First Half (1953), 3–54.

The role of the school psychologist inevitably will be to devote considerable time to discussing, explaining, and cooperating with teachers and others involved in establishing the most suitable time scheme for each mentally gifted child.

An effective procedure on the part of the school psychologist will be to spread a growing understanding of individual needs of children at all levels of mental growth throughout the school system and the community.

The Present Group and the Child's Eventual Status as an Adult

The psychologist needs at all times to be working within two frames of reference: the present needs of the individual child, and the child's possible future functioning.

In a school where the mean of the distribution is an IQ of 85, the child with an IQ of 120 needs very special placement care. Since presumably such a child would be found rarely in that neighborhood, one promising way of handling his case would be to place him in a grade nearer his mental age group (with an older chronological group).

If the same child appeared with an IQ of 120 in a school where the mean IQ was 115, no special placement would be needed. Such a child would be in the middle 50 percent of the class; at each stage he would be receiving work appropriate to his mental age, and he should have no difficulty in making friends with his classmates.

The child with an IQ of 140, 150, or 160 will require special care in the over-all planning of his progress through school, no matter what school he is in—excluding, of course, the two or three schools in the United States that limit their enrollments to just such children.

The child with an IQ of 120 and the child with an IQ of 150 will function quite differently in society when they reach adult years. The child with an IQ of 120, all other things being equal, will have earned his college bachelor's degree with some effort and will be out in the world earning his living in his chosen field. The child with an IQ of 150, all other things being equal, will have secured his master's degree and probably his doctor's degree, and will be functioning in some professional area of his choice. The child with an IQ of 150 will be in the top half of one percent of the adult population in intellectual functioning. The child with an IQ of 120 will be in the top ten percent of the population.

The school psychologist needs to cooperate with the school staff in adjusting the child's experience to his present child society; at the same time he must be projecting the child's life line in his mind to the adult roles in which the child is going to function.

Those rare minds, children with IQ's of 175 or 180 and up,[30, 31] will need very special arrangements and the constant supervision of their experiences by the psychologist. It is to be hoped that the psychologist will supervise so skillfully that the child and his teachers will not be much aware of the supervision.

It will require the utmost ingenuity on the part of the psychologist who is advising on the affairs of such a child to find him companions, as, for instance, in an art center, in a little theater, in the nearest university scientific laboratory, in a social agency in the community. It will also tax the ingenuity of the psychologist to see that the child secures adequate intellectual experiences in some fashion within the framework of his school. It may even be, in some rare cases, that the psychologist will be able to arrange the transfer of the child to one of the very few schools devoted to children of extremely high ability. Otherwise, some measure of flexibility within the school administration may be achieved to keep the child in touch with intellectual material difficult enough to be a real joy to him, or to arrange rescheduling that gives him a chance for satisfying social interaction.

The psychologist will also wish to work with the parents and help prepare them to deal with each later school unit, and to effect the child's entrance into each unit at the appropriate time. In fact, throughout the entire program the school psychologist will be in frequent consultation with the parents, aiding them in understanding the special talents of the child, the school program planned for him, and ways of confronting the various blocks and obstacles that almost inevitably develop for a child of exceptional talents.

The psychologist will remember that he might live out his whole professional life without ever once encountering a child at the 180 IQ level. Such children are extremely rare; presumably, also, their potential contributions to society, in whatever fields they enter, are of the same level of rarity and significance.

A Broad Appraisal of the Needs of the Intellectually Gifted Child

The placement of each individual child will take into account his total array of characteristics. Among other aspects, a clear picture will include the following:

a. *The child's present mental age and his rate of mental growth.* Several intelligence tests will give the psychologist and the school a better picture than one single test.

[30] Hollingworth, *op. cit.*
[31] Terman and Oden, *op. cit.*

b. *The child's present educational knowledge and skills.* Standardized educational tests in all of the appropriate school subjects will be necessary.

c. *Special abilities of the child.* Creativity in art, music, science, writing, etc., will be seen in the reports of teachers and records of special activities and experiences.

d. *The child's physical size.* Although friendships do not depend upon size, it will be of interest to see whether the child is approximately at the average height of other children of his mental age.

e. *The child's general state of health, including any sensory deprivations.*

f. *The child's present friendships and the opportunities for building friendships in a new placement.*

g. *The child's level of emotional adjustment.*

In considering a new grade placement for the child, the school psychologist will also want to know the attitudes of the teacher from whose room the child is moved, the attitudes of the receiving teacher, the attitudes of the school supervisors and administrators involved, and particularly, the attitudes of the child's parents.

Indeed, it will very often become the function of the psychologist to serve as a catalyst in unifying the efforts of all persons involved in meeting the child's needs, especially when new arrangements are being made. This may entail many conferences with parents, helping them to look ahead and to visualize the framework of a long-time plan for the child.

Educational Arrangements for the Intellectually Gifted Child

The school psychologist will need to be fully conversant with the many different types of educational provisions for the intellectually gifted child that have been utilized in one community and another.[32-51] With a full

---

[32] Walter B. Barbe and Dorothy Norris, "Special Classes for Gifted Children in Cleveland," *Exceptional Children*, 21 (1954), 55–58.

[33] Marie A. Flesher, and Sidney L. Pressey, "War-Time Accelerates Ten Years After," *Journal of Educational Psychology*, 46 (1955), 228–238.

[34] French, *op. cit.*

[35] Nelson B. Henry, ed., *Education for the Gifted*, National Society for the Study of Education, 57th Yearbook, Part II. (Chicago: 1958).

[36] John L. Holland, "Prediction of Scholastic Success for a High Aptitude Sample," *School and Society*, 86 (1958), 290–293.

[37] Jack A. Holmes and Carmen J. Finley, "Underage and Overage Grade Placements and School Achievement," *Journal of Educational Psychology*, 48 (1957), 447–457.

[38] Bernice M. Horrall, "Academic Performance and Personality Adjustments of

arsenal of administrative arrangements and educational procedures in mind, the school psychologist will be able to be of use to teachers, principals, supervisors, and superintendents, through individual conferences and group meetings, as they work out constructive provisions suitable to the particular school situation and to the needs of its intellectually gifted children.

One strong probability is that the intellectually gifted child may be capable of a depth and breadth of intellectual functioning that far surpasses any goals imagined by the educational world. As an illustration, one study [52] compared the reading abilities of two groups of children of comparable mental ages, eleven years three months, one group being fifteen years five months in chronological age (IQ 79) and the other, nine years two and one-half months in C.A. (IQ 126). The reading abilities were measured in eleven different aspects (word meaning, drawing inferences, reading rate, etc.). Of the eleven measurements, two showed almost no difference between the younger and the older children; four favored the younger children at about the 0.05 level of significance; the remaining five favored the younger children with much more highly significant differences. In testing comprehension it was hard to think of the younger and the older children as being in the same universe, the

---

Highly Intelligent College Students," *Genetic Psychology Monographs*, 55 (1957), 3–83.

[39] Joseph Justman, "Personal and Social Adjustment of Intellectually Gifted Accelerants and Non-accelerants in Junior High Schools," *School Review*, 61 (1953), 468–478.

[40] ————, "Academic Achievement of Intellectually Gifted Accelerants and Non-accelerants in Junior High School," *School Review*, 62 (1954), 143–150.

[41] ————, "Academic Achievement of Intellectually Gifted Accelerants and Non-accelerants in Senior High School," *School Review*, 62 (1954), 469–473.

[42] Miller, *op. cit.*

[43] Vera V. Miller, "The Dynamics of Establishing and Maintaining Programs for the Intellectually Gifted" Symposium, American Psychological Association, Division of School Psychologists, 1958, Mimeo.

[44] A. Harry Passow, and Others, *Planning for Talented Youth: Considerations for Public Schools* (New York: Teachers College, Columbia University, 1955).

[45] Carl W. Pegnato and Jack W. Birch, "Locating Gifted Children in Junior High Schools: A Comparison of Methods," *Exceptional Children*, 25 (1959), 300–304.

[46] Pennsylvania Department of Public Instruction, *Standards for the Organization and Administration of Special Classes* (Harrisburg: The Department, 1945).

[47] Dan C. Shannon, "What Research Says About Acceleration," *Phi Delta Kappan*, 39, 70–73.

[48] Martinson, *op. cit.*

[49] John M. Stalnaker, "National Program for Discovering Students of Exceptional Ability," *Exceptional Children*, 23 (1957), 234–237, 266.

[50] Paul A. Witty and Anne Coomer, "A Case Study of Gifted Twin Boys," *Exceptional Children*, 22 (1955), 104–108, 124–125.

[51] Dean A. Worcester, *The Education of Children of Above-Average Mentality* (Lincoln: University of Nebraska Press, 1956).

[52] Emery P. Biesmer, "Reading Abilities of Bright and Dull Children of Comparable Mental Age," *Journal of Educational Psychology*, 45 (1954), 321–331.

difference was so great (F_{05} = 4.04; in "listening" comprehension F = 47.57). It is to be remembered that the two groups were at the same mental age level on the Stanford-Binet Form L.

There is evidence that some schools have rid themselves of their blind spots with respect to their intellectually gifted children, and are endeavoring to find constructive ways of helping these children to reach a wider range of experience and a higher altitude in their intellectual endeavor, both today and in future years. Some valuable educational administrative procedures have been devised by some of these schools. Consideration can be given to the following:

1. Entrance to kindergarten and first grade by mental age and rate of mental growth.

2. Homogeneous grouping of first grade by mental age, especially when there are three, four, or five first grades in the same building.

3. Homogeneous grouping from first grade on, as in the "fast track" system.

4. Reducing the time spent on a unit in the school system, as, for instance, junior high school (grades 7, 8, and 9) in two years instead of three.

5. Entrance to college after the eleventh year.

6. "Enrichment" of the curriculum for the intellectually gifted child for whom none of the preceding arrangements has been established; in other words, provisions for more interesting work for him within his "regular" school grade.
   (How can the teacher find time to help a child of mental age twelve in a third grade where two-thirds of the group have mental ages of eight and a few children have mental ages only of six? [53])

With respect to the sixth point, the school psychologist will be hard pressed to find any studies showing improved academic status, increased motivation, or more successful social and emotional adjustment resulting from the type of "enrichment" that keeps the intellectually gifted child with his chronological age equals, but not with his mental age equals. Such studies as those of the Cleveland Major Work program,[54] which uses homogeneous grouping and holds to the usual course of study with only a little "enrichment," have found no such decisive improvement in academic and social adjustment as have the experiments dealing with early entrance, acceleration, homogeneous grouping without curriculum restrictions, a "fast track" system, and other more homogeneous approaches.

It is understood that "homogeneous" grouping does not mean that all of the children in the group will have exactly the same mental age. It does

[53] Martinson, op. cit., p. 184.
[54] Barbe and Norris, op. cit.

mean that the mental age range in a group will be greatly reduced, achieving a group where communication and interaction are more feasible.

Homogeneous grouping by mental age gives the teacher a much more favorable setting in which to help children with each one's special academic needs. Perhaps for all children, and certainly for the intellectually gifted child, there is greater freedom for continuity of thought and for whole-hearted purposeful activity within the group. Many experiments have demonstrated the measurable increase in learning and the more favorable attitudes resulting from such grouping.

One responsibility that the school psychologist must assume is to guard the continuity of whatever program is established for intellectually gifted children, and to see that it is maintained throughout each child's entire school career. Observational studies have shown the disrupting effect on intellectually gifted children when provisions made for them for a year or two are suddenly dropped.[55] Continuity is especially urgent when homogeneous groups are established, and when a "fast track" system is entered upon. To have these arrangements dropped in midstream may be more damaging to the child than if nothing had been done for him in the first place.

It may be that from the standpoint of the administrator, such arrangements as early entrance to kindergarten or to first grade, or placing the child in a higher grade are less demanding than are other procedures. The individual child's progress can usually be insured once he has been started at a younger chronological age or has been advanced somewhere in the grades because of his doing excellent school work. As has been suggested, such special arrangements as homogeneous grouping require long-time commitment on the part of the school board, superintendent, and principal.

Friendships for the Intellectually Gifted Child

One of the major concerns about intellectually gifted children that has caused much confusion is that of peer relations and friendships. It has long been considered an educational truism that a child profits most by being with his own chronological age group. The few research studies that are available, however, point to exactly the opposite conclusion, namely, that any child can interact most effectively and most wholesomely with other children who are of the same, or nearly the same, *mental age.*[56, 57, 58, 59]

[55] Miller, *op. cit.*
[56] Hollingworth, *op. cit.*
[57] Leon M. Lessinger and Ruth A. Martinson, "The Use of The California Psychological Inventory with Gifted Pupils," *The Personnel and Guidance Journal,* 39 (1961), 572–575.
[58] Horace Mann, "How Real Are Friendships of Gifted and Typical Children in a Program of Partial Segregation?" *Exceptional Children,* 23 (1957), 199–201, 206.
[59] Harriet E. O'Shea, "Friendship and the Intellectually Gifted Child," *Exceptional Children,* 26 (1960), 327–335.

Children in nursery schools, in forming their small spontaneous groups from hour to hour and from day to day, associate with children of closely similar mental age. Moreover, when primary and elementary school children of more advanced mental ages are grouped for half a day with their chronological-age peers and the other half-day with children of similar high mental ages, on sociometric tests the intellectually gifted children chose children of the same mental age rather than those of the same chronological age, even though they had spent an equal amount of time with both groups. Their involvement in the lives of other children who are their mental peers is further illustrated when they report that they do not like certain children in their mental-age group, and fail to mention those in their chronological-age group. It is evident that they have paid literally no attention to the lower mental age children; on the other hand, there is real interaction, satisfaction, and involvement, even in the sense of rejection, with those of their own mental ages. Hollingworth presented many records of the great changes that occur when intellectually gifted children are taken away from their chronological age groups and placed in groups closely resembling their own mental ages.

A recent broad study of intellectually gifted children ordered by the legislature of the state of California [60] has reported the level of personal maturity of intellectually gifted pupils compared to those of the same mental age who are older chronologically.[61] On the California Psychological Inventory, gifted boys completing the seventh grade showed maturity scores comparable to those of the composite high school and adult male norms. The same high maturity scores were shown for the intellectually gifted girls at the same grade level. Their scores fell in the high school norms, eleven of eighteen scales exhibiting no difference between the gifted seventh-graders and the high school girls. In the same way, the intellectually gifted boys and girls in high school showed significantly higher maturity on fourteen of eighteen scales for boys, and on thirteen of eighteen scales for girls compared to fellow high school students of the same chronological age.

Such findings mean that in arranging school placement the school psychologist must concern himself with the friendship possibilities of intellectually gifted children as well as with their academic achievement.

Educators and lay persons have wondered whether grouping a superior child with others of his own mental age and rate of mental growth will not make an insufferable prig of him, whether he will not "lord it over" children of lesser ability, and whether he will not sense a difference indicating that he is "better" than they.

The exact opposite is what does occur, apparently. In his own mental age group the gifted child has both necessary intellectual stimulation and

[60] Martinson, op. cit.
[61] Lessinger and Martinson, op. cit.

honest "competition." If he does not work hard, he will suddenly end up at the bottom of the class in situations where the classroom is structured as a competing organization. It is when the child is grouped with others two, three, or four years below his mental age that he stands out as obviously "superior" to the rest. There is no way he could escape knowing it. (Worse yet, the others know it, too, and do not like it; thus he is truly rejected, alone, and unable to enter into the group or to communicate with others.) With other children of his own mental age, he is one of the crowd, and he can succeed if he works hard.

A most serious penalty for keeping the child with children far below his mental age is the rigid inner distance he builds after repeated failures to establish a warm contact with other children; this is as poor a personal experience as one could possibly subject a child to.

If for no other reason, mental health considerations demand that the child be kept with his mental equals. Intellectually gifted children, also, have a right to life, liberty, and the pursuit of happiness.

Academic Achievement Relative to Intellectual Ability

The evidence is decisive in all experiments that have been published that early entrance, or homogeneous grouping, or "fast track," or grouping with chronologically older children, or early entrance to college all result in the child's receiving higher academic grades than before and scoring higher on standardized achievement tests than children of equal intelligence who were left behind with their chronological age mates.[62, 63, 64] The evidence is so clear-cut in this respect, that the school psychologist does well to keep these facts at all times before the appropriate educational groups with which he works.

Special questions arise about intellectually gifted children who do not achieve up to their level of ability.[65, 66, 67, 68, 69, 70] The school psychologist

[62] French, *op. cit.*

[63] Hobson, "Mental Age."

[64] Hobson, "Scholastic Standing."

[65] Marion E. Armstrong, *A Comparison of the Interest and Social Adjustment of Under-Achievers and Normal Achievers at the Secondary School Level*, Doctoral dissertation, University of Connecticut, 1955.

[66] Louis A. Fliegler, "Understanding the Underachieving Gifted Child," *Psychological Reports*, 3 (1957), 533–536.

[67] John C. Gowan, "Dynamics of the Underachievement of Gifted Students," *Exceptional Children*, 24 (1957), 98–101, 122.

[68] John C. Gowan, "The Underachieving Gifted Child—A Problem for Everyone," *Exceptional Children*, 21 (1955), 324–329.

[69] Holmes, *op. cit.*

[70] A. Harry Passow and Miriam L. Goldberg, "Study of Underachieving Gifted," *Educational Leadership*, 16 (1958), 121–125.

needs to "keep books" on the achievement of intellectually gifted children so as to throw into clear relief any intellectually gifted children who are working below their level of ability, even though they may not receive failing marks. Such "concealed failure" [71] is of utmost significance if these highly able individuals are to be salvaged before it is too late.

The psychologist can develop ways of making this discrepancy statistically clear for himself and for the teaching and administrative staffs of the school. One method is to express both the intelligence test results and the standardized educational achievement test results in terms of the standard deviation of each distribution. Each child's situation can then be visualized in terms of whether his intelligence (mental age) is more standard deviations above the mean than his educational achievement (educational age). The finding, in many studies from first grade through college, is that there is an appalling amount of underachievement on the part of intellectually gifted children, undoubtedly due in large part to unsuitable placement in school.[72]

In cooperation with the educational staff, the psychologist needs to seek out the causes of underachievement in each such individual intellectually gifted child. He will want to know how the school is handling the child, where he is placed in school, and the mental ages and rates of mental growth of the children with whom he is classified.

A second area of inquiry is the child's home life and his status with respect to friends and in general social activities inside and outside the school. The intellectually gifted child, has been shown to have the same chance as any other child of encountering deep-seated emotional troubles arising from the attitudes and behavior of parents toward him, toward his siblings, and toward each other.[73, 74] When appropriate, the school psychologist will assist in locating possible trouble spots and in instituting necessary service to the family, possibly with the assistance of or referral to some other qualified agency.

The academic achievement of the intellectually gifted child is closely related to the so called factor of "motivation." [75, 76, 77] The question of what inspires the child to do the work put before him must be answered in terms

[71] Horrall, op. cit.
[72] Ibid.
[73] French, op. cit.
[74] Thom and Newell, op. cit.
[75] James V. Pierce and Paul H. Bowman, "Motivation Patterns of Superior High School Students," in The Gifted Student (Washington, D.C.: U.S. Department of Health, Education, and Welfare, Office of Education, Cooperative Research Monograph No. 2, 1960).
[76] Leona E. Tyler, "Studies on Motivation and Identification of Gifted Pupils," Review of Educational Research, 27 (1957), 391–399.
[77] Donald D. Young, Parental Influence upon Decisions of Scholastically Talented Youth Concerning Higher Education, Doctor's thesis, University of Wisconsin, 1958.

of the individual child—perhaps the work is deadly dull because the child has covered the material two or three years earlier; perhaps his tastes and interests lie elsewhere; perhaps ineffective educational procedures are utilized within the classroom; perhaps children are not given experiences which illuminate the areas of thought being explored; or perhaps the day's work is concerned only with minimum, superficial aspects of subject matter,[78] presented in a deadening fashion. In the course of examining the child's situation and devising ways to institute desirable changes, the school psychologist may assist in improving educational procedures for all children, and not alone for a single intellectually gifted child.

As the causes of underachievement are located, they must obviously be reversed in whatever ways are necessary to produce a constructive and permanent change. The school psychologist often will be called upon to take the initiative in making the appropriate changes that will release the gifted child's abilities and enabled him to move forward on his own high level.

The Intellectually Gifted Child with Emotional Troubles

It is not improbable that individual intellectually gifted children have all of the emotional ills that afflict mankind, even though Terman's original findings and all of his follow-up studies [79, 80, 81, 82] have demonstrated that the incidence of emotional and social maladjustment among the intellectually gifted is less than in the population as a whole.

The recognition of those among the highly intelligent children who are over-anxious or over-conscientious may be more difficult than it is among children of lesser ability. The over-conscientious child will often be getting such high grades that no one in the school system pays him the slightest attention; the psychologist, perhaps, may have noted how alone he is or how disliked by the others, or with what alarm he reacts to small academic failures. The over-anxious, highly intelligent child is easier to recognize; he often gets low grades or engages in varieties of bizarre behavior. He boldly "whistles in the dark," and often no one is aware that there is trouble in his extreme apprehension.

---

[78] Holmes, *op. cit.*
[79] L. M. Terman, *et al., Mental and Physical Traits of a Thousand Gifted Children,* Genetic Studies of Genius, I (Stanford, Calif.: Stanford University Press, 1925).
[80] L. M. Terman, *et al., The Promise of Youth: A Follow-Up Study of a Thousand Gifted Children,* Genetic Studies of Genius, III (Stanford: Stanford University Press, 1930).
[81] Terman, *The Gifted Child Grows Up.*
[82] Terman, *The Gifted Group at Mid-Life.*

Creativity in the Intellectually Gifted Child

During the past decade or so, great interest has centered on how human beings perceive new relationships and create new constructs. While more study and experimentation has been expended on adult creative thinking than on creativity among children,[83, 84] especially in the area of science, some studies of childhood creativity have been completed, and more are under way.

One fact which appears to emerge is that, if creativity is defined and measured as "divergent thinking,"[85, 86, 87] and if children of satisfactory academic standing are sorted into fairly "pure" groups, high-school-level teachers do not like the children who show creativity. At the same time, they do like those who show intellectual traits that result in high intelligence quotients. In the elementary-school-age range[88] there appears to be the same uncomfortableness on the part of teachers towards "pure" creativity (divergent thinking) displayed by children. The other children also seem to like the high-IQ child better than the divergent-thinking child. In spite of this, those who are high in both traits are viewed as the "stars" of the elementary school population.

So far it has not been determined whether the intellectual characteristics measured as divergent thinking are closely related to the kind of creativity that can result in products of social value. Chapter 20 reviews in depth the role of the school psychologist in fostering creativity in the school.

Evaluation of Programs

It is highly desirable that the school psychologist arrange and carry out an annual evaluation of whatever programs for the gifted are under way in his school system. Such an annual evaluation is a necessity for a continuous, flexible improvement of the program and for demonstrating to the school board, to the superintendent, to the principals, to the teaching staff, to the parents and to the general public the worth of such enterprises.

The school psychologist will need to confer with the educational staff about the facets of the programs that would be most significant to appraise.

---

[83] Calvin W. Taylor, *Research Conference on the Identification of Creative Scientific Talent* (Salt Lake City: University of Utah Press, 1957).

[84] —————, *Research Conference on the Identification of Creative Scientific Talent* (Salt Lake City: University of Utah Press, 1959).

[85] J. W. Getzels and P. W. Jackson, "The Study of Giftedness: A Multidimensional Approach," *The Gifted Student* (Washington, D.C.: U.S. Department of Health, Education, and Welfare, Office of Education, Cooperative Research Monograph No. 2, 1960).

[86] Taylor, *op. cit.*, 1957.

[87] Taylor, *op. cit.*, 1959.

[88] *Ibid.*

He will contribute his technical knowledge and skills to implement an appraisal program that will satisfy the educators and the community.

Selection of Teachers for the Gifted

There are as yet few facts available as to whether there are special characteristics needed for the teachers of intellectually gifted children and almost no research has been done about how teachers should be trained for this responsibility. In the California Attitudes Surveys,[89, 90] all groups of respondents believed that teachers of the gifted should have a broader cultural background than teachers of average pupils. In this California sample, lay people, teachers, and psychologists thought that teachers of the gifted should have special credentials.[91] All groups also thought that teachers would meet the needs of the gifted more adequately if they had smaller classes.

A nation-wide survey of the education of teachers for the gifted [92, 93, 94] has shown that essentially nothing is being done along this line; however, a few in-service and undergraduate programs in the preparation of teachers have been described, and several states now have teacher education and certification programs for teachers of the gifted. California has recently passed special education legislation to give financial aid to local school districts which will establish programs for "mentally gifted minors."

The General Task

All of the school psychologist's professional knowledge and skills will be required in his work with and for intellectually gifted children. In this special field, in contrast to the psychologist's general work with children throughout the whole range of intelligence, at least two less usual functionings will come into play.

1. In almost all cases, the psychologist himself will need to initiate and develop most phases of the program for the intellectually gifted children. The initiative and the responsibility are not borne by any other educators in most school systems. If he does nothing, nothing will occur.

2. Initiation of any special provisions to help intellectually gifted chil-

[89] Reed, *op. cit.*

[90] Martinson, *op. cit.*

[91] Penn. Dept. Public Instruction, *op. cit.*

[92] Nelda Davis, "Teachers for the Gifted," *Journal of Teacher Education,* 5 (1954), 221–224.

[93] Frank T. Wilson, "Preparation for Teachers of Gifted Children in the United States," *Exceptional Children,* 22 (1953), 78–80.

[94] ————, "In-Service and Undergraduate Preparation of Teachers of the Gifted," *Educational Administration and Supervision,* 43 (1957), 295–301.

dren requires that the psychologist be occupied for untold hours in a vigorous effort, explaining, encouraging, and soliciting the understanding and cooperation of many persons, and developing their interested participation in the welfare of intellectually gifted children. More than in any other part of his work, he will need to acquire and utilize skills of "promotion" as he works for the gifted. It is only with the active support of educators and the community that successful programs can be developed.

Selected Supplementary Readings

Abraham, Willard, Common Sense About Gifted Children. New York: Harper & Row, Publishers, 1958.

American Psychological Association, Division 16, Subcommittee on Needed Research on Gifted Children, "Needed Research on Gifted Children," American Psychologist, 9 (February, 1954), 77–78.

Barbe, Walter B., "The Influence of Examiner–Child Interaction on Measurement of Giftedness," The Gifted Child Quarterly IX (Autumn, 1965), 145–148.

Bereday, George Z. F., and Joseph A. Lauwerys', eds., The Gifted Child: The Year Book of Education, 1962. New York: Harcourt, Brace & World, Inc., 1962.

Bettelheim, Bruno, and Kenneth Mott, "Grouping the Gifted," NEA Journal, 54 (March, 1965).

Birch, J. W., and M. C. Reynolds, "The Gifted," Review of Educational Research, 33 (February, 1963), 83–98.

————, W. David and W. J. Tisdall, "Early Admission of Able Children to School," The Warren Demonstration Project, School Life, 46 (June, 1964).

Blosser, George H., "Group Intelligence Tests as Screening Devices in Locating the Gifted and Superior Students in the Ninth Grade," Exceptional Children, 29 (1963), 282–286.

Carroll, H. A., "Intellectually Gifted Children," Teachers College Record, 42 (1940), 212–227.

Conant, James B., "Identification and Education of the Academically Talented Student in the American Secondary School," The Conference Report. Washington, D. C.: National Education Association, 1958.

Crow, Lester D., and Alice Crow, eds., Educating the Academically Able: A Book of Readings. New York: David McKay Co., Inc., 1963.

Cutts, Norma E., and Nicholas Moseley, Teaching the Bright and Gifted. Englewood Cliffs, N. J.: Prentice-Hall, Inc., 1957.

————, *Providing for Individual Differences in the Elementary School.* Englewood Cliffs, N. J.: Prentice-Hall, Inc., 1960.

DeHaan, Robert F., and Robert J. Havighurst, *Educating Gifted Children,* rev. ed. Chicago: The University of Chicago Press, 1961.

Durr, W. K., *The Gifted Student.* New York: Oxford University Press, 1964.

Ferguson, Donald, "Professional Roles in the Vocational Guidance of Gifted Children," *Vocational Guidance Quarterly* (Summer, 1963), pp. 241–246.

Fine, Benjamin, *Stretching Their Minds: The Exciting New Approach to the Education of the Gifted Child Pioneered by Sands Point Country Day School.* New York: E. P. Dutton & Co., Inc., 1964.

Freehill, Maurice F., *Gifted Children: Their Psychology and Education.* New York: The Macmillan Company, 1961.

Gallagher, Jane J., *Teaching The Gifted Child.* Boston: Allyn and Bacon, Inc., 1964.

————, "The Gifted," *Review of Educational Research,* **36** (February, 1966), 37–55.

Goertzel, Victor, and Mildred G. Goertzel, *Cradles of Eminence.* Boston: Little, Brown and Company, 1962.

Goldberg, Miriam L., "Recent Research on the Talented," *Teachers College Record,* **60** (December, 1958), 150–163.

————, and Associates, "A Three Year Experimental Program at De Witt Clinton High School to Help Bright Underachievers," in *Readings on the Exceptional Child,* ed. Trapp and Himelstein. New York: Appleton-Century-Crofts, 1962.

Gowan, John Curtis, and George D. Demos, *The Education and Guidance of the Ablest.* Springfield, Ill.: Charles C Thomas, Publisher, 1964.

Gross, Frank P., and David A. Sabatino, "Role of the School Psychologist in Evaluating an Experimental Program for Gifted Students," *Journal of School Psychology,* **3** (1965), 56–61.

Hildreth, Gertrude H., *Introduction to the Gifted.* New York: McGraw-Hill Book Company, 1966.

Hobson, James R., "A Failure in Retrospect," *Psychology in the Schools,* I (July, 1964), 285–287.

Hollingworth, Leta S., *Gifted Children, Their Nature and Nurture.* New York: The Macmillan Company, 1929.

Jordan, J. E., and J. P. Keith, "The Counselor's Role in Working with the Gifted," *The Gifted Child Quarterly* IX (Autumn, 1965), 136–141.

Kelley, Robert, "The Limits to Deviant Behavior in the Gifted," *School Life,* 47 (October, 1964).

Lesser, Gerald S., Frederick B. Davis, and Lucille Naheneow, "The Identification of Gifted Elementary School Children with Exceptional Scientific

Talent," *Educational and Psychological Measurement*, 22 (1962), 349–364.

Martinson, Ruth, Chariman, Gifted Child Committee, California Association of School Psychologists and Psychometrists, *The School Psychologist and the Education of Gifted Children.* Sacramento: California State Department of Education, 1962.

Newland, T. E., "A Critique of Research on the Gifted," *Exceptional Children*, 29 (1963), 391–398.

————, "Essential Research Directions on the Gifted," *Exceptional Children*, 21 (May, 1955), 292–296.

————, "Implications of Research in the Area of the Gifted," *Exceptional Children*, 25 (January, 1959), 195–198.

————, "Programs for the Superior: Happenstansical or Conceptual?" *Teachers College Record*, 62, No. 7 (April, 1961), 513–523.

Oswalt, Edna R., *The Role of the Parent in the Education and Training of of the Mentally Superior Child*, Revision of Conference on Mentally Superior Children, Warren G. Harding High School, Kent State University Bulletin. Kent, Ohio: Kent State University, 1957.

Passow, A. Harry, and M. L. Goldberg, "The Gifted," in *Behavioral Research on Exceptional Children*, ed. S. A. Kirk and B. B. Weiner. Washington, D. C.: The Council for Exceptional Children, NEA, 1963.

Roberts, H. E., "Factors Affecting the Academic Underachievement of the Gifted Child," *Journal of Educational Research*, 56 (December, 1962), 175–183.

Seashore, H. G., "The Identification of the Gifted," *Test Service Bulletin*, No. 55. New York: Psychological Corporation, 1963, pp. 1–7.

Sivers, W. A., "Psychologists Aid Gifted Children," *Bulletin to the Schools* (May, 1960), pp. 1–4.

Smith, D. W., "Identifying Gifted School-age Children," *Education*, 83 (February, 1963), 370–374.

Tannenbaum, Abraham, Jr., *Adolescent Attitudes Toward Academic Brilliance*. New York: Columbia University Press, 1962.

Tisdall, William J., and Jack W. Birch, "The School Psychologist in a Program of Early Admission for Mentally Advanced Children," *Journal of School Psychology*, 3 (1965), 48–55.

Weise, Phillip, J. K. Tuel, and C. E. Meyers, "Increasing the Efficiency of Identification of Gifted in Kindergarten," *CASSP Conference Proceedings* (1964), pp. 92–98.

Wilson, C. D., "Using Test Results and Teacher Evaluation in Identifying Gifted Pupils," *Personnel and Guidance Journal*, 41 (April, 1963), 720–721.

Witty, Paul, "The Gifted Child," in *Professional School Psychology*, Vol. I, ed. M. G. Gottsegen and G. B. Gottsegen. New York: Grune & Stratton, Inc., 1960, pp. 206–223.

Woods, Elizabeth, "Special Classes for Children who are Superior in Mental Ability," *Los Angeles Board of Education, Division of Psychology and Educational Research, Third Yearbook, Bulletin 185* (1929), pp. 22–43.

ELI M. BOWER

15

The School Psychologist's Role in the Identification and Adjustment of Socio-Emotionally Handicapped Children

The school psychologist is a recently adopted growing child in the educational family. As is often the case with growing children, little growth may take place in some years and much in others. In California, as late as 1950, there were less than 100 certified psychologists serving the schools of the state. Five years later, the number was 500, and in 1967 over 1000. Similar growth trends were taking place in other sections of the United States. As schools found themselves in need of persons with professional psychological training and experience, more and more psychologists began to find the school a vast frontier in need of services, programs, and research. There were, however, two major forces that affected the growth and status of school psychological services and that had their greatest impact on the school after World War II, *circa* 1945.

Over the years there had been gradual acceptance of the notion of providing educational opportunities for all children although few could conceive of this goal

446

being reached to any great degree in actual practice. However, the initiation and development of organized groups of parents whose children were not receiving an education, i.e., parents of cerebral palsied and mentally retarded children, gave impetus and support for the extension of educational services to these and other children. Within recent years most states have passed laws providing for the extension of school services to handicapped children so that, for example, in California in 1960, 97.8 per cent of school age children were attending a public school.[1] In essence, the implementation of the philosophy of providing educational opportunities for handicapped children has placed the school in a position of having to learn more about the educational assets and liabilities of such children often on an individual basis. At this point the school psychologist, as the specialist in psychological testing and individual study became a necessary part of the team in planning for the education of children with major learning handicaps.

While the school has been grappling with the problem of educating children with severe sensory, motor, and intellectual handicaps, increasing clinical and experimental evidence of the impact of emotions on learning has become available.[2] In the last decade much of the relationship between emotions and learning has been focused on the deviant or non-learner in an effort to discover educational means to help such children toward effective learning. Undoubtedly, there has been more general acceptance and utility of the psychodynamic concepts of behavior and learning by educators, especially in attempting to understand emotional factors in the learning process.[3, 4, 5] Again, this has led the schools to seek the services of persons who could help interpret and understand the emotional processes of children, especially those children who were having difficulty in school. The school psychologist was therefore called upon to study children who were unable to profit by school attendance and to assist the school in achieving a successful educational experience for the child. The school psychologist's clinical experience and training in understanding children with emotional handicaps was found to be extremely helpful to teachers and others in carrying out their educational responsibilities.

The psychologist who functions in a school setting must bear in mind the purpose of the institution he serves—the education of children. Although "understanding" the child may be an integral part of such instruction, it

[1] *Rankings of the States* (Washington, D.C.: NEA Research Division, 1960), 3.

[2] D. Prescott, *Emotions and the Educative Process* (Washington, D.C.: American Council on Education, 1938).

[3] F. Redl and W. Wattenburg, *Mental Hygiene in Teaching* (New York: Harcourt, Brace & World, Inc., 1951).

[4] R. Stewart and A. Workman, *Children and Other People* (New York: The Dryden Press, 1956).

[5] C. Buhler, F. Smitter, and S. Richardson, *Childhood Problems and the Teacher* (New York: Holt, Rinehart & Winston, Inc., 1952).

cannot be regarded, in a school setting, as a self-consummating act. Understanding the nature of a child's emotions must have meaning in terms of the child's education. This is especially true in the case of children with moderate or severe emotional handicaps. The relationship between emotions and intellectual growth must be understandably presented to the educators and community in an effort to assist the psychological unsophisticate to understand some of the following ideas and concepts about emotion as it relates to education.

Emotions and Learning

Emotions and intellectual achievement are bound by strong and intricate ties. Learning that results in mature behavior, communicative skills, economic productivity and wisdom cannot and does not take place without active emotional involvement in the experience. In most cases, this involvement is taken for granted as a necessary component of intellectual readiness. Often it is difficult for the average person to understand how emotional conflicts or defects affect intellectual learnings. Indeed, there are many who feel the thinking processes of man can best be activated in a neutral or cold emotional climate, and that emotions have been placed in the human personality to function at weddings, burials, and sad movies. One might consider the clarity and excellence of the thought processes of the paranoid individual that often lead him to the inevitable and logical conclusion that violence is necessary to protect himself. Or the girl in *Feelings of Hostility* [6] who secured little love from her parents, but a great deal of admiration for intellectual successes. For her, love and recognition could only be obtained by successful intellectual accomplishment. As an adult, this girl became a successful business woman, but a lonely and despondent person.

Man's capacity to create and use symbols as representations of reality makes possible not only his highest development as a rational time-binding organism, but his vulnerability to the distortions of these symbols. As Kubie points out, "Education has not yet attacked the problem of how to develop these highest capacities of *Homo Sapiens* while at the same time preventing their neurotic distortion." [7] Educational purposes such as self-realization, economic efficiency, and intellectual competence cannot be realized for any child in an emotional vacuum. It is probable that the development of the intellectual capacities of a child without concomitant emotional growth and maturation will produce empty and distorted persons whose brilliance and potential are only half realized. The prerequisite for sound thinking and

[6] *Feelings of Hostility*, 16mm. Sound Film (New York: McGraw-Hill Book Company).

[7] L. Kubie, "The Psychiatrist Considers Curriculum Development," *Teachers College Record*, 50 (January, 1949), 241–246.

effective participation in a democratic society rests on the ability of the school and the family to help children think on the basis of facts and realities, rather than on the basis of individual emotional conflicts or defects. As a student of human behavior has noted,

> Students of human nature and philosophers have long taught us that we are mistaken in regarding our intelligence as an independent force and in overlooking its dependence upon the emotional life. Our intelligence . . . can function reliably only when it is removed from the influences of strong emotional impulses; otherwise, it behaves merely as an instrument of the will and delivers the inference which the will requires. Thus . . . logical arguments are impotent against effective interests and that is why reasons which in Falstaff's phrase are "as plenty as blackberries" produce so few victories.[8]

If the basic vulnerability of the adult to emotional and learning disabilities is a result of early life experiences, to what extent can a school program repair or reduce this vulnerability? There are numerous examples of teachers who have had a marked effect on children's lives.[9] Schools provide organized social and intellectual experiences that have a powerful formative influence on the personality of the child. "Educators vary in the degree to which they are conscious of this total effect—but the effect of schools on personality development is great whether or not educators intend it to be so." [10]

What Are Emotional Handicaps?

Unlike other kinds of handicaps which are usually the result of physical or intellectual defects, emotional handicaps may be the result of an overabundance of emotions. The emotionally handicapped child may exhibit his difficulties in different ways. He may pour all his energies into school work as a way of avoiding relationships with himself or others; or, he may be able to muster only small bits of energy for educational activities. He may appear to be severely mentally retarded or extremely brilliant. A classic case of the latter was reported in the *New Yorker Magazine* several years ago.[11] This was a graduate of a California high school, Dale Maple, who had never received a grade below "A" in his high school career and had graduated first in a class of 585 seniors. Dale received a four-year scholarship to Harvard, majoring in comparative philology and graduating with an "A" average. Dale also had the unique distinction of being the first American soldier in World War II who was tried and convicted of treason. A psychiatric examination

---

[8] S. Freud, *Collected Papers* (London: Hogarth Press, 1950), V, 302.
[9] W. Gibson, *Miracle Worker* (New York: Alfred A. Knopf, Inc., 1957).
[10] *The Elements of a Community Mental Health Program* (New York: Milbank Memorial Fund, 1956), p. 13.
[11] E. J. Kahn, "Annals of Crime," *New Yorker Magazine*, March 11, 18, 25 and April 1, 1950.

at the time of his trial revealed an IQ of 152 in an infantile and distorted personality.

Our language, with its subject-predicate structure, tends to define as black or white qualities that are seldom either. The use of the term "emotionally handicapped," for example, in place of "emotionally disturbed," "socially maladjusted" or other similar term is designed to reduce somewhat the semantic problems inherent in delineations of states of emotion. The term "handicap" has a relatively more lasting and persistent quality; disturbances are often seen as transitory or temporary. The use of "disturbance" is usually indicative of the acting-out, overtly aggressive child; therefore, one tends to perceive emotional problems as resulting in one type of behavior. "Emotionally handicapped" has less of the black or white connotation of a disease and is more illustrative of the degree nature of emotional problems. Lastly, the term "emotionally handicapped" is often more realistically descriptive of the disability and is not an attempt to "gild the lily." Part of the problem, however, of any attempt at an adequate description or definition of the term, lies in the difficulty in cognitively describing the complex affective state, called "emotion." Indeed, one dictionary states that emotion is virtually impossible to define except in terms of conflicting theories.

Feelings and emotions are synonymous to most persons. Both are regarded as vague, misty things highly variable and situational. In part, this may be a result of not having any measurement devices or techniques comparable to those employed in measuring intellect, sight, hearing acuity, or academic achievement. Unlike sensory, intellectual, or physical handicaps that exhibit themselves along a single dimension primarily as a deficit, emotional handicaps can only be inferred from behavior that may be overly aggressive, inappropriate, overly withdrawn or combinations of these. One can, for example, be just as handicapped by an overabundance of emotion as by a lack of it. One can be said to be emotionally handicapped by demonstrating "normal" grief at the death of a loved one—for twenty years. One may consistently develop strong and overwhelming emotions in one relationship and be relatively self-contained in another. In addition, one can be economically successfully because of an emotional handicap or in spite of such a handicap just as one can be a blatant failure without benefit of neurosis or emotional conflict.

Handicap as Restriction of Choices

The concept of emotional handicap that would be of greatest utility to the school psychologist is one which is operationally related to the possibility of early detection and educational intervention in the school. One is trying to define and predict which children in the school population will be markedly handicapped by emotional problems as adolescents or adults. In this sense, perhaps, the term "handicapped" can best be understood as an increasing restriction of choice or alternatives of behavior. To be able to choose behavior freely and responsibly rather than being driven by impulses or emotion is a sign of healthy emotional development. When one's choices are markedly limited by emotional lacks or injunctions, one's behavior can be regarded as handicapped. The reduction of possible behavioral alternatives serves to further reduce the individual's degrees of freedom in social and educational endeavors. In addition, this reduced maneuverability or inflexibility in a changing world of mobile peers and events increases an individual's susceptibility to behavior difficulties and interpersonal friction. The emotionally handicapped child is, therefore, circumscribed as one having a higher degree of vulnerabiilty to behavior problems and one who, as an adult, will exhibit this vulnerability in general health problems, poor interpersonal relationships, inability to function sexually or economically, inability to profit from experience or lead a happy life. In its more pervasive form this vulnerability may lead to psychosis, neurosis, suicide, repetitive automobile accidents, alcoholism, narcotic addition, criminal behavior, or the inability to function or live happily.

Five Types of Behavior That Can Result from Emotional Handicaps

In terms of their visibility to the psychologist or teacher, emotionally handicapped children can be perceived as children who demonstrate one or more of the following characteristics *to a marked extent and over a period of time:*

1. AN INABILITY TO LEARN THAT CANNOT BE SOLELY EXPLAINED BY INTELLECTUAL, SENSORY, OR GENERAL HEALTH FACTORS

An inability to learn is, perhaps, the single most significant characteristic of emotionally handicapped children in school. Such non-learning may be manifested as an inability to profit from experience as well as inability to master skill subjects. The non-learner seldom escapes recognition by school personnel. Achievement tests often confirm what the teacher has long suspected. If all other major causative factors have been ruled out, emotional conflicts or resistances can be ruled in.

2. AN INABILITY TO BUILD OR MAINTAIN SATISFACTORY INTERPERSONAL RELATIONSHIPS WITH PEERS AND TEACHERS

It isn't just getting along with others that is significant here. Satisfactory interpersonal relations refer to the ability of the child to show sympathy and warmth toward others, his ability to stand alone when necessary, the ability to have close friends, to be aggressively constructive, and the ability to enjoy working and playing with others as well as enjoying working and playing by oneself. In most instances, children who are unable to build or maintain satisfactory interpersonal relationships are most visible to their peers and teachers.

3. INAPPROPRIATE TYPES OF BEHAVIOR OR FEELINGS UNDER NORMAL CONDITIONS

Inappropriateness of behavior or feeling can often be sensed by the teacher and peer groups. "He acts funny," another child may say. The teacher may find some children reacting disproportionately to a simple command such as "please take your seat." What is appropriate or inappropriate is best appraised by the psychologist, capitalizing on the teacher's professional training, her daily and long-term observation of the child, and her experience working and interacting with the appropriate behavior of large numbers of normal children.

4. A GENERAL, PERVASIVE MOOD OF UNHAPPINESS OR DEPRESSION

Children who are unhappy most of the time may demonstrate such feelings in expressive play, art work, written composition, or in discussion periods. They seldom smile and usually lack a *joie de vivre* in their school work or social relationships. In the middle or upper grades, a self-inventory is usually helpful in confirming suspicions about such feelings.

5. A TENDENCY TO DEVELOP PHYSICAL SYMPTOMS, SUCH AS SPEECH PROBLEMS, PAINS, OR FEARS ASSOCIATED WITH PERSONAL OR SCHOOL PROBLEMS

This tendency is often first noted by the parent. Illness may be continually associated with school pressures or develop when a child's confidence in himself is under stress. In some cases, such illnesses or fears may not be apparent to the teacher; peers, however, are often aware of children who are sick before or after tests, or have headaches before recitations. Speech difficulties that may be the symptoms of emotional distress are usually most visible to the parent.

The significant characteristics of children indicating a need for closer scrutiny by the school psychologist are: inability to learn, unsatisfactory interpersonal relationships, inappropriate behavior, unhappiness and physical symptoms or repetitive illness.

These characteristics can, of course, be said to be true of all children to some degree at different times. There seems to be little likelihood of by-passing the "how much is too much" issue in any descriptive attempt at separating the more vulnerable child from others. A more satisfactory and precise analysis can be made by assessing classes with some standardized process in which perceptions by teacher, peers, and self can be combined. Such a process has been employed with some success and will be discussed later in the chapter.

The Problem of Inferring Emotional Handicap from Behavior

A major caution in the use of descriptive definitions of the behavior of children to infer causation is the problem of differentiating incipient pathology from normal behavioral deviation. Marked differences in behavior are noted in children with emotional handicaps, but they are also noted in children who *choose* to behave somewhat idiosyncratically. Perhaps the key in differentiating the child whose behavioral deviation is caused by emotional problems and the child whose behavior is socially different is one of determining the source of the behavior. The behavior of the emotionally handicapped child is, to the extent of his handicap, not a matter of choice but necessity. The degrees of behavioral freedom for the emotionally handicapped individual may be restricted by internal conflicts or by a lack of inner controls. In any case, strange, unconventional, or deviant behavior cannot, in and of itself, be regarded as a sign of an emotional handicap. The film *Shyness* [12] contains an excellent illustration of the difficulty in inferring causes solely on the basis of observed behavior. Of the three children in the film referred to as being shy and withdrawn, only one could be said to be emotionally handicapped. On the other hand, Clare in *Feelings of Hostility,* although a successful and competent business woman, had pervasive feelings of loneliness and hostility toward men. Her overt behavior would hardly suggest the depth or intensity of her problem.

Relationship of Definition to Personality Theory

Teachers with the help of peer and self-perceptions are in the best position to act as screeners of those who may need help. They may note children whose behavioral temperature is rising or those who show no normal reaction under stress. In the final analysis, a diagnosis of emotional handicap rests on an inference of motivation of behavior based on personality dynamics. The

[12] *Shyness,* 16mm. Sound Film (New York: McGraw-Hill Book Company).

energy source of the behavior is the basic sought-after ingredient. Is the behavior motivated primarily by transient environmental forces or by personality factors?

What kinds of observations about personality would be most helpful in making inferences or professional guesses as to causes of deviant behavior? The behavior of the emotionally handicapped child will be "driven" behavior, i.e., the energy level of the child will seem to be inappropriate or disproportionate to the task or situation. The child may play with an intensity and frenzy which bodes ill to anyone or anything interfering. He may be unable to obey rules in school even after repeated and varied contacts with accepting or disciplining adults. The emotionally handicapped child has relatively little freedom to adapt. He is often regarded as especially stubborn and recalcitrant since the usual influence techniques of reward, punishment, recognition, praise, etc., are relatively ineffective in influencing his behavior. Or, he may be regarded as a "real pushover," i.e., influenced almost completely by the wishes and ideas of others. Here the self or ego may be regarded as underdeveloped as compared to other emotionally handicapped children who are immobilized or driven by inner conflicts.

In healthy emotional development, the individual has sufficient emotional strength to vary his personality appropriately in accordance with the situation but, at the same time, to maintain a sufficient core of self in all situations. For example, one is not expected to be the same at church as at a party, yet the differences cannot be so radical as to involve complete changes in personality.

The emotionally handicapped child seems not to profit from experience and appears to behave in an automatic, repetitive pattern. His ideas about the teacher or his peers may be somewhat distorted. For example, he may see the teacher as a punishing, threatening adult and classmates as unfair competitors constantly outdoing him in reading, drawing, or sports. One would infer that in the relatively unhandicapped child, behavior is motivated by forces at relatively greater levels of awareness; conversely, behavior motivated primarily by unconscious forces would be characteristic of the emotionally handicapped child. Thus, as Kubie notes,

> . . . the essence of normality is flexibility, in contrast to the freezing of behavior into patterns of unalterability which characterize every manifestation of the neurotic process whether in impulses, acts, thoughts, or feelings. Whether or not a behavioral event is free to change depends not on the quality of the act itself, but upon the nature of the constellation of forces that has produced it . . . Wherever unconscious forces play the preponderant role in this constellation, then behavior . . . is subject to a tendency to automatic and obligatory repetition.[13]

[13] L. S. Kubie, "Social Forces and the Neurotic Process," in *Explorations in Social Psychiatry*, ed. A. H. Leighton, J. A. Clausen, and R. Wilson (New York: Basic Books, Inc., Publishers, 1957), p. 81.

While the emotionally handicapped child might be characterized as having a greater load of problems and conflicts, in some cases he may appear to have little conflict, little concern with others and little, if any, conscience. Such individuals deal with emotional tensions by rapid action rather than by internalizing the subsequent anxiety. Whereas, most children develop a core of self and ego processes which can successfully mediate forces in the environment and in the organism, some children may have a deficiency of such processes. This may be manifested by an absence of normal anxieties about behavior or misbehavior and a pattern of behavior which is stereotyped, childish, and relatively uninhibited. A large number of the latter kinds of emotionally handicapped individuals are found among juvenile delinquents.

The Degree of Emotional Handicap

As in other handicaps, emotional handicaps may vary from transient to pervasive. To complete the definition, it would be necessary to establish a continuum in which the degree of handicap can be perceived and perhaps estimated, especially as it relates to possible action by the school. One could begin such a continuum with 1) children who experience and demonstrate the normal problems of everyday living, growing, exploration, and reality testing. There are some, however, who can be observed as 2) children who develop a greater number and degree of symptoms of emotional problems as a result of normal crises or stressful experiences such as death of father, birth of sibling, divorce of parents, brain or body injury, school entrance, junior high school entrance, puberty, etc. Some children move beyond this level of adjustment and may be described as 3) children in whom moderate symptoms of emotional maladjustment persist to some extent beyond normal expectations but who are able to manage an adequate school adjustment. The next group would include 4) children with fixed and recurring symptoms of emotional maladjustment who can, with help, profit by school attendance and maintain some positive relationships in the school setting. Beyond this are 5) children with fixed and recurring symptoms of emotional difficulties who are perhaps best educated in a residential school setting or temporarily in a home setting.

The school psychologist may be involved with children in each of these categories. One of his basic tasks, however, is to help the school act in a preventive fashion by identifying early those children who seem to be moving toward group 3, 4, or 5. The school is an agency of vast potential in the primary prevention of emotional and mental disorders. To the extent to which school psychologists can assist the school to be a more effective educational institution for all children including children handicapped by physical, mental, or emotional disabilities, to that extent will this potential of the school be realized. In part, the answer lies in working with the school, parents, pediatricians, health officers, nurses and others in finding problems in

their beginning states and planning appropriate school experiences where
necessary.

Some Implicit Assumptions in Early Identification [14]

Adults and children usually have a nostalgic and pleasing remembrance
of things magical, stemming in part from remnants of feelings of omnipotence developed in early childhood. To some extent these feelings are
often transformed, usually with some success, into feelings that science and
technology are the "open sesame" to problems of impossible magnitude and
complexity. Consider what can be done by the flick of a switch, the turn of a
dial, or the push of a button. Science, to some extent, has indeed provided
man with "magic" solutions to highly technological problems. It is not surprising, therefore, to find human beings thinking of "push-button" solutions
for complex social or personal problems.

At the present time, the solutions of the complex social problems of the
human organism in his society are not available in "push-button" form. In
fact, no problem seems to be less subject to solution through necromancy or
magic spells than the antisocial and asocial behavior of individuals in society.
However, small "magical" beginnings are being sought. One of the "yellow
brick" roads often suggested as a beginning path is early identification of
children with developing personality or behavior disorders. The search for a
kind of "psychological penicillin" by which personality disorders and delinquent behavior can be prevented or cured has been and continues to be
particularly intriguing. However, there are a number of major assumptions
upon which the success of such an activity rests.

One basic assumption is that if a child with a developing emotional
disorder can be detected early, he can be helped most economically and
effectively. Although the truth of this assumption seems logical, its psychological or scientific validity needs to be tested. Stevenson [15] discussed a variety
of assumptions, still unproved, related to the supposed greater malleability of
the child over the adult. It may not always be true that the younger an individual is, the more economical and effective his treatment. For example,
some psychotherapists are reluctant to begin treatment of disturbed adolescents of ten because the results are more effective and lasting if treatment is
started at a later time. Even if it is admitted that emotionally handicapped
children could be detected early, the problem would not be solved since it is
not known to what extent these peculiarly susceptible cases will respond to
prophylactic measures. "Or such cases may well be victims of constitutional

[14] This section is based on material prepared for the 1960 White House Conference on Children and Youth and used by permission of the Conference.
[15] I. Stevenson, "Is the Human Personality More Plastic in Infancy and Childhood?," American Journal of Psychiatry, 114 (August, 1957), 151–161.

factors which may render all preventive measures undertaken on a re-educational level illusory or very difficult." [16]

One study of children identified and helped early was made in the Cambridge-Somerville areas of Massachusetts. In this study 650 children, ages nine to eleven, all of whom were showing problem behavior in school or in the neighborhood, were divided into two comparable groups. One group received the services of nine trained professional persons for a period of eight years (1938–45). During these eight years, the service teams studied the children, counseled the families, and applied their professional skill and training to prevent delinquent behavior by the children. The other group of 325 children did not receive any special help or counsel. Despite the extenuating circumstances and difficulties of the project, especially during the war years, Witmer and Tufts concluded,

> . . . this experiment seems to indicate that the provision of the kind of friendly guidance and other service the C.S.Y.S. (Cambridge-Somerville Youth Study) afforded will not reduce delinquent acts or keep chronic delinquency from developing. . . The chief importance of the Cambridge-Somerville Youth Study, so far as evaluation is concerned, is its use of a control group for checking results. Had this been lacking, much greater claims for the effectiveness of the program as a delinquency prevention measure might have been made. . . It was only when the delinquency records of the treatment and control groups were compared that the inability of the study to prevent or reduce delinquency was revealed.[17]

Another later evaluation of the Cambridge-Somerville Youth project is somewhat more encouraging.[18] This study attempted to delineate more specifically the nature of "friendly guidance and other services" and to analyze factors that contributed to a successful adjustment of the child, i.e., absence of any record of delinquent acts. Such an analysis found the court records of the boys who had received treatment did not differ significantly from the control boys; nor did the number of counselors, length of treatment by first counselor, or total length of treatment seem to have any relationship to the outcomes. However, when the children were separated on the basis of intensity of contact with any counselor, it was found that those seen at least every week had a significantly smaller incidence of criminality. This, of course, could have been due to other factors such as better school attendance, better response on the part of these boys, or other factors that encouraged a more intense contact. Other factors significantly related to the reduction of

[16] L. Bovet, *Psychiatric Aspects of Juvenile Delinquency* (Geneva, Switzerland: World Health Organization, 1951), p. 44.

[17] H. Witmer and E. Tufts, *The Effectiveness of Delinquency Prevention Programs*, Children's Bureau Publication No. 350 (Washington, D.C.: U. S. Department of Health, Education, and Welfare, 1954), 30.

[18] W. McCord, J. McCord, and I. K. Zola, *Origins of Crime: A New Evaluation of the Cambridge-Somerville Youth Study* (New York: Columbia University Press, 1959).

criminality were age at which treatment was begun, and the sex of counselor during the adolescent period. The research findings of this study seemed to confirm the general ineffectiveness of those forms of counseling consisting of family assistance plus infrequent interaction with the boy. However, the findings suggest that frequent counseling contact with a pre-delinquent child —particularly if begun when the child is under ten, or by a female counselor after the boy has reached adolescence—may significantly prevent criminality.

There are only a small number of other studies in which positive results could be attributed to early identification and help. For example, the reduction of delinquency among Jewish minors in New York City when the over-all rate of delinquency was increasing was justifiably attributed to the comprehensive program of psychological outpatient clinic facilities for psychotherapy and in-patient treatment centers developed by the Jewish Board of Guardians. As Bovet points out, "The suggestion that this organization, the Jewish Board of Guardians, has contributed to the remarkable diminution of child delinquency in the Jewish community of New York is very possibly correct." [19]

Visibility of Developing Emotional Handicaps

A second assumption implicit in early identification of children with emotional handicaps is that personality disorders in adulthood are the result of a progressively developing condition *visible* in a child's behavior. Indeed, the recognition of normal personality growth, to say little of its measurement, is a problem of which the surface has only been scratched. Where normal behavior is equated with average behavior, it may be difficult to differentiate the child who is different from the child who is basically ill. Therefore, any appraisal of children with suspected emotional handicaps must differentiate between behavior pathology and the wide range of normal behavior. Jahoda [20] and other professional workers in mental health have emphasized that the criteria for mental health must be such that they do not automatically exclude everything but average behavior. To complicate this matter further, one can equate modal or average behavior with normal behavior but not necessarily with healthy behavior. For example, such disabilities as the common cold or dental decay cannot be regarded as a healthy condition despite their vast prevalence.

Often, one may observe a child who seems to be experiencing little difficulty until a psychological crisis initiates what appears to be an unexpected eruption. Management of emotional difficulties may be possible under the protective environment of a school, but environmental changes

[19] Bovet, *op. cit.*, p. 48.
[20] M. Jahoda, *Current Concepts of Positive Mental Health* (New York: Basic Books, Inc., Publishers, 1958).

may trigger a coiled spring. For example, a study of high school students who became mentally ill showed that some of them made excellent school records but ran into difficulty almost immediately after graduation.[21] The progress of a slow-learning child might well be within normal limits in the earlier years of elementary school, but may fall off sharply in the fourth or fifth grades when reading and arithmetic skills become the *sine qua non* of school success.

In addition to the problem of determining how to spot behaviors which are the beginning signs of delinquency or emotional disturbance, one needs to know how early is "early" in evaluating a child's mental health. Is early recognition often too late, too costly, or too ineffective if it is made by the pediatrician, well-baby clinic, or in the fourth grade? What can schools or pediatricians attempt by way of early recognition of mental health problems? Which factors are more important in helping teachers to recognize emotional problems comfortably and understandably? Does the process of identification carry with it the seeds by which the identified are helped? Are there economical and effective ways in which the school psychologist can help the school undertake a program designed to identify and help as early as possible those children seemingly unable to help themselves?

The Value Enigma in Appraising Behavior

Another problem in identifying children with serious personality difficulties is that the *same behavior* can and often is interpreted differently under different circumstances and at different times. What is considered maladjustment in one phase of development may be considered normal in another. For example, a boy who is being hostile and rebellious toward his parents when he is eleven years old may be considered a problem until he reaches the age of thirteen when he finds himself in a peer group where hostility and rebellion against adults is expected behavior. As has been repeatedly pointed out and emphasized, cultural and subcultural values tend to circumscribe the behavior norms of a population. Temporal change in values in our own culture have also affected our concept of normality. Whyte,[22] for example, describes as an emergent social value the belief in the group as the moving force in our society. To belong to the group and to work well with a group is behavior that is seen as normal—good behavior. The rugged individualist of the early years of the century would find his behavior regarded differently under the present value system.

[21] E. M. Bower, T. A. Shellhammer, J. M. Daily, and M. Bower, *High School Students Who Later Became Schizophrenic* (Sacramento: California State Department of Education, 1960).

[22] W. H. Whyte, *The Organization Man* (New York: Random House, Inc., 1956).

Effect of Past Experiences of Observer

The past experiences and unconscious conflicts of adults undoubtedly play a large role in determining which behavior is perceived as normal or abnormal. Adults who have had problems involving authority figures may be more sensitive to or avoid perceiving behavior which elicits authority-related conflicts. Some adults are upset by boys who appear to act effeminate or overly athletic. Others are more upset by children who don't work or prefer activities other than the subject matter being taught. Early studies by Wickman [23] and others that seemed to indicate a lack of congruity between the perceptions of teachers and mental health experts in evaluating problem behavior have been negated by recent studies which indicate a close relationship between the two perceptions. For example, in a recent study, it was found that teachers perceived as emotionally disturbed or maladjusted about the same children seen as emotionally disturbed by mental health personnel.[24] Often a professional person in a strategic position to recognize problems early is beset by role confusions and inconsistencies that make it difficult to carry out the function of early case finding. One possible result of such role confusions when mixed with high professional standards and a share of personal problems is reflected in part in the mental health problems of teachers themselves. Fenton [25] in a study of 241 teachers in California, found 187 or 77.6 percent to be in reasonably good mental health, 54 or 22.5 percent to be suffering from some form of personality disturbance. In 17 of these cases, the teachers were found not to be seriously handicapped in their classroom work. In 37 of the 54, their professional work showed evidences of their personal difficulties. A study at the Mayo Clinic of neurotic disturbances in its patients found teachers had the highest incidence among the various occupations represented in the sample of 1,164 patients.[26] No professional group is immune to mental or emotional disorders or illnesses. However, the presence of such disturbances or illnesses in teachers, psychologists, parents, or school administrators is most likely to affect perceptions as well as relationships.

[23] E. K. Wickman, "Children's Behavior and Teachers' Attitudes" (New York: The Commonwealth Fund, 1928).

[24] E. M. Bower, Early Identification of Emotionally Handicapped Children in School (Springfield, Ill.: Charles C. Thomas, Publishers, 1960).

[25] N. Fenton, Mental Hygiene in School Practice (Stanford: Stanford University Press, 1943).

[26] H. L. Smith and N. C. Hightower, "Incidence of Functional Disease (Neurosis) Among Patients of Various Occupations," Occupational Medicine, 5 (February, 1948), 182–185.

Social Conflicts in Prevention

If early identification and intervention is to be effective, a community agency such as the public school needs to intervene in a child's life at a point in time that may be regarded by some families as rank interference without adequate proof or cause. Indeed, the vast problem of prevention in the field of mental and emotional disorders has many conflicting roots in a free society. As Bellak pointed out, "At present, the governing of men and the raising of children seem to be among the very few occupations in civilized society for which no training or certified ability are required—and for fairly sound reasons. Imposition of laws on either activity could constitute a serious invasion of personal freedom." [27]

Laws, however, provide for compulsory school attendance of children between certain years, rules and regulations affecting the use of vehicles, standards for the provision of nutrition, sanitation, and care of children. As our society becomes more and more interdependent, each of us finds it necessary to depend more and more on the sane, rational behavior of the other. Any public agency that serves the general population in an effort to provide healthy growth and education for children cannot help invading, to some extent, the privacy of the child and his family. Since the certainty of identification of emotionally handicapped children is still a vexing problem, a parent may well question the basis for the prediction or the presumption of the school in labeling her child. Any program for early identification and intervention needs to anticipate such societal conflicts and plan to reduce or minimize their effects on the program. That such anticipation and planning is necessary is illustrated by Nettler's experience.

> Where the student of behavior works in a xenophobic or individualistic community, he cannot assume his scientifically honorable intentions will be considered morally justifiable by those whom he seeks to help. Even though the scientist says in effect "I am studying you and asking you these questions for your own good," his subject may respond, "It is part of my good that you desist from your intrusion of my privacy." [28]

Other Sources of Information for Early Identification

Only two institutions in our society, the family and the school, have contact with all children. Pediatricians, general practitioners, health departments, nursery schools also come into contact with many children. However, such contact is highly varied depending on the community and the services avail-

[27] L. Bellak ed., *Schizophrenia* (New York: Logos Press, 1958), p. viii.

[28] G. Nettler, "Test Burning in Texas," *American Psychologist,* **14** (November, 1959), 682–683.

able. In some communities, lower class children ordinarily unseen by pediatricians or well-baby clinics are visited regularly by members of welfare or health offices. In most cases, such contacts cannot be maintained regularly since the low ratio of staff to population served does not permit intensive contacts. Pediatricians and general practitioners who do note developing behavioral problems are usually pressed by time and patient load. In some instances, families who are most in need seldom come into consistent contact with any agency until their children are enrolled in school.

In theory, some early identification of children who are or will be most prone to personality or social difficulties is possible as early as the first trimester of pregnancy and soon after birth. In actual practice, obstetricians, general practitioners, pediatricians, well-baby clinics and other agencies in the pre-school period have not as yet fully crystallized, delineated and developed their roles in early identification.

Pre-School Histories and Agency Contacts of Emotionally Handicapped Children

The early recognition of children most prone to personality and emotional disturbances in the pre-school period is dependent on the scientific accuracy and interpretation of recognizable signs of such disorders and on the presence of some agency or professional person who can do something about such signs.

Pasamanick and others have been studying prenatal factors and their relationship to neuro-psychiatric disorders of children.[29, 30] Their findings can be summarized as follows: Inasmuch as prematurity and complications of pregnancy are associated with brain injury and in some cases with death, there must be some children who are so injured who develop disabling conditions ranging from cerebral palsy, epilepsy, mental deficiency, to conditions which produce lower thresholds to stress as a result of lesser degrees of damage. Such abnormalities of pregnancy are associated strongly with the socio-economic level of the family and are of greatest number in the lower class group. In addition, it was noted that the greater the abnormalities of pregnancy of mothers, the greater the reading disabilities of their children in school.

Many studies of the relationship of birth conditions and later adjustment have shown that children born prematurely may have minimal brain injuries which may have retarded their development. Yet as Schwartz noted,

29 B. Pasamanick, "The Epidemiology of Behavior Disorders of Childhood," in *Neurology and Psychiatry in Childhood* (Baltimore: The Williams & Wilkins, Co., 1956), Chap. 16.
30 A. A. Kawi and B. Pasamanick, *The Association of Factors of Pregnancy with the Development of Reading Disorders in Childhood* (Yellow Springs: Child Development Publications, 1959).

it may be presumed that birth, in general, produces circulatory disturbances that are transmitted to deeper parts of the brain. "In fact," says Schwartz, "investigations have shown that almost every baby born normally suffers some disturbance of the cranial and even the cerebral circulation as a result of the release effect." [31]

Approximately twenty percent of all children seen in the Bellevue Hospital Mental Hygiene Clinic were estimated by Silver to have suffered organic cerebral defects during prenatal, paranatal, or neonatal life.[32] The children were brought to the clinic for help because of behavior difficulties. A complete physical yielded no gross neurological defects and detailed neurological examinations in terms of reflexes, cerebellar signs, cranial nerves and sensory examinations gave normal results.

Silver and others suggest that the behavior of a child with brain damage is not only a function of the biologic damage itself but it also is dependent upon the child's psychological defense patterns and upon the environmental forces acting upon him. Eisenberg described the effects of brain damage as the result of three interacting factors: 1) altered neurophysiology of the brain; 2) reaction of the child to the damage and to the loss of function; and 3) the reaction of the social environment. Eisenberg emphasized that maladaptive behavior can result from damage to the cortical analyzer that mediates between the child and his world but that the psychosomatic highway is a two-way street. "Effects are no less forceful in the opposite direction. Disorder in the social setting to which the child endeavors to adapt will induce disorder in behavior and its neurophysiologic substrate." [33]

In summary, there seems to be ample evidence of the relationship of healthy birth to the mental health of the child and the major role of pre-birth maternal conditions on the subsequent presence or absence of emotional or behavioral problems in children.

The Pediatrician's Role in Early Identification

In any age of anxiety—especially anxiety surrounding the raising of healthy, normal children—the pediatrician is perceived as Merlin the Magician by mothers and fathers. Indeed, the magic wielded by Spock in his attempt to allay fears about the physical care of young children may refute in part the earlier statement about the absence of a magic button in parent-child relationships.

[31] P. H. Schwartz, "Birth Injuries of the Newborn," *Archives of Pediatrics*, 73 (December, 1956), 433.

[32] A. Silver, "Behavioral Syndrome Associated with Brain Damage in Children," *Pediatric Clinics of North America. Symposium on Handicaps and Their Prevention* (Philadelphia: W. B. Saunders Co., 1957).

[33] L. Eisenberg, "Dynamic Considerations Underlying the Management of the Brain Damaged Child," *GP*, 14 (October, 1956), 105.

Pediatricians have become more interested and concerned about the mental health of patients and their role in early case finding. Many work with teachers and school psychologists especially in problems of mental retardation, learning or behavior difficulties. Indeed, May, in an editorial in *Pediatrics,* commented on the need for pediatricians to get more training in the area of mental hygiene.[34] Physicians, psychologists, and pediatricians have been aware for some time of the effects of early parental separation on the child. Studies by Bowlby,[35] Spitz,[36] and others have helped emphasize the diagnostic significance of this fact—that early separation or detachment of the child from mother has a marked effect on the infant's instinctual balance and development. Brody, in her research, found signs of disturbance where there was a hyper-responsiveness by the mother to the child to the extent that the mother interfered with the child's spontaneous reactions.[37] Responses by the mother to the child may also be too frequent or infrequent or markedly inconsistent, oscillating between indulgence and strictness. The pediatrician's role, then, is to help the mother perceive the unbalance or excesses in one direction or another and correct them. The pediatrician can diminish anxiety, loosen up maternal overprotection and deal with some aspects of parental rejection. When the child gets to the toddling stage, he can help the mother who makes too many demands too soon; or one who makes too few demands too late.

Pediatricians are also aware that there is a reliable and positive relationship between the number, frequency, duration, and severity of symptoms as reported by mothers and the degree of sickness found in the child. As Glidewell and others noted, mothers' reports can be used with more confidence and effectiveness than was formerly supposed possible.[38]

A number of pediatricians have attempted to incorporate psychometric procedures into their examinations with some success. Two studies of the use of the Draw-A-Man Test proved that the average pediatrician could reliably score the test and that the results had significant value in predicting progress and achievement in school.[39, 40]

[34] C. D. May, "Mental Hygiene in the New Pediatrics," *Pediatrics,* 24 (1959), 355.

[35] J. Bowlby, *Maternal Care and Mental Health* (Geneva: World Health Organization, 1951).

[36] R. Spitz, "Problems of Infantile Neurosis," *Psychoanalytic Study of the Child,* 9 (1954), 16–71.

[37] S. Brody, "Signs of Disturbance in the First Year of Life," *American Journal of Orthopsychiatry,* 28 (April, 1958), 362.

[38] J. C. Glidewell, I. M. Mensh, and M. C. L. Gildea, "Behavior Symptoms in Children and Degree Sickness," *American Journal of Psychiatry,* 114, No. 1 (July, 1957), 47–53.

[39] J. M. Coleman, I. Iscoe, and M. Brodsky, "The Draw-A-Man-Test as a Predictor of School Readiness and as an Index of Emotional and Physical Maturity," *Pediatrics,* 24 (August, 1959), 259–263.

[40] A. A. Silver, "Diagnostic Value of Three Drawing Tests for Children," *Pediatrics,* 37 (January, 1950), 129–135.

In summary, the pediatrician represents a potent resource in early identification. He is a specialist in the normal growth problems of children; an authority to whom parents will listen; a potential liaison to other community agencies; a child-rearing specialist and often a leader in community affairs. However, the average pediatrician carries a high patient load and sees parents in lower class situations only occasionally.

The Pre-School Age

Studies of behavior disturbances of children in school and their relationship to the pre-school period reveal that many school behavior problems are recognizable in the pre-school period. Oppenheimer and Mandel found that of 60 older children seen in a clinic, in 32 cases the problem had been first noted prior to school entrance; in 20 cases it had been first noted in the kindergarten; in 5 cases it had been noted in the first grade, and in 3 cases in the second grade.[41] Bolten studied the early histories of 100 children of school age who had attended a child guidance clinic. She found that about 3 out of 4 had shown observable symptoms in the first 5 years of life.[42]

The importance of identifying children with major learning handicaps prior to school entrance has been emphasized by investigrtors. School failure can add a heavy burden to children already overwhelmed by stress and conflict. One investigator found a pocket of vulnerable children who came from government-run or foster homes and residential schools and suggested that intensive mental health assistance to such institutions is a must in the primary prevention of emotional disorders.[43]

Another group of investigators were interested in ways of assessing a child's emotional adjustment just prior to school entrance.[44] Their methods included a standardized clinical examination of the child, interviews with parents, systematized observation of the child, teacher ratings, teacher interviews and sociometric data. Using a standardized type of doll play, the investigators rated four kinds of behavior observed in this setting: 1) ease with which child separated from mother; 2) extent to which child controlled his emotions; 3) amount of unusual behavior; 4) number of special demands made on the experimenter. This doll play experiment proved to be a sucesssful predictor of success in kindergarten and provided a method that could be adapted for use with larger populations entering school.

[41] E. Oppenheimer and M. Mandel, "Behavior Disturbances of School Children in Relation to the Preschool Period," *American Journal of Public Health*, 49 (November, 1959), 1537–1542.

[42] A. Bolton, "A Prophylactic Approach to Child Psychiatry," *Journal of Mental Sciences*, 101 (July, 1955), 696–703.

[43] W. L. Neustatter, "An Experiment in Prophylactic Psychiatry in Children's Homes," *Lancet* (April, 1955), 807.

[44] E. Lindemann and A. Ross, "A Follow-up Study of a Predictive Test of Social Adaptation in Preschool Children," in *Emotional Problems of Early Childhood*, ed. Gerald Caplan (New York: Basic Books, Inc., Publishers, 1955).

Caplan summarized the essential problem of prevention of emotional disorders in early childhood as, first, the need for a body of systematic knowledge, identification of pathogenic forces, and attention to screening procedures at points which can bring whole populations under review.[45] Lastly, one needs to arouse community interest in prevention, a task as complex and delicate as the treatment of schizophrenias.

The Prerequisites of In-School Screening Procedures

Past research by Rogers,[46] Ullmann,[47] Smith,[48] and others, has demonstrated the feasibility of the use of certain instruments and information for mental health screening. Some of these procedures and information were subjected to research and developed into a screening process.[49] As part of this research, it was noted that although many instruments and ratings are available for screening purposes, few are or would be used by teachers and most are diagnostically, not screening, oriented. It was also noted that ratings or techniques that tapped and synthesized teacher, peer, and self-perceptions offered the best screening procedure. The problem, however, was to develop ratings and instruments that "fit" the teacher's role and task requirements. On the basis of this condition, the following prerequisites were set up for the screening instruments and procedure.

1. The information to be collected by the teacher would be usable with large samples of school children, and the instruments used would be capable of group administration.

2. The collection of the data would not involve as a necessary condition direct psychological or psychiatric assessments.

3. The administration and scoring of rating scales and tests should require a minimum amount of time and work.

4. The data should be obtainable as part of regular classroom routine and not involve the teacher in extra classroom duties, home visits, or individual test administration.

5. The data collected should help the teacher obtain a comprehensive, perceptual picture of the child from as many sources as would be economically possible.

[45] G. Caplan, "Recent Trends in Preventive Child Psychiatry," in Emotional Problems of Early Childhood.

[46] C. A. Rogers, "Mental Health Findings in Three Elementary Schools," Educational Research Bulletin, 21 (March 18, 1942), 13–29.

[47] C. A. Ullmann, Identification of Maladjusted School Children, Monograph No. 7 (Washington, D.C.: U.S. Public Health Service, 1952).

[48] L. M. Smith, "The Concurrent Validity of Six Personality and Adjustment Tests for Children," Psychological Monographs: General and Applied, 72, No. 457 (1958), 30.

[49] E. M. Bower, Early Identification of Emotionally Handicapped Children in School.

6. The data collected would not offend parents or involve questions of a highly personal nature to parents or children.

7. The major function of the data collected and the process utilized in obtaining the data should be one of screening, not diagnosis.

8. As a result of utilizing such a screening process, more positive and earlier referrals of children in need of help would be made.

9. Before making recommendations for educational placement or clinical referral, each pupil screened by this process would be given an individual psychological evaluation by school guidance staffs and/or mental health personnel to determine the most appropriate follow-up procedure.

Validity of School Screening Procedures

Using the instruments and process developed by Bower, Tashnovian, and Larson, a sample of 169 boys and 56 girls were screened and individually examined. The group was found to represent a wide variety of types of behavior problems. Approximately 90 per cent of the screened group were confirmed to be moderately or seriously emotionally handicapped by individual examination.[50]

Ullmann surveyed the nature and extent of the mental health problems presented by a group of children in the ninth grade of a public school system.[51] He was also interested in finding out to what extent the judgments of teachers could be relied upon as a means of identifying children who needed psychological assistance. Another question Ullmann wanted to answer was: To what extent are children who have been identified as maladjusted by the teacher the same as those who would be considered maladjusted by their classmates? He found a high correlation between the judgments of teachers and clinicians, and concluded that teachers and mental hygienists are at present much closer together in their judgments of the behavior problems of children than perhaps earlier studies had noted.

Smith investigated the validity of six group-administered personality and adjustment tests for children. He concluded that none of the tests discriminated well enough to be used singly. However, he noted that several of the tests had group differences extensive enough to allow for a limited amount of applicability when the test data were combined with other information. Satterlee found a low but definite correlation between sociometric choice of individuals in a group and the individual's self-appraisal.[52] He concluded that

---

[50] N. Lambert and E. M. Bower, *Technical Report on In-School Screening of Emotionally Handicapped Children* (Princeton, N.J.: Educational Testing Service, 1961).

[51] C. A. Ullmann, "Teachers, Peers, and Tests as Predictors of Adjustment," *Journal of Educational Psychology*, 48 (May, 1957), 257–267.

[52] R. Satterlee, "Sociometric Analysis and Personality Adjustment," *California Journal of Educational Research*, 6 (September, 1955), 181–184.

sociometric and self-appraisals are measuring different aspects of personality and that a relationship between the two measures might be indicative of an individual's reality testing. Gronlund and Holmlund studied sociometric scores of high school students as related to scores received in the sixth grade.[53] They found that pupils with low sociometric scores in the sixth grade do not blossom out in high school and that sociometric status is highly predictive of the high school adjustment of students. Tindall urged caution in using one type of measure for assessing the mental health of students and suggested that a number of indices were usually more effective than one.[54]

Griffiths studied 900 children, aged six to fourteen, who had behavior difficulties.[55] He found that young children of early elementary school age are aware of difficulties characterized by aggressive behavior but, as they get older, they become more aware of submissive or withdrawing difficulties. He also found that as children get older they judge behavior more like parents and teachers and that children of middle socio-economic groups have fewer aggressive behavior difficulties and more withdrawing problems.

A St. Louis County group asked the question—can directly observable behavior symptoms be taken as reliable evidence of difficulty? They hypothesized that if the mother's report of the behavior symptoms correlated reasonably well with the teacher's rating and if both agreed with the opinions of professional workers, there would be reason to believe some significant aspects of mental health were being measured. In their study of 830 families with at least one child in the third grade, the results were clear-cut—the greater the number of symptoms reported by the mother, the greater the likelihood that the child would be rated disturbed by the teacher. The same group of investigators using trained adult raters as independent criteria found that students' sociometric choices significantly differentiated among four levels of psychological adjustment of school children. Children with few classroom interactions were more negatively and less positively chosen by their classmates.

Ullmann found that teachers' ratings of adjustment showed a much closer relationship to sociometric ratings than to scores on personality tests. In using the teachers' appraisal of the adjustment status of children, Ullmann found that their ratings were more accurate when the teachers were not functioning under anxiety or pressure. He also noted that increasing the emphasis upon the use of data that were available to the teacher had the effect of

[53] N. E. Gronlund and W. S. Holmlund, "The Value of Elementary School Sociometric Status Scores for Predicting Pupils' Adjustment in High School," *Educational Administration and Supervision*, 44 (September, 1958), 255–260.

[54] R. H. Tindall, "Relationships Among Indices of Adjustment Status," *Educational and Psychological Measurement*, 15 (Summer, 1955), 152–162.

[55] W. Griffiths, *Behavior Difficulties of Children as Perceived and Judged by Parents, Teachers and Children Themselves* (Minneapolis: University of Minnesota Press, 1952).

increasing the breadth and depth of the teacher's understanding of the child. These studies offer substantial evidence that teacher ratings, self-descriptive data, and peer ratings when combined gave the clearest, most comprehensive, and economical picture of the adjustment status of children. Teacher ratings were found to be better predictors of emotional handicaps in children when the resultant behavior was manifested overtly or acted out; self-descriptive data appeared to be better for evaluating that aspect of personality which had to do with feelings, attitudes, and inner tensions.

Next to teacher judgment, research points to peer perception as the most valid and reliable indicator of pupil adjustment and personality development. There are a host of studies [56, 57, 58, 59, 60, 61, 62, 63, 64, 65] in addition to the ones already mentioned, that confirm the effectiveness of peer responses in noting those children who are becoming or have become alienated from self or group. There is also much evidence indicating that teachers are, in general, valid observers and raters of children's emotional status.[66, 67, 68, 69, 70, 71, 72]

[56] J. C. Glidewell, M. C. L. Gildea, H. R. Domke, and M. B. Kantor, "Behavior Symptoms in Children and Adjustment in Public School," *Human Organization*, 18 (Fall, 1959), 123–130.

[57] M. E. Bonney, "Social Behavior Differences Between Second Grade Children of High and Low Sociometric Status," *Journal of Educational Research*, 48 (March, 1955), 481–495.

[58] K. L. Cannon, "Stability of Sociometric Scores of High School Students," *Journal of Educational Research*, 52 (October, 1958), 43–48.

[59] N. E. Gronlund and W. S. Holmlund, "The Value of Elementary School Sociometric Status Scores for Predicting Pupils' Adjustment in High School," *Educational Administration and Supervision*, 44 (September, 1958), 255–260.

[60] N. E. Gronlund, "Generality of Teachers' Sociometric Perceptions: Relative Judgment Accuracy on Several Sociometric Criteria," *Journal of Educational Psychology*, 47 (January, 1956), 25–31.

[61] N. E. Gronlund, "Personality Characteristics of Socially Accepted, Socially Neglected, and Socially Rejected Junior High School Pupils," *Educational Administration and Supervision*, 43 (October, 1957), 329–338.

[62] N. E. Gronlund, *The Accuracy of Teachers' Judgments Concerning the Sociometric Status of Sixth Grade Pupils* (Boston: Beacon Press, 1951).

[63] R. G. Kuhlen and E. G. Collister, "Sociometric Status of Sixth and Ninth Graders Who Failed to Finish High School," *Educational and Psychological Measurement*, 12 (March, 1952), 632–637.

[64] I. Mensh and J. Glidewell, "Children's Perceptions of Relationships Among Their Family and Friends," *Journal of Experimental Education*, 27 (September, 1959), 65–71.

[65] B. N. Phillips and M. V. DeVault, "Relation of Positive and Negative Sociometric Valuations to Social and Personal Adjustment of School Children," *Journal of Applied Psychology*, 39 (December, 1955), 409–412.

[66] G. L. Andrew and H. Lockwood, "Teachers' Evaluations of the Mental Health Status of Their Pupils," *Journal of Educational Research*, 47 (April, 1954), 631–635.

[67] M. J. Fitzsimons, "The Predictive Value of Teachers' Referrals," in *Orthopsychiatry and the School*, ed. Morris Krugman (New York: American Orthopsychiatric Association, 1958).

[68] J. A. Mitchell, "A Study of Teachers' and Mental Hygienists' Ratings of Certain Behavior Problems of Children," *Journal of Educational Research*, 36 (December, 1942), 292–307.

Other factors related to the prediction of school adjustment have been found to be IQ,[73, 74, 75] achievement in school subjects,[76, 77, 78, 79, 80, 81] age-grade relationship,[82, 83] socio-economic status,[84, 85, 86, 87, 88, 89] and truancy.[90]

[69] P. B. Neubauer and E. K. Beller, "Differential Contributions of the Educator and Clinician in Diagnosis," in *Orthopsychiatry and the School.*

[70] W. C. Olson, *Problem Tendencies in Children: A Method for Their Measurement and Description* (Minneapolis: University of Minnesota Press, 1930).

[71] M. H. Schrupp and C. M. Gjerde, "Teacher Growth in Attitudes Toward Behavior Problems of Children," *Journal of Educational Psychology,* 44 (April, 1953), 203–214.

[72] G. A. W. Stouffer, "Behavior Problems of Children as Identified by Today's Teachers and Compared with Those Reported by E. K. Wickman," *Journal of Educational Research,* 48 (January, 1955), 321–331.

[73] J. Kagan, et al., "Personality and IQ Change," *Journal of Abnormal and Social Psychology,* 56 (March, 1958), 261–266.

[74] L. W. Sontag and C. T. Baker, "Personality as a Determinant of Performance," *American Journal of Orthopsychiatry,* 25 (July, 1957), 57–561.

[75] D. Wechsler, "Cognitive, Conative, and Nonintellective Intelligence," *American Psychologist,* 5 (March, 1950), 78–83.

[76] V. M. Axline, "Nondirective Therapy for Poor Readers," *Journal of Consulting Psychology,* 11 (March, 1947), 61–69.

[77] P. H. Bowman, et al., *Mobiziling Community Resources for Youth* (Chicago: University of Chicago Press, 1956).

[78] M. Buswell, "The Relationship Between the Social Structure of the Classroom and the Academic Success of the Pupils," *Journal of Experimental Education,* 22 (September, 1953), 37–52.

[79] R. F. DeHaan and J. Kough, *Helping Children with Special Needs* (Chicago: Science Research Associates, 1958).

[80] H. J. Fine, S. C. Fulkerson, and L. Phillips, "Maladjustment and Social Attainment," *Journal of Abnormal and Social Psychology,* 50 (January, 1955), 33–35.

[81] *Reducing Juvenile Delinquency: What New York Schools Can Do* (Albany: New York State Youth Commission, 1952).

[82] W. H. Bedoian, "Mental Health Analyses of Socially Overaccepted, Socially Under-Accepted, Over-age, and Under-age Pupils in the Sixth Grade," *Journal of Educational Psychology,* 44 (October, 1953), 336–371.

[83] J. I. Goodlad, "Some Effects of Promotion and Non-promotion Upon the Social and Personal Adjustment of Children," *Journal of Experimental Education,* 22 (June, 1954), 301–327.

[84] R. Bendix and S. Lipset, *Class, Status, and Power* (New York: Basic Books, Inc., Publishers, 1957).

[85] L. Freedman and A. B. Hollingshead, "Neurosis and Social Class," *American Journal of Psychiatry,* 113 (March, 1957), 769–776.

[86] R. N. Frumkin, "Occupation and Major Mental Disorders," in *Mental Health and Mental Disorder,* ed. A. M. Rose (New York: W. W. Norton & Company, Inc., 1955).

[87] H. G. Gough, "The Relationship of Socio-economic Status to Personality Inventory and Achievement Test Scores," *Journal of Educational Psychology,* 37 (December, 1946), 527–540.

[88] A. B. Hollingshead and F. C. Redlich, "Social Stratification and Psychiatric Disorders," in *Mental Health and Mental Disorder.*

[89] E. Leacock, "Three Social Variables and the Occurrence of Mental Disorder," in *Explorations in Social Psychiatry,* ed. A. H. Leighton, J. A. Clausen, and R. Wilson (New York: Basic Books, Inc., Publishers, 1957).

[90] S. Glueck and E. Glueck, *Unraveling Juvenile Delinquency* (New York: The Commonwealth Fund, 1950).

Summary on Early Identification

Past research in the evaluation of emotionally handicapped children tends to point in the direction of early identification as a reliable and profitable point of focus. Research confirms the usefulness of different kinds of information relevant and valid for use in making appraisals of a child's future adjustment. Different combinations of peer, teacher, and self ratings plus achievement and age-grade relationships in school are found to be effective in separating emotionally handicapped children from others.

There is little doubt that emotional disturbance cannot be studied as a discrete illness such as pneumonia or scarlet fever. It can only be regarded as a complex, interwoven relationship of the organism with himself and his environment. The ability of a school psychologist, teacher, pediatrician, or nurse to assimilate and use perceptual information other than that filtered through self will help him to be more accurate in confirming or rejecting suspicions about children. Therefore, early identification of children more vulnerable to emotional handicaps must be regarded as a process used by a professional person in which standardized data from other easily available sources can be synthesized into a total perceptual look at the child. All the psychologist or teacher may be able to say is, "On the basis of what information I have at this time, it looks as if so and so may be true. Let's have a closer look at this child to find out if my guess is correct."

Research points to the fact that given sound information, professional personnel can make good judgments about the adjustment capacities of children. The problem is how to synthesize the different kinds of information and put the various perceptual parts back together again.

Program Possibilities in the Education of Emotionally Handicapped Children

Educational adjustments for emotionally handicapped children who attend school can be aimed at 1) modifying the child's in-school experiences directly through special groupings, time spent in school, provision of remedial help, etc.; 2) assisting the teacher through direct or consultation services to plan more effective learning experiences for the child; 3) assisting the parents to understand how to best help their child learn in school, and, in general, represent ways of managing the school environment or the key adults in a child's life to enhance positive learning factors or reduce factors preventing such learning. The public school has not been given sanction or staff to treat or cure seriously emotionally handicapped children. It does, however, have the responsibility of educating handicapped children including those whose handicaps cause resistance to learning. An adjusted program for children functioning under moderate or serious emotional handicaps cannot realistically expect to markedly change a child's school achievement overnight nor should one be disappointed if, over a period of time, complete success is not obtained. On the other hand, one needs to constantly appraise the results of programs which are initiated on behalf of the emotionally handicapped child, especially in terms of those measures that are meaningful and observable to parents and teachers.

Programs, however, may vary somewhat as to purpose and effect in individual cases. In some instances, the major purpose of an adjusted program for an emotionally handicapped child may be to reduce the secondary effect of emotional conflict. At times, this can best be done by attacking the symptoms directly. For example, where early emotional trauma was a major factor in the cause of reading retardation, searching for causes may lead one down a long, wearisome, and unrewarding series of past events about which little can be done. If the meaning of the reading disability to the child indicates that a direct remedial approach can be successful, then one can proceed to help the child cope with this disability through individual and small group remedial reading programs. This reduction of secondary effects may be a primary factor in producing sufficient comfort and value to the student to enable him to make measurable changes in attitudes and feelings about himself and the school.

Another type of program may have as its objective helping children with impulse control problems to explore and gain better control of such behavior through structured play experiences.[91] Or, the school may plan to help parents whose children are having learning or behavior difficulties to meet once a week for two hours to discuss how they might best help their children in school. Help to teachers is, of course, a major necessity whether the teacher is working with a special group of emotionally handicapped children or with a child in a regular class. A description and rationale for some program possibilities will be outlined below.

The Adjustment or Special Class in the Elementary School

The adjustment class is composed of a group of 8–12 young emotionally handicapped children who are within transportable distance to the school where the class is established. The class is situated in a regular elementary school in a nonisolated but appropriate locality on the school grounds. The teacher is a regular elementary teacher with some special training for this

---

[91] M. Schiffer, "The Therapeutic Group in the Public Elementary School" in *Orthopsychiatry and the School.*

work. She is assisted by the school psychologist and other guidance and curriculum specialists who consult with her on a regular basis. The educational program is aimed at individualizing instruction and providing appropriate limits for each child. Some may need and get a rather tough regimen of work and discipline; with others, the teachers may move slowly within a more relaxed relationship. In any case, the content of the program is that of a basic educational program appropriate to the grade level of the child. Behavior standards are maintained by the teacher and referrals to principal or parents utilized when necessary. However, the teacher in many instances works with individual children or small groups of children when this relationship is found to be most productive for the child's learning. The great range of interests, abilities, and emotional needs may make the class a relatively heterogeneous group although the range of such heterogeneity may vary markedly from one group to another.

Improvement and growth are continually assessed by the teacher and psychologist. Children who show sufficient growth intellectually and emotionally are placed back in an appropriate regular class.

RATIONALE

The special class is aimed at obtaining increased individualization of instruction for those children who cannot be so served in a regular class. In addition to the fact that the teacher of the regular class is relieved of the child and the anxieties inherent in his presence, the special grouping provides an opportunity to reduce class size, to give expert help to one teacher and to provide a greater flexibility in educational program and classroom control procedures. For some children, the special class provides a haven from school pressures, peer conflicts, and continuing unsuccessful experiences in school. For others, it provides a safe, comfortable base to resolve conflicts and self-doubts, to make progress slowly, to be better understood, to receive more teacher time and learn more effectively.

ADMINISTRATIVE IMPLICATIONS

The special class program is most often seen as the most "natural" or obvious program for emotionally handicapped children. The small size of the group and the additional help given the teacher make it possible for the program to function. Its success in some schools seems to be predicated on securing volunteer teachers from the district for one or two years of service. In addition, careful screening and placement of children who stand a good chance of profiting from the experience seem necessary. If such a program is conceived or perceived as a "discipline barracks" or a place to send children when everything else has failed, it too will often fail. The administrator will need to protect and enhance the program by relating to it as to any other class and to assist other faculty to do so. The school psychologist will find the program highly demanding of his time and energies.

A special class requires an additional classroom and teacher and is often difficult to establish in districts where transportation is a problem or in smaller districts. The program places a great burden on the teacher who may be required to be a curriculum planner for up to twelve anxiety-ridden, hyperactive children during the day and a case worker by night. The teacher of this group will often be seen as apart from the staff, lack status in the eyes of the others and find little of the rewards of the regular teacher. Expert mental health consultation is required and staff must be available for careful placement of children. In most cases, the educational needs of the children are markedly heterogeneous and varied, lending support to the possibility that each child could be served as effectively in a regular class. In most cases, however, this does not occur.

The Adjustment or Special Class in the Secondary School

The special class in the junior or senior high school is a group of ten to fifteen students who meet with one teacher for approximately three hours or more, not necessarily in consecutive periods. During the rest of the school day the student may be programmed into selected electives with the help of the special class teacher and guidance staff.

The educational program in the special class usually consists of functional, integrated units based on real life needs that incorporate experiences in better use of language, mathematics, and other basic educational skills. Future employment, recreational, and human relation problems are also stressed. In addition, the special teacher may spend additional time with selected students in remedial work. The teacher attempts to find an educational anchor in each student from which he can sustain interest and perhaps broaden the student's educational horizon. The program is primarily aimed at improving the educational level of the student. The teacher's relationship to the psychologist is essentially one of translating clinical insights about the emotional problems of students into classroom management and educational procedures.

In some cases, such classes are integrated with work experience educational programs. Although such integration opens many educational possibilities, the extension of this aspect of the program that has many promising possibilities has been slow in developing. Psychologists who can find the time may find it fruitful to work with curriculum consultants and community agencies in developing this aspect of the program.

RATIONALE

Emotionally handicapped children in the high school are especially vulnerable in the basic academic courses of English, mathematics, and social studies. Many are ashamed of their educational retardation and are constantly and inadvertently reminded of this inadequacy by other students. Most are lost in the fragmentation of courses by departmentalized offerings and their need to relate to one or two teachers. The adjustment class is often one of the few havens in which the emotionally handicapped child can come without fear or shame and in which he can attempt to learn with some chance of success. Often, the emotionally handicapped student realizes his plight and his hostility toward the "school"; yet, he finds the special class teacher friendly, helpful, and instructive. He may feel free to discuss his self-doubts and his fears about the future with the special teacher and seek his help for remedial instruction.

ADMINISTRATIVE IMPLICATIONS

A special class for emotionally handicapped students in the secondary school may be the only means for providing an adequate education for some children. Such a program necessitates a teacher with skill in translating clinical and educational needs of adolescents into a core program. The teacher needs to be comfortable with students who may seek more intense and personal relationships and who may test such relationships repeatedly. He also must feel free to be imaginative and creative in his planning and know a great deal about the community in which most of his children reside. He must be free and skillful in liaison work with other staff, guidance personnel, probation officers, and parents. Lastly, he must be comfortable working with psychologists and other guidance personnel in modifying individual programs or relationships.

Mental Health Consultation

Mental health consultation as spelled out by the staff at the Harvard School of Public Health [92] and the Wellesley (Massachusetts) School project [93] needs to be understood as a specific discipline quite apart from psychotherapy, supervision, medical consultation, education, or nondirective coun-

[92] The consultation program described here is, with some slight modifications, based on the work of Gerald Caplan. See, for example, Caplan and Insley, *Concepts of Mental Health and Consultation* (Washington, D.C.: Supt. of Documents, 1959).

[93] E. Lindemann, *The Wellesley Project for the Study of Certain Problems in Community Health* (New York: Milbank Memorial Fund, 1953).

seling. Although it is best carried out by a psychiatrist, clinical psychologist, or psychiatric social worker, it entails the understanding and use of theory and technique that are not the logical outcomes of training in psychotherapy, projective testing, or case work.

Mental health consultation is defined as an interview process between two professional workers, a consultant (the mental health person) and a consultee, (the teacher) in which the consultant attempts to help the consultee solve a mental health problem of one or more students within the *framework of the consultee's usual professional functioning*. It has as its major objective the provision of a type of in-service training based in each case, on the consultee's professional interpersonal and intrapersonal biases, blind spots and anxieties. It needs to be differentiated in objectives and basic technique from other types of interview processes, and teacher relationships. In mental health consultation, the consultant is not in any administrative or authority relationship to the consultee and has no responsibility for implementing plans or solutions devised in the consultant-consultee meetings. Consultation is usually initiated by the teacher as a result of a current work problem or upset. The consultant usually enters the scene temporarily and leaves when the job is done. The consultant is not, under ordinary circumstances, a member of the guidance or psychological staff of a school. He is usually of a different professional background from the consultee and not just a senior or more experienced member of the same profession. Consultation services to teachers usually serve to abet a more productive and positive use of school psychological services which, in turn, help to increase the effectiveness of mental health consultation.

RATIONALE

The theory upon which consultation services of this kind are based is that the state of mental health of an individual may be anywhere on a scale from good to poor mental health but that the individual's relationship to his present state of adjustment is usually at an equilibrium—a seesaw balanced in each individual case along different points of the scale. As the individual faces new problems, his equilibrium may be temporarily upset. This often occurs during a period of problem solving. Under ordinary circumstances, his equilibrium is restored without changing his position on the mental health scale.

At certain times, however, the individual may be faced with a problem too difficult to solve with his resources and methods. A more lengthy and intense upset which is called a crisis may result. Such a crisis is often accompanied by a rise of inner tension, unpleasant feelings, and a loss in functioning effectiveness. Eventually, the crisis passes over or is resolved in some way and a new state of equilibrium is reached. This equilibrium may be as stable as the previous state but at a different position on the mental health scale. Two aspects of "crisis" are utilized in mental health consultation. First, the outcome of a crisis is, to a significant degree, dependent on key figures in the emotional milieu of the individual. Such key figures in addition to family and friends include the professional community or school workers whose "role" it is to help people in trouble. Second, during the period of crisis, the "seesaw" of forces is in greatest disequilibrium so that a minimal force can tip the balance one way or the other. Therefore, minimal help at these critical periods may be most effective and lasting for the mental health and functioning effectiveness of the teacher.

Teacher crises are usually derived of frustrations in teaching children who won't learn or who do not respond to ordinary classroom discipline. The crisis or upset as a result of the teacher's relationship to difficult children is almost universal. The consultant, therefore, focuses his professional relationship with the teacher on the crisis but has as his primary objective helping the teacher resolve the problem in such a way as to increase the teacher's mental health and level of functioning. It should be remembered that the symptoms referred to as a crisis are signs of healthy interaction of a person and his environmental problems and does not reflect a weakness or a tendency toward illness. Such crises are part and parcel of normal living.

ADMINISTRATIVE IMPLICATIONS

Mental health consultation seems to work best when the consultant is *not* related administratively to the school staff. However, he will need support and will need, from time to time, to discuss his work with the administrator. The school administrator who seeks a detailed account of the consultant's work may, in some instances, reduce the effectiveness of the consultant. Nor, should an administrator seek to obtain help from the consultant for teachers who have more than their share of personal problems. The consultant's job or function is not to treat the teacher but to help her do a better job of using her professional self in teaching.

School psychologists should understand the function of consultation, its relationship to their services, and how it fits into the total pattern of school mental health services. School psychologists may be working with the teacher in other ways and should encourage consultation services to teachers as supplementary help. One cannot and should not assume that any professional mental health worker can be an effective mental health consultant. Consultation competency demands some formal training in consultation and an attitude of respect for non-mental health professional personnel which permits a "sharing" relationship to develop between teacher and consultant.

As has been mentioned, there is at present a dearth of trained consultants available. There is also some confusion in delineating exactly what it is that the consultant does. Many teachers become defensively resistant or immobilized by the idea that they are being "psychoanalyzed." In the secondary school there is usually not enough identification or relationship between the regular subject matter teacher and the consultant to enable consultation to work. Consultation with special teachers who teach core classes is different. There is, also, a problem in helping the school staff to define the role of the consultant; what does he do, how is he related to the psychological staff, etc. Consultation is a program necessitating an active teacher-consultant relationship and can only be administered as a voluntary program.

In general, this program is easy to administer, inexpensive, affects many children by affecting teachers and can result in increased staff morale and communication.

Parent Group Counseling

Parents whose children are experiencing some difficulty in school are contacted and an effort is made to enlist both father and mother into separate counseling groups. The explicit reason given to parents for participating in such a group is to help their children be more effective learners in school. It is pointed out that relationships between parents and children can often be hindrances to a child's motivation and learning potential and that participation in the group might assist the family to work together more effectively. The group leader is a trained professional mental health worker, school social worker, or psychologist.

The counseling process varies from group to group. Some group leaders can manage to maintain discussion on a "feeling" level without direct educational exposition. Others feel it necessary to intervene and to work in more directive guidance and information. In any case, the group leader aims at increasing the awareness of the parents about their own feelings and enabling them to act with greater insight in their relationships to their children.

In the course of such group sessions, the group leader will often find it necessary to extricate himself from the perceived role of expert and oracle. The need to work through how the group functions and learns is a constant group crisis. For example, in one session, the parents have been discussing their children with the group leader who has been listening. Many questions have been directed at the group leader soliciting his help on what one ought to do in this situation or that. His replies have been an honest "I don't know" or "What do you think?" or silence. This has gone on for approximately thirty minutes; finally, one parent more harassed than the others in her inability to get ready answers, says:

Parent One: "I thought Mr. Smith was evasive, but I think that you take the cake."

Group Leader: "How do you mean?"

Parent Two: "He's just taking this all in, you see. He has already formulated his opinion."

Parent One: "Do you ever give your opinion?"

Group Leader: "Sometimes, when I can say something worthwhile."

Parent One: "I didn't understand exactly your position."

Group Leader: "Okay, let's get this settled. Let me be very clear about this. I am not here to tell you how to raise your kids. I am not here as an expert or as an authority to say this is what you do when. I don't believe that experts can solve your problems for you. I think you have to arrive at your own solution and develop your own confidence in your ability to solve your own problems, because you are not going to have an expert available, you know, in the kitchen or in the car or wherever it is. The idea of this sort of treatment is for you to learn to talk your problems over with other people like yourselves that you can confide in, maybe family, maybe husband, but to help you think through problems yourself so that you won't rely—have to rely—on experts. The idea is that there is more—that you know your child better, you see, and you love your child more and you have more experience with your child than any expert can have—and there's probably more experience, more love, and more wisdom in this group than there is in all my learning. The idea of my being here is to help you to help each other, rather than for me to tell you what to do. You can find your answers in the group. You can get your guidance, you can get your support, you can get your understanding from each other and, you are to look to each other for this, rather than to me."

This is followed by about five minutes of discussion and another question by the first parent.

Parent One: "Well, then, isn't this the blind leading the blind?"

Parent Three: "No, I don't think so. No, I believe in discussion. I think that it's good. I mean it has always been our policy at home between my husband and I, to discuss our problems and, consequently, we have never had any arguments or anything like that. We have always been able to solve most things at home by just discussing things. I found it true among my friends also, that different little problems come up and I've gotten a lot of help. I can't give you specific cases, I mean it's too general, but there's times when I have gotten a lot of help just by talking things over because, then, you can—you sort of pick the best out of everyone's opinion and try to see if it will work in your case to a specific end. But, I think if you can't—you can't really expect one person, such as you, to tell me or any of us around this table exactly what we can do to correct the problem that we have at home."

Parent Two: "Well, I agree with you to a certain extent; the only thing is, I mean—however, I'll put it this way. He is a specialist in his field and he knows what the recommended procedure for a certain situation that comes up or a procedure that could be tried—the same as myself or Jack. I'm a specialist in dentistry and Jack is a specialist in engineering."

Parent One: "Yes, but that's a lot different than the mind."

Parent Two: "Well, I mean, a situation arises and I would know how to cope with it but, if a situation arose in Jack's case—he being an engineer, I wouldn't know the first thing to do about it."

Parent One: "That's true, but this is . . ."

Parent Two: "It's the same in his case; he's a specialist in his field and I am sure that he has had a lot of training and study in youngsters and what not, so he probably could recommend a certain solution or a certain procedure to be used in a certain situation involving the youngster."

Parent Four: "But, he said he wouldn't do it."

Parent Two: "Well, that's quite true."

Parent Five: "Yes, but what will you all do when this thing is over?"

The tendency, then, to place the group leader in the position of an authority who will present prescribed formulae needs to be anticipated and dealt with in the group. This tendency to see the group leader as the depository of all psychological knowledge continues and is never completely dissipated in some members of the group.

Later, some of this disappointment and hostility engendered by the absence of a prescribed, magical formula is converted into dissatisfaction with the way the group is moving. Some complain that the discussion doesn't get anywhere and that the group leader should intervene—especially during periods of long silences.

Parent One: (to group leader) "Well, last time I was here, anyway, we chatted outside after you roared madly away to your next appointment. We all felt that we would like a little guidance when we bog down. You remember that last meeting that I attended—anyway, it was a dud. Remember, there were long silences?" (all talk at once)

Parent Two: "I mentioned it and, as I recall, he doesn't want to set forth any guide. He wants, he felt, that the group as a whole could get more out of this thing if everybody brought up whatever questions was bothering them, or whatever question they had in their mind. Is that correct? Something to that effect."

Group Leader: "Frankly, I think it's good that you're aware of what's happening in the group. You know when a group is moving and when it isn't, and then you take the responsibility for doing something about it."

Parent Three: "You mean of shifting. I mean, sometimes it's kind of rude. Say someone has something to say which has nothing to do with the price of rhubarb."

Group Leader: "Then, it's up to you to tell them. You see, one of the important things that can happen in a group is that if you are annoyed or you are bored, you can speak your mind and say exactly how you feel."

Parent One: "No, I leave that up to the leader, always. Don't you? For instance, that one particular meeting, I thought, was a complete waste of time."

There is general discussion about what the group thinks about this and what they feel their responsibility is and what the responsibility of the group leader ought to be.

Parent Two: "I think he'll speak up if we get on something he doesn't care for us to discuss. I think he'll intervene, probably."

Group Leader: "I'm not sure. I'm not sure, you see, because if you get troubled enough about what you're doing as a group, one of you is going to become upset enough or angry enough or responsible enough to say 'look, I'm sacrificing an evening away from my home, and I want something worthwhile to come out of this. Now, let's get down to business and talk about something that's important.' I think that the group member can do this. I don't have to play teacher, see to it that you keep your noses to the grindstone. The important thing is that if you feel that somebody is leading the group down the garden path, or somebody is stalling, or somebody is keeping you from talking about something that's worthwhile or important, that you be able to say it to that person. It's when you can speak freely this way, when you can both 'dish' it out and 'take' it, that the group will have real meaning."

The relationship of the group leader to the school staff needs understanding. The school needs to know what is going on in general, if only to relieve staff anxiety and curiosity. One cannot and should not expect the group leader to discuss individual parents. In general, group leaders work best when they are not members of the school staff. This makes it easier for the parent and the leader, and increases the freedom of both in the group, especially in school-related discussions. In using a non-school staff group leader, one needs to plan some liaison between the school staff and group worker.

RATIONALE

Some school systems have reported successful experiences with such parent counseling groups. Gildea described a five years' experience in St. Louis with this kind of program with parents of children with mild degrees of disturbance.[94] In the program in St. Louis, discussion was focused on

[94] M. C. L. Gildea, *Community Mental Health* (Springfield, Ill.: Charles C. Thomas, Publisher, 1959).

material initially presented in a mental health film or dramatic skit. Also, the leaders of these groups were lay persons who were trained to act as discussion leaders.

The probability that parents unknowingly (unconsciously) promote or encourage emotional conflicts and antisocial behavior in children is an assumption with some validity. Johnson and Szurek [95] and Brickman [96] have found that serious misbehavior in some children can be shown to derive its impetus from parental motivations and relationships with children. Supposedly, then, if parents are helped to become more aware of their relationships in some insightful way, the child will be freer to respond to more positive educational and social influences. In most cases, the subsurface motivations may be close to recognition; in some, the unconscious factors influencing the problem may be relatively deep. In any case, those parents who can be helped to gain insight about their interpersonal relationships and feelings will, in turn, reduce the emotional conflicts in their children. As parents gain, children will improve—not only in behavior but in achievement, perception by peers, and self-perception.

ADMINISTRATIVE IMPLICATIONS

One of the difficulties in the administration of parent counseling groups is that the need for professional distance between the school administrator and the group leader may, in some cases, cut the school off from the program. It is also evident that parents in the lower socio-economic groups do not find this type of program to their liking. In the main, this activity fits best the middle-class parent whose child is not performing up to par or is a behavior problem. In some cases, the pressure of other community activities makes for serious attendance problems and as a logical excuse for poor attendance and dropouts.

One needs to ascertain whether the school is the best or most appropriate agency to support such an activity. Most professional mental health workers seem to find sponsorship by the school the most promising and fruitful entry for such parent groups. The fulcrum of the helping relationship—a child with a school problem—comes at an earlier time than is usually possible using other agencies or symptoms. In addition, this service when provided by the school is regarded in a positive and helpful manner by the parents and one consistent with the school's interest in the education and welfare of their children. Such an intervention with parents where the problem is basically

---

[95] A. M. Johnson and S. A. Szurek, "Genesis of Antisocial Acting Out in Children and Adults," *Psychoanalytic Quarterly*, 21 (1952), 323–343.

[96] H. Brickman, "The Delinquent Child and the Family Doctor," *Journal of the American Medical Association*, 165 (September, 1957), 339–343.

one of poor parent-child relationships has great potential for effective preventive action in some families.

In preparation for this program there is a great need for detailed and explicit communication between parent and school, and parent and group leader. In some cases, it would seem best for the initial contacts with parents to be made by the group leader in conjunction with the school administrator. Some parents find it difficult to accept involvement in their child's problems and could better be prepared, at this initial session, for active participation by the group leader.

Activity Program

This program is usually structured as a club or after-school activity. In most cases, six to eight children meet about twice a week for a two-hour session. The children in the group are emotionally handicapped children who manifest a variety of problems—some are extremely hyperactive, others are timid and withdrawn children. A variety of expendable craft, painting, clay and wood work, and other expressive media are made available to the children. A teacher assumes the role of group leader. His role is to help the child to use the play materials and to provide a nonthreatening, nonpunishing atmosphere in which they can express and explore emotional conflicts that frighten or embitter them. During the play sessions he is an active "neutral"—providing help when asked, but avoiding any interference in or criticism of the child's work.

Each child is free to do whatever he wishes in the playroom provided he does not damage the building, injure himself or other pupils. It is also understood that the play program is limited to the area of the activity and does not continue into other classrooms or include relay races around the school buildings.

Play sessions can be developed with experienced professional persons or with selected teachers who are willing to undergo a short period of training for this purpose. In the New York City Schools a play program based on teacher-trained leaders produced encouraging results.[97] Such teachers must be intellectually alert, emotionally mature and be able to "tune in" to some of the unconscious needs of children. In addition, they need to be able to endure outbursts of hostility and relationship testing by children and their self-doubts and anxieties aroused in their work. Although the play leader may appear to be doing nothing, this kind of active nonparticipation does not come easy. Schiffer noted in the New York City program how uncomfortable and awkward the teachers felt in this role. He observed that "they begin to learn

[97] M. Schiffer, "The Therapeutic Group in the Public Elementary School," in *Orthopsychiatry and the School.*

what it means to remain peripheral to the group but readily accessible; permissive without sanctioning; dynamically neutral as opposed to studied noninterference." [98]

RATIONALE

Play is one of the most successful and universal methods for "blowing off steam." The energies bound by emotional conflicts, self-doubts and anxieties can be realistically expended in a play situation. In addition, realistic situations that are fraught with danger can be played out in comparative safety. Indeed, play offers a child a temporary victory over environmental difficulties and a chance to discharge feelings in a positive and socially approved manner. Children can get into a multitude of roles—father, mother, cowboy, villiain, baby brother, and work out some of their feelings with respect to the assumed role. For children, play is real; it is a form of activity that helps them define themselves and the world around them.

Emotionally handicapped children, in addition to being frightened of themselves or others, are also unable to play well. They find it difficult to express feelings impulsively or, when they do, they seem unable to control the limits of their activity. This is often reflected in their ostracization by other children and their dependence on adult supervision for control of impulses.

In play groups, emotionally handicapped children learn to play and learn to use play for many specific needs. The nonpunishing, nonthreatening atmosphere of the playroom encourages them to act more spontaneously and to explore feelings which up to now have been too frightening and too anxiety producing to be permitted to come to the surface. The child is also encouraged by the nonthreatening play climate to try new methods of response—to be freer in his responses and to add a few new ways of behaving to what was normally a rigid, constricted pattern of relationships. The children find they can retaliate against people who have hurt them without really hurting the objects of their fury. Such are the virtues of golf, tennis, and football rallies.

ADMINISTRATIVE IMPLICATIONS

For some impulsive-ridden and frightened children this may be the only school program with possibilities for help. It is possible to train some teachers to work effectively with play groups but the selection and training processes need careful attention. It is best programmed at the end of the day somewhere on the school grounds. Mental health consultation to the play leader is a necessary adjunct to the program as is staff co-operation and understanding. Chil-

[98] *Ibid.,* p. 77.

dren need to be carefully placed and tried out in the play group before permanent assignments are made.

On the negative side, one might well ask if such an activity is the responsibility of the school. Are there other community agencies that might better manage such programs? It is also well to understand that this type of permissive play group is not a simple, easily established, and administered program. This type of program cannot be "jury-rigged" or established without adequate professional help.

Of particular concern to the staff and the administrator is the fact that permissive play groups often, at first, bring out the worst in children. Since the children are permitted to act like children, they seize the opportunity to be as infantile as they need to be. Some of this may carry over into school behavior but should be replaced, in time, by more acceptable and promising behavior.

Selected Supplementary Readings

Bandura A., and R. H. Walter, *Social Learning and Personality Development.* New York: Holt, Rinehart & Winston, Inc., 1963.

Bennett, Ivy, *Delinquent and Neurotic Children: A Comparative Study With One Hundred Case Histories.* New York: Basic Books, Inc., 1961.

Berkowitz, Pearl H., and Esther P. Rothman, *The Disturbed Child—Recognition and Psychoeducational Therapy in the Classroom.* New York: New York University Press, 1960.

Blum, L., and J. Raths, "Can Kindergarten Teachers Be Trained to Identify Emotionally Handicapped Children?" *Elementary School Journal,* LXIV (February, 1964), 242–245.

Bower, Eli M., "The School Psychologist and the Emotionally Handicapped Child," *Ninth Professional Division 16 Institute Proceedings, The School Psychologist,* 19 (1965), 11–13.

————, ed., *The Psychologist in the School.* Sacramento, California: State Department of Education, 1958.

————, and Nadine M. Lambert, *Teachers Manual for In-School Screening of Emotionally Handicapped Children.* Princeton, New Jersey: Educational Testing Service, 1961.

Caplan, Gerald, and Virginia Insley, *Concepts of Mental Health and Consultation.* Washington, D.C.: Superintendent of Documents, 1959.

Cohen, Rosalyn S., "An Inquiry into Variations of Teacher-Child Communication: Implications for Treatment of Emotionally Ill Children," in *Educational Programming for Emotionally Disturbed Children: The Decade Ahead.* Syracuse: Syracuse University Press, 1965.

————, "Some Childhood Identity Disturbances: Educational Implementation of a Psychiatric Treatment Plan," *Journal of the American Academy of Child Psychiatry*, 3 (July, 1964), 488–498.

————, "Therapeutic Education and Day Treatment: A New Professional Liaison," *Exceptional Children*, 32 (September, 1965), 23–28.

————, and R. LaVietes, "Clinical Principles of Curriculum Selection," in *Educational Therapy*, I. Seattle: Special Child Publications, 1966.

Ekstein, Rudolf, and L. Motto Rocco, "The Borderline Child in the School Situation," in *Professional School Psychology*, Vol. I, ed. M. G. Gottsegen and G. B. Gottsegen. New York: Grune & Stratton, Inc., 1960, 249–263.

Gardner, George, ed., *Case Studies in Childhood Emotional Disabilities*. New York: American Orthopsychiatric Association, 1956.

Gildea, Margaret C. L., *Community Mental Health: A School Centered Program and a Group Discussion Program*. Springfield, Illinois: Charles C. Thomas Publisher, 1959.

Glueck, Eleanor T., "Distinguishing Delinquents from Pseudodelinquents," *Harvard Educational Review*, 36 (May, 1966), 119–130.

Goldfarb, William, *Childhood Schizophrenia*. Cambridge, Massachusetts: Harvard University Press, 1961.

Haring, Norris G., "The Emotionally Disturbed," in *Behavioral Research on Exceptional Children*, ed. S. A. Kirk and B. B. Weiner. Washington, D. C.: The Council for Exceptional Children, National Education Association, 1963.

————, and E. Lakin Phillips, *Educating Emotionally Disturbed Children*. New York: McGraw-Hill Book Company, 1962.

Henry, Marie, and James Rudder, "An Evaluation of a Process for Screening School Children with Emotional Handicaps," *Journal of School Psychology*, I, No. 1 (January, 1963), 28–32.

Herbert, W. L., and T. V. Jarvis, *Dealing With Delinquents*. New York: Emerson Books, Inc., 1962.

Knoblock, Peter, "Critical Factors Influencing Educational Programming for Disturbed Children," *Exceptional Children*, 30 (October, 1963), 124–129.

————, "Toward a Broader Concept of the Role of the Special Class for Emotionally Disturbed Children," *Exceptional Children*, 31 (March, 1965), 329–335.

Kotinsky, Ruth, and Helen L. Witmer, eds., *Community Programs for Mental Health*. Cambridge, Massachusetts: Harvard University Press, 1955.

Lambert, Nadine M., and Eli M. Bower, *Technical Report on In-School Screening of Emotionally Handicapped Children*. Princeton, New Jersey: Educational Testing Service, 1961.

Leighton, A. H., J. A. Clausen, and R. Wilson, eds., *Explorations in Social Social Psychiatry*. New York: Basic Books, Inc., 1957.

Leton, D. A., "Differential Teaching Techniques for Emotionally Disturbed Children, *Mental Hygiene* (April, 1964).

Lippman, Hyman S., *Treatment of the Child in Emotional Conflict*. New York: McGraw-Hill Book Company, 1962.

Loevinger, Jane, "The Meaning and Measurement of Ego Development," *American Psychologist*, 21 (March, 1966), 195–206.

Long, N. J., and R. G. Newman, "The Teachers' Handling of Children in Conflict," *Bulletin of the School of Education*, Bloomington, Indiana: Indiana University, XXXVII (July, 1961).

Long, N., R. Newman, and W. Morse, *Conflict in the Classroom*. Belmont, Calif.: Wadsworth Publishing Co., 1965.

Moller, Hella, "The Treatment of Childhood Schizophrenia in a Public School System," *Psychology in the Schools*, I, No. 3 (July, 1964), 297–304.

Morse, William C., and C. O. Dyer, "The Emotionally and Socially Handicapped," *Review of Educational Research*, XXXIII (February, 1963), 109–125.

Morse, W. C., R. L. Cutler, and A. A. Fink, *Public School Classes for the Emotionally Disturbed: A Research Analysis*. Washington, D. C.: Council for Exceptional Children, 1964.

Newman, R., F. Redl, and H. Kitchener, *Technical Assistance in a Public School System*. Washington, D. C.: Washington School of Psychiatry, School Research Program, PHS Project OM-525, 1962.

Papanek, Ernst, "The Delinquent Child," in *Professional School Psychology*, Vol. I, ed. M. G. Gottsegen and G. B. Gottsegen. New York: Grune and Stratton, Inc., 1960.

Quay, Herbert C., ed., *Research in Psychopathology*. Princeton, N. J.: D. Van Nostrand Co., Inc., 1963.

Spotnitz, Hyman, "The Neurotic Child," in *Professional School Psychology*, Vol. I, ed. M. G. Gottsegen and G. B. Gottsegen. New York: Grune and Stratton, Inc., 1960.

Stone, F., and V. N. Rowley, "Educational Disability in Emotionally Disturbed Children," *Exceptional Children*, 30 (May, 1964), 423–427.

Trippe, Matthew J., "Conceptual Problems in Research on Educational Provisions for Disturbed Children," *Exceptional Children*, 29 (March, 1963), 400–406.

Wall, W. D., *Education and Mental Health*. New York: Columbia University Press, 1955.

White, Mary Alice, and Myron W. Harris, "Techniques for Detecting Maladjustment Among Pupils," Chapter 9, *The School Psychologist*. New York: Harper & Row Publishers, 1961.

GORDON P. LIDDLE

16

The School Psychologist's Role
with the Culturally Handicapped

John is eleven years old. He is the third of Helena Robbins' four children. John spent his first seven years in
rural Alabama. His father was a tenant farmer until
mechanization, poor soil, and the hopes of a better life
brought the family to Midwest City four years ago. Now
John and his brother and sisters live in a federal housing
project in the city's Negro district.

When they first moved to Midwest City, William
and Helena Robbins hoped for a better life for themselves
and their children. Helena got a job cleaning chickens at
a packing plant. But William wasn't able to find steady
work although he did drive a coal truck occasionally during cold weather. In part, it was his inability to support the
family that led to the fights which broke up the marriage.

John liked Alabama better than Midwest City even
though their two-room shack in Alabama had neither
running water nor electricity. In Alabama, the family
worked together. When John was only five he began to
help his older siblings and parents when there was cotton

to be chopped or picked. When he stayed home he played hide-and-seek, mumbletypeg, and marbles, or went fishing with children his own age. Except when there was a lot of work to be done in the fields, he went to the one-room Negro school. His parents had only fourth-grade educations, owned no books, and seldom did any reading, but they told him they wanted him to do well in school. His teacher said he was an average student.

John was in the second grade when the family left the South for Midwest City; John, like his father, could no longer contribute to the family's income for there was no cotton to chop. The other children in the second grade were further along in their books than John. His parents knew this but did little about it. His mother worked during school hours, so she never had a chance to talk to the teacher. Neither she nor William felt they knew how they could help him.

Soon, squabbles about William's lack of a job, his drinking, other women, etc., dominated the family scene. For John, school became more and more dull and unsatisfying. Occasionally, he and a couple of his friends would skip school for a day to walk the alleys looking for things which could be "junked" so that they could get money for candy and the movies.

Although John found the city exciting, he sometimes longed to be out in the country again. He felt his teachers treated him pretty decently in school, but he found few satisfactions there. The older kids all said it did not make any difference how well you did in school anyway, for a colored boy would still get the same kind of "no good" job even if he finished high school.

Several million American children like John are seriously handicapped by their cultural background. Although many thousands of these children are seen by school psychologists, programs aimed at meeting their educational needs were all but nonexistent until 1960. In part, this is due to the fact that unlike the blind, the hard of hearing, the mentally defective, and other groups, the culturally handicapped or environmentally deprived had not been generally recognized as a separate diagnostic category in educational literature. Often, they were seen as mentally retarded or as emotionally disturbed. As a group they had not been claimed by special education.

In the past few years, however, the national spotlight has been turned on this group. Programs aimed at remediation of cultural handicaps or the primary prevention of learning difficulties have sprung up in almost all our larger cities and in some smaller ones as well. One illustration of the awareness of the importance of educating these children is California's 1964 law providing for special assistance for culturally disadvantaged children. The State Department of Education was authorized to provide grants to local school districts for "compensatory education" programs including broadening of cultural experience, stimulation of educational and cultural interests, guidance and counseling, work with community agencies, individualized instruction, and remedial assistance. This is the first state-wide special assistance program for culturally deprived children.[1] With the passage of the federal anti-poverty legislation in the Summer of 1964, education of the disadvantaged became one of the most discussed issues of the day.

There is a considerable body of research regarding the effects of cultural factors on intelligence and on learning. We should be aware of this research, should acquaint teachers and administrators with it, and should utilize this knowledge in helping to develop programs aimed at alleviating the problems caused by cultural handicaps.

A person may be said to be suffering from a cultural handicap if his values, customs, patterns of thought, language, or even his interests are significantly out of line with the prevailing pattern of the society in which he lives. Thus, the term "culturally handicapped" does not mean that a person lacks a culture, but that the cultural group from which he comes has certain values and ways of looking at the world that make it difficult for him to function adequately in our urban, industrialized society. We should think, therefore, of a cultural handicap as being relevant to certain problem situations within a particular culture.

Our beliefs and expectations, including those about intelligence, are based largely upon the cultural tradition within which we have grown up. The natives of a tribe in New Guinea would probably classify us as culturally handicapped, or perhaps just stupid, for not knowing how to grow yams, snare and cook rats, or propitiate their gods. They might also think it strange that we were not more interested in that portion of their educational curriculum dealing with methods of cooking wild boars. Similarly, an Indian or a Mexican boy may be regarded by his family as intelligent because he knows a great deal about the habits of the goats he tends. His teacher, in contrast, regards him as mentally retarded because he has no idea how far it is from New York to Paris, or who discovered America. Each cultural group has its own values, its own pattern of language and reasoning, and a somewhat different definition of intelligence than is commonly held in a second group, and may therefore be judged to be less intelligent by the second group.

The Extent of the Problem

It is among the culturally handicapped that we find our greatest waste of talent in this country. In several large subgroupings of American society, many (if not most) of the children are benefiting very little from their years in school. They are unhappy in school, leave it as soon as possible, and subsequently fail to make a very significant contribution to American society.

[1] E. S. Myers, *Community Mental Health Advances* (Bethesda, Md.: U.S. Department of Health, Education and Welfare, Public Health Service, National Institute of Mental Health, April, 1964), p. 7.

Dean Bond of Atlanta University reports that "culturally disadvantaged" families produce only one talented youngster for every 235 produced by "culturally advantaged" families.[2]

Richard Plaut, president of the National Scholarship Service and Fund for Negro Students, has another interesting finding. He reports that in minority-group slum neighborhoods, a child with a measured IQ of 105 in the third grade can be expected to measure 90 to 95 by the seventh grade. Masland demonstrated that class differences on intelligence measures increase in the later grades.[3] In a study of thirty-two northern schools in which a third of the graduates were Negroes, he reported that in terms of class standing, white students did fifteen times as well as the Negroes, and that less than one per cent of the Negro students were fully prepared for college.[4]

In programs for the gifted we spend considerable time trying to differentiate between the intellectual potential of a doctor's daughter with an IQ of 140 and a lawyer's son with an IQ of 127, but relatively little time attempting to identify those who are potentially gifted among the culturally handicapped. The psychologist may think it interesting that the culturally handicapped child's performance IQ is higher than his verbal IQ; he may use it to keep the child out of a class for the mentally handicapped; but we spend little time attempting to adapt the curriculum to meet the needs of a child who does poorly in the verbal areas of our tests, a group composed largely of under-achievers. Much evidence leads us to believe that there are many potentially gifted children among the laboring class and in minority groups. Projects such as the Higher Horizons Project in New York City have discovered many previously unrecognized talents among these groups. Studies show that IQs of rural Negroes moving to the urban North rise through time, and that children adopted into intellectually stimulating families in the early years of life tend to have IQs approaching those of their adopted parents.[5] But few programs for gifted children are set up to help the child whose ability is in a nonverbal area such as spatial reasoning, and high IQ non-achievers are almost always eliminated from action programs for the gifted. Failure to provide for these two groups eliminates most gifted culturally handicapped children from enrichment programs.

From what groups do most of our culturally handicapped children come; where is this loss of talent greatest? This question can be answered by replying, "Among the Negroes, Mexicans, Indians, Appalachian whites, Puerto Ricans, children of the foreign-born, migrant farm workers, and un-

---

[2] *Time Magazine*, November 21, 1960, p. 53.
[3] C. T. Rowan, "A Road Out of the Slums," *Saturday Evening Post*, February 4, 1961.
[4] R. L. Masland, S. B. Sarason, and T. Gladwin, *Mental Subnormality* (New York: Basic Books, Inc., Publishers, 1958).
[5] *Ibid.*

skilled laborers." It could also be answered in another manner, by saying that children will be culturally handicapped to the extent to which their group is outside the main stream of American life. In a group that is excluded from full participation in our society, certain of its values and traditions will be different from those of the majority of the American people, and its children will be handicapped. Of course, not all members of the aforementioned groups are culturally handicapped, but the vast majority are. As will be discussed later in this chapter, a child's language pattern and mode of reasoning may also be a culturally determined handicap.

We often think of the bilingual child as handicapped, but in many instances it seems that his handicap rises primarily out of his parents' low status and differing values, rather than from the language barrier itself. For example, a bilingual daughter of an immigrant German doctor may be far less handicapped by her cultural background than the daughter of a poor Kentucky farmer whose parents have spoken English for generations. This does not mean that Spanish-speaking pupils with little opportunity to hear and speak English are not handicapped by the language barrier. Rather it means that they have many handicaps in addition to the language handicap. Pablo Roca tested Puerto Rican children using individual intelligence tests translated into Spanish. He found that his pupils averaged twelve IQ points less than the average American child even after appropriate translation.[6]

Surely the several million Americans of Mexican extraction are handicapped for success in our schools and in the business and industrial world as well; so also are the majority of the American Indians who have left the reservation, and the one million Puerto Ricans living in our cities. Most of these people must do more than merely learn a new language. Most of them have lost their old identities, they are unsure of their place in American life, and therefore are unsure of their own personal worth. Among groups who feel unwanted as workers, neighbors, citizens, and school mates, the attitudes toward America, including its schools, will be somewhat different from those of other children. These differences influence motivation.

In addition to these racial and ethnic groups, educators and industrial people in cities such as Toledo and Detroit regard the average Appalachian mountaineer as culturally handicapped. When the author moved from West Virginia to Indiana during his high school days, he was automatically placed in the slow classes. In other parts of the country, recent migrants from the rural South, French Canadians, or other groups may be similarly viewed. Many children of lower class "old American stock" are also culturally handicapped, even though their parents may have lived in urban communities for several generations.

[6] P. Roca, "Problems of Adapting Intelligence Scales from One Culture to Another," *High School Journal*, 38 (1955), 124–131.

What then is the nature of this handicap? Usually a number of elements are involved, the effects of which are cumulative.

Basil Bernstein points out that linguistic form subtly affects cognitive, affective, and social experiences. His contention is that many of those groups we would classify as culturally handicapped speak a public language characterized by short, grammatically simple, often unfinished sentences of poor syntactical construction. The use of adjectives and adverbs is limited and rigid. If words such as "hell" or "nice" are frequently used in an attempt to communicate ideas and relationships that require a precise formulation, approximate terms become the equivalent of the appropriate logical distinctions.

Insensitivity to verb tense and a limited use of conjunctions are other characteristics of linguistic form commonly found among the culturally handicapped, which adversely affect the organization and communication of thinking. These characteristics make precise temporal relationships unclear and logical modification and stress can only be crudely expressed. Thus they affect the length and complexity of the ideas that can be expressed. Bernstein says that when

> . . . this form of language is continuously reinforced from the very beginnings of speech, and as the individual learns no other possibility, subjectively, there is little or no experience of adequate characterization. In fact when a more appropriate formulation is pointed out to the user of a public language, the latter may insist that this is precisely what he meant.[7]

If Bernstein's formulation of the problem is correct, the psychologist and the teacher face the problem, "should we attempt to eliminate the public language the child brings with him to school, with consequent major changes in his social relationships? Do we dare attempt to cut him off from communication with his family and neighbors by profoundly changing his language?" If not, how can we make accessible the values of the more precise formal language one needs to reflect upon and communicate his highly individual experiences, feelings and ideas; the type of language needed to indicate clear-cut logical, temporal and spatial relationships? After recognizing that formal English has many of the characteristics of a foreign language for these children, we are faced with this question: how can we most effectively teach these children to become more precise in their use of language?

In some cultural groups, fathers typically say, "Never mind why, just do what I say." Children from these families are often handicapped when critical thinking or creativity are called for. Not only can little learning take place when the reasons for behavior are not explained, but there is no room for an interchange of ideas. Every disagreement becomes a personal one. In-

---

[7] B. Bernstein, "A Public Language: The Sociological Implications of a Linguistic Form," *British Journal of Sociology*, **10** (1959), 311–326.

stead of a free conflict between differing ideas, disagreements become power struggles. To disagree with an idea threatens the emotional relationship with the other individual. In such families, curiosity and reflection about one's ideas and feelings may be very threatening, and most children will learn not to think for themselves.

Deutsch has suggested that another subtle factor is that of differences in auditory attention span. He thinks that these children lack experience in sustained attention to verbal communication. At home they hear unrewarding short commands or incomplete sentences with little explanation or elaboration. Thus, they are not used to giving any explanation their undivided attention, even for a short time.[8]

In interviewing parents of culturally handicapped children the author has been impressed with the continual blare of the TV set regardless of whether or not anyone is watching TV and regardless of conversation. Perhaps the meaningless background noise shuts out some of the unpleasantness of the world and gives these people some of the same sense of privacy that the suburbanite enjoys on his two acres. Nevertheless, continual inattention to speech and lack of reward associated with speech contributes to the short verbal attention span characteristic of this type of youngster.

In a study comparing English- and Spanish-speaking children in reading and arithmetic, Manual found that the Spanish-speaking pupils' achievement in reading averaged a year less than in arithmetic. In subsequent testing they fell even further behind their English-speaking classmates in reading but not in arithmetic.[9] In a related study, Tireman found that Spanish-speaking pupils had better visual than aural comprehension and a larger visual than aural vocabulary.[10] He concluded that this was because the Spanish-speaking children had little opportunity to hear and speak English outside of school. The farther children advanced through school the greater was the difference in favor of reading. Many Puerto Ricans, Indians, and others face the same problem, and even some English-speaking groups such as Appalachian whites or Southern Negroes only partially share the language of the school.

The hedonistic pattern of living widely found in some lower status groups is a cultural handicap. The educative process in our schools is largely an adult-directed procedure in which many of the rewards come only after a relatively long period of apprenticeship. When parents do not postpone their own gratifications, they are not in a good position to tell their children

---

[8] M. Deutsch, "Minority Group and Class Status as Related to Social and Personality Factors in Scholastic Achievement," Society for Applied Anthropology, Monograph #2 (1960), pp. 3–4.

[9] H. T. Manual, "A Comparison of Spanish-Speaking and English-Speaking Children in Reading and Arithmetic," Journal of Applied Psychology, 19 (1935), 189–202.

[10] L. S. Tireman, "School Problems Created by the Homes of Foreign-Speaking Children," California Journal of Elementary Education, 8 (1940), 235.

to study in order to get a scholarship, or to save their money in order to go to college. In many Indian, Spanish, and Negro groups, and among large numbers of lower class native-born whites, parents are essentially oriented to the present rather than to the future. Difficult work is to be avoided if possible, not sought as a challenge. The child is taught that the wise man takes time to get some enjoyment from every experience that comes along.

Postponing gratifications today so that in the future you can have position, wealth, or power makes much less sense logically as well as emotionally to a member of a spurned minority group. On the average, Mexican or Negro college graduates earn more than uneducated Mexicans or Negroes, but education makes a greater difference in position and money among the majority group of whites. On the average a Negro college graduate still makes less money than the white high school graduate. Such acute observers of the American scene as Edgar Friendenberg, S.M. Miller, and Frank Reissman have expressed the opinion that most of the students now dropping out of school would not have a better chance—even economically—if they stayed in school.[11]

The incidence of social disorganization is greater among these groups listed as culturally handicapped. Despised, unhappy, down-trodden people, separated from their old culture without being integrated into the new, typically exhibit more broken homes and psychiatric disorders than do members of dominant groups. Often, the emotional relationships with the family are superficial or distant. If a child's emotional relationships with adults are not good, he is much less ready for the adult-directed processs of education typically found in our schools.

Any unusual parental or familial religious adherence will have its deficit value, particularly if the embraced belief is one that is characterized as a cult or sect. Culturally deviant down-trodden groups often seek such solace. In the 1930's we had Father Divine; today the Black Muslims. The effort to avoid the pain which comes from social and/or economic inadequacy seems to be a factor attracting the down-trodden to cult groups that believe strongly that the tables will be turned in the next world. In an attempt to retain their beliefs in the face of a hostile world, these religious groups must be quite authoritarian; there must be no questioning of the revealed truths. Unfortunately, creativeness and critical thinking do not thrive in these surroundings. Religions that have maintained a sharp ideological discipline over their adherents have been noticeably unproductive in producing scientists and scholars.[12]

Many lower class children are taught that life is a long series of trying

[11] D. Schreiber, ed., *The School Dropout* (Washington, D.C.: National Education Association, 1964).

[12] S. S. Visher, "Scientists Starred 1903–1943," in *American Men of Science* (Baltimore: Johns Hopkins Press, 1947).

situations to be avoided whenever possible. Schooling, work, and even marriage are seen by the lower classes as less desirable. Middle class children are
taught that life is a series of hurdles to be jumped, and that true happiness is
to be found in clearing these hurdles. This puts the lower class child at a
disadvantage in such activities as learning to read or taking a test. He tries
to avoid the unpleasantness or to guess and get it over with, while the middle
class child is concentrating on doing what is expected of him because he is
reasonably sure that his efforts will be rewarded.

Thus we have seen that the term culturally handicapped is a relative
one that can be applied to many children from a variety of groups having
quite a diversity of values. Nevertheless, the term has value, even though to
a degree all of us are culturally handicapped. The principal characteristic
shared by individuals and groups commonly termed culturally handicapped is
that in some important ways they are unlike upper-middle class urban Americans. Consequently, they sometimes think differently and react differently
than do other children when faced with what may seem to be an identical
problem situation.

Schools Are Middle Class Institutions

Beginning at the age of five or six, children from culturally different
families begin to live in two somewhat different worlds. Their parents and
neighbors only partially share the prevailing values of the school as represented by the teachers. The child finds his teacher wants him not only to
learn certain things but also to change certain of his emotional patterns
and behaviors. He often finds that his teacher sees herself as not only
different from his parents, but superior to them. Since it is difficult for any
of us to be indifferent to the judgments of anyone with whom we have
more than peripheral contact, these conflicting standards are psychologically
threatening to the child and bring about some degree of anxiety.

While most teachers come from homes characterized by neither wealth
nor poverty, the vast majority hold strongly to middle class values. Even those
who grew up in poverty usually grew up in an atmosphere that valued thrift,
church-going, books, cleanliness, and speaking correctly. Most teachers have
learned to handle their aggressive tendencies, sexual impulses, and their
money in a very responsible manner. Lower class children find that school is
a middle class institution in which they can succeed only if they identify with
middle class values. Although they often come from families which live
largely in the "here and now," if they are to succeed they must work hard in
the hope that in the very long run they *may* be rewarded for their efforts.
For many culturally different children the hoped-for reward will never ma-
terialize.

Children learn best when they are in a rich setting full of new ideas, new situations, etc., and in the presence of warm, supportive, accepting, and creative individuals who have become significant persons in their lives. The support of teachers with these characteristics is especially important as the child tackles a complicated task such as learning to read or learning to play the violin. To what extent does the culturally handicapped child find such support? How can we give him greater support?

In any conflict between the values of the school and those of the home, with which values will the child identify? Many of the parents of culturally handicapped children are unhappy, insecure individuals. Consequently, often the emotional relationship is not what it might be. Nevertheless in all but the most inadequate of families, parents provide many gratifications—love, food, shelter, companionship, etc. Therefore, while most culturally handicapped children are under some pressure to identify with the school's values, they will probably do so only in the presence of warm, supportive, and accepting individuals. To the extent that they are made to feel different, stupid, and unattractive they will feel attacked and will resist change.

In dealing with the parents of culturally handicapped children we must bear in mind that they do not see their child as retarded. Bobby can probably do almost anything his father could do at the same age and knows far more about the world beyond the neighborhood than did his parents. He has no difficulty communicating with his parents; they feel that his vocabulary is quite adequate. The child's parents and friends think that he is a typical normal child, yet the school usually defines him as defective in some way. If we were in a similar situation, with whom would we identify? It is not surprising that we often find neither the parent nor the child has a very high opinion of the school or of the school psychologist and his tests.

Intelligence and Cultural Handicaps

School psychologists are often called upon to measure the intelligence and psychological adjustment of culturally handicapped children, particularly those who are doing poorly enough in school to warrant retention of placement in a special class. How adequately can these assessments be made? How can the results of the psychologist's testing be used most effectively?

When we compare upper and lower status children, those from the upper levels of society unquestionably get higher scores on intelligence tests and get higher grades in school. But are they more intelligent than lower class children, the group that includes the culturally handicapped? If they are more intelligent, were they at conception or at birth? Are their higher scores the result of genetic differences, differences in diet, differences in the level of language usage in the home, differences in the level of intellectual stimulation the children experience, differences in the amount of emotional support for mental growth? Or are they largely the result of intelligence tests drawing heavily on experiences with which upper status children are more familiar or more motivated to demonstrate their abilities? While not all the evidence is in, let's see what we now know and what remains to be discovered.

We are still not clear about what we mean by intelligence. Those who have studied intelligence see it as a group of abilities with some intercorrelational tendencies but with great individual differences in pattern; yet many people still think of intelligence as a single monolithic quality. At least they act as though they hold this view. While we may give tests to measure abstract reasoning or spatial ability, schools by and large are manipulators of verbal symbolism. We haven't learned what to do with these other abilities. We are sometimes amazed that the boy in the third row who still can't write a complete sentence repairs cars to get his spending money, but this doesn't really change our evaluation of his intellectual ability and doesn't modify our curriculum for this boy. Perhaps it should.

In any given individual it is exceedingly difficult to separate the relative influence of heredity and environment on his varied abilities and disabilities. It is nevertheless important that the school psychologist not close his eyes to the nature vs. nurture question, for upon his views and those of other educators rest our educational plans for children. If intelligence is a relatively fixed entity that cannot be modified by changes in environmental conditions or educational opportunities, one type of school program for low IQ children may be appropriate. This program may not be appropriate if intelligence can be shown to change significantly for particular groups of children with shifts in environmental influences.

The handicaps of the culturally different child are often accentuated by deprivation. In addition to growing up as a member of a group sharing only partly the values of the majority group, with the consequent threat created by discontinuities and conflicting loyalties, many culturally handicapped children also suffer from neglect. While the child who is only culturally different may be able to think clearly and maintain his emotional stability, particularly if he can live largely among his own subgroup, the deprived child has further problems. He grows up largely on his own, essentially lacking a consistent culture. He lacks close ties with other individuals and the mental stimulation that meaningful contacts with people and things create. He has not been talked to or listened to enough; he has not been loved enough; he has not been read to; he has not had much experience handling tools, paints, or even toys; he has not traveled, or if he has, he hasn't had the background to understand what he has seen. He has had to learn largely from his equally inexperienced and psychologically damaged peers. Lack of emotional security and intellectual stimulation injures a child of this type emotionally, as well as intellectually, for life in any cultural group.

Many culturally handicapped children suffer from a degree of environmental deprivation. The amount as well as the kind of intellectual stimulation found in their homes is different from that experienced by middle class children. In general the homes of the culturally handicapped are bare. There are fewer objects to manipulate; there is less talk and less variety in language; and the members of the family invest less emotional capital in one another.

While the great body of evidence indicates that genetic inheritance sets very broad limits on functional intelligence and almost everyone is an under-achiever to some extent, the culturally handicapped usually use much less of their native ability than most. Eli Ginzberg estimates that twenty-five per cent of our children could have IQs of 125 instead of our present six per cent were it not for cultural handicaps.[13] Dean Bond reckons that our talent pool would be increased fivefold if every child in the land had the same cultural opportunities as those in the wealthier classes.

Benjamin Pasamanick, who has spent years studying mental retardation, estimates that we could, through environmental manipulation, including the prenatal environment, prevent at least half of our cases of mental defect and mental retardation.[14] Alfred Binet himself recognized the vital influence of environment when he wrote, "A child's mind is like a field for which an expert farmer has advised a change in the method of cultivating, with the result that in place of desert land we now have a harvest."[15] It is apparent that the school psychologist would do well to bet on nurture. He should try to help the school improve the use of the child's intellect all he can; then there can be no errors of neglect.

Let's look at some of the evidence that leads these men and others to reject the conception of intelligence as a fixed entity. What has led them to take the view that intelligence tests do not strictly measure native ability, but rather native ability as it has been developed or inhibited by the child's experience in the home, the neighborhood, and the school?

During World War II nearly fourteen per cent of the draftees from some states were rejected as mentally unfit, while in other states the rate was only one-half of one per cent.[16] Since it was obvious that there were not twenty-eight times as many mentally retarded in a rural southern state as were found in an urban northern state, the tests must be measuring differences in schooling and differences in cultural expectations. We have known for a long time that the average IQ of Negro children moving north increases year by year for a number of years. Nationwide the Negro rate of rejection in World War II was six times that of whites; yet the rate of rejections for Negroes in

[13] E. Ginzberg, "Problems in Developing Human Potential," *Teachers College Record*, 48 (1956), 79–84.

[14] B. Pasamanick, *Regional Conference on Mental Retardation*, Illinois Department of Public Welfare (1958), pp. 89–92.

[15] A. Binet, *Les Idées modernes sur les enfants* (Paris: Ernest Flamarion, 1909), p. 146. Cited from Stoddard.

[16] E. Ginzberg and D. W. Bray, *The Uneducated* (New York: Columbia University Press, 1953).

the Northwest and Far West was below the white rate in the Southeast and Southwest.[17]

This evidence points up the importance of differentiating between mental deficiency and mental retardation. At the present status of medical science, mental deficiency is usually an essentially incurable condition caused by a massive central nervous system defect present at or shortly after birth. Mental retardation, on the other hand, is often heavily influenced by cultural factors.

It is important also to differentiate between various clinical groups of mentally defective children. Some children have suffered organic brain damage due to severe epilepsy or cerebral palsy; others are mongoloid, cretin, microcephalic, etc. Some mentally retarded children have a history of brain injury due to trauma or inflammation. Others were so neglected that their retardation appears to be solely due to an absence of mental stimulation or a failure to respond to stimulation due to deafness, blindness, or some other cause during early childhood. Some children suffering from severe emotional problems give the appearance of severe retardation. However, the culturally handicapped child, as we are speaking of him, usually fits none of the aforementioned categories. He is retarded but there is no history of brain injury and there is an absence of neurological signs. His siblings are usually also retarded. These children are not suffering from an essentially incurable condition caused by a massive central nervous system defect; rather they are thought to have had nearly average mental ability at birth.

Children of professional people seldom have IQs in the educable mentally retarded range; however, the professional class contributes a more expected proportion to the mentally deficient group. Prenatal defects or birth injuries can happen to any child regardless of social status, but our educable mentally handicapped classes are loaded with children of low social status. Studies correlating intelligence test scores with socio-economic status have consistently found a linear relationship between the two ranging from .25 to .50. In the author's ten year study of a cross sectional group of 1200 children growing up in a midwestern city the average social status of classrooms for the mentally handicapped was lower than the average social status of any of the community's fifteen elementary schools.

Kirk found it difficult to experiment with the early education of mentally retarded youngsters because social workers, doctors, and others working with young children were often unable to differentiate between a child's mental ability and his social position. He reports,

[17] P. H. Bowman, et al., Mobilizing Community Resources for Youth, Supplementary Educational Monographs, No. 85 (Chicago: University of Chicago Press, 1956).

the judgment of social workers, public health workers, and other agency personnel was more closely correlated with unsanitary home conditions or domestic difficulties of the parents than with the test results. It was somewhat surprising to find that so few of the children referred as subnormal actually were mentally retarded according to psychometric and other evaluations.[18]

Cyril Burt attempted to separate the effects of heredity and environment by studying twins.[19] He found that on group intelligence tests identical twins reared together correlated .94 in intelligence, while identical twins reared apart correlated only .77. Siblings reared together correlated .52. When he looked at scholastic achievement the correlations for identical twins were .90 if reared together, .68 if apart. For siblings reared together the correlation was .81; for unrelated children reared in the same households, .54. He concluded that there are "no such things as hereditary characters; there are only heredity tendencies."

The importance of growing up in a stimulating environment as a member of a social group is emphasized by some findings from experimental psychology. There is strong evidence to indicate that man and other mammals are stimulus-hungry creatures. Olds found that rats rewarded only by electrical stimulation in certain areas of their brains learned mazes as well as those motivated by hunger.[20] Hebb and others have been experimenting with the effects of lack of stimulation on the intellectual and emotional development of various animals. Hebb reared dogs in a barren dark room and found that, "the animal reared in isolation is a permanent screwball at maturity; motivationally, socially, intellectually abnormal." [21] No matter what experiences they had after puppyhood, they always appeared to be feebleminded. Studies of feral children and children raised in attic rooms in isolation have with one exception produced similar findings.[22]

Bexton, Woodburn, and Scott have been experimenting with the effects of sensory isolation on adults.[23] Alone in a bare room with diffuse lighting and padded clothing, their subjects began to hallucinate within a few hours. They

[18] S. A. Kirk, *Early Education of the Mentally Retarded* (Urbana, Illinois: University of Illinois Press, 1958), p. 13.
[19] C. Burt, "The Inheritance of Mental Ability," *American Psychologist*, 13 (1958), 115.
[20] J. Olds, "Runway and Maze Behavior Controlled by Basomedial Forebrain Stimulation in the Rat," *Journal of Comparative Psychology*, 49 (1956), 507–512.
[21] D. O. Hebb, "The Motivating Effects of Extroceptive Stimulation," *American Psychologist*, 13 (1958), 109–113.
[22] K. Davis, "A Case of Extreme Isolation," *American Journal of Sociology*, 57 (1947), 432–437.
[23] H. W. Bexton, H. Woodlawn, and T. H. Scott, in *Contributions to Modern Psychology*, ed. D. E. Dulany, Jr. (New York: Oxford University Press, 1958), pp. 72–79.

became confused in their self-perception and even their EEG record changed. Those who were given the privilege of hearing nursery rhymes upon request, asked for them over and over again. Upon emerging after a day or two in this extremely dull environment, the subjects' intelligence test performance had been temporarily impaired. They conclude that a person's motivation is largely a function of stimuli impinging on the organism from without. Totalitarian police have made this same discovery. After prisoners are isolated for a few weeks, Communist propaganda presented and discussed in a group setting becomes quite acceptable to many.

Pasamanick's research has indicated that mothers from lower class groups usually have more abnormal pregnancies and prematurely born children, factors which in turn are correlated with mental deficiency and retardation.[24] He has related this to dietary differences. Nevertheless, his studies of children in the first seven years of life indicate that during the first year of life there is only a small correlation between socio-economic or ethnic status and intelligence. By the age of three, however, significant differences have appeared, and this trend is accentuated throughout childhood.

Other researches have found that the relationship between intelligence test scores and socio-economic status or its correlate, parental education, increases as children grow older. Bayley reports a correlation of .59 between mid-parent education and the IQ of the child.[25] Honzik's findings are similar. She reports that:

> . . . the most marked increases in mental test scores between 21 months and eight years occurred in families where one or both parents went to college. A high school education was the least amount of schooling for any parent whose child showed marked gains in scores. In the case of children making markedly sub-average records, parents were usually found to have no more than a grammar school education.[26]

Eells found that among nine and ten year olds about 50 per cent of the items on a number of group intelligence tests showed significant differences between high and low status children. Four years later, 85 per cent of the items so discriminated, and the variability on IQ shown by low status children increased significantly. As higher levels of abstraction are demanded by tests and by the curriculum, more lower status youngsters are unable to meet the expected standards.[27]

Eells also found that the largest status differences were found on verbal symbolism items. Many such items involve words, concepts, or objects with

[24] Pasamanick, op. cit.
[25] N. Bayley, in Intelligence: Its Nature and Nurture, Part II, ed. G. M. Whipple (Bloomington, Illinois: Public School Publishing Company, 1940), p. 57.
[26] M. P. Honzik, Ibid., p. 204.
[27] K. Eells, "Social Status Factors in Intelligence Test Items," (Abstract of an unpublished Ph.D., dissertation) University of Chicago, 1948.

which high status children are familiar because of home and other non-school experience. "Items that show small differences are almost without exception either nonverbal in symbolism or involve simple everyday words which do not appear to be intended as testers of vocabulary knowledge." [28]

These studies and others aimed at changing the intelligence scores of children do not prove that there are no differences between various groups in the population, but they do show that ability is strongly influenced by environment.

The Psychologist Tests the Child

Culturally handicapped children, finding little reward for their attempts to understand the school's curriculum, may become behavior problems. Often they are then tested by the psychologist and find their way into special classes for mentally handicapped children. If asked how they got there they might say as one boy did, "Well I ain't so sure. The test report said I have a low IQ, but nobody noticed it till I couldn't get along with Miss Smith. She gave me some silly test and when I handed in my paper she looked at it and said, 'Just what I thought; he doesn't belong in here.'" While culturally handicapped children are often glad to get out of the regular classroom and into the class for mentally retarded children, such moves are unfortunate because they set our goals for these children too low. Movement into the special class makes it very unlikely that the culturally handicapped child will subsequently develop his abilities when he leaves school. Rather than taking this "easy way out," Sarason and Gladwin suggest that we should be attempting to identify in the early grades the particular defects of the culturally handicapped child. Then we should design a training program which from the beginning would prepare him for the gradually rising level of abstraction and conceptualization found in the curriculum in later years, for it has been widely recognized that the number of children classified as mentally retarded rises sharply as the curriculum demands more abstract thinking in the upper grades. If such a program can be developed we might save culturally handicapped children from fumbling and bluffing in the lower grades and later failing outright.[29]

If we do not develop such programs, psychologists will continue to be faced with the dilemma of either placing a culturally handicapped child in a special class for the mentally handicapped on the basis of functionally low verbal ability scores or of keeping him in a regular class on the basis of higher scores on the Leiter or WISC performance tests. If we do the first, we run the risk of setting the goals too low. If we leave him in the regular classroom,

[28] *Ibid.*
[29] Masland, Sarason, and Gladwin, *op. cit.*

the teacher often finds it difficult to find time to work with him and he becomes more and more lost.

Systematic Biases in Other Aspects of Psychological Evaluation

The biases against culturally disadvantaged children found on our intelligence tests are also found on the measures of adjustment used in psychodiagnosis. In the studies by the author and his associates in a Midwestern city, large numbers of the children from the lowest social class were identified as maladjusted.[30] On the California Test of Personality given late in grade school, less than nine per cent of the lower-lower class children had scores in the most favorable quarter of their age group while sixty-eight per cent were in the bottom half of the distribution. In high school the correlation between socio-economic status and adjustment as measured by the California Psychological Inventory was 0.22 for boys and 0.43 for girls. There would seem to be a need for different norms for children of various economic groups, and probably for the various cultural groups as well. When a middle class child says that he wishes his father had a better job, he may be indicating that his relationship with his father is not all that it should be, but a Puerto Rican's son may say this even though he and his father have a good relationship.

There is still another type of bias which may enter into our evaluating culturally handicapped children. How does the child view the psychologist and the testing situation? The culturally handicapped child, particularly if he has delinquent tendencies, has probably experienced the adult world as threatening and hostile. In the testing situation he is likely to feel that he has nothing to gain and everything to lose by revealing himself. The minute or two that we spend chatting with him in an attempt to gain rapport and gain his cooperation often does little to offset long established patterns. Yet the manner in which the child views the psychologist has a profound influence on his behavior in the testing situation.

Sarason has found significant differences in the amount of test anxiety experienced by children from varied cultural backgrounds, anxieties that affect test results.[31] Harari and Chwast report that some lower class youngsters, particularly delinquents, experience "their seeming freedom of choice in projective techniques as being extremely restrictive." [32] Surely we would expect the college-bound middle class high school student to have a very different

[30] Kirk, op. cit.
[31] S. B. Sarason, *Anxiety in Elementary School Children* (New York: John Wiley & Sons, Inc., 1960).
[32] C. Harari and J. Chwast, "Class Bias in Psychodiagnosis of Delinquents," paper given at the American Psychological Association Convention, 1959.

attitude toward intelligence, achievement, or projective tests than the dropout-prone student seated in the next row, with consequent influences on the test results. Yet in practice we often act as though their test scores are equally valid.

Considerations in Testing Culturally Deprived Children

In 1964, the Society for the Psychological Study of Social Issues, Division of the American Psychological Association, published an informative pamphlet entitled, *Guidelines for Testing Minority Group Children.* This publication was prepared by a work group of the Society under the chairmanship of Leonard Kogan.[33]

The committee identified the following critical difficulties in testing minority groups with the use of standard tests: 1) they may not provide reliable differentiation in the range of minority group's score; 2) their predictive validity for minority groups may be quite different from that for the standardization and validation groups; and 3) the validity of their interpretation is strongly dependent upon an adequate understanding of the social and cultural background of the group in question. For a detailed discussion of each of these issues, the reader is directed to this report.

The suggested remedies of the committee were as follows:

> One way might consist of measuring separate skills first, gradually building up to more and more complex items and texts which require the exercise of more than one basic skill at a time. With enough effort and ingenuity, a sizeable universe of items might be developed by this procedure. Special attention should also be given to the selection or development of items and tests that maximize criterial differentiations and minimize irrelevant discriminations. If a test is likely to be biased against certain types of minority groups, or if its validity for minority groups has not been ascertained, a distinct *caveat* to that effect should appear in the manual for the test.

> Furthermore, we should depart from too narrow a conception of purpose and function of testing. We should re-emphasize the concept of the test as an integral component of teaching and training whereby a floor of communication and understanding is established and *learning* capabilities are measured in repeated and cyclical fashion.

> Finally, we should think in terms of making more use of everyday behavior as evidence of the coping abilities and competence of children who do come from the cultural mainstream. Conventional tests may be fair predictors of academic success in a narrow sense, but when children are being selected for special aid programs or when academic prediction is not the primary concern, other kinds of behavioral evidence are commonly needed to modulate the results and implications of standardized testing.

[33] Leonard Kogan, "Guidelines for Testing Minority Group Children," *Journal of Social Issues*, XX, No. 2 (April, 1964), 129–149.

The publication concludes with the following statements:

Since the minority group child is so often handicapped in many ways his test scores may have meanings different from those of non-minority children, even when they are numerically the same. The task of the conscientious educator is to ponder what lies behind the test scores. Rather than accepting test scores as indicating fixed levels of either performance or potential, educators should plan remedial activities which will free the child from as many of his handicaps as possible. Good schools will employ well qualified persons to use good tests as one means of accomplishing this task. In testing the minority group child it is sometimes appropriate to compare his performance with that of advantaged children to determine the magnitude of the deprivation to be overcome. At other times it is appropriate to compare his test performance with that of other disadvantaged children—to determine his relative deprivation in comparison with others who have also been denied good homes, good neighborhoods, good schools and good teachers. In most instances it is especially appropriate to compare the child's test performance with his previous test performance. Utilizing the individual child as his own control and using the test norms principally as "bench marks," we are best able to gauge the success of our efforts to move the minority group child forward on the long, hard road of overcoming the deficiencies which have been forced upon him. Many comparisons depend upon tests, but they also depend upon *our* intelligence, our good will, and our sense of responsibility to make the proper comparison at the proper time and to undertake the proper remedial and compensatory action as a result. The misuse of tests with minority group children, or in any situation, is a serious breach of professional ethics. Their proper use is a sign of professional and personal maturity.

Experimental Attempts to Improve Children's Learning

Kephart worked with institutional borderline mental defectives who had no physical evidence of pathology. He spent a year and a half trying to stimulate ingenuity and spontaneous evaluation through generous amounts of social approval and recognition of ingenuity and initiative. Four-fifths of his children increased their IQ scores by at least five points and half showed an increase of at least ten points.[34]

The findings of Skeels and Dye are even more impressive. In a study of 25 mentally retarded children in an orphanage, thirteen were transferred prior to the age of three to an Iowa institution for the feeble-minded. There, each child was cared for by several of the brighter feeble-minded girls and women. Twelve similar children with somewhat higher initial intelligence scores stayed in the orphanage until they were four. The children being taken care

[34] N. C. Kephart, "The Effect of a Highly Specialized Program upon the IQ in High-grade Mentally Deficient Boys," proceedings and addresses of The American Association for Mental Deficiency, 1939.

of by the feeble-minded mothers showed an increase of 27.5 points and every child in the group showed a gain, while the average IQ of the control group dropped 26 points. In discussing this, Sarason points out that,

> the institutional girls were living a life devoid of excitement or any particular focus of emotional interest; they were able and delighted to shower upon the babies in their care endless affection and attention along with the minimal but adequate intellectual stimulation which created the increase in IQ.[35]

In severely inadequate homes we find conditions approximating the life of Skeel's orphanage children. In such homes, mental retardation is not primarily the result of differences in approaches to problem-solving or even of differences in motivation. Rather, in such families the absolute amount of problem-solving is not sufficient to stimulate intellectual growth. The barren, fatherless homes so often found among the culturally handicapped sometimes approximate this damaging environment. In these homes meals usually consist of individual raids on the icebox. Parents do not talk with the children during meals and sometimes forbid the children to talk to each other. When behavior of this type is combined with whipping as punishment, or only absence of beatings as a reward, children are ill prepared to enter an adult-controlled classroom atmosphere, an atmosphere which requires considerable self-discipline to be successful.

In another study, Skeels and Skodak studied the intelligence of children who had been placed in average and superior adoptive homes in infancy. They found that the average IQs of these children compared very favorably with the mean IQs of children from families of high socio-economic status and were considerably above those for the general population.[36]

In summary, it seems clear that intelligence tests do not do a good job of measuring the intellectual potential which the individual possessed at birth and probably do not do a very good job of measuring the intellectual potential of the child at the time he enters school. Rather they measure the developed intellectual abilities which school systems have felt to be important. It is clear that these measured abilities can be developed by favorable environment and depressed by environments which fail to stimulate, or actually repress, the abilities to verbalize, to conceptualize and to make generalizations from one's experiences. Thus the culturally handicapped child's native ability will often be greater than he is able to demonstrate on our present intelligence measures.

Nevertheless, IQ tests have value. Often it is important to know the child's present level of functioning with respect to the skills that are usually dealt with in school. Our present tests enable us to spot those who, if not

[35] Sarason, *op. cit.*
[36] M. Skodak, *Children in Foster Homes: A Study of Mental Development*, University of Iowa Studies in Child Welfare, Vol. 16, No. 1, 1939.

aided, will have difficulty learning to make generalizations from their experience. In interpreting intelligence test results to the teacher, it should be the function of the school psychologist to give a broader view of what the results may mean, and to help redefine the problem of individualizing instruction in such a way that an intelligent plan for action is forthcoming.

Cultural differences must also be taken into account in measuring the psychological adjustment of the culturally different child. Behaviors such as swearing, verbal and overt aggression, and even stealing may have differing meanings and consequences depending on the child's group memberships. There is much to be said for evaluating the child relative to his own subgroup and its values rather than the larger society.

Delinquency and the Culturally Handicapped

A number of researches have indicated that low socio-economic status, low scores on IQ tests, reading retardation, truancy, early school leaving, and delinquency all have a strong correlational tendency. In our study in a Midwestern city of 45,000 we found that seven-eighths of our delinquents came from lower class families, many of which would fall under our definition of culturally handicapped.[37]

Since communication, verbal and written, is the greatest academic problem of the culturally handicapped child, most such children are retarded in reading. Studies by Fabian and by Traxler have indicated that approximately ten per cent of our school population has a pronounced reading disability, but in a sample of delinquent and pre-delinquent children Fabian found that 83 per cent had reading disabilities.[38] Harrower reported that 76 per cent of first offenders she studied were retarded by two or more years in reading and almost 40 per cent were five or more years retarded.[39] Roman reports that 84 per cent of the cases carried by the Treatment Clinic of Manhattan's Children's Court were severely retarded in reading.[40]

School takes a large block of the child's time, and since we are all sensitive, to a degree, about the attitudes of anyone with whom we spend a considerable block of our time, it is difficult for the child who has difficulty with reading or other important areas of the curriculum to be seen, or to see himself, as an adequately functioning individual. In reading, and in other areas too, the culturally disadvantaged child has his disability constantly before

[37] Kirk, op. cit.
[38] A. Fabian, "Reading Disability—An Index of Pathology," paper presented at American Orthopsychiatric Association Conference, 1954.
[39] M. R. Harrower, "Who Comes to Court?", paper presented at American Orthopsychiatric Association Conference, 1954.
[40] M. Roman, Reaching Delinquents Through Reading (Springfield, Illinois: Charles C. Thomas, Publisher, 1957).

him. This destruction of the child's sense of worth may well be one of the causative factors in delinquency. It may be that the culturally handicapped child's negative self-image has more to do with his becoming a social, legal, or economic problem than the reading handicap itself.[41] There are many factors in our school system leading to rewards for the most successful, but we deprive the least successful of the rewards they need. As a result the culturally handicapped not only have lower than average IQs but are constantly under-achievers.

Cohen suggests that culturally handicapped children, having been defeated in the larger society, including the schools, gradually give up hope of ever being seen as adequate individuals and as a consequence strike out at society. He believes that this is responsible for the strong negativistic and nonutilitarian quality found in much of juvenile crime.[42]

No serious student of delinquency would dispute the fact that culturally handicapped groups contribute disproportionately to the delinquency problem, and that the children from the more disorganized of these families have an even higher delinquency rate. We would also have to conclude that the culturally handicapped child's defeating school experience contributes to his chronic dissatisfaction with himself and his world, a dissatisfaction often finding expression in hostility, some of which we label delinquency.

Bill, a moderately delinquent high school junior, was asked by his English teacher to write a story using as his last line, "and finally I gave up the search in despair." His story summarizes the fate of many culturally handicapped youngsters.

> When I was a boy in the first grade I was slow in most everything I did. I usual had to stay after school and finish my work. That was the first time I flunk. Flunk got to be a ugly word with me. The second year in the first grade didn't help me.
>
> The second and threeth grades went by and I didn't learning anything. The fourth grade I was flunk again. What was my trouble?
>
> It was reading. I never couldn't learn to reade. And no one saw to it that I did. We can skip the grads fifth thourth ninth. In the tenth grade I had fully realize that I had to learn to reade. I was seventeen and in the tenth grade. Mom got som outside help for me. It did som good for me but not enough. I still don't know how to read good. And went you can't read you soon get discouraged. And furthermore it would suit me to get kick right out of here. And when I use your sentence, "Finally I gave up the search in despair" I am talking of hope of learning to reade.

What can we do for Bill? For his younger sister? For his children?

[41] W. Reckless, S. Dinitz, and E. Murray, "Self Concept as an Insulator Against Delinquency," *American Sociological Review*, 21 (December, 1956).

[42] A. K. Cohen, *Delinquent Boys* (New York: The Free Press of Glencoe, Inc., 1955).

The Role of the School Psychologist
with the Culturally Handicapped

Many school systems began hiring psychologists first for psychometric functions only, but as school psychologists became better trained and as teachers and administrators became more aware of their skills, their role has broadened. He is tester of children, an interviewer of parents, a diagnostician, and sometimes a therapist. His effectiveness is largely dependent on his skills in interpersonal relations, for he must work largely through other persons in attempting to influence the lives of children. If he is to be successful, his diagnosis and suggestions must motivate others to take effective action. Therefore his role as a consultant is vitally important; he is a consultant not only to individual teachers and parents, but also to individuals and groups planning organizational and curricular modifications. He must have a broad view of the problems with which he is working, and he must be highly skilled in the art of building on the existing motivations of those with whom he works.

If the psychologist goes on testing and bailing out children, parents, and teachers without trying to modify the system causing or accentuating the problems he faces, he will not pass the old Cornish test of sanity. In this test a person was taken into a room in which a tap was slowly filling a pail. He was then given a cup and told to bail the bucket. If he did not turn off the tap before bailing, he was adjudged insane. If the psychologist doesn't· pass this test in his work, his value to the school system will at best be only moderate.

Now let us turn to some possible methods of dealing with the problem of educating culturally handicapped children and to the roles which the school psychologist can play in attempting to move toward solutions to their problems.

Bill's teachers sought at least a partial solution when they retained him in the first grade and again in the fourth, with obviously unsuccessful results. His teachers said he was retained, but Bill and his friends knew that he had failed. Most retained children remain near the bottom of their class and few ever finish high school. Their failure experience seems to produce inhibitions and poor attitudes toward learning and toward themselves as learners. Retention was unsuccessful because Bill faced the same curriculum and teaching methods the second year that were proven unsuccessful the first year.

Joyce comes from a barren substandard home. She is small for her age, and she greatly fears her father's aggressiveness. Her first grade teacher says of her,

> Joyce was very immature when she came to school. We should have told her
> mother to keep her at home for another year. Her vocabulary was very

limited; she couldn't keep her mind on anything for more than a minute; and she couldn't sit still. She surely wasn't ready to learn to read. Now she's so far behind that she knows and I know that she'll never catch up. She just came to school too soon.

There is something to be said for this point of view. Children do mature at differing rates, and the curriculum should not demand more maturity than they possess. In another year Joyce would have been somewhat more ready for school.

But should Joyce have remained at home for another year? Those who who say "yes" tend to see maturity as the primary factor to be considered. But Joyce came to school unprepared primarily because her home had not provided her with an intellectually adequate diet. Remaining at home for another year in the same inadequate atmosphere would have resulted not only in a greater amount of retardation relative to her age, but also would have demonstrated that once the optimal time for learning is past, the intellect is permanently handicapped. Thus each year's delay in enriching the life of a culturally handicapped child is detrimental.

What then is the solution? Should our goal be to change the over-all scholastic standards to fit the limitations of our marginal students? A professor once said that if our environmentally handicapped children could not understand the story problems in the arithmetic workbooks, the teacher should tear out these problems and give them problems at which they could be successful, such as additional pages of subtracting 2 from 5 or 4 from 6.

Unfortunately, if a child doesn't know whether to add or divide he can't use the computational skills he has acquired, so this is not a realistic solution. Although not every job calls for high verbal skills, and although we do need to find ways to utilize the nonverbal talents of children, ours will continue to be a verbal world in which the child who does not develop his verbal ability will be permanently handicapped. Therefore we cannot solve the problem of culturally handicapped children coming to school verbally handicapped by deemphasizing such skills. Rather we must recognize the need to identify the particular aspects of interpersonal or cultural experiences of these children that were inadequate for the development of the skills important in our society, and must then institute a remedial program.

Culturally handicapped children need more opportunity to hear and speak the language. In large families, especially those in which the father is seldom present and the mother has a job or is overburdened, there is a tendency not to talk with children unless talking is necessary. Thus the quantity as well as the quality of speech is often deficient. Since children learn to understand and manipulate verbal symbols only in social interaction, children isolated from speech cannot learn, and without language all knowledge is necessarily very limited. If the child is forced to learn the language largely from his inexperienced peers, we must expect that his grammar and pronunciation will be poor and his concepts and vocabulary limited. Psychologists should therefore encourage teachers of culturally handicapped children to have verbally active classrooms. These children need to be talked to, read to, and listened to. Dramatic plays should be encouraged.

Helping Teachers and Administrators

While we hope that the psychologist has the personal attributes that would make it possible for him to become a significant individual in the life of a culturally handicapped child, we do not usually expect him to play this role. Rather he should be a consultant to teachers and administrators.

While educators usually make some effort to individualize the instruction of a child who is badly out of step with the curriculum, we don't expect a school system to change its goals in order to accommodate a given individual. However, we may reasonably expect the system to try to reach a group of children sharing a common problem. Where there is one culturally handicapped child there are usually many more, for such children usually live in sections of the city in which almost everyone and everything suffers from neglect. In these neighborhoods, children do not have easy access to enrichment experiences. Even public institutions such as art galleries, libraries, and museums are economically and psychologically distant from these children and there is therefore little tendency to seek participation in their programs. The school then is often the only potentially stimulating spot in the community. If it does not see its role as a broad one, if it does not see itself as a community center, if its teachers do not become in some way substitute parents, the school will become merely a custodial institution for most culturally handicapped children.

If teachers are to accomplish anything with culturally handicapped children they must see some hope. If the psychologist merely reports that a child whom he suspects is culturally handicapped has an IQ of 82 and does not help the teacher to correctly interpret the child's strengths and weaknesses, he serves only the function of helping the teacher feel less guilty about the fact that she is not accomplishing very much with this child. Many culturally handicapped children can be spotted by giving an intelligence test which has both a verbal and a nonverbal component. Where the performance IQ is considerably above the verbal IQ, culturally handicapping conditions are suspected. In the Higher Horizons project the nonverbal IQ of the Negro and Puerto Rican children averaged 100, almost 20 points above their verbal level.[43]

Where it is thought to be important to identify nonverbal children, and

[43] D. Schreiber, "A School's Work With Urban Disadvantaged Pupils," paper published by the College Board, New York, N.Y., 1960.

the psychologist does not have time to give individual Wechslers or similar tests, the California Test of Mental Maturity or some similar test having verbal and nonverbal sections can be administered individually or in small groups by a classroom teacher. It is important, however, not to spend so much time attempting to identify the culturally handicapped that we have neither the time nor the energy left to institute programs aimed at meeting the handicaps.

New York's Higher Horizons program is an example of the type of program the school psychologist should encourage. The program began in 1956 in Junior High School 43. Whereas in 1953 only five per cent of the largely Puerto Rican and Negro student body at Junior High passed all their subjects, in 1959 fifty-seven per cent did so. The median IQ of the first year's class rose from 93 to 102 in four years. The twenty-five per cent of the 1960 high school graduating class going to college is at least five times as many as went from pre-project classes.

These results have been obtained because teachers, parents, and volunteers have taken the time to take children to college campuses, the theater, the opera, the art gallery, and the science laboratory. The school held book fairs, circulated its library on weekends, instituted group guidance and small classes for remedial reading, made awards for reading books, and held workshops for its teachers aimed at adapting the curriculum to the culturally underprivileged.

Other programs aimed at raising the child's and the parent's cultural sights and assisting each child in making and carrying out appropriate educational and occupational plans are underway in Detroit, Kansas City, Oakland, and other cities. It has been reported that Central High in Kansas City has increased the percentage of its graduates going to college from fifteen to forty-five per cent while changing from an all-white school to a school with more than fifty per cent Negro children.[44]

The role of the psychologist should be that of helping teachers redefine their problems on the basis of wider information about the children and their specific learning difficulties. He should also arouse their interest in and sympathy for these children and their problems. He must help them find ways to give school learnings the inner meaningfulness that make them worth remembering.

A psychologist must function largely through teachers. He is a member of the teacher's staff, not an administrative officer charged with evaluating teachers. Teachers hope that psychologists will be able to help them with their classroom problems by giving them suggestions as to how they might be more successful in reaching a given child or group of children. In short, psychologists can help teachers plan next steps, point out new uses for the

[44] Reckless, *op. cit.*

available resources, and other material or personal resources available to the teacher. The psychologist should be a member of a team of equals planning the best possible course of action within the classroom to meet children's needs.

When as a result of his testing and observation the psychologist has ideas that he thinks might be worth trying, he should come forward with them, although he should never attempt to take over responsibility for the teaching function. When he does not have ideas he may serve a useful function if he can ask significant questions, ones which spur the teacher to be a more acute observer and to take a more experimental attitude toward her attempt to reach these children.

In order to be of greatest help to teachers, the psychologist should have an adequate understanding of how a person learns his intellectual and emotional lessons. He must have an understanding of the limitations of the classroom situation and must be able to communicate this understanding to the teacher in a meaningful way.

In addition to his reports about the child from the teachers, the psychologist should have available to him at least three other sources of information: a home interview, the results of his testing of the child, and the results of his own observations of the child in the classroom and on the playground.

In the testing situation the psychologist sees several aspects of a child's performance, some of which may throw new light on the child's classroom behavior. He should then help the teacher to see that these are just two of the many environments in which the child performs, and that differences in the child's performance from one situation to another provide valuable materials for teacher-psychologist explorations of how a given child or group of children learns best.

The psychologist's own observations of the child in the classroom, on the playground, and if possible in the family, should supplement his sources of information from teachers, administrators, and others. He should be an acute observer of interpersonal relationships.

The teacher cannot be expected to be entirely objective about the child in the classroom, anymore than we would expect a husband to be entirely objective about his relationship to his wife, children, mother, or his boss. Therefore direct observation should be a part of the psychologist's standard procedure whenever possible. When observation is not possible this lack of objectivity should be taken into account.

Helping Parents Do a Better Job

While there are great variations in the emotional climate and even the intellectual climate of homes that are culturally handicapping, some reasonably accurate generalizations can be made. Most of the parents of these children had relatively unhappy experiences in school when they were children. Because of their frustrations in school and with other aspects of life as well, their view of life, a view that they pass on to their children, is apt to be biased and distorted. It will not be the official version of the culture. To the extent that the child also feels a sense of defeat, guilt, anxiety, shame, and resentment toward society, or toward certain groups in society, his views will be like his parents'. Many homes consciously or unconsciously encourage defiance. Aggressiveness and hostility are often encouraged, while social responsibility and group participation, if not actively discouraged, are at least not encouraged.

The parents of these children know that most people look down on them and that for the most part their opportunities for advancement are rather limited. Therefore, some hostility directed at majority groups in the society is to be expected, and parents make little effort to hide this hostility from their children. If the parent feels that the world is against him, he is apt to strike out aggressively. He may transfer his hostile feelings from those too powerful to attack, onto other individuals and groups. Further, some studies have shown that the emotional relationships in lower-lower class families are characterized by a lower level of emotional involvement with one another. That is, the parents do not invest as much emotional capital in their children or in the marriage relationship as is usually true in middle class families. As the result of these influences, as we might expect, it is more difficult for environmentally deprived children to learn to be socially responsible and vitally concerned about others in their group, two expectations which are highly valued in the school setting. Children lacking these characteristics are not likely to be highly valued by their teachers, and children who are not highly valued by the significant adults in their lives are not likely to put forth the sustained effort which mastering an academic discipline requires.

Nevertheless, the psychologist has a powerful ally in his battle against cultural handicaps. This ally has too often been forgotten and not used. I refer to the motivating force of hope. America for the most part was not founded by the rich and the powerful people of Europe and Africa; they stayed home. Rather we became great because the poor and the despised from other cultures saw in America a hope for a brighter future for themselves and their children. We must awaken this hope in our newer immigrants from Mexico, Puerto Rico, the Appalachian Highlands, the rural South, and the Navaho Reservation. We must also rekindle it in the hearts and minds of the second and third generation slum dwellers of our urban centers.

We often think of the parents of culturally handicapped children as hard to reach and hard to motivate. They think teachers have a soft job with short hours and high pay. They don't usually come to PTA meetings. They are sometimes hostile when called in because John has been failing in school or "smarting off" to the teacher. Why? Because they have given up hope for themselves and for the success of their children. When the fires of hope are rekindled, as in New York's Higher Horizons Program, it has been found that the hard-to-reach child and parent isn't really so hard to reach after all. In a single year the percentage of parents interested in seeing their child's counselor rose from thirty-eight per cent to eighty-four per cent. When hope of higher horizons for their children returned, the average attendance at daytime parents' meetings increased to thirty-four per cent, more than three times the city-wide average.[45]

Often the psychologist can serve as a mediator between the home and the school. The social distance and differing standards of parents and teachers need to be bridged if they are to work together effectively. He can help each group to see that their long range objectives for the child are similar in most instances, and that they hold many values in common.

The psychologist, particularly if he is a man, might well attempt to reach the fathers of these children and involve them in the education of their children, particularly the boys. Too often, schools contact only the mother because she is more available and possesses, at least on a verbal level, more middle class values. In many minority groups, the Puerto Ricans for instance, the man is supposed to be the head of the family, yet school people usually approach the woman of the family. What effect does this have on the father's involvement?

In working with parents the psychologist should adapt his vocabulary to the level of their understanding. He should work with them in an effort to arrive at some joint decisions as to how the home and the school can do a better job of making the child's educational experience meaningful. A child is often more strongly motivated when he finds that school people and his parents are singling him out for special attention. The culturally handicapped child's lack of the background experiences needed to make a subject exciting is another aspect of his lack of motivation. Experience is the food for intellectual growth, and some environments are much poorer in providing meaningful stimulating experience than are others; for this reason, children are not ready to learn the things they actually need to learn. In these instances, the school must be led to see the need for creating learning experiences by broadening the children's conceptions of the world and their future role in the world. The school must also teach the child the more exact languages of the intellectual world.

If he has the time, and admittedly few school psychologists do, he can help the parent or the teacher learn how to encourage in his child a questioning mind, a desire to know. Parents can learn to encourage exploration by their interest and by their questions. For instance, Esin Kaya has suggested that perceptual sensitivity can be developed by such seemingly simple ex-

[45] Ibid.

ercises as asking a child to tell you all he can about a leaf.[46] If the child's responses involve only visual cues, blindfold him to encourage the use of touch, smell, taste, etc. As a next step children can be asked to classify leaves according to their own systems of classification as to size, shape, texture, color, for example. This in turn will lead to comparison of classification systems, and could lead into a study of how biologists have classified plants and animals.

It is interesting to note that Braun has recently found a closer relationship between concept formation ability and reading achievement than between intelligence tests results and reading achievement at the third, fifth, and seventh grade levels.[47] Culturally handicapped children not only need more field trips and other direct learning experiences; they must be taught to make generalizations about their experiences, if they are to function adequately in school and in our complex urban society.

Future Developments

One way that the school psychologist who works in an area where there are concentrations of culturally deprived children can keep abreast of developments is by reading the major research studies appearing in this area. The accompanying Selected Supplementary Reading List at the end of this chapter contains many references which should be on the shelf of the school psychologist in the economically and educationally depressed areas.

Selected Supplementary Readings

Antonovsky, Aaron, and Melvin Lerner, *Occupational Aspirations of Lower Class Negro and White Youth*. New York: New York State Commission on Human Rights, 1959.

Association for Supervision and Curriculum Development, *Freeing Capacity to Learn*. Washington, D. C.: National Education Association, 1960.

———, *Learning More About Learning*, Washington, D. C.: National Education Association, 1959.

Ausubel, D. P., "Effects of Cultural Deprivation on Learning Patterns," *Audio Visual Instruction*, January, 1965.

[46] E. Kaya, "A Curricular Sequence Based on Psychological Processes Rather Than Subject Content," paper read before the American Psychological Association, Chicago, September, 1960.
[47] J. S. Braun, "An Investigation of the Relationship Between Concept Formation Ability and Reading Achievement At Three Developmental Levels," paper read before the Midwest Psychological Association, Chicago, May, 1961.

Baber, Eric R., *Programs for the Educationally Disadvantaged.* Washington, D. C.: U. S. Office of Education, 1963.

Beilin, Harry, "The Utilization of High Level Talent in Lower Socio-Economic Groups," *Personnel and Guidance Journal* (November, 1956), pp. 175–177.

Bower, J. R., and J. F. Magary, eds., *Education and Guidance of the Disadvantaged.* New York: Pitman Publishing Co., 1967.

Bowman, Paul, and Maurine Pellman, "Socially Underprivileged Youth and the Schools," *The High School Journal* (May, 1958), pp. 331–335.

Brim, Orville G., *Sociology and the Field of Education.* New York: Russell Sage Foundation, 1958.

Burchill, George W., *Work-Study Programs for Alienated Youth: A Casebook.* Chicago: Science Research Associates, Inc., 1962.

Clarke, Kenneth B., "Discrimination and the Disadvantaged," *College Board Review* (Winter, 1960), pp. 5–9.

————, "The Psychodynamic Implications of Prejudice toward Children from Minority Groups," in *Professional School Psychology,* I, ed. M. G. Gottsegen and G. B. Gottsegen. New York: Grune & Stratton, Inc., 1960, pp. 64–71.

————, Rossi, Peter, *et al., The Search for Talent.* New York: College Entrance Examination Board, 1960.

Coffman, William, "Developing Tests for the Culturally Different," *School and Society,* 93 (November, 1965), 36–41.

Conant, James Bryant, *Slums and Suburbs: A Commentary on Schools in Metropolitan Areas.* New York: McGraw-Hill Book Company, 1961.

Conference on Reading. Chicago: University of Chicago Press, 1964. A monograph on the disadvantaged student and reading curriculum and instruction.

Conference on Unemployed Out-of-School Youth in Urban Areas, *Social Dynamite.* Washington, D. C.: National Committee for Children and Youth.

Cutts, W. G., "Special Language Problems of the Culturally Deprived," *Clearing House,* XXXVII (October, 1962), 80–83.

Daugherty, L. G., "Working with Disadvantaged Parents," *NEA Journal* (December, 1963), 18–20.

Davis, Allison, *Social-Class Influences upon Learning.* Boston: Harvard University Press, 1948.

Delmo, Della Dora, "The Culturally Disadvantaged: Educational Implications of Certain Social Cultural Phenomena," *Exceptional Children,* XXVIII (May, 1962), 467–472.

Demonstrations Guidance Project, Annual Report (I–V). New York: New York City Board of Education, 1957–1961.

Educational Planning for Socially Disadvantaged Children and Youth, the 33rd Yearbook of the *Journal of Negro Education.* Washington, D. C.: Howard University, Summer, 1964.

Educational Policies Commission, *Education and the Disadvantaged American.* Washington, D. C.: National Education Association, 1962.

Ferguson, Harold A., and Richard L. Plant, "Talent: To Develop or to Lose," *Educational Record* (April, 1954), pp. 137–140.

Frost, Joe L., and Gleen R. Hawkes, *The Disadvantaged Child.* Boston: Houghton Mifflin Company, 1966.

Fusco, Gene C., *School-Home Partnership in Depressed Urban Neighborhoods.* Washington, D. C.: U. S. Department of Health, Education and Welfare, Office of Education, 1964.

Ginzberg, Eli, "Guidance, Limited or Unlimited," *Personnel and Guidance Journal* (May, 1960), pp. 707–712.

————, *The Negro Potential.* New York: Columbia University Press, 1956.

Gladwin, Thomas, "The School, Society, and the Child," *Psychology in the Schools,* I (April, 1964), 162–172.

Glazer, Nathan, and Daniel Moynihan, *Beyond the Melting Pot: The Negroes, Puerto Ricans, Jews, Italians, and Irish of New York City.* Cambridge, Mass.: M. I. T. Press and Harvard University Press, 1963.

Gordon, Edmund W., "Social Status Differences: Counseling and Guidance for Disadvantaged Youth," in *Guidance and the School Dropout,* ed. D. Schreiber. National Education Association, 1964.

Gowan, John C., and George D. Demos, *The Disadvantaged and Potential Dropout: Compensatory Educational Programs.* Springfield, Ill.: Charles C Thomas, Publisher, 1966.

Gray, W. W., R. A. Klaus, J. O. Miller, B. O. Forrester, *Before First Grade: The Early Training Project for Culturally Disadvantaged Children.* New York: Teachers College Press, 1966.

Guttentag, M., "The Problem of the Have-nots in Suburbia," *Journal of School Psychology,* 2 (Summer, 1965), 37–43.

Handlin, Oscar, *The Newcomers.* Garden City, New York: Anchor Books, 1962.

Harrington, Michael, *The Other America.* Baltimore: Penguin Books, Inc., 1962.

Havighurst, Robert J., "Conditions Favorable and Detrimental to the Development of Talent," *School Review* (Spring, 1957), pp. 20–25.

————, *Human Development and Education.* New York: Longmans, Green & Co., Inc., 1953.

————, and Bernice Naugarten, *Society and Education.* Boston: Allyn and Bacon, Inc., 1957.

Hess, R. D., and J. M. McKee, "Summary of Discussions on the Conservation of Human Potential: the Disadvantaged," *School Psychologist* (Summer, 1966), 37–40.

Hicks, R. A., and Pellegrini, "The Meaningfulness of Negro White Differences in Intelligence Test Performance," *The Psychological Record*, 16 (January, 1966), 65–72.

Hunt, J. McV., *Intelligence and Experience*. New York: The Ronald Press Company, 1961.

Jewett, A., J. Mersand, and D. V. Gunderson, eds., *Improving English Skills of Culturally Different Youth in Large Cities*. Washington, D. C.: U. S. Department of Health, Education, and Welfare Bulletin, Office of Education, 1964

John, Vera P., "A Brief Survey of Research on the Characteristics of Children from Low Income Backgrounds," *Urban Education*, Vol. 1, No. 4, 1965, The University of Buffalo Foundation, Inc.

Journal of Marriage and the Family, Vol. 26, No. 4 (November, 1964), entire issue.

Journal of School Psychology, Spring, 1966. Special issue on compensatory education.

The Journal of Social Issues, Vol. XX, No. 2 (April, 1964). Articles on the Negro personality plus a supplement entitled "Guidelines for Testing Minority Group Children."

Karp, J. M., and Irving Sigel, "Psychoeducational Appraisal of Disadvantaged Children," *Review of Educational Research*, December, 1965.

Katz, Irwin, "Review of Evidence Relating to Effects of Desegregation on the Intellectual Performance of Negroes," *American Psychologist*, XIX (June, 1964), 381–400.

Krugman, Judith I., "Cultural Deprivation and Child Development," *High Points* (November, 1956), pp. 5–20.

Lambert, Nadine M., "The Present Status of the Culture Fair Testing Movement," *Psychology in the Schools*, I (July, 1964), 318–330.

Landers, Jacob, "Higher Horizons-Quality Education," *Higher Horizons Bulletin*, April, 1962.

Lantz, Beatrice, "The School in the Deprived Neighborhood," in *Professional School Psychology*, pp. 44–53.

Larson, Richard, and J. L. Olson, "Method of Identifying Culturally Deprived Kindergarten Children," *Exceptional Children*, XXX (November, 1963), 130–134.

Lee, Frank F., *Negro and White in a Connecticut Town*. New York: Bookman Associates, 1961.

Lichter, Solomon O., Elsie B. Rapien, Frances M. Seibert, and M. A. Slansky,

The Drop-Outs: A Treatment of Intellectually Capable Students Who Drop Out of High School. New York: Free Press of Glencoe, Inc., 1962.

Loretan, Joseph O., and Shelley Umans, *Teaching the Disadvantaged.* New York: Teachers College Press, 1966.

Lott, Albert J., and Bernice E., *Negro and White Youth: A Psychological Study in a Border-State Community.* New York: Holt, Rinehart & Winston, Inc., 1963.

McClelland, David, et al., *The Achievement Motive.* New York: Appleton-Century-Crofts, 1953.

National Child Labor Committee, "Disadvantaged Children and the World of Work," *The American Child* (November, 1958), pp. 1–24.

National Education Association and American Association of School Administrators, Educational Policies Commission, *Education and the Disadvantaged American.* Washington, D. C.: The Association, 1962.

O'Connell, Charles D., Jr., "'GRITS': A Modest Experiment in Talent Searching," *Journal of the Association of College Admissions Counselor* (Winter, 1962).

Olsen, James, "Children of the Ghetto," *High Points,* XLVI (March, 1964), 25–33.

Passow, A. H., *Education in Depressed Areas.* New York: Columbia University Press, 1963.

Pearl, A., "As a Psychologist Sees Pressures on Disadvantaged Teenagers," *NEA Journal* (February, 1965), pp. 18–19.

Perkins, Keith J., "A School Preparation Project," *The School Psychologist,* **19** (1965), 5–9.

Plaut, Richard L., *Blueprint for Talent Searching.* New York: National Scholarship Service and Fund for Negro Students, 1957.

Rath, James, "Underachievement and a Search for Values," *The Journal of Educational Sociology* (May, 1960), pp. 707–712.

Reading Teacher, March, 1965. Entire issue on the disadvantaged—their characteristics, methods of teaching them, and the pre-service and in-service education of their teachers.

Review of Educational Research, December, 1965. Issue on education for socially disadvantaged children.

Riese, Hertha, *Heal the Hurt Child.* Chicago: University of Chicago Press, 1962.

Riessman, Frank, *The Culturally Deprived Child.* New York: Harper & Row, Publishers, 1962.

Roberts, Gene, Jr., "Negro Education—For What?", *New York Times Magazine,* November 19, 1961.

Rohrer, John H., and Munro S. Edmonson, *The Eighth Generation Grows Up: Cultures and Personalities of New Orleans Negroes.* New York: Harper & Row, Publishers, 1964.

Rose, Arnold, *The Negro in America: The Condensed Version of Gunnar Myrdal's An American Dilemma.* New York: Harper & Row, Publishers, 1964.

Savitsky, Charles, "Theory Advances on the Disadvantaged," *High Points,* Vol. XLVI (February, 1964).

Schreiber, Daniel, *The Higher Horizons Program: First Progess Report, 1959–1960.* New York: New York City Board of Education, 1960.

———, "Raising Sights to Higher Horizons," *Strengthening Democracy* (May, 1960).

Sexton, Patricia, *Education and Income.* New York: The Viking Press, 1964.

Smith, Herbert A., and Lawrence L. Penny, "Educational Opportunity as a Function of Socio-economic Status," *School and Society* (September 12, 1959), pp. 342–344.

Teachers College Record (November, 1956). The theme of this issue is Guidance and Conservation of Human Resources.

Today's Educational Programs for Culturally Deprived Children, Proceedings of Section II, Seventh Annual Professional Institute of the Division of School Psychologists, American Psychological Association, 1962.

Trueblood, Dennis, "Role of the Counselor in the Guidance of Negro Students," *Harvard Educational Review,* XXX (Summer, 1961), 252–260.

Warner, W. Lloyd, *et al., Social Class in America.* Chicago: Science Research Associates, 1949.

———, *Who Shall Be Educated?* New York: Harper & Row, Publishers, 1944.

Wechsler, D., "The IQ is an Intelligent Test," *New York Times Magazine,* June 26, 1966, pp. 12–17.

White, Mrs. Frederick E., "Career and Guidance Preparation for Minority Children," *The American Child* (January, 1961).

White, Mary Alice, and Myron W. Harris, "The School Psychologist in School Society," in *The School Psychologist,* pp. 75–91.

HAROLD F. POWELL

NORMAN M. CHANSKY

17

The Evaluation
of Academic Disabilities

The most important role that a school psychologist has is
to study the child who is not benefitting from regular
classroom instruction. Such a child is commonly referred
to as having an "academic disability." Academic disabilities are often symptomatic of mental retardation as well as
of personal and social maladjustments. Occasionally, they
result from the failure of the teachers to adjust the curriculum to a child's unique growth pattern. The problem
of proper labelling of academic disability, moreover, is
vividly observed when teachers evaluate as mentally retarded a child who does not adjust to common instructional techniques, yet, upon subsequent measurement of
his capacity for learning, a score is obtained that fails to
support the teacher's diagnosis. While teacher evaluation
of achievement is vital, the psychologist should be alerted
to the possible bias in teacher estimates of achievement.[1]

[1] H. J. Battle, "Relation Between Personal Values and
Scholastic Achievement," *Journal of Experimental Education*, 26
(1957), 27–41.

It is the primary responsibility of the psychologist to study the child with an academic problem by means of both standardized and informal testing techniques. This involves investigating the current symptoms as well as the related predisposing and precipitating conditions. As a result, the problem would be sharply defined and the subsequent recommendations as to school placement, classroom management, and remedial treatment would not merely palliate the symptom but would contribute to the child's growth.

Today a school psychologist is dedicated and bound ethically to preserve the basic dignity of each student. He must perceive himself as a professional scientist who specializes in the school life of children. As a result of his training he is called upon as a member of a special service team to fulfill diagnostic and remedial functions in guiding children toward realizing their potentialities so they may become responsible citizens in a democratic society.[2]

Identifying Academic Disabilities

At the present time the techniques available to a school psychologist permit only gross evaluations of academic problems. This, despite the availability of seemingly precise formulae determining the presence of disabilities in academic areas. The lack of uniformity among the criteria for determining a reading disability is exemplary. Durrell and Sullivan[3] suggest several criteria that may be used in assessing for severity of a reading disability. A moderately severe reading disability, they state, involves a difference of ten months between reading capacity and reading achievement status. A very severe reading difficulty, moreover, involves a discrepancy of at least fifteen months in favor of reading capacity. Johnson,[4] however, suggests using a combination of grade placement, mental-grade level, and reading index in determining eligibility for remedial reading. Bond and Tinker[5] depart somewhat from the mental-grade method of determining the presence of a reading problem. They estimate reading expectancy by adding the constant 1.0 to the product of the I.Q. times the number of years in school. In addition, they present data that reveal striking differences between incidence of reading problems when using their formula and the mental-grade method. Specifically, at I.Q. 140, seventy per cent of the children in one study were adjudged retarded in reading according to the mental-grade estimate, whereas no one

    2 Norma E. Cutts, School Psychologists at Mid-Century (Washington, D.C.: American Psychological Association, 1955).
    3 D. D. Durrell and Helen B. Sullivan, Manual for Durrell—Sullivan Reading Capacity and Achievement Tests (New York: Harcourt, Brace & World, Inc., 1945).
    4 G. O. Johnson, "A Critical Evaluation of the Problem of Remedial Reading," Elementary School Journal, 57 (1957), 217–220.
    5 G. L. Bond and M. A. Tinker, Reading Difficulties: Their Diagnosis and Correction (New York: Appleton-Century-Crofts, 1957).

was so adjudged according to their formula. At an I.Q. of 110, thirty per cent were deemed retarded according to the mental grade method but fourteen per cent qualified for remedial treatment according to their formula.

The utility of these formulae is yet to be established experimentally. The incidence of reading disability will not be stable as long as I.Q. is an element in a formula; there are several reasons for this. In the first place I.Q. is not explicit. For some tests, intelligent quotient is a proportion; for others, it is a standard score based on a fixed mean and a fixed standard deviation. In addition, the standard deviations and the standard error of measurements for the several intelligence tests may be dissimilar. The former indicates the percentile equivalent of an I.Q.; the latter, the limits of chance variation of a score. The standard deviation for the California Test of Mental Maturity is sixteen points but for the Otis Gamma it is thirteen points. An I.Q. of 132 on the former occupies the same percentile position as an I.Q. of 126 on the latter, namely plus two standard deviations from the mean. The standard error of measurement of both tests is approximately four points. As a result of random fluctuations of scores in both tests there will be a 50–50 chance that an I.Q. of 136 on the California will be equivalent to an I.Q. of 122 on the Otis. It is patent that in defining I.Q. one may get lost in a maze of numbers. Where intelligence test scores must be considered in a formula, treatment of scores would be simplified if the differences between intelligence tests themselves could be controlled. It is suggested here that the I.Q. score from different tests be transformed to a common distribution in which the mean equals 50 and the standard deviation equals 10. This is known as a T score. The statistical advantages to such transformations are unlimited. Personality and achievement test scores could likewise be transformed to T scores. Then a score of say 60 on intelligence, personality and achievement tests would signify the very same thing, namely, the 84th percentile.

Due to the youth of psychology as a science, simple functional models of behavior have yet to be worked out. A common model emulated by behavioral scientists is that found in medical research. In it a causative agent acts upon the organism predisposed by constitutional and environmental factors to respond to it. Symptoms appear and methods of treatment are developed to treat the symptoms and/or the cause. Eysenck [6] pointed out, however, many instances in medicine where no close link between cause and symptoms may be observed. Diagnosis of the former on the basis of the latter is of questionable value. Certainly in the behaviorial sciences where causes of behavior are so obscure or at least not responsive to current methods of investigation, a satisfactory classification of learning disabilities is yet to be formulated.

[6] H. J. Eysenck, "Classification and the Problem of Diagnosis," in *Handbook of the Abnormal Psychology. An Experimental Approach* (New York: Basic Books Inc., Publishers, 1961).

The mental testing movement has exerted an enormous influence on contemporary school psychology. It is little wonder, then, that I.Q. and M.A. are included in many definitions of academic problems. There is a growing literature, however, indicating correlations between such motivational variables as self-concept and need for achievement with academic attainments. Controlling I.Q., Walsh [7] found high achievers could be distinguished from children with academic problems on the basis of their self-concept. Keeping I.Q. constant Brookover and others [8] found high correlations between self-concept of ability in a subject matter area and achievement in that area. The value of including I.Q. in the definition of academic disability, moreover, would be derived not only from its delimiting power but also from its power of predicting outcome of remedial treatment. Yet in at least two studies the latter was not supported. Chansky and Bregman [9] found an inverse relationship between verbal ability and growth in a college remedial reading class. Later, Chansky,[10] studying elementary school children, obtained a correlation of $+.01$ between I.Q. and improvement of reading when age was controlled.

Each definition of an academic disability fails to account for those classified children who do not make the predicted progress in reading. Snygg [11] opines, "each inadequate assumption in the system forces the formulation of another inadequate assumption to explain why the predicted behavior did not occur. The effect of these errors is cumulative." To him a psychological concept is scientific and useful when it assists in the prediction of behavior. A conceptual scheme based on the widest range of phenomena is preferred in order to take into consideration all of the possible interrelationships between relevant behaviors.

In keeping with these dicta, Chansky [12] proposed a definition of reading ability relatively free of reading grade placement, percentile position, and I.Q. This definition is extended to the other academic areas and would be stated as follows: The able student (in arithmetic, spelling, reading, science) is one whose responses (in arithmetic, spelling, reading, science) at any given moment permit him to function in those situations (in arithmetic, spelling, read-

[7] Ann M. Walsh, *Self Concepts of Bright Boys with Learning Difficulties* (New York: Columbia University Teachers College, Bureau of Publications, 1956).

[8] W. B. Brookover, Ann Velinsky, and T. Shailer, "The Relationship of Self-image to Achievement in Junior High School."

[9] N. M. Chansky and M. Bregman, "Improvement of Reading in College," *Journal of Educational Research*, 51 (1957), 313–317.

[10] N. M. Chansky, "Age, I.Q., and Improvement in Reading," *Journal of Educational Research*, 8 (1963), 439.

[11] D. Snygg, "Scientific Method in Psychology," *Journal of General Psychology*, 52 (1955), 189–196.

[12] N. M. Chansky, "Reading Ability: An Organismic View," *Reading Service Bulletin #98* (Washington, D.C.: Association for Childhood Education International, 1956).

ing, science) necessary for growth of Self. Operationally then an academic disability occurs when a *child's responses do not permit him to realize his subject matter goals.*

Growth and Development

According to this point of view, the purpose of life is realization of the Self. The Self, moreover, is ever changing. This means then that the goals toward which a child aspires are altered too. The changes may constitute greater specificity of the existing goals or the formulation of new ones. A direct result to the child of these changes is increased search for perceptual-motor acts that are goal satisfying.

The child changes his goals as his organs grow larger, as new organs appear, and as existing organs differentiate in structure. Correlated with these changes are modifications in his capacity for skilled acts. The several significant people in a child's world not only stimulate a search for newer and more discriminating goals but feed back to him reinforcing information about his goals and his correlative instrumental acts. As a result certain goals become firmly established and the instrumental, perceptual-motor acts become increasingly more refined.

From this storehouse of perceptual-motor acts, the child selects those acts he judges befit the novel situations he encounters in school. This reserve includes sounds he knows, auditory discriminations he makes, visual discriminations he identifies, words whose meanings he explicates, number concepts he has developed, and numerals he has learned. At any way station in the school life of the child, measurements of the range of perceptual-motor responses as well as the degree of their refinement may be obtained. Links between degree of perceptual-motor skill and progress in different academic areas have been established.[13] That children acquire the need of knowledges, skills, and habit patterns at different chronological ages is no longer questioned. More important, however, is the observation that the *rate* and *pattern* of growth of each child is *unique.*[14]

Although all of the prerequisite perceptual-motor skills necessary to succeed at academic tasks are as yet not known, tentatively it may be stated that a child will perform those acts in school to the degree that he has both the antecedent physiological equipment and the prerequisite learned perceptual-motor acts.

The importance of the growth factor in determining readiness for school

[13] W. B. Olson, "Recent Research Finds in Human Growth and Development," in the Sixth Yearbook A. A. C. P. E. (1953), 46–53.

[14] L. W. Sontag, C. T. Baker, and Virginia L. Nelson, *Mental Growth and Personality Development: A Longitudinal Study.* Monograph for the Society for Research in Child Development, 22 (1958), Serial #68.

subjects has been emphasized by Olson.[15] Experimental studies range from the determination of an optimum mental age of six years six months for the initiation of reading instructions [16] and the determination of the mental age as necessary for learning arithmetic, e.g., additions with the sum of 10 (six to seven), recognition that an object is 2, 3, or 4 times as high, wide, or deep as a criterion object (seven to eight), subtraction of 3-digit numbers from 3-digit numbers (eight to nine) [17] to those dealing with the delay of formal training in arithmetic until grade six with no resulting loss of competence,[18] and to those dealing with the effect of special training on achievement in social studies.[19]

READING READINESS

An important principle in growth and development related to academic progress is the concept of reading readiness. It includes general intellectual, physiological, and motivational variables. Although some educators delimit the use of "reading readiness" to the initiation of the first reading experiences, others look upon it as a concept useful in predicting success at any reading level.[20]

Good general health, eye muscle balance, skill in making near point visual adjustments, and mature skeletal systems point to success in the first steps in reading. In addition, articulation of sounds, word knowledge, ability to follow instructions, ability to perceive likenesses and differences between sounds and among visual forms, and ability to recall details of a story heard betoken success, too. Such social transactions as sharing one's experiences before a group, following directions and engaging in conversations prepare the child for finding meaning in reading.

A lack of readiness for the beginning experiences in reading has many implications, especially for the personal and social development of the child. A failure may be interpreted in many ways by a child, but it frequently results in a lower self-concept and a loss of incentive to correct the very

---

[15] W. B. Olson, *Child Development* (Boston: D. C. Heath & Company, 1949).
[16] Mabel B. Morphett and C. Washburne, "When Should Children Begin to Read?", *Elementary School Journal*, 31 (1931), 496–503.
[17] C. Washburne, "The Work of the Committee of Seven on Grade Placement in Arithmetic," in *Child Development and the Curriculum*, the 38th year book, National Society for the Study of Education (Chicago: University of Chicago Press, 1939), 299–324.
[18] L. T. Benezet, "The Story of an Experiment," *Journal of National Education Association*, 25 (1935), 241–244, 301–303.
[19] M. J. Eaton, "A Survey of the Achievement at Social Studies of 10,226 grade pupils in 464 schools in Indiana," Bulletin 20, #3, Indiana University School of Education (Bloomington, Indiana: Bureau of Cooperative Research & Field Service, Indiana University, 1944).
[20] J. I. Goodlad and R. H. Anderson, *Ungraded Elementary School* (New York: Harcourt, Brace & World, Inc., 1959).

weaknesses that would prepare him for the next level of development. The child may withdraw from further learning experiences to avoid repeating the episodes which jeopardized his self esteem. He may compensate for his low reading self-concept on the other hand by bullying, by becoming inattentive, or by day dreaming. He may channel his energy, however, and develop excellence in other school areas, e.g., athletics, arithmetic, art. Adequate diagnosis in this readiness period prevents deep rooted difficulties from spreading and may spearhead the development of a wide range of intellectual resources and emotional outlets.

In the evaluation of reading readiness several approaches are used. These include written teacher observations, parent conference on the child's general interest and aptitudes, cumulative records, and the results of standardized tests. The psychologist should have the results of teacher observation including those on the conduct of the child and his attitudes toward reading. Information on a cumulative record would include comments about the child's general health and current disabilities, such as those involving eyes, ears, glands, and the brain. The growing incidence of stomach ulcers in children may be worthy of note here.[21] The records may also show group intelligence test results, although their prognostic value is limited by the only modest reliability in young children. Standardized reading readiness tests are of some predictive value, too.

In one study,[22] total score on the Metropolitan Readiness Test correlated +.53 with average reading in grade one. This was slightly higher than the +.48 obtained when the reading readiness score was used and the +.52 obtained when the numbers subtest score was used. While reading achievement in grade one had been predicted on the basis of readiness tests, approximately 75 per cent of the variability in achievement was not accounted for.

READINESS FOR ABSTRACTION

Skill in developing concepts signify attainment of the next level of development. Using a sorting test Reichard and others [23] found young children categorizing on the basis of concrete aspects of the experimental materials. Older children sorted on the basis of function of the materials. This reached a peak at about ages eight to nine. Skill in categorizing on the basis of an abstract quality appeared at age nine with maturity reached at age eleven.

While beginners in reading can handle such simple abstractions as

[21] A. R. Ramos, J. B. Kirsner, and W. L. Palmer, "Peptic Ulcers in Children," *American Medical Association Journal of Diseases of Children,* 99 (1960), 135–148.
[22] The Manual. *Metropolitan Readiness Test, Form R.* (New York: Harcourt, Brace & World, Inc., 1949).
[23] Suzanne Reichard, Marion Schneiber, and D. Rapaport, "The Development of Concept Formation in Children," *American Journal of Orthopsychiatry,* 14 (1944), 156–161.

"food" and "clothing," they are more apt to think in terms of concretistic or functional properties of materials until they are at least nine years old. The implications of these findings for the elementary school curriculum are wide. Courses of study recognize the child's propensity for abstract thinking. This is revealed in the type of stories children are required to read, their use of puzzles, and their developing appreciation of jokes and puns. Stating the similarity and differences between things as well as identifying incongruities appear as items on intelligence tests. In arithmetic the child learns about time, space, number systems, and refinements in arithmetic fundamentals.[24]

Historically this period of growth has been called the beginning of the age of reason. However, the expectation level in our culture for skill in conceptualizing has been poorly timed. We make demands upon children before they are ready for abstractions. A child can develop academic problems if these demands are so great that he perceives himself to be a failure. Because of the lack of satisfying experiences he may fixate or regress on a lower developmental level.

In a study by Levy and Cuddy[25] normal achievers and low achievers were matched for intelligence. They were asked to solve problems of the "oddity" type. In contrast to normal achievers, low achievers made more errors in solving the problems, reached the criterion later, and were unable to verbalize the concept.

The low-achieving child causes the greatest concern to teachers. As a result such a child is sent to the psychologist for evaluation. The psychologist can help the teacher by pointing out that the reason for the disability may be the lack of readiness for abstractions.

Girls go through each of the development levels ahead of boys. The majority of school problems appear to be in boys. This is true for the areas of reading, speech, and conduct. Often arithmetic is the least popular subject among children. A possible reason for this may be that the highly abstract material is presented to the average child when he is only ready to cope with concretistic or functional relationships. Failure is inevitable.[26]

PREPUBERTAL PERIOD

The third developmental level at which there is an increased incidence of academic disabilities is the prepubertal period. This period begins ap-

[24] Arithmetic Grade Placement Chart, *Learning to Use Arithmetic Series* (Boston: D. C. Heath & Company, 1958).

[25] N. M. Levy and J. M. Cuddy, "Concept Learning in Educationally Retarded Children of Normal Intelligence," *Journal of Consulting Psychology*, 20 (1956), 445–448.

[26] L. J. Brueckner and G. L. Bond, *Diagnosis and Treatment of Learning Disabilities* (New York: Appleton-Century-Crofts, 1955), p. 205.

proximately one year immediately preceeding the onset of adolescence. For many girls this is usually the sixth grade and for many boys it is the eighth grade. The exact age of onset differs however from child to child. In this prepubertal period there is a relatively rapid increase in height and weight and a relatively lower increase in academic achievement. Olson points out that these growth factors are interwoven and that intensive growth in one area may cause lowered growth in another area.[27] For example, if the energy being used is for physical growth, the organism does not show as much growth in intellectual and educational areas.

A child who has been achieving at a normal rate may suddenly find that he is unable to sustain his efforts. McCurdy [28] presented data on older adolescents in which the relationship between basal metabolism rate and achievement was found. Williams [29] found patterns of metabolic processes to affect mentation. More recently, Smith and Carrigan [30] presented persuasive evidence for the role acetylcholine-cholinesterase imbalance plays in causing certain types of reading problems. Each child adjusts to the new physiological eruptions but often at no small cost to the Self.

The problem of academic adjustment is further complicated by the change from elementary school to the junior or senior high school. Usually this means larger school buildings, more complicated school organization, new teachers and strange classmates. This period is stressful to the students and there is likely to be interferences with normal academic progress as well as exacerbations of existing academic disabilities.

A case in point is Mary who had done well in the elementary grades. She had suddenly failed in junior high school. The mother was asked if she had had a similar experience in school. The mother showed a great deal of confusion and physical signs of discomfort. Ultimately she admitted she had, but she asked the psychologist not to inform her husband. After further discussion it was discovered that she had gone through a similar phase but no one had understood her. She plodded through high school and refused to go to college although her parents were college graduates. The psychologist was able to interpret to the mother and to the teacher that this prepubertal lag was not unusual. With added understanding they were able to guide the child back to her former level of achievement. One may only speculate how far the mother could have gone in school had she been given similar guidance.

[27] W. C. Olson, "Recent Research Findings in Human Growth and Development," *Sixth Yearbook* (A.A.C.T.E. The Association, 1953), pp. 46–63.

[28] H. G. McCurdy, "Basal Metabolism and Academic Performance in a Sample of College Women," *Journal of Educational Psychology*, 38 (1947), 363–367.

[29] R. D. Williams, "Some Implications of Physiological Individuality," in *Feelings and Emotions: The Moosehart Symposium*, ed. M. L. Reymert (New York: McGraw-Hill Book Company, 1950).

[30] D. E. P. Smith and Patricia M. Carrigan, *The Nature of Reading Disability* (New York: Harcourt, Brace & World, Inc., 1959).

Sociological Factors

Many academic goals and interests that a child develops are learned in day to day transactions with the other members of one's ethnic and social groups.[31] Marks and grade attainments may reflect a realization of group inspired goals. Saltzman [32] indicated that children of high economic status could be distinguished from those of low on the basis of vocabulary and of verbal ability. This limited vocabulary may be due to the few books in the home and a lack of incentive to read. Many children of this low socioeconomic group in large cities have never visited the downtown area. Some of the children have never seen farm animals. This lack of nurturing experience limits a child in his academic attainments.

Dorothy is a case in point. She was a small seven-year old child who was taken to a farm in order to see the animals. She became very frightened when she saw a small calf. Later it was discovered that she thought that calves were about the size of a cat or a dog because this is the way that she had experienced them in her school textbook. The little girl had never been more than five blocks away from her slum area home. On the other hand, parents in the middle class will often have many books for their children and provide them with many travel opportunities that enrich their reading backgrounds. Expectations in this class, however, are high. These children may have disabilities growing out of their anxiety about their achievements. Extracurricular involvements play a role in academic achievements, too. While in one study high school extracurricular activities correlated $+.66$ with achievement,[33] excessive extracurricular activities, though resulting in status within the school community, may actually curtail productivity in school.

Another characteristic difference between children of the two major socio-economic classes is their attitudes toward aggressive behavior. The lower class child is apt to be permissive in his outlook; the middle class child, to exercise self-restraint. The aggressive behavior of the lower class children is correlated with low academic achievement. Since neither class condones aggression as a way of life, it is plausible that the high expectations of a middle class oriented curriculum are not attainable by means of their meager verbal ability. It is not unexpected, then, that the ensuing frustration instigates these children to act aggressively. Another aspect of social class is level of aspiration.[34] The child in the lower class appears not to be highly motivated toward

31 A. B. Hollingshead, *Elmtown's Youth* (New York: John Wiley & Sons, Inc., 1949).

32 S. Saltzman, "The Influence of Social and Economic Background of Stanford-Binet Performance," *Journal of Social Psychology*, 12 (1940), 71–81.

33 J. P. McQuarry, "Some Relationships Between Non-Intellectual Characteristics and Academic Achievement," *Journal of Educational Psychology*, 44 (1953), 215–228.

34 L. J. Cronbach, *Educational Psychology* (New York: Harcourt, Brace & World, Inc., 1962).

high academic achievement. Some of the boys look upon school success as being feminine. It is sometimes difficult for school psychologists to evaluate the part that aspiration and motivation play in bringing about academic disability. In extreme cases, a child may be improperly diagnosed as mentally handicapped because he has meager verbal ability.[35]

Another factor that a school psychologist should be aware of is the effect of moving from community to community and from school to school upon academic progress. Occasionally a child is confused because methods of teaching may vary from one community to another; marking systems also vary considerably. This problem is experienced primarily by the children of migrant workers who move into metropolitan areas. Not only is it a major adjustment for a child to get used to a new subcultural way of life, but he must also become used to new teaching methods in the school. In the schools these children are often in a psychological minority group; they do not have the feeling of belonging to "society" and, oftentimes, therefore, are not motivated to achieve at their capacity level.

A case in point is Ralph. He was insolent to the teachers. He struck them and he spoke profanity. When he got into difficulty he always blamed someone else. He had only recently moved to a large city from a small town. Ralph, as well as his family, found it difficult to adjust to the new city. Neither parent disciplined the children nor seemed concerned about Ralph's conduct or the quality of his work. Ralph, because of the lack of discipline at home and the lack of interest shown by the parents, became so unstable and resistant that he was unable to accept diagnostic teaching help. Because of the deep seated problem the psychologist was unable to give an adequate interpretation to the parents. Ralph made little progress in reading. It was the belief of the psychologist that intensive social case work was needed before remedial education could be started.

In the typical classroom the subject is often geared to one level presentation or at the most, some teachers are able to have two groups of children, the slow and the fast. It seems to be a well known fact that any typical grade in the upper elementary or junior high school has a wide range of achievement levels. For the over age child, the psychologist can often recommend a transfer to another school, transfer to another classroom of the same grade, and, sometimes, a transfer to a classroom in a higher grade.

One elementary school principal would promote the children from the sixth grade to the junior high school by measuring them and weighing them. If they were over five feet, six inches, and over 150 pounds, they were promoted automatically to the junior high school. This merely propelled the educationally retarded child into the secondary school. Although it is logical that a child cannot handle seventh grade material if he is reading only at the second grade level, educationally retarded children rarely benefit from

[35] A. W. Combs, "Intelligence from a Perceptual Point of View," *Journal of Abnormal and Social Psychology*, 47 (1952), 662–673.

non-promotion. They not only make as much progress academically by being promoted but often avoid developing the emotional and social problems which their non-promoted school mates acquire.[36, 37]

Psychologists can often recommend programs to the junior high school principal that may be used for both heterogeneous and homogeneous grouping. He often can direct the administrator to high experience but low vocabulary reading level materials. At this educational level it is often a fact that a child may have many more reading problems than his score on the standardized achievement test would indicate. The self-concept of such a child is to avoid reading situations. The lack of contact with reading prevents him from improving in reading. This results in reinforcing his self-concept as an inadequate reader. Since retention in a grade has little effect on such a child, frequently individual counseling and individual remedial reading treatment may penetrate the barrier the child has erected to protect himself from academic learnings. A study that opens new approaches to classroom management of such children was conducted by Smith and others.[38] Students described as permeable and anxious made progress under directive methods of teaching. Students described as impermeable and anxious, on the other hand, did not make the predicted progress under permissive teaching.

Because the psychologist can rarely change the home environment or the personality of teachers it is necessary, therefore, that he make recommendations that can rather easily be effected. His suggestions are geared frequently toward understanding of the child's pattern of growth as well as his motivational structure. As a result, parents and teachers frequently find within themselves techniques of managing such youngsters which eventuate in their realizing their potentialities.

Occasionally there is a problem of obtaining books adapted to a child's reading level. Where there is no library in the school or a meager library in the community, the psychologist may be able to make concrete suggestions to the school as to libraries through which loans could be arranged. In addition, it could be recommended to the teacher that such living experiences as field trips, planting seeds, and creative handicraft could be instituted.

By way of concluding this section, sociological variables have been found related to academic successes and failures. By understanding the plight of the child who is not a member of the prevailing culture, improved home and school management techniques could be found for more effective guidance

[36] A. A. Sandin, *Show an Emotional Adjustment of Regularly Promoted and Non-Promoted Pupils* (New York: Teachers College Columbia University, Bureau of Publications, 1944).

[37] A. J. Goodlad, "Research and Theory Regarding Promotion and Non-promotion," *Elementary School Journal*, 63 (1952), 150–155.

[38] D. E. P. Smith, R. L. Wood, J. W. Downer, and A. L. Raygar, "Reading Improvement as a Function of Student Personality and Teaching Methods," *Journal of Educational Psychology*, 47 (1956), 47–59.

of the child. Germane to the frequent faulty diagnosis of sociogenic academic disability is the high proportion of items in tests of intelligence [39] and tests of personality [40] showing socio-economic bias. Until methods of assessment can be developed which free test materials from culture bias, there will be a constant error in diagnosing children of certain groups.

Interviewing

Qualitative diagnostic findings are not based upon records or tests alone, but depend upon interviewing the child, parents, and the teacher. The purpose of interviewing them is to obtain information relative to the developmental history, family background, and attitudes of the child. Also one can make qualitative observations of the interviewee's relationship with the child.

It is essential to establish rapport with the child before any attempt is made to test him. The typical child who is referred to the school psychologist is apprehensive about being confronted by a relative stranger. The child who is referred for academic disability has doubts about his adequacy as a student. Frequently the teacher dispatches the child with misgivings herself. Her explanation for sending the child is not straightforward; this frightens the child further. Should the psychologist hold the Ph.D. degree, the title "Doctor" may, through generalization of fear from past experiences with hospitals and physicians, be stimulus for further alarm.

Many a child, then, comes to the school psychologist distraught. Immediate testing may increase the validity and reliability of the test results. Test-anxious children, moreover, perform poorly on formalized testing situations. This is not the case, however, for the more informal test like the Davis-Eells Games.[41] For test-anxious adolescents the interference effect of anxiety may only last for the first few minutes of testing,[42] thereafter interference will either increase or decrease as a function of the structure of the experience.[43]

The psychologist may not always penetrate the wall the client has

---

[39] A. Davis, *Social-Class Influence upon Learning* (Cambridge: Harvard University Press, 1948).

[40] J. Mitchell, Jr., and J. W. Mitchell, "The Identification of Items in the California Test of Personality that Differentiates Between Subjects of High and Low Economic Status at the 5th and 7th grade levels," *Journal of Educational Research*, 51 (1957), 241–250.

[41] F. S. Lighthall, B. Reubush, S. Sarason, and I. Zweibleson, "Changes in Mental Ability as a Function of Test Anxiety and Type of Mental Test," *Journal of Consulting Psychology*, 23 (1959), 34–38.

[42] D. P. Ausubel, H. N. Schiff, and N. Goldman, "Qualitative Characteristics in the Learning Process Associated with Anxiety," *Journal of Abnormal and Social Psychology*, 48 (1953), 537–547.

[43] N. M. Chansky, "Pre-examination Stress, Information Schedules, and Learning," *Journal of General Psychology*, 63 (1960), 219–228.

erected. In some cases testing may have to be postponed several weeks. Introducing oneself to the child with a sincere smile and then saying to him "I am the kind of doctor that helps children learn" sufficiently assures many a child that no harm will come to him. If anything the child clutches to the hope that he can realize the Self he has always aspired to become.

No set procedure is followed in interviewing parents. Some psychologists obtain a history of the child prior to testing him; others test first, relate the results to the parents, and inquire at that time about relevant personal history. Two interviews with parents of young children with learning problems may be desirable: one before testing and one after. This, however, is not always feasible. With older children the psychological evaluation may bring out problem areas that the psychologist would like to explore with the parents. This does not mean the interview should be limited to one contact. An interview should be structured to a degree but not so much that the parent is unable to talk freely about the problems pertaining to his child. By letting the mother talk freely the psychologist may ascertain her feelings about school. He will also get some indication as to the academic role she has engendered in her child. Sometimes a child's dislike of school is reinforced by the parent's negative attitudes. Many parents on the other hand, are aware of the child's problem and are willing to cooperate fully in developing procedures at home and in school to help the child remove his learning weaknesses.

Reporting to the referring teacher the results of the psychological testing is essential. Frequently the psychologist finds gaps in his own information about the child. The teacher will often volunteer information to clarify the psychologist's perception. Reciprocally the school psychologist relates information to the teacher to fill her information gaps.

The psychologist, parent, and teacher work together to develop a program that helps the child discover his weaknesses, regain his self-esteem, and then realize his Self.

Testing

The testing process should be looked upon as the sampling of a child's behavior in a standardized situation. It should be stated categorically that a psychologist never limits the evaluation of an academically handicapped child to an intelligence test. A battery of tests is chosen. It will include an individual intelligence test, a personality assessment, and, when indicated, an achievement test. Due to the large number of tests on the market, a psychologist must make a judicious decision as to which tests to include in his battery. Inasmuch as intelligence testing and projective testing are discussed in detail in other chapters, they will not be discussed in this presentation.

Typical individual intelligence tests are the *Stanford-Binet Scale of In-*

telligence, Form L-M,[44] *The Wechsler Intelligence Scale for Children,*[45] and the *Detroit Test of Learning Aptitude.*[46] Psychologists often use the performance part of the Wechsler in conjunction with the Binet. Projective tests of personality include the *Bender-Gestalt,*[47] *Draw-A-Person,*[48] and the *Symond's Picture Story Test.*[49] Objective tests of personal and social growth include the *Vineland Social Maturity Scale*[50] and the *California Test of Personality.*[51] An achievement test that may be used with clients in different age brackets is the *Wide Range Achievement Test.*[52] An achievement test that yields information specifically about weaknesses in reading problems, arithmetic, and fundamentals of English is the *California Achievement Test.*[53]

The psychologist in searching for the factors predisposing the child to academic disability, is primarily concerned with evaluating aptitude for learning. Therefore the initial step is usually the administration of an individual test of intelligence. This type of test evaluates four major areas of ability. These areas are visual imagery, auditory attention, kinesthetic or motor ability, and verbal ability including vocabulary and symbolic relationships. No one area is sampled independent of other areas. Pure scores on one of these areas can seldom be obtained.

VISUAL

The most important consideration in evaluating academic disability is the visuo-motor aspect of learning because reading is a visual process and is basic to all academic achievement. Ideally all children referred to the school psychologist for evaluation of academic disability should have a physical examination that includes a test of vision. The typical screening test for

---

[44] L. M. Terman and Maud A. Merrill, *Stanford-Binet Intelligence Scale: Manual for the Third Revision, Form L-M* (Boston: Houghton Mifflin Company, 1960).

[45] D. Wechsler, *The Wechsler Intelligence Scale for Children: Manual* (New York: Psychological Corporation, 1949).

[46] H. J. Baker and Bernice Leland, *Detroit Tests of Learning Aptitudes* (Bloomington, Illinois: Public School Publishing Company, 1935).

[47] Loretta Bender, *A Visual Motor Gestalt Test and its Clinical Use* (New York: American Orthopsychiatric Association, 1951).

[48] Karen Machover, *Personality Projection in the Drawing of the Human Figure* (Springfield, Illinois: Charles C. Thomas, Publisher, 1948).

[49] P. M. Symonds, *Symond's Picture Story Test* (New York: Teachers College Columbia University, 1948).

[50] E. A. Doll, *The Measurement of Social Competence* (Philadelphia: Educational Test Bureau, 1947).

[51] L. T. Thorpe, W. W. Clark, and E. W. Tiegs, *California Test of Personality* (Los Angeles: California Test Bureau, 1939–1940).

[52] J. Jastak, *Wide Range Achievement Test* (Wilmington, Delaware: Charles L. Story Company, 1946).

[53] A. W. Tiegs, and W. W. Clark, *California Achievement Test* (Monterey: California Test Bureau, 1957).

Diagnostic Analysis of Learning Difficulties[*]
California Achievement Tests—Lower Primary Battery

1. Reading Vocabulary

A. WORD FORM

- 1, 3, 4 ...... Identical words, lower case
- 2, 7, 12, 16, 17, 21, 24, 25 } Different words, lower case
- 14, 19, 23 ... Different words, capitals
- 6, 8, 9, 11, 13, 15, 22 } Identical words, mixed forms
- 20 ...... Different words, mixed forms
- 5, 10, 18 ..... Reversed words

B. WORD RECOGNITION

- 1, 11 ...... Gross differences
- 2, 3, 5, 7, 9, 12, 13, 18 } .... Final sounds
- 4, 6, 10, 16, 17 } .... Initial sounds
- 8, 14, 15, 19, 20 } ... Middle sounds

C. MEANING OF OPPOSITES

- 1-15 ...... Basic vocabulary

D. PICTURE ASSOCIATION

- 1-9 ...... Identification of objects
- 10-15 ...... Location of objects

2. Reading Comprehension

- 1, 2 ...... Simple directions
- 3, 4, 5 ...... Directions requiring choice
- 6, 7, 8, 11, 12, 13 } Directly stated facts
- 9, 10, 14, 15.. Inferences

[* Consult Part 2 of the Manual for uses.]

TEST OF LETTER RECOGNITION

- 1, 2, 3, 4, 5, 6 } ... Lower case
- 7, 8, 9, 10, 11, 12 } Capitals
- 13-24 ...... Mixed forms

3. Arithmetic Reasoning

A. MEANINGS

- 1, 2, 3 ...... Picture-symbol association
- 4, 5, 6, 7, 8, 9 } .... Recognizing numbers
- 10, 11, 16, 17, 18, 19 } .. Writing numbers
- 12, 20 ...... Sequence of numbers
- 13, 14, 15 ... Comparison of numbers
- 21, 22, 23 ... Value of coins
- 24, 25 ...... Telling time
- 26, 27, 28 ... Weight & time concepts
- 29, 30 ...... Symbols & abbreviations

B. PROBLEMS

- 1, 2, 3, 6, 8, 10, 11, 12, 15 } ... One-step problems
- 4, 7, 14 ..... Budgeting
- 5 ...... Sharing
- 4, 5, 7, 9, 13, 14 } .. Two-step problems

4. Arithmetic Fundamentals

C. ADDITION

- 1-20 ...... Number facts
- 6, 8, 11, 18 .. Adding zeros
- 21-25 ...... Two-place simple addition
- 22, 25 ..... Carrying

D. SUBTRACTION

- 1-15 ...... Number facts
- 1, 3, 5 ..... Subtracting zeros
- 16-20 ...... Two-place simple subtraction
- 20 ...... Borrowing

5. Mechanics of English

A. CAPITALIZATION

- 1, 2, 8, 14 ... Names of persons or animals
- 3, 11, 16, 19 . Pronoun "I"
- 4, 5, 17, 20 .. First words of sentences
- 6, 7, 9, 12, 18 } Names of months or days
- 10, 13, 15 ... Names of cities

B. PUNCTUATION

- 1, 3, 5, 8, 9, 15, 17, 20 } Periods
- 2, 4, 7, 10, 12, 14, 19 } Question marks
- 6, 11, 13, 16, 18 } Commas

C. WORD USAGE

- 1, 4, 8, 11, 14, 25 } Number
- 2, 3, 9, 10, 12, 19, 23, 24 } Tense
- 5, 7, 13, 15, 16, 17, 18, 20 } Good usage
- 6, 21 ...... Person
- 22 ...... Case

6. Spelling (1-20) .. See profile

FIGURE 1. *This chart accompanies the California Achievement Tests. Diagnoses of specific learning problems may be made. Numbers refer to subtest items which measure the designated functions. The test also yields age and grade scores.*

vision in schools may not be adequate and referral to an opthalmologist may be necessary.

In the evaluation process the psychologist can make several observations relative to visual factors. Holding reading materials too close, holding materials too far, or tipping the material may be symptomatic of visual disturbance.

All tests of intelligence have such visual material as designs, pictures, and blocks. These materials are duplicated or manipulated. These tests generally range from the five year mental age level to the adult level. The materials vary in complexity from the simple duplication of a design to the more advanced memory for complex designs.

On the *Stanford-Binet Intelligence Scale, Form L-M,* year seven, the child is asked to duplicate a diamond on the test booklet. Successful drawing of the diamond is approximately at the mental age of six years and six months. The average child, other things being equal, is ready to read at this age. Children who are unable to make a diamond are usually unable to read. Mere passage of the item does not signify success in reading, however, as there are other factors that should be evaluated.

One teacher learned that copying the diamond was an important diagnostic cue. She attempted to train her slow first grade children in duplicating the diamond. At the end of six weeks she discovered that added maturation and practice permitted only one out of thirty-two children to duplicate the diamond.

Observation of tests on visual imagery will reveal directional tendencies. This is important for determining whether the child has a left to right orientation. Without this orientation a child will not only reverse letters but small words and will further attempt to substitute words in order to make sense. Most young children beginning to read will show some tendencies to reverse letters. A typical child, however, will overcome this tendency with only modest teacher guidance. It should be noted that without help the child may continue to build up poor reading habits and become a serious disability case, later. At the higher, more complex level, a child with weaknesses in the visual area may find it difficult to succeed in map work, drawing, or geometry.

A closely related problem is confused laterality. This is not limited to handedness but may involve an absence of preference for one side. Children with these tendencies may duplicate designs or may make a series of marks in a sinistrad, or right-left direction. The normal child, however, performs in the same material in a left to right direction or dextrad direction.

One simple test of laterality which has been devised is to have two sheets of paper. The bottom one has a large inked-in circle, the top paper has a hole in the middle through which the child can see the inked circle. The child is then instructed to bring the top paper up to his eye at the same time looking through the hole to see the inked circle at all times. This is done two or three times and a child may go to his left eye or to his right eye. If the child asks to which eye he should take it, the answer should be either one. This may therefore indicate that the child has a dominent left eye. This may be related to a tendency to go from right to left. These children will often be confused with lower case letters "p" and "q," or "b" with "d." There is some evidence that children who are left-handed seem to have a tendency to go from right to left but it should be remembered that a child may be right-handed but left-eyed or left-legged. While some children with this problem are reading failures, Hilman [54] found no connection between the parameters of reading ability and handedness, eyedness, cross laterality, or lack of hemispheric dominance.

Children with average intelligence who confuse similar letters can often be trained to make the necessary corrections. Even children with mirror writing, other things being equal, can be taught to write in a normal fashion with sympathetic and understanding teaching. The psychologist should suggest to the school nurse that these children be referred to an eye specialist for exact diagnosis.

A case in point is Billy. He was referred to a psychological clinic. He was retarded in reading and presented symptoms of instability. His chronological age was seven years. According to the Detroit Test of Learning Aptitude his mental age was nine years and two months. The psychologist noticed that he was ambidextrous. It was recommended that the teacher emphasize spelling and writing from left to right, erasing words on the blackboard from left to right, and reading with finger pointing from left to right. An interpretation of the diagnosis was given to the father with the suggestion that no emphasis be placed on handedness. Billy gained a grade in reading level within a few months. Insistence upon good work habits did much to improve his behavior.

Another case is that of Herman. He showed confused laterality and was repeating the first grade for the fourth time when he was referred for special help. He was labeled a "cry baby." He withdrew and did a great deal of day dreaming. Neither his teachers nor the other pupils liked him. Herman was considered "stupid" by his parents and by his three older siblings. He hated school and built up tremendous antipathies toward reading. In the clinic, Herman liked the personal interest shown by the psychologist and by the reading teacher. At first only pictures were given to him and he was encouraged to tell about them. Soon pictures with single words printed at the bottom were presented; later kinesthetic methods with emphasis on left to right directions were used. In spite of Herman's personal unattractiveness, the teachers were not rejecting. They created situations in which Herman could experience success. There was an improvement in attitudes. The greatest gain,

[54] H. H. Hilman, "The Effect of Laterality upon Reading Ability," *Durham Research Review*, 7 (1956), 86–96.

however, was in reading. The family was pleased with the general improvement in school.

The second area in evaluation of scholastic aptitude is the auditory. Auditory skills are needed in order to profit from the explanation, directions, and instructions given by the teacher.

Auditory perception is assessed in different ways. In most tests of intelligence there are materials that are written at different semantic levels. At the beginning level there may be tasks which require auditory attention for unrelated materials such as isolated words and nonsense syllables or simple random numbers. At the next level one is asked to repeat sentences. Several things can be observed by the psychologist that have implications for reading readiness and academic progress in general. A pattern of substitution of sounds may be observed, when a child is asked to repeat words out of context. Specifically a child may substitute beginning sounds, beginning consonants or final consonants.

Often these children have speech difficulties, or if there is no obvious speech defect, then articulatory speech skills are retarded in developing. A child with speech problems either does not hear the difference between sounds or is unable to reproduce a sound as he hears it. One can readily see that this auditory difficulty would be the basis of incorrect pronunciation. Where incorrect pronunciation is associated with some fixed visual pattern only deficiencies in spelling and reading can be expected to develop.

Here the psychologist should be acquainted with the order of difficulty of pronunciation of letters in the English language. If the child is still mispronouncing certain sounds by the second grade he should be referred for a speech and hearing examination.

At the higher grade levels auditory weakness may be the basis of academic difficulty in history, science, foreign language, and geography. It would be difficult to perceive and repeat proper names, scientific terms, and new sounds such as in the conversational approach to the study of foreign language.

One can readily see the interrelationship of auditory and visual factors especially when the nonphonetic nature of spelling in the English language is considered. Generally speaking, children learn to spell after they have established some skill in basic reading. It is obvious that the spelling of sounds in the English language is difficult for children when one considers languages as Spanish or Italian where the phonetic value of alphabetic letters is fairly consistent.

The school psychologist can recommend the use of phonics in teaching reading to children with auditory weaknesses. Although the effect of using phonics varies with the individual, research shows that using phonics increases the efficiency of the reading in children with mental ages beyond seven.[55]

VERBAL

The third area is the verbal. Test of verbal ability usually includes a test of vocabulary, verbal absurdity, and symbolic relationships. In the vocabulary test it may take the form of defining a word, finding a synonym, or giving the opposite meaning of some stimulus word.

In presenting a vocabulary test it is often helpful with children in the third grade and above to ask them to write the answers to the first few vocabulary words. This may give a psychologist cues not only to the child's reading ability but also to his spelling skills. Such productions like "gril" for *girl* and "dab" for *bad* are of diagnostic significance. Also a child asking how to spell a word is worthy of note. After the stimulus words have been presented in this manner it is often well to go back and give the words orally in order to check whether the child has perceived the words correctly.

From a psychologist's standpoint it is necessary that all vocabulary words be pronounced in accordance with the local dialect. A psychologist from New England working in the Midwest asked "what do you mean by 'conquer'?" The child responded to this question by saying "to hit on the head." As was pointed out earlier vocabulary is often a reflection of the socio-economic cultural level of the child and the educational level of his parents, children from the higher levels knowing more words on standard vocabulary tests. Should a student be weak in verbal ability but relatively strong in other scholastic aptitude areas he may profit from vocabulary building exercises and as a result improve his functional reading ability.

MOTOR OR KINESTHETIC

The fourth area of intelligence testing is the kinesthetic or motor ability. This is often divided into gross motor skills and fine motor skills. Most tests measure acts executed with the smaller muscles. The test items often take the form of duplicated symbols or designs. For example, the Detroit Test of Learning Aptitude has one timed test in which the child is asked to put the letter "x" in a series of circles. One can observe if the child has the motor skill to be able to make the letter "x," if he keeps within the circle, and if the two lines cross. One may observe also if the child goes from left to right or from right to left.

A test of this type is often a good check on fatigue. Some children tire

[55] E. W. Dolch and Maurine Bloomster, "Phonic Readiness," *Elementary School Journal*, 38 (1937), 201–205.

rather rapidly and show this by cramping their hand or by moving the upper part of their torso. Other tests use such items as maze tracing or duplication of designs. Of course these measure areas other than the strictly kinesthetic. Here the psychologist may wish to use the Bender-Gestalt, not only for obtaining information about the child's projections but also for assessing the developmental aspects of perceptual motor abilities. Serious weaknesses in the kinesthetic area may have physiological origins, perhaps, brain damage. Many skilled school psychologists have other means of detecting the possibility of brain damage, however, it is generally wise to refer to a neurologist those children suspected of brain damage. The psychologist in the meantime may wish to recommend kinesthetic retraining techniques, for example, tracing, finger contact, or left to right orientation exercises.[56]

Of interest here is a case of a brain injured child with perseveration of orientation. An elementary pupil generalized to arithmetic tasks the left-right orientation he learned in remedial reading. He attempted to add, subtract, multiply by going from left to right. One can imagine the difficulty that he had in borrowing and carrying numbers forward, especially in subtraction and addition.[57]

Educationally speaking, motor skill is an important aspect of acceptable writing and spelling. If a pupil is weak in the kinesthetic area this may in part cause both handwriting and spelling disability. This weakness may also contribute to a reading disability. The lack of accuracy in forming numbers and in placing them in the correct position for computation may result in incorrect answers in arithmetic.

TEST SCATTER

The four major areas of intelligence tests have been discussed as well as their implications for diagnosing academic disabilities. Rarely does a child show excellence or disability in all areas. The pattern of abilities, however, not only reveals the areas of academc weakness but also serves as a guide to the psychologist in making suggestions about the academic areas in which the child can be expected to succeed. For example, a visual and an auditory child who lacks motor skills may succeed in reading but experience difficulty in physical education. Wide scatter of subtest scores such as could be found on the Wechsler, or a wide range between the basal age and the maximal age such as could be found on the Stanford-Binet can indicate several things. First it may indicate a physical defect. Second it may be symptomatic of

---

[56] Grace Fernald, *Remedial Techniques in Basic School Subjects* (New York: McGraw-Hill Book Company, 1943).

[57] H. F. Powell, "Specifics Disabilities in School Subjects," in *Clinical Psychology in Exceptional Children*, ed. C. M. Louttit (New York: Harper & Row, Publishers, 1957), 159–196.

emotional disturbance. Third it may be symptomatic of glandular imbalance. Fourth it could reveal a differential rate of growth of the aptitudes measured by the test. A specific pattern of scatter may indicate the presence of a certain learning disability. Low coding, low arithmetic, low information, and normal block design scores on the Wechsler Intelligence Scale for Children have been found to be related to reading disability.[58] To be sure, the experienced psychologist would look for other signs and make appropriate recommendations for further testing to confirm his diagnosis.

A teacher can indicate in his class book the strengths and weaknesses in terms of the foregoing areas and then group the children in terms of their strengths. In many classes grouping is on the basis of reading. Other teachers group on the basis of the child's dominant word recognition technique. For instance, there are children who have strong visual ability and remember the appearance of words; other children have to hear the word in conjunction with a visual presentation; still others seem to learn best by writing words.

OTHER TESTS

The use of the intelligence test in diagnosing academic disability is basic but it is not sufficient. This test uncovers mental retardation as well as mental superiority. It may point to other disabilities that necessitate referral to other specialists. This still leaves, however, the large percentage of children who cannot be so categorized but who are, nevertheless, disabled academically. Standardized achievement tests can be administered to help discover the symptoms of their academic disabilities. Many schools have group testing programs and these tests and their results will be available to psychologists. This is helpful, but observing the child as he is actually performing on the test yields valuable clues. The psychologist therefore may wish to administer another achievement test. For example, the standardized reading test reveals grade level only. By administering a test like the Gilmore Oral Reading Test [59] the examiner actually observes the child and his method of approach to the reading. Notice of avoidance and weaknesses can be made. The psychologist can observe the child using his finger to point out each word, if he hesitates, if he reads word by word, if he reads in phrases, and if he pays attention to details. The psychologist also can see if the child substitutes words and still retains the meaning. The psychologist may wish to refer to the remedial reading teacher for more specific reading evaluation. In the evaluation of educational disability the place of school records, physical factors, interviewing of parents and teachers, intelligence test scores, and

[58] Grace T. Altus, "A WISC Profile for Retarded Readers," *Journal of Counseling Psychology*, 20 (1956), 155–156.
[59] J. V. Gilmore, *Gilmore Oral Reading Tests* (New York: Harcourt, Brace & World, Inc., 1951).

scores on other tests have been discussed. Although these evaluation techniques are indispensable, the origin of the academic disability may be in the psychological history of the child.

4. Tom and Ned live near a large city park. They often visit it with their playmates. In the park are many shady maple trees. There is a pleasant picnic ground on the hill, and the valley below has a pretty little pond. The girls always enjoy watching the boys while they sail their tiny boats in the water. Mother and Father enjoy picnics in the park.

TIME——Seconds

—1. What kind of trees grow in the park?
—2. Where is the picnic ground?
—3. What is in the valley?
—4. What do the boys do at the pond?
—5. What do Mother and Father like to do in the park?

NUMBER RIGHT ——

ERROR RECORD	Number
Substitutions	
Mispronunciations	
Words pronounced by examiner	
Disregard of punctuation	
Insertions	
Hesitations	
Repetitions	
Omissions	
Total Errors	

5. On Saturday the two boys do things they enjoy. For them this is the nicest day of the week. Sometimes they help with different household duties. In warm weather Tom and Father mow the lawn. If Mother is especially busy cooking for Sunday, Ned is glad to run errands for her before lunch. The family does not always spend the day working. In summer they often visit a lake near the city, where they spend happy hours swimming and boating. In winter the boys sometimes attend a movie; or, in freezing weather, they skate with their parents. The family takes real pleasure in Saturday activities.

TIME——Seconds

—1. What is the most pleasant day of the week for the boys?
—2. What do Tom and Father do on Saturdays in warm weather?
—3. What does Ned do for Mother?
—4. Where does the family go in summer?
—5. What do the boys do with their parents in the winter?

NUMBER RIGHT ——

ERROR RECORD	Number
Substitutions	
Mispronunciations	
Words pronounced by examiner	
Disregard of punctuation	
Insertions	
Hesitations	
Repetitions	
Omissions	
Total Errors	

FIGURE 2. *Excerpts from the Gilmore Oral Reading Test.*

Emotional Factors

Research and practice reveal the growing appreciation of the role that emotional factors play in developing academic disabilities. Cognitive disabilities frequently have emotional correlates. The cause and effect are frequently so interrelated that the true etiology is difficult to ascertain. Therefore the psychologist needs to study the emotional factors by interviews, observations, and simple projective techniques. The psychologist has already formulated hypotheses from the scatter pattern on the intelligence tests, from the difference between verbal and performance tests, from the responses the child makes to test items, and from the manifest signs of anxiety displayed by the child.

Children exhibiting extreme symptomatic behavior, observed either on tests or interview, should be referred to childrens' clinics or mental health clinics for more intense evaluation.

For many children with less severe symptomatology the diagnosis and treatment can be furthered by an interdisciplinary team. After a case conference a school social worker may be asked to do case work: the school guidance worker, to counsel the child; the classroom teacher, to initiate remedial work; and the school psychologist, to do psychological counseling. Play therapy by qualified psychologists, it has been found, may have a beneficial effect on children with reading problems.[60] Through a process of continuous diagnosis, the remedial program may be suitably adapted to the child's changing goals and skills.

The psychologist will often find two general types of cases. One child may suddenly present problem behavior in academic achievement where there was none before. Another child may chronically show academic and behavioral problems. Generally speaking the first type may have a history of traumatic experiences such as death, divorce, separation, illness, or accident. The latter may be due to absence of early recognition of the problem.

John, a fourteen year old boy, is a case in point. He had an excellent academic record in the elementary school. Both his marks and scores on standardized achievement tests had suddenly gone down. He was also viewed as a conduct problem. The cumulative records showed that his group intelligence scores dropped from superior to average over a period of four years. The interview and observation seemed to indicate that he was a confused boy and had a "defeatist" attitude. Wide scatter on the intelligence test suggested the presence of a physiological problem. An interview with the mother brought out the fact that the boy had had a very severe case of measles about four years earlier. The boy was referred for complete physical and neurological examinations. The results indicated the presence of surface brain damage with progressive deterioration. The prognosis was not favorable. The neurologist predicted that the boy would continue to have difficulty in school.

In considering emotional factors as related to academic disability several concepts may be noted.

SELF-CONCEPT

In elementary school, achievement is highly correlated with ability and opportunity. Many children, however, have distorted or unrealistic pictures of themselves that may in part cause the low academic achievement. It has been pointed out that they will often see themselves as disabled or disturbed and therefore will perform poorly academically. This may occur in all subject matter areas or may be limited to one such as reading or arithmetic.[61] The

[60] Virginia Axline, "Non-directed Therapy for Poor Readers," *Journal of Consulting Psychology*, 11 (1947), 61–69.
[61] Emma N. Plank and R. Plank, "Emotional Components in Arithmetic Learning," in *Psychoanalytic Study of the Child*, IX (New York: International Universities Press, 1954), 274.

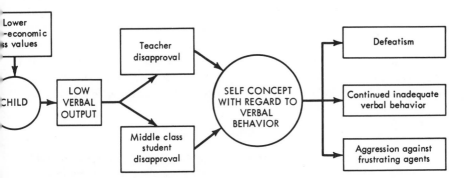

FIGURE 3. *Interaction between social class and learning.*

sources of this attitude may be the home, school, socio-economic group, or the ethnic group to which the child belongs.[62]

Invidious comparisons with siblings are often made by parents and teachers. At least two results of these unfavorable comparisons may appear. First, the older child seems always to be ahead of the younger sibling; and second, the younger child begins to see himself as inferior. Over a period of time he may find that if he acts inferior, little is demanded of him. While this defense permits him to meet the anxiety generated from sibling comparisons, his successes may motivate him to avoid learning in school.

Competition in school is beneficial for those who succeed but may harm those who fail. Even when the teacher does not make negative comparisons or does not instil competition in the teaching-learning situation, a child himself may deprecate his achievements. Loss of interest and withdrawal from participation in learning follows. It is not uncommon for the children to tear up papers and drawings when they see their productions downgraded. A child who has not been chosen for a team, elected to an office, or chosen to act in a school play, may perceive himself as unwanted.

If unfavorable comparisons and unsuccessful competitions seem to be related to academic disability, the psychologist may suggest to parents and teachers that the child will probably achieve more satisfactorily under less pressure.

The socio-economic factor also can reinforce a low self-concept; this is especially true if the child is made aware of his inelegant home and his threadbare clothes. Ethnic factors, too, may reinforce a low self-concept. Clark found that Negro children who saw themselves in inferior roles began to

[62] M. Deustch, "Minority Group and Class Status as Related to Social and Personality Factors in Scholastic Achievement," *Journal of Human Organization*, Monograph #2 (1960).

perceive themselves as inferior. This negatively affected their motivation to achieve at a level commensurate with their ability.[63]

Many students who have educational problems seem to have a distorted self-image. They believe themselves to be too thin, too fat, too tall, or too short. The slight deviations from the group norm become exaggerated. They often believe they are not accepted by their peers. Emotional reactions to perceived social rejection occasionally generalize to academic areas.

AUTHORITY FIGURES

Sensitive children may be easily frightened by exacting authoritarian teachers. Whether an academic disability develops depends upon whether or not the child avoids contact with the teacher-sponsored tasks. However, it should be emphasized that not all children see the same teacher in the same light. In one study with adolescents it was found that students assigned to teachers democratic or authoritarian tendencies that they themselves harbored.[64] Of significance here is the observation that rejected children find it difficult to identify with parents and teachers; as a result they fail to develop healthy self-concepts. In addition, they are unable to accept new learning because it is too threatening.[65]

Leonard is a case in point. He was six and a half years old. He had three older siblings. Their parents were dead. The children were being raised by their indulgent aunts and uncles. School was threatening to Leonard. To gain attention he resorted to fighting and "horse play." He needed prodding to do his work, and he was a year retarded in reading. This boy's homelife kept him immature and he was unprepared to take his place in a larger group. His lack of initiative in studying revealed the fact that he had little or no responsibility within the home. Frequent absences with inadequate excuses seemed to indicate a form of withdrawal. When Leonard was placed in the diagnostic teaching class he immediately responded to the security of a small group and made a good adjustment to the pupils. At first he tried to divert attention to extraneous matters. An interpretation of his problem was given to his aunt and uncle. After one semester of diagnostic teaching, Leonard gained a year in reading ability. His general school work was better too. His absences became infrequent and his classroom attitude improved.

[63] K. B. Clark, "Psychodynamic Implications of Prejudice Toward Children from a Minority Group," in *Professional School Psychology*, ed. M. G. Gottsegen, and G. B. Gottsegen (New York: Grune & Stratton, Inc., 1960), pp. 64–71.

[64] N. M. Chansky, "The Attitudes Students Assign to Their Teacher," *Journal of Educational Psychology*, 49 (1958), 13–17.

[65] D. B. Ausubel, "Ego Development and the Learning Process," in *Mental Hygiene*, ed. B. Hountras (Columbus, Ohio: Charles E. Merrill Books, Inc., 1961), pp. 48–48.

Klein pointed out that children, especially boys who had reading difficulty, often are strongly attached to their mother and fear a stern father.[66] These are the types of boys who withdraw from body contacts such as take place in games or in fights. He also pointed out that usually these children like to be dressed by their mother beyond the age that the average child dresses himself. This type of boy often makes a satisfactory adjustment to school initially, especially if there is a kindly teacher, but in response to a stern teacher the child often develops fears and avoidance techniques in order to stay away from school.[67] Then the reading or lack of reading actually becomes a disguised form of aggression directed against authority figures. It is believed, moreover, that girls are less apt to develop reading disabilities because they are more passive than boys. Passivity and femininity, however, were found to characterize intellectually superior educationally disabled adolescent boys in another study.[68]

Children from subcultural groups who highly value masculinity have difficulty identifying with women teachers. In one elementary school the children were largely of second generation Italian background. All of the teachers were women. There was difficulty among the older boys until a male principal was appointed. The school atmosphere improved. Also improved was the general level of school achievement.

Authoritarianism and punitive attitudes may have a pervasive effect on reducing academic achievement. Children affected by this to the point of reducing their academic achievement may be most effectively helped by being transferred to a different type of classroom or by building up their frustration tolerance levels. A case in point is that of an eight year old girl who was not achieving well. She was also truant. The psychologist discovered that she was avoiding a teacher who had a swinging ruler. A change to another classroom was made by the principal after a discussion with the psychologist. Attendance became nearly perfect and her academic record gradually improved.

SCHOOL PHOBIA

Today most children like school. There are children, however, referred to the psychologist, who have a fear of school.[69] This is known as school phobia. The child has anxiety about school and everything associated with it.

[66] E. Klein, "School Problems," *Psychoanalytic Study of the Child, III–IV* (New York: International Universities Press, 1949), 381.

[67] G. H. J. Pearson, "A Survey of Learning Difficulties," *Psychoanalytic Study of the Child, VII* (New York: International Universities Press, 1952), 329.

[68] Barbara Kimball, "Case Studies in Educational Failures During Adolescence," *American Journal of Orthopsychiatry, 23* (1953), 406–415.

[69] S. B. Sarason, K. Davidson, F. Lighthall, R. Waite, and B. Ruebush, *Anxiety in Elementary School Children* (New York: John Wiley & Sons, Inc., 1960).

He is afraid of being ridiculed by his teachers and by the other children. It often occurs with a small child facing a new experience, a large building, or too many children, that a feeling of confusion results. With some children it might occur after prolonged illness or absence. Fears associated with school may have their source outside of the school such as becoming lost on the way to school.

John is a case in point. At the age of six he was held down in a muddy ditch by some older boys on his way home from school. The next day he had an ear infection. A week later he was hospitalized. A month later he was sent, alone, to Arizona for convalescence. At thirteen when seen by the psychologist, he still hated school.

In contrast to the above, there are children who are afraid of success. They often perceive success as being aggressive and in their own upbringing, their aggressive tendencies have been held down but somehow or other they equate success with aggression.[70] Closely related to this is the fear of children that they will surpass their parents in achievement. There is the story of the famous baseball player who, when he was asked why he only finished fourth grade in school, replied he did not want to go beyond the level attained by his father. This suggests a need to evaluate more critically the effect of parental values on school achievement.

SYMBOLISM

Certain children with serious disability may give private meanings to letters and numbers.[71] It is well known that adults often consider individual numbers as lucky or unlucky. Historically numbers have been given significance by widely different cultures.

One child looked upon the letter "g" as an aggressive monkey. In fact, many of his associations with the actual letters were that the symbols were aggressive as shown by biting, and hanging on.

A ten year old boy, Fred, had been in several boarding homes and was unable to read. There seemed to be emotional factors present. As a result of intelligence tests, assessment of personality, and intensive psychiatric interviewing, it was discovered that the boy was unable to read any word in which the letters of his own short name occurred. One of the letters was "e." In the English language this is a very important letter in terms of its frequency of occurrence. To be sure, this finding alone was not the real basis of his problem. There were many other emotional problems present. His inability to read the letters of his name was a result of these problems. This

[70] Beulah Ephron, *Emotional Difficulties in Reading* (New York: Julian Press, 1953).

[71] Vivian Jarvis, "Visual Problems in Reading Disability," *Psychoanalytic Study of the Child*, XII (New York: International Universities Press, 1958), 470.

deficiency stimulated other problems to arise. Relevant studies of the emotional factors in reading have been ably summarized by Holmes.[72]

Although psychologists should remember that emotional factors may be as much a result as a cause, there are certain symptomatic behaviors that will give the psychologist further reason to hypothesize about the etiology of the specific difficulty. The psychologist can observe the child and then make inferences about his feelings of inadequacies or about his attitudes regarding school. One can look for such things as a confused way of responding, difficulty in relating to other people, and avoidance patterns. Of significance also are symptoms of indifference, or responses that seem to be unrelated to, or out of proportion to the stimulus. Other behaviors that should be observed are defensiveness, contentiousness, or disobedience. One can also see such obvious symptoms as day dreaming. With children above the second grade such symptomatic behavior as tattling on the other children may be significant of a child's own inadequacies.

Hugo was a boy who stole. He was very unhappy at home. His mother had been married when she was fifteen years old. The teacher described her as being immature and inadequate. Many household tasks were delegated to Hugo that an older brother, apparently more dominant, refused to do. The two boys quarreled continually. In school Hugo was shy until crossed by other children. Then he would fight viciously. In the class, visual discrimination was emphasized and approbation for good work was given. His oral reading and vocabulary improved greatly. He began to feel more self confident. Hugo's classroom behavior improved. Stealing had, at least in school, disappeared. Although interpretation was given to the mother, it was difficult to determine any appreciable change in the home situation.

Other symptomatic behavior that may have an indirect relationship to lack of achievement in school are thumb sucking, nail biting, stealing, and unwarranted fighting with others. In addition to these, lying and enuresis may be symptoms accompanying an academic disability.

A case in point is George who was considered a serious problem when he began to steal in school. Upon investigation the stealing was found to be symptomatic of sibling rivalry. This feeling of rejection in the home carried over into the school and influenced his reading. George began to feel rejected by his mother when his younger brothers were born. He failed in school at the time of their births. Although he was friendly to adults, he fought with other boys in school and in the neighborhood. The psychologist, through

---

[72] J. A. Holmes, "Personality Characteristics of the Disabled Reader," *Journal of Developmental Reading*, 4 (1961), 111–122.

interpretation to the parents, to the regular classroom teacher, encouraged more individual attention for George. At the end of six months he had emotionally developed so that he was able to accept other boys. He joined the Boy Scouts. His reading and academic work had improved to such a degree that he was promoted at the end of the year.

FOLLOW UP

After assessing the factors relative to the child's failure to develop the instrumental, perceptual motor responses to attain his goals, the psychologist will make recommendations for further study as well as for current management of the problem. Quite often this involves referral to the family physician or dentist through the school nurse, referral to the reading specialist, or referral to the speech therapist. Results of testing are given to the responsible administrative officer in the school. Recommendations are given to the parents and teachers which will tie closer together their efforts to help the child realize his Self. Finally, the psychologist may feel that he should counsel the child with his academic problems. Having such a student purge his ambivalent feelings about himself as an inadequate student may pave the way for greater precision in perception, the anticipated result being improved scholastic achievement.[73] The school psychologist may also use perceptual-motor discrimination and organization exercises to help establish precision in perception in those children with developmental deficiencies.[74]

Selected Supplementary Readings

Anderson, I. H., and W. Dearborn, *The Psychology of Teaching Reading.* New York: The Ronald Press Company, 1952.

Ashlock, P., and A. Stephen, *Educational Therapy in the Elementary School.* Springfield, Ill.: Charles C Thomas, Publisher, 1966.

Baker, H. J., and Bernice Leland, *In Behalf of Non-Readers.* Bloomington, Illinois: Public School Publishing Co., 1934.

Bender, Lauretta, "Specific Reading Disability as a Maturational Lag," *Bulletin of the Orton Society,* 7 (May, 1957), 4–14.

Bennett, C., *An Inquiry into the Genesis of Poor Reading.* New York: Bureau of Publications, Teachers College, Columbia University, 1938.

[73] D. Snygg, and A. Combs, *Individual Behavior* (New York: Harper & Row, Publishers, 1949).

[74] N. C. Kephart, *The Slow Learner in the Classroom* (Columbus, Ohio: Charles E. Merrill Books, Inc., 1960).

Bryan, Q. R., "Relative Importance of Intelligence and Visual Perception in Predicting Reading Achievement," *California Journal of Educational Research,* 15 (January, 1964), 44–48.

Burton, A. P., and J. H. Neely, "Failure in Boys: A Short Term Group Therapy and Educational Approach," *American Journal of Psychiatry,* 122 (April, 1966), 1211–1229.

Cassel, Russell N., "Counseling and Guidance for the Instructionally Ill Students," *Psychology in the Schools* (April, 1964), pp. 182–186.

Chansky, Norman M., "Problems of Research in Reading," *Journal of Developmental Reading,* 7, No. 2 (1964), 102–119.

————, *Untapped Good: The Rehabilitation of School Dropouts.* Springfield, Ill.: Charles C Thomas, Publisher, 1966.

————, and Margaret Taylor, "Perceptual Training with Young Mental Retardates," *American Journal of Mental Deficiency,* LXVIII, 4 (1964), 460–468.

Cleland, Donald L., "Clinical Materials for Appraising Disabilities in Reading," *Reading Teacher,* XVII (March, 1964), 428–434.

de Hirsch, Katrina, "Two Categories of Learning Difficulties in Adolescents," *American Journal of Orthopsychiatry,* IV (January, 1963), 87–91.

————, and J. Jansky, *Predicting Reading Failure.* New York: Harper & Row, Publishers, 1966.

Delacato, Carl H., *The Diagnosis and Treatment of Speech and Reading Problems.* Springfield, Ill.: Charles C Thomas Publisher, 1963.

Eiserer, Paul E., *The School Psychologist,* pp. 42–61. Washington, D. C.: The Center for Applied Research in Education, Inc., 1963.

Frost, E. P., "Some Personality Characteristics of Poor Readers," *Psychology in the Schools,* 3 (1965).

Fueller, Gerald B., "Perceptual Considerations in Children with a Reading Disability," *Psychology in the Schools,* I, No. 3 (July, 1964), 314–317.

Gallagher, J. R., "Reading Problems and Child Development," *The Sight Saving Review,* XXXIV (Summer, 1964), 88–91.

Harris, Albert J., ed., *Readings on Reading Instruction.* New York: David McKay Co., Inc., 1963.

Hellmuth, Jerome, ed., *Learning Disorders,* Vols. I and II. Seattle: Special Child Publications, 1965.

Henry, N. P., *Development in and through Reading.* National Society for the Study of Education, 60th Yearbook, Part I. Chicago: National Society for the Study of Education, 1961.

Hewett, Frank M., "Teaching Reading to an Autistic Boy through Operant Conditioning," *Reading Teacher,* XVII (May, 1964), 613–623.

Kirk, S. A., "Diagnosis and Remediation of Learning Difficulties," *Exceptional Children*, XXIX (October, 1962), 73–78.

————, and James J. McCarthy, "The Illinois Test of Psycholinguistic Abilities—An Approach to Differential Diagnosis," *American Journal of Mental Deficiency*, LXVI (November, 1961), 399–412.

Kornrich, M. *Underachievement*. Springfield Ill.: Charles C Thomas, Publisher, 1965.

Lambert, N. M., *The Prediction of School Adjustment*. Sacramento: State Department of Education, 1964.

McDonald, Arthur S., "Characteristics of Disabled Readers," *Journal of Developmental Reading*, VII, No. 2 (Winter, 1964).

Miller, Daniel R., and J. C. Westman, "Reading Disability as a Condition of Family Stability," *Family Process*, III (March, 1964), 66–76.

Mingoia, Edward, "Possible Causes of Underachievement in Reading," *Elementary English*, XL (March, 1962), 220–223.

Money, John, ed., *Reading Disability: Progress and Research Needs in Dyslexia*. Baltimore: The John Hopkins Press, 1962.

Nicholls, J. V. V., "Children with Reading Difficulties," *Sight Saving Review*, 36 (Spring, 1966), 27–31.

Pollack, M. F. W., and M. Piekarz, *Reading Problems and Problem Readers*. New York: David McKay Co., Inc., 1963.

Robinson, H. Alan, ed., *The Underachiever in Reading: Proceedings of the Annual Conference on Reading Held at the University of Chicago, 1962*. Chicago: University of Chicago Press, 1962.

Robinson, Helen M., *Why Pupils Fail in Reading*. Chicago: University of Chicago Press, 1946.

Robeck, Mildred C., "Intellectual Strength and Weaknesses Shown by Reading Clinic Subjects on the WISC," *Journal of Developmental Reading*, VII (Winter, 1964), 120–129.

Roswell, Florence, and Gladys Natchez, *Reading Disability: Diagnosis and Treatment*. New York: Basic Books, Inc., 1964.

Sampson, O. C., "Reading and Adjustment: A Review of the Literature," *Educational Research*, 8 (June, 1966), 163–183.

Spivack, George, "Toward an Understanding of a Specific Type of Academic Underachievement," *Forum*, 3 (Spring, 1966), 1–9.

Studholme, Janice M., "Group Guidance of Mother's Retarded Readers," *The Reading Teacher*, XVII (April, 1964), 528–530.

Symonds, P. M., *What Education Has to Learn from Psychology*. New York: Columbia University Teachers College Bureau of Publications, 1960.

Tien, H. C., "Use of the Organic Integrity Text with Children Who Cannot Read," *American Journal of Psychiatry*, 122 (April, 1966), 1165–1171.

Whipple, G. M., ed., "Educational Diagnosis," *National Society for the Study of Education, 34th Yearbook.* Chicago: National Society for the Study of Education, 1935.

White, Mary Alice, and Myron W. Harris, "Educational Adjustment of the Pupil Population," *The School Psychologist,* Chapter 6, pp. 92–118. New York: Harper & Row, Publishers, 1961.

Witham, A. D., "Clinical Tests for Diagnosis of Reading Difficulties," *Elementary English,* XXXIX (December, 1962), 824–827.

ELLEN V. PIERS

18

The School Psychologist
and Other Types
of Exceptional Children

In addition to his work with the mentally retarded, the gifted, and the socio-emotionally disturbed, the school psychologist will see many other types of exceptional children. These will include children with orthopedic handicaps, neurological handicaps, other handicapping medical conditions, vision, hearing, and language disorders. Sometimes these are grouped together under the term physically handicapped. One of the reasons the psychologist is called in, however, is that the primary physical handicap is only part of the problem. Not only may there be multiple physical handicaps that will affect the child's progress in school, but mental and emotional factors are very frequently involved.

Martmer says: [1]

[1] E. E. Martmer, ed., *The Child with a Handicap* (Springfield, Illinois: Charles C Thomas, Publisher, 1959), p. xii.

No clear-cut definition as to what constitutes a child with a handicap has been reached. In the past, when attention was focused on the child with an orthopedic defect, the term "crippled child" was adopted. Today orthopedic handicaps are recognized to be important; but many other conditions including rheumatic heart disease, congenital heart lesions, cerebral palsy, other types of brain damage, eye and ear defects, speech defects, craniofacial defects, and emotional disturbances are recognized as being equally important. One definition that has been suggested is that any child with a physical, mental, or emotional problem that interferes with normal growth and development is a child with a handicap. Such a definition, emphasizing the child as a whole individual, recognizes that handicaps may involve the mental and psychological well being as well as the physical health of the affected individual.

Meyerson on the other hand, says: [2]

Handicaps may or may not follow from a disability. In recent years it has become common to make this sort of distinction between the two terms. A disability is seen as an impairment having an objective or medical aspect while a handicap is seen as an impairment in a particular kind of social and psychological behavior. . . . In strictly objective terms it can be said only that variations in physique exist. Which variations will be considered disabilities, impairments, or handicaps is strictly relative to the expectations of the culture in which the person lives, the tasks that are required of him, and the meaning the person himself and others may assign to the variation.

Wright [3] makes the point that the term "physically disabled person" is a dangerous short cut, in that it implies that the whole person is disabled. She strongly urges using the longer term "person with a disability" that implies that here is a person with many abilities as well as a disability.

School-age children whose disabilities have a physical basis differ from others whom the psychologist sees in that the primary diagnosis has usually (although not always) been made by medical or other specialists. Other workers, such as physical or speech therapists may also be involved with the child. A team approach is, therefore, especially necessary in planning for these children.

The school psychologist's role involves not only the difficult task of assessing current intellectual and personality functioning. He may also be called on to make a differential diagnosis, and to use his findings to suggest differential educational procedures. Another very important function is that of interpreting to teachers and other school personnel, some of the psychological effects of disability in an effort to help the children make the best possible adjustment.

[2] L. Meyerson, "Somatopsychology of Physical Disability," Psychology of Exceptional Children and Youth, 2nd ed., William M. Cruickshank, ed. (Englewood Cliffs, N.J.: Prentice-Hall, Inc., 1963), p. 8.
[3] B. A. Wright, Physical Disability—a Psychological Approach (New York: Harper & Row, Publishers, 1960), p. 7.

To accomplish these functions, the school psychologist needs first of all to be thoroughly familiar with the literature on the psychology of exceptional children. He also needs to have as much information as possible on the physical and medical aspects of these conditions and a facility with medical terminology. This is not to say that the psychologist should in any way attempt to replace the physician, speech pathologist, etc. He is concerned with the behavior associated with the disability rather than the disability itself. But in order to function effectively as a psychologist, he needs to know how to interpret reports from specialists, anticipate reactions to various physical disorders, and make further referrals when necessary. He also needs to know the supplementary tools needed for the psychological assessment of these children, as well as the modifications in the use of his regular instruments.

The school psychologist's primary concern is that of determining the child's educational potential, and then of assisting the school system to give the child the type of program that will enable him to fulfill this potential in so far as possible.

Factors Affecting the Educability of the Handicapped

In considering the factors that may affect school progress, three stand out as of major importance: a) direct effects of the physical disability; b) mental handicaps; c) psychological reactions to the disability.

Under the first factor should be considered the objective physical or medical picture: Johnny has a loss of fifty decibels in his better ear; Ethel's corrected visual acuity is 20/100; Jimmy's right leg is shorter than his left; Mary's arms are very difficult to control due to severe athetoid movements; Charles cannot walk at all, and is in a wheelchair. These conditions may affect educability in two ways. First they imply the possibility that the child has been deprived of some kinds of normal experiences. This gap may, in some cases, affect his readiness to learn. Second, they indicate that ordinary teaching procedures will have to be modified, and that learning may be more difficult because of the necessity to work around the disability.

It is important to differentiate educational retardation that may arise as a direct result of the disability, as outlined above, from the educational retardation resulting from mental handicaps that may accompany the physical condition. This differentiation is often difficult to make, but some progress is evident. We no longer use the term "deaf-and-dumb" that implied not only inability to speak, but also carried the connotation of inability to think. We no longer assume that a cerebral palsied child with severe motor involvement is necessarily mentally retarded. We no longer assume mental deterioration in an epileptic.

It is the function of the school psychologist not only to know in general what types of physical disability are likely to be accompanied by intellectual disability, but to try to determine in a specific case whether or not intellectual impairment exists. Educational placement and procedures for physically handicapped children will vary, depending on this factor.

The psychological reactions to disability that interact with the first two factors constitute an important area in themselves and will be treated separately in this chapter. Their effects on school progress are often negative, and serve to increase educational retardation. However, in some instances the desire to compensate for the physical disability results in tremendous motivation to succeed in school, and thus facilitates learning. Whatever the direction of their effect, these reactions should be assessed by the psychologist as an important factor in educational planning for the child.

Potential Ability Versus Functioning Level

The problem of trying to distinguish potential ability from test scores or current functioning level has been evident with children of other cultures and those suffering severe environmental deprivation. This problem is equally evident with the physically handicapped. Much has been written concerning the inadequacy of many of our tests for assessing these children and the unfairness of comparing results with those of the general population. As a result modifications in tests have been made, or special tests have been devised. It is, of course, important to try to partial out the results due directly to the physical disability as described above, or to the emotional reactions to the disability. But to ignore their effects completely is to say: "let us pretend this disability does not exist."

Such a potential estimate of ability may be of theoretical interest, but is of practical interest only if there is a possibility that the disability may disappear or be lessened (i.e., conditions like cerebral palsy, where medical treatment and occupational therapy may, on occasion, reduce the extent of the physical disability). But for one who is permanently disabled, such as a deaf or blind child, the estimate of his basic capacity must inevitably be interwoven with the effects of his deafness or blindness. The psychologist is concerned with prediction. If, on the basis of a modified test he reports average intelligence for a disabled child, this is misleading unless it is also pointed out that special methods of teaching will be necessary, school achievement will probably take place at a slower rate, and vocational opportunities will be restricted.

IQ's and other results based on regular tests, without modification, may be equally misleading. Intelligence tests supposedly help to predict school performance. If test scores have been artificially depressed by items which will not necessarily affect learning, the error of prediction may be much greater than usual, and may result in poor educational planning.

In other words, with the physically handicapped especially, the school psychologist cannot be content with reporting just IQ scores, either from a regular or a special test. It might be preferable in some cases not to report an IQ at all. What is needed is a careful appraisal of the child's weaknesses and strengths by any and all means at hand, an interpretation of these in terms of effects on school learning (i.e., what differential effects would arm involvement as compared with leg involvement have in the classroom?) and some prediction of achievement based on the *interaction* of the mental, physical and emotional factors operating, along with recommendations for the most effective educational program.

Newland goes into this question in detail and reminds us to distinguish clearly between our frames of reference in interpreting the performance of exceptional children.[4] On the one hand, for most educational purposes we can consider how well the child is doing in terms of his own particular equipment. On the other hand, for vocational and certain research purposes we must compare his performance with the general population. Newland's point is well taken, but it applies not only to so-called exceptional children. It can and should be applied in interpreting the achievement of all children.

Psychological Reactions to Disability

From the large area of the psychology of disability, only a few general statements can be summarized here. Reactions specific to certain types of disability will be mentioned as they are discussed separately.

1. Little evidence has been found for special "personality types" within the various categories of disability. Although it has often been claimed and is still widely believed that certain disabilities have characteristic personality patterns associated with them, most of the studies have been inconclusive. Crowell, after reviewing the literature on an "epileptic personality" feels that the concept is a highly tenuous one and best dismissed.[5] Marzolf quotes Cutsforth as saying that the adjustive peculiarities of the blind are no more caused by blindness than are the adjustive peculiarities of the seeing caused by vision. Levine has come to similar conclusions about the deaf.[6]

2. Physical disabilities *may* lead to emotional handicaps. Meyerson makes the following generalizations: [7]

---

[4] T. E. Newland, "Psychological Assessment of Exceptional Children," *Psychology of Exceptional Children and Youth,* ed. William M. Cruickshank (Englewood Cliffs, N.J.: Prentice-Hall, Inc., 1963), p. 64.

[5] D. H. Crowell, "Neurological and Physical Disabilities," in *Clinical-Psychology of Exceptional Children* (3rd ed.), ed. C. M. Louttit (New York: Harper & Row, Publishers, 1957), p. 506.

[6] S. S. Marzolf, "The Physically Handicapped," in *An Introduction to Clinical Psychology* (2nd ed.), ed. L. A. Pennington and I. A. Berg (New York: The Ronald Press Company, 1954), p. 338.

[7] Meyerson in Cruickshank, *Psychology of Exceptional Children and Youth,* p. 17.

1. No variation in physique requires psychological maladjustment.

2. If an emotional handicap exists in a person who has a physical disability, it does not stem directly from the disability but has been mediated by social variables.

3. The mediation between physical status and psychological behavior occurs in the following way:

(a) The person lacks a tool that is required for behavior in the culture in which he lives, and he knows he lacks it.

(b) Other individuals perceive that he lacks an important tool and devaluate him for his lack.

(c) The person accepts the judgment of others that he is less worthy (or, to the degree that he is a product of his own culture, he judges himself as less worthy) and devaluates himself.

The (a) (b) (c) sequence is a unit. If (a) or (b) do not occur, (c) does not occur. If (c) does not occur, there is no emotional handicap.

3. Children who have disabilities, as a group, tend to have more frequent and more severe psychological problems than others. Meyerson, in line with his generalizations above, attributes these problems to the children's perception of the social reaction to them.

4. Parental attitudes appear to be particularly influential in determining the child's reaction to his disability. Studies reviewed by Barker et al., mention overprotection, indulgence, severity, neglect, pushing beyond capacity and rejection as the kinds of destructive emotional attitudes in parents that may lead to maladjustment in the child.[8]

5. Studies of factors such as institutionalization, degree of handicap, age of onset, etc., show conflicting results in their effect on the child's adjustment. Intelligence is usually regarded as a positive factor.

6. Frequent types of reactions to disability include: withdrawal, depression, resentment, anxiety, self-pity, suspicion, negativism, and compensatory behavior. However, attitudes of persons towards their disabilities vary widely. These attitudes have little relation to the degree of disability, but are often related to personality characteristics existing prior to the disability. Acceptance of the disability often requires changes in the person's value system and emphasis on the coping rather than the succumbing aspects.

Psychological Assessment of Physically Handicapped Children

No attempt will be made here to describe various handicapping conditions in detail. These topics are well covered by Louttit,[9] Michal-Smith,[10]

[8] R. G. Barker, B. A. Wright, L. Meyerson, and M. R. Gonick, *Adjustment to Physical Handicap and Illness: A Survey of the Social Psychology of Physique and Disability* (New York: Social Science Research Council, 1953), pp. 67–69.

[9] C. M. Louttit, *Clinical Psychology of Exceptional Children* (3rd ed.) (New York: Harper & Row, Publishers, 1957).

[10] H. Michal-Smith, ed., *Pediatric Problems in Clinical Practice* (New York: Grune & Stratton, Inc., 1954).

Martmer,[11] Goodenough,[12] Cruickshank [13] and many others. Instead the discussion will center around the contribution that the school psychologist can make in the assessment of these children. Handicaps, of course, frequently occur together. This is particularly true of speech and hearing problems, and of some cerebral palsied children with multiple handicaps. For the sake of clarity, however, the conditions will, in the main, be discussed separately.

It is assumed that the psychologist realizes the importance of obtaining, as well as the medical and other specialist reports, as complete a developmental history of the child as possible. The school rarely has this information on hand, which means that it will usually be both necessary and desirable to schedule parental interviews.

BLIND AND PARTIALLY SEEING CHILDREN

According to the most widely accepted definition, a child who has central visual acuity with correcting glasses of more than 20/200 or an equally disabling field defect, is considered eligible for education as a blind child. In January 1961, the American Printing House for the Blind reported 15,973 blind children and youth in the United States. Of this total number, 7,706 were enrolled in state or private residential schools for the blind, and 8,267 in public school programs.[14]

Children with visual acuity of better than 20/200 up to and including 20/70 or who have progressive eye difficulties or diseases are regarded as partially seeing and in need of sight-saving education. Approximately one child in 500 is so classified.

Knowledge of the extent of the visual handicap is essential before the psychologist can estimate the intellectual level. This means that a report from an ophthalmologist should be made available before the psychological study. Only after seeing this report can the psychologist properly plan his evaluation.

Blind children. In the past, the instrument most often used with blind children has been the Interim Hayes-Binet Intelligence Test developed by Hayes in 1942.[15] This is an adaptation of the 1937 Stanford-Binet,[16] with an

---

[11] Martmer, ed., *The Child With a Handicap.*

[12] F. L. Goodenough, *Exceptional Children* (New York: Appleton-Century-Crofts, 1956).

[13] W. H. Cruickshank, ed., *Psychology of Exceptional Children and Youth,* 2nd ed. (Englewood Cliffs, N.J.: Prentice-Hall, Inc., 1963).

[14] B. Lowenfeld, "The School Psychologist and the Visually Handicapped Child," *Professional School Psychology,* Vol. II, ed. M. G. Gottsegen and G. B. Gottsegen (New York: Grune & Stratton, Inc., 1963), pp. 165–167.

[15] S. P. Hayes, "A Second Test Scale for the Mental Measurement of the Visually Handicapped," *Outlook for the Blind,* XXXVII (1943), 37–41.

[16] L. M. Terman and M. A. Merrill, *Measuring Intelligence: a Guide to the New Revised Stanford-Binet Tests of Intelligence* (Cambridge, Mass.: Houghton Mifflin Company, 1937).

age range from five to fifteen years, although it is acknowledged to be unsatisfactory at both the lowest and highest ages. Visual material from the Stanford-Binet is replaced chiefly by oral and Braille material.

More recently, the verbal subtests of the Wechsler Intelligence Scale for Children (WISC),[17] have been widely used because they are better standardized. Only slight modifications are necessary, such as reading the three last arithmetic problems twice, instead of presenting them on a card.

For children over fifteen, the verbal subtests of the newer Wechsler Adult Intelligence Scale (WAIS) [18] are probably to be preferred to the Wechsler, Form I.[19] Hayes' suggestion that the Vocabulary Test replace Digit Span is no longer necessary with the WAIS since all six tests are included in the Verbal Scale. Items 2 and 7 of the Comprehension sub-test which needed alternatives are now items 5 and 9 on the WAIS. In the Arithmetic subtest of the Wechsler, Form I, items 9 and 10 should be read aloud twice, with extra credit given only if the solution is found within fifteen seconds of the second reading. Additional readings are permissible but no bonus credit is granted. The extra reading is to compensate for the fact that seeing subjects have the question on a card, as in the WISC. On the WAIS, however, all items are designed to be given orally, so that the questions are read only once and time bonuses given for questions 11 to 14 just as for seeing subjects. Other modifications of the WB-I such as giving all the Similarities, continuing the Vocabulary through eight failures, and spelling difficult words, can be retained on the WAIS.

An essential part of any evaluation of an exceptional child is the Vineland Social Maturity Scale as discussed in Chapter 12.[20] Although measuring social competence, rather than adjustment, it is useful in assessing the degree to which the disability has, in Meyerson's terms, become a handicap. Stressing habitual behavior rather than performance on demand or inferred intellectual potential, it can reflect not only direct effects, but also psychological reactions to the disability, such as withdrawal or compensatory behavior. The required interview with the informant, usually the mother, can also reveal the predominant attitudes to which the child is exposed, and which may be reflected in his self-attitudes. The Vineland looks deceptively simple to administer and score. Actually it requires considerable skill and experience to use properly, particularly in such matters as trying to separate what the child does not do because he cannot, from what he is not given a chance to do because of overprotection. The score would be the same in

---

[17] D. Wechsler, *Wechsler Intelligence Scale for Children* (Manual) (New York: The Psychological Corporation, 1949).

[18] D. Wechsler, *Wechsler Adult Intelligence Scale* (Manual) (New York: The Psychological Corporation, 1955).

[19] D. Wechsler, *The Measurement of Adult Intelligence* (3rd ed.) (Baltimore: The William & Wilkins Company, 1944).

[20] E. A. Doll, *Vineland Social Maturity Scale* (Manual) (Minneapolis: Educational Test Bureau, 1946).

either case, but the interpretation of the failure would be very different. Results from the Vineland, used in conjunction with estimates of intellectual ability, can give a considerably broader picture of the child and his functioning than can the intelligence tests alone, and can furnish tentative suggestions for management. An adaptation of the Vineland for blind pre-school children has recently been revised by Maxfield and Buckholz.[21]

Hayes has reported by far the greatest amount of material on the intelligence of the blind, not only from the Perkins Institution but, earlier, from other residential schools.[22] While he found mean IQ's around 100 with his Hayes-Binet, just as in the normal population, later studies report a consistent trend for the group with average scores to consist of fewer than fifty per cent of the total, while a slightly larger percentage of above average and a considerably larger percentage of below average scores were obtained.[23] He found, on the other hand, that on the average, blind children were at least two years retarded for their age in school achievement,[24] a finding substantially confirmed by Lowenfeld [25] and attributed to environmental deprivations and slower acquisition of knowledge due to lack of sight. (It is possible that an unmodified intelligence test that did not try to allow for these factors, would have shown scores more in line with achievement.) It is generally hoped that an increase in the use of radio, and Talking Books, will enlarge the environment of the blind, and reduce this educational retardation.

Cutsforth's book on "The Blind in School and Society" although originally published in 1933, still has much to offer on the effects of blindness on personality.[26] More recently, Barker et al.[27] and Lowenfeld [28] have each reviewed the growing number of studies in the area. Some of these suggest the possibility that the blind may be more neurotic, rigid, intropunitive, or more generally maladjusted than the seeing, on the average. Other studies have failed to demonstrate any significant differences in adjustment between the two groups.

The whole area of personality assessment of the blind needs further study. The validity of personality questionnaires has been questioned, due to the difference in their life situations, from those on whom the questionnaire

[21] K. B. Maxfield and S. Buckholz, A Social Maturity Scale for Blind Preschool Children: A Guide to its Use (New York: American Foundation for the Blind, 1957).
[22] S. P. Hayes, Contributions to a Psychology of Blindness (New York: American Foundation for the Blind, 1941).
[23] S. P. Hayes, "Measuring the Intelligence of the Blind," in Blindness, ed. P. A. Zahl (Princeton, N.J.: Princeton University Press, 1950), pp. 141–173.
[24] Hayes, Contributions, p. 216.
[25] B. Lowenfeld, Braille and Talking Book Reading: A Comparative Study (New York: American Foundation for the Blind, 1945), p. 11.
[26] T. D. Cutsforth, The Blind in School and Society: A Psychological Study (new ed.) (New York: American Foundation for the Blind, 1951)
[27] Barker, et al., Adjustment to Physical Handicap, pp. 282–308.
[28] Lowenfeld in Psychology of Exceptional Children.

was standardized, and obviously the usual projective techniques cannot be administered. Until further research studies demonstrate the validity of any assumptions about personality characteristics, psychologists should take nothing for granted in dealing with an individual child.

Partially seeing children. The testing of partially seeing children is usually conducted with standard instruments. Certain items may be enlarged or omitted but a valid estimate of intelligence can usually be obtained with the Stanford-Binet or WISC, even though the child may have to put his eyes very close to the paper or object. Some achievement tests are available in enlarged form. Most of the children can also respond to picture cards and other projective techniques. The Vineland Social Maturity Scale is useful to try to establish the effect of the child's impaired vision on his daily living.

Studies on either the intelligence or the achievement of the partially sighted are very few. Lowenfeld attributes this to the fact that they are considered, for all practical purposes, as seeing, and that they therefore would not be expected to differ markedly from other children who deviate slightly from the normal.[29] Such information as is available suggests that their group intelligence test performance was found to be a little below average. This finding may reflect lack of ability, lack of experience, or the fact that normal-sized tests penalized them unduly. Achievement showed the same slight retardation, and possibly for the same reasons. However, it has been suggested that for partially seeing children in regular classes, inadequate teaching methods may be responsible. The psychological effects of eye difficulties on achievement should also be considered. Lowenfeld suggests three factors stemming from their disability that may cause maladjustment: 1) limitation of activities; 2) actual pain or eyestrain; 3) facial disfigurements, such as strabismus, heavy glasses, or an artificial eye. Although individual children may react to these factors very differently, their effects should be considered in interpreting test scores and school performance.

Psychologists can help by calling these factors to the attention of the teacher and by suggesting specific ways in which a child can be made to feel part of the group. For example, the teacher might look for special skills in the child, such as a good singing voice, that she could play up in class performances.

DEAF AND HARD OF HEARING CHILDREN

Definitions of deafness are varied. Some authorities have defined it as hearing loss which occurs early enough to prevent establishment of speech and language, regardless of the degree of hearing loss. Others have spoken of

[29] Lowenfeld in *Psychology of Exceptional Children*, pp. 296–301.

it as hearing which is nonfunctional for the ordinary purposes of life. Some definitions and consequent educational practices have been based on degree of hearing loss. These range from mild (loss of twenty decibels or less in the speech range, in the better ear) through moderate, marked, and profound (loss of seventy to seventy-five decibels or more). Meyerson criticizes most of these definitions and suggests that the terms deaf and hard of hearing are outgrown for scientific use, since information on multiple parameters and much finer distinctions among the attributes of individuals are necessary. He feels that in terms of a psychology of impaired hearing, hearing for speech or *auding*, as he terms it, will become a central concept to psychologists and that children with auding difficulties will be studied just like children with reading difficulties.[30]

Recent figures do not tabulate degree of "functional" hearing. In 1961, the American Annals of the Deaf reported 28,529 children with hearing impairments.[31] Of these, 58 per cent resided in institutions, a decrease from previous years.

The deaf. Many deaf children cannot lip-read or use language functionally when first seen by the psychologist. As a result, nonverbal tests must be used. It is, of course, necessary to have an audiological report to be sure whether the lack of language is due to a hearing loss or to other factors to be discussed in the section on language disorders. In this section we are assuming that the diagnosis of peripheral deafness has been made.

Of the special tests devised, two of the best known are the Nebraska Test of Learning Aptitude [32] and the shorter Ontario School Ability Examination,[33] both standardized in schools for the deaf. The Nebraska Test also has norms for hearing children, which helps in making comparisons. The Revised Form II of the Grace Arthur Point Scale of Performance Tests has special instructions for use with deaf children,[34] but the California booklet "the School Psychologist" [35] suggests that the scale is more valid for these children if the Healy Test is omitted. Considering the fact that the pictures on the Healy are inexcusably out of date, it has probably lost a good deal of its valid-

[30] L. Meyerson, "A Psychology of Impaired Hearing," in *Psychology of Exceptional Children and Youth*, ed. W. M. Cruickshank (Englewood Cliffs, N.J.: Prentice-Hall, Inc., 1963), p. 138.

[31] Tabular Statements of American Schools for the Deaf, October 31, 1961, *American Annals of the Deaf*, 107 (1962), 158.

[32] M. S. Hiskey, *Nebraska Test of Learning Aptitude for Young Children* (Manual) (New York: The Psychological Corporation, 1941).

[33] H. Amoss, *Ontario School Ability Examination* (Toronto: The Ryerson Press, 1936).

[34] G. A. Arthur, *A Point Scale of Performance Tests, Revised Form II*, (Manual for Administering and Scoring the Tests) (New York: The Psychological Corporation, 1947).

[35] *The School Psychologist*, Bulletin of the California State Department of Education, Vol. XXIV, No. 12 (1955).

ity for testing any child. The Leiter International Performance Scale [36] can be given with pantomime directions and has many good features, although Cronbach warns that IQ conversions are of questionable accuracy at preschool levels.[37] If instructions can be understood, the Columbia Mental Maturity Scale [38] may be used, although some have felt that the test needs more work before it will live up to its promise. Correlation with the 1937 Stanford-Binet is about .75. Raven's Progressive Matrices [39, 40] also require no verbal responses. This test can be very useful to assess concept formation and possible perceptual disturbances, but norms are meager and come chiefly from English children. The Goodenough Draw-a-Man [41] is an excellent supplementary test, provided the child can understand directions. Harris [42] has revised the Goodenough point scale and has also developed a shorter "quality" scale. He reports information regarding the drawing of a woman, and separate norms for boys and girls, since persistent sex differences have been found.

Finally, the performance subtests of the WISC are frequently used with deaf children, and provide some of the most adequate norms, although standardized on hearing children.

In using nonverbal or performance tests of ability, it must be remembered that they do not predict school performance as well as do verbal tests. For that reason, verbal paper-and-pencil tests should be added as soon as the child can read, and individual verbal tests included as soon as possible.

The Vineland Social Maturity Scale is always helpful in evaluating deaf children. Other rating scales such as the Haggerty-Olson-Wickman [43] have been used in the past, and some paper-and-pencil tests, questionnaires and inventories can be completed by the children themselves. The Rogers Test of Personality Adjustment [44] is one of the better examples of these, even though it is not very well standardized. As long as scores in the various areas are not taken too literally, the test can be very useful in giving some idea of

[36] R. G. Leiter, *Leiter International Performance Scale* (Chicago: C. H. Stoelting Co., 1948).

[37] L. J. Cronbach, *Essentials of Psychological Testing* (2nd ed.) (New York: Harper & Row, Publishers, 1960), p. 207.

[38] B. Burgemeister, L. H. Blum, and I. Lorge, *Columbia Mental Maturity Scale* (Manual of Directions) (New York: Harcourt, Brace & World, Inc., 1959).

[39] J. C. Raven, *Guide to Using Progressive Matrices* (1947) Sets A, Ab, B. (London: Lewis, 1951).

[40] J. C. Raven, *Guide to Using Progressive Matrices* (1938) (London: Lewis, 1952).

[41] F. L. Goodenough, *Measurement of Intelligence by Drawings* (New York: Harcourt, Brace & World, Inc., 1926).

[42] D. B. Harris, *Measuring Psychological Maturity in Children's Drawings* (New York: Harcourt, Brace & World, Inc., 1963).

[43] M. E. Haggerty, W. C. Olson, and E. K. Wickman, *Haggerty-Olson-Wickman Behavior Rating Schedules* (New York: Harcourt, Brace & World, Inc., 1930).

[44] C. R. Rogers, *Test of Personality Adjustment* (Manual) (New York: Association Press, 1931).

the child's self-concept, and how he perceives the members of his family. Forms are available for both boys and girls.

Some psychologists use figure drawings extensively in the assessment of personality, even though positive validity studies are noticeably lacking in the literature. Besides the similar limitations in the Rorschach,[45] TAT,[46] and other projective techniques, Heider reports that their usefulness with deaf children is additionally complicated by language limitations. The picture of the personality becomes confused with the language difficulties and it is difficult to know what significance the results have.[47]

No consistency has been obtained in studies attempting to report the intelligence of the deaf. At least three factors might account for this: 1) vagueness in definitions of deafness; 2) selectivity of samples; 3) use of various types of instruments and different standardization groups. Most of the studies show mean scores lower than 100 (median of the means being 91) or around 100. An exception to this is a study by MacPherson and Lane where tests devised especially for the deaf produced mean IQ's of 113 and 116.[48] Most studies reporting normal intelligence utilize performance tests. Crowell lists twenty studies by various investigators which illustrate the variability of samples, instruments and results.[49]

Whether or not deaf children are retarded in performance abilities, results on verbal tests and measures of abstract thinking reflect their language handicap fairly consistently. Language teaching is thus the major educational problem, but there is still considerable controversy about what type of communication shall be taught.

Studies of educational achievement have consistently reported considerable retardation, often increasing with age. Early estimates of three to four years retardation on the average probably still hold, with the greatest retardation occurring in the understanding of paragraphs and words and the least in language (grammar, capitalization, etc.), arithmetic computation, and spelling. Factors that *may* influence amount of retardation are intelligence, degree of deafness, age of onset, placement in day or residential school, and methods of teaching, but the evidence is conflicting. However, there is considerable agreement that early diagnosis of hearing impairment and early

[45] H. Rorschach, *Psychodiagnostics*, trans. Paul Lemkau and Bernard Kronenberg (2nd ed.) (Bern: Huber, 1942).

[46] H. A. Murray, *Thematic Apperception Test* (Manual) (Cambridge, Mass.: Harvard University Press, 1943).

[47] G. M. Heider, "Adjustment Problems of the Deaf Child," in *The Exceptional Child*, ed. J. F. Magary and J. R. Eichorn (New York: Holt, Rinehart & Winston, Inc., 1960), pp. 309–310.

[48] J. MacPherson and H. S. Lane, "A Comparison of Deaf and Hearing on the Hiskey Test and on Performance Scales," *American Annals of the Deaf*, 93 (1948), 178–184.

[49] Crowell in Louttit, *Clinical Psychology of Exceptional Children*, pp. 468–471.

language training are desirable and can have a significant effect on educational achievement.

Some of the factors listed above seem also to influence personality adjustment. Although the literature is not extensive, results from questionnaires and inventories are in general agreement that the deaf are less well adjusted than hearing children. A more recent study by Bindon [50] using such personality tests as the Rorschach and an adaptation of the MAPS,[51] as well as the Wechsler Performance Scale, found no significant differences between rubella deaf and non-rubella deaf, but found that the deaf subjects in general appeared to be functioning at a less mature level than their hearing counterparts.

In spite of these findings, the school psychologist should again be warned against assuming maladjustment in any individual case, without adequate evidence.

Hard of hearing children. Less attention will be given to the hard-of-hearing since information in this area is generally what would be expected. Depending on the degree of loss and the amount of language, usual methods of assessment can be used or they can be supplemented by the nonverbal tests. If the psychologist is aware of the degree of loss there should be no problem. However, in spite of the fact that audiological screening is now carried on in most school systems, there still may be cases referred, usually for suspected mental retardation, which are actually cases of hearing loss, perhaps at certain frequencies only. The psychologist should be constantly alert to this possibility with all children, as he is to the presence of unsuspected visual defects. Apparent misunderstanding of directions or verbal items along with good non-verbal performance can be a warning signal and easily checked by the "watch" test or the "whisper" test as well as by asking the child if he hears. For purposes of the psychological evaluation itself, it is enough to be sure that the child can hear the psychologist, that is, that his hearing is acute enough not to directly affect test performance. This is not sufficient, however, to interpret failures on items dealing with school learning, or the fact that educational retardation exists in the face of normal intelligence. In all such cases it is important to refer the child for a complete audiological examination.

Investigations of the intelligence of hard of hearing children report slightly lower than normal IQ scores, especially on highly verbal tests such

[50] M. D. Bindon, "Personality Characteristics of Rubella Deaf Children: Implications for Teaching of the Deaf in General," *American Annals of the Deaf*, 102 (1957), pp. 264–270.
[51] E. Shneidman, *Make a Picture Story (MAPS): Manual* (New York: The Psychological Corporation, 1952).

as the Stanford-Binet. However, when both verbal and nonverbal tests were administered by Pintner and Lev, differences between hard of hearing and normals which appeared on the verbal tests disappeared on the nonverbal tests.[52] In line with these findings some educational retardation was found with hard of hearing children but not as much as with deaf children.

Studies of personality suggest that differences between hard of hearing and normal hearing children are slight. There appears, in general, to be a positive correlation between degree of loss and maladjustment, although this does not always hold true, since reaction to the disability seems to play a more important role in determining adjustment than the extent of the disability itself. The school could help more than it has in the past in such areas as teaching the hard of hearing child how to react in social situations when he cannot understand what is going on, how to react to people who are offended because he did not answer them, and so on.

CHILDREN WITH SPEECH AND LANGUAGE DISORDERS

The American Speech and Hearing Association Committee on the Midcentury White House Conference on Children and Youth estimated the total incidence of speech handicaps in children to be about five per cent.[53] This is considered to be a very minimal estimate, with perhaps another five per cent suffering from minor defects. The types of defects listed were: Functional Articulatory, Stuttering, Voice, Cleft Palate Speech, Cerebral Palsy Speech, Retarded Speech Development, and Impaired Hearing with Speech Defect. Of these, the functional articulatory disorders form by far the largest group, being approximately sixty per cent of the total.

The role of the school psychologist with speech defective children will vary, depending on the type of disorder, facilities within the school system, and community facilities. While he cannot often be expected to be an expert in the area of clinical speech, he should have some knowledge of the various clinical conditions, and of their relation to the educational progress of children. He will usually maintain close relations with the speech therapist and refer children to them as well as receive referrals for evaluation. His job is often one of interpreting to teachers and parents the psychological factors involved, and of making suggestions that will improve the child's psychological climate.

Functional articulatory disorders. The diagnosis of functional as opposed to organic articulatory disorder should be made before the child is seen by

[52] R. Pintner and J. Lev, "The Intelligence of the Hard-of-Hearing School Child," *Journal of Genetic Psychology,* 55 (1939), 31–48.
[53] ASHA Committee on the Midcentury White House Conference, "Speech Disorders and Speech Correction," *Journal of Speech and Hearing Disorders,* 17 (1952), 129–137.

the psychologist. Significant factors to be investigated by the latter are intelligence, emotional problems and possible history of faulty training.

Unless the disorder is so great as to make speech unintelligible, standard instruments can be used to assess ability. Additional performance tests may be included, since, even if speech is intelligible, the difficulties that the child has experienced in the verbal area may be reflected in lowered verbal scores.

Many studies have shown that faulty articulation is frequently associated with subnormal intelligence. Reid found, however, that in children with IQ's over 70 there was no significant relationship between intelligence and articulation difficulties.[54] If the psychologist finds average ability or only slight retardation, he should look elsewhere for the cause.

Intelligibility of speech must again be considered in choosing methods of personality assessment, since responses to the Rorschach and picture card tests require so much verbalization. Drawings are frequently used. If the child can read, Incomplete Sentences, the Rogers Test of Personality Adjustment and other pencil and paper tests may be employed. In many cases, however, parental interviews can yield the greatest amount of information, if faulty training seems to be involved, or if emotional problems are suspected.

Psychologists should be aware that many articulatory disorders seem to decrease with age, particularly during the primary school grades, and that as a result, speech therapy is often put off until it seems clear that improvement will not take place through maturation alone.

Organic articulatory disorders. These disorders involve structural abnormalities of the speech organs. With some conditions, such as cleft palate speech, the physical problem is primary and if the psychologist is called in, it is usually for the purpose of evaluating the psychological effects of the disability, or of helping parents or teachers with their planning. With such conditions as cerebral palsy speech, however, where the speech difficulty is only one of multiple handicaps, the child must be evaluated as a whole, as will be described in a later section.

Impaired hearing with speech defect. The difficulties in the development of language in deaf and hard of hearing children have already been touched on. Even if the loss is slight, articulatory disorders may result, or speech may be delayed. Speech sound discrimination should always be checked before attributing the difficulty to subnormal intelligence or other factors.

[54] G. Reid, "The Etiology and Nature of Functional Articulatory Defects in Elementary School Children," *Journal of Speech and Hearing Disorders*, 12 (1947), 143–150.

Stuttering. It is difficult to keep up with the many theories on the etiology of stuttering and its treatment. Texts by Hahn,[55] Johnson,[56] and Van Riper [57] are representative of some of the recent thinking in this field. Psychological evaluation is usually more concerned with assessing past and present environmental and personality factors than such apparently irrelevant factors as intelligence.

Most of the responsibility for the diagnosis and plan of treatment for stutterers is currently undertaken by speech clinics. Speech therapists within a school system may do some of the day-to-day treatment. Teamwork can be facilitated if the psychologist and speech personnel can agree on their point of view and interpret it similarly to teachers and parents. Unless the school system operates its own clinic, a school psychologist may not have time to undertake any of the psychotherapy frequently recommended for stutterers along with speech therapy, but he can make recommendations to available local facilities as was discussed by Ruzicka in Chapter 5.

Retarded speech development. So-called "delayed speech" is really a language rather than a speech disorder. Van Riper suggests at least eleven possible causes of this condition.[58] In the Cleveland Speech and Hearing Centre study of 1200 children, reported by Wood, somewhat broader classifications as to primary causal factor for the delay in speech were used: mental retardation (IQ below 70), hearing loss, emotional disturbance, environmental factor, delayed development, language disorder, multiple problems, and unclassified. Information was obtained from medical reports, hearing, psychological and language examinations. Of these 1200, 348 children remained unclassified after the first attempt, and it was only after considerable further study of most of the group by a team of specialists that agreement could be reached.[59] Although Goodwin [60] reported mental retardation as the most frequent causal factor in an earlier study of 454 cases, Wood's total figures show environmental factors such as parental handling to be equally important. The Cleveland study illustrates the frequent difficulty encountered in determining the cause, and serves as a warning to the school psychologist who may have to attempt an evaluation without adequate referral facilities. Myklebust [61]

[55] E. F. Hahn, *Stuttering: Significant Theories and Therapies* (Stanford: Stanford University Press, 1943).

[56] W. Johnson, ed., *Speech Problems of Children* (New York: Grune & Stratton, Inc., 1950).

[57] C. Van Riper, *Speech Correction: Principles and Methods* (4th ed.) (Englewood Cliffs, N.J.: Prentice-Hall, Inc., 1963).

[58] Van Riper, *Speech Correction.*

[59] N. E. Wood, *Language Disorders in Children* (Chicago, National Society for Crippled Children and Adults, Inc., 1959), pp. 2–3.

[60] F. B. Goodwin, "A Consideration of Etiologies in 454 Cases of Speech Retardation," *Journal of Hearing and Speech Disorders,* 20 (1955), 300–303.

[61] H. R. Myklebust, *Auditory Disorders in Children: a Manual for Differential Diagnosis* (New York: Grune & Stratton, Inc., 1954), pp. 352–353.

lists some useful differential psychological patterns characteristic of children with peripheral deafness, aphasia, psychic deafness and mental deficiency, but if at all possible the diagnosis should be the result of a team effort. The psychological testing itself will follow somewhat the same pattern as that outlined for deaf children, although verbal instructions should always be tried to see if they can be followed, and the psychologist should always be alert to the clues suggested by Myklebust.

Not only may psychological factors be involved in the development of many of the speech and language disorders, but the child's progress in and adjustment to the school may be affected by his emotional reactions to his disability. A large number of children with speech problems are in the regular classes, where their difficulty is immediately obvious, thus increasing chances for ridicule. There is also a definite tendency for disabilities in speech and reading (particularly oral reading) to be related, although experts differ in their interpretation of this relationship. Some feel that the two have a common cause, such as faulty auditory discrimination, or an emotional problem. Others think that the speech disability causes the reading disability, i.e. a child who cannot pronounce a word correctly cannot learn it correctly. A third interpretation might be that the emotional reaction to speaking results in an avoidance of reading. It is probable that any or all these factors may be involved in a given case.

Psychological damage due to ridicule may take place early. For this reason it is imperative that teachers, particularly in the primary grades, be alerted to the task of instilling in their pupils a tolerance for differences and an attitude of mutual helpfulness, rather than permitting the practice of laughing at one another's mistakes. An excellent instruction booklet, *Understanding the Disabled*,[62] is available for elementary school teachers. This tells how to introduce and discuss in the classroom the area of physical disability, with a view toward developing more adjustive attitudes.

CEREBRAL PALSIED CHILDREN

The neurologically handicapped child, without motor involvements, is, strictly speaking, outside the scope of this chapter. However, since cerebral palsy is a form of neurological involvement, some of the available information on the so-called brain-injured child is pertinent, and will be discussed briefly.

The work of Strauss and his colleagues has given us considerable data on the minimally brain injured child, with or without mental retardation. Their careful studies and ingenious tests have provided models for work with many

---

[62] *Understanding the Disabled,* prepared by National Foundation for Infantile Paralysis and the Citizen Education Project (New York: Columbia University Citizen Education Project, 1956).

types of exceptional children.[63] Sarason, however, while recognizing their contributions, has criticized Strauss' procedures for the diagnosis of the exogenous child on several grounds. In general he felt that the behavioral peculiarities which Strauss observed in his exogenous cases had not been conculsively shown to be the result of minimal brain injury, nor had it been shown that "exogenous" behavior was not found in the absence of such a presumptive brain injury.[64]

Birch has also commented on the lack of homogeneity of Strauss' group and noted that the "brain injured" child was not a "child" at all, but a statistical generalization derived as a composite from a population of children.[65]

One reason, now obvious, why results of studies on characteristics of the brain injured have been so contradictory, is that cases with neurological involvement are not homogeneous in terms of site and extent of lesion. "Brain injury" is not a single entity any more than mental deficiency is a single entity. Psychologists, must, therefore, avoid adopting a stereotyped picture of these cases, particularly on such frequently cited characteristics as perceptual disturbances, rigidity, perseveration, concreteness, hyperactivity, etc. For example, O'Connor in England found no significant differences in relationship between IQ and marble board performance in two groups with IQ's varying from 50 to 105, one group having known brain injury and the other not.[66] In another study, O'Connor and Haritos came to the conclusion that, in general, mental level was more relevant than the existence or absence of brain injury in explaining aspects of performance.[67] More recently Gallagher,[68] with matched groups of brain injured and familial mentally retarded children came to a very similar conclusion. In his factor analysis, general mental development was much more important in both groups than any unique and specific intellectual factors. More striking than perceptual disabilities, were differences in the details of language development between the two groups, something that Strauss and Kephart have noted.[69] Further

[63] A. A. Strauss and L. E. Lehtinen, *Psychopathology and Education of the Brain-Injured Child* (New York: Grune & Stratton, Inc., 1947).

[64] S. B. Sarason, *Psychological Problems in Mental Deficiency* (3rd ed.) (New York: Harper & Row, Publishers, 1959).

[65] H. G. Birch, "Problems in the Differential Diagnosis of Mental Retardation: Psychological Aspects," in *The Evaluation and Treatment of the Mentally Retarded Child in Clinics* (New York: National Association for Retarded Children, Inc., 1956), pp. 44–45.

[66] N. O'Connor, "Brain Damage and Mental Defect," in *Mental Deficiency, The Changing Outlook,* ed. Ann M. Clarke and A. D. B. Clarke (London: Methuen & Co. Ltd., 1958), p. 214.

[67] N. O'Connor in *Mental Deficiency*, pp. 214–215.

[68] J. J. Gallagher, "A Comparison of Brain Injured and Non-brain Injured Mentally Retarded Children on Several Psychological Variables," *Monograph of the Society for Research in Child Development,* 22, No. 2 (1957).

[69] A. A. Strauss and N. C. Kephart, *Psychopathology and Education of the Brain-Injured Child,* Vol. II: *Progress in Theory and Clinic* (New York: Grune & Stratton, Inc., 1955).

work in this area may yield information important for teaching some of the brain injured children.

All this is to say that while many of the signs usually listed as suggestive of brain pathology may be present in an individual child, the psychologist must remember that there will be wide individual differences and should not expect the same picture to emerge or insist on the same symptoms before coming to a tentative diagnosis of brain injury.

Differences in personality ratings between Gallagher's two groups were also striking. One explanation offered was that a brain injured child may not be able to perceive social situations correctly or distinguish between appropriate and non-appropriate behavior. Another was that a general lack of inhibition with its accompanying impulsivity and unpredictable behavior may make a brain injured child socially unacceptable to peers and adults. This, in turn, produces secondary effects of fearful behavior and demands for attention and affection as a result of the distrust and rejection brought about by the original disinhibition.

Many brain injured children *are* hyperactive and distractible. Rather than assuming that they cannot attend or concentrate, the general current opinion is that they are attending to too much. Specially trained teachers know this, and in many classes, bare little cubicles have been built to reduce distraction, and activities are much more restrained and methodical. But since this procedure is in direct contrast to the usual charge to the teacher to provide a lively, stimulating atmosphere for children, the psychologist may need to reeducate teachers of, say, a minimally brain injured child in a regular classroom, or even in a special education class, where the teacher has a mixed group.

The diagnosis of brain injury in the case of a cerebral palsied child is not in question. By definition the term implies a group of conditions that may have different manifestations, but which have in common lesions of the brain affecting motor control. The American Academy of Cerebral Palsy defines it as "any abnormal alteration of movement or motor function arising from defect, injury, or diseases of the nervous tissues contained within the cranial vault. Such a condition may occur before, during or after birth."

While cerebral palsy has long been known, usually under the name of Little's Disease, much of our definitive information about it dates only from the last two or three decades. Figures of incidence depend on diagnosis and age of sample and are hard to establish. Phelps says approximately seven new cases appear in every 100,000 of the population each year, in the United States.[70] Cruickshank and Raus [71] found 5.9 per 1000 in Schenectady County, N.Y. but other estimates range from 1.5–3 per 1000 population.

[70] W. N. Phelps, "The Cerebral Palsy Child," in *Pediatric Problems in Clinical Practice,* ed. H. Michal-Smith (New York: Grune & Stratton, Inc., 1954), p. 121.

[71] W. M. Cruickshank and G. M. Raus, *Cerebral Palsy* (Syracuse, N.Y.: Syracuse University Press, 1955), p. 4.

Illingworth quotes slightly lower figures for some European countries and suggests that about fifty per cent of cerebral palsy cases are usually diagnosed as spastic, fifteen to twenty per cent as athetoid, with the other types amounting to a very small percentage.[72] Hopkins in the New Jersey Study, suggests the following ratios: spastic 4, athetoid 2, rigidity 1, ataxia 1; others negligible. He also suggests a ratio of 5 boys to 4 girls.[73]

Problems in etiology and medical diagnosis cannot be gone into here but should be studied as fully as possible by the psychologist as background for his evaluations. Illingworth has some excellent chapters on these topics.[74] It is also important to know as much as possible about the various clinical syndromes. Perlstein says: [75]

> If you are aware that a child who has a form of cerebral palsy known as athetosis might also have difficulty in moving his eyes up and down or even laterally, then you cannot expect such a child to follow objects with his eyes. If in addition you are aware that some of the athetoids will either have a hearing loss or an auditory aphasia—in other words, they might have normal hearing but make no use of sound—then you cannot expect some of these children to respond well to auditory cues. In such children, the response to the visual cue is much more important. If you are aware of the fact, for instance, that a child who has a hemiplegia will walk at a normal age if he is of normal intelligence, then you will not attribute lateness in walking to the fact that he has something wrong with him physically; it will then have to be assigned to motivational, emotional or intellectual factors. In other words, although we have a lot of standardized scales for normal children, we do not have standardized scales for these children who have specific motor handicaps.

It can already be seen that the adequate psychological assessment of the cerebral palsied child is an extremely complex task. Besides possible motor involvement of the arms, to interfere with test performance, there may be speech disorders which have either a physical, neurological, or intellectual basis, visual and perceptual difficulties of many kinds, hearing difficulties, seizures, and intellectual retardation. The New Jersey Study on the Evaluation and Education of the Cerebral Palsied Child,[76] mentioned above, used medical records by Phelps in which he found approximately twenty-eight per cent out of some 1300 cases to have defective or questionable vision, thirteen

---

[72] R. S. Illingworth, ed., *Recent Advances in Cerebral Palsy* (Boston: Little, Brown and Company, 1958), p. 2.

[73] T. W. Hopkins, H. V. Bice, and Kathryn C. Colton, *Evaluation and Education of the Cerebral Palsied Child: New Jersey Study* (Washington, D.C.: International Council for Exceptional Children, 1954), pp. 1–3.

[74] Illingworth, *Recent Advances in Cerebral Palsy*.

[75] M. Perlstein, "Problems in the Differential Diagnosis of Mental Retardation: Pediatric Aspects," in *The Evaluation and Treatment of the Mentally Retarded Child in Clinics* (New York: National Association for Retarded Children, Inc., 1956), pp. 36–37.

[76] Hopkins, Bice and Colton, *Evaluation*, pp. 9–16.

per cent to have defective or questionable hearing, and sixty-eight per cent to have defective speech, with rather different patterns for the different types of cerebral palsy. Absence of intelligible speech, found in nearly sixteen per cent, seemed to be related to excessive incidence of seizures and lack of hand dominance. Their breakdown of physical and psychological findings into the four major types of cerebral palsy can be of considerable assistance to the psychologist in suggesting areas to check.

What has been said about any of the conditions mentioned so far in this chapter, may be pertinent for the cerebral palsied child, plus others, and plus the task of allowing for handicaps appearing in combination. Phelps points out the importance of evaluating the speech mechanism, the sight, the hearing and the motor handicap before trying to determine underlying mentality. He suggests that the diagnosis must first be made, chiefly through history and neurological examinations. The orthopedic examination would be next, followed by very careful eye examination, and examination by an otolaryngologist to determine hearing, possible pitch cut-off deafness and the status of the larynx and associated speech mechanism. Only after information from these are obtained should the psychologist begin his assessment.[77]

Many have questioned whether an accurate intellectual estimate can be obtained under these often difficult circumstances. It is true that psychologists need to know a great deal more to test and evaluate results from a cerebral palsied child than they do with normal children. But Perlstein, a medical authority in the field, says: [78]

> It is fallacious to think that a child with motor defects like cerebral palsy is not able to be evaluated by psychological tests, properly administered. This can often be defensive reasoning on the part of some parents. It has been shown that reliable estimates may be made in over ninety per cent of these children. An experienced psychologist is able to look at the results of the tests and say, "are the results right or wrong? Do they over-estimate or underestimate?" Often, clinical hunches are the important factors.

Crowell and Crowell come to much the same conclusion about the adequacy of psychological estimates.[79]

What then, constitutes an adequate psychological examination of a cerebral palsied child? Many suggestions have been made for the use of special instruments or various modifications of the standard instruments, but no one method can be followed in all cases because of differences in the medical picture.

[77] Phelps in *Pediatric Problems*, pp. 123–125.
[78] Perlstein in *Evaluation and Treatment of the Mentally Retarded Child in Clinics*, p. 37.
[79] D. H. Crowell and D. C. Crowell, "Intelligence Test Reliability for Cerebral Palsied Children," *Journal of Consulting Psychology*, 18 (1954), 296.

For school aged children, the 1937 Revision of the Stanford-Binet has stood up very well and has probably been the most frequently used instrument. The 1960 revision [80] is gradually replacing it. The WISC is also used, preferably with somewhat older children, since it does not go down as far as the Binet. The Ammons Full-Range Picture Vocabulary Test,[81] although not very well standardized, requires only pointing, as do the Columbia Mental Maturity Scale, Raven's Progressive Matrices, and other nonverbal tests previously mentioned in this text. The Bender Visual Motor Gestalt Test [82] and figure copying tests of various kinds such as were mentioned in Chapter 12 help to establish the existence or absence of perceptual disturbances. The Vineland is useful and should be included if at all possible.

Illingworth feels, as do others, that the importance of an exact IQ has been overestimated.[83] Particularly where multiple handicaps exist and few complete tests can be given, it may be much more meaningful to describe the child's performance in various areas, and then to give a rough estimate of his over-all performance, perhaps in terms of mental age, or degree of retardation. If the psychologist can free himself of the compulsion to give a complete test, once he has started, he can take suitable items from many tests, provided he has some idea what the items measure. Taylor, for example, who has had many years of experience with handicapped children, lists dozens of items of various types, age of success with which has been fairly well determined. Her case portraits of the evaluation of cerebral palsied children of several types over a period of years can also be of enormous assistance in illustrating developmental stages and their problems. She says: [84]

> Not only may the whole of the psychological examination resemble a psychological experiment, but also each individual test situation. The child himself, rather than the test that is being administered, is the subject of experimentation. Whenever possible each test item is presented in standard form first. This is a prerequisite wherever scoring with available norms is aimed at. Then the examiner introduces modifications, partial solutions, questions. These may help to show up how the child has understood the task. They may also uncover feelings and thoughts or demonstrate whether and how the child follows suggestions, adjusts to directions, changes. The skilled examiner avoids arbitrary modifications but manipulates with psychological insight.

[80] L. M. Terman and M. A. Merrill, *Stanford-Binet Intelligence Scale* (Manual for the Third Revision, Form L-M) (Boston: Houghton Mifflin Company, 1960).

[81] R. B. Ammons and H. S. Ammons, *Full Range Picture Vocabulary Test* (Louisville, Kentucky: University of Louisville, 1948).

[82] L. Bender, "A Visual Motor Gestalt Test and its Clinical Use," *American Orthopsychiatric Association Research Monographs*, No. 3 (1948).

[83] Illingworth, *Recent Advances in Cerebral Palsy*, p. 64.

[84] E. M. Taylor, *Psychological Appraisal of Children with Cerebral Defects* (Cambridge, Mass.: Harvard University Press, 1959), p. 15.

We have mentioned several times that, as much as possible, differentiation must be made between failure due to motor or other physical handicaps and failure due to mental retardation. This can be done in part by noting differences in success on items requiring, variously, the manipulation of objects, verbal responses, or just pointing, "looking" or nodding the head. It can also be done by observing items of the same type but of different levels of difficulty. For example, if the child has enough motor coordination to build the Stanford-Binet block tower but fails the block bridge, the failure cannot be attributed to motor handicap. Similarly, if he can name some of the items on Picture Vocabulary but not others, it must be assumed that his vision and speech are adequate for that item. Particularly with cerebral palsied children, any failure should be examined carefully to try to determine *why* it was failed.

Because of the fact that physical therapy, speech therapy, surgery, and other treatment may change the picture more with the cerebral palsied child than we expect with normals, it is essential that periodic re-evaluations take place. Results may be quite accurate at the time they are given, but predictive validity may be lower. A child, for example, who has been tested before he can walk without support, or before he can talk, should be seen again as soon as these skills have had a chance to affect his general life experience and his performance. There is also evidence that the hyperactivity and distractibility of some brain injured children decreases with age, particularly with the help of good educational methods. As they are able to concentrate better and use their ability more efficiently, scores may increase.

Former estimates of the intelligence of cerebral palsied children put the number of mentally retarded as low as thirty per cent. Cruickshank quotes more recent studies in which IQ's below 70 ranged from forty-five per cent to forty-nine per cent.[85] Illingworth on the basis of several studies, estimates that approximately fifty-five per cent fall below IQ 70.[86] The psychologist will probably not be too far off, if he considers about half of the children with cerebral palsy to have IQ's below 70, about one-quarter to be in the borderline-dull category and another quarter, average or above, with the mean IQ falling somewhere around 77. While no major differences have been found between the intelligence of spastics and athetoids, there is some evidence, chiefly from the New Jersey study,[87] that children with ataxia or rigidity have lower mean IQ's than the more frequent types. There also appears to be some relation between the extent of the handicap and the IQ, spastic quadriplegics, for example, being the lowest in their group.

---

[85] W. M. Cruickshank, "Psychological Considerations with Crippled Children," in *Psychology of Exceptional Children and Youth*, ed. W. M. Cruickshank (Englewood Cliffs, N. J.: Prentice-Hall Inc., 1955), p. 320.
[86] Illingworth, *Recent Advances in Cerebral Palsy*, pp. 64–68.
[87] Hopkins, Bice, and Colton, *Evaluation and Education*, p. 38.

Personality assessment of the cerebral palsied, as with other children, involves observations during interviews and testing, a study of the developmental history and parental attitudes, school history, and perhaps the administration of questionnaires or projective techniques. Cruickshank obtained interesting results with sentence completion tests in a study of the relation of physical disability to social adjustment.[88] Figure drawings and picture cards are frequently used, but the psychologist should apply the usual cautions in making interpretations based on these.

The interview was used extensively in the New Jersey study [89] and it was found that anger, resentment, shame, and fear were reported most frequently as disturbing experiences of the cerebral palsied.

From all the methods employed in the psychological evaluation of a cerebral palsied child, and it should be stressed that more valid estimates can often be made by using a wide variety of assessment procedures, the psychologist should be able to give a picture of the child's current functioning level with some partialing out of the direct effects of the physical handicap, the amount of mental retardation, if any, the presence of perceptual disturbances that may have a marked effect on the acquisition of such skills as reading, social competence, and a personality description. With this information, along with the medical picture, the team, composed of physician, physical, occupational and speech therapist, teacher, special educator, and psychologist, can formulate the best plan for the child.

OTHER HANDICAPPING CONDITIONS

Only a few of the handicapping medical conditions can be discussed, but the general psychological principles involved can be applied to all.

Epilepsy. The old term "epilepsy" is currently being referred to more often in terms of its pathology, as "paroxysmal cerebral disrythmia." While some experts consider that any person who has had a seizure is epileptic, most experts limit the term to those who are chronically affected. Incidence is difficult to establish but is usually estimated at about 1 per cent of the population. Two broad etiological categories are usually used: 1) idiopathic, where no cause has been found, but hereditary or constitutional tendencies are assumed; 2) symptomatic, presumably following injury to or lesions in the brain. Main seizure types include grand mal, petit mal, perhaps with myoclonic jerks, Jacksonian epilepsy, and psychomotor or psychic equivalent seizures. Since most seizures are obvious, diagnosis has usually been made and confirmed with EEG tracings before the child is seen by the psychologist, but he should be alert to the possibility of undiagnosed epilepsy in types

88 W. M. Cruickshank, "A Study of the Relation of Physical Disability to Social Adjustment," *American Journal of Occupational Therapy,* 6 (1952).
89 Hopkins, Bice, and Colton, *Evaluation and Education,* pp. 60–63.

without loss of consciousness or muscle spasms, such as some psychomotor seizures or autonomic seizures.

Intellectual level is important to determine and can be ascertained by the usual methods. Contrary to the old ideas that the disease implies progressive degeneration with mental deterioration as a necessary consequence, many epileptics have normal or superior intelligence. If deficiencies do exist, Lennox lists four possible causes: 1) the defect may be congenital and not related to the epilepsy; 2) it may be the result of the damage to the brain (which also produces the epilepsy); 3) it may be the result of a multitude of severe convulsions which could injure brain cells; 4) it could reflect excessive use of drugs or be the result of social and intellectual isolation and repression by the public.[90]

It has been found fairly generally, that children with symptomatic epilepsy do more poorly on psychological tests than do those with idiopathic epilepsy. Pattern analysis of test results has not been helpful, and the symptomatic group cannot be distinguished from other brain injured groups, indicating that it is the brain injury rather than the epilepsy which is responsible for the impaired intellectual functioning. It has also been found that the level of institutional patients tends to be significantly lower than that of epileptics outside institutions. Figures based on institutional groups are, therefore, not representative of the epileptic population at large.

It is generally accepted that emotional conflict or environmental stress can *precipitate* (not *cause*) seizures in an epileptic individual.[91] It may also be assumed that epilepsy leads to emotional, psychological, and social problems, even though the stereotype of the "epileptic personality" is no longer considered tenable. Rorschach studies have been so contradictory as to be of little help. Either the epilepsies have no common psychological denominators, or they are etiologically so heterogeneous as to produce a variety of personality pictures. Ordinary methods of personality assessment can be employed, however, to try to throw some light on the personality of a particular child.

Many emotional problems arise as a result, first, of parental reactions, and then of reactions from society. A three-point treatment program involves medical treatment, including drugs; psychological treatment, including counseling or psychotherapy; and social therapy, including the education and treatment of parents, and, ideally, the changing of prejudiced attitudes in society. Studies in Baltimore [92] and New York City [93] have shown that most intellectually normal epileptics can be retained in regular classes.

---

[90] W. G. Lennox, "The Epileptic Child," in *Pediatric Problems in Clinical Practice*, ed. H. Michal-Smith, p. 259.

[91] C. Kram, "Epilepsy in Children and Youth," in *Psychology of Exceptional Children and Youth*, ed. W. M. Cruickshank, p. 378.

[92] O. A. Whildin, "The Epileptic Child and the Public School," *Nervous Child*, 6 (1947), 99ff.

[93] Board of Education, *Epileptic Children*, Report of the Sub-Committee on Epileptic Children (New York: Board of Education, New York City, 1941), p. 59.

Apart from the psychological evaluation, the school psychologist can be of great help to both parents and teachers in helping to explain epilepsy in general and an epileptic child in particular. Much fear and prejudice vanish with knowledge, and teachers can learn to accept epileptic children and handle their infrequent convulsions calmly in the classroom situation.

Educational work in the community should also be undertaken, both with prospective employers and with the public at large so that they might urge their legislators to repeal or revise the restrictive laws regarding epileptics, some of which are grossly unfair.

Cardiac conditions. Heart disease in children may be divided into three main types: functional murmur, rheumatic heart disease, and congenital heart disease. Functional murmurs, due to turbulent flow of blood, occur in at least fifty per cent of children and cause no abnormal cardiac symptoms. It is important for the doctor to differentiate a functional from an organic murmur, not only because the latter does require treatment, but also to reassure the parents in the former case, that nothing is wrong. Much psychological damage can be done by treating such a child as though he had heart disease.

Rheumatic heart disease, following rheumatic fever, is a serious condition and one that causes many thousands of deaths each year. Those who survive have illnesses lasting many months. When the child finally returns to school, he has been through a great deal and usually shows it. In the first place, he has had to try to understand what it means to have heart disease, and adjust to his parents' reaction to it. There has often been great anxiety from the separation involved in hospitalization, and great frustration in the long, enforced idleness of the convalescent period. When he returns home, the over-concern of the parents may restrict his activities unnecessarily and add to his feelings of rejection. Congenital heart disease must, of course, be handled by a physician. The survival rate today is considerably higher than formerly due to advances in surgical treatment. The physician should undertake as complete an explanation as possible to the parents, particularly with respect to their attitudes and the handling of the child. Much of the psychological damage comes from parental fears and the consequent over-control of the child.

Most experts agree that only under certain conditions should the activity of a cardiac child be limited. First, during the acute and convalescent stages of rheumatic fever. Second, *competitive* sports should be avoided by the child with congenital heart disease. In most other cases the child learns to limit his own activity, and should not be constantly watched and admonished by parent or teacher.

In school, the cardiac child may show the effects of his illness both in his personality and his achievement. He may be neurotic, dependent, and unresponsive. Often he is over-age for his grade, due to missing time. He is apt to be an underachiever.

In the past, the practice in the larger cities has been to provide separate facilities for these children wherever possible. More recently results of the extensive New York study [94] and current medical thinking are changing the picture somewhat. White, for example, feels that most children with heart disease, once the disease is not active, can attend school in regular classes.[95] The only exceptions are the actual cardiac cripples, who may need special facilities in school or homebound instruction.

The school psychologists's role with the cardiac child may be one of evaluation, so as to help make an appropriate placement after time lost from school. He also needs to interpret to the teacher the medical and personality factors, and make suggestions for helping the child feel one of the group. For example, rather than constant admonitions to take care, or pointedly leaving a child out of games, the teacher might ask the child with congenital heart disease to be an umpire or scorekeeper. A better understanding of the psychological aspects can help the teacher to tolerate possible unsatisfactory work or behavior when a child first returns to school, and help her to concentrate on the relevant factors in overcoming these.

Approaches to the Psychology of Disability

Most discussions of the psychological effects of physical disability are limited to descriptions and explanations of the reasons for these effects. Very few make any attempt to suggest what can be done to prevent or reduce maladjustment in the group, beyond the usual attempts to have the child "accept" his handicap, while at the same time, society is exerting tremendous pressure on him to be as close to normal as possible. A notable exception in the literature springs from Lewin's field theory.[96] This theory has been applied to the physically handicapped by Barker and his colleagues,[97] and is ably expounded by Meyerson.[98] An even more complete discussion is contained in Wright's recent book,[99] that should be required reading for anyone working in the field. Only a few of the highlights from these points of view can be included here, to persuade the school psychologist that a more intense study

[94] *Children with Cardiac Limitations: Studies of Pupils Enrolled in Special Classes* (Board of Education of the City of New York, Bureau of Educational Research, December 1952).

[95] P. D. White, *Heart Disease* (New York: The Macmillan Company, 1951), p. 261.

[96] K. Lewin, *Principles of Topological Psychology* (New York: McGraw-Hill Book Company, 1936).

[97] Barker, et al., *Adjustment to Physical Handicap.*

[98] Meyerson in *Psychology of Exceptional Children and Youth*, Chaps. 1, 3.

[99] Wright, *Physical Disability.*

might be very fruitful and enable him to give to children, teachers, and parents help that is theoretically based, yet concrete and specific.

One of Meyerson's useful concepts is that of psychologically new situations which inevitably produce frustration and conflict. Since persons with physical disabilities are more frequently placed in these psychologically new situations than normals, behavior disruption is more frequent. Help, then, involves the reduction of the "newness" of situations, or, if absolutely necessary, the avoidance of them.

Another concept involves the overlapping roles which all individuals experience. Some of these roles are compatible with each other, some interfere, some are really antagonistic, and some are excluding. The latter occur when people reject the roles that are open to them, and strive for those which are relatively unattainable, experiencing, as a result, frustration and conflict. Persons with physical disabilities are exposed a great deal more frequently to overlapping excluding roles. It is proposed that adjustment involves reducing the frequency of occurrence of these situations.

Meyerson describes three possible patterns of adjustment. One is that of admitting the disability and withdrawing to the safe, restricted psychological world of persons with similar handicaps. This is not necessarily a maladjusted reaction, although it narrows the field. A second pattern is that of rejecting the world of the disabled and aspiring to the normal world. This is a difficult task; if not successful, the person is in constant conflict. Rewards are great for the few who succeed, but Meyerson feels that success in adjusting to society may, in these cases, be at the expense of personal adjustment. In a third pattern, the person shares many behavioral areas with others in the normal world, but does not try to participate in those activities that require the tools he lacks. He also participates in some special activities related to his disability. While this pattern encompasses many advantages, it is difficult to achieve and represents a problem not restricted to the disabled. Adjustment for the physically normal also is presumed to involve the acceptance of one's limitations as part of oneself, without devaluing oneself as a person.

Wright is inclined to doubt the generality of the assumption that persons with disabilities are more frequently frustrated than the nondisabled. Protection from frustration seems to arise both from environmental accommodations and adjustive changes in the person, and there is some evidence that they react just as adequately as normals to whatever frustrations do arise. In any case, she feels that some frustration in life is not only inevitable, but may sometimes lead to desirable results if channeled into adaptive rather than maladaptive behaviors.

To Wright, acceptance means accepting one's disability as nondevaluating. Ways to achieve this might include: 1) enlarging one's scope of values; 2) subordinating physique; 3) containing disability effects; and 4) transforming comparative values into asset values. These ideas can be communicated to a child from his earliest years by those who love him, along with knowledge of the negative and devaluating aspects with which he will have to cope. Wright calls this "realization amid interpersonal acceptance."

Other useful discussions deal with the handling of curiosity, pity, help, motivating children in rehabilitation programs, and coping with the heightened problems of adolescence. Perhaps most important of all, the book is filled with psychologically sound principles for those who live and work with persons who have physical disabilities—and that would include almost everyone in our society.

Selected Supplementary Readings

GENERAL

Allen, R. M., "The School Psychologist's Role in the Identification and Diagnosis of Exceptional Children," *Training School Bulletin,* **62** (August, 1965), 66–72.

Birch, J. W., "Patterns of Clinical Services for Exceptional Children," *Exceptional Children,* **19** (March, 1953), 214–222.

Capobianco, R. J., "Psychological Services in Special Education," *Education,* **77** (April, 1957), 480–482.

Garrett, J. F. ed., *Psychological Aspects of Physical Disability,* Federal Security Agency, Office of Vocational Rehabilitation, No. 210. Washington, D.C.: U.S. Government Printing Office, 1952.

———, and Edna S. Levine, eds., *Psychological Practices with the Physically Disabled.* New York: Columbia University Press, 1962.

Gowan, J. C., and G. D. Demos, eds., *The Guidance of Exceptional Children: A Book of Readings.* New York: David McKay Co., Inc., 1965.

Hylbert, Kenneth W., *Medical Information for Counselors.* State College, Penn.: Counselor Education Press, 1962.

Kanner, L., *Child Psychiatry,* 3rd ed. Springfield, Illinois: Charles C Thomas Publisher, 1957.

Karlsen, Bjorn, "Assessment of Handicapped Children," *College of Education Record,* **22** (May, 1966), 75–78.

Reynolds, M. C., "Psychologist in Special Education," *Minnesota Journal of Education,* **40** (1960), 22.

Ross, A. O., *The Exceptional Child in the Family.* New York: Grune and Stratton, Inc., 1964.

Trapp, E. Philip, and Philip Himelstein, *Readings on the Exceptional Child: Research and Theory.* New York: Appleton-Century-Crofts, 1962.

IMPAIRED VISION

Attitudes toward Blindness. New York: American Foundation for the Blind, 1951.

Ashcroft, S. C., and R. K. Harley, "The Visually Handicapped," *Review of Educational Research*, 36 (February, 1966), 75–93.

Bateman, Barbara, "Psychological Evaluation of Blind Children," *The New Outlook for the Blind*, 59 (June, 1965), 193–196.

Chevigny, H., and S. Braverman, *The Adjustment of the Blind*. New Haven: Yale University Press, 1950.

Cowen, Emory L., Rita P. Underberg, Ronald T. Verillo, and Frank G. Benham, *Adjustment to Visual Disability in Adolescence*. New York: American Foundation for the Blind, 1961.

Harnes, M. B., and J. P. Wollersheim, "An Intensive Differential Diagnosis of Partially Seeing Children to Determine the Implications of Education," *Exceptional Children*, 30 (1963), 17–25.

Hopkins, K. D., and L. McGuire, "Mental Measurement of the Blind: The Validity of the WISC," *International Journal of the Education of the Blind*, 15 (March, 1966), 65–73.

Lowenfeld, B., "The Visually Handicapped," *Review of Educational Research*, 33 (February, 1963), 38–48.

Nolan, C. Y., "The Visually Impaired," in *Behavioral Research on Exceptional Children*, ed. S. A. Kirk and B. B. Weiner. Washington, D.C.: Council for Exceptional Children, NEA, 1963.

Zahl, P. A., ed., *Blindness*. Princeton, N.J.: Princeton University Press, 1950.

IMPAIRED HEARING

Gardner, W. H., "Report of the Committee on Hard-of-Hearing Children of the American Hearing Society," *Hearing News*, 18 (1950).

Hiskey, M. S., "A Study of the Intelligence of Deaf and Hearing Children," *American Annals of the Deaf*, 101 (1956), 329–339.

Lane, H. S., "The Deaf and Hard of Hearing," *Review of Educational Research*, 33 (February, 1963), 48–62.

Lerman, A., *Vocational Adjustment and the Deaf: A Guide and Annotated Bibliography*. Washington: The Volta Bureau, 1965.

Levine, Edna Simon, *The Psychology of Deafness: Techniques of Appraisal for Rehabilitation*. New York: Columbia University Press, 1960.

Myklebust, Helmer R., *The Psychology of Deafness: Sensory Deprivation, Learning and Adjustment*. New York: Grune & Stratton, Inc., 1960.

Oleron, P., "A Study of the Intelligence of the Deaf," *American Annals of the Deaf*, 95 (1950), 179–195.

Rudloff, J. S., "Counseling Hearing Handicapped Children in School," *Exceptional Children*, 30 (February, 1964), 251–254.

Rosenstein, J., "The Deaf and Hard of Hearing," *Review of Educational Research*, 36 (February, 1966), 176–196.

SPEECH DEFECTS

Barbara, Dominick A., ed., *The Psychotherapy of Stuttering*. Springfield, Ill.: Charles C Thomas, Publisher, 1961.

Canter, G. J., and J. E. Trost, "The Speech Handicapped," *Review of Educational Research*, 36 (February, 1966), 56–74.

Daley, William T., ed., *Speech and Language Therapy with the Brain-Damaged Child*. Washington, D.C.: Catholic University of America Press, 1962.

Johnson, W., *et al.*, *The Onset of Stuttering: Research Findings and Implications*. Minneapolis, Minn.: University of Minnesota Press, 1959.

Johnson, Wendell, Frederick Darley, and D. C. Spriesterbach, *Diagnostic Methods in Speech Pathology*. New York: Harper & Row Publishers, 1963.

Kessler, Jane W., "Developmental Problems in Speech and Language," in *Psychopathology in Childhood*. Englewood Cliffs, N. J.: Prentice-Hall, Inc., 1966, pp. 129–165.

Morley, M., *The Development and Disorders of Speech in Childhood*. Baltimore, Md.: The Williams and Wilkins Company, 1957.

Myklebust, H. R., *Development and Disorders of Written Language*, Vol. 1: *Picture Story Language Test*. New York: Grune & Stratton, Inc., 1965.

Olson, D. R., "The Role of Speech in the Behavior of Children: A Theoretical Overview," *Ontario Journal of Educational Research*, 8 (Spring, 1966), 249–260.

Schiefelbusch, R. L., "Children with Speech and Language Impairments," in *Behavioral Research on Exceptional Children*, ed. S. A. Kirk and B. B. Weiner. Washington, D.C.: Council for Exceptional Children, N.E.A., 1963.

Taylor, I. K., "What Words are Stuttered?" *Psychological Bulletin*, 65 (April, 1966), 233–242.

Travis, L. E., ed., *Handbook of Speech Pathology*. New York: Appleton-Century-Crofts, 1957.

CEREBRAL PALSY

Allen, R. M., and T. W. Jefferson, *Psychological Evaluation of the Cerebral Palsied Person*. Springfield, Ill.: Charles C Thomas, Publisher, 1962.

Cruickshank, W. M., ed., *Cerebral Palsy: Its Individual and Community*

Problems, 2nd ed. Syracuse, New York: Syracuse University Press, 1966.

Denhoff, E., and T. P. Robinault, *Cerebral Palsy and Related Disorders*. New York: McGraw-Hill Book Company, 1960.

Linde, T., "Mental Evaluation in Cerebral Palsy," *Journal of Rehabilitation*, 30 (April, 1964), 17.

Psychological Problems in Cerebral Palsy: a Symposium. Chicago: National Society for Crippled Children and Adults, 1952.

Spencer, H., *A Glossary of Scientific Terms in the Field of Cerebral Palsy*. New York: Columbia University, College of Physicians and Surgeons, 1956.

OTHER NEUROLOGICALLY HANDICAPPING CONDITIONS

Agranowitz, Aleen, and Mildred Riddle McKeown, *Aphasia Handbook for Adults and Children*. Springfield, Ill.: Charles C Thomas, Publisher, 1964.

Benton, Arthur L., "Behavioral Indices of Brain Injury in School Children," *Child Development*, 33 (1962), 199–208.

Birch, H., *Brain Damage in Children*. Baltimore, Md.: The Williams and Wilkins Company, 1964.

Ellingson, R. J., "Relationship Between EEG and Test Intelligence: A Commentary," *Psychological Bulletin*, 65 (February, 1966), 91–99.

Ernhart, Claire B., Frances K. Graham, P. C. Eichman, Joan M. Marshall, and D. Thurston, "II. Comparison of Brain Injured and Normal Children," *Psychological Monographs: General and Applied*, 77 (1963), 17–33.

Garron, D. C., and D. I. Cheifetz, "Comment on Bender Gestalt Discernment of Organic Pathology," *Psychological Bulletin*, 63 (March, 1965), 197–200.

Reid, L. L., "Children with Cerebral Dysfunction," *Behavioral Research on Exceptional Children*, ed. S. A. Kirk and B. B. Weiner. Washington, D.C.: Council for Exceptional Children, NEA, 1963.

Rothstein, Jerome H., ed., *The Brain Injured and Neurologically Impaired: Readings and Resources*. New York: Holt, Rinehart & Wilson, Inc., 1965.

Strother, C. R., "Some Problems Involved in the Assessment and Training of Brain-Injured Children," *Research Bulletin of the Mental Health Research Institute*, Fort Steilacom, Washington, 5 (April, 1962), 73–76.

Summary of Progress in Childhood Disorders of the Brain and Nervous System, Research Profile Number 11. Washington, D.C.: U.S. Department of Health, Education, and Welfare, 1965.

OTHER HANDICAPPING MEDICAL CONDITIONS

Bennett, E. M., and D. E. Johanneen, "Psychodynamics of the Diabetic Child," *Psychological Monographs*, No. 382 (1954).

Fairfield, L., *Epilepsy: Grand Mal, Petit Mal, Convulsions*. New York: The Philosophical Library, 1957.

Hunt, J. T., "Children with Crippling Conditions and Special Health Problems," *Review of Educational Research*, 33 (February, 1963), 99–109.

Lennox, W. G., *Epilepsy and Related Disorders*, I and II. Boston: Little, Brown and Company, 1960.

Meyers, J. S., ed., *An Orientation to Chronic Disease and Disability*. New York: The Macmillan Company, 1965.

Swinyard, Chester A., "Problems of the Orthopedically Handicapped Child," in *Professional School Psychology*, Vol. II, ed. M. G. Gottsegen and G. B. Gottsegen. New York: Grune & Stratton, Inc., 1963.

TESTS AND TESTING

Kornrich, M., ed., *Psychological Test Modifications*. Springfield, Ill.: Charles C Thomas, Publisher, 1965.

Maslow, P., M. Frostig, D. W. Lefever, and J. R. B. Whittlesey, "The Marianne Frostig Developmental Test of Visual Perception, 1963 Standardization," *Perceptual Motor Skills*, 19 (1964), 463–499.

McCarthy, J. J., and S. A. Kirk, *Illinois Test of Psycholinguistic Abilities*. Urbana, Ill.: University of Illinois, Institute of Research on Exceptional Children, 1961.

WILLIAM ITKIN

19

The School Psychologist's Role in Research

The research role of the school psychologist is likely to differ widely from one working situation to another. It may also vary from time to time for the same psychologist within the same school system.

Research Functions of School Psychologists

The school psychologist may be considered as having three main research functions: 1) user of research; 2) conductor of research; and 3) research consultant.

As user of research, the school psychologist has a dual role as scholar and as applied scientist. His responsibilities to the school system include identification of exceptional children, consultation on educational provisions for exceptional children as individuals and in groups, contribution to curriculum development, in-service training of teachers, and parent education. His responsibilities to programs of special education and to exceptional children as individuals require that he periodically reappraise his diagnostic skills and reconsider his recommendations for actions and programs in the light of new research findings. He needs to be skillful in the use of his basic reference tools in order to keep up with important developments in theory and research. He must be able to think creatively and critically in order to draw implications from learning principles and learning theory for curriculum and instructional practices. To improve his own insight as well as to help teachers and parents understand children, he must augment his clinical experience with research findings on the needs of exceptional children, on the physical, emotional, and intellectual development of all children, on the influence of family relationships upon personality, and on the effect of social groups upon the behavior of group members. For the improvement of his own technical skills, the school psychologist needs to be aware of developments in sociology and statistics as well as those in educational, physiological, developmental, and clinical psychology.

As a researcher, one of the school psychologist's most important duties may be the gathering of data needed as a basis for administrative decisions. This is administrative research. Information on the rate of pupil transfers in and out of schools, on drop-outs, school enrollments, class size, teacher vacancies, and test results are examples of data needed as a basis for policy decisions.

The school psychologist may conduct research as an individual on educational problems having to do with curriculum or instruction, on psychological problems holding special interest for him, or on technological problems having to do with his skills as an applied psychologist. Typical problems studied by school psychologists include comparisons of educational methods, evaluation of instructional programs, methods of identifying children with special needs, and comparisons of the effectiveness of different diagnostic tools. During a recent school year, for example, the Bureau of Educational Research of a large city school system experimented with a Spanish translation of a widely used intelligence test, carried out a validity study of a mechanical aptitude test, evaluated aspects of its social studies curriculum, and studied factors influencing measures of IQ.

The school psychologist may also participate in research as a member of a cooperative research team, working with colleagues in universities, governmental agencies, private foundations, or other school systems on cooperatively designed and executed experiments.

Finally, the school psychologist may be called upon to act as a research consultant either to administrators of his school system in the planning of system-wide research programs or to administrators or teachers of local schools interested in more limited studies within single schools or school districts.

Research Frontiers

Although the usual function of a textbook is to summarize available knowledge of a subject, this chapter will attempt to draw attention to questions and problems relevant to the responsibilities of school psychologists upon which more knowledge is needed. This chapter will not attempt to review available research, but rather will identify areas needing further study. While other chapters in this text properly summarize accomplishments, this chapter will stress frontiers of educational and psychological research, problems presented by these frontiers, and tools needed to meet their challenges.

Man knows more today about the world in which he lives than ever before. Along with his greater knowledge, man has more control over his physical environment than he ever has had. Yet, every day, as individuals and as a society, we have to make important decisions based upon insufficient knowledge. In education, for example, in one decade greater consideration was given to age as a criterion for promotion, in another to academic standards. Many educators feel that evidence of the effect of pupil failure upon personality development is needed as a basis for a sound policy decision on promotion.

The relative effectiveness of different methods of instruction and of different ways of grouping children for instruction are other examples of educational issues on which more evidence is needed. During the 1930's, a great deal was heard about the unit method of instruction. Two decades later, much less emphasis was being given to this method. Opportunities, however, had been missed for gathering sound experimental evidence to answer questions as to the relative effectiveness of this and other methods for different categories of children and with different types of teacher personalities. Similarly, during the 1920's there was considerable experimentation with homogeneous grouping. This consisted of grouping children on the basis of their learning abilities, resulting in separate classes for academically talented children in some situations and for slow learning children in others. During the 1930's and 1940's many of these programs were discontinued, but not having been adequately evaluated, important questions about their advantages or disadvantages still await answers.

Education is a multibillion dollar business. Society has a great stake in the efficiency with which this business is being conducted and in the quality of its product. A relatively modest investment in research to evaluate how well the job is being done and to determine how the job could be done better would give a great stimulus to educational progress. There has been rich educational literature. Many creative ideas have been proposed. There has been too little follow-up in putting the theories and ideas of educational leaders to experimental test, however. Provision for the evaluation of new programs and procedures and for comparing their effectiveness with those of the programs they have superceded has been the exception rather than the rule. Thus, effective programs may have been discontinued not because they were found wanting, but because they were supplanted with others that might have been theoretically superior, but were actually untried.

The area of research with children of retarded mental development is illustrative of a field of educational research which had long suffered neglect. In 1951, Cruickshank surveyed state training schools, institutions of higher education, and public school systems of large cities to determine what research was being conducted on the education of children with retarded mental development.[1] He found that studies which only by a very liberal criterion could be classified as research were being done in eight of eighty state training schools, in three of forty-five institutions of higher education, and in two of eighteen public school systems. In 1953, Kirk and Kolstoe found a decrease of substantial research on educational problems of the mentally retarded during the years of 1944 to 1953.[2]

Until the latter half of the 1950's, research on mentally handicapped children was a seriously neglected area. There was almost no adequate evaluation of educational practices for the mentally handicapped. Many studies conducted at the time were inadequately designed, inadequately controlled, and inadequately analyzed. Evaluation instruments employed were often unsuited for educable mentally handicapped subjects. Little research was done in school systems. Many teachers were doing creative teaching jobs, but each seemed to take his own teaching techniques for granted, and there was relatively little exchange of information or of teaching methods. There were few longitudinal studies. There was a scarcity of appropriate instructional materials suitable for mentally handicapped children, and little research was being carried out by school psychologists.

During the latter half of the 1950's and through the 1960's, a great stimulus to research in the entire field of education was given by grants from the Cooperative Research Program of the Office of Education of the Department of Health, Education, and Welfare. In mental retardation, not only was more research initiated, but there were more studies dealing with practical problems. The design and execution of experimental studies improved. There were more large scale studies, more replications of experiments, and more multidisciplinary studies. Participation in research on the part of school systems and of school psychologists both in school systems and in institutions increased. Although the Cooperative Research Program gave impetus to research in this area, credit for progress both in quantity and quality of research was due also to university

[1] W. M. Cruickshank, "Research in the Education of Children with Retarded Mental Development," *American Journal of Mental Deficiency*, 56 (1951), 308–312.
[2] S. A. Kirk and O. P. Kolstoe, "The Mentally Retarded," *Review of Educational Research*, 23 (1953), 400–416.

training centers, private foundations, professional organizations, and school administrators having the vision and courage to evaluate their programs. Some of these trends in research on mental retardation were reflected in a recent report of Lipman, Blackman, and Stevens, who conducted a survey of then current research in institutions for mentally retarded.[3] These investigators sent questionnaires to ninety-five institutions for mentally retarded. Thirty-five of forty-seven responding reported research programs in progress, completed, or anticipated. Nine reported long-range coordinated efforts by personnel devoting fifty per cent or more of their time to research. Ninety-one per cent of the studies were conducted by Ph.D.'s, M.D.'s, and Ed.D.'s.

ILLUSTRATIVE QUESTIONS

This section will discuss questions in ten areas of research relevant to the functions of the school psychologist. The ten areas are not mutually exclusive; in a field as complex as education interrelationships among problems are inevitable. The areas are: 1) organization of instruction; 2) diagnostic tools; 3) gifted children; 4) retarded children; 5) prognosis; 6) curriculum; 7) mental health; 8) teacher personality; 9) evaluation of instruction; and 10) evaluation of psychological services.

Organization of instruction. In 1956, Stoddard suggested a creative departure in organization of instruction.[4] He proposed that home room teachers be given charge of two rooms, for one half day each. These teachers would be responsible for counseling and for instruction in reading and social studies. Mathematics, science, music, arts and crafts, and an optional sequence in language would be taught by special teachers on a longitudinal basis, through the elementary grades. This is an example of a creative idea suggested by an eminent educator that deserved to be tried out and compared with traditional methods rather than allowed to remain in the literature as interesting, but academic reading. Studies conducted by the Horace Mann-Lincoln Institute of Columbia University in cooperation with the New York City and Evanston, Illinois public schools on the effect of ability grouping on the intellectual, social, and personal development of both academically talented and normal children are examples of needed research on the effects of different methods of organizing instruction. Additional studies are needed comparing the effectiveness of instruction of academically retarded but not mentally handicapped children in special remedial classes as compared with instruc-

    [3] R. S. Lipman, L. S. Blackman, and H. A. Stevens, "A Survey of Research in Institutions for the Mentally Retarded," *American Journal of Mental Deficiency,* 63 (1959), 997–1000.
    [4] George D. Stoddard, "New Ways to Reach the Mind of the Child," in *Education 2000 A.D.,* ed. C. W. Hunnicutt (Syracuse, N.Y.: Syracuse University Press, 1956).

tion of such children in heterogeneous classes. A comparison of the effectiveness of individual tutoring in reading as compared with small group instruction in groups of different sizes for pupils with different degrees of reading disability is a similar problem having economic as well as educational significance.

Diagnostic tools. Additional research is needed on the effectiveness of the screening and diagnostic tools used by school psychologists, and new tools are needed for presently inadequately met measurement needs. Research on the screening effectiveness of widely used group tests is urgently needed in view of the uncritical use of such tests. More information is needed on the screening effectiveness of different group tests in different situations and for different purposes. Which group intelligence tests are best in predicting academic achievement for the upper end of the intelligence distribution for different ethnic and socio-economic groups? Which group tests are best for screening mentally retarded children from different socio-economic and ethnic groups? Which group tests are best for screening very young gifted and mentally retarded children, which for pre-adolescents, and which for adolescents? It may be that some group tests are better for some purposes and for some situations, and that other tests are superior for other purposes. A general comparison based upon correlations of group tests with individual tests of intelligence, or upon correlations of group intelligence tests with measures of achievement based upon heterogeneous samples may be misleading when applied to a specific screening situation for which the general findings do not apply.

Better screening measures for early identification of gifted and retarded are needed, both in terms of economy of testing time and in terms of efficiency of prediction. New tests of aptitude and ability are needed, tests of creativity, ingenuity, and initiative, tests measuring potentiality for creative achievement at the elementary school level as well as at the high school level. Mere proliferation of instruments will not solve these measurement problems; it should be understood that in pointing out needed diagnostic tools, the uncritical acceptance of untried, unreliable, or invalid instruments is not being advocated.

More research is needed on early identification of potentially underachieving gifted children. Attitudinal screening measures are needed to predict at an early age later attitudes toward advanced training on the part of gifted children. More information is needed on differential diagnosis of learning disabilities. Research on this problem would enable school psychologists to make more discriminating diagnoses of learning disabilities. It would help to identify better the role of intellectual, memory, perceptual, sensory, and personality problems in academic disabilities, and would contribute to more effective programs of remediation.

The promising work on delinquency proneness suggests similar studies on proneness for academic disability and susceptibility for neurotic adjustments and for psychiatric breakdowns.

GIFTED CHILDREN

In 1954, a subcommittee on Gifted Children of the Division of School Psychologists of the American Psychological Association designated a number of areas of needed research on gifted children. During the latter half of the 1950's, progress was made on research on some of the unanswered questions identified by that committee, but relatively little advancement was made during that period on curriculum research on gifted children. In 1959, Itkin posed a number of research challenges with respect to curriculum for gifted children: [5]

> Should gifted children be presented with the same curriculum as average children? How much may we expect of them with respect to quantity of work? How much may be expected of them in view of their mental ages and chronological ages? What is or are the most reasonable mental age grade expectancy formula or formulas with respect to different areas of the curriculum? What should be taught gifted children, and how should they be taught? To what extent may their relatively greater abstract thinking ability be utilized in programs to develop their critical thinking ability, problem solving ability, understanding of relationships, and drawing of inferences? How much stress on drill is optimum? How do ethical concepts develop in the gifted? Can ethical principles be taught, and how may they best be taught? Have any of us heard of an honors course in ethics and interpersonal relationships?

Other research challenges suggested by Itkin included modification of the attitudes of gifted girls toward professional careers, studies of the incidence of gifted children in below average socio-economic communities, parent-child relationships influencing the personality development of gifted children, and multidisciplinary sociological-educational experiments on modification of community and family attitudes toward academic achievement in below average socio-economic communities. The importance of evaluation research in the education of gifted children was stressed.

RETARDED CHILDREN

A number of unanswered questions on retarded children were raised by several Chicago school administrators in conference and correspondence: How should teaching methods differ for children of low mental ability as compared

[5] W. Itkin, "Research Challenges," Paper presented at a Symposium on Identifying and Providing for the Intellectually Gifted Child During the Elementary School Years, at meeting of Midwestern Psychological Association in Chicago, May 9, 1959.

with those of severe educational retardation? What effect does failure in school have upon the self-concepts of educable mentally handicapped children? What should be the educational program for educable mentally handicapped children after they reach their limitations for academic progress? What effect would a work-study program during the ages of sixteen to eighteen have upon the post-school adjustment of educable mentally handicapped? How do the post-school histories of educable mentally handicapped persons having had special education facilities compare with those not having had special education placement?

Dybwad,[6] also, has pointed out the need for experimentation in the areas of curriculum development and teaching materials, and for comparative studies of the effectiveness of a variety of curricula and of materials with the mentally retarded. He stressed the need for new diagnostic instruments for more effectively identifying factors in intelligence as a basis for the development of instructional materials and methods for the training of intellectual functions.

Capobianco suggested studies of socio-economic variables differentiating endogenous ("familial") and exogenous ("brain damaged") mentally deficient children. He pointed out that despite the fact that specific curricula have been established for brain injured mentally retarded children, few of these instructional materials and techniques have been experimentally tested.[7]

PROGNOSIS

Mullen and Itkin [8] have suggested longitudinal studies relating post-school adjustment of educable mentally handicapped children to educational, social, and psychological data recorded during their school histories. Results from such longitudinal studies would help predict at an early date which children are likely to have later adjustment problems. Such research would thus aid educators to identify children most in need of early therapeutic intervention.

University of Pittsburgh's Project Talent [9] inventoried the aptitudes and abilities of a sample of 500,000 high school students. This research program involved not only investigations of relationships between abilities,

[6] G. Dybwad, "Trends and Issues in Mental Retardation: Draft of a Working Paper for 1960 White House Conference on Children and Youth," (New York: National Association for Retarded Children, Inc., 1960).

[7] R. J. Capobianco, "Problems in Evaluating Programs for Mentally Handicapped," Paper presented at meeting of American Psychological Association in New York, August 30, 1957.

[8] Frances A. Mullen and W. Itkin, *Achievement and Adjustment of Educable Mentally Handicapped Children in Special Classes and in Regular Grades* (Chicago: Chicago Board of Education, 1961).

[9] "The Story of Project Talent," (Washington, D. C.: University of Pittsburgh Talent Office, Bulletin No. 1, 1959).

hobbies, and competence, but anticipated after-school follow-up prediction studies as well.

CURRICULUM

Problems in the teaching of mathematics identified by Brown and Kinsella [10] illustrate needed curricular research. These reviewers found the following questions asked or implied in research in mathematics: What concepts of algebra can be successfully taught in grades four to six? Are integrated mathematics courses at the tenth and eleventh grade level more effective than separate courses in plane geometry, advanced algebra, and trigonometry? To what extent should social applications of arithmetic be taught at the seventh and eighth grade levels?

MENTAL HEALTH

School psychologists are in an excellent position to make clinical studies of family background factors related to the mental health of children, but do not have equally good opportunities to carry out controlled experimental studies in this area. Research in family relationships having significance for mental health includes problems such as the influence of parental child-rearing practices and attitudes upon changes in IQ with age, the effect of parental harmony or discord, parental attitudes, and child rearing practices on the achievement and creativity of gifted children, parent-child relationships in achieving and non-achieving gifted children, and the effect of different manifestations of overprotection upon prognosis for school achievement and for post-school adjustment.

TEACHER PERSONALITY

The work of David G. Ryans [11] is illustrative of needed research on teacher effectiveness. More study needs to be given to the problem of teacher effectiveness in different types of teaching assignments, measured in terms of pupil achievements and pupil behavior, as related to the personality attributes of the teacher. Answers to questions such as the following are needed: What qualities in teachers distinguish the effective primary grade teacher from the effective upper grade teacher? How are teacher personality characteristics related to job satisfaction in different teaching assignments?

10 Kenneth E. Brown and John J. Kinsella, *Analysis of Research in the Teaching of Mathematics 1957 and 1958* (Washington, D. C.: U. S. Department of Health, Education and Welfare, Bulletin No. 8, 1960).

11 D. G. Ryans, "Some Correlates of Teacher Behavior," *Educational and Psychological Measurement* 19 (1959), 3–12.

What personality attributes characterize effective teachers of different categories of exceptional children—of the trainable mentally handicapped, the educable mentally handicapped, the socially or emotionally maladjusted, the gifted, and the physically handicapped? What characteristics prognosticate success in administrative assignments? Research on these problems may make important contributions not only to the effectiveness of educational programs, but to teachers' job satisfaction as well. While the reluctance of teachers to participate in personality research may be an almost insurmountable obstacle in cross-sectional research, the possibility of longitudinal research relating personality test data obtained during entrance examinations and teacher training to later job effectiveness and job satisfaction may be a feasible alternative to cross-sectional studies.

EVALUATION OF INSTRUCTION

It has already been suggested that additional evaluation research is needed to determine what kinds of educational programs best prepare educable mentally handicapped and gifted children for post-school adjustment. In the area of mental handicap, an example of such an evaluation problem would be a comparison of the academic progress and behavioral adjustment of educable mentally handicapped children (EMH) in heterogeneous EMH classes and in groupings based upon social background and behavioral criteria. Other evaluation problems needing investigation include evaluation of high school honors classes, evaluation of special classes for socially maladjusted children, and evaluation of tutoring provisions for mentally handicapped and non-mentally handicapped, but academically retarded children, and a comparison of the effectiveness of remedial instruction by teaching machines and by remedial teachers.

EVALUATION OF PSYCHOLOGICAL SERVICES

As applied scientists with a responsibility for evaluation research, one of the most important frontiers of research challenging both the courage and competence of school psychologists is that of evaluation of their own services. What constitutes good school psychological services? Number of cases tested per day or number of diagnostic instruments administered per case? Uniformity of testing procedures, or flexibility in the utilization of diagnostic tools? Thoroughness with which a few functions are carried out, or diversity of functions? All of the above are subjective criteria, dependent upon the evaluator's judgment as to what constitutes an adequate psychological service program. Subjective judgments are often relied upon for evaluation, but the real test of a program is in its effects. What are school psychologists trying to achieve in their work with schools, with children, and with parents? How well are these objectives being accomplished? How can psychological services be improved? Are some ways of giving service better than others? Are some methods of giving service better under some circumstances or with some types of cases than others? Answers to these questions require at least four steps: One, clear definition of objectives. Two, the selection or development of instruments to measure outcomes toward these objectives. Three, analysis of findings to determine whether changes in desired directions occur as a result of psychological services. Four, measurement of differences in amount of change under different conditions of operation to determine the effectiveness of different methods of operation. The complex problem of evaluation of psychological services has been selected to illustrate principles, problems, and methods of school psychological research, and will be treated in a more extensive discussion in a later section of this chapter.

Problems in Doing Research in a School Setting

School psychologists encounter very real, very practical, and sometimes insurmountable problems in conducting research in a school setting. Simply stated, these problems are time, money, administrative approval, rapport, and technical competence. The school psychologist's major responsibility is service. Very often, his service load is so heavy, and the requests for additional service so urgent and valid, that he is reluctant to spare even unexpectedly available free moments for any activities not directly related to service. One correspondent, in discussing proposed plans for collaborative research, described this obstacle as follows:

> The structure of the system in which I operate would almost preclude my participation in a cooperative venture unless the venture were initiated or eventually organized at the level of the local superintendent. In the State of . . . there are only five or six individuals employed by public schools who could be professionally categorized as psychologists. The pressures for psychological services of a school nature throughout the State are terrific. For those of us located directly in the course of the flood, there appears little to do but attempt to keep our heads above water.

School psychologists live the same twenty-four hour day as the rest of the population. This time must be allotted among primary job responsibilities, family responsibilities, civic responsibilites, in-service training, and recreation. From a realistic point of view, unless a school psychologist is in the fortunate position of having a definite proportion of his working day allotted to research, many brief vacations, late night and early morning hours are needed to accomplish any substantial research.

The problem of money is allied to that of time. Few school psychologists are in a position to be able to afford to pay for clerical help to carry out routine clerical and statistical chores concommitant to data processing in research. Only slight experience with the annual "Battle of the Budget" is necessary to convince one of the stringent economy with which the typical American school system is operated. There is much competition for each budgeted dollar. In the battle for the budgeted dollar, the advocates of research have not often found strong support.

It seems plausible to assume that research cannot be conducted in a school system without the approval and support of the top administration of that school system. If the local superintendent does not see value in research, time, funds, and personnel will not be made available for any substantial research program. If personnel are freed, either on a part-time or a full-time basis from instructional, service, or administrative duties to work on a research project, the top school administration must do so because of a belief that research will contribute to the improvement of instruction or of service.

Not only is the researcher's time an important consideration in the conduct of research in a school setting, the time of other school personnel is an even more vital consideration. Teachers and school administrators, like the service-oriented psychologist, are faced with time limitations. If the researcher makes unreasonable or insufficiently explained demands upon their time, he will not only meet with resistance, but will jeopardize the rapport which is essential to carrying out his service responsibilities. He will find that a majority of teachers and school administrators are as professionally oriented and as service-motivated as he. If he asks them to take time from their instructional or administrative responsibilities, or from their own well earned leisure, his demands must be stringently minimal, and the reasons for his requests clearly understandable. He must not ask a teacher or administrator to do anything that he cannot have done in any other way. He must not present them with a request for data, or with a psychological instrument requiring fifteen minutes of their time if by the expenditure of fifteen days of his own he can refine his data recording form or instrument so that the teacher or administrator can complete it in five, or even ten minutes.

Rapport with school personnel requires that even if no demands are being placed upon school personnel for time, and no inconveniences caused them, they be given the courtesy and consideration of an explanation of the objectives of the research being done in their school with their children, and of the hoped for benefits that might accrue to the school, the school system, or the public.

Just as the researcher should be considerate of teacher and administrator time, he must be considerate of the time of pupils as subjects. The primary purpose of the school is instruction. Pupil time, just as the appropriation dollar, is budgeted with the view of most effective accomplishment of educational goals. The researcher has the responsibility of exercising economy in the demands he makes upon pupil time. He will encounter school opposition, and even pupil opposition, if he does not use economically the time of the pupils who are allowed to serve as subjects. He must plan carefully, choose his instruments carefully, and make compromises with his own time rather than waste that of his subjects.

Finally, the school psychologist, as indeed all research psychologists, must recognize and accept the limitations of his own technological skills. New developments in statistics, in research design, and in measurement techniques, are, fortunately, constantly evolving. Keeping up with these developments is a challenge, and often an impossibility. Continued in-service training, attendance at professional meetings, and participation in professional institutes help him recognize his limitations. The school psychologist needs to know where to go for technical consultation and whom to approach for necessary help. To know when one needs to seek such consultation is a sign of professional maturity rather than of overdependence.

These obstacles to research in a school setting are not necessarily insolvable. During the late fifties, a number of large scale research projects and many small ones were carried out in school systems of all sizes throughout the country, both in urban and rural communities. The number of studies involving school systems, state departments of education, and universities increased. Although it continued to be more difficult for school systems than for universities to obtain grants for research, it was possible for even isolated researchers to obtain small grants from federal agencies and private foundations through cooperation with state departments of education or universities. School systems, also, showed an increasing inclination to allocate funds for research.

Several suggestions for increasing school psychological research were offered by Seashore: [12] 1) cooperative research among a number of school systems; 2) long-term collection of data on a problem over a period of years; 3) the harnessing of school psychologists and university professors into cooperative research teams; and 4) utilization of graduate students of education and psychology in research conducted by school psychologists. Research studies done in Illinois and Wisconsin illustrate the kind of collaborative research possible between universities and school systems. Studies of administrative provisions for gifted children conducted in California exemplified state-wide cooperation in research programs, and the Chicago Cooperative Research Project was an excellent example of teamwork involving a research staff, school administrators, and teachers.

Basic Principles

This section will present a number of principles basic to the conduct and utilization of educational research. It will be followed by a section on special problems in educational research, and, in turn, both principles and

[12] H. Seashore, "The School Psychologist and Research," *Exceptional Children*, 25 (1958), 147–150.

problems will be illustrated in a discussion of research on the evaluation of psychological services.

Research design consists of the outlining of a sensible plan for obtaining evidence for a relatively direct answer to a direct question. The first step is to have clearly in mind the question one wants answered. A vague question will usually elicit an ambiguous answer. The following are examples of questions which are not specific enough to suggest specific answers:

When is the best time to accelerate a pupil?

Under what circumstances do gifted children profit most from special class placement?

Under what circumstances, and with what types of gifted children are different degrees of separation in grouping most effective?

One starts with a general question, but it must be delimited, and expressed in terms of specifics which are capable of eliciting a specific answer. Just as the question should be expressed in specific terms, the possible answers should also be anticipated in concrete terms. Thus: For pupils with IQ's of 120 and above on the Stanford-Binet Form L-M, is early entrance in kindergarten, acceleration during grades one or two, acceleration during grades three or four, or acceleration during grades five or six best in terms of the following measures obtained at the end of grade eight: a) reading achievement, as measured by the X Reading Achievement Test; b) arithmetic achievement, as measured by the X Arithmetic Achievement Test; c) over-all adjustment, as measured by the Y Adjustment Rating Scale; d) self-concept, as measured by the Z Sociometric Rating Instrument?

The formulation of the question asked in a research plan is a creative mental process analogous to a research design. The expression of a hypothesis, or the formulation of a good researchable question, requires observations of data, insightful thinking about interrelationships among the data, and predictions of effects. A good hypothesis cannot come from a data vacuum, nor can it be derived from facts alone. It requires creative thinking about interrelationships among facts, accompanied by a critical attitude with respect to the inadequacy of the data and the tentative nature of the conclusions drawn. The more adequate data one has upon a problem, and the more insightful theorizing he has done about these data, the better, i.e., the more likely of verification, his hypothesis is likely to be. It is therefore important that a school psychologist contemplating research upon an educational problem work closely with subject matter specialists and review previous literature on related problems during the hypothesizing stage of his planning.

CONTROLS

Control in an experiment consists of those provisions in the experimental plan that have been made for the purpose of assuring that effects observed are the result of the experimental conditions rather than of extraneous circumstances. Let us suppose that an investigator treats a learning problem with medication and finds improvement. He must demonstrate that the improvement in learning was brought about by something intrinsic to the drug rather than by improvement in the subject's cooperativeness with the examiner, confidence of the subject in the efficacy of the medication, or to something in the therapeutic relationship between subject and examiner. Controls may be built into the experimental design by matching subjects on factors relevant to their performance on the measurement instruments, and by making measurements under comparable circumstances in the different conditions of the experiment. Controls may also be achieved by statistical means, as in analysis of covariance. Without adequate controls in an experiment, however, definite conclusions cannot be reached, while incorrect conclusions might be drawn.

The limitations of case history data for research use lie in the lack of uniformity in the conditions under which such data are usually collected. Different clinicians are likely to record different types of data. Those having a sociological orientation may be most impressed by factors such as living conditions, cultural influences, and attitudes; those with a medical orientation may be more likely to record health history and physical factors. Clinicians with one theoretical orientation may emphasize certain aspects of the parent-child relation, and those with another point of view may emphasize other aspects of family relationships. Two well trained clinicians using the same personality test may administer it differently and use different methods of scoring. Case history material may be very valuable in research, but for maximum usefulness it is necessary that it be collected under controlled conditions.

DATA PROCESSING

Accuracy and completeness of data and uniformity in the recording of data are the responsibility of every professional and clerical person involved in a research project. In the preparation of forms for the recording of data, data categories should be made as specific and concrete as possible. Explicit instructions for the recording of data should be written out. No instructions for recording of data should be left to memory. Subjectivity in coding of information should be minimized. Where subjective factors might influence the recording of data, the influence of subjectivity should be estimated by checks upon the consistency of recording and coding of data.

In collaborative research involving a number of researchers who are geographically separated, completeness and uniformity of data recording is a special problem. Under such circumstances, it is particularly important that great determination be exercised to insure completeness and meticulous accuracy in data collection, coding, and recording. In geographical separation, differences in procedure may easily arise if each participant allows himself to rely upon his judgment to reinterpret agreed-upon procedures. Temptations to make *any* changes in agreed-upon procedures should be scrupulously avoided. Strict uniformity is an absolute necessity. In data processing, compulsive accuracy is a virtue, flexibility a mistake. If judgments or ratings are required, judgments must be made. One should not decide that judgments asked for cannot be made validly. A participating researcher should accept as a limitation upon his role the making of decisions that certain data are or are not valid, that different categories or classifications of data than asked for would give better results. He may criticize, and make his criticisms a matter of record, but he must record all of the data in exactly the form agreed upon. There are ways of treating categorical data statistically, and there are methods of estimating the effect of subject factors in the recording of data, but the methods of recording data and the criteria for judgments must be uniform.

ANALYSIS OF DATA

The design or outline of an experiment should include plans for gathering the information, for insuring its uniformity, for controlling or estimating the effect of extraneous circumstances which might bias results, and for analysing the results so that specific answers to the hypothesis formulated or questions asked might be obtained. This is not to say that statistical plans may not be changed, but that there must be a planned direction for the entire investigation, including plans for analysis of results.

Statistics are tools of the researcher for analysing his data. A senior school psychologist at the Ph.D. level needs an adequate background in mathematics and statistics. Inadequacies in one's preparation in mathematics and statistics should be recognized. They may be overcome, to a degree, by proper in-service training, by post-doctoral study, and by consultation with experts in research design and statistics. It is always advisable, even in planning small scale studies, to consult experts in research design, data processing, and statistics. Progress in research demands that the most effective designs be employed and that the most efficient methods of data processing and of statistical analysis by utilized.

CRITERION MEASURES

Measures of effects of experimental conditions, or criterion measures, should be of satisfactory validity and reliability, and should be appropriate for use with the population of subjects studied. For mentally handicapped subjects, tests requiring reading should be avoided if possible unless it is reading that is being measured. For gifted subjects, it is important that tests employed have high enough ceilings to discriminate among high scorers.

QUALIFICATION OF FINDINGS

The research worker has a responsibility to assess the influence of circumstances that might have biased his results, and to caution the research user of the limitations that must be placed upon the application of the results of his experiment. The appropriateness of an experimental design is related to interpretation of findings. Efficient designs may allow interpretation of interrelationships among factors in an experiment not possible in less sophisticated designs. Punch card tabulation and use of electronic computers make possible the analysis of complex experiments not feasible with less efficient methods of data analysis.

COMMUNICATION OF FINDINGS

The research literature in psychology is so extensive and so specialized that no one school psychologist can be expected to keep up with the reading of all of the primary sources. Periodic reviews of the research literature on various topics are needed. School psychologists should accept greater responsibility for preparation as well as for the reading of such reviews. Sources such as *Annual Review of Psychology, Contemporary Psychology,* and *Review of Educational Research* help one to keep up with the literature.

Reviews of the literature for school psychologists and for teachers and other educators should be written in a clear manner, with an applied slant. One need not apologize for the applied slant of such reviews, since the failure of education and psychology to apply research findings in educational practice is a serious problem of long standing. The school psychologist, trained in psychology, close to the school situation, and typically an individual with a practical bent, can render a much needed service in spelling out the implications and applications of the research findings of the academic psychologist.

APPLICATION OF A SCIENTIFIC ATTITUDE IN SCHOOL
AND CLINICAL PSYCHOLOGICAL PRACTICE

When a school psychologist makes recommendations for action, it should be clear in his own mind and apparent to others whether his recommendations are based upon verified knowledge or upon unverified hypotheses. It is too easy to become such a firm believer in one's hypotheses that one begins to confuse them with verified facts. An inadequately confirmed hypothesis should be recognized as having the same status as experimental findings that require qualification and may be applied only with reservations and restrictions. Many scientists who are cautious in interpreting the results of their experiments tend to be very incautious about the strength of their convictions about their theoretical orientations.

A clinician should apply an objective appraisal and an ongoing reappraisal of his own clinical skills and practices. He should have a critical attitude not only toward his diagnostic tools, but also toward his own diagnostic and prognostic skills. He should recognize that he is himself a clinical instrument of less than perfect reliability and validity.

Special Problems in Educational Research

Because of the multiplicity of conditions both within the school situation and external to the school that affect learning, the educational research worker is faced with a number of peculiarly complex problems. These difficulties include problems in selection of a sample, control of bias, collection and processing of data, and measurement of effects.

PROBLEMS IN SELECTION OF SAMPLES

For the investigator to be able to generalize his findings from the particular subjects in his study to a larger population of which his subjects are a sample, it is necessary for him to demonstrate that his subjects adequately represent the larger population about which he desires to generalize. Representative samples are not always available to the relatively isolated investigator. The subjects available to him may be unrepresentative in important respects related to the effects he is trying to measure. If the only subjects available to him reside in a college town, for example, a suburban neighborhood of high socio-economic status, an urban slum area, or in a neighborhood populated by a single ethnic group, it may not be possible for him to apply conclusions from his learning experiments to groups of different cultural backgrounds.

Some experimental designs require random selection of subjects. Subjects chosen at random may, however, be unwilling to cooperate, or may be otherwise unavailable. Similarly, classroom groups chosen at random may be unavailable to the experimenter.

PROBLEMS IN CONTROLLING BIAS

It is difficult to determine to what extent progress toward educational objectives may be attributed to educational programs and to what extent attainment or failure to attain these objectives may be due to home and community influences or to initial differences between pupils. Presumably, teaching ability affects pupil learning, and different methods of instruction may be more effective than others in bringing about pupil achievement in different areas of the curriculum. Academic aptitude, socio-economic factors, cultural attitudes toward learning, and sex are also known to affect school achievement. In addition, unknown subtle influences may affect outcomes of educational experiments. The control of biasing factors and the estimation of the influence of such factors upon the results of educational experiments is therefore a complex problem in educational research.

PROBLEMS OF DATA COLLECTION AND DATA PROCESSING

Decisions on the background information to be collected on subjects in an educational experiment, and upon classroom and school factors, experimental conditions, and outcomes must be made before any data are gathered. The data to be collected depend upon the hypothesis being investigated. The planning of an experiment requires information, creativity, and foresight. Because data relevant to the investigation of one hypothesis may be irrelevant to another, reviews of the literature on related problems, and consultation with subject matter specialists need to be employed in the planning stage of an experiment. In collaborative research, loss of data because of the failure of a single participant to supply needed information or ratings may render much other painstakingly collected data useless.

PROBLEMS IN MEASUREMENT

The objectives of educational programs are often expressed in general terms such as development of economic competence, good citizenship, adequate human relations, aesthetic and spiritual values, and productive use of leisure time. Obtaining or developing reliable and valid measures of such factors is a challenging problem. Even standardized tests of academic skills must be carefully considered with respect to their suitability for the particular sample used in an educational experiment.

SPECIAL PROBLEMS IN METHODS EXPERIMENTS

In addition to the problems general to educational research, there are a number of additional problems peculiar to educational methods experiments. The basic problem is defining the methods of instruction in specific terms and determining how adequately experimental conditions are carried out. Teachers participating in methods experiments may have to be given training in the experimental methods. Appropriate instructional materials of uniform quality for the different experimental groups may be difficult to obtain. In addition, there is the problem of uniqueness. Each teacher carries out a particular method of instruction in ways unique to her, that reflect her intelligence, creativity, and her background of training and experience. This may be fortunate for instruction, but it makes it difficult for the research worker to interpret his results.

Loss of data because of pupil, and especially of teacher mobility, is a particularly vexing problem in methods experiments. The loss of teachers because of transfer or illness may mean the loss of an entire group of children from an experiment, and possibly the loss of an entire methods group.

In methods experiments, differences between classrooms magnify the problem of differences between individuals. Classrooms may differ in age, IQ, sex, initial school achievement, socio-economic backgrounds, and adjustment. In turn, these factors may affect performance on the criterion or outcome measures. These factors, however, are fairly objective, and relatively easy to identify. The factor of teacher effectiveness is one that is extremely difficult to control. It is more difficult to identify than these more readily measurable factors, and it may have an even more important influence upon results.

Other problems in methods experiments relate to the measurement problem. Comparable time intervals must be maintained in testing subjects from different experimental groups. Absence of pupils, unavailability of adequate testing space and time, and conflicts in the examiner's own testing schedule complicate the measurement problem.

An Illustrative Problem: Evaluation of Psychological Services

Let us now take the problem of evaluation of psychological services to illustrate some of the basic principles and several of the major methodological questions in educational research.

Let us suppose that a school psychology department wishes to determine how effective its services have been and whether its services may be improved. Basically, this question asks: Are psychological services having any effect? If so, how much effect, and can different methods of providing or organizing these services produce greater desired effects?

The evaluator may begin with subjective methods of evaluation. He may ask: What constitutes good psychological services? Several criteria may suggest themselves:

1. A good psychological program is one of wide scope. The evaluator accepting this as a criterion may list the functions his department has carried out during a designated year, i.e.; individual testing, group testing, individual counseling, group counseling, curriculum development, in-service training of teachers, parent education, research, etc.

2. A good psychological program is staffed by well trained professional workers. Using this criterion, the evaluator may list the number of psychologists on his staff having certain graduate degrees or having designated numbers of hours of graduate training in certain fields of study.

3. A good psychological program is one which carries out a large number of studies of individual children. If the evaluator considers this an adequate criterion, he may produce a count of the number of individual psychological examinations made by his bureau in a given year.

4. A good psychological program is one that communicates its findings to teachers and parents. On the basis of this criterion, the evaluator might provide counts of the number of teacher and parent contacts made by his staff.

5. A good psychological program is one which provides intensive individual and group counseling.

6. A good psychological program provides for systematic follow-up.

7. A good psychological program utilizes community facilities.

8. A good psychological program serves pupils with a wide range of referral problems.

9. A good psychological program is one that is highly regarded by school personnel, pupils, and community agencies.

All of the above criteria are subjective. Applying such criteria to a school psychology program may answer in general terms the question whether a given program is consistent with a particular evaluator's conception of what a good school psychology program should be. Different evaluators having different conceptions of what constitutes adequate psychological service may use the same data to arrive at a different set of conclusions. Finally, none of the above criteria, with the possible exception of the last, answer the question: Is the psychological program being evaluated having any desired effect?

The fundamental tasks of a research program on the evaluation of the effectiveness of school psychological services are to formulate the objectives of a school psychological program and to determine how well these objectives are being accomplished. Carrying out these fundamental tasks requires at least four steps: One, the objectives of the psychological program must be defined clearly, in terms specific enough to be testable, yet general enough to be important. Two, instruments have to be selected or criteria established for measuring progress toward these goals. Determining the reliability and validity of such instruments or criteria is part of this step. Three, criterion measures have to be employed to determine whether changes in desired directions occur as a result of psychological services. Four, these criterion measures may be used to measure differences in the amount of change under different conditions of service to determine the relative effectiveness of different types of service.

The general purpose of an evaluation study of the effectiveness of psychological services, then, is to determine which methods of organizing or of providing psychological service are most effective, or under which circumstances some methods are superior to others with respect to accomplishing certain objectives. As thus stated, however, such a general purpose is not testable. Objectives need to be spelled out; services rendered must be described in specific terms; the effects of the psychological services must be measured; effects need to be related to service or treatment variables (to different aspects of the services rendered) and to problem variables (to different categories of problems).

What, then, are school psychologists attempting to accomplish in their work with schools and with children? We shall not attempt, in this discussion, to deal with the question of the efficacy of services rendered to a school system as a whole, nor to the community as a whole, but shall limit ourselves to the problem of evaluation of services to individual children.

Objectives of the school psychologist's work with children may be inferred from statements such as *The Psychologist on the School Staff.*[13] Objectives stated or implied in that report include the following:

1. Screening of cases for individual study. This objective refers to the process of selection of cases for individual study.

2. Diagnosis. Diagnosis involves a number of aspects: evaluating the current intellectual functioning of the child; appraising his academic aptitude and readiness for learning; his motivation, interests, vocational aptitudes, and adjustment; determining his difficulties in terms of intelligence, personality, achievement, and relationships with peers, with adults at school, and within his family; classifying him according to accepted criteria of exceptionality; and identifying factors contributing to his problems.

3. Interpretation and communication of findings to school, parents, and pupil.

4. Determination of appropriate educational placement.

5. Treatment. Treatment may include individual counseling, group counseling, interpretation of findings to school personnel or to parents, parent counseling, placement, remedial instruction, or referral to community guidance, recreational, or social service agencies.

---

[13] Frances A. Mullen *et al., The Psychologist on the School Staff: Report of the Committee on Reconsideration of the Functions of the School Psychologist* (Phoenix, Arizona: Division of School Psychologists, American Psychological Association, October, 1958).

In his services to schools, then, the psychologist is working toward a number of objectives: He aims to screen his referrals in such a way as to insure that those children needing psychological service most are given priority in service. He attempts to give an accurate and comprehensive diagnosis, in which he identifies the different aspects of a problem and the factors contributing toward it. He tries to communicate his diagnosis in such a way as to broaden teachers' understanding not only of the child referred, but of other similar exceptional children. He aims to change teachers' attitudes toward individual children and toward children's behavior. Through counseling and through remedial measures, he hopes to effect modifications of parental attitudes and child reading practices and of children's behavior. Focusing upon objectives brings us closer to expressing our research problem in testable terms.

Let us begin with our first objective, screening of referrals, and let us further limit our question to the effectiveness of our procedures for screening referrals for special class placement of mentally handicapped children. How effectively is testing time available for diagnosis of mental handicap being used? What are the criteria for referral that are being used? These criteria would have to be specifically designated, e.g., group test, plus teacher nomination, plus principal approval. With the use of these criteria, what proportion of cases tested for special class placement are found eligible for placement? How would the addition of several criteria, let us say, four discrete facts about a child's social and educational background, and an adjustment rating scale filled out by his teacher, change the proportion of screened cases qualifying for placement? How would the further addition of a brief individual test of general information and general comprehension in cases meeting certain of the second set of screening standards change the proportion of screened cases qualifying for placement? Are these differences in proportions statistically significant? In this illustrative problem, the criterion measure might be a psychologist's recommendation for special class placement based upon an individual examination and clinical judgment. The hypotheses serving as the basis for the selection of the additional screening measures would be derived from the results of previous research. Background information on sex and socio-economic status of subjects would be pertinent to this problem.

Assessing the accuracy of diagnosis is a more complex evaluation problem. An evaluator may be interested in determining the accuracy of general classifications of exceptionality, i.e., educable mentally handicapped, socially maladjusted, or gifted. In such instances, he would be faced with a criterion problem. Whose diagnosis should serve as a criterion of exceptionality? If he uses one psychologist or one test as a criterion against which to judge another, how is he sure that the criterion is more accurate than the diagnosis whose validity is being assessed? A partial solution to this problem may be to regard his experiment as a test of consistency of diagnosis rather than of validity. Thus, he might compare the consistency of two concurrent diagnoses or of two diagnoses separated by a period of time.

Assessing both the accuracy and comprehensiveness of diagnoses renders the evaluation problem more complex. With an increase in the number of aspects of diagnosis that are being validated, the criterion problems become magnified.

Evaluating the effectiveness of the school psychologist's communication of findings to teachers and parents requires designating the types of communication utilized and measuring the effect of such communications. For example, it may be desired to compare four types of communications: 1) written report; 2) brief individual contact; 3) single case conference, and 4) a series of case conferences. The experimenter may attempt to measure the effect of his communication upon teachers and parents through instruments such as tests of insight into the dynamics of deviant child behavior, attitude scales, or rating scales. He may attempt to measure the effect of his communication upon child behavior through rating instruments, anecdotal records of critical incidents, or personality tests. One of his major problems in interpreting his results would be to determine, if possible, which effects could be attributed to communication, and which to other aspects of the psychological services rendered.

Measuring improvement in pupil behavior as a result of psychological services is an evaluation problem which illustrates the difficulties inherent in the complex variables which affect pupil behavior. The criterion problem is only one of the problems faced by the evaluator in designing such an experiment. Difficult as it is to measure effects in terms of pupil behavior, attitudes, and personality, the problem of determining which effects are a result of treatment and which may be attributable to conditions external to the treatment may be an even more difficult problem.

The experimenter would find it necessary to record data not only on pupil behavior or test performance before and after treatment, but also data on specific treatment variables, pupil variables, psychologist variables, family variables, and school variables. Treatment variables would involve a description of the actions taken by the psychologist and of the steps carried out as a result of his recommendations. In recording pupil factors, methods would probably have to be developed for categorizing levels of pupil adjustment, personality attributes, intelligence, and socio-economic status. Psychologist variables would probably need to include level of training, theoretical orientation, sex, and relevant personality attributes. Family factors might include intact or non-intact homes and specific parental attitudes. School variables might include average class size, pupil turnover, and measures of classroom climate.

The design of an experiment on the effect of psychological services upon pupil behavior would probably require the group planning of a team of psychologists meeting over a period of time. Not only would collaborators in such an experiment need to formulate hypotheses on interrelationships between treatment and effect variables, but it would probably be necessary for them to hypothesize relationships between psychologist, subject, and family variables and effects of treatments. Hypotheses concerning interrelationships among so many variables might be derived from clinical experience and previous research. Discrete pilot studies might have to be carried out to reduce the possibilities of false steps and wasted data in the major experiments. An evaluation problem of such complexity would probably be researchable only by means of electronic methods of data processing and computation.

Selected Supplementary Readings

American Educational Research Association, "Educational and Psychological Testing: Reviews the Literature for the Three-Year Period since February, 1962," *Review of Educational Research*, 35 (February, 1965), 1–10.

Bachrach, Arthur, *Psychological Research: An Instruction.* New York: Random House, Inc., 1962.

Boyer, T. H., "School-University Cooperation: Implications for Educational Research," *California Journal of Educational Research*, 16 (January, 1965), 23–28.

Carpenter, Finley, and Eugene E. Hadden, *Systematic Application of Psychology to Education.* New York: The Macmillan Company, 1964.

Castaneda, Alfred, and Leila S. Fahel, "The Relationship Between the Psychological Investigator and the Public Schools," *American Psychologist*, 16 (April, 1961), 201–203.

Cochran, William G., and Gertrude M. Cox, *Experimental Design*, 2nd ed. New York: John Wiley & Sons, Inc., 1957.

Collier, Raymond O., and Stanley Elam, eds., *Research Design and Analysis: Second Symposium on Educational Research.* Bloomington, Ind.: Phi Delta Kappa, 1961.

Dixon, Wilfrid J., and Frank J. Massey, Jr., *Introduction to Statistical Analysis*, 2nd ed. New York: McGraw-Hill Book Company, 1957.

Edwards, Allen L., *Experimental Design in Psychological Research.* New York: Holt, Rinehart & Winston, Inc., 1963.

Eiserer, Paul E., "Research Roles," in *The School Psychologist.* Washington, D. C.: The Center for Applied Research in Education, Inc., 1963, pp. 93–100.

Gage, N. L., ed., *Handbook of Research on Teaching.* Skokie: Rand McNally & Co., 1963.

Gray, Susan W., "The Data-Oriented Problem Solver: I. The Research Role of the School Psychologist," in *The Psychologist in the Schools*. New York: Holt, Rinehart & Winston, Inc., 1963, pp. 54–79.

Hare, Paul A., *Handbook of Small Group Research*. New York: Free Press of Glencoe, Inc., 1962.

Hilgard, E. R., "Perspective on the Relationship between Learning Theory and Educational Practice," *National Social Study Education Yearbook*, 63 (1964), 402–415.

Hirst, Wilma E., "Research," in *Know your School Psychologist*. New York: Grune & Stratton, Inc., 1963, pp. 203–212.

Hobson, James R., William Itkin, Tom A. Lamke, and Harriet E. O'Shea, "How Research on Intellectually Gifted Children Can Be Done," *The University of Kansas Bulletin of Education*, 16 (May, 1962), 107–116.

Kerlinger, Fred N., *Foundations of Behavioral Research*. New York: Holt, Rinehart & Winston, Inc., 1964.

Krathwohl, David R., ed., "Methodology of Educational Research," *Review of Educational Research*. 27, No. 5 (December, 1957).

Lighthall, F. K., and R. C. Diedrich, "The School Psychologist, The Teacher, and Research Willing and Reluctant Cooperation," *Psychology in the Schools*, 2 (April, 1965), 106–110.

Lindquist, E. F., *Design and Analysis of Experiments in Psychology and Education*. Boston: Houghton Mifflin Company, 1953.

McAshan, Hildreth H., *Elements of Educational Research*. New York: McGraw-Hill Book Company, 1963.

"Methodology of Educational Research," *Review of Educational Research*. 27, No. 5 (December, 1957).

Mussen, Paul H., *Handbook of Research Methods in Child Development*. New York: John Wiley & Sons, Inc., 1960.

Reger, R., "The School Psychologist and Research for the Future," *Psychology in the Schools*, I (October, 1964), 38–53.

Scott, William A., and Michael Wertheimer, *Introduction to Psychological Research*. New York: John Wiley & Sons, Inc., 1962.

Schutz, R. E., "The Control of Error in Educational Experimentation," *School Review*, 74 (Summer, 1966), 150–159.

Siegel, Sidney, *Non Parametric Statistics for the Behavioral Sciences*. New York: McGraw-Hill Book Company, Inc., 1952.

Travers, Robert M. W., *An Introduction of Educational Research*, 2nd ed. New York: The Macmillan Company, 1964.

Van Dalen, Deobold B., *Understanding Educational Research: An Introduction*. New York: McGraw-Hill Book Company, 1962.

Wert, James B., Charles O. Neidt, and J. Stanley Ahmann, *Statistical*

Methods in Educational and Psychological Research. New York: Appleton-Century-Crofts, 1954.

White, Mary Alice, and Myron W. Harris, "Research," in *The School Psychologist.* New York: Harper & Row, Publishers, pp. 366–377.

Wrightstone, J. Wayne, "Research in School Psychology," in *Professional School Psychology,* Vol. I. New York: Grune & Stratton, Inc., 1960, pp. 264–274.

NEWTON S. METFESSEL

20

The School Psychologist's Role
in Developing Creativity

The Zeitgeist of Creativity in
Historical Perspective

An empirical analysis of historical writing indicates that chroniclers have attempted to capture the *Zeitgeist* (spirit of the times) of recent centuries with characteristic labels. The Seventeenth Century, for example—the period of Sir Isaac Newton in Science, Rembrandt in painting, and Dryden in literary criticism—has been referred to as the Age of Enlightenment.[1] The Eighteenth Century—the time of Rousseau, Haydn, and Priestly, the "fathers" of the French Revolution, the symphony, and carbon dioxide, respectively, has been termed the Age of Reason.[2, 3]

[1] Antonino Bruno, *Cartesio e l'illuminismo: Rene Descartes, 1596–1650*. Bari: G. Laterza, 1949.
[2] Sir Harold George Nicolson, *The Age of Reason, 1700–1789*. London: Constable, 1960.
[3] Robert B. Mowat, *The Age of Reason: The Continent of Europe in the Eighteenth Century*. Boston: Houghton Mifflin Company, 1934.

Historians label the Nineteenth Century as the Age of Progress [4] with the mid-point of the century designated as both the end of the industrial revolution and the beginning of scientific-metallurgy. The young student of today will not have to wait the turn of the century (today's kindergartener will be in his forties) to find what "catch word" has been applied to his time. Newspapers and other communicative media have *already* labeled the Twentieth Century with a plethora of pronouncements. Presently, public air terminals are erected in tribute to the "Jet Age." Research laboratories representing a variety of academic disciplines are dedicated to the "Age of Space." Public fairs and armed forces displays emphasizing the "Age of Rocketry" are commonplace. These are some manifestations of the *Zeitgeist* of creativity from which the psychologist's role in developing creativity has emerged.[5] A perspective of the societal *Zeitgeist* in general and the professional (psychological and educational) *Zeitgeist* in particular provides the necessary framework for discerning what is perhaps the newest role expectancy of psychologists in education.

The Societal Zeitgeist in National Perspective

The heredity of the *Zeitgeist* of creativity may be conceptualized by integrating recognized probabilities into a multiple-causation model.

Possibly conceived with the explosion of the atomic bomb in 1945 [6, 7] the *Zeitgeist* was probably born *circa* 1950.[8, 9] Ten major "god parents" are identifiable during the neonatal period, all of which, it must be emphasized, are still forces sustaining and expanding the *Zeitgeist* today:

1. The international struggle for the sustainment of our democratic way of life.

2. Heavy political-military demands for innovative weapons and weapon systems.

3. Economic pressures for new processes and markets.

4. Social changes, in that creative expressions formerly minimized by class and caste protocols are being released by the *avant garde* of minority groups.

[4] A. A. Ekirch, *Idea of Progress in America, 1815–1860*. New York: Columbia University Press, 1944.

[5] J. P. Guilford, "Traits of Creativity," in *Creativity and Its Cultivation*, ed. H. Anderson. New York: Harper & Row, Publishers, 1959.

[6] C. R. Hulbeck, "The Creative Personality," *American Journal of Psychoanalysis*, 5 (1945), 49–58.

[7] Frank Barron, "The Creative Individual," *Conference Report, California Educational Research and Guidance Association* (October, 1959).

[8] E. G. Boring, "Great Men and Scientific Progress," *Proceedings of the American Philosophical Society*, 94 (1950), 339–351.

[9] J. P. Guilford, "Traits of Creativity," in *Creativity and Its Cultivation*, p. 142.

5. Industrial discoveries of the industrial revolution in modern technology.

6. Increased automation that demands less thinking of a problem-solving nature on the job, often causing boredom that seeks creative outlets.

7. Creative release from boredom caused by increased leisure time off the job.

8. The personal recognition that innovation, invention, and discovery have value in increasing one's material well-being.

9. Rebellion against demands for conformity and social adjustment.

10. The broad emphasis on the "good life" stemming in part from democratic ideals which hold that every man is entitled to an opportunity to express himself freely and be his most individual self.

Further elaboration and discussion on contributing causes may be found in the analyses of Barron,[10] Boring,[11] Guilford,[12] Snow,[13] and Wilson.[14]

The Zeitgeist in Professional Psychology and Education in Brief Perspective

The first systematic attack of significance on the problem of creativity was inaugurated in 1950 by J.P. Guilford.[15] He found that, of approximately 121,000 titles listed in the previous twenty-three years of *Psychological Abstracts*, only 186 were indexed as definitely pertaining to the subject of creativity. Quantitatively, this represents less than two-tenths of one per cent of the articles in professional psychology for a quarter century. Although research knowledge about creativity is still scanty, some of the major research centers expanding the *Zeitgeist* may be identified as follows:

1. *The University of Southern California.* Over a decade of research by Guilford [16, 17, 18, 19, 20, 21, 22, 23, 24] and his co-workers [25, 26, 27, 28] has been de-

---

[10] Frank Barron, "The Creative Individual," *Conference Report, Calif. Educational Research and Guidance Assn.* (October, 1959).

[11] E. G. Boring, "Great Men and Scientific Progress," *Proceedings of the Amer. Phil. Soc.*, 94 (1950), 339–351.

[12] J. P. Guilford, "Traits of Creativity," in *Creativity and Its Cultivation*, p. 142–161.

[13] C. P. Snow, *The Two Cultures and the Scientific Revolution*. New York: Cambridge University Press, 1960.

[14] R. C. Wilson, "Creativity," in *Education for the Gifted*, National Society for the Study of Education, 57th Yearbook, Part II, pp. 108–126. Chicago: University of Illinois Press, 1958.

[15] J. P. Guilford, "Creativity," *American Psychologist*, 5 (1950), 444–454.

[16] J. P. Guilford, *et al., A Factor-Analytic Study of Creative Thinking*, Vol. I: *Hypotheses and Description of Tests*. Los Angeles: University of Southern California, 1951.

voted to the factor analytic investigations of human intellectual abilities. Primary emphasis today is the validation of Guilford's model of the "Structure of Intellect." [29, 30, 31] This three-dimensional schematic proposes that there are 120 different kinds of intelligence. It will be discussed in detail later in this chapter. The monumental findings from adult males in a military population have been increasingly generalized to school age subjects.[32]

2. *The University of Minnesota.* The largest amount of research directly applicable to subjects of school age has been provided by E. P. Torrance and associates at the Bureau of Educational Research. The major contributions appear to be in the three areas: 1) the description of the nature, development, and sustainment of creative thinking and talent; [33, 34, 35, 36, 37, 38,]

[17] "The Nature of Creative Thinking," *The Meaning of Creativity,* Research Bulletin, pp. 5–9. Kutztown, Pa.: Eastern Arts Association, 1954.

[18] "Factors in Problem Solving," *ARTC Instructors' Journal,* 4 (1954), 197–204.

[19] "Creative Abilities in the Arts," *Psychological Review,* 64 (1957), 110–118.

[20] "Can Creativity Be Developed?" *Education Digest,* 24 (December, 1958), 49–51.

[21] "Creative Intelligence in Education," *Conference Report, California Educational Research and Guidance Association* (November, 1958).

[22] "Frontiers in Thinking Teachers Should Know About," *Reading Teacher,* 13 (1960), 176–182.

[23] J. P. Guilford, et al., "The Measurement of Individual Differences in Originality," *Psychological Bulletin,* 50 (1953), 362–370.

[24] J. P. Guilford, J. W. Frick, P. R. Christensen, and P. R. Merrifield, "A Factor-Analytic Study of Problem-Solving Abilities," *Reports from the Psychological Laboratory,* No. 24. Los Angeles: University of Southern California, 1960.

[25] R. C. Wilson, J. P. Guilford, P. R. Christensen, and D. J. Lewis, "A Factor-Analytical Study of Creative Thinking Abilities," *Psychometrika,* 19, No. 4 (1954), 297–311.

[26] R. M. Berger, J. P. Guilford, and P. R. Christensen, "A Factor-Analytic Study of Planning Abilities," *Psychological Monographs,* 71, No. 6 (1957), 1–31.

[27] P. R. Christensen, J. P. Guilford, and R. C. Wilson, "Relations of Creative Responses to Working Time and Instructions," *Journal of Experimental Psychology,* 53 (1957), 82–88.

[28] P. R. Merrifield, "A Factor-Analytic Study of Problem-Solving Abilities." Unpublished Ph.D. dissertation, University of Southern California, 1959.

[29] J. P. Guilford, "The Structure of Intellect," *Psychological Bulletin,* 53 (1956), 277–279.

[30] ————, "Three Faces of Intellect," *American Psychologist,* 14 (1959), 469–479.

[31] ———— and P. R. Merrifield, *The Structure of Intellect Model: Its Uses and Implications,* Reports from the Psychological Laboratory, No. 24. Los Angeles: University of Southern California, 1960.

[32] ————, P. R. Merrifield, and A. B. Cox, *Creative Thinking in Children at the Junior High Levels,* Reports from the Psychological Laboratory, No. 26. Los Angeles: University of Southern California, 1961.

[33] E. P. Torrance, "Factors Affecting Creative Thinking in Children: An Interim Research Report," *Merrill-Palmer* Quarterly, 7 (1961), 171–180.

[34] "Current Research on the Nature of Creative Talent," *Journal of Counseling Psychology,* 6, No. 4 (1959), 309–316.

[35] *Sex-Role Identification and Creative Thinking.* Minneapolis: Bureau of Educational Research, University of Minnesota, 1959.

[39, 40] 2) the important, largely verifying replications of the Chicago studies of Getzels and Jackson; [41, 42] and finally 3) the development of assessment devices for creativity.[43, 44] In the latter instance, the school psychologist may be particularly interested in the "Ask-and-Guess-Test." [45] Torrance's volume, *Guiding Creative Talent* [46] represents an excellent summary of his research.

3. *The University of Chicago.* The various University of Chicago investigations into giftedness have included the studies on creativity conducted by Getzels and Jackson,[47, 48] and summarized in one volume, *Creativity and Intelligence.*[49] This work probably represents the most important single source of information for school personnel on this issue. The major focus of their work was on:

. . . The identification of two groups of students each exhibiting as its salient characteristic a different type of cognitive excellence—the one high in

---

[36] E. P. Torrance, F. B. Baker, and J. E. Bowers, *Explorations in Creative Thinking in the Early School Years*, Vol. IV: *Manipulation of Objects and Inventiveness.* Minneapolis: Bureau of Educational Research, University of Minnesota, 1959.

[37] ————, K. N. DeYoung, S. N. Ghei, and J. Kincannon, *Explorations in Creative Thinking in Mental Hygiene*, Vol. I: *Alone or in Groups?* Minneapolis: Bureau of Educational Research, University of Minnesota, 1958.

[38] "Explorations in Creative Thinking in the Early School Years," *Research Memoranda.* Minneapolis: Bureau of Educational Research, University of Minnesota, 1960.

[39] E. P. Torrance and J. E. Bowers, *Explorations in Creative Thinking in the Early School Years*, Vol. III: *Sex Roles and Appropriateness of Stimuli.* Minneapolis: Bureau of Educational Research, University of Minnesota, 1959.

[40] E. P. Torrance, K. N. DeYoung, S. N. Ghei, and H. W. Michie, *Explorations in Creative Thinking in Mental Hygiene*, Vol. II: *Some Characteristics of the More Creative Individuals.* Minneapolis: Bureau of Educational Research, University of Minnesota, 1958.

[41] *Educational Achievement of the Highly Intelligent and the Highly Creative: Eight Partial Republications of the Getzels-Jackson Study.* Minneapolis: Bureau of Educational Research, University of Minnesota, 1960.

[42] *Explorations in Creative Thinking in the Early School Years*, Vol. VI: *Highly Intelligent and Highly Creative Children in a Laboratory School.* Minneapolis: Bureau of Educational Research, University of Minnesota, 1959.

[43] E. P. Torrance, *et al.*, *Assessing the Creative Thinking Abilities of Children.* Minneapolis: Bureau of Educational Research, 1960.

[44] "Measurement and Development of the Creative Thinking Abilities," in *The 1961 Year Book of Education.* London: Evans Brothers Ltd., 1961.

[45] E. P. Torrance and H. H. Radig, *The Ask-and-Guess-Test: Scoring Manual and Rationale.* Minneapolis: Bureau of Educational Research, 1959.

[46] E. P. Torrance, *Guiding Creative Talent.* Englewood Cliffs, N. J.: Prentice-Hall, Inc., 1962.

[47] J. W. Getzels and P. W. Jackson, "The Study of Giftedness: a Multidimensional Approach," in *The Gifted Student*, Cooperative Research Monograph, No. 2, pp. 1–18. Washington, D. C.: U. S. Government Printing Office, 1961.

[48] ————, "The Meaning of 'Giftedness'—an Examination of an Expanding Concept," *Phi Delta Kappan*, 40 (1958), 75–77.

[49] ————, *Creativity and Intelligence.* New York: John Wiley & Sons, Inc., 1962.

intelligence but not concomitantly high in creativity, the other high in creativity but not concomitantly high in intelligence.[50]

Other objectives [51] included the analyses of these two groups as it related to their morality and psychological adjustment, school behavior, including tested abilities, values, fantasies, aspirations, and career planning. Important studies of the differential parental and teacher perceptions of these subjects was also undertaken.

The works of Stein [52, 53] have also been of consequence to school psychologists, particularly his bibliographical text, *Creativity and the Individual*.[54]

4. *The University of California*. Research into five major areas of importance has emanated from the *Institute of Personality Assessment and Research* as follows: 1) the determination of a definition of creativity; 2) a description of the creative process; 3) an analysis of the qualities of creative individuals; 4) the ascertainment of the qualities that distinguish creative products; and 5) an investigation into the nature of environments that facilitate and inhibit creative thought and action.[55] Findings by MacKinnon,[56, 57, 58, 59] Barron,[60, 61, 62, 63, 64, 65, 66, 67] and Crutchfield [68, 69, 70] have been based on assessments and evaluations of adult subjects from all walks of life.

[50] *Ibid.*, p. 11.

[51] *Ibid.*

[52] M. I. Stein, "A Transactional Approach to Creativity," in *The 1955 University of Utah Research Conference on the Identification of Creative Scientific Talent*, pp. 171–181. Salt Lake City: University of Utah Press, 1956.

[53] ———— and B. Meer, "Perceptual Organization in a Study of Creativity," *Journal of Psychology*, 37 (1954), 39–43.

[54] ———— and Shirley J. Heinze, *Creativity and the Individual*. New York: The Free Press of Glencoe, Inc., 1960.

[55] Lake Tahoe Conference on "The Creative Person." Berkeley, California: Institute of Personality Assessment and Research, University of California at Berkeley, 1961.

[56] Donald W. MacKinnon, "The Highly Effective Individual," *Teachers College Record*, 41 (1960), 367–378.

[57] "What Do We Mean by Talent and How Do We Test for It," in *The Search for Talent*, pp. 10–29. New York: College Entrance Exam Board, 1960.

[58] *The Identification of Creative Scientific Talent*, Proceedings of the 1957 Research Conference, University of Utah. Salt Lake City: University of Utah Press, 1958.

[59] "Some Variables Functioning in Productivity and Creativity," in *The Second University of Utah Research Conference on the Identification of Creative Scientific Talent*, ed. C. W. Taylor. Salt Lake City: University of Utah Press, 1958.

[60] Frank Barron, "Creativity, A Symposium," *National Education Association Journal*, 50 (March, 1961), 17–27.

[61] "The Psychology of Imagination," *Scientific American*, 119, No. 3 (1958), 150–166.

[62] "Originality in Relation to Personality and Intellect," *Journal of Personality*, 25 (1957), 730–742.

[63] "The Disposition Towards Originality," *Journal of Abnormal and Social Psychology*, 60 (1955), 478–485.

[64] "Threshold for the Perception of Human Movement in Inkblots," *Journal of Consulting Psychology*, 19 (1955), 33–38.

[65] "Some Relationships Between Originality and Style of Personality," *American Psychologist*, 9 (1954), 326.

5. *The University of Utah.* Several research conferences on the identification of creative scientific talent, coordinated by C. W. Taylor [71, 72, 73, 74, 75, 76] have attempted to provide opportunity for interaction among those from varied disciplines engaged in research programs involving creativity. Another from this center, Brewster Ghiselin [77] contributed *The Creative Process,*[78] a summary of the views of thirty-eight well known individuals, e.g., Jung and Einstein, on the subject of creativity.

6. *The Pennsylvania State University.* This center was under the leadership of a major authority in the area of art education, the late Viktor Lowenfeld. His early works [79, 80] were followed by a significant volume for educators interested in child psychology and esthetics, *Creative and Mental Growth.*[81] One of the most important works for school psychology was his replication

[66] "Some Personality Correlates of Independence of Judgment," *Journal of Personality,* 21 (1953), 287–297.

[67] Frank Barron and G. S. Welsh, "Artistic Perception as a Possible Factor in Personality Style: Its Measurement by a Figure Preference Test," *Journal of Psychology,* 33 (1952), 199–203.

[68] R. S. Crutchfield, *The Gottschaldt Figures Test.* Palo Alto, California: Consulting Psychologists Press, 1962.

[69] "Conformity and Character," *American Psychologist,* 10 (1955), 191–198.

[70] R. S. Crutchfield, D. G. Woodworth, and Ruth E. Albrecht, *Perceptual Performance and the Effective Person,* Technical Note WADC-TN-58-60, ASTIA No. 151039. Lackland Air Force Base, Texas: Personnel Laboratory, Wright Air Development Center.

[71] C. W. Taylor, ed., *The Second University of Utah Research Conference on the Identification of Creative Scientific Talent.* Salt Lake City: University of Utah Press, 1958.

[72] *The 1955 University of Utah Research Conference on the Identification of Creative Scientific Talent.* Salt Lake City: University of Utah Press, 1956.

[73] *The Third University of Utah Research Conference on the Identification of Creative Scientific Talent,* p. 324. Salt Lake City: University of Utah Press, 1959.

[74] C. W. Taylor and J. L. Holland, "Development and Application of Tests of Creativity," *Review of Educational Research,* 32, No. 1 (1962), 91–102.

[75] C. W. Taylor, W. R. Smith, and Bernard Ghiselin, "Analyses of Multiple Criteria of Creativity and Productivity of Scientists," in *The Third University of Utah Research Conference on the Identification of Creative Scientific Talent,* ed. C. W. Taylor, pp. 5–28. Salt Lake City: University of Utah Press, 1959.

[76] C. W. Taylor, et al., *Explorations in the Measurement and Prediction of Contributions of One Sample of Scientists,* Technical Report ASD-TR-61-96. Lackland Air Force Base, Texas: Personnel Laboratory, Aeronautical Systems Division, Air Force Systems Command, 1961.

[77] B. Ghiselin, "The Creative Process and Its Relation to the Identification of Creative Talent," in *The 1955 University of Utah Research Conference on the Identification of Creative Scientific Talent,* pp. 195–203. Salt Lake City: University of Utah Press, 1956.

[78] ————, *The Creative Process.* New York: Mentor, 1955.

[79] Viktor Lowenfeld, *The Nature of Creative Activity.* New York: Harcourt, Brace & World, Inc., 1939.

[80] "The Meaning of Creativity for Art Education," in *The Meaning of Creativity,* Research Bulletin, pp. 15–16. Kutztown, Pa.: Eastern Arts Association, 1954.

[81] ———— and W. L. Brittain, *Creative and Mental Growth,* 4th ed. New York: The Macmillan Company, 1964.

of Guilford's findings which indicated that creativity in scientific disciplines has much in common with the esthetic arts.[82]

7. *The University of Buffalo.* The Creative Education Foundation Program, led by Parnes and Meadow [83, 84] has import in the investigation of the relationship of group dynamics, "brainstorming," etc., to creative output.

As Taylor [85] has pointed out, until a few years ago, research studies were not undertaken in creativity because of the complexities involved. Today is a transitional period in research in that many of the most formidable research projects are not yet published or are still in process.

The Zeitgeist in Today's Schools

It is apparent that one of the most exciting and expanding concepts identifiable in the schools today is the creative process. Without implying generalizations to the total population it is clear that school administrators receive training from recent texts titled *Creative School Administration,*[86] teachers read bibliographies which cite *Creative Teaching,*[87] and students in English receive assignments in anthologies such as *The Creative Vision.*[88] From what directions has this ebullient spirit developed and why should the school psychologist be concerned?

The primary source of interest in creativity has been and will probably continue to be related to interest in the gifted child.[89] Differential diagnosis of these two attributes, intellect and creativity, represents one of the most challenging needs in education—a need of direct concern to the school psychologist. The development of this task has a brief though significant history.

In 1950, when school psychology as a discipline was in its infancy, public school interest in making special provision for the gifted began to be perceptible. In that year the Educational Policies Commission [90] issued a

[82] "Current Research on Creativity," *NEA J.,* 47 (1958), 538–540.

[83] S. J. Parnes and A. Meadow, "Effects of 'Brainstorming' Instructions on Creative Problem Solving by Trained and Untrained Subjects," *Journal of Educational Psychology,* 50 (1959), 171–176.

[84] ————, "Evaluation of Persistence Effects Produced by a Creative Problem-Solving Course," *Psychological Reports,* 7 (1960), 357–361.

[85] C. W. Taylor and J. L. Holland, "Development and Application of Tests of Creativity," *Review of Educational Research,* 32, No. 1 (1962), 91–102.

[86] Harold G. Shane, *Creative School Administration.* New York: Holt, Rinehart & Winston, Inc., 1954.

[87] H. Zirbes, *Spurs to Creative Teaching.* New York: G. P. Putnam's Sons, 1959.

[88] M. Block, ed., *The Creative Vision.* New York: Grove Press, Inc., 1960.

[89] J. P. Guilford, *et al., Creative Thinking in Children at the Junior High School Levels,* Reports from the Psychological Laboratory, No. 26. Los Angeles: University of Southern California, 1961.

[90] Educational Policies Commission, *Education of the Gifted.* Washington, D. C.: National Education Association, 1950.

strong declaration indicting the waste of human resources resulting from neglect of those with superior intellect. The commission also made strong proposals for remediation of the problem.

In 1950, only thirty-six cities had special programs for the gifted.[91] In comparison, according to Harris,[92] in 1940, there were 604 cities in the United States reporting special educational attention to the mentally retarded and deficient. In 1954, a nation-wide survey of secondary schools indicated an upswing in all varieties of special programs designed to meet the needs of the academically talented.[93] In general, however, the schools of the nation were still oriented towards a heterogeneous pattern of grouping and "enrichment" for the gifted.

In October, 1957, however, with the launching of Sputnik I, the educational dictum of "equal experiences for all" was sent perambulating in orbits of controversy. For the first time in American history, education was cited by political and military leaders as a cause of political-military-scientific failure. Professional educators countered that the United States had the necessary humans and hardware for a pre-Sputnik satellite launching but lacked the political-military-scientific harmony, coordination, and subsidy for an effective space program.

Notwithstanding the lack of resolution of these arguments, the general demand for special programs for the gifted was both widespread and immediate. As a result, the school psychologist was soon brought face to face with the *Zeitgeist* of creativity from *both* societal and professional founts. Recent research [94] had isolated and identified many abilities labeled as "creative" as separate from those termed "intellectual." Other findings [95, 96] indicated that a major attitudinal retooling among many educators was necessary for creativity to develop in the classroom. The roots of creativity as a separate discipline of knowledge became firmly established. Indeed, in Fleigler and Bish's 1959 summary of research and comment on the gifted to that time, the task of the school psychologist was exemplified with the statement, "Development of creativity is the crux of educating the gifted." [97]

[91] Dale B. Harris, "A Psychologist Looks at the Issues," in *Talent and Education,* ed. E. P. Torrance, p. 126. Minneapolis: The University of Minnesota Press, 1960.

[92] *Ibid.*

[93] Abraham J. Tannenbaum, "History of Interest in the Gifted," in *Education for the Gifted, National Society for the Study of Education, 57th Yearbook,* Part II, pp. 21–38. Chicago: University of Chicago Press, 1958.

[94] Getzels and Jackson, "The Meaning of 'Giftedness'—An Examination of an Expanding Concept," *Phi Delta Kappan,* 40 (1958), 75–77.

[95] E. P. Torrance, *et al., Explorations in Creative Thinking in Mental Hygiene: I* (Minneapolis: University of Minnesota Press, 1961).

[96] ———, *Explorations in Creative Thinking in Mental Hygiene: II* (Minneapolis: University of Minnesota Press, 1961).

[97] L. A. Fieger and C. E. Bish, "The Gifted and the Talented," *Review of Educational Research,* 29 (1959), 408–450.

Towards a Definition of Creativity

Probably no single term in recent pedagogical history has been so widely applied and yet so infrequently defined as "creativity." Strang [98] referred to it as the "educational catch word of the year," with the admonition to all concerned that it must not be allowed to degenerate into "jargon." Confucius, in the fifth century B.C., was purportedly asked by one of his students, "Master, what is needed to change the world?" Confucius replied, "A proper definition of things." It appears, however, at this time, that no one definition of creativity will ever be universally accepted. This problem is comparable to the lack of a satisfactory verbal formula for terms such as "intelligence" and "personality." As in these instances the school psychologist will have to develop a definitive model that is compatible with his operational objectives. To this end the resolution of the following problem areas is recommended.

THE QUALITATIVE DIFFERENCES IN CREATIVITY

As the Carnegie Report on *Creativity* [99] has emphasized, creativity differs in kind as well as degree. Creativity encompasses the spectrum of sensory experiences, e.g., it may be heard in the sixteen bar "riff" of a jazz pianist, seen in the symbolic description of a new theory, tactually appraised at a synthetic fabric exhibit, gustatorially assessed with a novel soufflé, and kinesthetically experienced on the dance floor. These facts emphasize the point that creativity is within the province of all subject matter.

THE PROBLEM OF OPERATIONAL DEFINITION

For many school psychologists, problems of definition are resolved through utilization of operational definitions. That is, "intelligence" is defined as the score on a scholastic aptitude test, "scientific interest" is defined as the score on the sub-test of an inventory such as the Kuder, and "personality" is often the sum total of the "Assets" and "Liabilities" sub-scores on the California Test of Personality. Since with tests of creativity, adequate validity coefficients, reliability indices, and normative data are frequently lacking in terms of generalizability to school age children, the problem of defining creativity operationally by "The score on test X" has many limitations at present.

[98] Ruth Strang, "Developing Creative Powers of Gifted Children," in *Creativity of Gifted and Talented Children.* New York: Bureau of Publications, Teachers College, Columbia University, 1959.

[99] "Creativity," *Carnegie Corporation of New York Quarterly,* 9, No. 3 (1961).

The problem of operational limitations is aggravated in subjective contexts. For example, assume that you, as the school psychologist, have been asked to be one of the judges at a "Creative Cake Baking Contest." If you are to pursue operational criteria for making judgments you would not judge a cake on its taste, odor, coloring, or texture but only on the specific operations performed in following the recipe. This would reward conforming behavior perhaps. And it could well be argued that a truly creative cake would not follow a rigorous recipe.

For pupil personnel workers interested in operational definitions of entities, the attitude should not be one of discouragement. The school psychologist may find a presently developed test of creativity which appears to meet his objectives without rigorous criteria of applicability to school age children. Through careful research over a period of time, the school psychologist could well develop his own coefficients of prediction and precision along with local normative data for judgmental evaluations.

Original thinking and creative thinking. As Whiting [100] has indicated, creative thinking involves the production of ideas that are both new and valuable. Orginal thinking simply involves the production of new ideas. This view is corroborated by the Carnegie report on "Creativity" as follows:

> We understand that to be creative means to be original—although on thinking about it that can't be all there is to it. The hallucinations of a madman are often highly original, but we do not call them, or him "creative." [101]

Duplicative imagination and creative imagination. Imagination has been defined by Swartz as, "The recall to consciousness of mental pictures originally produced through the senses, without the present stimulation of these senses in the original way." [102] He then differentiates between "duplicative imagination" which is synonymous with simple mnemonics, and "creative imagination" which is the *recombination* of elements from previous experience.

Systematic thinking and creative insight. In the case of systematic thinking, according to Hutchinson [103] the objective, problem, and method are clearly defined. The process involved is characterized by slow deliberation and orderly methodological protocols. Little frustration or emotion is consciously felt. Creative insight is accompanied by the appearance of the unpredicted,

---

[100] C. S. Whiting, *Creative Thinking.* New York: Reinhold Publishing Corp., 1958, p. 168.

[101] "Creativity," *Carnegie Corp. of N. Y. Quarterly,* 9, No. 3 (1961), 1.

[102] D. Swartz, "Developing Creative Imagination," *High Points,* 14 (1932), 43–46.

[103] E. D. Hutchinson, *How To Think Creatively,* p. 237. New York: Abingdon Press, 1949.

the perception of novel relationships, intense feelings of frustration, and finally, adequacy and exhilaration. There are four essential stages in creative insight: preparation or orientation, frustration, period or moment of insight, and finally, the stage of verification, elaboration, or evaluation.

Ingenuity and creativity. Flanagan [104] regards ingenuity as a process of ingenious problem-solving characterized by neatness, cleverness, or surprise. He indicates that ingenuity is much narrower than creativity in that it is statistically independent of other traits and is the result of an innate quality of the individual. Flanagan has developed a test of "ingenuity" for use with high school students.

Productivity and creativity. Although quantity has been found to be related to quality, Dennis,[105] in a study of variations in productivity among scientific authors, found ten per cent of the men did roughly fifty per cent of the work output. Also, Taylor,[106] in an investigation of variables related to creativity and productivity among research men in laboratory settings, found correlations in the 0.60's. However, it is axiomatic to state that quantity *per se* is no guarantee of qualitative value in production.

A Proposed Definition for School Psychologists

Perhaps the most intensive analysis of the problem of definition was the six and one-half year study of this issue conducted at the Institute of Personality Assessment and Research at the University of California. The director of the institute, MacKinnon, summarized the problem area and their findings as follows:

> The first task that must be faced by any group who would study creativity is to decide what they will consider creativity to be, since creativity has been so variously described and defined. It has seemed to us that true creativity fulfills at least three conditions. It involves a response that is novel or at least statistically infrequent. But novelty or originality of behavior, while a necessary aspect of creativity, is not sufficient. If a response is to lay claim to being a part of the creative process, it must be adaptive, or of, reality. It must serve to solve a problem, fit a situation, or accomplish some recognizable goal. And thirdly, true

[104] J. C. Flanagan, "The Definition and Measurement of Ingenuity," in *The Second Research Conference on the Identification of Creative Scientific Talent*, pp. 109–118. Salt Lake City: University of Utah Press, 1958.

[105] F. W. Dennis, "Age and Productivity Among Scientists," *Science*, 123 (1956), 724–725.

[106] D. W. Taylor, "Variables Related to Creativity and Productivity among Men in Two Research Laboratories," in *The Second Research Conference on the Identification of Creative Scientific Talent*, pp. 20–54. Salt Lake City: University of Utah Press, 1958.

creativity involves a sustaining of the original insight, an evaluation and elaboration of it, and developing it to the full.[107]

The complexities of definition are compounded by those of identification.

Creativeness and Giftedness

The *Zeitgeist* of creativity, as indicated previously, has emanated from a spirit of concern for the gifted. The great majority of contemporary programs for creative youngsters are closely allied or congruent with programs for the gifted. The view that the crux of educating the gifted is the development of creativity is being increasingly advanced. This concept is important to the school psychologist who may find himself confronted with students who are gifted but not especially creative, along with those who are both intellectually and creatively eminent. Certainly concern for the intellectually gifted should not preclude the school psychologist from identifying those whose tested abilities do not indicate giftedness and yet *are* creative. The import of these statements is reflected in the great interest shown by psychologists in the "classic" work on this issue, *Creativity and Intelligence,*[108] by Jacob Getzels and Philip Jackson. This work is basically a summation of three related investigations commencing in 1958 and representing a major portion of the research conducted on "giftedness" undertaken at the University of Chicago.

The major objective of their research was to investigate possible differences between the *creative* child and the *intelligent* child. The instruments employed by Getzels and Jackson are here described in some detail as they indicate important directions in responding to the query, "How is the creative child identified?" These tests were taken or adapted from Guilford or Cattell or constructed especially for the study. They were described as follows:

> WORD ASSOCIATION. The subject was asked to give as many definitions as possible to fairly common stimulus words (e.g., 'bolt,' 'bark,' 'sack'). His score depended on the absolute number of definitions and the number of different categories into which these definitions could be put. For example, a student obtaining a low score on this instrument might reply to the stimulus word "bolt" by saying, "To fasten down; to secure; bolt a door; bolt a hatch on a ship." A student obtaining a high score might say in response to the same stimulus, "To fasten down; to run away quickly; to eat food rapidly; a bolt of cloth; a horse bolts; a bolt of lightning."

> USES FOR THINGS. The idea for this test derives from a description of two similar tests used by J. P. Guilford in his factor analytic studies of

---

[107] Donald W. MacKinnon, "The Study of Creativity," in *The Creative Person,* Lake Tahoe Conference Proceedings. Berkeley: Institute of Personality Assessment and Research, University of California at Berkeley, 1961.

[108] J. Getzels and P. Jackson, *Creativity and Intelligence.* New York: John Wiley and Sons, Inc., 1962.

cognitive ability. The subject was required to give as many uses as he could for objects that customarily have a stereotyped function attached to them, for example, "brick," "paper-clip," "toothpick." His score depended on the number and originality of the uses he mentioned. A student obtaining a low score on this test might reply to the object "brick" by saying, "Bricks can be used for building purposes. You can build a wall with brick, or you can build a sidewalk or a fireplace with a brick." A student obtaining a high score might say to the same item, "Bricks can be used for building. You can also use a brick as a paperweight. Use it as a doorstop. You can heat a brick and use it as a bed warmer. You can throw a brick as a weapon. You can hollow out the center of a brick and make an ashtray." Whereas the number of responses to the World Association Test is restricted by the universe of meanings commonly attached to the given word, the number of responses that can be given to the Uses Test is almost limitless, depending only on the respondent's ingenuity and inventiveness.

HIDDEN SHAPES. This test is part (G37) of Cattell's Objective-Analytic Test Battery and consists of eighteen simple geometric figures each of which is followed by four complex figures. The subject was required to find the geometric figure that was hidden in the more complex form or pattern.

FABLES. The subject was presented with four fables in which the last lines were missing. He was required to compose three different endings for each fable: a "moralistic," a "humorous," and a "sad" ending . . . The subject's score depended on the number, appropriateness and originality of the endings.

MAKE-UP PROBLEMS. The subject was presented with four complex paragraphs each containing many numerical statements. He was required to make up as many mathematical problems as he could with the information given. He himself did not have to solve the problems or know how to solve them. The point of the task was to be able to see varied and new problems and relationships in a single set of data . . . The subject's score depended on the number, appropriateness, complexity, and originality of the problems.[109]

A composite score on "creativity" was obtained by using the mean of the five tests. A Stanford-Binet, a WISC, or a Henmon-Nelson score was available for each of the adolescent subjects as a measure of "intelligence." The scores obtained from the WISC and the Henmon-Nelson were converted by regression equation to comparable Stanford-Binet IQ's.[110] Secondary students in the top twenty per cent in "creativity" but not in IQ were compared with a "high intelligence group" composed of seventeen boys and eleven girls in the top twenty per cent in IQ but not in creativity. A crucial fact is that students in the upper twenty per cent in *both* IQ and creativity were

[109] *Ibid.,* pp. 17–20.
[110] "The Study of Giftedness: A Multidimensional Approach," in *The Gifted Student,* Cooperative Research Monograph No. 2, pp. 1–18. Washington, D. C.: U. S. Government Printing Office, 1961.

not included in this study. The authors reported that there were "many such individuals."

The major findings [111] were as follows:

1. *School Achievement.* Despite a difference of 23 IQ points in the means of the two groups, both were found to be equally superior to the total population of students, the conclusion being that both the High-IQ Low-Creativity, and the High-Creativity Low-IQ groups are equally effective on standardized achievement tests.

2. *The Achievement Motive.* As measured by McClelland's n-Achievement Test, there were no significant differences in achievement "drive" between the two groups.

3. *Preference by Teachers.* The teachers exhibited a "clear-cut" preference for the high-IQ child over the high-creative child in that the ratings given the high IQ group were significantly higher than for the total population. The ratings given the "high creative group" did not differ from the total group. This finding, of course, is of paramount importance to school psychologists.

4. *Fantasy Production.* The investigators felt that a distinct difference existed between the two groups in fantasy production in that the "creative group" exhibited much more humor, novelty, and unexpected endings, in their written responses to six stimulus pictures.

5. *Personal Qualities.* It was found that the "creative" child rated wide range of interest, emotional stability, and sense of humor much higher than the "intelligent" child. In the latter instance, sense of humor, the investigators felt such a differential existed as to make it one of their most important findings. Members of the "intelligent" group rated IQ, high marks, character, and goal-directness much higher than their "creative" counterparts.

6. *Success Variables.* Distinct differences appeared in the fact that the "high IQ" child desired to introject those qualities which would lead to success in adult life; the "creative" child did not have "success in adult life" as a crucial criterion in his present perceptions.

The relationship between "intellectual" and "creative" abilities may not be as dichotomized as suggested by these findings. Metfessel, Handler, and Hall [112] studied twelve matched pairs of subjects with eminent intellect. Junior high school students with tested abilities on the Stanford-Binet (Form L) of 170 IQ and over were matched on the basis of identical sex, grade, chronological age (within four months), time of testing (within four

111 *Ibid.*
112 Newton Metfessel, Harry Handler, and James Hall, "A Comparative Investigation into Creative Abilities of Subjects from Two Domains of Eminent Intellect." Paper read at the State Convention, California Association of School Psychologists, Los Angeles, California, March 16, 1962.

months), and socio-economic level with counterparts with tested abilities between 140 and 155. The latter group significantly exceeded the former on three Guilford tests of creativity, "Different Uses," "Obvious Consequences," and "Remote Consequences." The 170 IQ group was significantly superior to the 140–155 group on the "Match Problems" test. Both groups were superior to the normative population for all of these tests. These findings suggest that creativity as measured by the Guilford tests should be conceptualized as within the province of all gifted students in varying degrees from high to low. In a related study, Schmadel [113] contrasted the scores of "gifted" students on Guilford tests of creativity with the total school population of which they were a part and found that the "gifted" students were significantly higher in tested creative abilities. In summary, from both the Metfessel and Schmadel studies, giftedness, *per se*, was no guarantee of creativeness, but neither were these factors to be conceived of as negatively correlated.

The Structure of Intellect

One approach for school psychologists to this problem of identification is where creative abilities and intellectual abilities are incorporated into one model. This is afforded by Guilford's *Structure of Intellect*.[114, 115]

The structure of intellect model briefly discussed previously proposes that there are 120 different kinds of intelligence. Nearly seventy of these have presently been identified. This first definite system of organizing the intellectual abilities proposes that intellectual abilities can be classified, first, according to the kind of operation involved. Four kinds of operations are proposed: cognition, memory, production (convergent thinking and divergent thinking), and evaluation. The cognitive abilities have to do with the discovery of information and with its recognition. These are ways of understanding or comprehension. A parallel group has to do with the retention of information in various forms classified as abilities of memory. Productive-thinking abilities involve the generation of new information out of given or known information. The original productive-thinkng abilities hypothesized by Guilford were later dichotomized into convergent production and divergent production. Divergent production is the most important single area of the Guilford model pertaining to creativity. In divergent production the objective

[113] Elnora Schmadel, "The Relationship of Creative Thinking Abilities and School Achievement." Doctoral dissertation, University of Southern California, 1960.

[114] J. P. Guilford, "The Structure of Intellect," *Psychological Bulletin*, LIII (1956), 277–295.

[115] ————, "Three Faces of Intellect," *American Psychologist*, XIV (1959), 469–479.

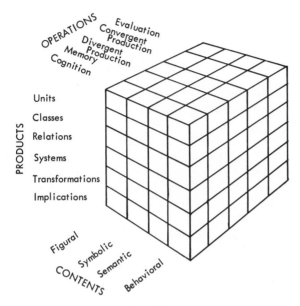

FIGURE 1. *Theoretical model for the complete "Structure of Intellect."*

is to produce a variety of ideas, all of which are logically possible. Convergent thinking pertains to the production of conclusions or other information that are fairly circumscribed and in some instances uniquely determined by the given information. In the instance of divergent thinking the person tends towards the unique, the novel, the speculative. Convergent thinking tends towards the normative and predictable. It has been proposed that Guilford's "convergent thinking" and "divergent thinking" are closely approximated by Rogers' concepts of "openness" and "defensiveness" and Maslow's "growth" and "safety" terms.[116, 117] Getzels and Jackson [118] then propose that divergency represents "intellectual inventiveness and innovation," while convergency typifies "intellectual acquisitiveness and conformity." Emphasis is made that the first instance emphasizes discovering what is yet to be known, while the latter focuses on knowing what is already discovered. Another parallel could also be made between the "open system" and "closed system" models proposed by Anderson.[119] Guilford's final category, evaluative abilities, have to do with decisions or judgments regarding "the correctness, soundess, consistency, or

116 H. A. Anderson, "Creativity in Perspective," p. 252.
117 Getzels and Jackson, *Creativity and Intelligence*, p. 14. New York, John Wiley & Sons, Inc., 1962.
118 *Ibid.*
119 Anderson, *op. cit.*, pp. 252–253.

suitability of information that is discovered, remembered, or produced." [120] These abilities are essentially those related to what is commonly termed "critical thinking."

THE DIMENSION OF CONTENTS

Intellectual abilities are here classified according to four kinds of content or material with which we have to interact: 1) figural, 2) symbolic, 3) semantic, and 4) behavioral.

When information is concrete and dealing in properties of form, size, shape, and texture, for example, it is termed "figural." When symbols are verbal such as numbers, letters, and words information is termed "symbolic." These abilities it must be emphasized do not pertain to the *meanings* or *representations* of things for which these symbols stand, for this is the "semantic" category. In other words, the ability to recognize the individual letters that make up a word would be an example of a "symbolic" ability. To be able to determine the meaning of that word is "semantic." "Our thoughts, desires, feelings, and intentions, and those of other individuals" [121] refers to the attempt to account for the information that we have concerning the "behavior" of ourselves. These abilities are closely related to what has been termed "social intelligence."

THE DIMENSION OF PRODUCTS

This dimension pertains to the products or forms into which the individual molds his information, and includes units, classes, relations, systems, changes, and implications. As Guilford [122] has indicated the technical meanings of these terms as applied in his model are nearly synonymous with their common meanings.

In using the Guilford model as a theory, it is important to state that a model is here proposed as a set of constructs specified in such a way that their connections are empirically evident. These constructs are represented by the individual cells in the three dimensional matrix, and represent the individual abilities. The formal connections between the constructs are deductible from the major categories of operations, contents, and products. These three are considered as formally independent in that no combination of operation, content, or product is logically excluded from the system. A model is used as a theory when connections between its constructs and the

[120] P. J. Guilford, "Creative Intelligence in Education," Conference Report, California Educational Research and Guidance Association (November, 1958), p. 2.
[121] _____, "Frontiers in Thinking that Teachers Should Know About," *Reading Teacher,* XIII (1960), 176–182.
[122] *Ibid.*

empirical world are hypothesized. The acceptance of the Guilford theory depends on the verification of such hypotheses. Factor analysis can be an hypothesis testing procedure through continued replications of assessments to divergent populations. The fact that many factors found with subjects from military and college populations have been increasingly found with subjects from school populations [123] indicates that the Guilford factors may represent a future source of tests of creative abilities for school psychologists. At the present time the school psychologist must realize that all tests of creative reasoning or complex problem solving are at the experimental level. Through research in his own school district the psychologist in the schools may find that these present tests, although experimental in nature, do measure criteria of creativity propounded by school personnel.

Standardized Tests of Creativity in Subject Areas

Anne Anastasi's intensive survey of contemporary tests identified only three as measures of creativity in subject areas, and all of these were in the field of art. These three measures of "creative artistic ability" were the Knauber, Lewerenz, and Horn instruments.[124] As Anastasi herself states the matter, "It is too early to know what will be the final outcome of current research on creativity." [125]

Conformity and Creativity

The issue of "creativity vs. conformity" is filled with many contradictions and very little research. Beatniks and Bohemians are not noticeably productive. Criminals, even the worst kind, are law-abiding *most* of the time. The child in our society is often told by his parents, "Be an individual." "Be creative." Minutes later, following the child's attempts at rugged individualism and/or divergency the parents may remonstrate, "Stop that this minute! Why can't you be like the other boys and girls—nice and quiet!"

Similarly, in the schools, the student often finds that he is pressured on the one hand to be an individual who is competitive, inventive, innovative, productive, resourceful, and indeed, "creative." On the other hand he must not forget that he is a "gentleman" who is a team-member, group-oriented, careful not to argue or question, and self-effacing—indeed, "conforming."

Creativity is honored by many. To others creativity is the offspring of eccentricity, mental aberrations, and even madness. This contemporary view

[123] Guilford, Merrifield, and Cox, *Creative Thinking in Children at the Junior High Levels,* No. 26.

[124] Anne Anastasi, *Psychological Testing,* p. 406. New York: The Macmillan Company, 1961.

[125] *Ibid,* p. 420.

has a long history. John Dryden, during the Seventeenth Century, the "Age of Enlightenment," wrote, "Great wits are to madness near allied." It is generally recognized that creativity is within the province of all human beings. That is to say that all human beings have the potential to be creative *some* of the time. Some individuals, however, have the proclivity to be creative in *most* situations that demand creative output to the extent that they are labeled as "creative individuals."

This involves the problem of *norms*. The juvenile delinquent, the drunk, the homosexual, the psychotic—all of these have been referred to as deviates. Many people have difficulty in applying the term deviate, even in a constructive opprobrium, to the creative individual. The fact exists, however, that the richly-endowed, highly-creative individual *does* deviate from a society of less-richly endowed, less-creative persons.

The appraisal of a deviation is inevitably made in the context of the social environment. The judgment that an individual is creative necessarily involves a comparison of the "creative" individual with some normative sample. The fact that an individual may be creative in art, but not in science or music, for example, increases the complexity of the problem, as does the fact that an individual may be designated as creative in one locale and not in another. Expert evaluations within the same locale may also vary.

Conformity, for our purposes here, is the *norm* of what is customary and expected within the limitations suggested above. The child is born unknowing and unconcerned about conformity, and seeks to wrest the satisfactions of his needs without regard to the group about him. As he develops, he is gradually initiated into group living; the belief being that what is best for the group is, over time, also best for the child. The group hopes to make a conforming individual out of the child by bending him towards acceptable group living so that they can endure him, nurture him, suffer little if any from his acts, and ideally, to make him a fruitful partner in cooperative living with his fellow man. Learning the graces of society is one of the major developmental experiences of the growing child. Some children learn their lessons too well. Others not at all. Extreme conformity costs the child his individuality. Extreme individuality costs the child the benefits to be gained from continued interactions with others.

THE "MODEL" CHILD VS. THE "ADJUSTED" CHILD [126]

Children's behavior, ostentatiously, often hides as much as it reveals. The ultra-conforming "model" child is often not the model adult. Children manifesting behavior characterized by "model" obedience, attentiveness, circumspect behavior, and mindfulness are often anxious, fearful, inhibited,

[126] Barney Katz and George F. J. Lehner, *Mental Hygiene in Modern Living.* New York: The Ronald Press Company, 1953.

and self-deprecating. "Adjusted" children who are impulsive, independent, assertive, and energetic are often found to be amiable, relaxed, secure, and confident.[127]

The Highly Creative Child

The intensive and voluminous research by Torrance and his associates describing the highly creative child may be summarized as follows:

HIGHLY CREATIVE CHILDREN

Personality characteristics: [128]

1. Have reputation for having wild, silly, and "naughty" ideas.
2. Produce ideas "off the beaten track, outside the mold."
3. Produce work characterized by humor, playfulness, relative lack of rigidity, and relaxation.

But often

1. Alienate their friends [129]
2. Are not well rounded [130]
3. Diverge from sex role expectancy [131]
4. Prefer to learn on their own [132]
5. Undertake difficult and dangerous tasks [133]
6. Have different values [134]
7. Can't stop working [135]
8. Try consciously to be different (search for their uniqueness) [136]

THE HIGHLY CREATIVE CHILD AND CONFORMITY

The highly creative child has a dual and difficult role because outward conformity and creative needs wage frequent and devastating wars upon each other. The child must learn to live with his peers, teachers, and the visual world around him. The pressure to conform in the school is constant, ever-present, vigorous. The pressure for creative expression is just as constant,

---

[127] *Ibid*, p. 8.
[128] E. Paul Torrance, *Guiding Creative Talent*, p. 78. Englewood Cliffs, N. J.: Prentice-Hall, Inc., 1962.
[129] *Ibid*, p. 108.
[130] *Ibid*, p. 109.
[131] *Ibid*, pp. 111–114.
[132] *Ibid*, p. 114.
[133] *Ibid*, pp. 116–117.
[134] *Ibid*, pp. 118–120.
[135] *Ibid*, p. 120.
[136] *Ibid*, pp. 120–121.

ever-present, and vigorous. The highly creative child may hear rhythms, beats, and tonal patterns that more crass ears do not. He may attempt to make explicit what he feels should not be left implicit. He may grow nervous or apathetic over routine and what he considers obvious. As one authority states the problem:

> . . . It is inevitable that highly creative individuals experience some unusual problems of adjustment. Thus the highly creative child must either repress his creativity or learn to cope with the tensions that arise from being so frequently this minority of one. Repression of creative needs may lead to actual personality breakdown. Their expression leads to loneliness, conflicts, and other problems of adjustment.[137]

SOME INDIVIDUAL CORRELATES OF CONFORMITY

As indicated earlier, research on conformity is both sparse and tentative. Replicative studies will be needed before the following points may be regarded as finalized:

1. The higher a person ranks within a group the greater his activities will conform to the norm of the group.[138]

2. Females are more conforming than males.[139]

3. Males are more variable (more heterogeneous) than females in their conformity patterns.[140]

4. Conforming females in college receive better grades than nonconforming females.[141]

5. No significant differences are found in the grade point averages of conforming and non-conforming male college students.[142]

6. Members of organizations and groups who place a high value on group membership are more conforming than those members who place a low value on membership.[143]

7. Non-conformists tend to be more distrustful and questioning than conformists.[144]

---

[137] Ibid, p. 104.

[138] George C. Homans, The Human Group. New York: Harcourt, Brace & World, Inc., 1950.

[139] Richard S. Crutchfield, "Conformity and Character," American Psychologist, 10 (1955), 191–198.

[140] Everett D. Erb, "Conformity and Achievement in College," Personnel and Guidance Journal, 39 (1961), 361–366.

[141] Ibid.

[142] Ibid.

[143] H. H. Kelley and M. N. Shapiro, "An Experiment on Conformity to Group Norms where Conformity is Detrimental to Group Achievement," 19 (1954), 667–677.

[144] David Marlowe, "Some Personality and Behavioral Correlates of Conformity." Unpublished doctoral dissertation, Ohio State University, 1959.

8. Subjects with high esthetic values are less conforming than subjects with low esthetic values.[145]

9. Juvenile delinquents frequently perceive conformity to the mores, customs, and laws of the community as a threat to their individual self concepts.[146]

10. Conformity is inversely related to the amount of information one has about a given topic.[147]

RIESMAN'S MODEL [148]

Well validated theoretical models regarding creativity and conformity are lacking. Reisman's model of conformity, though widely cited, has comparatively little research backing. He proposes three qualitative types: 1) the *tradition*-directed individual who is conditioned and oriented toward approaching new problems through the filter of past cultural rituals. The tradition-directed person is found more in other cultures than those in the United States; 2) the *inner*-directed person who is trained to conform to internalized goals of long-range value such as wealth, fame, and achievement; and 3) the *other*-directed individual trained to conform ". . . to the ever-changing expectations of ever-changing contemporaries." [149] These individuals, represent the most "conforming" type of the three and are characterized by high variability in their values (when conditions are changing) and expediency, rather than principle, as a guiding force in much of their behavior. The attainment of short-range rather than long-range goals is also typical of this individual.

The "ideal" person has been characterized by Riesman as ". . . an autonomous person, aware of others, responsive to them, but capable of making choices in accordance with his own individuality." [150]

Brodbeck [151] found that mothers of conforming children were more "inner-directed" than "other-directed" in applying discipline. Gross [152] found

[145] Aaron F. Snyder, *et al.*, "Value, Information and Conformity Behavior," *Journal of Personality*, 28 (1960), 333–341.

[146] T. A. Ringness, *et al.*, *Psychology in Theory and Practice*. Boston: Houghton Mifflin Company, 1959.

[147] Snyder, *et al., op. cit.*

[148] David Riesman, *The Lonely Crowd*. New Haven: Yale University Press, 1950.

[149] *Ibid.*

[150] *Ibid.*

[151] Arthur J. Brodbeck, P. Nogee, and A. DiMascio, "Two Kinds of Conformity: A Study of the Riesman Typology Applied to Standards of Parental Discipline," *Journal of Psychology*, 41 (1956), 23–45.

[152] Herbert W. Gross, "The Relationship between Insecurity, Self-Acceptance, Other-direction, and Conformity under Conditions of Differential Social Pressure." Unpublished doctoral dissertation, University of Buffalo, 1959.

that the "other-directed" individual conformed under conditions of both weak and strong social pressure. Thus far the relationship between Riesman's "types" and creative output has not been systematically investigated but probably represents the most appropriate theoretical model for further study.

ARE CREATIVITY AND CONFORMITY COMPATIBLE?

Creativity and conformity as entities are difficult to assess. Both are processes, matters of degree, subject to fluctuations of time, place, age, situation, and changes in normative contexts. Restrictions, and even some regimentation, are a necessary part of our closely-knit expanding population. Conformity may be regarded as a social pressure, inhibiting and stifling the creative process. Conformity may be perceived as a necessary societal grace.

The school psychologist should not let these many problems and limitations prevent him from determining if, for example, an individual is creative or simply non-conforming. He should, however, strive for continued growth in empirical accuracy in the frame of reference of these problems and limitations.

Our task as psychologists in education is to keep creativity and conformity in a *relationship* where inhibitions, fears, anxieties, and rigidity do not destroy flexibility. Our goal is a climate where each and every person may be more fully and freely himself.

The School Psychologist's Role in Developing Creativity

ESTABLISH OBJECTIVES

The school psychologist should delineate his short-range and long-range objectives in the development of creativity within his school district as early as possible. These objectives should be in the context of the contemporary societal and professional *Zeitgeist* in general, and the specific needs, personnel, facilities, and present programs of his school district in particular.

FACILITATE THE FORMATION OF INTEREST GROUPS

A leadership role in bringing school personnel together, particularly administrators and teachers who are or may be interested in the development of creativity, is essential. Without the formation of identifiable interest groups, it is highly probable that creativity will remain a nebulous "ghost" immersed in the curricular and guidance programs. Through cooperation with interest groups the ghost may be unmasked, the implicit made explicit, and the program for the development of creativity in terms of needs, roles, curriculum, and facilities identified.

ORGANIZE AND DISSEMINATE INFORMATION ON CREATIVITY

In the office of the school psychologist a reservoir of materials regarding creativity should be readily accessible to district personnel. Important printed materials should probably be made available (sent) to all appropriate individuals. This information, such as the following, should be couched in terms of probabilities (rather than "facts" or "fictions" *per se*):

Creativity is within the province of everyone.

Creativity is a process adaptable to all subject matter.

Creative abilities can be identified and assessed.

Creative processes can be taught.

Intellectual abilities and creative abilities are neither synonymous nor negatively correlated.

Creativity is not limited to the esthetic arts.

Creative abilities that are implicit may be made explicit through effective classroom climates.

Creativity must always be inferred from behavior.

Creativity differs in kind as well as degree.

Research on creativity is ongoing and tentative rather than final and conclusive.

SERVE EXTENSIVELY IN AN IN-SERVICE PROGRAM WITH TEACHERS, INDIVIDUALLY AND IN GROUPS

By working with as many teachers as possible the school psychologist expands the identification and nurture of creativity to a larger number of students. By acting as a "lecturer" and "consultant" in in-service settings he can both discuss and put into practice general and specific programs for the development of creativity. The specific action programs should probably be preceded by general orientation discussions in four areas: 1) identification, 2) records, 3) curriculum and grouping practices, and 4) evaluation.

Specific action programs imply that the school psychologist work *with* teachers in the following areas: 1) Determining how creativity may be defined in their teaching area(s); 2) Describing the components of creativity in their teaching field(s); 3) Developing effective work-sample methods for the assessment of creativity; 4) Developing criteria for the evaluation of the work-samples or other assessments; and 5) Describing what teachers can do to develop creativity—such as the following:

Place a high value on creative output.

Reinforce creative performance in a positive manner.

Emphasize divergent rather than convergent thinking.

Assist students in the development of methods of inquiry and discovery.

Guide students in the use of multi-disciplinary approaches.

Assist students in the crossing of subject-matter lines.

Allow students to initiate, carry out, and evaluate their own research projects.

Establish climates of flexibility and openness by exemplifying warmth, permissiveness, and acceptance.

Provide a rich variety of materials and experience opportunities.

Strive for a fine balance between individual enterprise and cooperation in creative endeavors.

IDENTIFY AS MANY CREATIVE STUDENTS AS POSSIBLE

Emphasis should be placed on teacher identification of creative students through anecdotal records, autobiographies, easily administered and scored tests of creativity, both informal and standardized, personality and life-experience inventories, rating scales, and behavior check-lists. In addition to these, the school psychologist would employ the more sophisticated tests of creativity that demand great finesse and sensitivity in handling the intricate and delicate scoring systems.

The use of projective techniques in the identification of creative individuals is controversial at present due to lack of research on what determines "creative" human responses to ambiguous stimuli. Certainly projective techniques should never be used alone in the assessment of creative abilities. When utilized in cautious context with extensive non-projective data the information obtained from projective or semi-projective approaches may provide corroborative data or lead to the development of hypotheses for further investigation.

The identification of the creative individual must necessarily involve a wide-spectrum assessment and evaluation procedure in which physical-mental-emotional-social assessments are cross-evaluated in a larger global appraisal.

WORK WITH PARENTS AND COMMUNITY GROUPS

Presentations by the school psychologists at PTA and other meetings in which the lay public may be informed of the program in the school for developing creativity is important. The school psychologist might advance a "community sponsor plan" in which an interested authority outside of the school would meet with interested students and sponsor materials and activities for creative research projects in conjunction with the regular school program.

ADVANCE DIFFERENTIAL PATTERNS OF GROUPING
FOR INSTRUCTION

Besides the "community sponsor plan" explored above, the school psychologist may want to recommend alternative grouping patterns of creative youngsters for instruction. These alternative patterns, of course, must be both feasible and compatible with the present curricular structure of the school district. By working cooperatively with all concerned the total instructional program ("curricular," "co-curricular," and "extra-curricular") may be greatly strengthened in the development of creativity by placement of students in special groups. With the possible exception of the multi-grade (interage) grouping plan, all of the following programs are designed to *supplement*—not suffice for—dynamic programs of developing creativity in the regular classroom(s):

1. *Multi-grade (interage) plan.* Students from different grades, e.g., the fourth, fifth, and sixth, are placed in the same classroom with one teacher on the principle that when differences, rather than similarities are emphasized that creative output is facilitated.[153] The multi-grade grouping pattern should not be confused with the "little red schoolhouse" or "combination grades" formed on the basis of expediency rather than philosophy.

2. *Saturday class plan.* Students are brought together on Saturday for a two- or three-hour period for creative activities involving painting, singing, reading, dancing, talking, or experimenting.

3. *Honors classes.* These classes would involve students who are both gifted and creative brought together for the purposes of sharing, interacting, and developing new ideas.

4. *Part-time interest groups.* Interested teachers or other school personnel sponsor special interest groups with the specific objective of developing creativity in a subject area, e.g. science. These groups generally meet once a week after school.

5. *Cluster grouping.* This plan is basically a pattern of student classification in which a homogeneous group is added to a heterogeneous group. For example, ten demonstrably creative youngsters would be added to a "regular" class of twenty students.

6. *Special homogeneous classes.* Although it may well be argued that a homogeneous group is one child this pattern of classification attempts to reduce the variability of a given group in a given characteristic. This pattern of student classification is at the opposite philosophical pole from the multi-grade grouping plan. The subjects for special homogeneous grouping need not be gifted.

---

[153] Newton S. Metfessel, "The Saugus Experiment in Multigrade Grouping," *California Journal of Educational Research*, 2, No. 4 (September, 1960), 155–158.

7. *Independent Study Plan.* Copied after the European model, a student may be given a two-hour period to do such things as personal research, library reading, and esthetics.[154]

PERFORM ORIGINAL AND REPLICATIVE RESEARCH

The person most qualified and available to perform research services in a school district is generally the school psychologist. If he does not assume responsibility for research it is probable that little research will be performed. Research knowledge in creativity represents an important need in education. The school psychologist may desire to perform original research. A great service may also be rendered in the replication of other studies. Roe,[155] for example, in an intensive survey of scientists found that the only consistent factor differentiating the "creative" scientist from the "non-creative" was perspicacity, the ability to work long and hard, a finding reminiscent of Edison's definition of genius as "one per cent inspiration and ninety-nine per cent perspiration." But psychologists and educators do not *really* know if her study of adulated mature scientists has findings that are generalizable to elementary school subjects.

Many important questions about the nature and nurture of creativity remain largely unanswered. Replication of studies performed with school age subjects are also needed. Torrance's [156] research indicating a "fourth grade slump" in creativity is a case in point. Theoretical models also need exploration, such as Anderson's [157] delineation of the "closed" and "open" educational systems that purportedly stifle and facilitate creativity.

The design, execution, and publishing of quality research represents one of the most significant contributions a school psychologist can make to his profession.

EVALUATE THE EFFECTIVENESS OF THE PROGRAM

Evaluation is a procedure that is basic to and part of any human endeavor attempting to determine the value or meaning of an undertaking.[158] Evaluation in the schools has been characterized [159] as having five basic processes: 1) the goals and objectives of the program are developed; 2) the

[154] Ruth Martinson, *Educational Programs for Gifted Pupils.* Sacramento, California: Calif. State Dept. of Education, 1960.
[155] Anne Roe, *The Making of a Scientist.* New York: Dodd, Mead & Co., 1957.
[156] E. P. Torrance, *Guiding Creative Talent*, p. 103. Englewood Cliffs, N. J.: Prentice-Hall, Inc., 1962.
[157] H. H. Anderson, "Developing Creativity in the Child." Paper presented for the 1960 White House Conference on Children and Youth.
[158] Richard Harsh, "The Evaluation Process," *Curriculum Exchange,* Office of the Los Angeles County Superintendent of Schools, 3, No. 5 (February, 1961), 1.
[159] *Ibid,* pp. 1–3.

objectives are explained and described in behavioral terms which are as meaningful and operational as possible; 3) the situations, experiences, or means by which it is planned to achieve the objectives are identified; 4) the selection of procedures for gathering data is stated; and 5) the summarization and interpretation of the data is delineated with recommendations carefully made on the basis of the facts gathered (assessments, summary) and the values placed on these facts (evaluation, interpretation). Evaluation without assessment is pure subjectivity. In the realm of creativity the school psychologist must be especially careful to be as scientific as possible. The subjective nature of creativity lends itself to the making of interpretations without factual bases. Through careful evaluation and assessment procedures desired aspects of the program may be retained, non-positive aspects of the program eliminated or modified, and new problem areas identified, hypotheses made, and experimentation developed in the light of the evaluative experiences.

Summary

The full complex of qualities that identify creative individuals from less endowed counterparts are yet to be identified. Yet the concept of creativity represents one of the most exciting and expanding concepts in our society today.

Over ninety-nine per cent of all of the research on creativity that has ever been performed has been conducted since 1950. This is one aspect of the professional *Zeitgeist* from which the educator's recent role in developing creativity has emanated. The great majority of school programs emphasizing creativity are allied with or congruent to school programs for the intellectually gifted. Giftedness, however, as measured by standardized tests is neither synonymous nor negatively correlated with creativity.

The term "creativity" is one of the most frequently cited yet infrequently defined terms in pedagogical circles—a "catch word" which is in danger of degenerating into jargon unless meaningfully defined. The most satisfactory definition appears to be that culminating from seven years of investigation at the Institute of Personality Assessment and Research at the University of California, Berkeley:

> It has seemed to us that true creativity fulfills at least three conditions. It involves a response that is novel or at least statistically infrequent. But novelty or originality of behavior, while a necessary aspect of behavior related to creative output, is not sufficient. If a response is to lay claim to being a part of the creative process, it must be adaptive, or of reality. It must serve to solve a problem, fit a situation, or accomplish some recognizable goal. And thirdly, true creativity involves a sustaining of the original insight, and evaluation and elaboration of it, and developing it to the full.

Identification is a continuing problem. Guilford's USC research on his "Structure of Intellect" model appears to represent the best present and future source of tests of creativity. At several research centers throughout the nation, particularly the Bureau of Educational Research at the University of Minnesota, assessment devices are being continually refined. The most appropriate single method of identification of creative students at this time appears to be the *work-sample* method in which a student's productivity is carefully evaluated by considered criteria of creativity in a given subject or discipline area.

The creative individual is invariably a minority of one. The issue of conformity and creativity is a crucial one. Extreme conformity costs the child his individuality. Extreme individuality costs the child the benefits to be gained from continued interactions with others. In a philosophical vein the creative gift belongs to the creative individual in an entrusted stewardship only—for creativity in the highest sense is a process which is mutually enhancing for the individual and the society in which he lives.

Those who would exert leadership roles in the developing of creativity in the schools must formulate programs, organize and disseminate information, work in in-service capacities, identify as many creative students as possible, work with parents and community groups, advance differential patterns of grouping for instruction, and exert leadership in research and evaluation programs.

Selected Supplementary Readings

Anderson, Harold H., "Creativity and Education," *Educational Horizons* (Winter, 1961–1962), pp. 123–129.

————, "Creativity as Personality Development," in *Creativity and Its Cultivation*, ed. H. H. Anderson. New York: Harper & Row Publishers, 1959.

Andrews, Michael F., ed., *Creativity and Psychological Health*. Syracuse: Syracuse University Press, 1961.

Arnheim, R., "The Creative Mind and Method," in *The Creative Mind and Method*. Cambridge, Massachusetts, 1959.

Ausubel, D. P., "Creativity, General Creative Abilities and the Creative Individual," *Psychology in the Schools*, 1 (October, 1964), 344–348.

Barlow, F., *Mental Prodigies*. New York: Philosophical Library, 1952.

Barron, Frank, *Creativity and Psychological Health*. Princeton, N. J.: D. Van Nostrand Co., Inc., 1963.

Biber, Barbara, "Premature Structuring as a Deterrent to Creativity," *American Journal of Orthopsychiatry*, 29 (1959), 280–290.

Bloom, B. S., "Report on Creativity Research at the University of Chicago," *The 1955 University of Utah Research Conference on the Identification of Creative Scientific Talent*, ed. C. Taylor. Salt Lake City: University of Utah Press, 1956.

_____, "Some Effects of Cultural, Social and Educational Conditions on Creativity," *The Second University of Utah Conference on the Identification of Creative Scientific Talent*, ed. C. Taylor. Salt Lake City: University of Utah Press, 1958.

Bond, J. A., "Analysis of Observed Traits of Teachers Rated Superior in Demonstrating Creativeness in Teaching," *Journal of Educational Research*, 53 (1959), 8–12.

Bromiley, D. B., "Some Experimental Tests of the Effect of Age on Creative Intellectual Output," *Journal of Gerontology*, 11 (1956), 74–82.

Brown, G. I., "A Second Study in the Teaching of Creativity," *Harvard Educational Review*, 35 (Winter, 1965), 39–54. See also Friedlander, B. I., "A Psychologist's Second Thoughts on Concepts, Curiosity, and Discovery in Teaching and Learning," pp. 18–38 in the same issue.

Chorness, M. H., "Increasing Creativity in Problem-Solving Groups," *Journal of Communication*, 8 (1958), 16–23.

_____, and D. A. Nottelmann, *The Predictability of Creative Expression in Teaching*. Research Report AFPTRCTN-56–130. Lackland Air Force Base, Texas: Air Force Personnel and Training Research Center, 1956.

Cook, R. H., "Look at Creativity," *School Science and Mathematics*, 60 (1960), 417–423.

Crawford, R. P., *The Techniques of Creative Thinking*. New York: Hawthorne Books, Inc., 1954.

Creative Education Foundation, *Compendium of Research on Creative Imagination*. Buffalo: Creative Education Foundation, 1958.

Dauw, D., "Personality Self-Descriptions of Original Thinkers and Good Elaborators," *Psychology in the Schools*, 3 (January, 1966), 78–80.

Davis, E. M., "The Condition of Growth and the Act of Creation," *Studies in Art Education*, 6 (Spring, 1965), 24–35.

Drevdahl, J. E., "Factors of Importance for Creativity," *Journal of Clinical Psychology*, 12 (1956), 23–26.

Dreyer, A. S., and M. B. Wells, "Parental Values, Parental Control, and Creativity in Young Children," *Journal of Marriage and the Family*, 28 (February, 1966), 83–88.

Ellinger, Bernice, "The Genesis of Creativity," *Reading Teacher*, 19 (April, 1966), 493–497.

Getzels, J. W., P. W. Jackson, and G. Joncich, "Culture-Bound Concepts of Creativity: A Social Historian's Critique," *Educational Theory*, 14 (July, 1964), 133–143.

Ghiselin, B., *The Creative Process*. New York: Mentor, 1955.

Goldman, R. J., "The Minnesota Tests of Creative Thinking," *Educational Research*, 7 (November, 1964), 3–14.

Gowan, J. C., *An Annotated Bibliography on Creativity and Giftedness*. Northridge, California: San Fernando Valley State College Foundation, 1965.

Gruber, Howard E., Glenn Terrell, and Michael Wertheimer, eds., *Contemporary Approaches to Creative Thinking: A Symposium Held at the University of Colorado*. New York: Atherton Press, 1962.

Gruen, W., "Utilization of Creative Potential in our Society," *Journal of Counseling Psychology*. 9 (Spring, 1962), 79–83.

Haefele, John W., *Creativity and Innovation*. New York: Reinhold Publishing Corp., 1962.

Hammer, Emanuel F., *Creativity: An Exploratory Investigation of the Personalities of Gifted Adolescent Artists*. New York: Random House, Inc., 1961.

Herr, E. L., G. D. Moore, J. G. Hansen, and C. Castelli, "Creativity, Intelligence, and Values: A Study of Relationships," *Exceptional Children*, 32 (October, 1965), 114–116.

Hildreth, Gertrude H., *Introduction to the Gifted*. New York: McGraw-Hill Book Company, 1966, Chap. 6, "The Assessment of Unusual Abilities," and Chap. 15, "Explorations of Creativity."

Hyman, R., *Creativity and the Prepared Mind*. Washington, D. C.: NEA, 1965.

Jackson, E. W., "Hunting Yardsticks for Creativity," *SK and F Psychiatric Reporter*, 6 (January, 1965), 402–404.

Johnson, D. F., "Creativity, A New Challenge," *School Arts*, 58 (1958), 23–25.

Kettner, N. W., J. P. Guilford, and P. R. Christensen, "A Factor-Analytic Study Across the Domains of Reasoning, Creativity and Evaluation," *Psychological Monographs*, 73 (1959).

Kneller, G. F., *The Act and Science of Creativity*. New York: Holt Rinehart, & Winston, 1965.

Landis, Mildred A., "Creativity, A Precious Possession," *Childhood Education*, 37 (1960), 155–156.

Leuba, Clarence, "A New Look at Curiosity and Creativity," *Journal of Higher Education*, 29 (1959), 132–140.

Levinger, Leah, "The Teacher's Role in Creativity," *American Journal of Orthopsychiatry*, 29 (1959), 291–297.

Link, Frances R., "When They Are Gifted," *Education*, 81 (1960), 158–162.

Mackinnon, P. W., "Identifying and Developing Creativity," *Journal of Secondary Education*, 38 (March, 1963), 166–174.

Maltzman, I., "On the Training of Originality," *Psychological Review,* 67, No. 4 (1960), 229–242.

Marksberry, M. L., *Foundation of Creativity.* New York: Harper & Row Publishers, 1963.

Maw, Wallace H., and Ethel W. Maw, "Differences in Preference for Investigatory Activities by School Children Who Differ in Curiosity Level," *Psychology in the Schools,* 2 (July, 1965), 263–266.

McWhinnie, H. J., "A Review of Some Research in Aesthetic Measurement and Perceptual Choice," *Studies in Art Education,* 6 (Spring, 1965), 34–42.

Meadow, A., "Evaluation of Training in Creative Problem Solving," *Journal of Applied Psychology,* 43, No. 3 (1959), 189–194.

Meer, B., and M. L. Stein, "Measures of Intelligence and Creativity," in *Creativity and the Individual.* New York: The Free Press of Glencoe, Inc., 1960.

Mooney, R. L., "Cultural Blocks and Creative Possibilities," *Educational Leadership,* 13 (1956), 273–278.

Mosing, Lionel W., "Development of Multi Media Creativity Test," *Dissertation Abstracts,* 19 (1959), 2137.

Murphy, Gardner, *Human Potentialities.* New York: Basic Books, Inc., 1958.

Nicholson, P. J., "An Experimental Investigation of the Effects of Training upon Creativity," *Dissertation Abstracts,* 20 (1959), 1071.

Ohnmacht, F. W., "A Note of Indices of Creativity," *Perceptual and Motor Skills,* 22 (April, 1966), 370–372.

Parnes, Sydney J., "Education and Creativity," *Teachers College Record,* 4 (1963–1964), 331–339.

_____, and Harold F. Harding, eds., *A Source Book for Creative Thinking.* New York: Charles Scribner's Sons, 1962.

Palm, H. J., *An Analysis of Test-Score Differences Between Highly Creative and High Miller Analogies Members of the Summer Guidance Institute.* Minneapolis: Bureau of Educational Research, University of Minnesota, 1959.

Pine, Fred, "Thematic Drive Content and Creativity," *Journal of Personality,* 27 (1959), 136–151.

Rivlin, L. G., "Creativity and the Self-Attitudes and Sociability of High School Students," *Journal of Educational Psychology,* 50, No. 4 (1959), 147–152.

Rogers, C. R., "Toward a Theory of Creativity," *ETC: A Review of General Semantics,* 11 (1954), 249–260.

Ruitenbeeck, H. M., *The Creative Imagination.* New York: Quadrangle Books, 1965.

Rush, Reuben, and David Denny, "The Development of a Test of Creativity in the Dramatic Arts," *Journal of Educational Research,* 57 (January, 1964).

Spindler, G. D., "Our Changing Culture, Creativity and the Schools," *California Journal for Instructional Improvement,* 9 (May, 1966), 78–94.

Stauffer, R. G., "Productive Reading-Thinking at the First Grade Level," *Reading Teacher,* 13 (1960), 183–187.

Taylor, Calvin W., *Creativity: Progress and Potential.* New York: McGraw-Hill Book Company, 1964.

————, and Frank Barron, eds., *Scientific Creativity: Its Recognition and Development.* New York: John Wiley & Sons, Inc., 1963.

Taylor, I. A., "The Nature of the Creative Process," in *Creativity,* ed. P. Smith. New York: Hastings House, 1959, 51–82.

Thurstone, L., "Creative Talent," in *Applications of Psychology.* New York: Harper & Row, Publishers, 1952.

Torrance, Paul E., *Education and the Creative Potential.* Minneapolis: University of Minnesota Press, 1963.

True, G. H., *Creativity as a Function of Idea Fluency, Practicability, and Specific Training.* Unpublished Doctoral dissertation, State University of Iowa, 1956.

Wallach, M. A., and N. Kogan, *Modes of Thinking in Young Children: A Study of the Creativity-Intelligence Distinction.* New York: Holt, Rinehart & Winston, Inc., 1965.

Wertheimer, M., *Productive Thinking.* New York: Harper & Row Publishers, 1959.

Wilson, R. C., and J. P. Guilford, "The Measurement of Individual Differences in Originality," *Psychological Bulletin,* 50, No. 5 (1953), 362–370.

Witty, Paul, J. B. Conant, and R. Strang, *Creativity of Gifted and Talented Children.* New York: Teachers College, Columbia University, 1959.

Yamamoto, Kaoru, "Creative Thinking: Some Thoughts on Research," *Exceptional Children,* 30 (1964), 403–411.

————, "Validation of Tests of Creative Thinking: A Review of Some Studies," *Exceptional Children,* 31 (February, 1965), 281–290.

JAMES F. MAGARY

21

The California School Psychologist: Professional Description and Status

In the surveys discussed in detail in Chapters 2 and 3 regarding the growth of school psychology in the last decade it became readily apparent that California, the most populous state in the United States, had also the greatest share of school psychologists. In fact, these studies revealed that approximately one out of every four school psychologists in the nation in 1960 was employed by a school system in California. Fourteen California institutions of higher education were training school psychologists in 1967; California began credentialing school psychologists and psychometrists on April 28, 1948.

If a cliché of "as California (in school psychological services) goes, so goes the nation," has any bearing, the editor has included many details regarding the school psychologist in California as well as the membership of the California Association of School Psychologists and Psychometrists (CASPP), the largest state association of school psychologists in the nation, in order that school psychologists in other states might evaluate their status in terms of the California perspective. California with approximately 19,000,000 persons in 1967 and approximately 1500 school districts, has the most highly developed network of school psychological services. Thus an entire chapter is devoted to a description of the status and functions of the approximately 1000 school psychologists employed in California.

For the interested reader, the status of the school psychologist in many other states has been carefully documented in journals, newsletters and state office of education documents. For information relative to the following states, Massachusetts,[1] Ohio,[2] Michigan,[3] Texas,[4] Colorado,[5] the reader is directed to the footnotes. For a discussion of the role of the psychologist in various countries, the reader is directed to a volume edited by W. D. Wall [6] in 1956. This work provides overview presentations of existing conceptions and services of psychologists in the schools of the following countries: Austria, Belgium, Denmark, France, Italy, Spain, Sweden, Switzerland, the United Kingdom and Yugoslavia. Articles relating to school psychological services in Japan, USSR, Germany and India are listed in the footnotes.[7]

[1] Louise Keenan, "A Job Analysis of School Psychologists in the Public Schools of Massachusetts," Psychology in the Schools, I (April, 1964), 185–186.

[2] Hazel C. McIntire, The School Psychologist in Ohio (Columbus Ohio Superintendent of Public Instruction, 1959), p. 10; and The Organization of Pupil Services— Guidelines for Ohio Schools, Division of Special Education, Columbus, Ohio, 1964; see also Donald G. Ferguson, "Training, and Certification of Ohio School Psychologists," Doctoral Dissertation, Western Reserve University, 1956; S. J. Bonham and E. C. Grover, The History and Development of School Psychology in Ohio (Columbus: State Department of Education, 1961).

[3] James A. Dunn, "Michigan's School Psychologists: A Profile Analysis of Personal and Professional Characteristics of School Psychologists in The State of Michigan," Psychology in the Schools, 2 (October, 1965), 340–344; and also, "The Employment of School Diagnosticians in Michigan," Journal of School Psychology, 3 (1964), 32–34.

[4] Frances M. Carp, "Sub-Doctoral Training in School Psychology: A Lesson on Failure," Psychology in the Schools, I (July, 1964), 215–223.

[5] M. L. Flax, and D. E. Anderson, "A Survey of School Psychologists in Colorado," Psychology in the Schools, III (January, 1966), 52–54.

[6] W. D. Wall, ed., Psychological Services in Schools (New York: New York University Press, 1956).

[7] L. Secrest, "School Psychology in Japan," Psychology in the Schools, I (October, 1964); U. P. Allahabad, The School Psychologist (Allahabad, India: Bureau of Psychology, 1956); H. Chauncey, "Some Notes on Education and Psychology in the Soviet Union," American Psychologist, 14 (1959), 307–312. See also, School Psychologists, International Bureau of Education Publication 105, Eleventh International Conference on Public Education, UNESCO and the IBE (Geneva, 1958). (Reports on the status, function, and orientation of school psychology in forty-two countries.) Also, Helmut Hofmann, "School Psychology in Germany," Comparative Education Review, III (1959), 23–25; Norma E. Cutts, "Professional Status and Problems," in School Psychologists at Mid-Century (Washington, D.C.: American Psychological Association, 1955), pp. 94–107.

California Association of School Psychologists and Psychometrists

In 1962, CASPP had an active and inactive membership of 856; and 61 per cent of this number completed a rather detailed questionnaire regarding their status as school psychologists.[8] By 1967, the membership was well over 1000.

In regard to job title, the study revealed that 45 per cent of the CASPP respondents had the title, psychologist; 16 per cent director of guidance; 11 per cent guidance coordinator, supervisor, or consultant, and 10 per cent were designated as psychometrists.

A study in 1961 [9] of the CASPP membership had resulted in the discovery that there were 57 specific occupational titles in use in California for individuals performing the broad spectrum of pupil personnel services and who were qualified to be members of CASPP.

In regard to the size of the employing district, the 1962 study revealed that 21 per cent worked in districts with from 5,000 to 10,000 students, (average daily attendance) while 19 per cent were employed in districts with 2000 to 5000 students; and 15 per cent were employed in districts with 10,000 to 15,000 students; 11 per cent were employed each in districts of 0 to 2000 and from 15,000 to 25,000 students.[10] Forty-four per cent of the sample characterized their locale as urban while 33 per cent felt it was suburban and 20 per cent classified their area as semi-rural or rural.

During school year 1964–65 California's four million pupils were served by approximately 900 school psychologists.[11] This was a 1 to 4,000 ratio which was an improvement over 1958 when the ratio was between 1 to 5225 in the elementary schools and about 1 to 4500 in the secondary schools. Thus, California would appear to have the best statewide ratio of school psychologists to student population. However, if the ratio recommended by the *Thayer Report* were implemented, California would have to quadruple its number of school psychologists and then some to keep up with the population increase. Table 1 presents a breakdown of these ratios in California based on school year 1962–3 data.

[8] K. D. Hopkins, N. Lambert, and J. F. Magary, "The C.A.S.P.P. Professional Status Inventory: A Descriptive Study," *Toward a Professional Identity in School Psychology*, Report of Fourteenth Annual Conference of the California Association of School Psychologists and Psychometrists, March, 1963.

[9] H. S. Johnson, "An Analysis of the Occupational Titles of Certain School Personnel Workers in California," Unpublished paper, Ranchito School District, May, 1961, p. 7 (mimeo.)

[10] Hopkins, Lambert, Magary, *op. cit.*, p. 2.

[11] Richard Carey, "What is an acceptable Psychologist Student Ratio," *California Guidance Newsletter*, 19 (November, 1964), 4–7.

TABLE 1

Ratio of Psychologists-Psychometrists to School
Population in California (1963)

	Total
500	5 (1%)
501–1,000	25 (7%)
1,001–2,000	57 (15%)
2,001–3,000	68 (18%)
3,001–4,000	69 (18%)
4,001–6,000	89 (24%)
6,001–8,000	25 (7%)
8,001–10,000	25 (7%)
10,001–15,000	8 (2%)
15,001+	4 (1%)
	374

In 1965, the CASPP research committee again collected data relating to a statistical description of the school psychologist and psychometrist in California. In terms of time devoted to various activities, the total sample revealed the following: Thirty per cent of the time was devoted to testing while ten per cent of their time was devoted to each of the following activities: counseling, parental interviews, work with teachers, work with administrators, professional activities, research and writing, and administration and supervision. This group averaged 12.5 years in the profession of school psychological services and 3.9 years on their present job.[12]

In regard to the job year, 57 per cent of the respondents were employed for ten months; 20 per cent for twelve months; 17 per cent for eleven months and 6 per cent for nine months. Forty per cent of the respondents were on a separate salary schedule from the teachers, while 41 per cent were on the teacher's salary schedule plus a fixed percentage. The median salary for the school psychologist during the school year 1962–1963 in this study as can be seen in Table 2 was $9500.

In terms of the educational background of these California school psychological services workers, in 1962 69 per cent had the masters, 11 per cent the Ph.D., 8 per cent the Ed.D., and 11 per cent only the bachelors. In regard to those with the Ph.D., nineteen had their doctoral major in psychology as did four of the Ed.D.'s and one hundred forty-seven of the masters. Twenty of the Ph.D.'s had majors in educational psychology, twenty-five of the Ed.D.'s, and ninety-six of the masters. Nine of the Ph.D.'s had their

12 CASPP Newsletter, 13 (March, 1966), 27.

TABLE 2

Salary 1962–63. (Prorated for a 10-month schedule. To adjust to another contract year add or subtract 10%.) (From Hopkins, Lambert, and Magary)

	Psychologists (N = 211)	Psychometrists (N = 45)	Director of Gu., etc. (N = 73)	Counselors (N = 39)	Gu. Consultants, Super. etc. (N = 56)	Others (N = 32)
High	13,700	12,400	20,200	11,000	13,200	15,700
Q3	10,500	9,200	11,500	10,300	10,900	11,800
Mdn	9,500	8,600	10,600	9,600	10,000	9,800
Q1	8,400	7,500	9,600	8,500	9,100	8,500
Low	6,400	5,800	6,400	6,500	7,900	6,300

major in educational guidance, eleven of the Ed.D.'s, and fifty of the masters.

In regard to certification by the California State Board of Medical Examiners, 62 per cent of the 517 CASPP respondents were certified, 38 per cent were not. This certification allows the individual to offer psychological services directly to the public for which he is qualified and he may use the word, "psychologist" after his name. This certification is separate from that issued by the State Department of Education.

In regard to organizational memberships, 32 per cent of the respondents were affiliated with the American Psychological Association with only 16 per cent belonging to Division 16. Seventy-seven per cent belonged to the California Teachers Association, 54 per cent to the National Education Association, 36 per cent to the California State Psychological Association, and 25 per cent each to the American Personnel and Guidance Association and the Council for Exceptional Children.

Fifty-six per cent of the sample had taught classes or conducted workshops in adult education, or taught in university extension or in colleges and universities. Twenty per cent had worked as consultant to a school district in addition to their regular employment while 49 per cent had engaged in psychological services (broadly defined as diagnostic, remedial, and therapeutic) on a paid basis in addition to their regular employment. It is important to point out, however, that the plurality, or 78, stated that they engaged in less than two hours of outside psychological services each month, and 30 per cent stated that this supplementary income had been less than $500 during 1961. And finally, 27 per cent of the total respondents reported that they had undergone therapy or analysis whereas 37 per cent of those who were engaged in psychological services beyond their school related duties revealed this experience in their background.

In 1958, the median California school psychologist [13] held a teaching credential and had had teaching experience as well. He also possessed the California State Pupil Personnel Services Credential, was on the faculty salary schedule, and was under contract for a ten month work year. He had to travel about ten per cent of his time and had a full time clerical aid. He had worked as a school psychologist for four years and was earning a median salary of $7500. By 1966, his median salary was $10,500.

In a 1959 California School Psychological Services Survey Questionnaire,[14] the following additional characteristics based on a sample of CASPP members were identified. Referrals of children to school psychologists were initiated by teachers, administrators, and parents, in this rank order. Referrals were most frequently screened by a school administrator or a guidance

[13] Verdun Trione, "Description of the School Psychologist," CASPP Newsletter XI (May, 1958).

[14] Verdun Trione, "School Psychological Services Survey Questionnaire," Report, Research Committee, Asilomar, California, March, 1959, (mimeo.).

director. The following problem situations were most frequently listed; emotionally disturbed children and educationally retarded children. However, in a study in Santa Barbara Schools of reasons for teacher referrals to school psychologists in thirteen elementary schools during 1959–1960, there were a total number of 547 children referred and 872 reasons stated. The four reasons for referral most frequently stated were educational difficulties, educational placement, personality disorders, and gifted identification.[15]

Referral Aspects

In terms of the types of referrals to the central office of the Riverside Public Schools, a very recent study [16] revealed the following characteristics of 1231 pupils referred during a recent year. 1) The rate of referrals was much higher for elementary pupils; in fact, the rate of referrals for elementary school children was about 7 per cent; 2) There were great differences in referral rate from the various school buildings; the significant variables appeared to be related to size of the school and attitude of the principal; 3) Contrary to expectations, referral rate was not related to the socioeconomic or ethnic composition of the school; 4) Boys far outnumbered girls in total referrals reaching a peak in the middle and later elementary grades while the peak for girls occurred in the last years of high school; 5) Most referrals originated within the school system as a result of teacher-principal team decision and most dispositions were handled by the school personnel. However, community resources were utilized in the management of many individual cases and families were frequently contacted; 6) The two peak periods during which students were referred for outstanding traits (giftedness) were kindergarten and grades two and three.

In an analysis of 289 cases referred for pupil personnel diagnostic services during school year 1964–65 in the Pomona Unified School District, boys outnumbered girls by almost two to one.[17] The greatest number of referrals for evaluation came for children in grades two to five. The reasons for referral were as follows: one-third experienced difficulty with school work; one-third were considered candidates for a special class and the remaining third were displaying inadequate personal adjustment or undersirable social behavior. Generally, the results of the evaluation were interpreted to the parent during a conference. About one-half of these conferences were

[15] Department of Guidance, "Distributions of Reasons for Teacher Referrals in Thirteen Elementary Schools in Order of Frequency," Santa Barbara City Schools, 1960 (dittoed).

[16] R. C. Robbins, J. R. Mercer, and C. E. Meyers, "The School as A Selecting-Labelling System: A Study of One Year's Referrals to the Central Office," *Journal of School Psychology* (1967).

[17] E. George Sitkei, "An Analysis of the Referral Process in Psychological Studies in the Pomona Public Schools," *Exceptional Children*, 32 (December, 1965), 256–258.

attended by the mother only and about 8 per cent by the father only. Only one-half of the referred children lived with both the natural parents. Fourteen per cent of the parents failed to keep their appointment or did not call after receiving a letter requesting them to make an appointment. The parents who did come for interviews received the recommendations in the following manner; 72 per cent displayed a favorable attitude while 7 per cent were negativistic and another 7 per cent were apathetic. To check to see if the parents followed through with the recommendations, referral agencies were contacted. Out of 102 questionnaires sent out to various agencies where children had been referred, the actual contacts with all agencies amounted to 30 cases. Of these only one-half remained with the agency, and one-fourth dropped before the recommended treatment was completed.

These discouraging results have strong implications for a need to improve the efficiency of the process of referral at its inception. A better understanding on the part of the parents concerning the serious nature of the problem and the imperative need for attention would appear to be required.

The case of Lee Harvey Oswald could be mentioned in this instance. He was diagnosed as a severely disturbed boy and therapy was recommended in the New York City psychological evaluation and yet his mother chose to ignore the recommendation and move to another state only to have this disturbed youth change the course of history in a very tragic way. As was pointed out in Chapter 5, agency representatives and school psychological services workers may need to improve their lines of communication and work together to build as Sitkei states "a greater sense of confidence and appreciation by those utilizing the existing services." [18]

Special Education, Consultation, Research

In terms of services to special education departments, in the statewide 1959 study [19] the school psychologist was most frequently called upon to evaluate educable mentally retarded children, gifted children, and trainable children, in this order. In terms of frequency of conferences, the study revealed that the school psychologist most frequently conferenced with teachers, secondly with pupils, and thirdly with administrators and parents. In terms of the type of intelligence tests used by these school psychologists, the most frequently utilized was the Stanford-Binet, followed by the WISC, Goodenough Draw-A-Man and the WAIS. The following projective tests were listed in terms of frequency of use: Bender-Gestalt, TAT, CAT, Rorschach, and H-T-P.

In terms of the frequency of advising teachers, administrators, parents, and committees, the following topical areas were most often listed: classroom climate; pupil classification and progress, use of records, studying pupil

18 *Ibid.*, p. 258.
19 Verdun Trione, *op. cit.*

behavior, and curriculum relationship to child growth and development. The most common routing pattern for the school psychologist's report was from the psychologist to the child's principal to the child's teacher. The school psychologists stated that in regard to their responsibility for the group testing program they most frequently served as members of group testing committees.

The school psychologists stated in regard to their research responsibilities that there was a rare incidence of experimental work conducted in their schools, although occasionally they advised other educational personnel on the psychological implications of current research findings.

In regard to time allotted for their various functions, the following percentages were listed (the first percentage represents the actual mean amount of time committed to the function while the second percentage listed represents what these 200 school psychologists stated they thought should be the mean desired amount of time allotted for the function): diagnosis, 35 per cent, 33 per cent; remedial and corrective endeavors 15 per cent, 17 per cent; advisory function 11 per cent, 13 per cent; preparing reports and records 12 per cent, 10 per cent; group testing, 5 per cent, 4 per cent; in-service teaching 3 per cent, 3 per cent; administration 7 per cent, 5 per cent; research 4 per cent, 7 per cent; and public relations 3 per cent, 4 per cent.

In a study of twenty psychologists who were members of the Sacramento County Association of School Psychologist in 1961,[20] the following can be added to our description of the role and functioning of the school psychologist in California. In terms of rank order, the referral resources utilized were as follows: family service agency, state mental hygiene clinic, and private practitioners.

The books the Sacramento psychologists felt were most helpful at that time were: Anderson and Anderson, *Introduction to Projective Techniques;* Cronbach, *Essentials of Psychological Testing;* Arieti, *American Handbook of Psychiatry;* Caplan, *Mental Health Consultation;* and English and English, *Comprehensive Dictionary of Psychological and Psychoanalytical Terms.* The journals most frequently read by the group were: the *American Psychologist, Exceptional Children,* and the *American Journal of Orthopsychiatry.*

Their retrospections regarding their graduate courses considered "most important" with respect to their present job resulted in the following list in descending order of importance: personality development, tests and measurements, projective techniques, mental retardation, and guidance.

In a more recent study California school psychologists were asked to identify the psychologist who most represented the profession. This was a difficult question because as Nadine Lambert,[21] former President of CASPP, has pointed out:

[20] Sacramento Association of School Psychologists, *Report on Questionnaire* (April, 1961, mimeo.).
[21] Nadine M. Lambert, "Toward A Professional Identity in School Psychology," A Report of Fourteenth Annual Conference, CASPP, 1963, 10–18.

The school psychologist has no parent image. Freud belongs to the analyst, . . . Rogers to counseling, Klopfer to the clinical psychologists. As we develop professional skills and competencies specific to the profession of school psychology, we will eventually have parent images; however, for the present we are an organization of peers only with sibling groups rivaling each other for status and power to guide the development of school psychological services.

However, when psychologists and psychometrists in California were given an opportunity to respond to this query Carl Rogers ranked first, David Wechsler and Eli Bower followed in this order.[22]

Smith's 1961 Role Analysis

A further study in California by Smith[23] attempted to determine expectations for school psychologist's performance, attributes, and participations. Smith was concerned with the importance of the functions and the frequency of performance of each function. An opinionnaire was distributed in 1961 to school superintendents, school psychologists, and college or university school psychologist trainers. Data was received from 354 school psychologists, 178 superintendents and 27 faculty members. Variance scores were computed to determine intrapositional consensus among the three groups; intrapositional consensus was established by use of the Kolmogorov-Smirnov Two Sample Test. These scores provided a comparison of opinions among and between the groups of role-definers (psychologists, superintendents, and trainers) for each item of the opinionnaire.

The use of the school executive studies model[24] as the basis for the research design to explore role analysis was an appropriate choice by the investigator. The design as originally formulated by a Harvard group (Gross, Mason, and McEachern) was an attempt to use the methodological tools of the behavioral sciences to analyze strategic public policy problems (role and role conflict analysis for the position of school superintendent and school board members). Smith's investigation was concerned with analyzing the perceptions of school psychologists, school superintendents, and university faculty members toward the role of the school psychologist in California.

The length of the opinionnaire (94 items) may have influenced the number of respondents, however, it was well organized and answers could be appropriately checked in most areas in a minimum amount of time. Ap-

---

[22] James C. Bennett, "A Critical Analysis of Issues Confronting School Psychologists" (Doctoral Dissertation, University of Southern California, 1965).

[23] T. E. Smith, "An Analysis of the Role of the School Psychologist in the State of California" (Unpublished doctoral dissertation, University of Southern Calif., 1962).

[24] Neal Gross, Ward S. Mason, and Alexander W. McEachern, *Exploration in Role Analysis: Studies of the School Superintendency Role* (New York: John Wiley & Sons, Inc., 1958).

proximately 80 per cent of those persons contacted in each of the three professional groups completed the opinionnaire. This opinionnaire type instrument, "Expectations for the School Psychologist's Performance," was developed from an analysis of the report of the APA Committee on Reconsideration of the Functions of the School Psychologist which had found considerable agreement in definition of the functions of the school psychologist.[25]

As those individuals holding a school psychologist's credential and employed in California in 1961 in school psychological services work were used as subjects, one must assume that they would see themselves behaving in the role of the school psychologist. This appears to involve an attitude that may or may not have been acquired at a training institution as well as the community attitudes toward their role. However, it is questionable if those individuals with titles similar to school psychologist would see their role expectations to be the same as the school psychologist.

By obtaining variance scores for frequency distributions of each item of the three expectation instruments and for each group of role-definers, the scores could be ranked and those falling in the top 27 per cent and the bottom 27 per cent noted. If the item fell in the top 27 per cent it was said to have high consensus, in the lowest 27 per cent it was said to have low consensus. This method of tabulating data to determine variance has been used by a number of investigators in role analyses studies.

Smith found that one-third of the items about school psychologist's performances had statistically significant differences between superintendents and psychologists. These differences resulted from one of the groups having opinions of greater intensity rather than opinions in an opposite direction. For example, the superintendents had stronger expectations regarding the personal attributes of school psychologists than did the psychologists. Differences also occurred regarding statements about psychologists belonging to, or participating in professional organizations. These differences appeared between the college trainers and superintendents. A statistically significant difference was also found between psychologists and college trainers on this item. More faculty members believed the school psychologist should be a member of the American Personnel and Guidance Association, than did the psychologists themselves. It appears quite obvious that the faculty group see this situation as they see their own position in relation to the usual community organizations which school personnel are expected to join.

Significant interposition differences between faculty members and the school psychologists were found on only a few items, and the differences that did exist were not the result of direction of opinion, but rather in intensity of opinion. The faculty members were less demanding than the school psy-

[25] Frances Mullen, *The Psychologist on the School Staff*, Report of the Committee on Reconsideration of the Functions of the School Psychologist (Washington, D. C.: American Psychological Association, Inc., 1958).

chologists in the areas of grooming, classroom teaching experience, even temper, good health, and possession of the Doctor of Philosophy degree. The superintendent group held stronger opinions than the psychologists and the college trainers on the above items.

Intraposition consensus of each group of role definers showed agreement on conducting diagnostic studies of children. This finding completely coincides with the past forty years of literature on the function of the school psychologist which has always placed diagnostic studies in the top group of expected role behaviors. However, school superintendents were more strongly negative than the psychologist's group on a statement in the opinionnaire regarding the school psychologist carrying on therapy in the schools with individual children.

The school psychologists in Smith's study ranked the frequency of performance of their duties from high to low as 1) diagnostic studies of individual children, 2) conferences with pupils and parents, 3) special placements for children, 4) consultation with teachers, 5) consultation with administrators, 6) follow-up studies 7) community services, 8) research, 9) group testing programs and 10) curriculum development.

Smith found that school psychologists were actually performing most often those tasks to which they and other role-definers attached the most importance. From the findings in this study it appeared that the role of the school psychologist in California has developed to the point where there was substantial agreement among the different role-definers about the many aspects of the role of the school psychologist.

Although these status studies were confined to California, similar findings would probably be found in our other heavily populated states. One factor which is not true of all states however, is that in California most of the psychological services workers have been trained primarily in schools of education usually in a department of guidance and/or educational psychology with a few courses in "liberal arts" psychology. A second factor is that four areas of services make up the professions commonly known as pupil personnel services in California. These service disciplines are: counseling, rehabilitation, psychology, and social work. A third factor unique to California school psychological services is that all pupil personnel services workers ideally have a common body of information in their training before specialization occurs.

Bennett's 1964 Critical Issues Survey *

One final study of great importance nationally was recently completed in California. In 1965, James C. Bennett completed a doctoral dissertation

* Some of the following is taken verbatim from this dissertation with the permission of James C. Bennett.

at the University of Southern California entitled, *A Critical Analysis of Issues Confronting School Psychologists.*[26] In this study endorsed and supported by CASPP, Bennett attempted to identify and present alternatives to the possible resolution of major issues which have a bearing on the identity of the school psychologist.

He stated his specific objectives as follows: 1) to determine critical issues confronting school psychologists and 2) to present solutions and alternative solutions to those critical issues as viewed by the majority of the respondents.

He developed the following taxonomy of critical issues.

    I. Issues involving Functions of a School Psychologist: (A) Diagnosing Physical and Mental Conditions, (B) Testing, (C) Placing Students in Special Classes and Programs, (D) Consulting with Administrators, (E) Participating in Curriculum Development, (F) Acting as Liaison Person Between the School and Other Community Agencies, (G) Initiating and Participating in Research, (H) Writing Reports, and (I) Providing Follow-up Services for Students Studied.

    II. Issues Involving Priority of Functions for School Psychologists: (A) Specializing in Case Practice, (B) Specializing in Consultation, and (C) Emphasizing (1) Case Practice or (2) Consultation.

    III. Issues Involving Consultation Practices for a School Psychologist: (A) Selecting Techniques for Psychotherapy, (B) Using Psychotherapy with Students, Teachers and Parents, (C) Utilizing a Counseling Orientation, (D) Giving More Time to Group Counseling, (E) Revealing I.Q. Scores, (F) Asking Students Questions of an Intimate Nature.

    IV. Issues Involving a School Psychologist in Private Practice: (A) Working with Students, (B) Working with Parents, (C) Emphasizing Psychotherapy, (D) Using School Facilities, (E) Rejecting the Idea of Private Practice.

    V. Issues Involving Qualifications, Experience, Credentialing and Certification for a School Psychologist: (A) Determining Degree Requirements, (B) Determining Major Field Requirements, (C) Determining Experience Requirements for the School Psychologist Credential, (D) Credentialing, (E) Certifying a Psychologist.

    VI. Issues Involving Standards of Pay and Work for a School Psychologist: (A) Establishing the Work Year, (B) Establishing Salary Considerations, (C) Gaining Recognition for Quality Performance, (D) Determining Ratio Between Number of Students and Number of School Psychologists, (E) Determining Grade Level Emphases for School Psychological Services, (F) Supervising the School Psychologist.

    VII. Issues Involving Professional Affiliations and a School Psychologist: (A) Affiliating at the National Level, (B) Affiliating at the State Level, (C) Holding Membership in Local Professional, Service and

---

[26] James C. Bennett, "A Critical Analysis of Issues Confronting School Psychologists" (Doctoral Dissertation, University of Southern California, 1965), p. 2.

Community Groups, (D) Having Membership in the American Psychological Association.

VIII. Identifying a School Psychologist Representative of the Profession.

Bennett reviewed the literature for the past ten years in each of the above areas; most of the studies have been covered in this text. Bennett then developed a questionnaire to assess opinion in each of these eight areas. The entire membership of CASPP or 684 school psychologists and psychometrists in 1964 were contacted and a 68 per cent response was received. All responses were treated to exhaustive statistical analysis in order to determine whether statistically significant differences occurred between observed and expected responses. Male respondents were compared with female respondents; respondents over forty were compared with those under forty; persons with the title school psychologist were compared with those with another title; Ph.D.'s were compared with Ed.D.'s; California certified psychologists were compared with those who were not certified; psychometrists were compared with psychologists; university trained school psychologists were compared with those who received their training elsewhere. Null hypotheses were advanced on the basis of the preceding interactions.

Two significant variables that Bennett neglected to consider were rural versus urban school psychologists and socio-economic-educational level of the community in which the school psychologist was employed.

In terms of his findings, there was a significant consensus that the school psychologist should *not* diagnose neurological impairment, functional aphasia or organic aphasia. Also significant was the finding that the school psychologist should *not* diagnose mental illness. The placement of students in classes for the educable mentally retarded was accepted as his province. At a significant level the sample indicated that a school psychologist should neither administer nor score group intelligence and achievement tests, however, he should interpret group intelligence and achievement test results to counselors, parents, teachers, and students and he should be the person assigned to the overall responsibility for a group testing program. The respondents accepted the use of projective tests in the realm of their competency.

Further the respondents in the study indicated that the school psychologist should play an important classroom role in the actual implementation of his findings and that he should send individual test information about a student to a new school only when such information was requested. Respondents indicated by a significant consensus that a school psychologist should base the interpretation of test data for Mexican-American students upon both national norms and separate district norms developed from the local Mexican-American student population rather than relying solely upon either national norms or separate district norms.

In regard to special classes and programs for emotionally disturbed students, the consensus as to the preferred situation was a special class with special individual counseling offered by trained personnel. The major findings relating to consulting with administrators indicated that a school psychologist should not consult with administrators on whether a teacher's behavior justified employment with tenure, dismissal, or promotion out of the classroom. Major findings also indicated that a school psychologist should not consult with administrators on evaluating candidates for teaching and/or administrative positions. Significant consensus obtained in regard to participation in curriculum development. It was felt that the school psychologist should act as the liaison person between the school and other community agencies in the areas of psychiatric services and disciplinary services but not in the area of medical health services. Further, the respondents agreed that a school psychologist should exchange verbal and/or written information about a student with professional agencies *only with parental consent.*

In regard to research, these California school psychologists felt that the school psychologist should *not* initiate and develop large scale research projects but rather he should initiate and develop action research. He should, however, encourage a research attitude among staff members in his district.

In terms of writing reports, the respondents felt that the school psychologist should state exactly what he believes about a case regardless of the possibility that his report may be read by an unauthorized person. They were also in significant agreement with the concept that a school psychologist should engage in follow-up studies even if it means fewer new cases.

In terms of priority of function for the school psychologist, statistically significant findings indicated that case practice, consisting of consulting with students, diagnosis and individual testing and consultation with administrators and teachers ranked equally high in importance.

The respondents felt that 1) nondirective counseling, 2) catharsis, and 3) suggestion were the three psychotherapeutic techniques to be used in descending order. In terms of actually using psychotherapy with students, teachers, and parents, the significant findings were as follows: A school psychologist, if he so desires, should employ psychotherapy on school time when working with students within his school district, but only with parental consent, and 2) he can employ psychotherapy on school time when working with disturbed parents. They rejected the idea of carrying out psychotherapy with disturbed staff members.

The respondents favored an eclectic approach to counseling and most felt that group counseling should be emphasized in order to provide more services in line with the preventive and remedial needs of students.

Respondents favored interpreting IQ scores to both students and parents on the basis of general statements, but the respondents favored interpreting IQ scores on the basis of percentiles to teachers.

The respondents accepted the idea that school psychologists should, if necessary, ask students questions of an intimate and personal nature, but as to whether consent from parents was needed, a decisive judgment was not evident.

In terms of private practice, two major findings evolved: 1) he should *not* accept in private practice those students who are in need of psychotherapy and who are enrolled in the school district in which he is assigned and 2) he should *not* accept in private practice those parents who are in need of psychotherapy and who have children enrolled in the school district where the school psychologist is employed. Furthermore, he should *not* use public school facilities for a private practice.

These California professionals felt that the basic degree for the school psychologist should be the masters and preferably taken in the field of school psychology and if not this specialty then educational or clinical.

In terms of experience requirements a statistically significant group felt that public school counseling experience, clinical experience, and teaching experience should be experience requirements for the school psychologist credential. Consensus was that there should be two credential levels based on education and experience with each carrying different levels of responsibility. Furthermore, the Californians felt that credentialing requirements for school psychologists should be similar in all states with automatic reciprocity.

In terms of standards of pay and work, they felt that the work year should be eleven months and that the salary schedule for a school psychologist should be based on a principal's salary schedule. The respondents supported a school psychologist ratio of between 1000 and 2000 students for each school psychologist with an equal emphasis upon all grade levels (K–12). The director of psychological services should be the supervisor of the school psychologist and the person to whom he should be responsible. Furthermore, they rejected the idea that an individual should be allowed merit pay for outstanding service.

The respondents felt that the school psychologist should hold membership in the APA, APGA, and the CEC, in that order of preference. The four most appropriate divisions of APA for membership were the divisions of school, counseling, educational and clinical psychology.

Bennett feels the following recommendations are justified on the basis of his study: 1) Institutions of higher learning offering credential training programs in school psychology should offer a degree major in school psychology; 2) School psychologists should widen their scope of curricular functions to include, for example, the determination and evaluation of curricular objectives, participation in teacher workshops designed to help teachers understand better the behaviors of children and youth; 3) School psychologists through individual, group, and professional organizations should exert influence on legislation affecting the educational program, such as programs for students with superior creative abilities, and for the mentally gifted to involve an increase in State allowed amounts for excess costs; 4) States should develop reciprocity agreements enabling persons who hold a school psychologist's credential or certificate to automatically transfer and work in any state. This implies, of course, that standards and requirements would be equalized. 5) School districts should make a determined effort to meet the ratio between number of students and a school psychologist as recommended by respondents in this study. The recommended ratio was one psychologist not to exceed 2000 students. Smaller school districts might work cooperatively with other school districts in order to meet this ratio; 6) School psychologists should take a more active part in research projects, especially projects that relate directly to the school psychologist's district (action research). School psychologists also should encourage a research atttiude among staff members; 7) Students with IQ's of 80 and above should not be placed in classes for the educable mentally retarded; 8) School psychologists should not diagnose conditions of neurological disorders and mental illness; 9) School psychologists should encourage school districts to develop local norms for certain bilingual ethnic groups to be used with national norms; 10) School psychologists, if engaged in private practice, should not overlap the two fields of activity in any way including using school facilities, and working with students and parents who are a part of the school psychologist's responsibility within the school district of his employment; 11) Because respondents accepted the concept that a school psychologist should, if he so desires, use psychotherapy, and because psychotherapy is ruled out (as treatment) by the California State Department of Education, it is recommended that the issue, "Should a school psychologist engage in psychotherapy?" be opened for further and considered study.

Public Relations for School Psychologists

In 1966, a CASPP committee under the chairmanship of Stuart J. Mandell published an attractive folder for public relations purposes entitled *School Psychology in California*. The contents of this brief statement are reproduced with minor editing as it gives an overview of the role of the school psychologist in California.

A school psychologist is a psychologist with training and experience in the behavioral sciences and education. He applies his specialized competencies in assessment and remediation to the understanding of the learning process, interpersonal relationships and personality dynamics. He not only gives direct help to students, he assists parents and school personnel in their efforts to make school more profitable for ALL children.

School Psychology in California:
The school psychologist works primarily in a collaborative relationship with other school staff members. Principals and teachers retain the basic responsibility for the education and control of children; school psychologists

assume a consultative responsibility in the educational management of the child.

Two levels of psychological service are recognized by the Association and appear in the credential requirements covering pupil personnel services.

The first level, school psychometrist, denotes special training and skills in educational and diagnostic appraisal.

The school psychometrist ordinarily works under the supervision of a school psychologist whose broader competencies and greater training can provide for a more effective application of the psychometrist's findings.

To assist school administrators to understand the kinds of responsibilities school psychometrists and school psychologists are ready to assume, the California Association of School Psychologists and Psychometrists has appended statements of purpose to the several services offered by these specialists.

School Psychometrist: Functions and Purposes:

Assesses intellectual and educational characteristics of children, including the administration of individual psychological tests, and assists in the planning, evaluating and interpreting of group testing programs in order to describe learning aptitudes more accurately and to evaluate the achievement of skills and knowledge.

Gathers basic information necessary for the understanding of the pupil in order to interpret his present learning status in terms of the pupil's educational history and his motivation patterns.

Makes verbal and written reports that organize information about a pupil in order to assist school staff in formulating and specifying appropriate plans for educational and behavioral management.

School Psychologist: Functions and Purposes:

In additions to those services which a school psychometrist performs, the school psychologist may provide the following:

Studies and assists the individual pupil, using extensive and intensive psychological techniques in order to assess his psychological functioning and to assist him with critical learning or behavioral problems.

Recommends appropriate educational and psychological remediation for exceptional children in order to accomodate their unique learning and psychological needs.

Determines eligibility for or recommends pupil placement in special programs or classes in order to evaluate educational strengths and weaknesses of a student and recommend means of dealing with them in the particular school setting.

Participates in planning, executing and assessing programs of education and re-education for pupils in order to aid in developing the best possible learning programs for all children and to evaluate the product of the educational effort.

Provides appropriate inservice training and consultative services to assist school staff members to better understand behavior and learning patterns of children and to apply these understandings in promoting an improved climate for learning.

Plans and executes research projects for the improvement of the educational program to obtain a foundation of accurately interpreted facts upon which future programs can be built.

Serves in a liaison relationship between the school, the community and community agencies in the understanding and treatment of learning and behavior problems in order to interpret the school to the community and to utilize fully all community resources in helping youth lead full and wholesome lives.

All activities that involve extensive or intensive psychological study of children are conducted on the basis of parental request and permission. The psychologist takes therapeutic measures through conferences with parents, teachers and students. In certain settings psychotherapy may become the function of the school psychologist, provided that such service is within the boundaries of his competence and is conducted with parental permission.

The essential role of the school psychologist is to offer his specialized training and background to other members of the school staff, students, parents and community resource personnel, in order to make the learning process more effective.

A chapter has been devoted to the topic of school psychological services in California because over one quarter of the nation's school psychologists are employed in California and very likely other states will look to California for leadership and will wish to draw upon the accumulated experience of California school psychologists as they forge ahead in this relatively new field.

Selected Supplementary Readings

Action Patterns for School Psychologists, CASPP Conference Proceedings, 1964.

Bower, Eli M., ed., *The Psychologist in the School,* A Report of a Workshop for School Psychologists. Sacramento, Calif., State Department of Education, August, 1958.

————, *The School Psychologist.* Sacramento: California State Department of Education, 1955.

California Association of School Psychologists and Psychometrists, *The Role of the School Psychologist Defined in Terms of Functions and Purposes,* (mimeo.), May 24, 1963.

CASPP Newsletters, Volumes I–XIII.

Clowes, Richard M., "Education Code Section 11804." A communication to District, City, and County Superintendents of Schools from California State Department of Education.

Howe, John W., *An Exploratory Study of Children with Neurological Handicaps in School Districts of Los Angeles County.* Los Angeles: Los Angeles County Superintendent of Schools, April, 1963.

Human Growth and Diversity, CASPP Conference Proceedings, 1965.

Lambert, Nadine M., ed., *Toward A Professional Identity in School Psychol-*

ogy. A report of Fourteenth Annual Conference, California Association of School Psychologists and Psychometrists, 1963, pp. 10–18.

Levine, L. S., "School Psychologists Training Programs in California," *California Journal of Educational Research,* 6 (1955), 123–126.

Martinson, Ruth A., et al., *Special Programs for Gifted Pupils.* Sacramento: State Department of Education Bulletin, 31 (January, 1962).

McIntosh, D. K., *Teacher and Administrator Perceptions of the School Psychologist.* Los Angeles: University of California Masters Thesis, 1964.

Rauch, Stephen, "Schools of School Psychology and the Action Patterns of School Psychologists or Teaching, Treating, Training and Trauma," *CASPP Conference Proceedings,* 1964, 24–33.

————, "Introduction," *Toward a Professional Identity in School Psychology.* Report of Fourteenth Annual Conference, California Association of School Psychologists and Psychometrists, 1963, pp. iii–iv.

————, "Selection Procedures for Early Admissions under S.B. 723," *The California Association School Psychologists and Psychometrists,* October 1, 1963, 2 pp. (Mimeo.).

Standard Designated Services Credential with a Specialization in Pupil Personnel Services. (Sacramento: California State Department of Education, 1964).

State of California, Department of Professional and Vocational Standards, *Directory of Certified Psychologists.* Sacramento: Psychology Examining Committee, 1962–63.

Valett, Robert E., *The Practice of School Psychology.* New York: John Wiley & Sons, Inc., 1963.

Wagner, Elmer E., "Responsibilities of School Psychologists, School Psychometrists, and School Counselors that Have Legal Implications." University of Southern California, 1961 (mimeo.).

JAMES F. MAGARY

22

Emerging Viewpoints in School Psychological Services

"Look to the Schools. Schools are important and exciting places for psychologists to spend their time."
Jerome S. Bruner, Presidential Address
American Psychological Association, 1965

School Psychological Services Workers in the 1960's and 1970's, as the preceding chapters have indicated, will be called upon to perform in many ways by various school systems throughout the nation. The psychological services specialist in the late 1960's, however, will have many more fellow workers, as the number of individuals employed in this specialized area of educational and psychological employment has expanded by six or sevenfold in the last fifteen years and the number will continue to grow. In 1965, an additional psychological services worker for the schools was proposed to Congress—namely, the child development specialist. The number of school psychological services workers will continue to expand as the national school enrollment soars past the fifty million mark, in the next decade.

As was stated in March, 1966 in the *American Psychologist* "The demand for personnel to perform psychological services in schools is expanding explosively, and will continue to do so due to the enormous stimulus provided by billion-dollar federal funding. Evidence suggests that there is increasing competition for the services of psychologists in the schools."[1] Presently approximately eight per cent of the national school budget is allocated for pupil personnel services of which school psychology is an important part.

Furthermore, changes in American society discussed by Mullen in Chapter Two and Meacham and Trione in Chapter Three will make for greater need for psychological services workers in the schools. Additional influences that will affect society and education in general and school psychological services in particular in the future have been ably presented by Wrenn and a Committee of the American Personnel and Guidance Association in *The Counselor in a Changing World*.[2] Some of Wrenn's projections will be repeated here with additional projections provided by the author that appear to be especially relevant to all school psychological services workers in the decades ahead:

1. There will be a continued emphasis upon achievement and excellence; this will remain largely as a reaction to the Communist challenge but also as a reaction to present research which suggests that high achievement and individually established patterns of excellence contribute greatly to an individual's sense of self-esteem.
2. There will be a greatly increased awareness of the value to American society of the diversity of human abilities. The psychologist, thus, becomes very important in such a society because he is the individual who researches, describes, and assesses individual differences. In 1965, for the first time in the history of the United States, a member of the American Psychological Association, John W. Gardner was appointed to a federal cabinet post, namely, Secretary of Health, Education and Welfare, perhaps an indication at this high level of what the discipline of psychology can contribute. Society values diversification in human talents and skills today more than in the past, partly because our occupational spectrum requires such diversification.
3. Increasing political responsibility and power will be transferred to larger units. This is certainly true of the public schools as was discussed by Meacham and Trione.
4. The national emphasis upon material comfort will continue, and probably increase; special federal programs and various assistance

---

[1] "State and Local Affairs," *American Psychologist*, 23 (March, 1966), 256.

[2] C. G. Wrenn, *The Counselor in a Changing World* (Washington: American Personnel and Guidance Association, 1962).

programs will be developed for the indigent and physically, mentally, and emotionally incompetent sector of our population.

5. The desire for personal security will increase, sometimes at the expense of individualism as social pressures for conformity increase.

6. A continuing uncertain international situation will create a future which will tend to promote a "pleasure in the present" philosophy.[3]

7. Population movements in the United States will continue toward urban and suburban areas, toward the West, and away from rural areas and the South. The United States will continue to have a high annual population increment with the nation increasing by about eighty million in the next twenty years. For the school psychological services worker this will mean as Wrenn [4] has stated, "students who live more closely together . . . will have to fight harder for a sense of personal identity." It means preparation of students for conflicts brought about by the presence of more people who will be competing for available schooling, houses, and jobs.

8. There will be changes occuring in the traditional American family structure with the husband and wife becoming equal partners in earning and spending and in the making of many family decisions. Families will live more closely together and there will be fewer family chores for teenagers.

9. There will be changes in America's patterns of sexual behavior brought about by the availability of wide-spread oral contraceptives and by the increasing need for population control and changed religious sanctions and legal statutes regarding sexual practices.[5]

10. The school in the future will be called upon to become more and more a multi-purpose institution with "multifold functions in developing intellectual, social, and vocational competencies in children and youth." [6] Extension of functions will be greatly increased in terms of preschool programs, work-study programs, cooperative programs with the vocational rehabilitation organizations, special programs in cooperation with other societal agencies for the dropouts, and programs for mentally, physically and emotionally handicapped youth throughout the years of late adolescence and young adulthood.

11. The school and the American people will be much more concerned about the people and developments in all spheres of life beyond the United States and international travel, study, and employment will be greatly expanded with increased federal aid available.

12. Classrooms of the future will be general learning centers and will contain many specialized electronic learning devices. There will be

[3] *Ibid.,* p. 11.

[4] *Ibid.,* p. 17.

[5] A. Heron, *Towards a Quaker View of Sex* (London: Friends Home Service Committee, 1963).

[6] Wrenn, *op. cit.,* p. 78.

more team teaching and generally American education will be characterized by the words flexibility and innovation.[7]

13. Teachers will be more carefully trained and will be more sophisticated regarding psychological and sociological concepts. Teachers will be more knowledgeable regarding evaluation of educational competence and the promotion of mental health than were our school psychologists of the 30's and 40's.

14. More flexible grouping patterns will become standard, the progression of subject matter in terms of level of complexity will become more important than specific grade levels. The lines between grade levels and educational levels will become less distinct.

15. More opportunities will be available for students, teachers, and psychologists to work with the culturally deprived both at home and abroad.

16. The future of measurement and evaluation would suggest that we will begin to talk about many aspects of intellectual competence, social competence, educational competence, and emotional competence rather than continue to refer to scores in these areas as global, generic unities as we have in the past, in the case of intelligence, educational and social quotients. The work of Guilford, Kirk and McCarthy, Frostig, MacKinnon and many others discussed in this text already points in this direction. Thus, teachers and school psychological services workers will begin to talk about human abilities and characteristics in the plural.

17. The psychological services profession will become more concerned about the area of values and the self concept. Certain writers now see the conflicts over poorly integrated value systems as the chief source of difficulty of troubled adolescents and adults.[8] In the

[7] G. C. Fusco, "Technology in the Classroom: Challenges to the School Administrator," Reprint *School Life* (March and May, 1960); Washington, D. C., U. S. Department of Health, Education and Welfare, 1960; see also, L. F. Carter, "The Impact of Automation and Technology on Education" (Santa Monica: Systems Development Corp., 1961); see also Ernest Hilgard, "Recent Contributions of Psychological Theory to Our Understanding of the Learning Process," 23–35; J. E. Bell, "Recent Contributions of Clinical Psychology to our Understanding of the Learning Process," 35–59; and Barbara Biber, "The Implications of Research in Learning for Public Education," 87–96, in *New Directions in Learning*, ed. Nadine M. Lambert and Ann G. Caffrey, California Association of School Psychologists and Psychometrists, Asilomar, Calif. 1959. See also, E. R. Hilgard, "Issues within Learning Theory and Programmed Learning," 129–140; and Yvonne Brackbill and J. E. Wagner and Dorothy Wilson, "Feedback Delay and the Teaching Machine," in *Psychology in the Schools*, I (1964), 140–156. See also, Robert E. Silverman, "The Evaluation of Programmed Learning: A Problem in Decision Making," 74–78; and W. C. Trow, "The New Media and the Obsolescent Classroom," 78–82. See also, L. M. Stolurow, Section Leader, "Learning Theory: The School Psychologist and Curriculum," *Newsletter*, 16 (1961), 7–11. See also, John Caffrey, "The Role, Responsibility and Training of School Psychologists in Relation to Electronic Data Processing," Paper read at the 1961 meeting of the American Psychological Association.

[8] Rudolf Ekstein, "Psychoanalysis Looks at the Origins of Values in Children," *Educational Leadership*, XXI (May, 1964), 523–526. The entire issue is devoted to

writer's opinion, Western society is moving away from the direction of externally imposed authoritarian, extrinsic valuative patterns for the individual toward the gradual establishment of internal, intrinsic, rationally-validated valuative patterns for each individual which have been cautiously established through careful discussion and thought on the part of each individual. The school psychological services worker in the future will not be able to remain neutral in the face of student's valuative conflicts in a culture that is changing rapidly. Every age sees old values fading and new values being sought. Ours is no different except in the rate of speed which historic changes are happening.

18. New concepts in learning will continue to influence educational and psychological thinking. The teacher and school psychological services worker will more carefully think through required behavior changes in children and as to whether suitable reinforcement is provided. This change owes a debt to B. F. Skinner and his concepts of operant conditioning. On the other hand, the work of Rogers, Combs, and Bruner, who emphasize the interrelationships of the cognitive and perceptual processes of the child in the learning situation, will become of major importance. Thus educational personnel will become cognizant of these two important domains within the learning process.

19. Factor analyses of psychological, psychiatric, and social worker data on normal school children will greatly improve our examination procedures. In the future there will be further carefully conducted normative studies on the development of cognition in children. "We have many normative studies which document what the child can do but few which deal with what the child knows." [9] Such studies as *The Prediction of School Adjustment* by Lambert reported at the APA convention in 1964 will greatly improve our examination procedures. [10]

Personal and Social Values. See also, R. F. Peck and R. J. Havighurst, *The Psychology of Character Development* (New York: John Wiley & Sons, Inc., 1962). This study, the first significant empirical work in this area since the Hartshore and Mays study of the 1920's traces five persisting patterns of attitudes and motives which produce a rather predictable kind and quality of moral behavior. The five styles are characterized as (1) Conforming, (2) Expedient, (3) Amoral, (4) Irrational-Conscientious, and (5) Rational-Altruistic. To me it seems doubtful that any human being can ever be satisfied with just "functioning" and "coping" with difficulties as they arise. A person cannot live for long without goals and without hope and be happy or even content. He needs a future to look forward to, believe in, to build on. In my opinion merely coping with current problems is not a goal, and adjustment is not enough. See also, Charlotte Buhler, *Values in Psychotherapy* (New York: Free Press of Glencoe, Inc., 1962).

[9] Statement made by Professor Maurice Freehill of the University of Washington in discussion with the editor.

[10] N. M. Lambert, *The Prediction of School Adjustment,* Coop. Res. Proj. 1980, USOE, 1963–64. See also Elizabeth Drews, "Report: 1960 White House Conference on Children and Youth," *Newsletter, Div. 16 APA.,* 14 (1960), p. 6. See also, Kaya Esin,

The Impact of Recent Federal Legislation and Programs Relating to School Psychological Services

Special education and psychological services in the schools have received more attention and financial support from the federal government in the past ten years than at any previous period in our nation's history.[11] The reader who wishes to keep abreast of federal legislation and its impact upon school psychological services is directed to the regular column by W. L. Hodges, in the quarterly publication, *The School Psychologist*, the Newsletter of Division 16.

The first White House Conference on Children and Youth was convened by President Theodore Roosevelt in 1909 and subsequent White House Conferences have been held about every ten years, since that time with the most recent taking place in 1960; thus there has been demonstrative federal interest in the special problems of children for well over fifty years.

With the passage of the National Defense Education Act of 1958, which provided for funds for training of secondary school counselors in short term and year long institutes at various universities, and for programs, materials and for research in the pupil personnel services with grants made directly to the state departments, who in turn distributed funds to various school districts, the federal government took a giant step forward in a committment to psychological services in the schools. The writer of this chapter views school psychology as one aspect of guidance, or pupil personnel or psychological services in the schools and he strongly favors close cooperation and coordinated training programs for persons with differing occupational titles within the spectrum of pupil personnel services.

More recent legislation that has influenced the development of school psychological services has been Public Law 85–926 (1960) that provided

"A Curricular Sequence Based on Psychological Processes Rather than Subject Content," Paper presented at the American Psychological Association Convention in 1960. Kaya emphasized three things in this paper: (1) the idea of having psychological operations determine the curricular process; (2) the intellectual operations should receive emphasis in the development of curricular theory; (3) when sequence is established it should take into account individual differences in rate of learning and intellectual functioning. See also, C. W. Taylor, B. Ghiselin, J. A. Wolfer, L. Loy, and L. E. Bourne, *Development of a Theory of Education from Psychological and Other Basic Research Findings* (Salt Lake City: University of Utah, 1963, mimeo.).

11 W. C. Geer, L. E. Conner, and L. S. Blackman, "Recent Federal Legislation: Provisions and Implications for Special Education," *Exceptional Children*, XXX (1964), 411–422. See also, E. S. Myers, *Community Mental Health Advances*, Public Health Service Publication No. 1141 (Bethesda, Md.: U. S. Government Printing Office, 1964). See also, Community Mental Health Centers Act of 1963, Title II, Public Law 88–164, *Federal Register* (Washington, D. C.: U. S. Department of Health, Education and Welfare, 1964).

for graduate fellowships for individuals desiring to become specialists in the area of mental retardation. Some individuals trained under this program have now found their place in various state or city psychological services programs especially in leadership positions relating to the mentally retarded. This act was extended in 1963 to include most areas of exceptionality.

The National Institute of Mental Health, through its USPHS fellowships played an initial role in supporting certain university programs that are providing leadership in the development of school psychology. Such a grant was made to George Peabody College in 1957 which developed one of the first four year doctoral programs in the country; the Peabody program emphasizes teaching students to use a wide scope of psychological knowledge productively in school settings.

Although President Kennedy will be remembered for many outstanding accomplishments, not the least of these will be his great concern and assistance to the mentally retarded and the mentally ill in America. Franklin Roosevelt is remembered as the champion of those afflicted with poliomyelitis while John F. Kennedy will be remembered as a spokesman for the cause for better educational, institutional and rehabilitative services for the retarded and mentally ill. The following statement represents the great compassion and dignity that Kennedy felt for the mentally disabled.

We as a Nation have long neglected the mentally ill and the mentally retarded. This neglect must end, if our Nation is to live up to its standards of compassion and dignity and achieve the maximum use of its manpower.

This tradition of neglect must be replaced by forceful and far-reaching programs carried out at all levels of government, by private individuals, and by State and local agencies in every part of the Nation. We must act—

To bestow the full benefits of our society on those who suffer from mental disability;

To prevent the occurrence of mental illness and mental retardation wherever and whenever possible;

To provide for early diagnosis and continuous and comprehensive care, in the community, of those suffering from these disorders;

To stimulate improvements in the level of care given the mentally disabled in our State and private institutions, and to reorient those programs to a community-centered approach;

To reduce, over a number of years, and by hundreds of thousands, the persons confined to these institutions;

To retain in and return to the community the mentally ill and mentally retarded, and there to restore and revitalize their lives through better health programs and strengthened educational and rehabilitation services; and

To reinforce the will and capacity of our communities to meet these problems, in order that the communities, in turn, can reinforce the will and capacity of individuals and individual families.

We must promote—to the best of our ability and by all possible and appropriate means—the mental and physical health of all our citizens.— JOHN F. KENNEDY, Message to the Congress, February 5, 1963.

Public Law 88–164, the Mental Retardation Facilities and Community Mental Health Centers Construction Act, was passed by the Eighty-eighth Congress and signed by President Kennedy on October 31, 1963. The final form of the law incorporated a bill on research centers and facilities for the mentally retarded and the development of community mental health centers.

Title I of Public Law 88–164 provides for the construction of research centers and facilities for the mentally retarded and related aspects of human development as well as project grants for the construction of university affiliated facilities for the mentally retarded. The first objective under Title I is administered by the newly created National Institute on Child Health and Human Development.

Title II authorizes a total of $150 million for fiscal years 1965 through 1967 for the construction of community mental health centers, which form the core of the new national program. When fully developed, a community mental health center will include the following elements to help complement school psychological services programs: 1) community services including consultation to community agencies and professional personnel; 2) diagnostic services; 3) rehabilitative services including vocational and educational programs; 4) inpatient and outpatient services; 5) training, research and evaluation.[12]

Needless to say, the presence of a community mental health center in America's smaller cities will provide additional referral resources for many emotionally disturbed children and adolescents which, as Meacham and Trione have pointed out in Chapter 3, are sadly lacking.

Title III relates to the training of teachers for the mentally retarded and other handicapped children and also provides for research and demonstration projects in the education of handicapped children.[13] In effect, this law amends former Public Law 85–926 and extends to all areas of the handicapped the provisions that were provided only for the mentally retarded.

Of great significance to the mentally retarded is Public Law 85–156, termed the Maternal and Child Health and Mental Retardation Planning Amendments of 1963. The import of this law is to determine what action is needed: 1) to combat mental retardation; 2) to develop public awareness to mental retardation; 3) to coordinate state and local activities relating to the prevention, treatment, and amelioration of mental retardation.

School psychological services workers will be affected by the major revisions and expansion of the Office of Education's program for vocational education (P.L. 88–210) of 1963 and the Manpower Development and Training Act. Dropouts, the unemployed, as well as eligible handicapped men and women will be assisted by research and demonstration projects under these

[12] E. S. Myers, *op. cit.,* pp. 1 and 4.
[13] W. C. Geer, L. E. Conner, and L. S. Blackman, *op. cit.,* p. 412.

statutes. The Vocational Education Act of 1963 (P. L. 88–210) authorized vocational education programs for persons in high school, for those out of high school available for full-time study, for persons who are unemployed or underemployed, and for persons who have academic or socio-economic handicaps that prevent them from succeeding in the regular vocational education program.

In July of 1964 the Anti-Poverty legislation (Public Law 88–142) was passed. This will undoubtedly improve services to the culturally deprived children and youth in the schools. Better assessment and evaluation, as well as educational and psychological remediation of the culturally deprived child is likely to result.

Susan Gray stated in reference to this law, the Economic Opportunity Act of 1964, commonly referred to as the Poverty Program:

> the part of the act of most interest to the school psychologist is Title II: Urban and Rural Community Action Programs. A community action program is broadly defined and includes programs which provide services, assistance and other activities of sufficient scope and size to give promise of progress toward elimination of poverty or a cause or causes of poverty through . . . improving human performance, motivation, and productivity, or bettering the work. Section 206 of the law authorizes the director to provide technical assistance to communities in developing, conducting, and administering community action programs, and also for training specialized personnel needed for such activities.
>
> At present the law seems broad and flexible, and would include many types of intervention programs for youth of all ages from the cradle upward that are directed toward the intent of the act and that involve maximum community participation. Many of these could involve school psychologists in important roles.
>
> If ever there was a time when school psychologists have an opportunity to use their special knowledge of culturally deprived children, their learning capacities and deficits, their patterns of motivation, and of ways of working with such children, that time is now. Let us hope that school psychologists will be equal to the challenge.[14]

Two specific aspects of the war on poverty which have further relevance to school psychological services workers are as follows: 1) *Job Corps,* providing residential centers for young men and women, 16 through 21, in a program of basic education, skill training and constructive work experience; 2) *Work-Training Program,* providing full or part time work experience and training for youth, 16 through 21, enabling them to stay in or return to school, or increase employability.

---

[14] Susan W. Gray, "School Psychologists and the Poverty Program," *School Psychologist,* Newsletter, Div. 16, **20** (February, 1965), 3–5. See also, C. L. Marburger, "The Economic Opportunity Act—and the Schools," *Educational Leadership,* **22** (May, 1965), 547–591.

Aspects of the Elementary and Secondary Education Act of 1965 [15] which have a relationship to school psychological services are as follows: *Title I—Education of Children of Low Income Families* is designed to encourage and support the construction of school facilities where needed, to meet the special needs of educationally deprived children of low-income families. Public school districts are eligible for payments for programs designed to meet the special educational needs of children in school attendance areas having high concentrations of disadvantaged children. In these areas, the school district would design special educational services and arrangements, including those in which all children in need of such services could participate. These special programs include dual enrollment (shared services) arrangements, educational radio and television, mobile educational services and equipment, remedial education, preschool or afterschool programs, additional instructional personnel, equipment and facilities, and others judged necessary for improving the education of disadvantaged children.

Title III—Supplementary Educational Centers and Services authorizes a five year program to provide vitally needed educational services not available in sufficient quantity or quality in elementary and secondary schools and to develop and establish exemplary elementary and secondary school educational programs to serve as models for regular school programs. Special personnel such as school psychological services personnel, equipment, and other costly educational services not normally available in most schools would be made available in centers for the widest possible participation of the entire community.

Title IV—Educational Research and Training; Cooperative Research Act authorizes the training of research personnel and improved dissemination of information derived from educational research development. Authority would be granted to utilize the research competence of research organizations not now eligible to contribute to the program, such as private non-collegiate research organizations and professional associations. In addition, the program provides for the construction and operation of research facilities to improve the quality of teaching in our schools and for the purchase of research equipment.

Title V—State Departments of Education authorizes a five year program to stimulate and assist in strengthening the leadership resources of state educational agencies. The state educational agency would identify educational needs of the state and design programs to meet these needs.

The 1965 federal legislation provides for the development of regional educational research laboratories. The laboratories planned on the West Coast will be independent entities and will have as their objective the improvement

[15] *Education '65. A Report to the Profession* (Washington, D.C.: Office of Education, U.S. Department of Health, Education, and Welfare, 1966). Contains a superb analysis of all federal programs in education.

of the quality of education for all levels of education within the region of operation. Each laboratory will select a program of educational research problems most germane to the schools in its area and will concentrate on them.

Dean James Jarrett of the University of California at Berkeley indicated that the laboratory that was being planned on his campus would have the following aims: 1) collaboration between university and public school; 2) plan research and development activities heretofore missing in public schools; 3) emphasize the use of the public schools; 4) emphasize communication and dissemination of research in practical form; 5) attempt to develop basic research to the point where it can be demonstrated in the classroom; and 6) carefully plan for administrative structures, community outcomes, design projects, evaluative criteria, and priority determination to facilitate plans and programs.[16]

The influence that such labs will have throughout the country on the coordination and particularly the emphasis on certain kinds of educational research affecting the public school is likely to be very significant. School psychological services personnel are the logical individuals in most school districts to participate in cooperative research activities with the labs.

Another significant advance sponsored by the United States Office of Education is the plan for the Educational Research Information Center (ERIC) which will be a unit in the Division of Research Training and Dissemination of the Bureau of Research. ERIC represents a decentralized nationwide network of information clearinghouses or research documentation centers coordinated by the Office of Education. ERIC will acquire, abstract, index, store, retrieve, and disseminate nationally the most significant educational research and research-related documents. This service which has as its basic objective to provide reliable, current educational research and related information promptly and inexpensively will be a great boon to school psychologists conducting research in their local districts.[17]

In August of 1965, the Community Mental Health Centers Act Amendments became law. In his statement concerning PL 89–105, President Johnson emphasized the following: "Under this law our colleges and our universities are providing this year's traineeships and fellowships to 4,900 students that are preparing to become teachers of handicapped children. But with these amendments we will now be able to double the number by 1967." The law also provides additional funds for research and demonstration projects for the education of handicapped children and for the construction of at least one research facility. These provisions of the amendments increase federal assistance for all areas of exceptionality with the exception of giftedness.

16 "News and Notes," *CASPP Newsletter* (May, 1966), 14.
17 *The Guidepost,* 8 (March, 1966), 3.

Finally, the Joint Commission of the Mental Health of Children under Public Law 88–97 became a reality in 1965. The purpose of the commission is to study the mental health needs of the nation's children. This legislation under Section 231 provided for a two-year study and a budget of a million dollars from the National Institute of Mental Health. Mary Alice White is representing school psychology on this interdisciplinary commission. Hodges commented on this commission as follows:

> School Psychologists, in particular, should be able to raise some pertinent issues for evaluation in regard to mental health and illness among our school children. Some of these issues might be those of definition of disorders, of the causative factors, of how effective our services are, of the role of learning in mental health and of the role of the school as an agent for mental health. . . . Here is an opportunity for school psychologists to offer incisive ideas and fresh approaches.[18]

The National Teacher Corps, launched in the summer of 1966, is an effort to improve education at its weakest point. By providing money, training and opportunity, the Teacher Corps will bring together qualified committed persons who want to use education to defeat poverty. They will go, in President Johnson's words, "to the places in this country that need them the most," to bolster the staffs of ghetto and back-country schools which customarily have the largest teacher turn-over. In school year 1966–67, the goal is to enroll 3,750 members to participate. School psychological services personnel will be called upon to help identify schools and children who should receive the assistance of the NTC as well as to participate in the training of Corpsmen.

The proposed federal budget for fiscal year 1967 for education programs administered by the United States Office of Education calls for a $174.1 million increase over 1966; this would bring the total federal appropriations for education to $3.4 billion for 1967.[19]

These federal laws offering large scale financial aid will greatly enhance all types of programs for handicapped and deprived children and youth as well as bolster research in the schools. School psychological workers will be called upon to play various roles in diagnosis, remediation, and research to evaluate these various federally initiated projects, and to help to select participants from local school districts.

Interprofessional Research Commission on Pupil Personnel Services

In September of 1961 a dozen associations formed an Interprofessional Research Commission on Pupil Personnel Services. Since that date four

18 *The School Psychologist,* Newsletter, Div. 16, 20 (January, 1966), 52.
19 *The Guidepost,* 8 (March, 1966), 2.

additional organizations have been added. The original group included the American Personnel and Guidance Association, the American Medical Association, and the American Psychological Association. In July of 1962, the National Institute of Mental Health issued a grant slightly more than one million dollars to underwrite this Commission in support of a five year program of research and demonstration.

The purpose of the commission is the promotion of more effective pupil personnel services. It was the thinking of many workers in psychological services around the nation that the present state of pupil personnel services left much to be desired.

> Their representatives in the schools often dealt with the same child; the discipline on the left frequently not knowing what the one on the right was doing; occasionally, for that matter, they seemed almost to be working at cross-purposes. Services sometimes overlapped, sometimes left gaps. If pupil personnel service workers frequently misunderstood one another, they and the educators did so perhaps even more often. Patterns of pupil personnel service organization abounded, yet none had been evaluated. Clearly, there was a plethora of issues awaiting clarification.[20]

The program thus set as its objectives as the promotion of more effective pupil personnel service, in their proposal as follows:

> 1) by providing through research a body of knowledge that will increase the effectiveness of all professions and services collaborating to provide the total learning experience . . . 2) by demonstrating efficient programs of pupil personnel services for various sizes and types of communities . . . 3) by carrying on and stimulating research on preventive mental hygiene related to the schools. . . .
>
> The national scope of the program will give it leverage on practice throughout the country, while its multidisciplinary character will help in the solution of major problems of coordination of services now out of phase making for readier focus on the instructional program of children and youth.

The hope is:

> to maximize the positive mental hygiene values of good schooling . . . to bring pupil personnel services to bear on such major socio-educational problems as juvenile delinquency, school drop-outs identification, and utilization of various kinds of talent and improved programs for the educationally disadvantaged . . . to provide demonstration centers and research findings that will strengthen the training programs of the future. . . .

Gordon P. Liddle, author of Chapter 19 in this volume is presently the General Director of the Commission. The following three colleges are serving

---

[20] E. L. Hoch, "The Interprofessional Research Commission on Pupil Personnel Services," *Psychology in the Schools,* 1 (January, 1964), 27–30; see also C. Merville Shaw and John K. Tuel, "A Focus for Public School Guidance Programs: A Model and Proposal," *Personnel and Guidance Journal,* 18 (April, 1966), 824–830.

as regional centers: Chico State College, the University of Michigan, and the University of Texas.

Albert Harris, former president of Division 16 of the APA has great hopes for the commission. He feels the findings of this new commission will have tremendous impact on pupil personnel services and particularly influence the nature of future federal and state legislation. The commission's findings may well strengthen the profession of school psychology and help to define more clearly the complex of interprofessional and interpersonal relationships in which the school psychologist must function.[21]

Divergent Role Conceptualizations

Wallin and Ferguson in Chapter 1 traced the history of school psychological services and presented some of the role models suggested and adopted by various committees, organizations and state credentialing agencies. Their historical discussion of these developments ended in 1960 while this chapter discusses the changes which have occurred up until 1967 and projects the role of the psychological services worker into the future.

Just as there have been a rash of the fanciful "Is" books, *Happiness is a Warm Puppy,* or *Security is a Thumb and a Blanket,* there have also been many statements over the past five years regarding a "School Psychologist is . . ." These serious statements suggest a multitude of divergent roles, however; some statements may impress you as chimeric proposals. At any rate, they confirm the viewpoint that school psychology is in an early stage of development in which its future direction and form have not fully emerged.

> The SP is a specialist in the area of child growth and development. . . .[22]

> The SP is one with competency in psychological techniques and skills in their application to the educational setting. . . .[23]

> The SP is a diagnostician who is concerned with integrating and coordinating the total facilities of the school and community toward meeting the psychological needs of students. . . .[24]

> The SP is an educational specialist who focuses his attention on the factors that enable students to gain the greatest possible advantage from their school experiences. . . .[25]

[21] A. J. Harris, "School Psychology Moves Ahead," Presidential Address, *Division 16 Newsletter,* **XVII** (1962), 3–5.

[22] Seattle Public Schools, *Standards for Preparation of Specialized Personnel* (State Board of Education, April, 1960), p. 1.

[23] R. M. Cassell, "Clinical Diagnostic Case Study, Procedure for the School Psychologist," *National Association of Women Deans and Counselors Bulletin,* **XXIV** (1960), 23.

[24] O. G. Mink, "The Role of the School Psychologist," *Cornell Miscellaneous Bulletin,* **LIV** (1963), 1.

[25] Beatrice Lantz, "The School Psychologist in the Inner City," in *Professional School Psychology,* ed. M. G. and G. B. Gottsegen (New York: Grune & Stratton, Inc., 1960), p. 47.

The SP is primarily a clinical psychologist specializing in diagnosing and suggesting remedial techniques through which to help the deviate child in school. . . .[26]

The SP is one who ties together the instructional program and the necessary clinical services whenever the latter are needed in helping the student solve his problem. . . .[27]

The SP is one who works in the school as a psychologist applying his professional training in testing and therapy to the needs of the school system. . . .[28]

The SP is a specialist in child study and development as it relates to learning in a school setting. . . .[29]

The SP is a specialist in guidance of children and youth. . . .[30]

The SP is a pupil personnel specialist who applies psychological principles and skills to learning and adjustment problems as found in schools. . . .[31]

The role of the SP is facilitating interaction between the teacher and pupil in order to make optimal use of the pupil's association with the teacher. . . .[32]

The SP is a professional who must be deeply involved with the total school system in such a way that he will be forever restless and will constantly try to help the teachers and administrators to improve the total system of teaching and learning.[33]

The SP is a member of a team of teachers, administrators and parents who are producing for the child the most fruitful, wholesome, and interesting conditions possible to further his development. . . .[34]

The SP is one who has many of the same functions of the counseling and clinical psychologist but these functions are performed exclusively in a school setting.[35]

The writer will add his "is statement" to the above compilation:

The SP is one who brings a psychological frame of reference to bear upon a set of school-related observations or behaviors of individuals or groups,

[26] *Doctoral Program in School Psychology,* University of Miami (c. 1962), p. 1.

[27] J. C. Fuchel, "Observations in Educational Psychology," *Educational Psychologist,* I (May, 1964), 4.

[28] Department of Guidance, Richmond Public Schools, *Introducing the School Psychologist,* Guidance Talks, No. 3 (1963), p. 1 (mimeo.).

[29] *Graduate Study and School Psychology,* "The Profession of School Psychology" (New York: Teachers College, Columbia University, 1961, mimeo.).

[30] W. F. Johnson, B. Stefflre, and R. A. Edelfelt, *Pupil Personnel and Guidance Services* (New York: McGraw-Hill Book Company, 1962), p. 138.

[31] Martha Montgomery, "School Psychologist in Princeton, N. J.," in *News and Views,* V (1963), 8.

[32] Harriett O'Shea, "The Future of School Psychology," in *Professional School Psychology,* p. 287.

[33] Rudolph Eckstein, "The School Psychologist," *Division 16 Newsletter,* 20 (January, 1966), 47.

[34] Liaison Committee Report to the Executive Board of CASPP (January 19, 1962), p. 4 (dittoed).

[35] Anne Anastasi, *Fields of Applied Psychology* (New York: McGraw-Hill Book Company, 1964), p. 484.

with the end in view of facilitating learning, creativity, and self-actualization for as many school children as possible.

There is no dearth of materials relating to the role or conceptualization of the school psychologist. Various individuals take the position that the school psychologist is primarily a clinical psychologist functioning in the school [36] while others see the role as that of one of "general educational psychologist" in the schools.[37]

This chapter reviews a number of divergent views regarding the role, services offered, and underlying purpose of the school psychologist. Authorities discuss issues that go beyond definitions and revolve around basic theoretical positions within psychology, the philosophical underpinning of school psychology as well as the dimensions of his services in the schools.

SUSAN W. GRAY: ROLE FLEXIBILITY AND RESEARCH COMPETENCE

Professor Gray of George Peabody College asserts in her excellent 1963 book, *The Psychologist in the Schools*,[38] that school psychology has been dominated by two general approaches, both of which have been limiting factors in the development of the profession. These two approaches are the "testing-placement function" that has grown up from the need to place exceptional children in special classes provided by state statutes, while the second general approach has limited his role to the definition that has been modeled after the clinician. Because of the prestigeful nature of the clinical field, especially after World War II, many school psychologists have emulated this role very closely. Gray, however, states that the "potentials of psychology for serving the schools are far broader than either of these two narrow approaches might suggest." [39]

For example she states, "there is considerable knowledge available in various segments of psychology that is not customarily utilized in school settings. Much of what social psychology has learned about the functioning of groups and the nature of social organization has found little place in the school's program of psychological services." [40]

---

[36] A. C. Coladarci, "A Note on the Role of the School Psychologist," *California Journal of Secondary Education*, XXVII (1952), 445–446.

[37] S. W. Gray, "Psychologists for the Public Schools: A Training Program," *American Psychologist*, XIV (1959), 701–704.

[38] S. W. Gray, *The Psychologist in the Schools* (New York: Holt, Rinehart and Winston, 1963).

[39] *Ibid.*, p. 389. See also, Susan W. Gray, "1984 or Twenty Years on," CASPP Annual Conference Proceedings, 1964, 1–12.

[40] Susan W. Gray, "Broader Roles for School Psychologists," *Educational Leadership*, XVIII (January, 1960), 226–229; see also, Susan W. Gray and R. Harris, "Psychologists for Tomorrow's Schools," *The Peabody Reflector*, XXXII.

Thus the solution of role definition lies in each psychologist and training institution adapting itself to the special resources and particular setting in which individuals work always keeping in mind the delicate balance between the role conceptualization of the scientist and the professional. Gray suggested that in the future two roles in which the school psychologist must demonstrate competence are 1) the data-oriented problem solver and 2) as consultant to teachers and ancillary personnel. To Gray, psychology has come to regard research competence, or a data-oriented approach to problems and a sense of what is researchable within them, as the very hallmark of the profession of psychology, and thus research competence should also be the forte of the school psychologist.

She further indicates that the psychologist must be a highly talented transmitter of psychological knowledge and skill. The school psychologist must today develop the role of consultant with teachers and ancillary school personnel. It is imperative that the school psychologist be able to communicate his special points of view concerning school learning and child development to those most directly concerned with the learning behavior of children. In a sense, he must be able to make meaningful psychological interpretations in the context of the school.

In an earlier paper, Gray had stated,

> . . . The model of the school psychologist we are attempting to develop at Peabody, then, is that of a specialist with flexibility and creativity in adapting his particular knowledge and skills to the demands of school situations. . . . Together with the front line personnel of schools—the teachers, with other specialists on the school staff, and with the school's administrative officers, they can work towards that comprehensive and difficult but most essential goal of the school, that of promoting the optimum educational, social, and personal growth of the children in its charge.[41]

Gray [42] has been criticized for possessing a heavily academic or idealistic orientation and for stressing the future of the school psychologist as a scientist-professional rather than a service-oriented individual. For Gray, the school psychologist should play an important role in research. However, in actual practice "there is little question as to which is the primary role for the school psychologist."

WHITE AND HARRIS: A WHOLISTIC VIEW

In a 1961 book, *The School Psychologist*, White and Harris give their definition of school psychology,

---

[41] *Ibid.*, p. 291.
[42] R. E. Valett, "What is the Role?", *Contemporary Psychology*, IX (July, 1964), 290–291.

as that branch of psychology which concerns itself with the personality of the pupil in interaction with the educational process . . . school psychology encompasses not only the learning process, as part of education, but also the personality of the learner as a member of school society, as a member of a family unit and as a member of a community. . . . We would stress that the school psychologist needs to be trained in education as well as clinical psychology.[43]

One especially perceptive portion of this book is where the authors discuss the problem of psychologists with diverse backgrounds adapting to the role of the school psychologist, for example, in the case of the clinician or experimentalist who enters the field of school psychological services.

White and Harris [44] classify the current major services of school psychology to pupils as follows: 1) educational diagnosis; 2) educational remediation; 3) personality diagnosis; 4) personality remediation.

Another outstanding aspect of this text is the authors' synthesis of relevant research findings regarding socio-economic variables and their impingement on school achievement and adjustment. The chapters, "Educational Adjustment of the Pupil Population," and "Mental Illness in Relation to the Pupil Population" are excellent. This material cannot be found elsewhere with economy of time and effort and these sections merit the book finding its place on the school psychologist's five foot shelf and for its use in all school psychologist training programs.[45]

ROGER REGER: EDUCATIONAL PROGRAMMER

Roger Reger [46] in his 1965 book *School Psychology* views the role of the school psychologist as an individual who is "intimately involved in the deliberate development of school activities and programs . . ." ". . . the school psychologist is to *help plan educational programs for children*. . . . A school psychologist is an educational engineer, a specialist who is well equipped to help plan educational programs for children." He feels that a school psychologist can perform in this manner if he is freed from the limitations of the clinician-tester-practitioner model and becomes aligned with the educator-research-academic model. He states:

The school psychologist of tomorrow is likely to closely resemble a "practicing academician" in his self-image and in his actions. He is likely to be research-oriented, helping the educational system develop, understand, and integrate new ideas in educational philosophy and technology. He probably will be

[43] Mary Alice White and M. W. Harris, *The School Psychologist* (New York: Harper & Row, Publishers, 1961), p. 13.

[44] White and Harris, *Ibid.*, p. 7.

[45] J. F. Magary, "On an Old Frontier, Review of White and Harris," *Contemporary Psychology*, 8 (1963), pp. 166–167.

[46] Roger Reger, *School Psychology* (Springfield, Ill.: Charles C Thomas, 1965).

viewed as a teacher, as one who, in a broad sense, helps to provide the conditions for professional growth on the part of other educational personnel within the school system. His most important function, however, and one upon which all other functions depend, is that of helping with the planning of effective educational programs for children.[47]

The school psychologist is a practitioner, but he is also a scientist, and he is an educational engineer, a designer of educational plans that use the latest methodologies and techniques. He has a great deal in common with the educational administrator and the classroom teacher in that he tries to use the educational system most effectively for individual children and groups of children. Like his colleagues in education, he should accent children's growth and development rather than "pathology". He differs from a family unit and as a member of a community. . . . We would stress that the school psychologist needs to be trained in education as well as clinical tional problems.[48]

Furthermore, Reger suggests a restructuring of the school psychologist's role on the basis of a growth-oriented direction rather than what he calls its present "pathology-centered mold."

For Reger the fundamental requirements for the school psychologist are a background in educational philosophy, educational curriculum, history of psychology, nature, philosophy and techniques of science, psychological testing and general psychology, apparently in that order.

Reger states that traditional medical conceptions of diagnosis in school psychology are largely irrelevant and makes a strong case for grounding the diagnosis in the discipline of education. His position on psychotherapy is a somewhat negative one as was discussed by Smith in Chapter 6. He feels that if the psychologist undertakes psychotherapy this may result in "an alienation of the school psychologist from the school system."

Reger suggests that the school psychologist forget his aura of secrecy and develop much more openness regarding his reporting. The school psychologist should be in a position of power and authority in the educational administrative hierarchy.

He suggests that the school psychologist play an active role with kindergarten children in terms of observations, locating problems, and establishing early parent contacts. Dr. Reger develops a rationale for special education, discrediting former extraneous medical classifications, which he feels were often only tangentially related to educational problems. Thus the focus of special education should be on the educational handicap of the child. His thoughts relating to the role of the school psychologist with the "brain-damaged" is an interesting section of this volume and, in general, he feels that this syndrome is often, at best, a spurious diagnosis.

In this breezy volume, Reger comes out as anti the establishment in

[47] *Ibid.*, p. 10.
[48] *Ibid.*, p. 27.

school psychology. On the other hand, his ideas are provocative and he should be read by the novitiate school psychologist.

GRUBBE: FACILITATOR OF ADJUSTMENT VIA ADLERIAN THEORY

Theodore E. Grubbe,[49] District Psychologist in Castro Valley, California has taken Adlerian theory [50] as the underpinning for his practice of school psychology. Grubbe states, "the school psychologist's main concern should be effecting through some means a more positive adjustment for the student and . . . other areas of concern should take a secondary position." Grubbe feels that generally the school psychologist is trained along Freudian or neo-Freudian concepts. He feels that in the clinic setting the traditional psychoanalytic framework may be effective; however, this framework is much less effective in the school.

Grubbe feels that the following limitations are inherent in applying the orthodox Freudian viewpoint in the school situation: 1) the school psychologist normally receives more referrals than he can handle; 2) referrals to outside agencies cannot always be effected; 3) communication is sometimes difficult with lay people and teachers using the Freudian framework; 4) Freudian theory does not provide the steps or program that the teacher or parent can put into effect.

Grubbe suggests that since Adlerian psychology is essentially a social psychology with the basic premise that all behavior is goal directed, this viewpoint has much relevance to the child in the school setting. Adler postulates that the individual is striving from a felt minus situation towards a plus situation based upon feelings of inferiority. According to Adler this is the one basic force behind all human activity. Grubbe maintains that this psychological frame of reference was most helpful in understanding the practical problems in the school setting. It is a psychology that if properly understood, is not going to create additional problems by a misdiagnosis of the dynamics of a child. In a diagnosis of a problem, the professional is determining the "life style" of the individual. He is looking for the "individual's own conception of himself as he sees himself in relation to society." The psychologist is looking for the purpose of the child's behavior rather than categorized predetermined factors.

Grubbe has found that the acceptance of Adlerian principles on the

---

[49] T. E. Grubbe, from an unpublished paper prepared for the editor in 1961 entitled, "The Changing Role of the School Psychologist."

[50] Heinze L. Ansbacher and Rowena R. Ansbacher, *The Individual Psychology of Alfred Adler* (New York: Basic Books, Inc., Publishers, 1956). Probably the best text which systematically presents Adler's writings and interpretations.

part of parents and teachers has been very encouraging. Poor school achievement, stealing, rebellion, withdrawing, lying, bedwetting, and speech problems are discussed in terms of what does this behavior mean to the child and does the refractory behavior help the child gain his goal toward striving toward "equality."

In the process of helping the child, the teacher does not take second place to the psychologist in working out behavior problems. The teachers are in a position to make tentative diagnoses themselves. The role of the school psychologist, moreover, becomes that of supporting the teacher diagnosis and elaborating on specific points and suggesting specific measures to be taken. Grubbe's experience suggests that the classroom teacher through the use of Adlerian psychology is able to detect the psychological and educational pathology more readily and with a greater degree of understanding. With such understanding on the part of teachers the referrals that reach the psychologist's office are those problems that require the more specialized skill and draw upon the background of a highly trained psychologist.

Thus, Grubbe feels that it is imperative that the school psychologist develop a functional theory of personality that is compatible with the reality of the school situation. Grubbe favors the Adlerian approach because it is a psychology that more realistically appraises the reasons for misbehavior in individuals, takes account of social interactions, has a firm foundation in the inherent right of the individual as a part of a social group, has practical and realist meaning *vis à vis* a democratic society, does not evade the real meaning of behavior and lends itself to a functional use within any existing problem situation.

PIELSTICK: SCHOOL PSYCHOLOGIST, FACILITATOR OF LEARNING

Norval L. Pielstick [51] takes the viewpoint that since the fundamental responsibility of schools is to promote learning and since this constitutes one of the major areas of psychology, it is fully appropriate for the school psychologist to direct his efforts primarily toward problems related to facilitation of learning.

Pielstick states his position as follows:

> Any point of view on school psychology, to be significant, must have direct relevance to both education and psychology. When one examines the aims of education, it becomes apparent that the achievement of its aims rests upon the learning processes which schools are able to effect. In general, one can consider the basic function of schools as that of bringing about

[51] Norval L. Pielstick, "School Psychology: A Focus on Learning," *Journal of School Psychology*, I, No. 1 (January, 1963), 15–17.

certain learnings. To do so effectively requires an understanding of how learning takes place and the factors which facilitate or impair learning efficiency. Although we are still far from a complete understanding of these matters, considerable psychological research and theoretical effort have been devoted to them. In fact, the field of psychology has built the foundation upon which we may erect a more thorough understanding of the nature of learning. By selecting learning as his point of focus, a school psychologist relates himself to the central function of a school system and at the same time concerns himself with an area of human behavior which has received considerable attention in the science of psychology since its earliest beginnings. Therefore, it seems both appropriate and promising to consider the possibilities likely to result from the school psychologist as a specialist in human learning. . . .[52]

The school psychologist who orients his efforts in a school system to problems related to learning may be as much concerned with individual children as a school psychologist who, for example, adheres to a mental health orientation. That is, his focus on learning which, after all, is the primary concern of the teacher leads the psychologist to a study of the pupil's learning situation and how he responds to it, an analysis of the particular learning abilities and disabilities of the child, the history of his learning patterns in and out of the school situation, and culminates in hypotheses or predictions (recommendations, if you wish) about what changes would be most likely to further the pupil's learning efficiency. This, of course, may constitute only the beginning point in work of the pupil, his teacher, and his parents.[53]

What has been suggested here should not be interpreted to mean that a school psychologist ignores the emotional components of behavior in a school setting. He may, in fact, be vitally concerned about how various social and personality factors impinge on learning processes and outcomes and undoubtedly he will need to use well established methods for the study of personality. The difference resides in his maintaining a focus on the impact of such factors on the learning of school children.[54]

For the school psychologist who is oriented in this manner, a useful publication that attempts to translate learning theory into classroom terminology in a very clear manner, is a 1964 publication of the Wisconsin State Superintendent of Public Instruction entitled *Learning Principles*.[55] It was prepared by a Learning Principles Committee which had representation from various school psychologist training programs as well as practicing school psychologists.

[52] *Ibid.*, p. 15.
[53] *Ibid.*, p. 16.
[54] *Loc. cit.*
[55] See also, David Ausubel, *The Psychology of Meaningful Verbal Learning: An Introduction to School Learning* (New York: Grune & Stratton, Inc., 1962); and Benjamin Wright, "On Behalf of a Personal Approach to Learning," *Elementary School Journal*, 58 (April, 1958), 365–375.

PETER: SCHOOL PSYCHOLOGIST COORDINATOR
OF PRESCRIPTIVE TEACHING

For Lawrence J. Peter of the University of Southern California, the school psychologist is the logical person to coordinate the prescriptive teaching process for any pupil. Peter in his book, *Prescriptive Teaching*[56] defines the process in this way: "Prescriptive teaching is a method of utilizing diagnostic information for the modification of educational programs for children with problems. It accomplishes this purpose by determining the education relevance of the child's disability, and devising teaching procedures to yield desirable changes in the child's academic progress, emotional condition, and/or social adjustment." In this respect, Peter parallels Reger in his regard for education as the central and most relevant discipline in planning for atypical youngsters.

Certainly the most egregious breach in professional effort in school psychological services has been the failure to extrapolate psychological and sociological findings into day-to-day classroom practices for the individual child studied. The interdisciplinary team has all too often been a convenient euphemism when specific educational recommendations were needed. *Prescriptive Teaching* provides a rationale for efforts to coordinate and operationalize psychological test findings and case history data regarding children referred so that they can be more adequately helped in the context of the school. Peter has developed a theoretical model for a *rapprochement* among the various specialists who work with the various groups of handicapped children. This multi-dimensional model provides a structure for medical, psychological, and social-work diagnoses to be converted into relevant educational terms and, furthermore, provides for adequate follow-through on specific recommendations. The author's chapters on "Translating diagnostic findings," "Communication and General Semantics," and "Follow-up" will be of special help to school psychological services personnel. Peter is a bit remiss in overlooking many of the prescriptive teaching regimens which have recently been developed around the United States, for example, the work of Marianne Frostig, Elsa Hauesserman, Katrina de Hirsch, Sophia T. Salvin, Elena Boder, Rosalyn Cohen and others.

M. S. Kaplan, Director of Psychological Services, in the Lansing schools would appear to agree with Peter's emphasis on school related variables when making an educational diagnosis and prescription as indicated in the following statement, "I want to learn how to diagnose and use the class, the teacher, the school and the child's environment in general, more effectively, rather

---

[56] Lawrence J. Peter, *Prescriptive Teaching* (New York: McGraw-Hill Book Company, 1965), p. 1. See also, L. J. Peter, "Effective Communication for School Psychologists," *Division of School Psychology Newsletter,* I (May, 1964), 1–8.

than continue the perseveration of our traditional analysis of the inner dynamics and aptitudes of the child (which often appears to be an intellectual exercise)." [57]

MOK: SCHOOL PSYCHOLOGY AS SOCIAL FACILITATION

Perhaps Paul B. Mok, formerly school psychologist in Bronxville, New York, represents the angry young man's view in school psychology today. A reading of his book, *A View from Within*,[58] will provoke a professional who holds either a traditionalist or a liberal view regarding the spectrum of school pupil personnel services. A few salty quotes from this book will whet the appetite of the reader.

> . . . Desperately the teacher wishes he had a wedge to place in the negative conditioning pattern in the hope it might deflect the pupil's energy from going into furthering of the maladaptive or socially undesirable pattern into constructive academic and social channels.

> *The school psychologist is just such a wedge.* He is a specialist in the area of human behavior. He has been trained as a diagnostician of academic, social, and personal learning problems of children. He has been trained in the theory and practice of techniques aimed at remedying such problems. If his training is superior, he has worked under careful supervision in clinical settings in helping children and their parents to alter negative conditioning patterns. He has been trained in large group settings and offers skills in understanding and helping the pupil in relation to both small and large group activities.[59]

> He is not a one-time coach who specializes in locker-room pep-talks as the means toward more successful learning. He is not the white-haired lady who has grown up in this town and knows everybody in it and who used to teach civics and now chats with the pregnant high school girls about their immediate and future plans and layettes. He is not the sullen, hatchet-faced young man with the glasses who is working on his master's degree in life adjustment and who comes reluctantly into the school for a sustaining paycheck to talk to high school freshman boys about their pimples and masturbation and nocturnal emissions. He is not the overworked principal who discusses next steps with Johnny's parents after their son has been arraigned in juvenile court. . . .[60]

However, later in his discussion, Mok parallels the emphases of Pielstick when he states:

> As a school psychologist, my first commitment is to promote learning. To promote learning is my task and to promote the ability to learn. In

[57] *The School Psychologist,* Division 16 Newsletter, 19 (July, 1965), 12.

[58] P. B. Mok, *A View from Within* (New York: Carlton Press, 1962). The psychologist's prime consideration, his prime aim, is to help individuals lead more socially constructive and productive lives.

[59] *Ibid.*, p. 125.

[60] *Ibid.*, p. 33

order to do this one of my main functions is to identify pupils who are experiencing apparent difficulty in learning. Thus, one of my basic functions is in identification and diagnosis. With a background of training and practice in the area of learning theory, learning difficulties, and disabilities, I endeavor to help teachers spot learning problems early.[61]

BARDON, MCNEIL, CUTLER, LONG, AND MORSE: SPECIALIST IN PREVENTIVE MENTAL HEALTH

According to the above individuals the primary function of a school psychologist is in the area of preventive mental health. This means he is *not* a high level intelligence tester, an administrator's assistant, director of testing and research, therapist, or curriculum developer.

Nicholas Long,[62] Associate Director of Hillcrest Center, in Washington, D. C. and formerly director of the school psychologist's training program at Indiana University, has stated that when the term school psychologist is used we should refer to a person whose basic identification is in psychology but whose training makes him vitally aware of and sensitive to the educational problems of the classroom teacher. Any other orientation, according to Long, dilutes the effectiveness of the school psychologist. He further feels that the question of whether the school psychologist should have a teacher certificate is not an important one. To be effective in a public school, the school psychologist should have the diagnostic and therapeutic training of the clinical psychologist and the knowledge and skills of the educational psychologist.

Long avers that there is no question that it is absolutely essential that a number of children receive individual psychotherapy. They need it. But, perhaps this should not be the function of the school psychologist. Individual psychotherapy is too time consuming and usually makes the teacher more dependent than independent, unless additional time is spent with the teacher clarifying her role with the child during treatment. However, if a school has the money and wants to provide this needed service, Long contends that, since in the past schools have provided many other supportive services, then there are no understandable reasons why a clinical psychologist cannot be hired by the school as a *clinical psychologist* to do clinical work with children. Why disguise a clinical psychologist under the name of school psychologist? Long asks.

The approach for the school psychologist that Long feels is most successful is the development of didactic case conferences. The goal of this approach being that by helping one teacher and one child you have helped all the children who are and will be in the teachers' classes who attend these

---

[61] *Ibid.*, p. 34.

[62] Nicholas J. Long, *A Rationale for Developing a New Graduate Training Program for School Psychologists* (Bloomington, Indiana; Indiana University, 1961, mimeo.).

learning sessions. A second approach he suggests is mental health screening programs during critical periods of personal development, e.g., kindergarten, third grade, eighth grade.

Elton McNeil, Richard Cutler, and William C. Morse [63] of the University of Michigan conceptualize the school psychologist as the managing director of the school mental health program. They divide his role into four parts: 1) sensitizing teachers to the existence of individual and group psychological problems; 2) teaching teachers how to be more sophisticated educational diagnosticians; 3) helping teachers manage learning according to good mental health principles; 4) helping the school translate psychological principles into educational programs.

Jack I. Bardon [64] and others have also looked upon mental health education as providing the overreaching framework for school psychological services. For Bardon, it makes the greatest sense to consider the total role of the school psychologist within the context of mental health education. He further feels that at the present time the climate is as good as it has ever been for major changes in mental health efforts.

More recently Rich and Bardon have written,

> The fundamental work of the school psychologist is to strengthen the efforts of the school through the broad application of mental health concepts. . . . Given our present knowledge in the behavioral and social sciences, learning and maturing cannot be separated. It is the psychologist's responsibility to share with teachers his appreciation that the teacher encourages the total growth of the child through the learning process. The psychologist is one agent in promoting mental health in the school; the teacher is another.[65]

VALETT: A TRADITIONAL VIEW

Robert Valett in his 1963 book, *The Practice of School Psychology*, states that, "The scientific study of the behavior of children and their educational problems with the purpose of facilitating learning and total human adjustment is the central concern of school psychology." [66] He later states that

---

[63] E. B. McNeil, R. L. Cutler, and W. C. Morse, "The School Mental Health Program," in *Professional School Psychology*, Vol. II, pp. 102–122.

[64] J. I. Bardon, "Mental Health Education: A Framework for Psychological Services in Schools," *Journal of School Psychology*, I (1963), 20–28.

[65] J. Rich and J. I. Bardon, "The Teacher and the School Psychologist," *Elementary School Journal*, LXIV (March, 1964), 318–323.

[66] R. E. Valett, *The Practice of School Psychology: Professional Problems* (New York: John Wiley & Sons, Inc., 1963). See E. M. Bower, "A Role Found or Sought?" *Contemporary Psychology*, IX (August, 1964), 315–316, for a review of Valett's book. Bower generally finds the book lacking excitement and contributing to the conservative portrayal of what a "mythical" school psychologist might be up to.

. . . his emphasis is primarily centered on preventive, educational, and remedial procedures rather than on the usual therapeutic and rehabilitative measures. . . . For purposes of clarification, it may be best to think of the school psychologist as a professional person especially well trained in clinical, counseling, and educational psychology, who also has extensive professional preparation and experience in education.[67]

Valett sees the school psychologist functioning in the three traditional areas: psychological counseling and guidance, consultation and individual evaluation, including responsibilities for case studies and follow-up. Valett takes a strong position when it comes to previous teaching experience for the school psychologist. . . . "It is not uncommon for teachers to ask the psychologist, either directly or indirectly, what teaching experience the psychologist has had. When the psychologist can informally mention and discuss some of the teaching problems he has had it is amazing to notice the greater ease whereby rapport is developed." [68]

The issue of teaching experience is a relatively dead issue in the late 1960's, while in the early 50's this was the source of burning controversy of the field. Most school psychologist trainers would feel that teaching experience would be helpful, as would many other kinds of practicum activities in working with children and adolescents. Some trainers would feel that practicums in child guidance clinics, state hospitals, sheltered workshops would add a significant dimension to the school psychologist's competence. However, it would appear today that teaching experience *per se* is not the *sine qua non* for entrance or success as a school psychologist.

LIVIE-NOBLE: SCHOOL PSYCHOLOGIST, A BRITISH VIEWPOINT: SPECIALIZED SCHOOL MASTER

Livie-Noble in his 1947 book, *The School Psychologist*,[69] the first book published in the pupil personnel services field that confined itself to a discussion of the school psychologist, presented a rather disparate role conceptualization, at least to an American reader. In some ways, Livie-Noble perceives the school psychologist as a special kind of school master, perhaps a more powerful and benign "Mr. Chips." A few quotations from his book will illustrate his characterization of this role.

What is the work which a Public School psychologist should be expected to do? First and foremost he must be a friend. He must not be regarded as a master nor as an official. He must be able to understand what the teachers mean when they describe the difficulties that they have with children: and

[67] *Ibid.,* p. 5.
[68] *Ibid,* p. 46.
[69] F. S. Livie-Noble, *The School Psychologist* (London: Gerald Duckworth & Co., Ltd., 1947).

he must also understand the reason for the difficulties which the children have with teachers: and for this he must be an experienced teacher and a child psychologist. He must be able to give the relevant tests and form an assessment of intellectual ability, and therefore he must have the equipment of laboratory training. He must be capable of recognizing and diagnosing early stages of psychological disorder, know when to refer a case to a medical psychiatrist, and be capable of giving psycho-therapy to appropriate cases; and therefore he must be a competent psychotherapist.[70]

I believe that an experienced psychologist, who has been a schoolmaster, can be of the greatest help and benefit in a school, where his contacts with boys and masters are free and his assistance and advice are readily sought and given.[71]

Education is not a matter of mechanics. It is not backwardness, dullness or misbehavior which should concern the school psychologist: it is with the personality of the child that he should be dealing.[72]

The American reader will be surprised when he reads the detailed training program proposed for the British school psychologist. Dr. Livie-Noble states that the school psychologist's preliminary instruction should consist of elements of logic, social anthropology, comparative religion, human anatomy, physiology, and body mechanics. The qualifying or second part of his professional education should consist of normal psychology, educational theory and practice, abnormal psychology, social psychology, psychotherapy, and parapsychology. (sic.) [73] For additional British viewpoints relating to the role of the school psychologist, the interested reader is directed to the footnote.[74]

TRACHTMAN: NEW DIRECTIONS FOR SCHOOL PSYCHOLOGY

Gilbert M. Trachtman [75] of New York University and formerly school psychologist and research coordinator in Long Beach, New York, contends that the schools of the future cannot possibly provide all the academic,

---

[70] Ibid., p. 28.

[71] Ibid., p. 8.

[72] Ibid., p. 21.

[73] Ibid., pp. 236–239.

[74] Eric Hopkins, "The School Psychological Service," Where, 23 (January, 1966), 24–25; D. M. Lee, "The School Psychological Service—an educational viewpoint," Bulletin of the British Psychological Society, 16 (1963), 27–31; Times Educational Supplement, "Educational Psychologist, School and Clinic," August 26, 1944; W. D. Wall, ed., Psychological Services in Schools (New York: New York University Press, 1956); Noel E. Whilde, The Application of Psychological Tests in Schools (London: Blackie and Son Limited, 1955); and H. J. Wright, "The School Psychological Service," Bulletin of the British Psychological Society, 16 (1963), 2–8.

[75] G. M. Trachtman, "New Directions for School Psychology," Exceptional Children, XXVIII (November, 1961), 159–164. This article was written specifically at the request of the editor of this book, and the editor writes to thank Professor Trachtman for this assistance. The paragraphs that follow are from the original manuscript.

clinical, and social services required by the children of the seventies. Thus he subscribes to the viewpoint that the schools should be especially charged with the intellectual development of the child. He feels that the schools should not abandon all noninstructional services but rather that such services should focus primarily on education, with matters of health and welfare being generally assigned to other community agencies. Philosophically this point of view suggests new directions for school psychology—a need Trachtman feels has already become evident from a casual inspection of manpower needs in the mental health professions, and in terms of the shortage of school psychologists.[76] Thus, Trachtman develops four priorities or hierarchies of function for school psychologists, as stated in the following paragraphs:

> In the school of the future the greatest concentration of school psychologists will be found in the primary grades . . . and the school psychologist's major function will be screening, early detection, and prevention. Academic and intellectual potential will be evaluated much earlier, and appropriate provisions for each child considered. . . .
>
> The psychologist will work with all children, and will spend much less time in intensive case work. Observational skills and techniques will have been sharpened and refined and more time will be spent in observing groups of children and consulting with teachers and parents. Although the complete and time consuming diagnostic work-up will still be warranted on occasion, the psychologist will more frequently refer to outside agencies for this purpose. The clinical tools will still be part of his armamentarium, but they will no longer be his chief stock-in-trade. . . .
>
> The second major emphasis for our school psychologist of the future will be evaluation and research. The school psychologist himself will conduct research studies and this will be a recognized and accepted aspect of his role. . . . Research conducted, supervised, or encouraged by the school psychologist will include practical and applied studies of immediate relevance to the local educational program as well as fundamental research on theoretical problems of child development, learning theory, etc. . . .
>
> The third major responsibility of the school psychologist will be his efforts to improve the mental hygiene atmosphere of school and community. Parent education and orientation programs may range in scope from academic lectures to group therapy with mothers of retarded readers. In-service programs for teachers may also range the gamut from academic to dynamic. Administrative consultation and participation in planning and policy making is also included here. . . .
>
> Fourth in Trachtman's hierarchy of major school psychological functions will be individual case work, the current front runner. In our dynamic reality-oriented profession of the future, the clinical approach with individual children will have been delegated mainly to other agencies of the

[76] See D. G. Salten, V. B. Elkin, and G. M. Trachtman, "Public School Psychological Services: Recent Growth and Further Potential," *Educational Administration and Supervision,* **XLII** (1956), 100–107, 162–169; and G. W. Albee, *Mental Health Manpower Trends,* Joint Commission on Mental Illness and Health Monograph Series, No. 3 (New York: Basic Books Inc., Publishers, 1959).

community and relegated to luxury status in the schools. . . . The routine processing of large numbers of individual referrals, so common today, will be found only in school systems boasting unusually large psychological departments in ratio to pupil population. Thus, the individual case approach will have become a luxury which only a few schools can afford. . . .

The future of school psychology, then, as it is pictured by Trachtman, does not entail any dramatic new concept of role, but rather a reality-oriented reassessment of priority of function. The most effective use of the limited number of psychologists available to the school is seen to lie in the deemphasis of the clinical approach and in the greater specialization of training and assignment for school psychologists. In the framework presented here school psychology becomes a distinct and definable field. . . .

With the exception of Gray [77] and Trachtman [78] few authorities have taken a clearly defined stand on the hierarchy of value in terms of services or functions which the school psychologist could possibly offer to American education.

LETON: TWO FUTURE FOCI

In discussing future directions for the specialty of school psychology, Donald Leton of the University of Hawaii has clearly stated that the traditional classification role will eventually become outmoded.[79] Recently the school psychologist has become involved in the prescription of special classes, remedial programs, and classroom treatments. Leton predicts that the traditional classification of assessment of mentality and educability will be supplanted by analyses of specific variables that will influence or alter these functions.

He projects several foci around which school psychologists might direct their future services. The first is to bring clinical skills to the diagnosis and treatment of students' problems. Leton affirms that "the school psychologist should be allowed, and even encouraged, to undertake the psycho-educational treatment of a problem." A second focus for the school psychologist of the seventies will be to provide psychological consultation to school personnel. In this latter respect, Leton supports the views of Gray, White, Harris, Trachtman, and others.

LEVY: PSYCHOLOGICAL INTERPRETATION IN THE SCHOOLS

In 1963, Professor Leon H. Levy of Indiana University published a book entitled *Psychological Interpretation*. This book, although written from

---

[77] Gray, *op. cit.*, 1963.

[78] Trachtman, *op. cit.*, 1961.

[79] Donald A. Leton, "School Psychology: Its Purposes and Directions," *Psychology in the Schools*, I (April, 1964), 187–189.

a clinical vantage point, conceptualizes a very important aspect of the school psychologist's role. Levy states:

> Interpretation is the most important single activity engaged in by the clinician. Whether engaged in overtly or covertly, intentionally or unintentionally, interpretation underlies every decision, diagnostic formulation, and therapeutic act. . . . Psychological interpretation, viewed as a behavior, is engaged in whenever a state exists that seems refractory to other efforts at mitigation or understanding. In essence, it consists of bringing an alternate frame of reference, or language system, to bear upon a set of observations or behaviors, with the end in view of making them more amenable to manipulation.[80]

Professor Levy continues his discussion *vis-à-vis* the logic and assumptions underlying the interpretative process and the nature of interpretation in psychodiagnosis, in the use of tests, and in psychotherapy.

The school psychologist is continually confronted with children, whose behavior is defined by teachers or parents as refractory or resisting ordinary methods of education or treatment. The *raison d'être* of the school psychologist in his diagnostic role then becomes that of the skilled behavioral scientist who can bring to the difficult situation a psychological point of view that he can communicate to the teacher, other educational personnel, or parent, in working with the child or children with the end in view of making the child's learning ability less hampered by adjustment problems or psychological complications.

Although psychological interpretation may not be the most important single activity of the school psychologist, for his role encompasses much beyond diagnosis, certainly interpretation, broadly defined as Levy defines the term, provides an organizing concept for much of the day-to-day activity of the school psychological services.

EISERER AND HIRST: INTERPRETING THE ROLE OF THE SCHOOL
PSYCHOLOGIST TO TEACHERS, ADMINISTRATORS, AND PARENTS

In 1963 Wilma E. Hirst [81] wrote a book which is an attempt to clarify and define the school psychologist's role. The book is written at a relatively unsophisticated level and has a use only in helping to interpret the role to those outside the specialty. Hirst defines the purposes and objectives of the school psychologist as follows:

> The school psychologist helps ascertain if the child is developing and utilizing his academic abilities to the fullest extent. He helps uncover causes of

[80] L. H. Levy, *Psychological Interpretation* (New York: Holt, Rinehart & Winston, Inc., 1963), viii.

[81] Wilma E. Hirst, *Know Your School Psychologist* (New York: Grune & Stratton, Inc., 1963).

failure in this development and utilization of the child's academic talent, and suggests ways of overcoming obstacles in the learning process. He helps school children discover and develop special interests and abilities. He helps children in the tremendously important task of becoming socialized—of learning to live and work with other people—of becoming an individual the rest of humanity cannot only tolerate but also admire.

Hirst neglects a consideration of the role of the school psychologist as mental health consultant and several other important areas of endeavor usually considered in a book on school psychology. Her definition of the school psychologist would seem to parallel that of the good teacher.

Professor Paul E. Eiserer of Columbia Teachers College also wrote a book, *The School Psychologist*, in 1963, primarily for the teacher and administrator. This brief book of about 100 pages presents a very coherent, readable statement regarding the various roles of the school psychologist. Eiserer emphasizes the fact that the school psychologist must work democratically with other educational personnel. He cautioned that the school psychologist rarely works alone. He feels the role of the school psychologist is influenced by the following factors: the community, the expectancies of the school, the particular training program, the certification requirements, and the individual's idiosyncratic professional self-image. He sees the school psychologist of today performing assessment, remedial, consultant, educator, and research roles. By educator role, Eiserer refers "to the role of providing more formal opportunities for the teacher to improve her knowledge of the theories and practices of psychology which will enable her better also to discharge her functions as a teacher." [82]

ARBUCKLE: ARBITER FOR SCHOOL PSYCHOLOGICAL
SERVICES WORKERS

Dugald S. Arbuckle in his 1966 book, *Pupil Personnel Services in the Modern School*,[83] reviews the place of psychological services in the American school and discusses the roles of the school counselor, the classroom teacher, the school social worker, and the school psychologist as well as of the attendance services, health services, psychometrist and other advisers in the guidance enterprise of a contemporary American school.

Writing from the vantage point of a counselor educator at Boston University, Arbuckle raises some provocative points.

In many ways, the school counselor and the school psychologist might both be described as counseling psychologists, since their orientation and their true expertise is, or should be primarily psychological in nature . . .

82 Paul E. Eiserer, *The School Psychologist* (Washington, D. C.: Center for Applied Research in Education, Inc., 1963), p. 82.

83 D. S. Arbuckle, *Pupil Personnel Services in the Modern School* (Boston: Allyn and Bacon, Inc., 1966).

they could be called educators if one means one who works in an educational milieu and is concerned in a broad sense with the education of children. The broad purpose of the school counselor and the school psychologist is the same as that of the teacher . . . the basic and primary function is to either help the child so that he may benefit more from his educational experience or to modify the educational experience so that it will be a valuable one for him.[84]

Arbuckle sees the school psychologist as still retaining his most central role of chief diagnostician, particularly for those children who might be considered atypical. He states: "The school psychologist is the one to whom the teacher will turn with the question, 'What is the matter with him?' and 'What can we do about it?' "[85]

He later raises the question as to whether the schools should have a counselor and a school psychologist and further wonders whether the schools might benefit from a combination of the two, namely "a counseling psychologist working in a school milieu." He further adds, ". . . the school counselor who has taken a few courses is no more a counselor than the "school psychologist who has taken a few courses is a psychologist." In a two year program for school psychological services workers there could be a broad core of courses and then a selection of courses which would determine the specific direction for the school psychological services worker. California approximates such a pattern now. Arbuckle feels that after this common core of training some individuals would move toward vocational theory and development and vocational counseling while others would see themselves as primarily diagnosticians for the normal or atypical child and many others would choose other specific roles based on training, competence and inclination.

He notes that the scope and standards of preparation in psychology for school counselors as presented by a committee of the Division of Counseling Psychology of the American Psychological Association parallels the training for school psychologists in many states and for the doctoral level person whom he has termed the school counseling psychologist.[86] He ends his discussion by stating, "The current doctoral graduates in school counseling and school psychology differ very little, and maybe the time has come to stop pretending that they represent two different professional areas and give them a new, more valid title." Arbuckle further states, "How the school psychologist uses what he knows is more important than what he knows." Arbuckle suggests that the "school psychologist is a professional and any professional worker should be able to develop the skills and competencies which make him effective in whatever direction he may wish to move."

He feels his proposal is in line with the recommendation of the 1963

[84] *Ibid.*, p. 170.
[85] *Ibid.*, p. 176.
[86] The Scope and Standards of Preparation in Psychology for School Counselors," *American Psychologist*, 17 (March, 1962), 149–152.

Peabody Conference, namely the point that "we should not be concerned with one model of school psychologist, but with several different models, each of whom might be highly effective in his own way, in furthering the optimal adjustment of school children." [87]

Arbuckle points out that the "openness" aspect of the school psychologist's function is in keeping with the Peabody Report's descriptions of the following functions: 1) bringing psychological knowledge to a situation as a resource person for helping others with problems, 2) facilitating communication among people, 3) facilitating the gathering of new knowledge to contribute to the solution of problems, 4) developing an inquiring attitude and a particular set of values that will guide him to look at situations objectively and to find solutions to problems in an objective way, 5) varying his approach as an attitude changer so that he uses procedures found to be effective through research in social psychology, 6) understanding that his ultimate concern is for the children of the school.

Arbuckle demonstrates that in terms of numbers the school psychologist is certainly junior to the school counselor. In 1967 the American School Counselor Association, a division of the American Personnel and Guidance Association had a membership of over 11,000 while Division 16 of the American Psychological Association had less than 1000. He opines that "psychologist" is not one of the accepted words in many school systems over the country while counselor is. Parenthetically, it is interesting that the City of Los Angeles requires its elementary *counselors* to have the *school psychologist* credential. Arbuckle has probably placed his finger on the reason.

Certainly the word "psychologist" is much more accepted in this decade than last and his prestige among school administrators and parents has risen substantially.

Congressman Sam Gibbons in his legislation proposed to Congress in 1966 would have us add another psychological services worker to the already expanding genre, namely the "Child Development Specialist." His bill, entitled the *Elementary and Preschool Child Development Act,* would provide scholarships for trainees in a two year graduate program. The explicit goal of the program is . . . "to help the school personnel to become more effective in the management and education of all children in the school, and especially to be a major support and resource to the teacher and to the parent in the education of children with beginning, moderate, or serious learning, behavior, or emotional problems." At the time of publication of this book, this bill had not yet become a law.

As Susan Gray has pointed out "we should all agree with Representative Gibbons that persons to provide those functions in the schools are needed

[87] *The Internship in School Psychology,* Proceedings of the Peabody Conference, March 21–22, 1963, 8.

sorely—and in large numbers." [88] This writer would question the advisability of a new professional. The general public, teachers and administrators are already confused with such a large number of pupil personnel services specialists. The writer tends to agree with Arbuckle that the professions of counseling and school psychology should consider a merger with the specificity in training and public school requirements for a distinctive type of psychological services worker to be left up to the training institutions, the knowledge of the employing official, the needs of the situation, and the conscience of the candidate.

The School Psychologist as a Teacher: Public Relations for Psychology

Among his other duties the school psychologist may be asked either to establish or to teach a course, or series of courses, in high school psychology. If this is the case, then the psychologist may well have reached the limits of his own ability, as this does indeed go beyond the training typically received by most school psychologists.

Several avenues are open to the school psychologist-teacher, according to Kenneth E. Coffield.[89] He may revert to his own first course in psychology in an attempt to ferret out those objectives, techniques, content, etc., that he can recall. This is, in all probability, one of the least productive of all the moves that he can make. It will only take him up blind alleys, and he will create without doubt a version less powerful than his own first course. Rather than search one's memory for material that has long since been forgotten, there are at least two productive steps in establishing a high school course. First, contact might be made with other teachers who have had success in the teaching of high school psychology. In some cases, these will be fellow school psychologists who have had similar problems, and whose aid will facilitate the immediate resolution of obstacles. Secondly, Division 2 of the APA maintains a Committee on High School Psychology which can be contacted for suggestions, bibliographic materials, mailing addresses, and general information that might be of assistance.

Once this initial step is taken, and it is established that the new course is to be added to the curriculum, there are at least three long-range objectives

[88] Susan W. Gray, "The President's Message," *The School Psychologist* (January, 1966), 33. For additional information relative to this proposed legislation, see, Eli M. Bower, "Washington News Notes," *Psychology in the Schools*, 3 (January, 1966), 88–90. For an analysis of the role of the CDS the reader is referred to: L. S. Levine, H. B. Gelatt, L. G. Nowlin, W. M. Littell, and H. Lahaderne "The Use of the Child Development Specialist in the Elementary School," *Psychology in the Schools*, 2 (July, 1965), 255–262.

[89] The writer of this chapter is indebted to Professor Kenneth E. Coffield for providing some of the material for this section relating to high school psychology.

to be set up for any first course in psychology. These objectives are: 1) the development of a more accurate image of the science of psychology; 2) recruitment into the profession; and 3) the creation of a better-informed public with regard to the nature and scope of psychology at large. Let it be stated from the outset that these are not to be considered the only objectives of the first course.

Although these objectives are set down in random order, the development of a more accurate image of psychology must be placed very high on the list of any instructor who is teaching a student's first class in psychology. Coffield feels the subject must be presented as a science.[90] Many of our high school students are now leaving their psychology classes with no more understanding of scientific psychology than when they entered. In fact, they often leave with a reinforced impression that "this is nothing but common sense." In effect, we are working against ourselves. The public at large must be aware of psychology the science, and one valuable avenue for disseminating this information is through the high school population. Certainly, as Valett [91] has stated, "The future of school psychology depends on the public image and understanding of the profession." This same statement can, of course, be made for the entire psychological field.

Eiserer [92] in discussing the recruitment problem, stated,

> Psychology must recruit into its ranks more young men and women with the talent to become highly qualified psychologists and the desire to use their competence in the service of education. In so doing, psychology must compete with other professions in placing before young people a bold conception of public service, excellent training facilities, and the challenge to contribute to the growing stature of a profession.

Mullen in 1963 [93] wrote an occupational information prospectus on the school psychologist. Such a publication is a useful introduction for high school or junior college students considering the specialty of school psychology.

There are two general areas around which the high school psychology course is typically taught: 1) the scientific, with a heavy emphasis on the biological aspects, and 2) the social. At this time we will not debate the issue of which is the proper orientation, but will point out that, despite the system followed, the scientific aspects of psychology can be presented. This approach, however, does place some unique demands upon any teacher, for he must be

[90] This is a statement of Professor Coffield's bias. Engle found from a random sample of Division 2 members that 48 per cent believed that high school psychology should be taught as a science, 29 per cent thought it should be taught as a social study, and 23 per cent thought it should be taught as either. T. L. Engle, "Preparation for Teaching Psychology," *American Psychologist*, 15 (1960), 353–355.

[91] R. E. Valett, *op. cit.*, p. 284.

[92] P. E. Eiserer, *The School Psychologist*, p. 107.

[93] Frances A. Mullen, *American Occupations, No. 26—Public School Psychologist* (Boston: Research Publishing Company, Inc., 1963).

capable of presenting scientific subject matter as does the biology, physics, or chemistry teacher. The school psychologist who attempts to teach a high school psychology course should, however, be far better prepared than many who are now teaching these classes. He should have had the advantage of a substantial psychological background and probably will have had at least some contact with psychological research. With a minimal shift in orientation, the school psychologist will be prepared to meet this demand and be able to present psychology, the science, in its best light.

The second broad objective, that of recruitment into the profession, is an ever-pressing problem that must be considered. The very rapid growth of this discipline has extended its sphere of influence across many fields. The science is very much in need of talented youth. Psychology is a vast field and should be capable of satisfying the diverse needs of many young people. A large number of students, however, are turning away from psychology and school psychology because they have not had the proper introduction at the high school level, or perhaps even the grade school level. This same comment can be made, to some degree, concerning the first course at the college level.

The able youth enters his first psychology class, whether in high school or college, finds, first of all, that it is not what he expected, and then often finds further that his instructor does not have a scientific orientation in spite of the fact that he is being told that it is a science. Before long he may begin to wonder; and, if his ambiguity tolerance is not great, he leaves this course and the field still wondering just what psychology is all about. Thus, as a result of faulty instruction, we may be turning away many potential psychologists, and losing them to the other fields. This is ability and talent that psychology cannot afford to lose.

The third broad objective is the development of a public better informed as to the total scope and the scientific basis of the discipline. We know that if we are going to have an impact on the "broad scene," the public must know just what psychology is. Approximately 50 per cent of our high school students go on to college, and of this group only some will take even the introductory course in psychology. If we are to reach the majority of people, therefore, it must be done at the high school level. These youth whom we teach in our high schools today are the potential recipients of psychological services tomorrow. They will one day be supporting or failing to support psychology and school psychological services, and mass support for much of psychology is of vital importance at all times. These are our future controlling agents, and it is Coffield's view that they should have as accurate an image of psychology as possible.[94]

[94] For an extended discussion of this topic as well as a detailed bibliography on this topic see T. L. Engle, "Teaching Psychology in the High School," in *Professional School Psychology*, II, 76–101.

Robert Belensky,[95] psychologist in the Newton Public Schools, Massachusetts, in a recent letter to the *American Psychologist*, suggested that instruction in psychology be extended to the elementary schools, for after speaking to a fourth grade class on "Psychology as a Science," he was rewarded for his efforts in terms of enthusiastic student response. Belensky kept a list of the questions these children asked. The following reflect the charm and honesty of childhood as well as psychological relevancy:

Why do cat's eyes get bigger when it is dark?
What does your bran do for you?
Why does fathers yell at you?
What part of the head lets you see?
Does an animal have as many parts in the brain as a human?
How come some people are smart and some aren't?
Why do boys and girls hate each other?
Why do people fight?
What makes people go to sleep?
Could you kid become a genus after he or she have many years of college?
Why do you get ideas faster than others?
Can you hipmalize (hypnotize) a bird?
Why don't I like to read?

Belensky raised the following concerns regarding this experience:

1. Might not psychology be taught as a major scientific area in the elementary grades?
2. Perhaps the psychologist's function in the schools can legitimately go beyond the now traditional (in some school systems at least) bounds of diagnosis and therapy. We are supposed to be experts in learning and behavior in general. We already conduct human relations seminars for parents or teachers. Why not teach more basic material and why not teach children—a rather appropriate thing to do in a public school, one would think?
3. Children seem to have a remarkable "built-in" capacity to respond enthusiastically to cognitive stimulation generously applied. I suspect that we who see children when they are primarily patients, or sources of data in a research endeavor, do not fully appreciate this.

Thus the above discussion suggested that the extension of the role of the school psychologist in some school districts to that of teacher of psychology at the elementary and secondary level can be a personally rewarding role and one that can serve the entire profession of psychology in a positive way. In 1966, Hingham, Massachusetts as well as other school districts had developed ele-

[95] Robert Belensky, "Psychology in a Suburban School System," *American Psychologist*, 18 (1963), 669–670.

mentary school courses of study in psychology. Several books which introduce the science of psychology to the grade school reader are now available.

Ethical Issues in School Psychological Services

A profession is often judged by the ethical standards of its members and by its contribution to the welfare of mankind. One of the ingredients of a profession according to Tiedeman and Field [96] is a "social mandate to use, within certain limits, the considerable power inherent in the possession of its expertise." Other attributes of a profession are 2) an ever-developing body of knowledge; 3) a desire to achieve certain general conditions in and through specific instances; and 4) persons capable of creatively achieving the desired general condition in particular instances.[97]

Ethical issues [98] cannot be separated neatly from legal issues although important distinctions can be made. Law is generally defined as a body of rules or conduct enforced by the courts. Ethics as a field of investigation is commonly defined as the study of the nature of the action of responsible human beings, these actions being considered in relation to their moral qualities. The ethical code of a profession represents the formulation by consensus derived from within the profession itself of the general rules of professional conduct and moral obligation to which the members by affiliation are held responsible. However, the profession alone cannot effectively control the standards of practice of those outside the professional organization if legal control of the unqualified is not an actuality.[99] Certification for school psychologists existed in 43 states including the District of Columbia in 1967.

Susan W. Gray [100] in her recent book discussed the ethical position of the school psychologist in considerable depth and summarized the origin of ethical codes. The ethical code of the American Psychological Association was developed by a committee under the chairmanship of Nicholas Hobbs.[101] This code, unlike the Hippocratic Oath, was developed through an analysis

[96] D. V. Tiedeman and F. L. Field, "Guidance: the Science of Purposeful Action Applied Through Education," *Harvard Educational Review*, **XXXII** (Fall, 1962), 483–502.

[97] *Ibid.*, p. 485.

[98] The writer acknowledges his debt to an unpublished paper prepared in 1961 by Dr. Elvet Glyn Jones of Western Washington College, Bellingham, Washington, entitled "Ethical Considerations in School Psychological Services," for some of the ideas contained in this section of the chapter.

[99] W. H. Nelson, "Variations in Patterns of Certification for School Psychologists," *Journal of School Psychology*, **II** (1964), 47–53.

[100] Gray, *op. cit.*, pp. 364–385.

[101] American Psychological Association, *Ethical Standards of Psychologists* (Washington, D. C.: American Psychological Association, 1953). See also, American Psychological Association, "Social Influences on the Standards of Psychologists," Report of the Committee on Scientific and Professional Responsibility, Washington, D. C., 1961.

of critical incidents and a generation of general principles regarding these incidents. This code, first published in its complete form in 1953, was derived in an empirical way, and has made great contributions in its applicability and immediacy in everyday decisions of the psychologist. The code was revised in 1959 and in 1963.[102]

Inasmuch as the preamble of this APA statement provides a brief summary of the responsibilities of the psychologist to society, to the profession, and to himself, it is reproduced here in its entirety:

> The psychologist believes in the dignity and worth of the individual human being. He is committed to increasing man's understanding of himself and others. While pursuing this endeavor, he protects the welfare of any person who may seek his service or of any subject, human or animal, that may be the object of his study. He does not use his professional position or relationships, nor does he knowingly permit his services to be used by others, for purposes inconsistent with these values. While demanding for himself freedom of inquiry and communication, he accepts the responsibility this freedom confers; for competence where he claims it, for objectivity in the report of his findings, and for consideration of the best interests of his colleagues and society.[103]

From a study of the revised APA Code the professional worker will become informed that: 1) his primary obligation is to the welfare of society and the individuals he serves (Principle 1); 2) if he becomes aware of improper practices of other psychological personnel he attempts to correct the situation at first informally and with the attitude of professional growth in mind. If he is unable to alter the situation informally he directs it to the attention of the appropriate authorities (Principle 2a); 3) even if under pressure by officials, he does not undertake to offer services for which he is neither qualified nor competent (Principle 2b); 4) information obtained in professional relationships is discussed only for professional purposes and only with authorized persons clearly involved with the case (Principle 6b). If case material is used at professional meetings the anonymity of the subject must be strictly preserved; 5) he does not normally offer assistance to a person who is presently receiving similar assistance from another professional worker unless he obtains permission from the other worker or unless the other relationship is voluntarily terminated by the client or guardian (Principle 11); 6) in research and publication involving cooperation of others he assigns credit in proportion to the contribution offered (Principle 17).

Important as it is to have a code that sets forth in written form the empirically derived standards of practice, no code can be expected to resolve or to encompass all the specific problems of practice. Each practitioner needs to

---

[102] American Psychological Association, "Ethical Standards of Psychologists," *American Psychologist*, **XIV** (1959), 279–282; American Psychological Association, "Ethical Standards of Psychologists," *American Psychologist* **XVIII** (1963), 56–60.

[103] *Ibid.*, 1963, p. 56.

develop the attitude of critical discussion of the unresolved issues among his colleagues.[104]

In addition to state legislative and judicial statutes relating to the ethical performance of psychologists in private practice and psychological services workers in the schools, a number of state school psychologist's associations have codes of ethics, as well as established committees which review evidence concerning the misconduct of their members. Gray [105] pointed out that school psychologists may be especially vulnerable to pressures that would lead them away from developing the highest quality in their work. Such pressures in this role are the long waiting list, possible administrative coercive behavior, and working in isolation, to mention only a few.

CASPP has had a very active ethics committee [106] which has formulated guidelines for school psychological services personnel based upon the APA ethical standards. It was the feeling of the CASPP committee that the APA ethical standards, although not phrased in language wholly appropriate to a public school setting, do express in spirit the ethical posture that school psychologists might wish to adopt as their own.

The following statements represent the CASPP committee amplifications of the APA code regarding special class placement:

> 1) A school psychologist realistically describes the values and limitations of a special class placement to a parent and/or child. . . . 2)He understands the importance of on-going evaluation in the placement of children in special classes. . . . 3) The school psychologist may be expected to give to the educational staff such clinical information as they, by virtue of their professional training and competence, are able to understand and use in the best interest of the child. . . . 4) He must be aware of his own limitations in the diagnosis of specific problems such as a possible existence of a neurological handicap or other condition which may involve consultations or referral to an appropriate resource specialist.[107]

Regarding the school psychologist who engages in psychotherapy the CASPP committee felt that he must recognize that this service requires functions and responsibilities differentiated from those usually performed by him. Thus the committee drew the following guidelines:

> 1) It is the responsibility of the school psychologist to assist the administration and others in defining his own professional competencies before determining the therapeutic activities he will perform. 2) The individual may feel external or internal pressures to perform services for which his training and experience are inadequate; the individual should recognize his ethical responsibility in response to these pressures. 3) In recognizing the limitations

104 *Ibid.*, pp. 56–60.
105 Gray, *op. cit.*, p. 385.
106 Dwight Goodwin, Committee Chairman, CASPP, Report of Ethics Committee, presented at the Annual Conference, Los Angeles, March, 1962 (mimeo.).
107 *Ibid.*, p. 11.

of his competencies, he may find it necessary to refer a client to a practitioner or agency more able to provide the appropriate treatment for the client.[108]

Regarding confidentiality, the CASPP committee proposed the following embellishment to the APA code:

> It is recommended that a public school staff may not be fully aware of the possible injury that could result from misuse of confidential information. It is therefore the responsibility of the school psychologist to reveal to appropriate school staff members, information which they may find useful in helping the child who has been referred to the school psychologist.[109]

The CASPP amplification of the APA statement concerning referral was as follows:

> When a referral to another agency is refused by the child's parent, the psychologist must consider the possible harm to the child that might result. If, in the judgment of the psychologist, the welfare of the child is endangered, the psychologist should either: 1) help the parents to understand and accept the referral, or 2) refer the child to an agency which can intervene to provide the needed assistance.[110]

The issue of parental consent for school psychological services has been handled in different ways by different districts in various cities and states. The CASPP committee statement in this respect had two addenda to the APA Code:

> 1) The school psychologist recognizes the importance of the parent-child relationship. Therefore, it is considered a sound and ethical practice to elicit the support of the parent when providing services for a child. 2) In a setting where self-referrals are not uncommon, the student should be made aware of responsibilities which require the school psychologist to advise the parents of the existence and nature of the relationships into which the student may be entering.[111]

The ethics committee endorsed the APA statement regarding private practice. The APA Principle 2.42–1 states:

> It is not good practice for a psychologist to accept a private fee or any other form of remuneration, for professional work with a person who is entitled to his services through an institution or agency (in this case the public schools).[112]

The issue of a private practice is a thorny one, as Katherine D'Evelyn [113] indicated in her Division 16 Presidential Address in 1961, where she discussed

---

[108] Ibid., p. 12.
[109] Ibid., p. 12.
[110] Ibid., p. 13.
[111] Ibid., p. 14.
[112] American Psychological Association, Ethical Standards of Psychologists, p. 72.
[113] Katherine E. D'Evelyn, "Running Twice as Fast," Newsletter, Division 16, November, 1961.

the ethical dimension of the school psychologist's role at some length. She especially concerned herself with the problem of ethics relating to private practice of the school psychologist. She asked the question: "How much time can the school psychologist give to private practice and not do harm to his work in the schools?"

As was documented in the California status studies reviewed in Chapter 21, some school psychologists do engage in a part-time private practice in communities other than the one where the school district is located in which they are employed. Thus many school psychologists hold both a credential from a State Department of Education as well as certification by an appropriate state licensing agency for private practitioners in psychology. In the case of California, this is the Board of Medical Examiners.

Even though the school psychologist does not intend to seek such a supplementary license in order to engage in private practice, Itkin [114] feels there are a number of reasons why school psychologists should be concerned in regard to certification of practicing psychologists. Itkin suggests that first the school psychologist wants to know that every psychologist who offers his service to the public for pay is adequately trained to give the service he offers. Secondly, the school psychologist wants to know that psychologists in private practice are the type of individuals who a) practice within the limitations of their competence; b) know when they need to depend upon the physician for medical diagnoses; c) know when to refer for psychiatric diagnosis and treatment and do so, and d) respect and use the service of other professional persons in the mental health services. Itkin points out that increasingly the school psychologist must make referrals for services to psychologists in private practice, and even though the school psychologist typically does not engage in private practice, he must be certain that those who do offer their services are competent and ethical.

The most persistent ethical problems confronted by one State school psychological association's committee on ethics were listed as follows: 1) private practice undertaken by school psychologists within the boundaries of the school district in which they are employed; 2) pressures on school psychologists to compromise their professional judgment for administrative expediency, and 3) communication of information to unauthorized persons.[115]

That ethical decisions are not always easy is illustrated in a study by Wiskoff [116] that presents some of the complexities faced by psychologists regarding divided loyalties. The problem of divided loyalties is of particular

[114] William Itkin, "Why Should School Psychologists and Educational Psychologists Care About Certification?" *Psychology in the Schools,* I (1964), 89.

[115] California Association for School Psychologists and Psychometrists, *Newsletter,* 7 (June, 1960).

[116] M. Wiskoff, "Ethical Standards and Divided Loyalties," *American Psychologist,* XV (1960), 656–660.

concern in school psychological services and those accepting a position in this area must realize and accept the nature of their multiple obligations. As stated in the report of the Thayer Conference:

> In all phases of his work the school psychologist must weigh the welfare of children, the welfare of staff members, and the welfare of the school as an educational organization, keeping the welfare of the children central in his consideration. He must avoid getting himself into situations which involve betraying a child (or staff member) on the one hand and disloyalty to the school on the other.[117]

One concern involving both legal and ethical considerations is that of safeguarding professional confidences. Since very few States have clearly defined legal provisions granting privileged communication and the confidentiality of records in school psychological services, each practitioner must study the legal rules that apply to his local situation and operate within these limitations. Defining one's limits of operation in advance can do much to prevent the development of conflicts concerning the safeguarding of professional confidences.

Trachtman[118] authored a chapter in 1963 that is well documented and presents in detail the situation and events leading up to the present position on confidentiality of school records and privileged communication in the State of New York. Guidelines for a policy concerning the confidentiality of psychological records and test data in the New Rochelle Schools were also recently published.[119]

Trachtman summarized his viewpoint as follows:

> Privileged communication is vital to the psychologist-client relationship and by-and-large recognition of this by judicial, legislative, and administrative officials seems to be increasing.[120]

Regarding confidentiality of records, he stated:

> The school psychologist should be dedicated to the theme of communication. Knowledge of a child which the psychologist keeps in his head or in a locked file benefits no one. But communication itself is a highly technical skill and the psychologist should be trained to determine *how* he may best communicate certain information, to *whom* he may most suitably communicate, and *when* it is most appropriate to communicate. At the parent's request he should gladly send his technical reports to another psychologist or clinic, or anyone with suitable training to use the material properly. He should be eager to sit down with the parent and interpret

---

[117] Norma E. Cutts, ed., *School Psychologists at Mid-Century* (Washington, D. C.: American Psychological Association, 1955), p. 90.
[118] G. M. Trachtman, "The School Psychologist and Confidentiality of School Records," *Professional School Psychology*, II, 306–329.
[119] Irving Zweibelson, "Who Shall Interpret Individual Test Results to Parents?", *Journal of School Psychology*, II (Winter, 1964), 82–85.
[120] Trachtman, *op. cit.*, p. 325.

findings. Then, with the best interests of the child at heart, he must exercise all his professional skill to make sure he communicates.[121]

Differences of opinion as to how professional ethics should be inculcated exist; however, there is wide agreement that increased attention should be given to systematic presentation of ethics during professional education.[122, 123, 124] DePalma and Drake,[125] in a study that reports on the extent of instruction in ethics at certain selected schools offering graduate work in psychology, suggest the following: "Ethics is handled best on a graduate level, in a seminar or colloquium, preferably on a required basis for all students, and definitely so for clinical students." The editor of this text feels very strongly that ethical considerations should also be an important substantive aspect of the graduate training of all school psychological services workers. However, in the final analysis sound ethical decisions must be based upon intelligent action involving individual conscience and informed experience.

Education, Training Standards, and Certification

Since 1920, the Bulletin of Teachers College, Columbia University has listed courses for the training of school psychologists even though New York State, the first state to certify school psychologists did not begin this practice until 1935. Many of the courses listed in the 1920's still perform an important propaedeutic role as for example, Psychology of Exceptional Children and Mental and Educational Tests.

The viewpoint of the author of this chapter is that training for *all* school psychological services personnel draws upon a common body of information, in fact, one can safely say that training for all of the helping professions, facilitative professions, or mental health professions draws upon this common body of information from the behavioral sciences, ethics, and other fields. Thus psychiatrists, clinical psychologists, psychiatric nurses, psychiatric social workers, school counselors, visiting teachers and others draw upon scientific and humanistic wisdom held in common in their day to day endeavors.

The differences among the various roles of the helping professions are primarily related to 1) geography or place of employment, 2) jurisdictional and/or certification standards, and 3) the intensity and specificity of psychological need in a certain place and time as related to the training and to the background skills of the professional person employed.

---

[121] *Ibid.*, p. 327.

[122] R. Creegan, "Concerning Professional Ethics," *American Psychologist,* 6 (1958), 272–275.

[123] National Educational Association, *Code of Ethics of the NEA.* (Washington: D. C.: NEA, 1952).

[124] M. Wiskoff, *op. cit.,* 656–660.

[125] N. DePalma and R. Drake, "Professional Ethics for Graduate Students in Psychology," *American Psychologist,* 6 (1960), 343–349.

The writer feels that in order to alleviate the power struggle presently existing in the psychological services field or for that matter in all of the mental health facilitative specialities, there should be a common core of training.

Mental health in America is too important an area of concern to be bogged down by internecine power struggles. If some training in all "helping professions" was truly interdisciplinary, perhaps we could achieve a more cooperative effort.

In this respect the concluding comment of the UNESCO report regarding psychological services for the schools of the world is relevant:

> It is for this reason that the committee recommends that all workers concerned with mental, emotional, and social well-being of children should in their training be given some acquaintance with specialities other than their own; and that as much as possible of the training of those who make up child guidance and similar teams should be conjoint. (sic.) [126]

In contrast, a school psychology training program where there is a strong role definition and commitment is described by Gray.[127] The findings of the Interprofessional Research Commission on Pupil Personnel Services [128] may provide further clarification regarding those areas of common knowledge and skills that the various pupil personnel services specialists hold in common and those areas where there should be training in common.

The writer supports the views of the Division 16 Report regarding two levels of training and the need for many sub-doctoral psychological examiners. Clark in 1957 writing of sub-doctoral workers in the field of psychology concluded:

> They are performing services that definitely need performing and we would expect, as more and more Ph.D. psychologists enter the field that the number of persons they will need to recruit as their assistants (with M.A.'s or less) will increase. Thus psychology needs to include in its recruiting process, not merely persons of various interest, but persons of varying levels of ability, in order to meet the demands of the future.[129]

In the Miami Conference on Graduate Education in psychology, the following summarizing statement was made:

> . . . we must now give serious attention to preparing persons for some of the functions which concern us by means of training programs which are less costly in time and personnel than in doctorate education. One

126 W. D. Wall, ed., *Psychological Services for Schools* (New York: New York University Press, 1956), p. 143.

127 Susan W. Gray, "Psychologists for the Public Schools," *American Psychologist,* XV (1959), 701–704.

128 E. L. Hoch, *op. cit.,* pp. 27–30.

129 K. Clark, *America's Psychologists: A Summary of a Growing Profession* (Washington: American Psychological Association, 1957), p. 18.

of these is the conviction that for some roles appropriate adequate training can be given in one or two years of graduate work.[130]

The demand for psychologists continues to grow disapproportionately to the output of Ph.D.'s. Albee in 1963 [131] projected a demand for 8,000 to 10,000 new psychologists in nonacademic positions during the 1960's. In regard to the number of school psychologists the present supply is far short of demand. Ferguson [132] estimated the need, based on a ratio of one psychologist to each 3,000 school children, which is an equally conservative figure. He indicated on this basis a shortage of at least 10,000 school psychologists in 1963.

One writer in 1964 [133] described a failure in sub-doctoral training in school psychology in Texas. This failure in part was attributed to the fact that in Texas a "school psychologist" had not been defined by the Texas Education Agency. Thus nothing prohibited school district administrators from hiring a "school psychologist," as long as he was paid out of local funds. Unfortunately, in the past, many school administrators have "anointed" or "knighted" individuals with the title school psychologist—individuals who had little professional training. Thus, there were few individuals who wished to undertake a rigorous two year pre-doctoral training in school psychology when many positions were available for persons with less than this amount of education.

Bindman [134] stated in 1964 that since the suggested certification standards have been made widely available by Division 16, universities may be able to develop high level training programs even in those states where the state certification standards are rather low.

> As the university training staffs become somewhat more homogeneous in their orientation and training in school psychology and as the profession becomes more standardized, it is expected that there will be an increased interest in working on standards and maintaining them.

White [135] in a survey of school psychology training programs existing in 1961–1962 found that at least three types of training emerged: 1) programs that met state certification only; 2) programs that led to a diploma or masters

---

[130] Ann Roe, J. W. Gustad, B. V. Moore, S. Ross and Marie Skodak, eds., *Graduate Education in Psychology* (Washington: American Psychological Association, 1959), p. 39.

[131] G. Albee, "American Psychology in the Sixties," *American Psychologists,* **XVIII** (1963), 90–95.

[132] D. G. Ferguson, "Training Programs in School Psychology," *Professional School Psychology,* **II**, 289.

[133] Frances M. Carp, "Sub-doctoral Training in School Psychology: a Lesson on Failure," *Psychology in the Schools,* I (July, 1964), 215–233.

[134] A. J. Bindman, "University Training of School Psychologists and Certification Standards," *Journal of School Psychology,* II (Winter, 1964), 43–48.

[135] Mary Alice White, "Graduate Training in School Psychology," *Journal of School Psychology,* II (Winter, 1964), 34–42.

degree including state requirements but representing an integrated professional training; and 3) programs leading to the Ph.D. or Ed.D. covering state requirements but representing a higher level of training.

In a survey by Smith [136] during school year 1964–65, he discovered that seventy-nine colleges and universities reported training programs in school psychology while two reported having training programs in the planning stage. (In contrast in a 1957–58 survey only nine programs *in toto* were located.) Sixty-five schools did not return the questionnaire; however, it was known that at least four of these colleges had training programs from the data collected annually by the APA. The administration of these seventy-nine programs was located in the department of psychology in thirty-seven schools, the department of education in twenty-two, eight in departments of educational psychology while twelve programs were administered by inter-departmental committees from both psychology and education.

Fifteen institutions granted a doctoral degree only while thirty schools offered only subdoctoral degrees. Thirty-four programs offered an option between a doctoral or subdoctoral training. Students in school psychology were receiving aid from United States Public Health Service Stipends while seven universities had NDEA stipends for students, as well as many local sources for fellowships and scholarships.

Smith leaves the prospective school psychologist trainee with the following advice: "*Caveat emptor* (let the buyer beware) would be a good maxim to remember. Students should write directly to each university for information concerning the goals and philosophy of the program, the curriculum and internship arrangements, admission procedures, and financial aid." A perusal of the December issue of the *American Psychologist* of the current year will provide up-to-date information on training programs.

White [137] concluded from her survey that a total of 1,005 students were reported in the field of school psychology in 1962–1963 in all three of the above mentioned programs. White felt that four-fifths of those school psychologists were in sub-doctoral training programs. Out of the thirty-eight programs surveyed only one program required teacher training, two implied it, and the rest made no reference to it. White assumed that "although many of those training to become school psychologists may have had teaching ex-experience, it is no longer the hallmark of their candidacy."

One study by Ferguson revealed that 134 institutions had played a part in the training background of those individuals who were members of Division

[136] Donald C. Smith, "Institutions Offering Graduate Training in School Psychology," *Journal of School Psychology*, 3 (Winter, 1965), 58–67. See also, M. A. White, "Graduate Training in School Psychology," *Journal of School Psychology*, 2 (1964), 34–42; S. Ross and J. Jacqueline, "Educational Facilities and Financial Assistance for Graduate Students in Psychology: 1964–65," *American Psychologist*, XIX (1964), 814–845.
[137] White *op. cit.*, p. 39.

16 in 1960. The five leading universities in terms of the number of persons trained who became school psychologists were: Columbia University, New York University, Ohio State University, University of Minnesota, and the University of Southern California.

Ferguson listed the problems and issues in training school psychologists as the following: 1) providing for students with great variations in background; 2) achieving a cooperatively developed training program; 3) defining the field; 4) providing a carefully supervised internship; 5) the issue of levels of title and training; and 6) the issue of required teaching experience.[138]

A brief description of the doctoral program at the University of Wisconsin follows:

> The doctoral program in school psychology is sponsored jointly by the department of Psychology and Educational Psychology. Graduate students do their major work in one department and complete a minor in the other. The decision as to whether the major is to be in psychology or educational psychology is determined primarily by the student's undergraduate major. In either case, the courses taken are essentially the same, and specific courses are required only to the Master's level. Beyond this level, courses, seminars, and independent reading and research are decided upon in terms of each student's special needs and interests.

> The school psychology program is strongly child-clinical in orientation but places considerable emphasis on personality and social psychology. The goal of the program is to prepare psychologists to serve as consultants, researchers, and practitioners in schools, and particularly, to equip them to deal with the psychological problems of school children, their parents, and their teachers, and such psychological problems as exist in curriculum planning and school administration.[139]

A November, 1965 statement from Rutgers University, in regard to the recruitment of beginning graduate students for a four year full time doctoral program in school psychology contained the following statement, "Applicants should have good undergraduate records and be able to perform at a high level on admission tests. We are not particularly concerned about the undergraduate major of these students, but rather, are interested in persons with a sense of commitment to working in an educational setting as psychologists." [140]

For descriptions of fourteen representative training programs for school psychologists, psychometrists, and diagnosticians containing purposes, academic and field experiences, administrative organization and admission policies, the reader is directed to the Winter 1965 issue of the *Journal of School Psychology*.

---

[138] D. G. Ferguson, *op. cit.*, pp. 291–300.
[139] Personal correspondence from Paul H. Whiteman, dated January 31, 1962.
[140] Letter to the author from Jack Bardon, dated November, 1965, mimeo.

In a recent article, "The Training of School Psychologists," Michael [141] poses a number of myths surounding training. First he describes the layman's myths as follows: all school psychologists' have the same training, all have the same type of job, school administrators have the same expectations, all can make themselves understood and can make sense to those with whom they talk. He characterized the myths within the profession as a) agreement on what they should be doing in the schools, b) university agreement on training standards and programs. However, more importantly he highlighted the training dilemmas: 1) How do you train school psychologists when you know that out in the field they will do different things? 2) How do you train someone to be a consultant? 3) How long should training take? 4) Should the training be clinically or educationally oriented? 5) Whom do you select to train the school psychologist?

As in the case of many new somewhat insecure professions, school psychology looks to older more well established professions for direction. Clinical psychology between 1940 and 1960 looked to medicine for help in training, internship programs, licensing, professional boards and for other concerns. Likewise, school psychology has looked to its elder brother clinical psychology for direction and support. In fact, it would appear that some school psychological services trainers work overtime attempting or perhaps struggling to see how clinical psychology can be adapted to the school, rather than looking at the school and determining how best a behavioral scientist can contribute in this setting.

A conference on "New Directions in School Psychology" [142] sponsored by the National Institute of Mental Health was held in June, 1964 through the joint efforts of the APA central office, Division 16 and the Training and Manpower Resources Branch and the Community Research and Services Branch of the NIMH. This conference was the first major national meeting since the Thayer Conference of persons involved in the training and utilization of school psychologists. The planning committee for the conference consisted of Joseph Margolin, Jack Bardon, Joseph Speisman and Eli Bower. The specific objectives of the conference as stated by Bower were to: "assess the various conceptual frameworks in which doctoral programs in school psychology are set; to see how these conceptualizations are implemented in the training programs; to explore the nature of the core concepts and experiences as well as the unique features of the programs; and finally, to appraise the directions and emphases which these programs might take in the future."

[141] D. C. Michael, "The Training of School Psychologists," *Psychology in the Schools*, 2 (October, 1965), 345–349.

[142] Jack L. Bardon, ed., "Problems and Issues in School Psychology—Proceedings of a Conference on New Directions in School Psychology June 22–24, 1964," *Journal of School Psychology*, 3 (Winter, 1965), 1–42.

It was hoped that guides for the future development of this field would emerge.

Bardon summarized the four models of current university training which he assessed after reading brief working papers of ten school psychologist trainers submitted prior to the conference: 1) Clinical in orientation—50 per cent, 2) An extension of the clinical model but one which gets changed in the process—a distinct specialty within psychology with content area of its own. The product, the person trained, is to be an expert on the child in interaction with the school. 3) This is based on the idea that school psychology is too narrow a framework in which to assist the school with its multitude of problems. What is needed is a "psychologist for the schools." "The need at this time is not for a sharper definition of the appropriate functions for school psychologists, but for imaginative ways of using all aspects of the science of human behavior in the attainment of the objectives of the schools." 4) The "educational human factors engineer" based on the belief that this type of psychologist will perform the same functions for education that the human factors engineer has performed for industry and for the military.

There was a concensus of the conferees that "research activity in some form will play a larger part in the training and in the field activities of the school psychologist while psychometrics will be relegated to a less important position than is true at present."

Bardon poses the issues in school psychology in terms of a series of dichotomies: practical emphasis vs. theoretical emphasis; emphasis on immediate need vs. emphasis on future goals; clinical orientation vs. research orientation; school centered vs. community centered; school psychologist vs. psychologist in the schools. It should be added that many of these issues within school psychology are now major concerns and the basis of schisms within the entire American Psychological Association.

Some of the conclusions and recommendations of the conference were as follows: 1) school psychology is not clearly defined at this time; 2) the role of the school psychologist will continue to broaden with emphasis on primary prevention of emotional and learning difficulties through demonstration, consultation, research and administration of the services of other specialists; 3) it is reasonable to assume that psychologists of different orientations and backgrounds will play an increasingly important part in public education; 4) the unsolved issues of manpower shortage, the desirable level of training and the innovative versus the evaluative functions of school psychologists remain important; 5) diverse opinions about role, trends, and training need buttressing with intensive self study of training programs; 6) if school psychology is to remain useful to a changing school structure, it must become more concerned with both the broad and local issues affecting its existence; 7) publication of research on self study and professional problems in school psychology, symposia, consensus and minority reports of local and state groups is vital to the development of the field.[143]

In May, 1965, the Division 16 Committee on Education and Training made a report to the APA Education and Training Board asking that E. and T. consider approving training programs in school psychology just as it now does in clinical and counseling. The APA board unanimously approved this suggestion and recommended this suggestion to the APA Board of Directors. Although the accreditation of training programs by the APA has not yet become a reality, it is very likely that this step will be taken in the future.[144]

The Division 16 committee discussed what should be the relevant criteria to appraise the quality of training programs in school psychology. In September of 1965, they adopted the following five criteria of quality training; "all of which are based on the premise that there should not be any one model of training." The five criteria adopted were: 1) the commitment of the faculty to a training program, 2) an integrated program of studies, 3) exposure of students to professional school psychologists, 4) well supervised practice and 5) true involvement of both psychology and education in training.

1962 APA Statement on Certification

In February 1962, the executive committee of the Division 16 of the APA approved a statement regarding the education and certification of school psychologists.[145] The document was prepared by Jack I. Bardon, Chairman, Paul L. Hill, Allan F. Rosebrock, Arthur J. Bindman, Allen Hodges, and Winifred Scott, who served on the committee on training standards and certification of Division 16 during the years 1959–1962. This document is reproduced in its entirety inasmuch as it was prepared primarily to assist state department of education certification officers and those responsible for university training programs who have requested guidelines to use in their attempts to establish or improve standards for the education and certification of school psychologists. It will also be of great assistance to school boards, superintendents, and principals interested in employing school psychologists and to individuals considering entering the field. This committee report, which now has the endorsement of the American Psychological Association as a whole, will undoubtedly have far reaching effects on the role of the school psychologist in the decade ahead.

Standards suggested for the education and certification of school psychologists are based on the following assumptions:

[143] Ibid., 42–44.

[144] School Psychologist, Newsletter of Division 16, 20 (January, 1966), 54.

[145] Division 16, Committee Training Standards and Certification, Jack F. Bardon, Chairman, "Proposals for State Department of Education Certification of School Psychologists," American Psychologist, XVIII (November, 1963), 711–714.

1. School Psychologists are dually oriented professionals who need to be well educated in both psychology and education. The objective of training is to develop a psychologist who is interested in and knowledgeable about schools, one whose contributions are meaningful to and utilized by the teacher because they are based on understanding of the classroom situation and teacher problems as well as on sound psychological knowledge and skills.

   a. The development of competencies needed by a fully qualified school psychologist requires at least the education represented by a doctoral degree or three years of graduate training in a planned sequence of courses, laboratory, and supervised work experiences offered by a recognized training institution.

   b. There are several alternative ways to achieve the desired objective of appropriate attitudes toward and understanding of the educational environment in which the school psychologist functions as a psychologist. Teacher training and certification and teaching experience are often effective. A program of training in school psychology, oriented as it is toward schools and including graduate work in education and supervised experience in a school setting, is considered to be an equally effective means of attaining the objective.

2. The need and demand for school psychological services are such that psychology as a profession as well as education should make mutual and reasonable adjustments in an effort to help schools solve their problems. It is reasonable to support a procedure whereby individuals who are not fully qualified may function as school psychologists, provided they have completed at least two-thirds of the full training and are considered by their training institution to be competent to function satisfactorily in a school setting while continuing their training toward full qualification.

3. There are psychological services that can be provided satisfactorily by people with less training than that considered essential for a school psychologist.

   a. Because of the knowledge and understanding needed for the judgments involved in psychological services, individuals with less than the minimal training as stated in 2a above should be employed only when there is provision for adequate supervision by a qualified school psychologist.

   b. The certificate and title under which these services are performed should help the school and the professional worker recognize training and function limitations.

4. Students entering a school psychology training program are likely to have had an undergraduate major in either psychology or education.

   a. The training program should build on such preparation, having enough flexibility to allow students to develop competence in their areas of initial weakness without having to duplicate adequate groundwork.

   b. Students who have not had the expected undergraduate foundation should have an opportunity to enter the field; but they will need more training in psychology and education than will those who already have the appropriate foundation.

Suggested certification standards are as follows:

FULL CERTIFICATION

Requirements

An applicant for full certification as a School Psychologist must, in addition to all of the requirements listed below for Provisional certification, present evidence of successful completion of requirements for the doctoral degree, or three years of graduate work, in a school psychology program or equivalent planned sequence of study.

Term

A School Psychologist certificate issued to an applicant who has not had approved experience as a school psychologist is valid for (three) years. A permanent School Psychologist certificate may be issued to an applicant who has completed (three) years of successful experience under a School Psychologist certificate, or, on completion of the required training, to an applicant who has completed (three) or more years of successful experience under a Provisional School Psychologist certificate.

PROVISIONAL CERTIFICATION

Requirements

1. Successful completion of an approved college or university program consisting of at least two academic years in *graduate* courses, and the recommendation of the preparing institution, or equivalent training and qualifications as determined by the authorized State certification agency.

The applicant's total *undergraduate and graduate* program of study shall have included at least two and one-half academic years of work, in separate or integrated courses in appropriate sequence, in the Areas of Study indicated below. (It is emphasized that these are areas of study or competence and not course titles.) *Graduate* credits must be presented in each of the starred fields.

AREA A. *Psychological Foundations*—Theoretical and Experimental
A minimum of 24 semester-hour credits or approximately thirty per cent of the student's work (but including not more than 6 semester hours at the undergraduate level) selected from fields such as:

Advanced general psychology; experimental psychology; history of psychology
Advanced educational psychology; developmental psychology; psychology of the exceptional; social psychology.
Learning theory; psychology of motivation.
Physiological psychology; comparative psychology.
Personality theory; abnormal psychology; approaches to psychotherapy.
Theoretical foundations of statistical and testing techniques; research methods.

AREA B. *Psychological Methods and Techniques*—Studies designed to insure competence in interviewing and counseling; evaluation in the intellectual, social and emotional areas; and remediation in the basic educational skills and in behavior.

A minimum of 27 semester-hour credits or approximately thirty-five per cent of the student's work (but including no more than 6 semester hours at the undergraduate level) selected from fields such as:

* Individual intelligence testing.
* Group intelligence and achievement testing.
* Assessment of personality, projective and non-projective.
* Statistical techniques.
* Interviewing and counseling techniques.
    Behavior problems of children.
    Case studies; social case work techniques.
* Play therapy; group therapy.
    Mental health education; community consultation services.

AREAS C and D. A minimum of 18 semester-hour credits or approximately twenty-five per cent of the student's work in Areas C and D, of which at least four-semester-hour credits in Area C and eight in Area D must be at the graduate level.

AREA C. *Educational Foundations*—Social, philosophical, historical. Selected from fields such as:

    History of education; philosophy of education, educational sociology; comparative education.

AREA D. *School Organization and Program.*

Selected from fields such as:

* Remedial instruction—speech, arithmetic, reading.
    School administration, supervision, curriculum, and extra-curriculum programs.
    School practices and methods of teaching.
    School guidance programs—principles, organization, techniques.
    Research methods.
* Educational programs for exceptional children; organization administration, methods, materials.

AREA E. *Electives.* Nine semester-hour credits or approximately ten per cent of the student's work at the graduate level selected from the above or closely related areas.

2. Supervised field experience in the duties of a school psychologist (internship or externship) consisting at the very least of one semester full time or 525 clock hours, under the direction of a certified school psychologist or other qualified personnel approved by the college or university. This experience shall be in addition to laboratory work done in connection with courses in the regular approved program. In exceptional circumstances a program of supervised experience not under the direction of a college or university may be approved by the State certifying agency.

At least fifty per cent of the supervised field experience must be in the psychological services division of a public school system, or in such a division of a college or university demonstration center, serving a cross section of school-age children. As much as fifty per cent of the supervised field experience may be obtained in an approved hospital, institution, clinic, or agency established for the study and/or treatment of special problems of children and adults.

Term and Renewal. Completion of the foregoing requirements will entitle the applicant to a Provisional School Psychologist certificate valid for (three) years, renewable when the applicant presents a minimum of (six) semester-hour credits, or its equivalent, acceptable toward full certification.

PSYCHOLOGICAL ASSISTANT

A certificate authorizing service *only under the supervision of a certified school psychologist employed by the same school district,* may be granted if the applicant for a certificate presents one and one-half academic years of graduate credit acceptable in meeting the requirements for a school psychologist's certificate, and evidence of enrollment in an approved college or university program for the preparation of school psychologists. The graduate training shall include work in each of the outlined Areas of Study and all starred courses shall be included. Also, an externship of at least 350 clock hours or equivalent experience shall be required. This certificate may be renewed annually when the applicant presents a minimum of four semester-hour credits, or its equivalent, in the approved program in which he is enrolled.

LONG AND ROGERS: DISSIDENT VOICES VIS A VIS TRAINING

Carl Rogers [146] in a paper written in 1964 challenged the entire basis of graduate education in psychology. Rogers felt that when the "day comes that psychology wishes to make a thoughtful appraisal of its methods of professional preparation, it will I believe, throw out most of our current assumptions and procedures." Rogers felt that in the present research literature of psychology are the facts and findings upon which a graduate program could be built that would foster "freely independent, openly curious psychologists, unafraid in their search for genuinely new and deeply significant approximations to the truth." Rogers felt a number of outmoded assumptions are found in graduate programs such as "Evaluation in education"; and "Method is science"; "Weeding out of 85 per cent of our selected applicants is proof of high standards."

Rogers and R. E. Farson suggested nine principles also relevant to the training of school psychologists: 1) the objective of the graduate program is to develop psychologists who can make original, significant, and continuing

[146] Carl R. Rogers, "Graduate Education in Psychology: A Passionate Statement" (La Jolla, Calif.: Western Behavioral Sciences Institute, unpublished paper).

contributions primarily to the science of psychology but also to the professional practice related to this science; 2) the selection of graduate students should be based on three criteria: originality, intelligence and independence of thought; 3) the best background for a psychologist is a broad education including the humanities, arts, and sciences; 4) significant learning takes place when the subject matter is seen by the student to have relevance for his own purposes and development; 5) learning is facilitated when the student participates responsibly in the learning process; 6) students have the potentiality for learning, developing, and making suitable educational choices. This potentiality can be released by a suitable psychological climate, whose principal ingredients are freedom and stimulation; 7) the time of the faculty member is best spent in providing resources that stimulate the desire to learn rather than in planning a guided curriculum; 8) learning is most likely to occur in the students when the faculty member approaches the interaction as learner rather than teacher; 9) creativity of thought is facilitated when self-criticism and self-evaluation by others is relegated to a position of minimal importance.

Nicholas J. Long [147] summarizes some of the present problems and issues facing existing graduate training programs in school psychological services. One of the real dilemmas is the fact that there are no consistent expectations or real limitations among these training programs regarding the basic function of a school psychologist.

Long opines, in general, the school psychologist seems to be an omnipotent he-man who is the master of all psychological and educational skills. He can develop curriculum guides, weed out "sick teachers," diagnose children with social and emotional disorders, counsel with parents, teachers and children, work with social agencies, direct research programs at the grassroots level, consult with school board members regarding personnel matters, develop remedial programs and special educational facilities, organize, administer and interpret group testing programs, administer and interpret individual intelligence tests, train and supervise interns, publish scholarly articles, participate in educational and psychological associations on a county, state and national level and present research evidence to protect the schools from pressure groups who want to crack down, ease up, or reorganize the educational system. In addition to these services, the school psychologist's psychodynamics should be such that he is free from feelings of superiority, can easily protect himself from over-idealization by parents and teachers, and can develop immediate rapport with children and adults of all ages. The results of trying to prepare a student for such a diversified role often leads to an everything and nothing program according to Long. *It seems that any institution that pretends it can train a person to have all the information, skills, and*

[147] Long, *op. cit.*, p. 2.

attitudes that are essential to function adequately in the foregoing areas is not only over-estimating its own ability but also the ability of the graduate student.

Certification in California and Elsewhere

A new credential law went into effect for California teachers and psychological services workers in January, 1964. The new credential structure extended the area of concern of pupil personnel services to the rehabilitation counselor in the schools in addition to the following areas covered in preceding legislation: child welfare and attendance counselor, school psychologist, and school social worker.

Under the new law, a masters or two years of postgraduate work in the area of pupil personnel services is required for the school psychologist for California schools. A number of professional courses are recommended as areas to be covered in the core for all pupil personnel services specialists. These areas are: pupil personnel services concepts and procedures, dynamics of individual behavior, counseling theory and procedure, measurement theory and procedure, group process theory and procedures, educational and career planning, research methodology, remedial and special education, laws relating to children, and organization of pupil personnel services. A completion of a post graduate pupil personnel services internship program is also required or 480 hours of supervised field experience rendered under the supervision of an approved professional to persons between four and twenty-one years of age; and at least one-half of this experience shall be gained in a public or private school.

In regard to the school psychologist, he additionally must have verification from an approved institution that he is competent to administer an individual examination of a child for special class placement. Preparation for this role must include course work in theory and supervised practice in administering and interpreting the following: 1) diagnostic tests of learning difficulties; 2) individual tests of intelligence; 3) tests for determining whether and to what extent a child varies from the normal with respect to mental and emotional characteristics; 4) case studies of children who vary from the normal with respect to mental or emotional characteristics and preparations of reports regarding the above children.

Certainly the training and requirements for school psychologists in California are idiosyncratic in certain ways. The reader should be directed to the state credentialing office for further information regarding specific requirements in the state in which he is seeking employment.

Nelson [148] reviewed the national variations in patterns of certification in

[148] W. H. Nelson, *op. cit.*, 17–33.

1963. Nelson summarized his 1963 study by stating that much variation was evident in regard to levels of training and designated titles, degree requirements and teacher training requirement. There were also great differences in the type of internship experience, prescribed course work, and the agency responsible for certification. Nelson noted the following trends: a) a tendency to reserve the title psychologist for the doctorally trained individual; b) provision for more than one level of certification; c) a minimizing of the demand for a teacher's certificate and prior teaching experience; and d) dependence of the certifying agency upon the training institution for an assessment of the competency of the applicant.

The Internship

School psychologist trainers in the State of Ohio have developed an Inter-University Council on School Psychology. This organization coordinates the education of all future school psychologists trained in Ohio and works in cooperation with the Division of Special Education for the State. The Council in February 1962, developed an excellent set of recommendations for internships. The report suggests that the intern is both an employee in the local school and an active participant in the graduate training program of his University.

The Ohio council attempted to remediate the problem so often encountered in practicum situations by insisting that there be a single-on-the-job supervisor who must be employed as a *certified school psychologist* with two years of experience. The college supervisor should have an individual conference with both the intern and the local supervisor at three week intervals. Supervision of the student psychologist in training involves at least four functions: planning of the intern's over-all program, assignment of tasks, observation of the individual's performance and a shared evaluation with the student.

The purposes of the internship program as well as the skills and competencies that should be developed during the internship year are presented in the following excerpt from the Ohio Inter-University Council on School Psychology publication on the Internship: [149]

A. *An orientation to the organization of psychological services in the public schools, and the relation of these services to the school and community.*
  1. To develop a broad understanding of the organizational framework of the public schools.
  2. To provide a general orientation to administrative policies and personnel practices in the public schools.
  3. To thoroughly acquaint the intern with the role and function of the

[149] Inter-University Council on School Psychology, Committee on Internships, *Recommendation on Internship* (Columbus, Ohio, Feb. 26, 1962, mimeo.).

the various specialists on the school staff in the areas of child study, guidance, pupil personnel, curriculum development, etc.

4. To familiarize the intern with the office and clerical procedures involved in the organization of psychological services in the schools.

5. To develop an understanding of the unique and common problems involved in the organization of psychological service programs in urban and rural areas, in city and county school districts, etc.

6. To enlarge the understanding of the intern regarding the place of the school and its psychological program in the community, especially the relation of the school psychologist to community referral resources and community social welfare structure.

B. *Skills in the diagnostic study of the individual child.*

1. To broaden the experience of the intern in the diagnostic evaluation of exceptional children of all age levels.

2. To broaden the experience of the intern in working with children who present a wide range of problems in terms of school placement and programming.

3. To enlarge the experience of the intern with various diagnostic tests, tests, including intelligence and educational achievement tests, special tests used in the assessment of children with physical, sensory, and mental handicaps, developmental scales, and projective approaches to the study of personality.

4. To provide close supervision in the techniques of administration, scoring and interpretation of individual diagnostic tests and in the techniques of interviewing pupils and their parents for facts of diagnostic significance.

5. To assist the intern in the integration of all diagnostic findings into a useful and understandable written report.

C. *Orientation to the teacher's classroom role and function.*

1. Develop skill in interpreting classroom behavior through the eyes of the teacher.

2. Develop skill in establishing and maintaining communication with teachers and principals.

3. Develop skill in working with teachers.

4. Familarize intern with instructional materials and techniques.

5. Develop an awareness of the developmental sequence of academic skills.

6. Develop an awareness of the realistic perception of the problems of group management.

7. Develop an understanding that the goals of the psychologist are the same as those of the school and its professional staff. His contribution rests in the uniqueness of his goals.

8. Develop an understanding that the value of the school psychologist lies in his ability to facilitate the efforts of the other members of the school staff.

9. Develop an appreciation that while the focus of the work of the school psychologist is the child, his ultimate client is the Board of Education and its delegated professional workers.

D. *Skills in consultation, teamwork, and in-service training.*

1. To develop skills in the oral interpretation of test findings to children, parents, teachers, building principals, and other members of the school staff.

2. To help the intern function more effectively as a member of a team of professional specialists, representing a variety of skills, training, philosophy, and modes of operation.

3. To develop an understanding of the group dynamics and interactions involved in case conferences, and to help the intern develop effective methods of presenting his findings and planning cooperatively in the case conference.

4. To develop familiarity with the routine procedures involved in follow-up of the plans and recommendations formulated for individual children.

5. To develop skill in the effective referral and follow-up of cases with child guidance clinics and other community agencies; to provide experience in interagency conferences and in other liaison functions between the school and community agencies.

6. To permit the intern to observe and eventually to participate actively on various committees within the schools, in such areas as pupil personnel, special education, evaluation, pupil mental health, teaching method and classroom management, curriculum planning, etc.

7. To provide the opportunity for the intern to participate in programs of in-service training organized by administrators or teachers and dealing with topics related to psychology.

8. To promote skills in public speaking, through participation in conferences, workshops or discussion groups and serving as a panel member, discussion leader or in other similar capacities.

E. *Skills in interviewing and counseling.*

1. To augment skills in interviewing and short-term counseling with individual pupils or groups.

2. To develop skills in parent interviewing and counseling in the process of discussing the meaning and significance of diagnostic studies and deciding on treatment plans.

F. *An understanding of the group testing program in the schools.*

1. To orient the intern to the problems involved in the organization and administration of the group testing program in the schools.

2. To broaden knowledge of achievement, intelligence, personality, aptitude, and other group tests, and procedures for their administration, scoring, and tabulation.

3. To orient the intern to such problems as reporting and evaluation of group test results, the preparation of test calendars and bulletins, the

training of teachers and building principals in group test administration, etc.

G. *Skills in initiating and conducting research in schools.*

1. To alert the intern to the opportunities and limitations of research in the school setting and the practical problems involved in initiating research.

2. To develop skills in research design and planning and in the identification of significant research problems in the school.

The internship program at the University of Michigan for school psychologists in-training was described by Trow in 1961 as follows:

All students will enroll for a practicum requiring three hours a day for a minimum of one semester in the University School. During this time under the guidance of a special supervisor they will attend a number of different grades and classes ranging from the kindergarten through grade twelve, participate in instructional as well as measurement and guidance activities, and study and follow through on individual instructional and adjustment problem cases. We believe that this range of experience will be even more valuable than that of teaching a particular grade or subject for a year or two.[150]

For further discussion of the internship program, the reader is directed to the Proceedings of a Peabody Conference,[151] held in 1963 as well as a discussion by Ferguson.[152] In general, the internship experience should provide the predoctoral trainee an opportunity to observe and participate in a well rounded school psychology program.[153]

Professional Affiliations and Identity

"When individuals in any particular group discover that they are using a common body of knowledge which has been developed and is identified and communicable through an intellectual process of higher education, inevitably they band together to form a professional association." [154]

This statement by Selden certainly applies to school psychological ser-

150 William Clark Trow, "Diagnostician, Ed.S., and Ph.D. Programs for School Psychologists in Michigan," *American Psychologist,* XVI (February, 1961), 84–85.

151 Susan W. Gray, ed., *The Internship in School Psychology,* Proceedings of the Peabody Conference, Nashville, Tennessee, George Peabody College for Teachers, March 21–22, 1963.

152 D. G. Ferguson, "Training Programs in School Psychology," in *Professional School Psychology,* II, 287–305.

153 R. C. Morris, "Issues in the Training of School Psychologists: Practicum and Internship Experiences." Paper read at the 1959 American Psychological Association meeting.

154 W. H. Seldon, *Accreditation: A Struggle Over Standards in Higher Education* (New York: Harper & Row, Publishers, 1960).

vices, as will be apparent in the following pages. The writer feels that there actually are too many associations, books, and journals relating to school psychological services, and he sometimes wishes a moratorium were called on all printed material in this field for a year or so. However, he feels, it is important that all practicing school psychological services workers belong to one or two associations, subscribe to several professional journals, attempt to read a book every month or so, and attend one or two professional meetings per year.

Although school psychology is a smaller field at present than either clinical or counseling psychology, there are indications that it will someday overtake both of these areas of psychological practice, especially if districts in the decades ahead implement the recommendation of one psychologist to every 1500 or 2000 school children. In 1963,[155] 320 students in the United States received doctorates in clinical psychology, 43 in counseling psychology and only 15 in school psychology, however, by 1967, the number in school psychology had greatly increased.

In terms of the professional identification of 9,521 psychologists who were respondents to an inquiry sent out by the National Science Foundation in 1964, 3,441 identified themselves as clinical psychologists, 1000 counseling psychologists and 633 identified themselves as school psychologists.[156]

The novitiate school psychologist will certainly wish to affiliate himself with his state and local association of school psychologists. The second most important affiliation would be the American Psychological Association and especially Division 16, the division concerned with school psychology.

Although the American Psychological Association was founded in 1892, Division 16 was born only in 1947 when 167 applications for membership were received and acted upon by the membership committee of APA. The original by-laws expressed the objectives of Division 16 as: a) to provide opportunities for professional fellowship and for the exchange of professional ideas among school psychologists; b) to advance the professional status of school psychologists; c) to promote and maintain high standards of professional service among its members.

Division 16 membership in 1967 was approximately 1100, or about five per cent of the total membership of the APA; this division has been however, one of the fastest growing over the past decade.

The following excerpt from the Constitution provides the prospective school psychologist with answers to many of his questions concerning membership requirements:

ARTICLE II. MEMBERSHIP

1. Membership in the Division of School Psychologists shall be limited to Associates and Members in good standing of the American Psychological Association who are actively engaged as school psychologists or who have a major interest in that field. A school psychologist is a psychologist a major portion of whose work is a) the application of clinical psychological techniques to children and adolescents presenting problems in school, or b) the psychological supervision of psychologists doing such work. A major interest in this field shall be defined as major research, teaching, or administrative functions directly and specifically related to the work of school psychologists.

2. The Division shall consist of three classes of members: a) Associates, b) Members, and c) Fellows.

3. An Associate of the APA shall be eligible for election as an Associate of the Division of School Psychologists if he or she holds a master's degree or its equivalent in graduate training and if he or she has had two years of acceptable experience as a school psychologist.

4. A Member of the APA shall be eligible for election as a Member of the Division of School Psychologists if he or she a) holds the doctoral degree based in part upon a psychological dissertation and conferred by a graduate school of recognized standing, and b) has had two years of acceptable experience as a school psychologist.[156]

One important function of Division 16, in addition to the publication of a newsletter and an annual convention program, with many papers and symposia relating to school psychological services, is the annual professional institute that precedes the APA convention. This institute provides the opportunity for practicing school psychologists to upgrade their skills in various areas. In 1965, the institute concerned the following topics: Diagnostic Problems in the Personality Assessment of School Children; Brain Damage: Implications of Diagnosis for Educational Remediation; Implications of Human Learning Research; Learning Disabilities: Diagnosis, Prevention, and Re-education and Preventive and Therapeutic Approaches in the Classroom. The 1966 professional institute, the eleventh, had as its general theme, "The School Psychologist as a Consultant and Educator."

The APA in 1966 had a membership of 24,473 and there were 26 divisions to which the appropriately trained and qualified psychologist could make application for membership. Many school psychologists in addition to Division 16 hold memberships in related divisions, such as educational, clinical, teaching of psychology, counseling, or rehabilitation. The headquarters of the APA, where further information regarding membership requirements and the addresses for the divisional memberships secretaries can be obtained, is 1200 17th St. N.W., Washington, D.C. 20036.

[156] Constitution By-laws, Division 16, *American Psychological Association* (Washington, D. C.: APA, as amended through 1962).

Other organizations with which the school psychologist may wish to affiliate or at least to read their publications are the following:

American Personnel and Guidance Association. The APGA was founded in 1952, bringing together in a professional unity several guidance and personnel groups. The APGA is now composed of seven divisions that span personnel and guidance work in elementary and secondary schools, measurement theory and practice, higher education, community agencies, and organizations, and encompass many personnel interests in government, industry, and business. The purposes of the association are: 1) to provide leadership for the profession and liaison with other related groups; 2) to issue journals and other publications of significant leadership in research, thinking, and practices in guidance and personnel work; 3) to serve branches in their professional work in local regions; 4) to join together the persons who are engaged in professional personnel services and to provide a professional identity for them; 5) to endeavor continually to improve standards of guidance and personnel work and to enhance the service of the profession to the public; 6) to encourage the development of a personnel point of view toward all persons and to endeavor to express this view in practice. The national headquarters of the group are located at 1605 New Hampshire Ave., N.W., Washington, D. C. 20009

American Association on Mental Deficiency. This organization is one of the oldest professional groups, as it was founded in 1876. An interesting aspect of the association is that it is an interdisciplinary group composed of persons engaged in work pertaining to the care, treatment, and promotion of the mentally retarded. Thus the membership includes administrators, teachers, medical doctors, psychologists, and others associated with the care, education, training, or supervision of the mentally retarded. Three of the eight objectives of the AAMD relevant to school psychologists are: 1) The establishment of special classes for the mentally retarded in all cities and towns having ten or more retarded children, vocational instruction and special supervision of the mentally deficient leaving regular classes for special classes at the age of 16 years up to the age of 21; 2) Research in the psychiatric, social, psychological, educational, and pathological field to determine and inaugurate better methods of scholastic education and the industrial instruction and training of mental defectives; 3) The adoption of uniform standards for use in all Training Schools, including diagnostic nomenclature and uniform statistical tables. The AAMD publishes 1) the *American Journal of Mental Deficiency,* and 2) a new periodical, *Mental Retardation.* The headquarters of the AAMD are located at 5201 Connecticut Ave. N.W., Washington, D.C. 20015.

American Orthopsychiatric Association. This organization was founded forty years ago. Its membership includes psychiatrists, psychologists, psychiatric social workers, and other professional persons whose work and interests lie in the study of personality and behavior and in the treatment of disorders. The purposes of the association are: 1) To unite and provide a common meeting ground for those engaged in the study and treatment of problems of human behavior; 2) To foster research and spread information concerning scientific work in the field of human behavior including all forms of abnormal behavior. This organization publishes the *Journal of Orthopsy-*

chiatry. The headquarters of the association are located at 1790 Broadway, New York, New York 10019.

Council for Exceptional Children is a department of the National Education Association and publishes the journal *Exceptional Children.* The CEC is open to special educators, school psychologists, and other interested persons. There are several divisions of the CEC including the Association for Gifted Children. By 1967, the membership of the NEA numbered close to 1,000,-000 while the CEC had a membership of approximately 28,000. The organization's headquarters are at 1201 16th St. N.W., Washington, D.C. 20036.

National Society for the Study of Education. The purposes of this group are to carry on the investigation of educational problems and to publish their results and to promote discussion concerning educational research. The NSSE has published yearbooks since 1902. A number of these yearbooks have direct relevance to the work of the school psychologist; for example, the *Fifty-Seventh Yearbook,* 1958, Part II concerned the Education of the Gifted, while the *Fifty-Eighth Yearbook,* 1959, Part II was Personnel Services in Education. The organization's headquarters are located at the University of Chicago at 5835 Kimbark Avenue, Chicago 37, Illinois.

Many additional organizations could be listed, such as the National Association for Retarded Children, and the National Association for Mental Health, and the National Council on Measurement in Education. However, the busy school psychologist will not have time to devote to reading the publications of all relevant organizations nor the money to invest in membership fees.

On the American academic scene, a measure of the identity of a discipline or a curriculum is the periodical publications available relating to this area of study in addition to the professional associations. The specialty of school psychology was rather late in developing journals specifically relating to the role of the psychologist in the schools. However, since 1963 two such journals have been launched, largely through the personal efforts of such leaders in the field as Donald Leton, Donald Ferguson, Samuel Bonham, T. Ernest Newland, William A. Hunt, and others.

Journals Relating Specifically to School Psychology

In 1963 the first journal specifically devoted to school psychology, the *Journal of School Psychology,* was launched by the Ohio Department of Education, under the editorship of Donald C. Smith of the Department of Psychology, Ohio State University. The decision to publish such a journal was made by a group of professionals concerned with the training and professional development of school psychologists in Ohio who felt that the journal would provide an effective means of stimulating research by school psychologists. It is a scientifically oriented journal devoted to the publication of original research, reports, reviews, and articles with the aim of fostering the expansion of school psychology as an applied science.

The journal accepts the following types of material for publication: 1) action research on the organization and development of school psychological services and the evaluation of various aspects of school psychology programs; 2) reports of surveys or questionnaire studies of school psychologists; 3) descriptions and evaluations of experimental or demonstration projects in school psychology; 4) original research on psychological diagnosis, test construction, group measurement, counseling, exceptional children, and other subject matter related to the role and function of the school psychologist; 5) authoritative articles dealing with the role and function of the school psychologist; 6) evaluative reviews of research and theory in school psychology; 7) theoretical contributions.

A second journal, entitled *Psychology in the Schools,* a quarterly devoted to research, opinion, and practice, and especially concerned with school psychology as a practicing discipline, appeared in January, 1964. The editor is William A. Hunt of Northwestern University and the publisher is the Psychology Press, Inc. of Brandon, Vermont. The journal contains reports of research, expressions of opinion, reviews of literature, theoretical contributions, case histories and, in general, content designed to stimulate thinking about the application of psychology to education. The journal provides an outlet for the expression of school psychologists, educational psychologists, and others who are interested in bridging the gap between the practical problems of the classroom and the relevant findings of psychology.

School Psychology: A Time for Pluralism

The writer feels that despite the fact that the respective spheres of guidance, counseling, school psychology, school social case work, school adjustment counseling have not yet been clearly defined and delineated, there are certain unifying elements in all roles in the school psychological services. The viewpoint expressed here is that the school psychologist should be a part of the total pupil personnel services program (although he would prefer the generic rubric, school psychological services) and that he must work cooperatively and uncondescendingly with other specialists. Thus the writer would agree with William Sivers, State Director of Psychological Services for the New York Schools, when he stated: The school psychologist, as a member of the pupil personnel services team and of the school faculty, shares with teachers, school administrators, and other school personnel the basic goal of making adequate provisions for meeting individual pupil needs in the educational setting."

The writer would disagree with those school psychologist trainers who emphasize a "strong role commitment" to only the role of the school psychologist *per se*. The writer would feel that there is a large common body of knowledge important to both educators and psychologists, and to all others in the helping professions. Furthermore, he would not be dismayed for an individual carefully trained in the common core of psychological services to move from one specialty to the other after further specialized training; thus, a teacher who becomes a counselor may wish later to take additional course work in an approved sequence leading to the doctorate in school psychology.

In the smaller districts and rural areas, the school psychologist may function as school guidance worker with secondary youth, school social worker, and rehabilitation counselor. In the large city, the school psychologist may become a specialist in intellectual, social, perceptual, and emotional appraisal of the cerebral palsied child. The point of view of the author of this chapter is that both individuals, one in the rural area, one in the large city, are school psychologists, even though the specific behaviors that they exhibit daily in carrying out their professional obligations are widely disparate. And according to the author's definition both can legitimately think of themselves as school psychologists.

The writer is opposed to the "hardening of the categories approach in the pupil personnel services," and feels that there should be a substantive common course background for all those working in the helping professions or facilitative services. He further feels that all pupil personnel services specialists, whether they be school social workers or school psychiatrists, should have some understanding and course work in educational philosophy and curriculum theory; however, he further feels that they need not be certified as teachers. Perhaps in the years ahead, as the pupil personnel services pass into adolescence and maturity, we will see more cooperative effort and less power struggle.

Thus, when asked the question, "What is a school psychologist or what is his identity?", the writer would have to say that presently he is performing many different roles in many different places. This role is determined by the conditions discussed in Chapter 1. He would hope that all future school psychologists have adequate training, as suggested in the recent Division 16 report. He would also hope that psychological services workers would not assume roles for which they are neither professionally nor personally suited.

As Lambert [157] has stated, "Being a scientist by profession, the school psychologist who renders any of these services (those discussed in this text) must be able to tell others what he is doing, why he is doing it, and he must search his professional conscience to be sure that he has the training and

[157] Nadine Lambert, "The School Psychologist," Paper prepared in 1962 for the CASPP Conference.

experience to provide the service. An old adage applies here: 'If in doubt, leave it out.'"

The writer would say that like the clinical psychologist [158] and the psychiatrist who play widely varying roles in various settings, the school psychologists of the nation will continue to be omnibus workers and will play many roles. Some skills for which the school psychologist has received training may lie dormant in his professional repertoire, while other skills will have to be developed to meet the needs of his position through various in-service training, further professional education, and reading.

All professional people must regularly evaluate themselves in terms of whether their professional repertoire of skills does take into account accumulated knowledge gained through new research and practice advances. Thus the late 1960's and early 1970's will continue to be a time for pluralism in the school psychological services field.

Personal Development of the School Psychological Services Worker

You have been subjected to a voluminous quantity of substantive material regarding a professional role you now have or one to which you aspire. At times, in your reading, you have probably felt that the school psychologist's role required the patience and fortitude of Job, the clinical wisdom of Freud, the educational acumen of Horace Mann, and the energy of Jason. Certainly all of these traits would be helpful. However, we must be realistic about the personal characteristics and professional role of school psychological services workers.

Although, this text has discussed many diverse roles for the school psychologist, it is unlikely that you will be called upon in your professional life to be a specialist in all of them. Rather, there will be certain skills which you will have to develop to meet the needs of your particular school environment after a careful assessment of yourself as a person.

The school psychological services worker who has had his professional training in the behavioral sciences and is applying this knowledge in one institutional setting—the school—does have a great responsibility. So far, in this text, we have not emphasized the school psychologist as a person.

What about your development as a person and its relationship to your effectiveness as a school psychological services worker?

A recent Illinois publication [159] states that the prospective school psy-

---

[158] N. D. Tyler and L. E. Tyler, *Clinical Psychology* (New York: Appleton-Century-Crofts, 1962), pp. 451–458.

[159] Genevieve Drennen, *Here's the Job For Your Future* (Springfield, Illinois: Office of the Superintendent of Public Instruction, 1959), p. 26.

chologist should ask himself the following questions concerning his personality. . . . Do I like children? . . . Am I patient? . . . Can I establish rapport with people? . . . Am I alert and sensitive to behavior of people around me? . . . Am I tolerant of the ideas, beliefs, and peculiarities of others? . . . Am I flexible? . . . Can I see the humorous side of a situation?. . . Can I share ideas and information with other people? . . . Do I have good mental health?

The writer feels that the school psychologist should be characterized first and foremost by an interest in wishing to help children. Thus, the commitment to a service orientation based upon and with a respect for the need for research in the school setting would seem to be paramount. Certainly, new methods of reaching more children through group counseling, in-service training programs for teachers, careful selection of teachers, child study groups, are all ways to help children reach a higher level of development, and the writer in his service commitment is thinking of much more than the testing-placement function or the vestigial role of the school psychologist.

One of the best ways toward reaching an understanding of a child in the school environment is through observation of that child in as many natural school situations as possible which might sharpen one's insights about the children with whom we work. George M. Kaiser,[160] School Psychologist in the Glencoe, Illinois, Public Schools has stated, "Testing, individual counseling, parent conferences, and other techniques employed by school psychologists will be viewed as aids, rather than as primary tools, as we approach our main business . . . and that is to work as closely as possible with classroom teachers in order to assist them and the children in question improve their relationships so that more effective learning can take place."

To work closely with many classroom teachers representing differing personal styles and backgrounds and to feel comfortable while sitting in the back of a classroom or participating in an activity in a gymnasium is a skill many new psychologists in the schools must learn.

In a statement prepared by the Teachers College staff entitled "Who Should Become a School Psychologist?" [161] school psychologist trainers at Columbia discussed interest and personality characteristics of the future school psychologist as follows:

> *Interest.* It is important for a school psychologist to be interested in children, but simply to want "to know more about children" is not sufficient motivation for the scientific work required as a psychologist. Motivation for successful work in this field requires ability to think objectively on the basis of broad

[160] G. M. Kaiser, "The School Psychologist and the Total School Program," Unpublished paper read at the American Psychological Association meeting, Division of School Psychologists, 1958.

[161] *Program in School Psychology,* "Who Should Become a School Psychologist?" (New York: Teachers College, Columbia University, undated, about 1962), p. 2.

knowledge in the areas of education, interpersonal relationships, child development, and sociology. Above all the psychologist must be able to check his ideas through reliable techniques of thought and measurement to be assured that his ideas are sound and unbiased insofar as possible. In other words, he must be interested in scientific thinking. The candidate who is interested in parents, teachers, and children, and also interested in obtaining fundamental theoretical knowledge of all aspects of human development will make the best school psychologist.

Personality. There is probably no one pattern of "personality" that is essential to success as a school psychologist. The profession of psychology, like all other professions, includes many different kinds of people. Experience indicates, however, that two qualifications of personality seem essential for successful work in this field.

The school psychologist accomplishes the major part of his work through securing cooperation from educators, parents and children. He must, therefore, not only be able to work *with* people but must also be able to encourage and at times inspire his colleagues in education to venture into heretofore unknown areas of experience.

Another important qualification for the school psychologist is ability to tolerate frustration in a mature manner. Graduate study involves many difficulties and frustrations. In professional work also, colleagues, individual parents, or children with whom the school psychologist works are often "uncooperative" and thus try his patience. Both as a student and as a professional worker, a psychologist has to be able to take criticism, to regard antagonistic attitudes calmly, and to resolve conflicting viewpoints, and to retain poise, self-control, and objectivity. School psychology is not a profession for a person who, when frustrated, becomes angry and blames other people or who, on the other hand, becomes depressed and loses his self-confidence under such conditions. In other words, people interested in this field must be free of personal difficulties that hamper constructive interpersonal relationships.

In the *Information Manual for the School Psychology Program* at Rutgers University prepared in September, 1965, the following statement regarding the attitude of the school psychologist appears.

> The attitude of the school psychologist must be one of "positive skepticism." A school psychologist must be a skeptic because this reflects understanding of the imperfections of his knowledge and tools. Since he works primarily with real-life situations, the school psychologist must often act without the benefit or the security of a scientifically determined body of knowledge or precise instruments upon which to base his actions. In order to insure that he remains open to change and benefits from his own successes and failures, it is necessary that he develop a critical, cautious approach to the assessment of his own findings and deliberations.
>
> The school psychologist must also be concerned about what happens to people. He must be capable of genuine identification with all kinds of people and their modes of behavior. He must have a sincere and positive attitude toward humanity which will enable him to try new approaches and to persist even in the face of discouragement, lack of results, and frustrations.

A humanistic philosophy of life and rigorous scientific training are therefore both essential to the school psychologist's atttiude toward all his professional endeavors.

The editor of this text concurs completely with these sentiments.

Philip W. Jackson of the University of Chicago feels that student discontent is widespread and the school psychologist is the individual most skilled in assessing this discontent and recommending and accomplishing changes in the schools. He describes the role of the school psychologist as an agent of educational and social change as follows and charges this profession with a personal challenge.

> With respect to these attempts at change, the role of the psychologist in the schools is particularly crucial. He, more than any other professional on the school staff, can or should, stand for the wholeness of the human experience. He, more than any other, should be most sensitive to the forces that whittle away at the integrity of teachers and students. Although his help is clearly needed in dealing with the misfits—the students who are unable to function adequately within the system—he is needed even more urgently to examine the institution of which he is a part and to speak out against those elements of the system that might have a detrimental effect on all who experience them. The students who need his services are far greater in number than those who come hobbling into his sound-proof testing room.[162]

In his 1963 book, *On Becoming A Person*,[163] Carl Rogers described the characteristics of a helping relationship. In this book, "a must" for required reading for future school psychologists, Rogers extends his viewpoints regarding counseling and psychotherapy to the realm of ends and goals in human life generally. It is Rogers' most philosophical book, and the impact of recent existential writers is apparent. Reading of this book might very well contribute to the personal development of many school psychological services workers as they search for personal self-understanding as well as a professional understanding of others.

The writer concurs with the bias of Carl Rogers that ". . . in a wide variety of professional work involving relationships with people—whether as a psychotherapist, teacher, religious worker, guidance counselor, social worker, clinical psychologist—it is the *quality* of the interpersonal encounter with the client which is the most significant element in determining effectiveness." [164] For Rogers, the quality of the relationship with a child or an adult is more important than the scholarly knowledge, professional training, one's counsel-

162 Philip W. Jackson, "Student Discontent and the Schools," Ohio School Psychologist's Association, *Newsletter* (November, 1965).

163 Carl Rogers, *On Becoming A Person*. New York: Houghton Mifflin Company, 1963.

164 C. R. Rogers, "The Interpersonal Relationship: The Core of Guidance," *Harvard Education Review*, 32 (1962), 416–428.

ing orientation, or the techniques used in the interviewing process. Rogers further states, "I suspect that for a guidance worker also the relationship he forms with each student—brief or continuing—is more important than his knowledge of tests and measurements, the adequacy of his record keeping, the theories he holds, the accuracy with which he is able to predict academic success, or the school in which he received his training." [165]

The writer would mildly disagree with Rogers in his emphasis in the preceding statement; however, he would have to concur that graduate schools generally devote little time to training the student's sensitivity or communications quotient, but rather a great deal of time to techniques. Sometimes the techniques of guidance courses are taught with such emphasis on artificial structuring or interviewing trivia, such as how neat the office should be, the type of furniture, a rigid sequence for the interview, rigid report writing styles, and so forth, that little consideration and time are left for the more basic attributes. One writer has felt we have tended to train "phony" psychological services workers by emphasizing a preconceived set of personality traits to the point that the psychologist no longer is himself and is incapable of communicating his true feelings with the client.[166]

On the other hand, the writer would disagree with Rogers to some extent, for in school psychology there is a good deal more to the role than being a genuine self-actualizing adult. The skills discussed in this text, assessment, consultation, and research, when learned by a person who is capable of the attributes discussed by Rogers, would develop into the ideal school psychological services worker.

A sound, genuine, caring interpersonal relationship is basic to any psychological encounter. In his day-to-day work as a school psychologist the writer realizes first and foremost, in diagnosing, assessing, evaluating, remediating, or counseling, that the quality of the relationship determines the degree of communication with principal, parent, teacher, and child.

In the case of a spastic quadriplegic child, the school psychologist must communicate to the child that he is a worthy individual and that the psychological encounter can be a happy, mutually rewarding one. It is important to point out that not all psychologists are able to achieve this dimension in their interpersonal relationships. However, to the degree that he can achieve, in Rogers' terms, *congruence*, when the relationship with the child is genuine and without a front or facade; *empathy*, a sensing of the client's inner world of private meanings; *positive regard*, when the counselor is experiencing a warm, positive, acceptant attitude toward the client, and an *unconditionality of regard*, the school psychologist services worker will be able to communicate verbally and nonverbally more effectively and thus help the child to grow

---

[165] *Ibid.*, p. 417.
[166] Joan Chennault, "The Phony Counselor," *Phi Delta Kappan* (1964).

and change.[167] One further statement is necessary, and that is that the counselee, or child being evaluated, or administrator being consulted, must be communicated to and received by the other person—in the language of "linguistics," both encoded and decoded. The principle is easy to grasp; the achievement of it is difficult and complex.

The school psychological worker of the future has to feel comfortable in his interaction both with teacher and child, and he must be secure in promoting optimal use of the child's association with the teacher for the child's development. He must realize that it is important that his findings get into the lifespace of the adults who can most help the child make the desirable change in behavior, and these are the adults who provide the reinforcement of behavioral patterns during the greatest number of hours of the child's life—the teacher, the parent, or the parent-surrogate, and the child's peers.

In the future, report writing will hopefully assume a secondary role, and clear, verbal communication of complex ideas to those individuals directly concerned with the child will become of paramount importance. A talent all psychological services workers should develop is the ability to express complex psychological ideas in a simple, straightforward manner. It is all too easy to slip into the language of diagnosis and psychological jargon which only blocks communication with most persons with whom the school psychologist will be working.

William James when he was asked to give a series of lectures to the Cambridge teachers in 1892 which was later published in the penetrating classic, *Talks to Teachers*,[168] made a statement which has great relevance to school psychological services at this time.

> You make a very great mistake, if you think that psychology, being the science of mind's laws, is something from which you can deduce definite programs and schemes and methods of instruction for immediate schoolroom use. Psychology is a science, and teaching is an art; and sciences never generate arts directly out of themselves. An intermediary inventive mind must make the application, by using its originality.

It is hoped that the school psychologists of the next decade will themselves develop such minds and will be able to help teachers develop "intermediary inventive minds" in order that the science of psychology can be effectively utilized in service of the school and the child in a creative manner.

To be a school psychologist is to understand and love children and to be opposed to expediency, egocentrism, and compromise in the treatment of children. The worth of a profession is measured by its contribution to Man and the school psychologist is in a position to make a great contribution, to "the father of the man," in the child's formative years. The central educational

---

[167] Rogers, *op. cit.*, pp. 417–421.
[168] William James, *Talks to Teachers on Psychology* (New York: Holt, Rinehart & Winston, Inc., 1939), pp. 7–8.

problem of our time is how the individual can be helped to develop most adequately as a human being. The responsible psychological services worker in the school has a great contribution to make to this central educational problem in the years ahead.

Summary

In this chapter, the potpourri or *pastiche* chapter, the editor attempted to cover a number of concerns which had not been previously discussed. The chapter outlined the developments in school psychology since 1960 and projected the role of the school psychologist into the future.

The editor defined school psychology as follows: The school psychologist brings an alternative frame of reference to bear upon a set of school related observations or behaviors, with the end in view of facilitating learning and adjustment for as many school children as possible. Given this psychological frame of reference, it is important for the school psychologist to remember that the teacher is the central person in the school setting and, when possible, he should effect behavioral changes of pupils by working with and through their teachers. To achieve a productive working relationship with teachers, the school psychologist needs to develop the skill and diplomacy of the psychological consultant.

The position was taken that the school psychologist is one of many psychological services or pupil personnel workers in the schools. He emphasized teamwork and cooperative training programs among the helping professions in the school and in society at large. The point was made that all persons in the mental health fields should have some training in common and preferably have studied together in an interdisciplinary core of graduate courses. Psychological knowledge *per se* is not in the eminent domain of any one specialty. The school psychologist throughout the sixties and early seventies will continue to be an omnibus worker and his role will be determined by the following factors: the community, the school, the demands of the administration, the training and certification requirements in his State, and the personal image and professional image of the school psychologist himself.

Divergent role conceptualizations of school psychological services were summarized. One such role, the possibility of teaching psychology in the elementary and secondary schools, was explored. In this role, the school psychologist can contribute to creating in some detail a more accurate image of contemporary psychology.

The impact of Federal legislation over the last nine years on school psychological services of the future was discussed. Ethical issues in school psychological services, vis-à-vis confidentiality of records, privileged communication, and other matters, were presented.

Professional organizations and journals in this field were presented in terms of their contribution to professional affiliation and identity. Training standards and certification guidelines were discussed. The school psychologist's personal development in terms of Rogerian concepts was developed.

Selected Supplementary Readings

Adams, James F., "Ethical Responsibilities of the Counselor," *The School Counselor,* 12 (May, 1965), 197–205.

Adler, M. J., "Some Educational Implications of the Theories of Jean Piaget and J. S. Bruner," *Canadian Educational Research Digest,* 4 (December, 1964), 291–305.

Albee, G. W., "American Psychology in the Sixties," *American Psychologist,* 18 (October, 1963), 90–95.

Alexander, Irving E., "Postdoctoral Training in Clinical Psychology," *Handbook of Clinical Psychology.* New York: McGraw-Hill Book Company, 1965.

Alevy, D. I., "A Psychologist in the Schools," *Psychology in the Schools,* I (October, 1964).

Allen, Robert M., "The School Psychologist—Image and Role in Process," *The Training School Bulletin,* 56 (May, 1959), 136–139.

Allport, G. W., "Psychological Models for Guidance," *Harvard Education Review,* XXXII (Fall, 1962), 373–382.

Ames, Robert, "The Psychologist's Role in Programs for Exceptional Children," *Educational Perspectives,* 5 (May, 1966), 8–9.

Angrilli, Albert, and Bernard O. Leibman, "The Cooperative Relationship between the Educational Clinic and the Graduate Program in School Psychology at Queens College," *Psychology in the Schools,* 2 (April, 1965), 159–161.

Ashrer, M. J., and C. E. Bisch, eds., *Productive Thinking in Education.* Washington, D.C.: National Education Association, 1965.

Bardon, Jack I., and Virginia D. C. Bennett, "The Perception of the Role of the School Psychologist as Related to Teaching Experience and Educational Background," *Journal of School Psychology,* 4 (Summer, 1966), 52–58.

Barnhart, R. E., and R. J. Baldauf, "Role of the School Psychologist," *Nations Schools,* 11 (April, 1958), 49–51.

Bindman, Arthur J., "University Training of School Psychologists and Certification Standards," *Journal of School Psychology,* II (Winter, 1963), 43–48.

————, "Bibliography on School Psychology," *Journal of Education*, 146 (February, 1964), 53–56.

Blodgett, Harriet E., and Mary Lou Boice, "Putting Psychological Findings to Work," *Minnesota Journal of Education*, 40, 22–23.

Bloom, B. S., *Stability and Change in Human Characteristics*. New York: John Wiley & Sons, Inc., 1964.

Blum, Sam, "Are School Psychologists Helping or Hurting Your Child," *Redbook*, 122 (April, 1964), 76ff.

Bower, Eli M., "The Emerging School Psychologist," *Toward a Professional Identity in School Psychology*, Fourteenth Annual Conference, CASPP, March, 1963.

————, "Psychology in the Schools: Conceptions, Processes and Territories," *Psychology in the Schools*, 1 (January, 1964), 30–34.

Brayfield, A. H., "Human Effectiveness," *American Psychologist*, 20 (1965), 645–651.

Breakthroughs to Better Teaching. Compiled by the editors of the *Harvard Educational Review*, 1966.

Bruner, Jerome S., *The Process of Education*. New York: Random House, Inc., 1963.

————, *Toward a Theory of Instruction*. Boston: Belknap Press, 1966.

Buhler, C., "Values and Beliefs in Our Time," *Educational Leadership*, XXI (May, 1964), 520–523.

Cassel, Russell N., "A Clinical Diagnostic Case Study Procedure for The School Psychologist," *Journal of the National Association of Women Deans and Counselors*, 24 (October, 1960), 23–27.

Castaneda, Alfred, and L. Fahel, "The Relationship Between the Psychological Investigator and the Public Schools," *American Psychologist* (1961), pp. 201–203.

Chickering, Arthur W., "Improving Psychological Services in the School," *Journal of School Psychology*, 3 (1965), 36–42.

Compton, Bertita, "Psychology's Manpower: Characteristics, Employment, and Earnings," *American Psychologist*, 21 (March, 1966), 224–229.

Cook, Walter W., *et al.*, "Why a School Psychologist?" *Minnesota Journal of Education*, 40 (November, 1959), 14–15.

Copel, Sidney L., *Cross Sectional Study of School Age Clinical Case Material*. Ed.D. dissertation, Temple University, 1958.

Cornell, Ethel, "The Psychologist in the School System," *Journal of Consulting Psychology*, 6 (1952), 185–195.

Coxe, W., "The Function of the School Psychologist," *Psychology in the Schools*, I (October, 1964).

Cramer, Stanley H., "The Roles of the Secondary School Counselor and the

Secondary School Psychologist as Perceived by Educators of Counselors and Educators of School Psychologists," *Journal of School Psychology,* 4 (Summer, 1966), 37–42.

Cummins, L. R., "The Helping Professions: An Intergroup Relations Problem," *School and Society,* 80 (November, 1954), 161–165.

Dauterman, J. A., "A Study Comparing the Principal's Perception of the School Psychologist's Role and Function in the Columbus Public Schools with that of Child Study Personnel," unpublished ms., 1965.

David, Henry P., "International Trends in Clinical Psychology," *Handbook of Clinical Psychology.* New York: McGraw-Hill Book Company, 1965.

Derner, Gordon F., "Comments on the Emerging Role in School Psychology," *Psychology in the Schools,* 2 (October, 1965), 350–351.

The Diagnostic Process in Child Psychiatry, Report No. 38 of the Committee on Child Psychiatry. New York, 1957.

Dizney, Henry F., and Kaoru Yamamoto, "A Look at Educational Psychologists," *Psychology in the Schools,* 2 (October, 1965), 334–339.

Duhl, Leonard J., "Crises, Adaptive Potential, and the Schools," *Psychology in the Schools,* I (July, 1964), 263–266.

Dunlap, James M., "A School Psychologist Views His Own Responsibilities," *Psychology in the Schools,* I, No. 1 (January, 1964), 17–19.

Dunn, James A., "On the Growth of School Psychology," *Psychology in the Schools,* 2 (April, 1965), 110–112.

————, "School Psychology: Past, Present, and Future," *University of Kansas Bulletin of Education,* 20 (November, 1965), 12–16.

Eiserer, Paul E., "Factors Influencing and Limiting the Roles of School Psychologists," "Educator Roles," "Organization and Administration of Psychological Services," and "Future Perspectives," in *The School Psychologist.* Washington, D.C.: The Center for Applied Research in Education, Inc., 1963.

Ekstein, Rudolph, "Origins of Values in Children," *Educational Leadership,* XXI (May, 1964), 523–526.

————, "The School Psychologist's Quest for Identity—Premature Commitment of Growth Crisis," *Toward a Professional Identity in School Psychology,* Fourteenth Annual Conference, CASPP, March, 1963.

Elkin, Victor B., "Structuring School Psychological Services: Internal and Interdisciplinary Considerations," in *Professional School Psychology,* Vol. II, ed. M. G. Gottsegen and G. B. Gottsegen. New York: Grune & Stratton, Inc., 1963, pp. 200–226

Engle, T. L., "Teaching Psychology in the High School," in *Professional School Psychology,* Vol. II.

Erikson, Erik H., ed., *Youth: Change and Challenge.* New York: Basic Books, Inc., Publishers, 1963.

Farber, Nathan, "The Psychologist in the School System," *Merrill-Palmer Quarterly,* **2** (1956), 173–178.

Ferguson, Donald G., *Pupil Personnel Services.* Washington, D. C.: The Center for Applied Research in Education, 1963.

————, "Training Programs in School Psychology," in *Professional School Psychology.*

————, and Donald C. Smith, "School Psychology (1960–1963): An Annotated Bibliography," *Journal of School Psychology,* **2** (1963–64), 72–81.

Flair, Merrel D., "The School Administrator and Pupil Personnel Services," *Psychology in the Schools,* **2** (October, 1965), 369–372.

Frisch, Paul, "A Program in School Psychology," *Mental Hygiene,* **40** (1956), 258–266.

Fry, Edward B., *Teaching Machines and Programmed Instruction: An Introduction.* New York: McGraw-Hill Book Company, 1963.

Garfield, Sol L., "Clinical Psychology and the Search for Identity," *American Psychologist,* **21** (April, 1966), 353–362.

Geary, James J., "Administering Psychological Services," *Minnesota Journal of Education,* **40,** No. 15 (April, 1960), 37.

Gottsegen, Monroe G., "The Role of the School Psychologist," *Professional School Psychology,* Vol. I.

Graham, Frances K., Claire B. Ernhart, Marguerite Craft, and Phyllis W. Berman, "I. Performance of Normal Children," *Psychological Monographs: General and Applied,* **77** (1963), 1–16.

Gray, Susan W., "Broader Roles for School Psychologists," *Educational Leadership,* **17** (January, 1960), 226–229, 253.

————, "Prospect: The New Psychologist in the Schools," "The Training of Psychologists for the Schools," "Organization and Administration of Psychological Services," "Professional Development," "The Ethical Position of the School Psychologist," and "The Wide Prospect," *The Psychologist in the Schools.* New York: Holt, Rinehart & Winston, Inc., 1963.

————, "1984—or Twenty Years On," *Action Patterns for School Psychologists,* CASPP, 15th Annual Conference Proceedings, 1964, 1–12.

Gross, F. P., S. J. Bonham, and Venus Bluestein, "Entry Requirements for State Certification of School Psychologists: A Review of the Past Nineteen Years," *Journal of School Psychology,* **4** (Summer, 1966), 43–51.

Gross, Neal, and Robert E. Herriott, *Staff Leadership in Public School: A Sociological Inquiry,* New York: John Wiley & Sons, Inc., 1965.

"Guidance—An Examination," *Harvard Education Review,* **XXXII** (Fall, 1962), entire issue.

Guttentag, M., "A Newcomer Looks at School Psychology: The Problem of the 'Have-nots' in Suburbia," *Journal of School Psychology,* 3 (Summer, 1965), 6–10.

Hadley, J. M., and E. J. Asher, "Clinical, Counseling and School Clinical Psychology at Purdue University," *American Psychologist,* 10 (February, 1955), 71–74.

Halpern, F., "Challenge to School Psychologists," *Journal of the National Association of Women Deans and Counselors,* 26 (June, 1963), 19–24.

Hammer, E. F., "Functions of a Psychological Consultant at a High School," *High Points,* 36 (November, 1954), 5–15.

Harrower, Molly, "Clinical Psychologists at Work," in *Handbook of Clinical Psychology.* New York: McGraw-Hill Book Company, 1965.

Hathaway, Virginia, and Vernon Olson, "The Psychologist On the School Staff," *Minnesota Journal of Education,* 40 (December, 1959), 13.

Henriquez, Vera S., "A School Psychotherapist Reports on Her Work," *Psychology in the Schools,* I, No. 1 (January, 1964).

Higgins, Conwell, "Prospectus: Psychological Service Staff," *School Executive,* 78 (July, 1959), 42–43.

Higgins, Robert E., "Issues in School Psychology: The School Psychologist Versus the School Counselor?" *Journal of School Psychology,* 4 (Summer, 1966), 59–64.

Hobbs, Nicholas, "Ethics in Clinical Psychology," *Handbook of Clinical Psychology.* New York: McGraw-Hill Book Company, 1965.

Hoch, Erasmus L., "The Profession of Clinical Psychology," *Handbook of Clinical Psychology.* New York: McGraw-Hill Book Company, 1965.

Hodges, W. A., and B. E. Balow, "Guidance Services and the School Psychologist," *Minnesota Journal of Education,* 40 (January, 1960), 15.

Hodges, Walter L., "Certification of School Psychologists," *Professional School Psychology,* II.

Hunt, J. McV., *Intelligence and Experience.* New York: The Ronald Press Company, 1961.

Hunt, William A., "Relations with Other Professions," *Handbook of Clinical Psychology.* New York: McGraw-Hill Book Company, 1965.

Itkin, William, "The School Psychologist and His Training," *Psychology in the Schools,* 3 (October, 1966).

Kasanjian, Vard, "Some Experiences in the Development of an Identity as a School Mental Health Consultant," *Toward a Professional Identity in School Psychology,* Fourteenth Annual Conference, CASPP, March, 1963.

Keliher, Alice, "You, the Psychologist and the Child," *Grade Teacher,* 74 (April, 1957), 143.

Knowles, Richard T., and Bruce Shertzer, "Attitudes of School Psychologists

Toward the Role of the School Counselor," *Journal of School Psychology,* 4 (Summer, 1966), 30–36.

Lawhead, V. B., "Values Through Identification," *Educational Leadership,* XXI (May, 1964), 515–519.

Leton, Donald A., "Psychologist's Views on What is Good in American Education," *Teachers College Journal,* 36 (October, 1964), 7–10.

Levin, E. S., "An Ex-School Psychologist Looks at School Psychology," *Journal of School Psychology,* 3, 14–19.

Levine, Louis S., Harry B. Gelatt, Lois G. Nowlin, William M. Littell, and Henriette Lahaderne, "The Use of the Child Development Specialist in the Elementary Schools," *Psychology in the Schools,* 2 (July, 1965), 255–262.

Liddle, Gordon P., and Gary W. Reighard, "Directors of Pupil Personnel Services, Who Are They? Where Are They Going?" *Psychology in the Schools,* 3 (October, 1966).

Liebman, O. B., "A Training Program Coordinator Looks at School Psychology," *Journal of School Psychology,* 3, 11–13.

Los Angeles County Superintendent of Schools Office, *Guiding Today's Youth.* Los Angeles: Office of Los Angeles County Superintendent of Schools, 1962.

Losen, Stuart M., "The School Psychologist—Psychotherapist or Consultant," *Psychology in the Schools,* I, No. 1 (January, 1964).

Lucas, A. F., "Guide to Upgrade the High School Psychology Course," *Clearing House,* 37 (May, 1963), 523–528.

Luckey, Bertha, M., "The Administrative and Professional Functions of the School Psychologist," *Professional School Psychology,* II.

Maslow, Abraham, *Toward a Psychology of Being.* Princeton: D. Van Nostrand and Co., 1962.

McCandless, Boyd R., "Significant Developments in School Psychology," *Newsletter,* Division 16, 14 (1959), 6–11.

McDaniel, Leonard J., and A. Edward Ahr, "The School Psychologist as a Resource Person Initiating and Conducting In-service Teacher Education," *Psychology in the Schools,* 2 (July, 1965), 220–223.

McHugh, Ann F., "Potential Contributions of the School Psychologist," *Psychology in the Schools,* I (April, 1964), 190–193.

McIntosh, W. J., "School Psychologist," *Special Education, Canada,* 40 (February, 1966), 15–17.

Miles, Matthew B., ed., *Innovation in Education.* New York: Teachers College, Columbia University, 1964.

Miller, C. H., *Guidance Services: An Introduction.* New York: Harper & Row, Publishers, 1965.

Mullen, Frances A., "The School as a Psychological Laboratory," *American Psychologist,* 13 (February, 1959), 53–56.

Nelson, Williard H., Don F. Driggs, eds., *Contributions of the Behavioral Sciences To Quality Education,* School Psychology Conference, Florida State University, 1964. Contains papers by Susan Gray, Eli M. Bower, and Gordon L. Lippitt.

Newland, T. Ernest, "Psychological Services—Elementary and Secondary," in *Encyclopedia of Educational Research,* 3rd ed. New York: The Macmillan Company, 1961, pp. 1067–1073.

Oldridge, O. A., "An Experimental Study of Two Guidance Emphases in the Elementary School," *Toward a Professional Identity in School Psychology,* Fourteenth Annual Conference, CASPP, March, 1963.

O'Shea, Harriet E., "Shall School Psychologists Conduct Psychotherapy?" *Psychology in the Schools,* I (January, 1964).

————, "The Future of School Psychology," in *Professional School Psychology.*

Perkins, Keith J., "School Psychology: From Identification to Identity," *Journal of School Psychology,* II (Winter, 1964), 7–18.

"Personal and Social Values," *Educational Leadership,* XXI (May, 1964), entire issue.

Phillips, Beeman N., ed., *Perspectives on School Psychology.* Austin: The University of Texas Press, 1966.

Porter, T. L., and T. E. Cook, "Comparison of Student and Professional Prestige Ranking of Jobs in Psychology," *Journal of Counseling Psychology,* 11 (Winter, 1964), 385–387.

Post, P. D., "The School Psychologist," *Education,* LXXXII (1962), 339–341.

Powell, Marvin, "Teacher Certification," *American Psychologist* (1960), 218–219.

Purl, Mabel C., "The Roles of the School Psychometrist and School Psychologist," *CASPP Newsletter,* 10 (March, 1963), 21–23.

"Psychologists in the Schools," *American Psychologist,* 23 (March, 1966), 256.

Raferty, Gerald, "I Don't Mistrust *All* Psychologists," *The Clearing House,* 34 (December, 1959), 211–213.

Reger, Roger, *School Psychology.* Springfield, Ill.: Charles C Thomas, Publisher, 1965.

————, "School Psychology: An Emerging Profession," *National Elementary Principal,* 45 (January, 1965), 52–54.

————, "The School Psychologist: Friend or Foe?" *The Michigan Elementary Principal,* 39 (June, 1965), 9.

Rice, J. P., Jr., "Types of Problems Referred to a Central Guidance Agency at Different Grade Levels," *Personnel and Guidance Journal,* 42 (September, 1963), 52–55.

Rogers, C. R., "Significant Learning: In Therapy and in Education," *Education Leadership,* **XVI** (1959), 232–242.

―――――, "The Interpersonal Relationship: The Core of Guidance," *Harvard Education Review,* **XXXII** (Fall, 1962), 416–429.

Rosenbaum, Dorothy S., and Conrad F. Toepfer, Jr., *Curriculum Planning and School Psychology, The Coordinated Approach.* Buffalo, N. Y.: Hertillon Press, 1966.

Ross, Alan O., "The School Psychologist's Role Seen From the Child Guidance Clinic," *Psychology in the Schools,* **I,** No. 1 (January, 1964).

Ross, Sherman, and Robert F. Lockman, *A Career in Psychology,* rev. ed. Washington, D. C.: American Psychological Association, 1965.

Rotter, Julian, *Clinical Psychology.* Englewood Cliffs, N.J.: Prentice-Hall, Inc., 1963.

Scheibe, James N., "The School Psychologist: Clinical, Coordinator, Consultant," *The National Elementary Principal,* **45** (September, 1965), 43–51.

Schmidt, K. M., and F. Pena, "The Psychologist as a Consultant in the Schools," *Psychology in the Schools,* **I** (October, 1964).

Schmidt, Lyle D., "Some Ethical, Professional, and Legal Considerations for School Counselors," *Personnel and Guidance Journal,* **44** (December, 1965), 376–383.

Schofield, William, "Clinical and Counseling Psychology: Some Perspectives," *American Psychologist,* **21** (February, 1966), 122–131.

Shakow, David, "Seventeen Years Later: Clinical Psychology in the Light of the 1947 Committee on Training in Clinical Psychology Report," *American Psychologist,* **20** (May, 1965), 353–362.

Shaw, M. C., "A Focus for Public School Guidance Programs: A Research Design and Some Preliminary Results," *Human Growth and Diversity,* CASPP Conference Proceedings, 1965.

Shipley, Joseph T., *The Mentally Disturbed Teacher.* Philadelphia: Chilton Books, 1961.

Simmons, John, "Role Playing as a Method of Teaching Psychology in the Elementary School," *Journal of School Psychology,* **4** (1965), 13–15.

Sivers, W. A., and R. D. Salman, *The School Psychologist in Action.* Albany: University of the State of New York, the State Education Department, Bureau of Psychological Services, 1961.

Smith, E. W., *et al.,* "The School Psychologist," in *The Educator's Encyclopedia.* Englewood Cliffs, N. J.: Prentice-Hall, Inc., 1961, pp. 183–187.

Smith, H. R., and L. O. Eckerson, *Guidance Services in Elementary Schools.* Washington: U. S. Office of Education, 1966.

Starkman, Stanley, "The Professional Model: Paradox in School Psychology," *American Psychologist,* **21** (August, 1966), 807–808.

Sternlicht, Manny, "Some Notes Concerning the Roles of School and Clinical Psychologists," *Psychology,* 2 (1965), 37–39.

Stiller, A., "School Guidance Needs Research," *Personnel and Guidance Journal,* 41 (May, 1963), 798–802.

Stolurow, Lawrence M., *Teaching by Machine.* Washington, D.C.: U. S. Department of Health, Education, and Welfare, 1961.

Sundberg, Norman D., and Leona E. Tyler, *Clinical Psychology: An Introduction to Research and Practice.* New York: Appleton-Century-Crofts, 1962.

Tindall, Ralph H., "Problems of Clinical Supervision," in *Professional School Psychology,* II.

———, "Trends in Development of Psychological Services in the School," *Journal of School Psychology,* 3 (1964), 1–12.

Trachtman, Gilbert M., "The School Psychologist and Confidentiality of School Records," *Professional School Psychology,* II.

———, Victor B. Elkin, Marcia Guttentag, O. Bernard Liebman, and Edward S. Levin, "The Blind Men and the Elephant: Four Perceptions of School Psychology," *Journal of School Psychology,* 3 (1965), 1–22.

Trow, William Clark, "The Future of School Psychology by Extrapolation," *Psychology in the Schools,* III (April, 1966), 131–139.

———, *Teacher and Technology: New Designs for Learning.* New York: Appleton-Century-Crofts, 1963.

Valett, Robert E., "A Formula for Providing Psychological Services," *Psychology in the Schools,* 2 (October, 1965), 326–329.

———, "Problems in the Administration of School Psychology," and "Professional Development," *The Practice of School Psychology.* New York: John Wiley & Sons, Inc., 1963.

———, "Psychological Market Place," *Psychology in the Schools,* 3 (October, 1966).

von Mering, G. A., *A Grammar of Human Values.* Pittsburgh, Pa.: Univ. of Pittsburgh Press, 1961.

Webb, Wilse B., ed., *The Profession of Psychology.* New York: Holt, Rinehart & Winston, Inc., 1962.

University of the State of New York, The State Education Department Bureau of Psychological Services, "How Many School Psychologists Does A School System Need," 1959 (mimeo.).

Weinberg, William, "Mental Health Consultation Techniques in School Psychology," *Toward a Professional Identity in School Psychology,* Fourteenth Annual Conference, CASPP, March, 1963.

White, Mary Alice, and Myron W. Harris, "Objectives of School Psychology." "The Psychologist Becomes a School Psychologist," "Related Professional

Roles of the School Psychologist," in *The School Psychologist*. New York: Harper & Row, Publishers, 1961.

Woltman, B. B., ed., *Handbook of Clinical Psychology*. New York: McGraw-Hill Book Company, 1965.

Wylie, Ruth C., *The Self Concept: A Critical Survey of Pertinent Research Literature*. Lincoln: University of Nebraska Press, 1961.

Yamamoto, Kaoru, "Psychological Testing: Invasion of Privacy," *Educational Leadership*, **23**, No. 5 (February, 1966), 363–368.

Index

Index

A

A-B-C Vision Test, 402
Abel, Theodora, 409
Abt, L. E., 312, 341
Achievement tests, 184, 202
Adjustment Inventory, 372
Adler, Alfred, 155
Adler, Irving, 236
Adlerblum, Evelyn D., 163
Affleck, D. C., 269
Albaugh, William, 225
Albee, G., 717
Alexander Performance Scale, 290
Allen, Frederick H., 155
Allen, Jeremiah M., 223–224
Allen, R. M., 53, 85, 360, 371–372,
        375–376, 378
Allessi, Salvatore, 224
Allport, Gordon, 214, 310–311
Allport Vernon Scale of Values, 242